2895½31

4TH EDITION
MANAGERIAL
ECONOMICS

JAMES L. PAPPAS University of Wisconsin
EUGENE F. BRIGHAM University of Florida
MARK HIRSCHEY University of Wisconsin

DRYDEN PRESS   CHICAGO   NEW YORK   PHILADELPHIA   SAN FRANCISCO   MONTREAL
TORONTO   LONDON   SYDNEY   TOKYO   MEXICO CITY   RIO DE JANEIRO   MADRID

THE DRYDEN PRESS
SERIES IN ECONOMICS

Acquisitions Editor: Elizabeth Widdicombe
Editorial Assistant: Judy Sarwark
Senior Project Editors: Kathy Richmond/Julia Ehresmann
Design Director: Alan Wendt
Production Manager: Mary Jarvis
Managing Editor: Jane Perkins

Text and cover design by Barbara Gibson
Copy editing by Linda McIntosh
Indexing by Lois Oster

Compositor: G & S Typesetters, Inc.
Text type: Times Roman

Address orders to:
383 Madison Avenue
New York, New York 10017

Address editorial correspondence to:
One Salt Creek Lane
Hinsdale, Illinois 60521

Library of Congress Catalog Card Number: 82-72179
ISBN 0-03-062441-X
Printed in the United States of America
345-016-9876543

CBS College Publishing
The Dryden Press
Holt, Rinehart and Winston
Saunders College Publishing

PREFACE

In the decade since the first edition of *Managerial Economics* was published, the practice of successful management has become ever more challenging and complex. The world in which managerial decisions must be made undergoes continuous and dramatic change. Inflation remains a significant factor, impacting on individuals, firms, and governments. Uncertainty about resource limitations and availability, coupled with substantial price increases for such basic goods as food, energy, and credit have changed lifestyles and purchasing patterns. These same factors, along with rapid technological change and increased international competition, have given rise to major transformations in production and distribution systems. An expanded participation by governments in the workings of the private economy adds to the complex nature of the environment in which managers function. In such an environment sound economic analysis has taken on even greater importance in managerial decision making—whether the decision-making unit is an individual, household, firm, nonprofit organization or government agency.

Managerial Economics is designed to provide a foundation of economic understanding for use in managerial decision making. The text offers a rigorous treatment of economic theory and analysis with a focus on the tools and techniques that make it useful and usable for decision-making purposes. Examples and problems are used to illustrate the application of theory to a variety of decision situations. The nature of the decision process and the role that economic analysis plays in the process are emphasized throughout.

Although both micro- and macro-economic relationships have important implications for managerial decision making, this revision of *Managerial Economics* continues to concentrate primarily on a set of micro-economic topics that are particularly important. The book begins by developing an economic model of the firm. The rationale for using this model to examine firm behavior and the important role of profits are examined. The demand for a firm's goods and services plays a major role in determining the profitability of operations. Thus, the economics of demand and techniques for estimating and analyzing demand form an important area of study in managerial economics. The efficiency with which resources are acquired and utilized is also an important determinant of a firm's success and value. Production theory and cost analysis, which examine the economics of resource allocation and employment, offer insight into this important area of managerial decision making. The markets in which a firm operates also significantly impact on managerial decisions. Market structure analysis provides a foundation for examining the pricing practices required for successful management of an enterprise. Capital is a fundamental economic resource; its importance to both the firm and the economic system as a whole is such that investment analysis is included in the study of managerial economics. Finally, the importance of government activity in determining the environment wherein managerial decisions are made, and the constraints under which management must operate, requires that regulation and antitrust be examined.

Managerial decision making revolves around attempts to optimize under conditions of risk or uncertainty. Numerous optimization and risk-analysis procedures have been developed for use in economic analysis, and we develop the basics of them early in the text and use them throughout, where appropriate. Although *Managerial Economics* takes a problem-solving approach, the focus is on the economics, not the mathematics, of the managerial decision process. Quantitative tools are introduced to assist in gaining greater insight into the economic relationships as well as facility in actually employing economic analysis in decision situations.

A particularly important feature of *Managerial Economics* is its attempt to depict the firm as a cohesive, unified organization. A basic valuation model is constructed and used as the underlying economic model of the firm. Each topic in the text is then related to an element of the model. In this process, management is seen to involve an integration of the accounting, marketing, production, personnel, and finance functions. This integrating process is particularly valuable for consolidating the materials and for demonstrating that important business decisions are *interdisciplinary* in the truest sense of the word. Our students have found that setting forth the interrelationships within a business firm—or a business administration curriculum—as a unified whole, rather than as a series of discrete, unrelated topics, is one of the most valuable aspects of the study of managerial economics.

CHANGES IN THE FOURTH EDITION

Just as the world in which managerial decisions are made is ever-changing, so too a textbook must continually be modified and updated to maintain its value as an educational resource. This revision of *Managerial Economics* contains several substantial changes, in addition to the typical smoothing out of materials that have proven most difficult to students using prior editions. Some materials have been eliminated, others were shifted to provide an improved flow. Several chapters incorporate new topics or expanded treatment of existing ones which strengthen the text. The use of illustrations has been increased and problem sets have been revised to reinforce the relationship between economic analysis and managerial decision making. Several of the more significant changes are noted below:

1. The end-of-chapter problems have been extensively revised. The problem sets now are broader both in terms of the *variety* of decision situations covered and the *range* of difficulty encountered. The end-of-chapter questions and problems are designed to assist the reader in acquiring a working facility with the tools and techniques of economic analysis.

2. A new study guide is now available. It contains a short statement of the major concepts of each chapter, an outline specifying the most important relationships developed, and a set of solved problems similar to those in the text.

3. The chapter on demand theory has been shortened slightly by eliminating the treatment of the acceleration principle and reducing the material on time characteristics of demand. This has improved both the flow of the chapter and the transition to the subject of demand estimation.

4. The material on interpreting regression equations and the use of regression statistics in Chapter 5 have been extensively revised. The new coverage is both more complete and somewhat more user-oriented than in past editions.

5. In the chapter on production, the development of optimal input combinations has been modified to emphasize the relationships among factor productivity, value of output, and resource employment. Additionally, output elasticities have been introduced as a means of analyzing the returns to scale in a production system.

6. Chapter 9, on linear programming, has been placed following the chapters on cost theory and cost analysis. This change improves the transition from production to cost topics and allows for discussion of a wider range of linear programming applications. An appendix covering the formulation of the dual linear programming problem statement has also been added to the linear programming chapter.

7. Material on market concentration has been incorporated into the chapter on market structure. This enables us to deal more explicitly with the issue of identifying and analyzing the market in which a firm sells its products.

8. Chapter 12, on regulation and antitrust, has been extensively revised with a more complete treatment of both equity and efficiency issues in regulating the economy. Questions of property rights and the role of government in both assisting and directing the private economy are examined.

9. Chapter 14 is a new, integrated case built around the interesting topic of robotics. The case provides an extensive summary while demonstrating an application of the theory and methods of economic analysis developed throughout the text.

ACKNOWLEDGMENTS

We are grateful to the many individuals who aided in the preparation of *Managerial Economics*, fourth edition. Many helpful suggestions and valuable comments have been received from instructors (and students) who have used previous editions. Additionally, numerous reviewers provided insight and assistance in clarifying difficult presentations. Among those who have been especially helpful in the development of this edition of *Managerial Economics* are: Bruce T. Allen, Michigan State University; Steven M. Crafton, Emory University; Joseph P. Magaddino, California State University, Long Beach; Edward J. Mathis, Villanova University; John R. McKean, Colorado State University; and Peter M. Schwarz, University of North Carolina at Charlotte. Special thanks go to Jay C. Foggy who assisted with the development of the new summary case (Chapter 14).

The universities of Wisconsin and Florida, and our students and colleagues on these campuses, provided us with a stimulating environment and general intellectual support. We are indebted to The Dryden Press staff—particularly Julia Ehresmann, Kathy Richmond, Judy Sarwark, and Elizabeth Widdicombe—for their special efforts. Finally, we want to thank our wives, Bonnie, Sue, and Chris, for their support and assistance with this project.

Although every effort has been made to minimize errors in the text, we recognize that some undoubtedly will have slipped through. We are anxious to eliminate them and invite readers to correspond with us concerning corrections, suggestions for further improvements of clarity, or other related matters.

Economic efficiency is an essential ingredient in the successful management of both private- and public-sector organizations. Its importance to the well-being of the entire economic system cannot be overstated. The field of managerial economics continues to undergo significant changes in response to the challenges imposed by the complexities of managerial decision making in a rapidly shifting environment. It is stimulating and exciting to participate in these developments. We sincerely hope that *Managerial Economics* will contribute to a better understanding of the application of economic theory and methodology to managerial practices, and thus help lead to a more efficient economic system.

September 1982

James L. Pappas   *Madison, Wisconsin*
Eugene F. Brigham   *Gainesville, Florida*
Mark Hirschey   *Madison, Wisconsin*

CONTENTS

CHAPTER 1

INTRODUCTION: THE NATURE AND SCOPE OF MANAGERIAL ECONOMICS

Although one finds the term *managerial economics* defined in a variety of ways, the differences are typically more semantic than real. Some define managerial economics as applied microeconomics. Others define the field in terms of management science and operations research concepts. There are also those who see managerial economics as primarily providing an integrative framework for analyzing business decision problems. In actuality, all of those views are correct, for each provides an important insight into managerial economics.

Managerial economics applies economic theory and methodology to business and administrative decision making. More specifically, managerial economics uses the tools and techniques of economic analysis to analyze and solve managerial problems. In a sense, managerial economics provides the link between traditional economics and the decision sciences in managerial decision making, as is illustrated in Figure 1.1. While we focus throughout the text on business applications, it is important to recognize that the concepts of managerial economics apply equally to other types of organizations. The principles of managerial economics pertain to the effi-

FIGURE 1.1

The Role of Managerial Economics in Managerial Decision Making

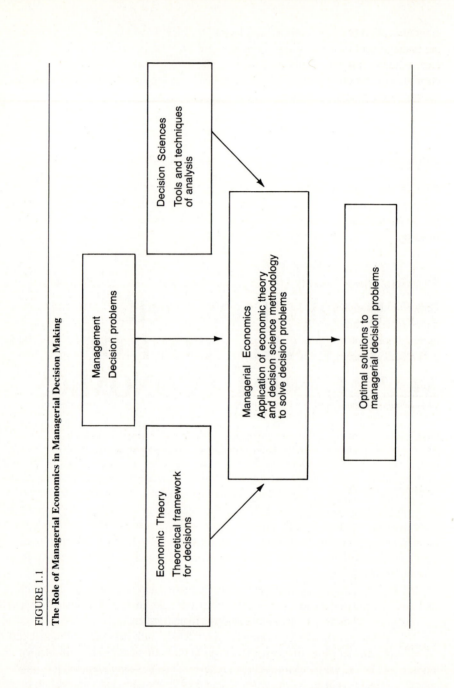

cient allocation of scarce resources. As such, these principles are equally relevant to the management of nonbusiness, nonprofit organizations such as government agencies, schools, hospitals, museums, and similar institutions. This point will become clear from the examples and problems drawn from the government and nonprofit sectors in the chapters that follow.

THE SCOPE OF MANAGERIAL ECONOMICS

We can more clearly understand the generality of the concepts of managerial economics by examining the relationship of managerial economics to (1) economics, (2) decision sciences, and (3) related fields that have impact on managerial decision making.

Relationship of Managerial Economics to Traditional Economics

Understanding the relationship between managerial economics and more traditional fields in economics is facilitated by considering the structure of traditional economic studies as shown in Table 1.1. The traditional fields of economic study presented in the table overlap to some extent. Not only are micro and macro theory

TABLE 1.1

Classification of Traditional Economic Studies

Theory:	*Microeconomics* focuses on individual consumers, firms, and industries.
	Macroeconomics focuses on aggregations of economic units, especially national economies.
Traditional Fields:	Agricultural economics
	Comparative economic systems
	Econometrics
	Economic development
	Economic history
	Industrial organization
	International trade
	Labor economics
	Money and banking
	Public economics
	Urban and regional economics
Emphasis:	*Normative economics* focuses on prescriptive statements; that is, establishes rules to help attain specified goals.
	Positive economics focuses on description; that is, describes the manner in which economic forces operate without attempting to state how they should operate.

interrelated, but there are also micro and macro aspects of each area listed. More-over, the areas themselves overlap; for example, econometric techniques provide a common set of tools of analysis that apply to each other area. Similarly, economic systems as studied in positive, or descriptive, economics must be understood before meaningful normative rules can be formulated. Nevertheless, the focus of each field of study is sufficiently well defined to warrant the breakdown suggested.

Since each area of economics has some bearing on managerial decision mak-ing, managerial economics draws from them all. In practice, some are more rele-vant to the business firm than others, and hence to managerial economics. To illus-trate, both microeconomics and macroeconomics are important in managerial economics, but the microeconomic theory of the firm is especially significant. It may be said that the theory of the firm is the single most important element in man-agerial economics. However, because the individual firm is influenced by the gen-eral economy, which is the domain of macroeconomics, managerial economics draws from this area as well.

The emphasis of managerial economics is certainly on normative theory. We want to establish decision rules that will help managers attain the goals of their firm, agency, or organization; this is the essence of the word normative. If managers are to establish valid decision rules, however, they must thoroughly understand the en-vironment in which they operate. For this reason positive or descriptive economics is important.

Relationship of Managerial Economics to the Decision Sciences

Economics provides the theoretical framework for analyzing managerial decision problems. Similarly, the decision sciences provide the means to actually construct decision models, analyze the impact of alternative courses of action, and evaluate the results obtained from the models. Managerial economics draws heavily upon *optimization techniques*, including differential calculus and mathematical program-ming, which help management to achieve the firm's established goals. *Statistical tools* are used to estimate relationships between important variables in decision problems. Because most managerial decision problems involve activities and events that occur in the future, *forecasting techniques* also play an important role in man-agerial decision making and, therefore, in the study of managerial economics.

As in economics, the dichotomy used here to classify the decision sciences is not absolute. Optimization procedures are inherent in statistical relationships, and both optimization techniques and statistical relationships play important parts in de-veloping forecasting methodologies.

In addition to the overlaps within the classifications of economics and decision science, there is substantial overlap between them. For example, many of the basic corollaries of economics—including the well-known microeconomic axiom which states that profit maximization requires operation at the activity level where mar-

TABLE 1.2

Classifications of Business Administration Studies

Functional areas:	Accounting
	Finance
	Marketing
	Personnel
	Production
Tool areas:	Accounting
	Management information systems
	Managerial economics
	Organizational behavior
	Quantitative methods: operations research, statistics
Special areas:	Banking
	Insurance
	International business
	Real estate
	Regulation
Integrating courses:	Business policy
	Managerial economics

ginal revenue equals marginal cost—are derived from the optimization procedures of differential calculus. Because of these interrelationships the differences in the definitions of managerial economics are largely semantic in nature.

Relationship of Managerial Economics to Business Administration

Now that we have established the role of economics and the decision sciences in managerial economics, it should prove useful to place managerial economics in perspective as a part of the study of business administration. In general, business administration is organized into four major categories, as is illustrated in Table 1.2. The functional areas are well situated because both businesses and business schools are generally structured to include these departments. The special areas are also fairly well defined, and their place in the business administration curriculum is relatively clear-cut. The tool areas and integrating courses are not so easily categorized. Accounting, for example, is a function within the firm, but it is also a tool used throughout the firm. Accordingly, accounting is listed both as a functional area and as a tool.

The real question is this: Where does managerial economics fit into the picture? Again, the answer is not clear-cut. Although many firms have economics departments, these departments are usually small, and economics per se is not a major function within the firm. One possibility is to include managerial economics as a special area, but in our judgment it would be somewhat out of character there.

As we see it, managerial economics fits into the classification of business administration studies in two places. First, it serves as a *tool course*, wherein certain economic theories, methods, and techniques of analysis are covered in preparation for their later use in the functional areas. Second, managerial economics serves as an *integrating course*, combining the various functional areas and showing not only how they interact with one another as the firm attempts to achieve its goals, but also how the firm interacts with the environment in which it operates.

THE THEORY OF THE FIRM

A useful way to begin studying managerial economics is to develop a theory of firm behavior with which to analyze managerial decision making. A business enterprise is a combination of people, physical assets, and information (technical, sales, coordinative, and so on). The people directly involved include stockholders, management, labor, suppliers, and customers. In addition to these direct participants, all of society is indirectly involved in the firm's operations, because businesses use resources that are otherwise available for other purposes, pay taxes if operations are profitable, provide employment, and generally produce most of the material output of our society.

Firms exist because they are useful in the process of allocating resources—producing and distributing goods and services. They are basically economic entities. As such, their activities can best be analyzed in the context of an economic model of the firm.

The basic model of the business enterprise is derived from what economists call the *theory of the firm*. In its earliest version, the goal of the firm was assumed to be profit maximization—the owner-manager of the firm was assumed to strive single-mindedly to maximize the firm's short-run profits. Later, when the emphasis on profits was shifted or broadened to encompass uncertainty and the time dimension, the primary goal became wealth maximization rather than short-run profit maximization. This goal of wealth or value maximization is recognized today as the *primary* objective of a business.

Definition of Value

Since the basis of the economic model is maximization of the value of the firm, it is appropriate to clarify the meaning of value. Actually, a number of definitions of the term are found in economic and business literature—book value, market value, liquidating value, going-concern value, and so on. For our purposes *value* can be defined as the present value of the firm's expected future cash flows. Cash flows may, for now, be equated to profits; therefore the value of the firm today, its *present value*, is the value of its expected future profits, discounted back to the present at an appropriate interest rate.[1]

The essence of the model with which we are concerned throughout the book may be expressed as follows:

Value of the Firm = *PV* of Expected Future Profits **(1.1)**

$$= \frac{\pi_1}{(1 + i)^1} + \frac{\pi_2}{(1 + i)^2} + \ldots + \frac{\pi_n}{(1 + i)^n}$$

$$= \sum_{t = 1}^{n} \frac{\pi_t}{(1 + i)^t} \ .$$

PV is the abbreviation for present value; π_1, π_2, and so forth represent the expected profits in each year, t; i is the appropriate interest rate.[2]

Since profits are equal to total revenues (*TR*) minus total costs (*TC*), Equation 1.1 may be rewritten as follows:

$$\text{Value} = \sum_{t = 1}^{n} \frac{TR_t - TC_t}{(1 + i)^t} \ . \qquad \textbf{(1.2)}$$

The marketing department of a firm has a major responsibility for sales; the production department a major responsibility for costs; and the finance department a major responsibility for acquiring capital to support the firm's activities and, hence, for the discount factor in the denominator. There are many important overlaps among these functional areas—the marketing department, for example, can help to reduce

---

[1] We assume that the reader is familiar with the concepts of present value and compound interest. For those who are not, we have included a detailed treatment of the subject in Appendix A at the end of the textbook. This material is useful for a complete understanding of Chapter 3, "Risk Analysis"; it is essential to an understanding of Chapter 13, "Capital Budgeting."

To understand Chapter 1, however, one merely needs to recognize that $1 in hand today is worth more than $1 to be received a year from now; because the $1 today can be invested and, with interest, can grow to an amount larger than $1 by the end of the year. If we had $1 and invested it at 5 percent interest, it would grow to $1.05 in one year. Thus, $1 is defined as the present value of $1.05 due in one year when the appropriate interest rate is 5 percent.

[2] The second form given for Equation 1.1 is simply a shorthand expression in which sigma (Σ) signifies "sum up" or add the present values of n profit terms. If $t = 1$, then $\pi_t = \pi_1$, and $(1 + i)^t = (1 + i)^1$; if $t = 2$, then $\pi_t = \pi_2$, and $(1 + i)^t = (1 + i)^2$; and so on, until $t = n$, the last year the project provides any profits.

The term $\sum_{t=1}^{n}$ simply says: Go through the following process. Let $t = 1$, and find the *PV* of π_1; then let $t = 2$, and find the *PV* of π_2; continue until the *PV* of each individual profit has been found; then add the *PV*s of these individual profits to find the *PV* of the firm.

the costs associated with a given level of output by affecting customer order size and timing, and the production department can stimulate sales by improving quality and making new products available to sales personnel. Further, other departments within the firm—for example, accounting, personnel, transportation, and engineering—provide information or services vital to both sales expansion and cost control. These activities all affect the risks of the firm and thereby the discount rate used to determine present values. We see, therefore, that various decisions in different departments of the firm can be appraised in terms of their effects on the value of the firm as expressed in Equations 1.1 and 1.2.

A fundamental assumption then in managerial economics is that the firm seeks to maximize its value as expressed in Equations 1.1 and 1.2, subject to constraints imposed by technology, resource scarcity, contractual obligations, and government restrictions. This statement is highly simplified; the remainder of this book will amplify and qualify it, and will show how economic theory can be used to help management achieve the value maximization goal.

Constraints and the Theory of the Firm

Managerial decisions are seldom, if ever, made in isolation. In order for any decision to be value maximizing, managers must consider both short- and long-run implications, as well as how various external restrictions or constraints affect their ability to achieve organizational objectives. Managerial decision making typically involves optimizing the value of some objective function subject to one or more constraints.

While a tremendous variety of constraints can arise in managerial decision problems, most fall within three broad categories, namely resource constraints, output quantity or quality constraints, and legal constraints. Given the important role that constraints play in managerial decision making, we will briefly examine some examples of constrained decision problems.

Firms and other organizations, such as hospitals, schools, and government agencies, frequently are faced with limited availability of essential inputs. Examples of such resource constraints include limitations on the availability of skilled labor, key raw materials, energy, machinery, warehouse space, and other such factors. Managers often face similar capital constraints due to limitations on the amount of capital resources available for a particular project or activity.

Managerial decisions can also be constrained by contractual output requirements. A specific minimum level of output often must be produced to meet delivery requirements. In other instances, output must meet certain minimum quality requirements. Some common examples of output quality constraints are nutritional requirements for feed mixtures, audience exposure requirements for media promotions, reliability requirements for measurement devices, and requirements for minimum customer service levels.

Legal restrictions that affect both production and marketing activities can also play an important role in managerial decisions. Laws that define minimum wages, health and safety standards, pollution emission standards, fuel efficiency requirements, and fair pricing and marketing practices all limit managerial flexibility.

The important role played by constraints in managerial decision making makes the topic of *constrained optimization* a basic element of managerial economics. In later chapters we examine two powerful approaches to constrained optimization—the Lagrangian technique and linear programming. We will focus on solution techniques for these important decision techniques and will also consider important economic implications of the constraints themselves. This analysis is important because both value maximization and productive and allocative efficiency in society depend upon the efficient use of scarce (limited) economic resources.

Limitations of the Theory of the Firm

Many critics have questioned why the assumed profit or wealth maximization criterion is used as a foundation for the study of firm behavior. Are not the managers of firms interested, at least to some extent, in power, prestige, leisure, employee welfare, community well-being, and society in general? Further, do managers really try to *maximize*, or do they *satisfice*? That is, do they seek satisfactory results rather than *optimal* results, as the economic theory asserts? Would the manager of a firm really seek the *sharpest* needle in a haystack (maximize), or would he or she stop upon finding one sharp enough for sewing (satisfice)?

It is extremely difficult to determine whether management is trying to maximize firm value or whether it is merely attempting to satisfy owners while pursuing other goals. For example, how can one tell whether a community benefit activity undertaken by a firm leads to long-run value maximization? Are high salaries and substantial perquisites really necessary to attract and retain managers who can keep the firm ahead of the competition? When a risky venture is turned down, how can one say whether this reflects conservatism or risk avoidance on the part of management, or whether it in fact reflects an appropriate decision from the standpoint of value maximization, given the risks of the venture compared with its potential return?

It is impossible to give definitive answers to questions like those above, and this problem led to the development of numerous alternative theories of firm behavior. Some of the more prominent alternatives are models in which sales maximization is the assumed primary objective of management, models which assume managers are most concerned with their own personal utility or welfare maximization, and models which treat the firm as a collection of individuals with widely divergent goals rather than a single identifiable unit.

Each of these theories, or models, of managerial behavior has added to our knowledge and understanding of the firm. Still, none could supplant the basic microeconomic model of the firm as a basis for analyzing managerial decisions. It is worthwhile to examine this somewhat further.

The economic theory of the firm, as it has evolved to date, states that a manager seeks to maximize the value of the firm, subject to constraints imposed by resource limitations, technology, and society. The theory does not explicitly recognize other goals, including the possibility that managers might take actions that would benefit someone other than stockholders—perhaps the managers themselves or society in general—but would *reduce* stockholder wealth. Thus, the model seems to ignore the possibilities of satisficing, managerial self-dealing, and voluntary social responsibility on the part of business.

Given that firms assert the existence of multiple goals, engage in active "social responsibility" programs, and exhibit what appears to be satisficing behavior, is the economic model of the firm really adequate as a basis for our study of managerial decision making? We think it is. First, we believe that the typically vigorous competition both in product markets, where firms sell their output, and in the capital market, where they acquire the funds necessary to engage in productive enterprise, force managements to heed value maximization in their decisions. In addition, stockholders are, of course, interested in value maximization since it affects their rates of return on common stock investments. Managers who pursue their own interests instead of those of the stockholder run the risk of being replaced. While stockholder revolts are relatively rare among large established firms, buyout pressure from unfriendly firms ("raiders") has been significant during recent years. Unfriendly takeovers are especially unfriendly to inefficient managements who are replaced. Further, recent studies of managerial compensation indicate a strong correlation between firm profits and managers' salaries. Thus, managers appear to have a strong economic incentive to consider value maximization in their decisions.

Second, even if value maximization oversimplifies some multi-goal objective of firms, the concepts and understanding developed from a study of the economic theory of the firm help improve managerial decisions. This will become clear as the theory is developed and explained in the text. Further, the foundation provided by such study forms the basis both for extending the model and for evaluating alternative models that are proposed for use in managerial decision making.

Third, the costs as well as the benefits of any action must be considered before a decision can be made. This rule applies to any decision to satisfice rather than to maximize. In other words, before a firm can decide on a satisfactory level of achievement, a manager must examine the costs of such an action. The analysis involved in the maximizing model provides information on such costs.

Fourth, the value maximization model provides insight into the firm's voluntary social responsibility activities, though at first glance the model seems to preclude this possibility. The criticism that the microeconomic theory of the firm emphasizes profits and value maximization while ignoring the issue of social responsibility is important enough to warrant a slightly extended discussion.

ROLE OF BUSINESS IN SOCIETY

As suggested above, an important element in the study of managerial economics is the interrelationship between the firm and society. Managerial economics can clarify the vital role firms play in society and can point out ways of improving their benefits to society.

The evidence that business in the United States has contributed significantly to the social welfare is both clear and convincing. Not only has the economy sustained a significant and unprecedented rate of growth over the past hundred years, but the benefits of that growth have been widely distributed. Suppliers of capital, labor, and other resources have all received substantial returns for their contributions. Consumers have benefited from both the quantity and quality of goods and services available for consumption. Taxes on the business profits of firms, as well as on the payments made to suppliers of labor, materials, capital, and other inputs, have provided the revenues for government to increase its service to society. All of these contributions to social welfare stem directly from the efficiency of businesses that serve the economy.

Does this mean that firms do not or should not exercise social responsibility in a broader, perhaps more philanthropic, sense? Not necessarily. Firms exist by public consent to serve the needs of society. Only through the satisfactory execution of this mandate will business survive. As the needs and expectations of society (and hence the social requirements placed on the economic system) change, business must adapt and respond to its changing environment.

If social welfare could be measured, business firms might be expected to operate in a manner that would maximize some index of social well-being. The maximization of social welfare leads to important yet unanswerable questions. For example, how should the goods be produced? What combination of goods and services should be produced (including negative by-products such as pollution)? And how should the goods and services be distributed? These are some of the most vital questions faced in a free enterprise system, and as such, they are important issues in managerial economics.

In a market-oriented economy, the economic system produces and allocates goods and services through the market mechanism. Firms determine what consumers desire, bid for the resources necessary to produce these products, then make and distribute them. The suppliers of capital, labor, and raw materials must all be compensated out of the proceeds from the sale of the output, and competition (bargaining) takes place among these groups. Further, the firm competes with other firms for the consumer's dollar.

Although this process of market-determined production and allocation of goods and services is for the most part highly efficient, there are inherent difficulties in a totally unconstrained market economy that can prevent maximization of social welfare. Society has developed a variety of methods to alleviate these problems through the political system.

One of the difficulties with an unconstrained market economy is that certain groups can gain excessive economic power, permitting them to obtain too large a share of the value created by firms. To illustrate, the economics of producing and distributing electric power are such that only one firm can efficiently serve a given community. Further, there are no good substitutes for electric lighting. As a result, the electric companies are in a position to exploit consumers; they could charge high prices and earn excessive profits. Society's solution to this potential exploitation is direct regulation. Prices charged by electric companies and certain other monopolistic enterprises are controlled and held down to a level just sufficient to provide stockholders with a fair rate of return on their investment. The regulatory process is simple in concept; in practice it is costly, difficult to operate, and in many ways arbitrary. It is a poor substitute for competition, but it is a substitute that is sometimes necessary.

A second problem in a market economy occurs when, because of economies of scale or other conditions, a limited number of firms serve a given market. If the firms compete with one another, no exploitation occurs; however, if they conspire with one another in setting prices, they may be able to restrict output, obtain excessive profits, and thereby reduce social welfare. Antitrust laws are designed to prevent such collusion, as well as to prevent the merging of competing firms whenever the effect of the merger would be to lessen competition substantially. Like direct regulation, antitrust laws contain arbitrary elements and are costly to administer, but they, too, are necessary if economic justice, as defined by the body politic, is to be served.

A third problem is that under certain conditions, workers can be exploited. As a result, laws have been developed to equalize the bargaining power of employers and workers. These labor laws require firms to submit to collective bargaining and to refrain from certain unfair practices.[3]

A fourth problem faced by the economic system is that firms may impose costs on society through their production activities. For example, they may dump wastes into the air or the water or deface the earth, as in strip mining. If a steel mill creates polluted air, which causes people to paint their houses in three years instead of five or to clean their clothes more frequently or to suffer lung ailments or other health impairments, the mill imposes a cost on society in general. Failure to shift social costs back onto the firm—and, ultimately, to the consumers of its output—means that the firm and its customers gain because the firm does not pay the full costs of its activities. This results in an economically inefficient allocation of resources between industries and firms. Currently, much attention is being directed to the prob-

---

[3] In recent years the question of whether labor's bargaining position is too strong in some instances has been raised. For example, can powerful national unions such as the Teamsters use the threat of a strike to obtain "excessive" increases in wages, which may in turn be passed on to consumers in the form of higher prices and, thus, cause inflation? Those who believe this is the case have suggested that the antitrust laws should be applied to labor unions, especially to those bargaining with numerous small employers.

lem of internalizing social costs. Some of the practices used to internalize social costs include the establishment of emissions limits on manufacturing processes and on products that pollute (for example, autos), as well as the imposition of fines or outright closures of operations that do not meet the established standards.[4]

All the measures discussed above—utility regulation, antitrust laws, labor laws, and pollution control restrictions—are examples of actions taken by society to modify the behavior of business firms and to make this behavior more consistent with broad social goals. As we shall see, these constraints have a most important bearing on the operations of a business firm.

What does all this mean with respect to the microeconomic theory of the firm? Is the model too narrow in scope and thus inadequate for examining issues of social responsibility and for developing models of business decisions that adequately incorporate the role of business in society? On the contrary, the model not only provides an appropriate framework for analyzing the social responsibility of business, but it also helps us determine the cost to society of changing the requirements imposed on business.

Business firms are primarily economic entities, and as such can be expected to analyze social responsibility in the context of the economic model of the firm. This is an important consideration in examining the set of inducements that can channel the efforts of business in new directions that society desires. Similar considerations should also be taken into account before political pressures or regulations are imposed on firms to constrain their operations. For example, from the consumer's standpoint it is preferable to pay lower rates for gas, electric, and telephone services; but if public pressures on these regulated firms drive rates down too low, then profits will fall below the level necessary to provide an adequate return to investors; capital will not flow into the industries, and service will deteriorate. When such issues are considered, the economic model of the firm provides useful insights. The model emphasizes the close interrelationship between the firm and society. This in turn indicates that business must participate actively to develop and formulate its role in helping to achieve society's goals.

NATURE OF PROFITS

In order to understand both the theory of firm behavior and the role of the firm in a free enterprise economy one must understand the nature of profits. Indeed, profits are such a key element in the free enterprise system that it would fail to operate without profits and the profit motive. Given its importance, it is appropriate to analyze the nature of profits in some detail.

---

[4]Given the difficulty of estimating social costs, including the long-run effects on life itself, it is easy to see why political discussions of the subject run more toward prevention than toward compensation fines.

Business versus Economic Profit

The controversy about *profit* extends even to the definition of the term. The general public and the business community define profit using an accounting concept. To these groups *profit* is the residual of income minus the explicit (accounting) costs of doing business. It is the amount available to the equity capital position after payment for all other resources used by the firm. For clarification this definition of profit is often referred to as *business profit*.

The economist also defines profit as the excess of revenues over the costs of doing business. To the economist, however, equity capital is viewed as just another resource that must be paid if it is to be employed by the firm. Thus, the economist includes a normal rate of return on equity capital as a cost of doing business. This normal rate is the minimum return on capital necessary to obtain its use in a particular activity. Profit, then, to an economist is the excess of business profit over the normal or required return on the equity capital invested in a firm. This profit concept is frequently referred to as *economic profit*, to distinguish it from the business profit concept.

Recognizing the difference between the concepts of business profit and economic profit helps to sharpen one's focus on the questions of why profits exist and what their role in a free enterprise economy is. The concept of economic profit requires payment for the use of a valuable resource—equity capital. There is a normal rate of return, or profit, which is necessary to induce individuals to save and invest some of their funds rather than to spend their entire income for current consumption. This normal profit is simply a price for capital. It is no different than the price for other resources, such as labor, materials, and energy.

The existence of economic profits is a more complex issue. What explains the difference between the economist's concept of normal profits as a price of equity capital and the actual business profits earned by firms? In long-run equilibrium, economic profits would be zero if all firms operated in perfectly competitive industries. In other words, all firms would report business profit rates reflecting only a normal rate of return on equity investment. We know, however, that reported profit rates tend to vary widely among firms. Profit rates range from very low in the railroad and textile industries, for example, to very high in the pharmaceutical, office equipment, and other high-technology industries. While we can explain some of this variation by examining differences in the riskiness of doing business, economic profits (or losses) are undoubtedly earned by various firms at any point in time.[5] Several alternative theories have been proposed to explain why some firms earn economic profits.

---

[5] In Chapter 3 it is shown that if one business is inherently riskier than another, its normal profit rate should exceed that of the low-risk firm.

Frictional Theory of Economic Profits

A common explanation of economic profits (or losses) offered by economists is that markets are seldom in long-run equilibrium, but often in disequilibrium because of unanticipated changes in product demand or cost conditions. In other words, shocks occur in the economy, producing disequilibrium conditions that lead to nonnormal profits for some firms. For example, the emergence of a new product such as the automobile might lead to a marked increase in the demand for steel, and this might cause profits of steel firms to rise above the normal level for a period of time. Alternatively, a rise in the use of plastics might drive the steel firms' profits down. In the long run, barring impassable barriers to entry and exit, resources would flow into or out of the steel industry, driving rates of return back to normal levels, but during interim periods profits might be above or below normal because of frictional factors that prevent instantaneous adjustment to new market conditions.

Monopoly Theory of Economic Profits

A second rationale, the monopoly theory, is an extension of the frictional theory. It asserts that some firms, because of such factors as economies of scale, capital requirements, or patent protection, can build monopoly positions that allow them to keep their profits above normal for long periods. Monopoly, a most interesting topic, is discussed at length in Chapters 10 and 12 of this book, where we consider in detail why it exists, its effects, and how it can be controlled.

Innovation Theory of Economic Profits

A third theory of profit, the innovation theory, is also related to frictions. Under the innovation theory, above-normal profits arise as compensation for successful innovation. For example, the theory suggests that Xerox Corporation, which historically earned a high rate of return because it successfully developed and marketed a superior copying device, continued to receive these supernormal returns until other firms entered the field to compete with Xerox and drive its high profits down to a normal level.

Compensatory Theory of Economic Profits

The compensatory theory of economic profits holds that above-normal rates of return may simply constitute a reward to firms that are extraordinarily successful in meeting customer needs, maintaining efficient operations, and so forth. For example, if firms that operate at the industry's average level of efficiency receive normal rates of return, it is reasonable that firms that operate at above-average levels of efficiency will earn above-normal rates of return. Similarly, inefficient firms can be expected to earn relatively unsatisfactory (below-normal) rates of return. It is important to note that if the compensatory theory explains the bulk of economic profits earned at any one point in time, then such profits might be quite desirable. Penalties in the form of excess or windfall profits taxes may have the unfortunate consequence of stifling improvements in operating efficiency.

Interaction of the Various Theories

It should be obvious that each theory has elements of truth; one theory applies in one instance, another in another instance, and perhaps many are applicable in some cases. To illustrate, a very efficient farmer may earn an above-normal rate of return in accordance with the compensatory theory, but during a wartime farming boom already above-average profits may be augmented by abnormal or frictional profits. Similarly, Xerox's profit position might be explained in part by all four theories: The company is exceptionally well managed and has earned compensatory profits; it earned high frictional profits while 3M, IBM, Savin, and other firms were tooling up to enter the office copier field; it is earning monopoly profits, because it is protected to some extent by its patents; and it has certainly benefited from successful innovation.

Economic profits are an important keystone to a market-based economy. First, above-normal profits serve as a valuable signal that firm or industry output should be increased. Indeed, expansion by established firms or entry by new competitors often occurs quickly during periods of high profit. Just as above-normal profits provide a signal for expansion and entry, below-normal profits provide a signal for contraction and exit. Without economic profits we would lose one of the most important indicators affecting the allocation of scarce economic resources. Also, above-normal profits can constitute an important reward for efficiency, just as below-normal profits can constitute a necessary penalty for inefficiency. Thus, profits play a critical role both in providing an incentive for innovation and productive efficiency and as an allocator of scarce resources.

STRUCTURE OF THIS TEXT

Objectives

Reflecting the concept of managerial economics developed above, this text is designed to accomplish the following objectives:

1. To present those aspects of economics and the decision sciences that are most important and relevant in managerial decision making.

2. To provide a rationale or framework to help the student understand the nature of the firm as an integrated whole, as opposed to a loosely connected set of functional departments.

3. To demonstrate the interrelation between the firm and society and to illustrate the key role of business as an agent of social and economic welfare.

Outline of Topics

In this chapter we presented the basic economic model of the firm and we introduced value maximization, the central focus of the firm. Chapter 2 deals with optimization—the process of seeking the best way of accomplishing a stated objective. In Chapter 3 the basic model is expanded to include risk. We shall examine how to measure risk and how to incorporate it into the model.

Chapters 4 and 5 explore demand theory as well as the application of the economic theory of demand to business decisions. Chapter 6 discusses production theory. Chapter 7 develops theoretical aspects of cost analysis. Chapter 8 explores how to estimate cost functions and points out some difficulties in the estimation process. Chapter 9 discusses linear programming, an important tool for constrained optimization. Chapter 10 relates the roles of demand, production, and costs in determining market structures and explains the manner in which this relationship affects the nature of competition in an industry.

Chapter 11 sets forth the pricing policies called for under different market structures. The chapter shows the limitations of economic theory in a world of uncertainty, and it shows the ways firms actually establish price policies. Chapter 12 discusses how price-output decisions taken by firms operating in a completely unconstrained manner are not always in the public interest. The chapter also details how certain rules and regulations, including antitrust laws, have been developed to help make business decisions more consistent with the public interest.

Chapter 13 explores long-run investment decisions, or capital budgeting, showing how firms combine demand analysis, production and cost theory, and risk analysis—all under constraints imposed by society—to make the strategic long-run investment decisions that shape the future of individual firms and of society itself.

SUMMARY

In the first section of this chapter we defined *managerial economics* as the application of economic theory and methodology to the practice of managerial decision making. We also discussed the contributions from traditional economic study and the decision sciences.

As a first step in our analysis of managerial decision making, this chapter examined the *economic theory of the firm* as the basic model of how a firm operates. This model is based on the premise that managers seek to maximize the value of their firms, subject to a variety of constraints. Although we briefly discussed alternative models, including satisficing and multiple-goal models, we stressed the constrained economic model, which has proved most useful for analyzing the behavior of the firm.

We also examined the role of business in society and concluded that the interaction of the firm with society is an important aspect of managerial decision making. Understanding how business activities support the goals of society is a key component of managerial economics.

An important element in the model is the firm's profit stream—the value of the firm is the present value of expected future profits. Because profits are so critical to understanding both the theory of the firm and the role of the firm in a free enterprise economy, the nature of profits, including both the theories used to explain their existence and problems encountered in defining and measuring them, received attention.

The reader should always have in mind the overall nature of managerial economics, because only in this way can one see how each individual topic fits into the general scheme of things and how each section builds toward a general model of business behavior. To help provide a road map for managerial economics, we presented a topical outline in the final section of the chapter.

QUESTIONS

1.1 Why is it appropriate to view firms as primarily economic entities?

1.2 Explain how the valuation model given in Equation 1.2 could be used to describe the integrated nature of managerial decision making across the functional areas of business.

1.3 In terms of the valuation model discussed in this chapter, explain the effects of each of the following:

   a. The firm is required to install new equipment to reduce air pollution.

   b. The firm's marketing department, through heavy expenditures on advertising, increases sales substantially.

   c. The production department purchases new equipment which lowers manufacturing costs.

   d. The firm raises prices. Demand in the short run is unaffected, but in the longer run unit sales can be expected to decline.

   e. The Federal Reserve System takes actions that lower interest rates dramatically.

   f. The firm is confronting inflation in the general economy by exactly passing increased costs through to sales so that business profits (sales minus costs) remain constant. At the same time inflation is causing generally higher interest rates, and hence the discount rate increases.

1.4 It is sometimes argued that managers of large publicly-owned firms make decisions so as to maximize their own welfare as opposed to that of stockholders. Does the existence of such behavior create problems in using the microeconomic theory of the firm as a basis for examining managerial decision making?

1.5 Do you feel that it is reasonable to expect firms to take actions that are in the public interest but are detrimental to stockholders? Is regulation always necessary and appropriate to induce firms to act in the public interest?

1.6 How is the popular notion of business profit different from the economic concept as described in this chapter? What role does the idea of normal profits play in this difference?

1.7 What factors should one consider in examining the adequacy (or excesses) of profits for a firm or industry?

SELECTED REFERENCES

Asakura, Kanji. "Management in Japanese Society." *Managerial and Decision Economics* 3 (March 1982): 16–23.

Baumol, William J. *Business Behavior, Value and Growth*. New York: Macmillan, 1959.

Beasley, W. Howard. "Can Managerial Economics Aid the Chief Executive Officer?" *Managerial and Decision Economics* 2 (September 1981): 129–132.

Ciscel, David H., and Carroll, Thomas M. "The Determinants of Executive Salaries: An Econometric Survey." *Review of Economics and Statistics* 62 (February 1980): 7–13.

Carroll, Archie B. "A Three-Dimensional Conceptual Model of Corporate Performance." *Academy of Management Review* 4 (October 1979): 497–504.

Edwards, Franklin R. "Managerial Objectives in Regulated Industries: Expense Preference Behavior in Banking." *Journal of Political Economy* 75 (February 1977): 147–162.

Friedman, Milton. "The Methodology of Positive Economics." *Essays In Positive Economics*. Chicago: University of Chicago Press, 1953.

Goodin, Robert, and Waldner, Ilmar. "Thinking Big, Thinking Small, and Not Thinking At All." *Public Policy* 27 (Winter 1979): 1–24.

Goodpaster, Kenneth E., and Mathews, John B., Jr. "Can a Corporation Have a Conscience?" *Harvard Business Review* 60 (January–February 1982): 132–141.

Hirschey, Mark, and Pappas, James L. "Regulatory and Life Cycle Influences on Managerial Incentives." *Southern Economic Journal* 48 (October 1981): 327–334.

Jensen, Michael C., and Meckling, William H. "Theory of the Firm: Managerial Behavior, Agency Costs and Ownership Structure." *Journal of Financial Economics* 3 (1976): 305–360.

Lewellen, Wilbur G., and Huntsman, Blaine. "Managerial Pay and Corporate Performance." *American Economic Review* 60 (September 1970): 710–720.

Machlup, Fritz. "Theories of the Firm: Marginalist, Behavioral, Managerial." *American Economic Review* 57 (March 1967): 1–33.

Rappaport, Alfred. "Executive Incentives vs. Corporate Growth." *Harvard Business Review* 56 (July–August 1978): 81–88.

Shubik, Martin. "Approaches to the Study of Decision Making Relevant to the Firm." *Journal of Business* 34 (April 1961): 101–118.

———. "A Curmudgeon's Guide to Microeconomics." *Journal of Economic Literature* 8 (June 1970): 405–429.

Williamson, Oliver E. *The Economics of Discretionary Behavior: Managerial Objectives in a Theory of the Firm.* Englewood Cliffs, NJ: Prentice-Hall, 1964.

Wong, Robert E. "Profit Maximization and Alternative Theories: A Dynamic Reconciliation." *American Economic Review* 65 (September 1975): 689–694.

CHAPTER 2
ECONOMIC OPTIMIZATION

Rational decision making is the process of determining the best possible solution to a given problem. If only one solution, or action, is possible, and if we know what this solution is, then no decision problem exists, and decision making is not involved. However, if a number of alternative courses of action are available, the alternative that produces a result most consistent with the decision maker's goal is the optimal action. The process of finding this best action, or decision, is the essence of managerial economics.

In this chapter we introduce a number of basic economic concepts and fundamental principles of economic analysis. This material is essential to all aspects of managerial economics. In addition to providing an introduction to the tools and techniques of optimization, Chapter 2 provides insight into both the theory of the firm presented in the preceding chapter and the complexities of goal-oriented managerial activities.

MAXIMIZING THE VALUE OF THE FIRM

In managerial economics the primary objective of management is assumed to be maximization of the firm's value.[1] This objective, which was introduced in Chapter 1, is expressed in Equation 2.1:

$$\text{Value} = \sum_{t=1}^{n} \frac{\text{Profit}_t}{(1 + i)^t} = \sum_{t=1}^{n} \frac{\text{Total Revenue}_t - \text{Total Cost}_t}{(1 + i)^t}. \qquad \textbf{(2.1)}$$

Maximizing Equation 2.1 is a complex task, involving the determinants of revenues, costs, and the discount rate in each future year of some unspecified time. Revenues, costs, and the discount rate are interrelated, complicating the problem even more. A closer inspection of the relationships involved in Equation 2.1 should help clarify both the concept and the complexities.

A firm's total revenues are directly determined by the quantity of its products sold and the prices received. This is nothing more than a recognition that total revenue (*TR*) is the product of price (*P*) times quantity (*Q*), i.e., $TR = P \times Q$. For managerial decision making, the important considerations relate to factors that affect prices and quantities, and to the interrelationships between them. These factors include the choice of products the firm designs, manufactures, and sells; the advertising strategies it employs; the pricing policy it establishes; the general state of the economy it encounters; and the nature of the competition it faces in the marketplace. In short, the revenue relationship encompasses both demand and supply considerations.

The cost relationships involved in producing a firm's products are similarly complex. An analysis of costs requires examination of alternative production systems, technological options, input possibilities, and so on. The prices of the factors of production play an important role in cost determination, and thus factor supply considerations are important.

Finally, there is the relationship between the discount rate and the company's product mix, physical assets, and financial structure. These factors affect the cost and availability of financial resources for the firm, and ultimately determine the discount rate used by investors to establish a value for the firm.

To determine the optimal course of action requires that marketing, production, and financial decisions—as well as decisions related to personnel, product distribution, and so on—be combined into a single integrated system, one which shows how any action affects all parts of the firm. The economic model of the firm pro-

---

[1]In Chapter 1 it was pointed out that the firm operates subject to such constraints as antitrust laws, labor contracts, pollution-control requirements, and so on. We might also note that the firm seeks to maximize the wealth of its *existing owners*, so an action that raises the value of the entire firm but reduces the wealth of present owners would not be optimal. In subsequent chapters these and other qualifications are made more explicit, and the matter of wealth versus utility or satisfaction is considered.

vides a basis for this integration and the principles of economic analysis enable one to analyze the important interrelationships.

The complexities involved in the fully integrated decision-analysis limit its use to major planning decisions. For many day-to-day operating decisions, much less complicated *partial optimization techniques* are employed. Partial optimization abstracts from the complexity of the integrated decision process and concentrates on more limited objectives within the firm's various departments. For example, a marketing department is often required to determine the minimum cost advertising policy that will achieve some sales goal, given the firm's product line and constraints on market prices. Similarly, the production department is expected to minimize the cost of producing a specified quantity of output at a stated quality level. Here too, economic analysis can help managers reach optimal decisions.

The decision process involved in both fully integrated and partial optimization problems takes place in two steps. First, one must express the economic relationships in a form suitable for analysis—generally, this means expressing the problem in analytical terms. Second, one must apply various techniques to determine the optimal solution. In the material that follows, we first introduce a number of concepts that are useful for expressing decision problems in an economic framework. Then, we examine several economic relationships frequently used in the second part of the decision making process.

METHODS OF EXPRESSING ECONOMIC RELATIONSHIPS

Economic relationships are expressed in equations, tables where relationships are enumerated, and graphs where these relationships are plotted. A table or a graph may be sufficient for the purpose at hand, but when the problem is complex, equations are necessary so that one may employ the powerful tools of math analysis and computer simulation.

Functional Relationships: Equations

Perhaps the easiest way to examine various ways of expressing economic relationships and, at the same time, gain insight into the economics of optimization is to consider several functional relationships which play key roles in the basic valuation model. Consider first the relationship between units sold, Q, and total revenue, TR. Using functional notation, we can express the relationship as follows:

$$TR = f(Q). \tag{2.2}$$

Equation 2.2 is read "total revenue is a function of units sold." The value of the dependent variable, total revenue, is determined by the independent variable—units sold.[2]

Equation 2.2 does not indicate the specific relationship between units sold and total revenue; it merely states that a relationship exists. A more specific expression of the functional relationship is provided by the equation:

$$TR = P \times Q. \tag{2.3}$$

Here P represents the price at which each unit is sold, and the relationship between the dependent variable and the independent variable is more precisely specified. Total revenue is always equal to price times the number of units sold. If, for example, price is constant at \$1.50 regardless of the quantity sold, then the relationship between units sold and total revenue is precisely stated by the function:

$$TR = \$1.50 \times Q. \tag{2.4}$$

Functional Relationships: Tables and Graphs

In addition to equations, tables and graphs are often used to express economic relationships. The data in Table 2.1, for example, express exactly the same functional relationship specified by Equation 2.4, and this same function is graphically illustrated in Figure 2.1. All three methods of expressing relationships help one analyze data for managerial decision making.

TOTAL, AVERAGE, AND MARGINAL RELATIONSHIPS

Total, average, and marginal relationships are very useful in optimization analysis. The definitions of totals and averages are too well known to warrant restating, but it is perhaps appropriate to define the term *marginal*. A *marginal relationship* is defined as the change in the dependent variable of a function associated with a unitary change in one of the independent variables. In the total revenue function, marginal revenue is the change in total revenue associated with a one-unit change in units sold.

Because the essence of the optimizing process involves analysis of differences or changes, the marginal concept is of critical importance. Typically, we analyze an objective function by changing the various independent variables to see what effect these changes have on the dependent variable. In other words, we examine the *mar-*

---

[2] In an equation such as this one, the variable to the left of the equals sign is called the *dependent variable*, as its value *depends* on the size of the variable or variables to the right of the equals sign. The variables on the right-hand side of the equals sign are called *independent variables*, because their values are assumed to be determined outside, or *independently*, of the relationship expressed in the equation.

TABLE 2.1

Relationship between Total Revenue and Units Sold: Total Revenue = $1.50 × Units Sold

Units Sold	Total Revenue
1	$1.50
2	3.00
3	4.50
4	6.00
5	7.50
6	9.00

FIGURE 2.1

Graph of the Relationship between Total Revenue and Units Sold

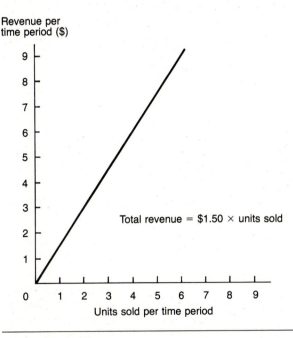

ginal effect of changes in the independent variables on the dependent variable. The purpose of this analysis is to determine that set of values for the independent, or decision, variables which optimizes the decision maker's objective function.

Relationship between Totals and Marginals

Table 2.2 shows the relationship between totals, marginals, and averages for a hypothetical profit function. Columns 1 and 2 show the output and profit relationship;

TABLE 2.2

Total, Marginal, and Average Relationships for a Profit Function

Units of Output Sold	Total Profits	Marginal Profits	Average Profits
Q	π^a	$\Delta\pi^b$	$\bar{\pi}^c$
(1)	(2)	(3)	(4)
0	$ 0	—	—
1	19	$19	$19
2	52	33	26
3	93	41	31
4	136	43	34
5	175	39	35
6	210	35	35
7	217	7	31
8	208	−9	26

[a] The Greek letter π (pi) is frequently used in economic and business literature to denote profits.

[b] The symbol Δ (delta) denotes difference or change. Thus, marginal profit is expressed as: $\Delta\pi = \pi_Q - \pi_{Q-1}$

[c] Average profit ($\bar{\pi}$) equals total profit (π) divided by total units (Q): $\bar{\pi} = \pi \div Q$.

column 3 shows marginal profits for each unit change in output, and column 4 gives the average profit at each level of output.

Marginal profit refers to the change in profit associated with each one-unit change in output. The marginal profit of the first unit of output is $19. This is the change from the $0 profits related to an output of 0 units to the $19 profit earned when one unit is produced. Likewise, the $33 marginal profit associated with the second unit of output is the increase in total profits ($52 − $19) that results when output is increased from one to two units.

The relationship between marginal and total values in decision analysis is important because when the marginal is positive, the total is increasing, and when the marginal is negative, the total is decreasing. The data in Table 2.2 can also be used to illustrate this point. The marginal profit associated with each of the first seven units of output is positive, and the total profits increase with output over this range. Since the marginal profit of the eighth unit is negative, however, profits are reduced if output is raised to that level. Thus, maximization of the profit function, or any function for that matter, occurs at the point where the marginal relationship shifts from positive to negative. This important relationship is examined again later in this chapter.

Relationship between Averages and Marginals

The relationship between average and marginal values is also important in managerial decision analysis. Since the marginal represents the change in the total, it follows that when the marginal is greater than the average, the average must be increasing. For example, if ten production workers average 200 units of output per day, and an eleventh worker (the marginal worker) producing 250 units is added to the work force, the average output of the workers increases. Likewise, if the marginal production worker produces fewer than 200 units per day, the average will decrease.

The data in Table 2.2 can be used to illustrate the relationship between marginal and average values. For the second through fifth units of output, marginal profit is greater than average profit and at each output average profit increases. Note that in going from four units of production to five, marginal profit, although declining from $43 to $39, is still greater than the $34 average profit at four units; hence, average profit *increases* to $35. So long as the marginal remains above the average, the average will rise. The marginal profit associated with the sixth unit, however, is $35, the same as the average at five units, so average profit remains unchanged between five and six units. Finally, the marginal profit of the seventh unit is below the average profit at six units, causing average profit to fall.

Graphing the Total, Marginal, and Average Relationships

The relationships between totals, marginals, and averages can also be demonstrated geometrically. Figure 2.2(a) presents a graph of the profit to output relationship given in Table 2.2. Each point on the curve represents an output-total profit combination taken from columns 1 and 2 of Table 2.2. The marginal and average profit data from Table 2.2 are plotted in Figure 2.2(b).

Just as there is an arithmetic relationship between the totals, marginals, and averages in the table, so too is there a corresponding geometric relationship on the graph. To see this relationship, consider first the average profit per unit of output at any point along the total profits curve. Average profit is always equal to total profit divided by the corresponding number of units of output. Geometrically, this relationship is represented by the slope of a line from the origin to the point of intersection on the total profits curve. For example, consider the slope of the line from the origin to point *B* in Figure 2.2(a). Slope is a measure of the steepness of a line, and it is defined as the increase (or decrease) in height per unit of movement out along the horizontal axis. The slope of a straight line passing through the origin is determined by dividing the *Y* coordinate at any point on the line by the corresponding *X* coordinate.[3] Thus, the slope of the line *OB* can be calculated by dividing $93 (the *Y* coordinate at point *B*) by 3 (the *X* coordinate at point *B*). Notice, however, that in this process we are dividing total profits by the corresponding units of output. This is the definition of average profit at that point. *Thus, at any point along a total curve, the corresponding average figure is given by the slope of a straight line from the origin to that point.* These average figures can also be graphed directly as in

---

[3]In general, slope $= \Delta Y/\Delta X = (Y_2 - Y_1)/(X_2 - X_1)$. Since X_1 and Y_1 are zero for any line going through the origin, slope $= Y_2/X_2$ or, more generally, slope $= Y/X$.

FIGURE 2.2

**Geometrical Representation of Total, Marginal, and Average Relationships: (a) Total Profit;
(b) Marginal and Average Profits**

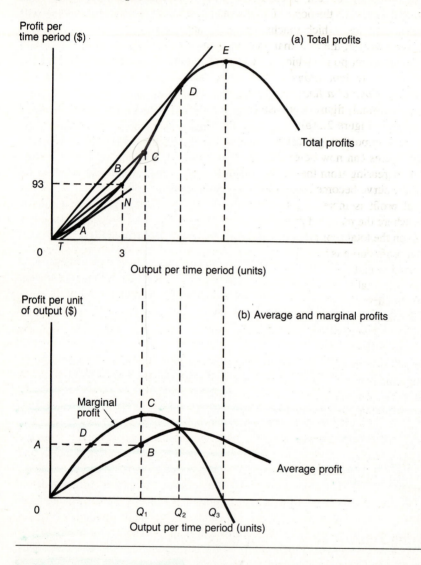

Figure 2.2(b). There, each point on the average profit curve is the corresponding
total profit divided by the output quantity.

The marginal relationship has a similar geometric association with the total
curve. In Table 2.2 each marginal figure was shown to be the change in total profit
associated with the last unit increase in output. This rise (or fall) in the total profit

associated with a one-unit increase in output is the *slope* of the total profit curve at that point.

Slopes of nonlinear curves are typically found geometrically by drawing a line tangent to the curve at the point of interest and determining the slope of the tangent. (A tangent is a line which touches but does not intersect the curve.) In Figure 2.2(a), for example, the marginal profit at point A is equal to the slope of the total profit curve at that point, which is equal to the slope of the tangent labeled TAN. *Therefore, at any point along a total curve, the corresponding marginal figure is given by the slope of a line drawn tangent to the total curve at that point.* These slope, or marginal, figures can also be graphed directly as shown by the marginal profit curve in Figure 2.2(b).

Several important geometric relationships between the total, marginal, and average figures can now be examined. First, note that the slope of the total profit curve is increasing from the origin to point C. That is, lines drawn tangent to the total profit curve become steeper as the point of tangency approaches point C, so marginal profit is increasing up to this point. This is also illustrated in Figure 2.2(b), where the marginal profit curve increases up to output Q_1, corresponding to point C on the total profit curve. At point C, called an *inflection point*, the slope of the total profit curve is maximized; thus, marginal (but not average or total) profit is maximized at that point. Between points C and E total profit continues to increase because marginal profit is still positive even though it is declining. At point E the total profit curve has a slope of zero and thus is neither rising nor falling. Marginal profit at this point (output Q_3 in Figure 2.2(b)) is therefore zero, and total profit is maximized. Beyond E the total profit curve has a negative slope, and marginal profit is negative.

In addition to the total-average and total-marginal relationships, the relationship between marginals and averages is also demonstrated in Figure 2.2(b). At low output levels, where the marginal profit curve lies above the average, the average is rising; the higher marginal profits are pulling up the average profits. Although marginal profit reaches a maximum at output Q_1 and declines thereafter, the average curve continues to rise as long as the marginal lies above it. At output Q_2, marginal and average profits are equal, and here the average profit curve reaches its maximum value. Beyond Q_2, the marginal curve lies below the average, and the average is falling.

Deriving Totals from the Marginal or Average Curve

Just as we can derive marginal and average profit figures from the total profit curve in Figure 2.2(a), we can also determine total profits from the marginal or average profit curves of Figure 2.2(b). Consider first the derivation of total profits from the average curve. Total profit is simply average profit times the corresponding number of units of output. The total profit associated with Q_1 units of output, for example, is average profit, A, times output, Q_1, or, equivalently, total profit is equal to the area of the rectangle $OABQ_1$. This relationship holds for all points along the average profit curve.

A similar relationship exists between marginal and total profits. Recall that the total is equal to the sum of all the marginals up to the specified output level. Thus, the total profit for any output is equal to the sum of the marginal profits up to that output quantity. Geometrically, this is the area under the marginal curve from the Y axis to the output quantity under consideration. At output Q_1, the total profit is equal to the area under the marginal profit curve, or the area OCQ_1.

Because these average/marginal/total relationships are the basis for many important microeconomic principles, they should be thoroughly understood. The most widely known example of their use is in short-run profit maximization: Marginal cost and revenue curves are derived from average or total figures, and profits are maximized where marginal profit (equal to marginal revenue minus marginal cost) is zero. Thus, profit is maximized where marginal revenue is equal to marginal cost. This is only one illustration of the use of these concepts; we will encounter others in the study of managerial economics.

First, however, it is useful to consider some elementary calculus, which is extremely valuable for finding optimal solutions to economic problems. The calculus concepts also further clarify the relationships between marginals, averages, and totals and the importance of these relationships in the optimization process.

DIFFERENTIAL CALCULUS[4]

Although tables and graphs are useful for explaining concepts, equations are frequently better suited for problem solving. One reason is that the powerful analytical technique of differential calculus can often be employed to locate maximum or minimum values of an objective function very efficiently through marginal analysis. Additionally, the basic calculus concepts are easily extended to decision problems where the options available to the decision maker are limited by one or more constraints. Thus, the calculus approach is especially useful for the constrained optimization problems which characterize managerial decision making.

Concept of a Derivative

Earlier, we defined a marginal value as *the change in the value of the dependent variable associated with a one-unit change in an independent variable*. Consider

---

[4]This section will be quite straightforward for readers who are familiar with the techniques of differential calculus. While a knowledge of calculus is not necessary to follow the main ideas presented in the text, because we provide both verbal and geometric interpretations of calculus formulations, we encourage all readers who do not have a good grasp of calculus to go through this section carefully. Calculus was developed specifically for handling problems such as those

FIGURE 2.3

Illustration of Changing $\Delta Y/\Delta X$ over the Range of a Curve

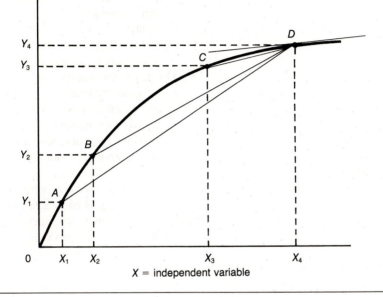

the unspecified function $Y = f(X)$. Using Δ (read delta) to denote change, we can express the change in the value of the independent variable, X, by the notation ΔX and the change in the dependent variable, Y, as ΔY.

The ratio $\Delta Y/\Delta X$ provides a very general specification of the marginal concept:

$$\text{Marginal } Y = \frac{\Delta Y}{\Delta X} . \qquad (2.5)$$

The change in Y, ΔY, divided by the change in X, ΔX, indicates the change in the dependent variable associated with a one-unit change in the value of X.

Figure 2.3, which is a graph of a function relating Y to X, illustrates this relationship. For values of X close to the origin, a relatively small change in X provides a large change in Y. Thus, the value of $\Delta Y/\Delta X = (Y_2 - Y_1)/(X_2 - X_1)$ is relatively large, showing that a small increase in X induces a large increase in Y. The situation is reversed the farther out one moves along the X axis. A large increase in X, say

---

found in managerial economics, so some concepts can be understood much more easily when expressed in these terms. Furthermore, the level of calculus we use is quite elementary and therefore not difficult to learn.

from X_3 to X_4, produces only a small increase in Y, from Y_3 to Y_4, so $\Delta Y/\Delta X$ is small.

It is clear that the marginal relationship between X and Y, as shown in Figure 2.3, changes at different points on the curve. When the curve is relatively steep, the dependent variable Y is highly responsive to changes in the independent variable; but when the curve is relatively flat, Y does not respond as significantly to changes in X.

In concept, a *derivative* is a precise specification of the general marginal relationship; $\Delta Y/\Delta X$. Finding a derivative involves finding the value of the ratio $\Delta Y/\Delta X$ for extremely small changes in the independent variable. The mathematical notation for a derivative is:

$$\frac{dY}{dX} = \lim_{\Delta X \to 0} \frac{\Delta Y}{\Delta X},$$

which is read: "The derivative of Y with respect to X equals the limit of the ratio $\Delta Y/\Delta X$, as ΔX approaches zero."[5]

This concept of the derivative as the limit of a ratio is precisely equivalent to the slope of a curve at a point. Figure 2.4 presents this idea, using the same curve relating Y to X shown in Figure 2.3. Notice that in Figure 2.4 the *average* slope of the curve between points A and D is measured as:

$$\frac{\Delta Y}{\Delta X} = \frac{Y_4 - Y_1}{X_4 - X_1},$$

and is shown as the slope of the chord connecting the two points. Similarly, the average slope of the curve can be measured over smaller and smaller intervals of X and shown by other chords, such as those connecting points B and C with D. At the limit, as ΔX approaches zero, the ratio $\Delta Y/\Delta X$ is equal to the slope of a line drawn tangent to the curve at point D. *The slope of this tangent is defined as the deriva-*

---

[5] A limit can be explained briefly in the following manner: If the value of a function $Y = f(X)$ approaches a constant Y^* as the value of the independent variable X approaches X^*, then Y^* is called the limit of the function as X approaches X^*. This would be written as:

$$\lim_{x \to x^*} f(X) = Y^*.$$

For example, if $Y = X - 4$, then the limit of this function as X approaches 5 is 1; that is:

$$\lim_{x \to 5} (X - 4) = 1.$$

This says that the value of X approaches but does not quite reach 5; the value of the function $Y = X - 4$ comes closer and closer to 1. This concept of a limit is examined in detail in any introductory calculus textbook.

FIGURE 2.4

Illustration of a Derivative as the Slope of a Curve

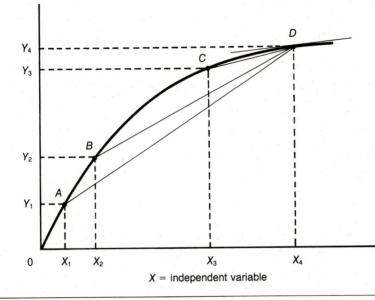

Y = dependent variable

X = independent variable

tive, dY/dX, *of the function at point* D; *it measures the marginal change in* Y *associated with a very small change in* X *at that point.*

For example, the dependent variable *Y* might be total revenue, and the independent variable might be output. The derivative *dY/dX* then shows precisely how revenue and output are related at a specific output level. Since the change in revenue associated with a change in output is defined as the marginal revenue, the derivative of the total revenue provides a precise measure of marginal revenue at any specific output level. A similar situation exists for total cost: The derivative of the total cost function at any output level indicates the marginal cost at that output.

Derivatives provide much useful information in managerial economics. Other illustrations of their usefulness will be considered later, but first the rules for finding the derivatives of certain frequently encountered functions are provided.

RULES FOR DIFFERENTIATING A FUNCTION

Determining the derivative of a function is not a particularly difficult task; it simply involves applying a basic formula to the function. The basic formulas or rules for

FIGURE 2.5

Graph of a Constant Function: Y = Constant; dY/dX = 0

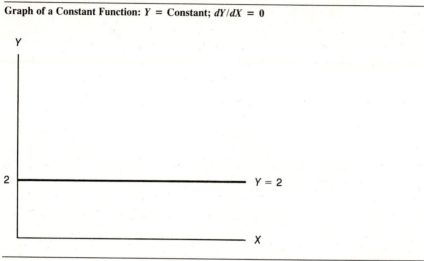

differentiation are presented below. Proofs are omitted here, but they can be found in any introductory calculus textbook.

Constants

The derivative of a constant is always zero; that is, if Y = a constant, then:

$$\frac{dY}{dX} = 0.$$

This situation is graphed in Figure 2.5 for the example $Y = 2$. Since Y is defined to be a constant, its value does not vary as X changes, and hence dY/dX must be zero.

Powers

The derivative of a power function such as $Y = aX^b$, where a and b are constants, is equal to the exponent b multiplied by the coefficient a times the variable X raised to the $b - 1$ power:

$$Y = aX^b$$

$$\frac{dY}{dX} = b \cdot a \cdot X^{(b-1)}.$$

For example, given the function:

$$Y = 2X^3,$$

then:

$$\frac{dY}{dX} = 3 \cdot 2 \cdot X^{(3-1)}$$

$$= 6X^2.$$

Two further examples of power functions should clarify this rule. The derivative of the function $Y = X^3$ is given as:

$$\frac{dY}{dX} = 3 \cdot X^2.$$

The exponent, 3, is multiplied by the implicit coefficient, 1, and in turn by the variable, X, raised to the second power.

Finally, the derivative of the function $Y = 0.5X$ is:

$$\frac{dY}{dX} = 1 \cdot 0.5 \cdot X^{1-1} = 1 \cdot 0.5 \cdot X^0 = 0.5.$$

The implicit exponent, 1, is multiplied by the coefficient, 0.5, times the variable, X, raised to the zero power. Since any number raised to the zero power equals 1, the result is 0.5.

Again, a graph may help to make the power function concept clear. In Figure 2.6, the last two power functions given above, $Y = X^3$ and $Y = 0.5X$, are graphed. Consider first $Y = 0.5X$. The derivative of this function, $dY/dX = 0.5$, is a constant, indicating that the slope of the function is a constant. This can be seen readily from the graph. The derivative measures the *rate of change*. If the rate of change is constant, as it must be if the basic function is linear, then the derivative of the function must be a constant. The second function, $Y = X^3$, rises at an increasing rate as X increases. The derivative of the function, $dY/dX = 3X^2$, also increases as X becomes larger, indicating that the slope of the function is increasing or that the rate of change is increasing.

Sums and Differences

The following notation is used throughout the remainder of this section to express a number of other important rules of differentiation:

FIGURE 2.6

Graphs of Power Functions

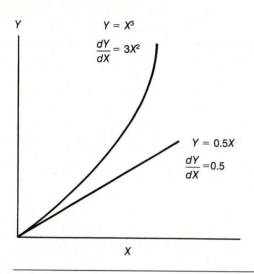

$U = g(X)$: U is an unspecified function, g, of X.

$V = h(X)$: V is an unspecified function, h, of X.

The derivative of a sum (difference) is equal to the sum (difference) of the derivatives of the individual terms. Thus, if $Y = U + V$, then:

$$\frac{dY}{dX} = \frac{dU}{dX} + \frac{dV}{dX}.$$

For example, if $U = g(X) = 2X^2$, $V = h(X) = -X^3$, and $Y = U + V = 2X^2 - X^3$, then:

$$\frac{dY}{dX} = 4X - 3X^2.$$

Here the derivative of the first term, $2X^2$, is found to be $4X$ by the power rule; the derivative of the second term, $-X^3$, is found to be $-3X^2$ by that same rule; and the derivative of the total function is the sum of the derivatives of the parts.

Consider a second example of this rule. If $Y = 300 + 5X + 2X^2$, then:

$$\frac{dY}{dX} = 0 + 5 + 4X.$$

The derivative of 300 is 0 by the constant rule; the derivative of $5X$ is 5 by the power rule; and the derivative of $2X^2$ is $4X$ also by the power rule.

Products

The derivative of the product of two expressions is equal to the sum of the first term multiplied by the derivative of the second, *plus* the second term times the derivative of the first. Thus, if $Y = U \cdot V$, then:

$$\frac{dY}{dX} = U \cdot \frac{dV}{dX} + V \cdot \frac{dU}{dX}.$$

For example, if $Y = 3X^2(3 - X)$, then letting $U = 3X^2$ and $V = (3 - X)$:

$$\frac{dY}{dX} = 3X^2 \left(\frac{dV}{dX} \right) + (3 - X) \left(\frac{dU}{dX} \right)$$

$$= 3X^2(-1) + (3 - X)(6X)$$

$$= -3X^2 + 18X - 6X^2$$

$$= 18X - 9X^2.$$

The first factor, $3X^2$, is multiplied by the derivative of the second, -1, and added to the second factor, $3 - X$, times the derivative of the first, $6X$. Simplifying the expression results in the final expression shown.

Quotients

The derivative of the quotient of two expressions is equal to the denominator multiplied by the derivative of the numerator *minus* the numerator times the derivative of the denominator—all divided by the square of the denominator. Thus, if $Y = U/V$, then:

$$\frac{dY}{dX} = \frac{V \cdot \dfrac{dU}{dX} - U \cdot \dfrac{dV}{dX}}{V^2}.$$

For example, if $U = 2X - 3$ and $V = 6X^2$, then:

$$Y = \frac{2X - 3}{6X^2}$$

and

$$\frac{dY}{dX} = \frac{6X^2 \cdot 2 - (2X - 3)\,12X}{36X^4}$$

$$= \frac{12X^2 - 24X^2 + 36X}{36X^4}$$

$$= \frac{36X - 12X^2}{36X^4}$$

$$= \frac{3 - X}{3X^3}\,.$$

The denominator, $6X^2$, is multiplied by the derivative of the numerator, 2. Subtracted from this is the numerator, $2X - 3$, times the derivative of the denominator, $12X$. The result is then divided by the square of the denominator, $36X^4$. Algebraic reduction results in the final expression of the derivative.

Function of a Function (Chain Rule)

The derivative of a function of a function is found as follows. If $Y = f(U)$, where $U = g(X)$, then:

$$\frac{dY}{dX} = \frac{dY}{dU} \cdot \frac{dU}{dX}\,.$$

For example, if $Y = 2U - U^2$, and $U = 2X^3$, then we find dY/dX as follows:

Step 1

$$\frac{dY}{dU} = 2 - 2U.$$

Substituting for U, we have:

$$\frac{dY}{dU} = 2 - 2(2X^3)$$

$$= 2 - 4X^3.$$

Step 2

$$\frac{dU}{dX} = 6X^2.$$

Step 3

$$\frac{dY}{dX} = \frac{dY}{dU} \cdot \frac{dU}{dX}$$

$$= (2 - 4X^3) \cdot 6X^2$$

$$= 12X^2 - 24X^5.$$

Further examples of this rule should indicate its usefulness in obtaining derivatives of many functions.

Example 1

$$Y = \sqrt{X^2 - 1}.$$

Let $U = X^2 - 1$. Then, $Y = \sqrt{U} = U^{1/2}$.

$$\frac{dY}{dU} = \frac{1}{2}U^{-1/2}$$

$$= \frac{1}{2U^{1/2}}.$$

Substituting $X^2 - 1$ for U in the derivative results in:

$$\frac{dY}{dU} = \frac{1}{2(X^2 - 1)^{1/2}}.$$

Since $U = X^2 - 1$:

$$\frac{dU}{dX} = 2X.$$

Using the function of a function rule, $dY/dX = dY/dU \cdot dU/dX$, so:

$$\frac{dY}{dX} = \frac{1}{2(X^2 - 1)^{1/2}} \cdot 2X$$

$$= \frac{X}{\sqrt{X^2 - 1}}.$$

Example 2

$$Y = \frac{1}{X^2 - 2}.$$

Let $U = X^2 - 2$. Then $Y = 1/U$, and, using the quotient rule, we find:

$$\frac{dY}{dU} = \frac{U \cdot 0 - 1 \cdot 1}{U^2}$$

$$= -\frac{1}{U^2} \cdot$$

Substituting $(X^2 - 2)$ for U we obtain:

$$\frac{dY}{dU} = -\frac{1}{(X^2 - 2)^2} \cdot$$

Since $U = X^2 - 2$:

$$\frac{dU}{dX} = 2X.$$

Therefore:

$$\frac{dY}{dX} = \frac{dY}{dU} \cdot \frac{dU}{dX} = -\frac{1}{(X^2 - 2)^2} \cdot 2X$$

$$= -\frac{2X}{(X^2 - 2)^2} \cdot$$

Example 3

$$Y = (2X + 3)^2.$$

Let $U = 2X + 3$. Then $Y = U^2$, and:

$$\frac{dY}{dU} = 2U.$$

Since $U = 2X + 3$:

$$\frac{dY}{dU} = 2(2X + 3)$$

$$= 4X + 6,$$

and

$$\frac{dU}{dX} = 2.$$

Thus:

$$\frac{dY}{dX} = \frac{dY}{dU} \cdot \frac{dU}{dX} = (4X + 6)2$$

$$= 8X + 12.$$

USE OF DERIVATIVES TO MAXIMIZE OR MINIMIZE FUNCTIONS

The process of optimization frequently requires one to find the maximum or minimum value for a function. For a function to be at a maximum or minimum, its slope or marginal value must be zero. The *derivative* of a function is a very precise measure of its slope or marginal value at a particular point. Thus, maximization or minimization of a function occurs where its derivative is equal to zero. To illustrate, consider the following profit function:

$$\pi = -\$10,000 + \$400Q - \$2Q^2. \tag{2.6}$$

Here π = total profit, and Q is output in units. As shown in Figure 2.7, if output is zero, the firm incurs a $10,000 loss (fixed costs are $10,000); but as output rises,

FIGURE 2.7

Profit as a Function of Output

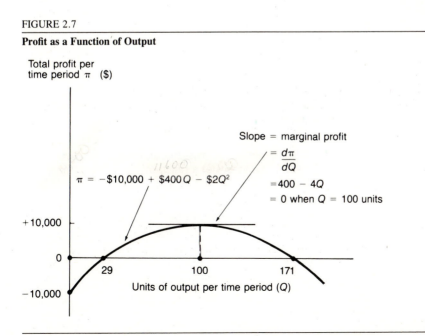

Total profit per
time period π ($)

Slope = marginal profit

$= \dfrac{d\pi}{dQ}$

$\pi = -\$10,000 + \$400Q - \$2Q^2$

$= 400 - 4Q$

$= 0$ when $Q = 100$ units

+10,000

0

29   100   171

−10,000

Units of output per time period (Q)

profit also rises. A breakeven point (the output level where profit is zero) is reached at 29 units of output; profit is maximized at 100 units and declines thereafter.

The profit maximizing output could be found by calculating the value of the function at a number of outputs, then plotting these as is done in Figure 2.7. The maximum can also be located by finding the derivative, or marginal, of the function, then determining the value of Q that makes the derivative (marginal) equal to zero.

$$\text{Marginal Profit } (M\pi) = \frac{d\pi}{dQ} = \$400 - \$4Q.$$

Setting the derivative equal to zero results in:

$$\$400 - \$4Q = 0$$

$$\$4Q = \$400$$

$$Q = 100 \text{ units}$$

Therefore, when $Q = 100$, marginal profit is zero and total profit is at a maximum. Even in this simple illustration it is easier to locate the profit maximizing value by calculus than by graphic analysis; had the function been more complex, the calculus solution might have been the only efficient means of determining the profit maximizing output level.

Distinguishing Maximums from Minimums

A problem can arise when derivatives are being used to locate maximums or minimums. The first derivative of the total function provides a measure of whether the function is rising or falling at any point. To be maximized or minimized, the function must be neither rising nor falling; that is, the slope as measured by the first derivative must be zero. However, since the marginal value or derivative will be zero for both maximum and minimum values of a function, further analysis is necessary to determine whether a maximum or a minimum has been located.

This point is illustrated in Figure 2.8 where we see that the slope of the total profit curve is zero at both points A and B. Point A, however, locates the output that minimizes profits, while B locates the profit-maximizing output.

The concept of a *second-order* derivative is used to distinguish between maximums and minimums along a function. The second-order derivative is simply the derivative of the original derivative; it is determined in precisely the same manner as a first derivative. If total profit is given by the equation $\pi = a - bQ + cQ^2 - dQ^3$, as in Figure 2.8, then the first-order derivative which defines the marginal profit function is:

FIGURE 2.8

Locating Maximum and Minimum Values of a Function

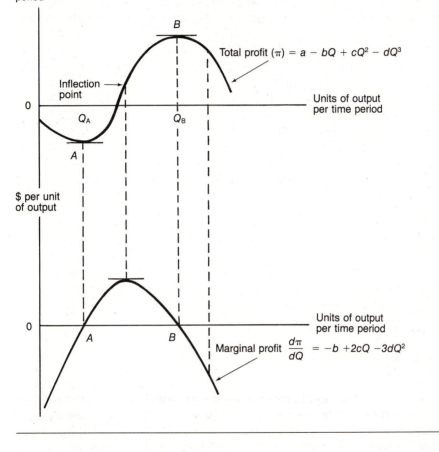

$$\frac{d\pi}{dQ} = M\pi = -b + 2cQ - 3dQ^2. \qquad (2.7)$$

The second-order derivative of the total profit function is the derivative of the marginal profit function, Equation 2.7:

$$\frac{d^2\pi}{dQ^2} = \frac{dM\pi}{dQ} = 2c - 6dQ.$$

Just as the first derivative measures the slope of the total profit function, the second derivative measures the slope of the first derivative or, in this case, the slope of the marginal profit curve. We can use the second derivative to distinguish between points of maximization and minimization because the second derivative of a function is always *negative* when evaluated at a point of *maximization* and *positive* at a point of *minimization*.

The reason for this inverse relationship can be seen in Figure 2.8. Note that profits reach a local minimum at point A because marginal profits, which have been negative and therefore causing total profits to fall, suddenly become positive. Marginal profits pass through the zero level from below at point A and hence are increasing or positively sloped. The reverse situation holds at a point of local maximization; the marginal value is positive but declining up to the point where the total function is maximized, and it is negative after that point. Thus, the marginal function is negatively sloped (that is, *its* derivative is negative) at the point of maximization of the total function.

A numerical example should help clarify this concept. Assume that the total profit function illustrated in Figure 2.8 is given by the following equation:

$$\text{Total Profit} = \pi = -\$3{,}000 - \$2{,}400Q + \$350Q^2 - \$8.333Q^3. \quad \textbf{(2.8)}$$

Marginal profit is given by the first derivative of the total profit function:

$$\text{Marginal Profit} = \frac{d\pi}{dQ} = -\$2{,}400 + \$700Q - \$25Q^2. \quad \textbf{(2.9)}$$

Total profit is either maximized or minimized at the points where the first derivative (marginal profit) is zero; that is, where:

$$\frac{d\pi}{dQ} = -\$2{,}400 + \$700Q - \$25Q^2 = 0. \quad \textbf{(2.10)}$$

Output quantities of 4 and 24 units satisfy Equation 2.10 and are therefore points of either maximum or minimum profits.[6]

---

[6] Any equation of the form $O = aX^2 + bX + c$ is a quadratic, and its two roots can be found by the general quadratic equation:

$$X = \frac{-b \pm \sqrt{b^2 - 4ac}}{2a}$$

Substituting the values from Equation 2.9 into the quadratic equation, we obtain:

$$X = \frac{-700 \pm \sqrt{700^2 - 4(-25)(-2{,}400)}}{2(-25)} = \frac{-700 \pm \sqrt{490{,}000 - 240{,}000}}{-50}$$

$$X = \frac{-700 \pm \sqrt{250{,}000}}{-50} = \frac{-700 \pm 500}{-50}.$$

Evaluation of the second derivative of the total profit function at each of these output levels will indicate whether they are minimums or maximums. The second derivative of the total profit function is found by taking the derivative of the marginal profit function, Equation 2.9:

$$\frac{d^2\pi}{dQ^2} = \frac{dM\pi}{dQ} = \$700 - \$50Q.$$

At output quantity $Q = 4$:

$$\frac{d^2\pi}{dQ^2} = \$700 - \$50 \cdot 4 = \$500.$$

Since the second derivative is positive, indicating that marginal profits are increasing, total profit is *minimized* at 4 units of output. In other words, total profit at 4 units of output corresponds to point A in Figure 2.8.

Evaluating the second derivative at 24 units of output, we obtain:

$$\frac{d^2\pi}{dQ^2} = \$700 - \$50 \cdot 24 = -\$500.$$

Since the second derivative is negative at 24 units, indicating that marginal profit is decreasing, the total profit function has reached a *maximum* at that point. This output level corresponds to point B in Figure 2.8.

Use of Derivatives to Maximize the Difference between Two Functions

The very important and well-known microeconomic corollary that marginal revenue equals marginal cost at the output level where profits are maximized has its basis in the calculus of optimization. It stems from the fact that the distance between two functions is maximized at the point where their slopes are the same; Figure 2.9 illustrates the point. Here hypothetical revenue and cost functions are shown. Total

---

The plus root is:

$$X_1 = \frac{-700 + 500}{-50} = \frac{-200}{-50} = 4 \text{ units,}$$

and the minus root is:

$$X_2 = \frac{-700 - 500}{-50} = \frac{-1,200}{-50} = 24 \text{ units.}$$

FIGURE 2.9

Total Revenue, Total Cost, and Profit Maximization

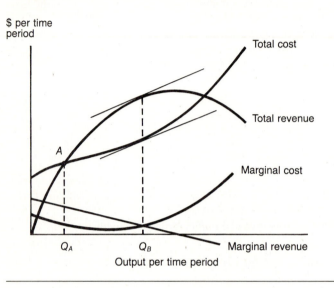

profit is equal to total revenue minus total cost and is, therefore, equal to the vertical distance between the two curves at any output level. This distance is maximized at output Q_B, where the slopes of the revenue and cost curves are equal. Since the slopes of the total revenue and total cost curves measure marginal revenues, MR, and marginal costs, MC, where these slopes are equal, $MR = MC$.

The reason that Q_B is the profit maximizing output can be seen by considering the shapes of the two curves to the right of point A. At A total revenue equals total cost, and we have a breakeven point; that is, an output quantity where profits are zero. At output quantities just beyond Q_A, total revenue is rising faster than total cost, so profits are increasing and the curves are spreading farther apart. This divergence of the curves continues as long as total revenue is rising faster than total cost; in other words, as long as $MR > MC$. Once the slope of the total revenue curve is exactly equal to the slope of the total cost curve—in other words, where marginal revenue equals marginal cost—the two curves will be parallel and no longer diverging. This occurs at output Q_B. Beyond Q_B the slope of the cost curve is greater than that of the revenue curve (marginal cost is greater than marginal revenue), so the distance between them is decreasing and total profits decline.

A numerical example will help to clarify this use of derivatives. Consider the following revenue, cost, and profit functions. Let:

$$\text{Total Revenue} = TR = 41.5Q - 1.1Q^2.$$

Total Cost $= TC = 150 + 10Q - 0.5Q^2 + 0.02Q^3$.

Total Profit $= \pi = TR - TC$.

The profit-maximizing output can be found by substituting the total revenue and total cost functions into the profit function, then analyzing the first and second derivatives of that equation:

$$\pi = TR - TC$$

$$= 41.5Q - 1.1Q^2 - (150 + 10Q - 0.5Q^2 + 0.02Q^3)$$

$$= 41.5Q - 1.1Q^2 - 150 - 10Q + 0.5Q^2 - 0.02Q^3$$

$$= -150 + 31.5Q - 0.6Q^2 - 0.02Q^3.$$

Marginal profit, the first derivative of the profit function, is:

$$M\pi = \frac{d\pi}{dQ} = 31.5 - 1.2Q - 0.06Q^2.$$

Setting marginal profit equal to zero and using the quadratic equation to solve for the two roots, we obtain $Q_1 = -35$ and $Q_2 = +15$. Since negative output quantities are not possible, Q_1 is a nonfeasible output level and can be discarded.

   An evaluation of the second derivative of the profit function at $Q = 15$ will indicate whether this is a point of profit maximization or profit minimization. The second derivative is given by:

$$\frac{d^2\pi}{dQ^2} = \frac{dM\pi}{dQ} = -1.2 - 0.12Q.$$

Evaluating this derivative at $Q = 15$ indicates a value of -3.0; therefore, $Q = 15$ is a point of profit maximization.

   To see the relationships of marginal revenue and marginal cost to profit maximization, consider once again the general profit expression $\pi = TR - TC$. Using the sums and differences rule of differentiation, note that a completely general expression for marginal profit is:

$$M\pi = \frac{d\pi}{dQ} = \frac{dTR}{dQ} - \frac{dTC}{dQ}.$$

Given that dTR/dQ is by definition the expression for marginal revenue, MR, and that dTC/dQ represents marginal cost, MC, we have:

$$M\pi = MR - MC.$$

Now, since maximization of any function requires that the first derivative be equal to zero, profit maximization will occur where:

$$M\pi = MR - MC = 0,$$

or where:

$$MR = MC.$$

Continuing with our numerical example, marginal revenue and marginal cost are found by differentiating the total revenue and total cost functions:

$$MR = \frac{dTR}{dQ} = 41.5 - 2.2Q.$$

$$MC = \frac{dTC}{dQ} = 10 - Q + 0.06Q^2.$$

At the profit-maximizing output level, $MR = MC$; thus:

$$MR = 41.5 - 2.2Q = 10 - Q + 0.06Q^2 = MC.$$

Combining terms, we obtain:

$$-31.5 + 1.2Q + 0.06Q^2 = 0,$$

which is identical to the expression obtained when the first derivative of the profit function is set to zero. Solving for the roots of this equation (again using the quadratic equation) results in $Q_1 = -35$ and $Q_2 = 15$, the same values found above. This confirms the fact that marginal revenue does equal marginal cost at the output where profit is maximized.[7]

To conclude the example, Figure 2.10 presents graphs of the revenue, cost, and profit functions. The upper section of the graph shows the revenue and cost functions; at 15 units of output, the slopes of the two curves are equal, and $MR = MC$. The lower section of the figure shows the profit function, and the profit maximizing output is shown to be 15 units, at which output $d\pi/dQ = 0$ and $d^2\pi/dQ^2 < 0$.

---

[7]This example also illustrates that while MR must equal MC at the profit-maximizing activity level, the converse does not hold. Profits are not necessarily maximized at a point where $MR = MC$, as for example at $Q = -35$ in the current problem.

FIGURE 2.10

Profit-Maximizing Output Conditions

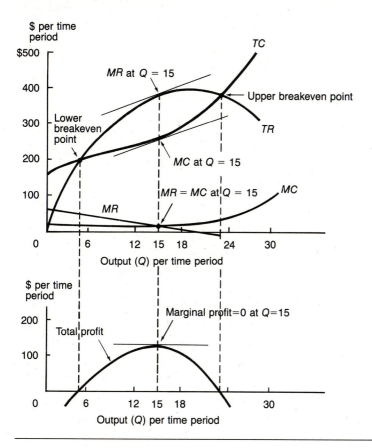

MULTIVARIATE OPTIMIZATION

Since most economic relationships involve more than two variables, it is necessary to extend the concept of differentiation to equations with three or more variables. Consider the demand function for a product where the quantity demanded, Q, is determined by the price charged, P, and the level of advertising expenditure, A. Such a function would be written as:

$$Q = f(P,A). \tag{2.11}$$

When analyzing multivariable relationships, such as the one in Equation 2.11, we need to know the marginal effect of each independent variable on the dependent variable. In other words, optimization in this case requires an analysis of how a change in each independent variable affects the dependent variable, *holding constant the effect of all other independent variables*. The partial derivative is the calculus concept used for this type of marginal analysis.

Using the demand function of Equation 2.11, we can examine two partial derivatives:[8]

1. The partial of Q with respect to price = $\partial Q/\partial P$.

2. The partial of Q with respect to advertising expenditure = $\partial Q/\partial A$.

The rules for determining partial derivatives are essentially the same as those for simple derivatives. Since the concept of a partial derivative involves an assumption that all variables except the one with respect to which the derivative is being taken remain unchanged, those variables are treated as constants in the differentiation process. Consider the equation $Y = 10 - 4X + 3XZ - Z^2$. In this function there are two independent variables, X and Z, so two partial derivatives can be evaluated. To determine the partial with respect to X, note that the function can be rewritten as:

$$Y = 10 - 4X + (3Z)X - Z^2.$$

Since Z is treated as a constant, the partial derivative of Y with respect to X is:

$$\frac{\partial Y}{\partial X} = 0 - 4 + 3Z - 0$$

$$= -4 + 3Z.$$

In determining the partial of Y with respect to Z, X is treated as a constant, so we can write:

$$Y = 10 - 4X + (3X)Z - Z^2,$$

and the partial with respect to Z is:

$$\frac{\partial Y}{\partial Z} = 0 - 0 + 3X - 2Z$$

$$= 3X - 2Z.$$

---

[8]The symbol ∂, called delta, is used to denote a partial derivative. In oral and written treatments of this concept, the word derivative is frequently omitted. That is, reference is typically made to the *partial* of Q rather than the *partial derivative* of Q.

Another example should help clarify the technique of partial differentiation. Let $Y = 2X + 4X^2Z - 3XZ^2 - 2Z^3$. Then, the partial with respect to X is:

$$\frac{\partial Y}{\partial X} = 2 + 8XZ - 3Z^2 - 0,$$

and the partial with respect to Z is:

$$\frac{\partial Y}{\partial Z} = 0 + 4X^2 - 6XZ - 6Z^2.$$

Maximizing Multivariable Functions

The requirement for maximization (or minimization) of a multivariate function is a straightforward extension of that for single variable functions. All first-order partial derivatives must equal zero.[9] Thus, maximization of the function $Y = f(X,Z)$ requires:

$$\frac{\partial Y}{\partial X} = 0,$$

and

$$\frac{\partial Y}{\partial Z} = 0.$$

To illustrate this procedure, consider the function:

$$Y = 4X + Z - X^2 + XZ - Z^2, \tag{2.12}$$

whose partial derivatives are

$$\frac{\partial Y}{\partial X} = 4 - 2X + Z,$$

and

$$\frac{\partial Y}{\partial Z} = 1 + X - 2Z.$$

---

[9]Because the second-order requirements for determining maxima and minima are somewhat complex and are not necessary for the materials that follow in this text, they are not developed here. A full discussion of these requirements can be found in any elementary calculus text.

To maximize Equation 2.12, the partials must be set equal to zero:

$$\frac{\partial Y}{\partial X} = 4 - 2X + Z = 0,$$

2 + 2x − 4z = 0

6 − 3z = 0   z = 2

and

$$\frac{\partial Y}{\partial Z} = 1 + X - 2Z = 0.$$

8 − 4x + 2z = 0

9 − 3x = 0   x = 3

Here we have two equations in two unknowns. Solving them simultaneously, we find that the values $X = 3$ and $Z = 2$ maximize the function.[10] Inserting these values for X and Z into Equation 2.12, we find the value of Y to be 7; therefore, the maximum value of Y is 7.

The process involved here can perhaps be clarified by referring to Figure 2.11, a three-dimensional graph of Equation 2.12. Here we see that for positive values of X and Z, Equation 2.12 maps out a surface with a peak at point A. At the peak the surface of the figure is level. Alternatively stated, a plane that is tangent to the surface at point A will be parallel to the XZ plane, meaning that the slope of the figure with respect to either X or Z must be zero; this is the requirement for locating a maximum of a multivariate function.

CONSTRAINED OPTIMIZATION

In a great many of the decision problems faced by managers, there are constraints imposed that limit the options available to the decision maker. For example, a production manager may be charged with minimizing total cost, subject to the requirement that specified quantities of each of the firm's products be produced. At other times the production manager may be concerned with maximizing output from a particular department, subject to limitations on the quantities of various resources (labor, materials, or equipment) available for use.

Other functional areas of the firm also face constrained optimization problems. Marketing managers are often charged with the task of maximizing sales, subject to the constraint that they not exceed a fixed advertising budget. Financial officers, in their efforts to minimize the cost of acquiring capital, must frequently work within constraints imposed by investment financing and cash balance requirements and by creditors.

[10] Since $4 - 2X + Z = 0$, $Z = 2X - 4$. Substituting this value for Z into $1 + X - 2Z = 0$, we obtain $1 + X - 2(2X - 4) = 1 + X - 4X + 8 = -3X + 9 = 0$, or $X = 3$. Substituting this value of X into $Z = 2X - 4$, we obtain $Z = 2(3) - 4 = 2$.

FIGURE 2.11

Finding the Maximum of a Function of Two Variables: $Y = 4X + Z - X^2 + XZ - Z^2$

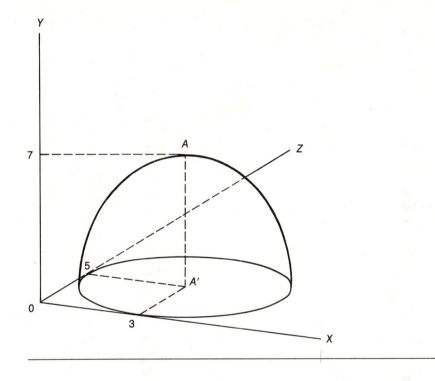

In general, constrained optimization problems fall into one of two classes:

Maximization Problems	Minimization Problems
Maximize: Profit, Revenue, or Output	Minimize: Cost
Subject To: Resource Constraint(s)	Subject To: Output Quantity or Quality Constraint(s)

There is a close relationship between the maximization and minimization formulations of constrained optimization problems, and either problem specification will lead to the optimal employment of a firm's scarce resources. This relationship, called *duality*, is discussed in Chapter 9.

Constrained optimization problems may be solved in several ways. In some cases, where the constraint equation is not too complex, one may solve the constraint equation for one of the decision variables, then substitute for that variable in the objective function—the function the firm wishes to maximize or minimize.[11] This procedure converts the problem to one of unconstrained maximization or minimization, which can be solved by the methods outlined above.

The procedure can be clarified by examining its use in a constrained minimization problem. Suppose a firm produces its product on two assembly lines and operates with the following total cost function:

$$TC = 3X^2 + 6Y^2 - XY,$$

where X represents the output produced on one assembly line and Y the production from the second. Management seeks to determine the least-cost combination of X and Y, subject to the constraint that total output of the product must be 20 units. The constrained optimization problem can be stated as follows:

Minimize

$$TC = 3X^2 + 6Y^2 - XY,$$

subject to

$$X + Y = 20.$$

Solving the constraint for X and substituting this value into the objective function results in:

$$X = 20 - Y,$$

and

$$TC = 3(20 - Y)^2 + 6Y^2 - (20 - Y)Y \qquad \textbf{(2.13)}$$

$$= 3(400 - 40Y + Y^2) + 6Y^2 - (20Y - Y)^2$$

$$= 1,200 - 120Y + 3Y^2 + 6Y^2 - 20Y + Y^2$$

$$= 1,200 - 140Y + 10Y^2.$$

Now we can treat Equation 2.13 as an unconstrained minimization problem. Solving it requires taking the derivative, setting that derivative equal to zero, and solving for the value of Y:

[11] In this section we examine techniques for solving constrained optimization problems in those cases where the constraints can be expressed as equations. Frequently, constraints impose only upper or lower limits on the decision maker and, therefore, may not be "binding" or effective at the optimal solution. Constraints of this second, more general, type

$$\frac{dTC}{dY} = -140 + 20Y = 0$$

$$20Y = 140$$

$$Y = 7.$$

A check of the sign of the second derivative evaluated at that point will insure that a minimum has been located:

$$\frac{dTC}{dY} = -140 + 20Y$$

$$\frac{d^2TC}{dY^2} = +20.$$

Since the second derivative is positive, $Y = 7$ must indeed be a minimum.

Substituting 7 for Y in the constraint equation allows us to determine the optimal quantity to be produced on assembly line X.

$$X + 7 = 20$$

$$X = 13.$$

Thus, production of 13 units of output on assembly line X and 7 units on line Y is the least-cost combination for manufacturing a total of 20 units of the firm's product. The total cost of producing that combination will be:

$$TC = 3(13)^2 + 6(7)^2 - (13 \cdot 7)$$

$$= 507 + 294 - 91$$

$$= \$710.$$

Lagrangian Multipliers [12]

Unfortunately, the substitution technique used above is not always feasible; the constraint conditions are often too numerous or too complex for substitution to be employed. In these cases, the technique of *Lagrangian multipliers* must be used.

---

are properly expressed as inequality relationships, and in these cases another optimizing technique, mathematical programming, is often used to analyze the problem. Mathematical programming is discussed in Chapter 9.

[12] This section can be omitted without loss of continuity.

The Lagrangian technique for solving constrained optimization problems is a procedure that calls for optimizing a function that combines the original objective function and the constraint conditions. This combined equation, called the Lagrangian function, is created in a way that insures (1) that when it has been maximized (or minimized) the original objective function will also be maximized (minimized), and (2) that all the constraint requirements will have been satisfied.

A re-examination of the constrained minimization problem illustrated above will clarify the use of this technique. Recall that the firm sought to minimize the function $TC = 3X^2 + 6Y^2 - XY$, subject to the constraint that $X + Y = 20$. Rearranging the constraint to bring all the terms to the right of the equals sign, we obtain:

$$0 = 20 - X - Y.$$

This is always the first step in forming a Lagrangian expression.

Multiplying this form of the constraint by the unknown factor λ[13] and adding the result to the original objective function creates the Lagrangian expression. For the example:

$$L_{TC} = 3X^2 + 6Y^2 - XY + \lambda(20 - X - Y). \tag{2.14}$$

L_{TC} is defined as the Lagrangian function for the constrained optimization problem under consideration.

Because it incorporates the constraint into the objective function, the Lagrangian function can be treated as an unconstrained optimization problem, and the solution to that problem will *always* be identical to the solution of the original constrained optimization problem. To illustrate this, consider the problem of minimizing the Lagrangian function constructed above in Equation 2.14. At a minimum point on a multivariate function, all the partial derivatives must be equal to zero. The partials of Equation 2.14 can be taken with respect to the three unknown variables, X, Y, and λ, as follows:

$$\frac{\partial L_{TC}}{\partial X} = 6X - Y - \lambda,$$

$$\frac{\partial L_{TC}}{\partial Y} = 12Y - X - \lambda,$$

$$\frac{\partial L_{TC}}{\partial \lambda} = 20 - X - Y.$$

---

[13] λ is the Greek letter *lambda*, which is typically used in formulating Lagrangian expressions.

Setting these three partials equal to zero results in a system of three equations and three unknowns:

$$6X - Y - \lambda = 0, \tag{2.15}$$

$$\dagger X \dotplus 12Y + \lambda = 0, \tag{2.16}$$

and

$$20 - X - Y = 0. \tag{2.17}$$

Notice that Equation 2.17, the partial of the Lagrangian function with respect to λ, is the constraint condition imposed on the original optimization problem. This result is not mere happenstance. The Lagrangian function is specifically constructed so that the derivative of the function taken with respect to the Lagrange multiplier, λ, will always give the original constraint. So long as this derivative is zero, as it must be at a local extreme (maximum or minimum), the constraint conditions imposed on the original problem will be met. Further, since under such conditions the last term in the Lagrangian expression must equal zero, that is, $(0 = 20 - X - Y)$, the Lagrangian function reduces to the original objective function, and thus the solution to the unconstrained Lagrangian problem will always be the solution to the original constrained optimization problem.

Completing the analysis for our example will clarify these relationships. We begin by solving the system of equations to obtain the optimal values of X and Y. Subtracting Equation 2.16 from Equation 2.15 gives:

$$7X - 13Y = 0. \tag{2.18}$$

Then, multiplying Equation 2.17 by 7 and adding Equation 2.18 to this product allows us to solve for Y:

$$
\begin{array}{ll}
140 - 7X - 7Y = 0 & 7 \times \textbf{(2.17)} \\
\phantom{140 - {}} 7X - 13Y = 0 & \textbf{(2.18)} \\
\hline
140 - 20Y = 0 & \\
140 = 20Y & \\
7 = Y. &
\end{array}
$$

Substituting 7 for Y in Equation 2.17 yields $X = 13$, the value of X at the point where the Lagrangian is minimized.

Since the solution of the Lagrangian is also the solution to the firm's constrained optimization problem, 13 units from assembly line X and 7 units from line

Y will be the least-cost combination of output that can be produced subject to the constraint that total output must be 20 units. This is the same answer that we obtained previously by solving the constraint for one of the decision variables and substituting for it in the objective function.

The Lagrangian technique is a more powerful technique for solving constrained optimization problems than the substitution method; it is easier to apply to a problem with multiple constraints, and it provides the decision maker with some valuable supplementary information. This is because the Lagrangian multiplier, λ, has an important economic interpretation. Substituting the values of *X* and *Y* into Equation 2.15 allows us to determine the value of λ in our example:

$$6 \cdot 13 - 7 - \lambda = 0$$

$$\lambda = +71.$$

Here we can interpret λ as the marginal cost of production at 20 units of output. It tells us that if the firm were required to produce only 19 instead of 20 units of output, total costs would fall by approximately \$71. Similarly, if the output requirement were 21 instead of 20 units, costs would increase by that amount.[14] More generally, any Lagrangian multiplier, λ, indicates the marginal effect on the original objective function solution of decreasing or increasing the constraint requirement by 1 unit. Often, as in the above example, the marginal relationship described by the Lagrangian multiplier provides economic data that helps a manager to evaluate the potential benefits of relaxing a constraint. This use of the Lagrangian variable is further examined in Chapter 9, where the linear programming approach to constrained optimization is introduced.

SUMMARY

Optimization is the process of determining the best possible solution to a given problem. In this chapter we first introduced a number of methods used to express economic relationships, and then examined several related tools of analysis used in the optimizing process.

Economic relationships may be expressed as tables, graphs, or equations. The key variables involve totals, averages, and marginals, and these values are themselves related in a unique way. Given any one set of variables, the other two can be developed on the basis of the basic relationships that hold among the different variables.

[14]Technically, λ indicates the marginal change in the objective function solution associated with an infinitesimally small change in the constraint. Thus, it provides only a rough estimate of the change in total costs that would take place if 1 more (or less) unit of output were required.

Frequently, optimality analysis involves locating the maximum or the minimum value of a function. Values for the function can be calculated and entered in a table or plotted on a graph, and the point where the function is maximized (minimized) can be observed directly. It is frequently more convenient, however, to use calculus to locate the optimum point, simply calculating the derivative of the total function and setting it equal to zero; that is, $dY/dX = 0$. Accordingly, the use of derivatives for determining points of maximization and minimization was explained in some detail.

A function may have several values at which the derivative is zero, with some points representing maximums and others minimums. To determine whether a maximum or a minimum has been found, the second derivative is calculated. If d^2Y/dX^2 is negative, a maximum has been found; if it is positive, a minimum has been located.

If a function contains more than two variables, partial differentiation is used, and the process of finding partials was examined. To maximize a function of two or more variables, the partial with respect to each variable must be calculated, and these partials must simultaneously be set equal to zero.

The final topic covered was constrained optimization, the process of maximizing or minimizing a function subject to a set of constraints. Here we examined the Lagrangian multiplier concept and demonstrated how it is used to solve constrained optimization problems. We also noted the interpretation of the Lagrangian multiplier as the marginal change in the objective function associated with a unit change in the constraint limit.

The tools developed in this chapter are used in all types of economic analysis, especially in managerial economics. Accordingly, they are employed throughout the remainder of the text.

QUESTIONS

2.1 The values of the derivative of a function, the slope of the graphed curve of the function, and the marginal (rate of change) of the real economic quantity represented by the function are all the same. What can be said about the values of the function itself, the graphed curve, and the total economic quantity when the derivative, slope, and marginal are equal to zero?

2.2 What is the key relationship between totals and marginals that makes an understanding of the marginal concept so important in optimization analysis?

2.3 Why must a marginal curve always intersect the related average curve at either a maximum or a minimum point?

2.4 Considering the optimization procedures outlined in this chapter, what hazard does one encounter in setting marginal revenue equal to marginal cost to solve for the profit-maximizing output level of a firm? Is the point at which marginal revenue equals marginal cost always a point of maximum profit? Is the point of maximum profit always a point where marginal revenue equals marginal cost?

2.5 Economists have long argued that if you want to tax away excess profits from a firm without affecting the allocative efficiency of market-determined price/output relationships, you should use a lump-sum license tax instead of an excise or sales tax. Use the materials developed in this chapter to support this position.

PROBLEMS

2.1 a. Given the total revenue (*TR*) and output (*Q*) data shown in the table below, calculate the related marginal revenue (*MR*) and average revenue (*AR*) figures needed to complete the table.

Q	TR	MR	AR
0	$ 0	$ —	$ 0
1	499	499	499
2	984	485	492
3	1,437		479
4	1,840	403	
5		335	435
6	2,424		404
7	2,569	145	367
8		23	
9	2,475	−117	275
10	2,200		

b. Using a two-part graph, like Figure 2.2, plot the total revenue, marginal revenue, and average revenue curves indicated by the data in the table constructed in Problem 2.1a. (*Note*: The relationships among totals, averages, and marginals are typically more accurately depicted by graphing the marginal values midway between the two output levels to which they relate. For example, the $499 marginal revenue associated with the first unit of output should be plotted at *Q* = 0.5.)

c. Locate on the total revenue curve graphed in Problem 2.1b the points at which marginal, average, and total revenues are maximized.

d. Locate the points of maximum total, average, and marginal revenues, using the average and marginal revenue curves constructed in Problem 2.1b.

e. Compare the relationships between the total, average, and marginal curves on your graph in Problem 2.1b and the table in Problem 2.1a with the relationships indicated in the chapter.

(*Note*: The total revenue function used to develop the data for this problem is shown in Problem 2.3. You may want to compare the solutions of this problem with those of Problem 2.3.)

2.2 Determine the first and second derivatives for the following:

a. $Y = 3 + 4X$

b. $Y = 5X - 6.3X^2$

c. $Y = 10 + 2X - X^2 + 3X^3$

d. $Y = (2X + 3)(X - 1)$

e. $Y = \dfrac{4X^2 - 2}{X^3}$

f. $Y = (5 + 2X)^3$.

2.3 Given the total revenue function $TR = \$500Q + \$2Q^2 - \$3Q^3$, where Q represents the quantity of a particular product sold:

a. Determine the output quantity that maximizes total revenue.

b. Determine the output quantity at which marginal revenue is maximized.

c. Determine the output quantity at which marginal and average revenue are equal.

d. This total revenue function was used to construct the data for Problem 2.1. Check to see that your solutions to both problems are reconcilable.

2.4 Lisa Paulson is a student at Minnesota State University. She is preparing for the final exams and has decided to devote five hours to the study of managerial economics and finance. Paulson's goal is to maximize the average grade earned in the two courses, and she must decide how much time to spend on each. According to her best estimates, Paulson's grades will vary according to the schedules shown below. (*Note*: Maximizing the average grade in the two courses is equivalent to maximizing the sum of the grades.)

Managerial Economics		Finance	
Hours of Study	Grade	Hours of Study	Grade
0	25	0	50
1	45	1	62
2	65	2	72
3	75	3	81
4	83	4	88
5	90	5	93

a. Describe the manner in which Paulson could make use of the marginal-total relationship she has studied in managerial economics to assist in determining the optimal allocation of the five hours between the two courses.

b. How much time should Paulson spend studying each subject?

c. In addition to managerial economics and finance, Paulson is also taking a marketing course. She estimates that each hour spent studying marketing will result in an eight point increase on the marketing examination score. She has tentatively decided to spend three hours preparing for the marketing exam. Is Paulson's attempt to maximize her average grade in all three courses in three hours devoted to marketing and five hours devoted to managerial economics and finance (allocated as in Part b) an optimal decision? Why?

2.5 Determine the partial derivatives for the following functions:

a. $Y = 2 - X - 3Z + XZ + 2Z^2$

b. $Y = 3X + 2Z + 4XZ - X^2 - 0.5Z^2$

c. $Y = 10 + X^2 + WXZ - 1.5WZ^2 + Z$

d. $Y = 6X^{0.4}Z^{0.6}$.

2.6 Leonard Manufacturing Company has developed and test marketed a highly energy efficient home heating and cooling system. The Leonard system is unique, and preliminary indications suggest that a substantial share of the new home and retrofitting markets can be obtained if the firm acts quickly in expanding its production. Data from independent marketing consultants indicates that the demand relationship for the Leonard system is:

$$P = 6000 - 3Q.$$

In addition, Leonard's own accounting department has estimated variable costs per unit as:

$$VC = 1000 + 2Q.$$

And finally, fixed costs allocated to the program total $800,000 yearly.

a. Determine the sales maximizing price and output levels.

b. Determine the profit maximizing price and output levels.

c. Calculate the implied future benefit to Leonard's of pursuing a one-year policy of sales rather than profit maximization.

2.7 The manager for quality control of Maguire Tool and Die has determined that quality control costs for the firm have two components, an inspection cost and a production repair cost. Both costs are a function of the number of inspections performed during the manufacturing process. The inspection cost per unit of production is given by the expression:

$$C_I = 2 + 10X - 0.3X^2,$$

where X is the number of inspections performed. Production repair cost is given as:

$$C_R = 70 - 2X + 0.8X^2.$$

Assuming the quality control manager wants to minimize the firm's average cost per inspection, what are the optimal number of inspections per unit of production?

a. Write the total, average, and marginal quality control cost functions.

b. What number of inspections will minimize the average cost per inspection?

2.8 Inventory management is an area where the calculus tools of optimization provide a valuable technique for decision making. Assume that in a specific inventory problem, usage of the item is evenly distributed over time, and delivery of additional units is instantaneous once an order has been placed. Under these conditions the costs associated with the purchase and inventory of the item are

a. Purchase Costs $= P \cdot X$,

b. Order Costs $\quad = \Theta \cdot \dfrac{X}{Q}$,

c. Carrying Costs $= C \cdot \dfrac{Q}{2}$,

where P is the price per unit of the item, X is the total quantity of the item used annually, Θ is the cost of placing an order for the item, Q is the quantity of the item ordered at any one point in time, and C is the per-unit inventory carrying cost of the item. Thus, the total costs associated with this inventory item are given by the expression:

$$TC = P \cdot X + \Theta \frac{X}{Q} + C \frac{Q}{2}.$$

The cost of carrying this item in inventory can be minimized by selecting an optimal order quantity, Q, sometimes called the economic order quantity, or *EOQ*. Develop an expression for determining the optimal *EOQ* by minimizing the above-cost function with respect to Q, the order quantity.

2.9 Designed for Sales is a centralized processor of promotional coupons for firms in the food products industries. A key aspect of the Designed for Sales operation is its sophisticated records division which monitors promotional and sales data in order to highlight effective promotions, limit coupon fraud, etc. A production function for the records division has been estimated as follows:

$Q = 4x^2 + 2xy + y^2$

$Q =$ coupons processed (in units)

$x =$ computer staff input (in worker weeks)

$y =$ minicomputer time input (in machine weeks).

Furthermore, computer staff earn an average of \$400 per week, while machine rentals (including software and service costs) average \$200 per week.

a. Use the Lagrangian technique to determine optimal levels for x and y if total expenses must be limited to \$100,000 per week.

b. Determine and interpret the Lagrange multiplier.

2.10 Lakewood College, a private institution, has been suffering from declining revenues and increasing costs for several years. In a cost reduction effort you have been asked to examine the school's basic accounting course to determine if the increase in enrollment that has taken place over the past two years has been cost effective. Your analysis indicates that students taught in the course are related to staffing by the following function:

$$students = 200P + 50A + 10P \cdot A - 0.5A^2$$

where P measures the number of professors teaching the course and A is the number of teaching assistants assigned to assist with that teaching. Lakewood's staffing costs are $8,000 for each professor assigned to the course and $2,000 for each teaching assistant.

> **a.** Currently Lakewood is using 3 professors and 24 teaching assistants to teach the basic accounting course. The expenditure (budget) for the course is $72,000. Is the current combination of professors and teaching assistants optimal if Lakewood's objective is to maximize the number of students taught subject to the budget constraint? If so, explain how you know this. If not, determine the appropriate combination.
>
> **b.** What is the average cost of teaching this accounting course to a student, assuming Lakewood uses the optimal combination of professors and teaching assistants?
>
> **c.** Use your knowledge of the Lagrangian multiplier to determine whether average costs would increase or decrease with increased enrollment in the course.
>
> **d.** Assuming Lakewood charges $25 for a three-credit course, will increased enrollment in the basic accounting course help or hinder with respect to the school's revenue shortfall problem? Explain. (The accounting course is a three-credit course.)

2.11 Jeannette Braun runs a regional financial consulting firm that deals mostly with small businesses. Braun is considering expanding her firm by opening a new office. An engineering analysis of Braun's operation reveals that the number of clients served per office, Q, is a function of the number of finance, X, and accounting, Y, staff employed, where

$Q = 6X + XY$

Q = clients served (output)

X = finance personnel

Y = accounting personnel.

Braun expects to pay market rates for new hires of $20,000 for finance and $30,000 per year for accounting personnel. Braun anticipates having a maximum of $300,000 available for the new office salaries during the coming year.

    a. Calculate optimal employment levels of finance and accounting personnel assuming Braun's objective is to maximize the number of clients served subject to the budget constraint described above.

    b. Are average salary costs per client served rising or falling at this optimal employment level?

2.12 The State Department of Revenue (DOR) provides taxpayer assistance to help in the preparation of individual income tax returns. The amount of assistance (A) that can be provided is a function of the number of professional accountants (P) and trained tax preparers (T) employed. The function relating assistance provided by any one office to the level of employment is:

$$A = 20P + 5T + 10PT.$$

    a. Assume DOR has budgeted $200,000 for a new taxpayer's assistance office. Employment costs per professional accountant are $20,000, and costs per trained tax preparer are $15,000. What is the optimal staff combination for the office, assuming the objective is to maximize the assistance provided?

    b. Assume the DOR staffs five offices as indicated by your solution to Part a above, and that virtually all service is provided over the phone so that actual location is unimportant in determining the amount of assistance provided by any one office. Could DOR provide more taxpayer assistance per dollar spent by operating fewer offices? Use your knowledge of the Lagrangian multiplier to answer and explain.

CASE 2.1
_____

JPB ENGINEERING CORPORATION: OPTIMIZATION IN PRODUCT RELIABILITY DESIGN
_____

JPB Engineering Corporation is one of several manufacturers producing electrical switching equipment for petroleum refining plants. JPB's management is currently examining one standard switch, model JPB-5, with the objective of optimizing its market position and maximizing the profit from this product. The management believes that, given the nature of the market within which the JPB-5 is sold, price competition would be an ineffective way to increase profits. The standard price of $200 is well established. Previous attempts to raise the price of similar products have resulted in substantial declines in market share, while attempts to increase market penetration by lowering price have always led to retaliatory price reductions by competing firms.

    On the basis of discussion with its sales representatives, JPB's management believes that product reliability holds the key to increasing profits on the JPB-5. JPB's sales force has long claimed that there is an important relationship between product reliability and sales volume. While top management had considered this proposition indirectly in the past, no effort was made to determine the true parameters of this relation-ship. Now, Paul Joseph, president of JPB, has requested such an analysis as part of the review of the JPB-5 profit position. Specifically, he has requested that Bonnie Chris-tianson, an administrative assistant, prepare a report that will answer the following questions:

1. What relationship exists between sales volume and the reliability level of the product?

2. What is the relationship between product costs and reliability?

3. Assuming that the current $200 price is to be maintained, what reliability level re-sults in maximum profits for the JPB-5?

Christianson began the analysis by examining the relationship between demand and re-liability. Reliability problems with earlier design of the JPB-5 provided data on re-liability and sales for a number of years. Because of the stability of price and the lack of growth in the total market for the JPB-5 switch over the period covered by the data, Christianson felt that these data accurately reflected the effect of variation in reliability on demand.

The data are shown in the following table. A graph of the data indicated a cur-vilinear relationship, and Christianson fitted a quadratic equation to it, using the least squares regression technique. (This statistical method is discussed in Chapter 5.) The resulting equation was:

$$Q(000) = 42 - 2.25F - 0.092F^2.$$

Reliability Level	Sales Volume
(F = percent failure per year)	Q
1	39,700
3	34,400
5	28,450
7	21,750
9	14,250

Christianson sought help from JPB's engineering staff to determine the production costs/reliability relationship for the JPB-5 switch. The engineering personnel deter-mined that total costs should be separated into three relevant categories for the analysis:

1. *Per unit production costs* (C_p), which are defined as all costs that remain constant (per unit) regardless of the reliability level of the product. These production costs were estimated to be $75 a unit, and this cost figure is not expected to vary significantly with respect to the quantity produced over the output range that appears relevant to JPB's decision problem—15,000 to 40,000 units.

2. *Per unit warranty costs* (C_w). The model JPB-5 switch is warranted for five years. On the basis of past service costs, it is estimated that warranty repair or replacement costs will average $100 for each failure. Thus, the warranty costs can be expressed as a function of the annual failure rate (F) by the following expression:

$$C_w = \text{Cost per Failure} \times \text{Number of Years Warranted}$$
$$\times \text{Failure Rate per Year}$$

$$= (\$100)\,(5)\,(F/100)$$

$$= 5F.$$

3. *Per unit reliability costs* (C_f). An extensive study by the engineering department of engineering alternatives that would provide different levels of product reliability as measured by the failure rate resulted in the following data:

Engineering Alternative	Reliability Level (F)	Reliability Costs per Unit (C_f)
1	1	$117
2	3	103
3	5	87
4	7	73
5	9	57

A graphical plot of these data indicated that a linear expression of the relationship between C_f and F would be acceptable for the decision problem at hand. Calculations of the linear regression equation resulted in the following relationship:

$$C_f = \$125 - 7.5F.$$

Christianson received these cost equations from the engineering department and was preparing to calculate the optimal reliability level when Paul Joseph called with an invitation to join his Friday afternoon golf foursome. Christianson could not refuse this offer, but since she knew that the completed report would be needed for a Monday morning meeting of the executive committee, she asked you, a new management trainee, to complete the analysis. The following points should be covered in your work:

1. The profit-maximizing reliability level.

2. The sales volume that will result from that reliability level.

3. The total profits from the JPB-5 switch, given that optimal reliability level.

SELECTED REFERENCES

Allen, R. G. D. *Mathematical Analysis for Economists*. London: Macmillan, 1956.

Budnick, Frank S. *Applied Mathematics: for Business, Economics, and the Social Sciences*. New York: McGraw-Hill, 1979.

Cain, Jack, and Carman, Robert A. *Mathematics for Business Careers*. New York: John Wiley & Sons, 1981.

Chiang, Alpha C. *Fundamental Methods of Mathematical Economics*. 2d ed. New York: McGraw-Hill, 1974.

Draper, Jean E., and Klingman, Jane S. *Mathematical Analysis, Business and Economic Applications*. 2d ed. New York: Harper & Row, 1972.

Funk, Jerry. *Business Mathematics*. Boston: Allyn & Bacon, 1980.

Henderson, James, and Quandt, Richard E. *Microeconomic Theory: A Mathematical Approach*. 2d ed. New York: McGraw-Hill, 1971.

Intriligator, Michael D. *Mathematical Optimization and Economic Theory*. Englewood Cliffs, N.J.: Prentice-Hall, 1971.

Khoury, Sarkis J., and Parsons, Torrence D. *Mathematical Methods in Finance and Economics*. New York: Elsevier-North Holland, 1981.

Roueche, Nelda W. *Fundamentals of Business Mathematics*. Englewood Cliffs, N.J.: Prentice-Hall, 1979.

Takayama, A. *Mathematical Economics*. Hinsdale, Ill.: Dryden Press, 1974.

Thorn, Richard S. *Business Mathematics*. 2d ed. New York: Harper & Row, 1979.

CHAPTER 3
RISK ANALYSIS

Many simple managerial decisions are made under conditions where the outcomes associated with each possible course of action are known with certainty. A firm with $100,000 in excess cash that can be invested in a thirty-day treasury bill yielding 11 percent ($904 interest for thirty days), or that can be used to prepay a bank loan, saving $936 in interest, can determine with certainty that prepayment of the loan will provide a $32 higher return. Similarly, a manufacturer needing 500,000 units of an industrial fastener that can be purchased from one distributor at 74¢ per unit and from a second at 74½¢ per unit knows with certainty that a cost savings of $2,500 will result by purchasing from the first distributor. Even for decision problems where events and results cannot be exactly predicted, substantial insight into decision making procedures can be gained by treating the problem as though management had complete information concerning the outcomes of all possible decisions. Understanding the rationale for decisions under certainty conditions provides a strong foundation for the somewhat more complex analysis required for decision making under uncertainty. For these reasons, much of the analysis and many of the optimality conditions developed in managerial economics relate to decision making where perfect information about all events and outcomes is assumed.

In reality, however, virtually all major managerial decisions are made under conditions of uncertainty. Managers must select a course of action from the perceived alternatives with less than perfect knowledge about the occurrence of events affecting the outcome. There is also uncertainty about the effect of the outcome should some particular event occur. In some cases uncertainty also exists about the ultimate consequences of the outcome itself.

The pervasiveness of uncertainty in managerial decision situations and the risk entailed by such uncertainty dictate that the concepts of risk and risk analysis be explored in the study of managerial economics. Risk analysis can be related directly to the basic valuation model underlying the microeconomic theory of the firm.

When both risk levels and decision maker attitudes toward risk taking are known, the effects of uncertainty on the basic valuation model can be reflected through adjustments to the model's numerator or denominator. The certainty equivalent adjustment factor method converts expected risky profit streams to their certain sum equivalents in order to eliminate value differences that result from different risk levels. Therefore, the certainty equivalent adjustment factor method adjusts the numerator of the basic valuation model so that present values for projects are risk adjusted and, thereby, comparable. A second method for directly reflecting uncertainty in the basic valuation model is through risk-adjusted discount rates. In this method, the interest rate used in the denominator of the basic valuation model depends upon the level of risk associated with a given cash flow. Thus, discounted expected profit streams once again reflect risk differences among projects and are directly comparable. We can use the certainty equivalent adjustment factor and risk-adjusted discount rate methods as well as other less precise methods to directly reflect the effects of uncertainty in the basic valuation model. We begin this chapter by defining risk and discussing methods for measuring it. We then examine the two primary methods for adapting the basic valuation model to account for uncertainty. And finally, we discuss the use of probability theory, decision trees, and simulation as aids to decision making under uncertainty. Simple game theory constructs and an analysis of the value of reducing uncertainty are examined in Appendix 3A at the end of the chapter.

RISK IN ECONOMIC ANALYSIS

Risk is defined as a hazard or peril; as an exposure to harm; and, in commerce, as a chance of loss.[1] Thus, risk refers to the possibility that some unfavorable event will

---

[1]Some writers distinguish between risk and uncertainty, but for our purposes this distinction is unnecessary. Accordingly, we define any decision whose outcome is less than certain as being risky, and we say that such decisions are subject to risk or uncertainty.

occur. For example, if one buys a $1 million short-term government bond priced to yield 11 percent, then the return on the investment, 11 percent, can be estimated quite precisely, and we define the investment as risk free. If, however, the $1 million is invested in the stock of a company being organized to prospect for natural gas in the Gulf of Mexico, the return on the investment cannot be estimated precisely. The return could range from minus 100 percent (a complete loss) to some extremely large figure. Because there is a significant danger of loss, we define the project as relatively risky. Similarly, sales forecasts for different products might exhibit differing degrees of risk. For example, The Dryden Press may be sure that sales of a fifth edition introductory finance text will reach the projected level of 70,000 copies, but the company may be uncertain about the number of copies it will sell of a new first edition statistics text. The greater uncertainty associated with the sales level of the statistics text increases the chance that the firm will not profit from publishing that book. Thus, the risk of that project is greater than that of revising the finance text.

Risk is associated with the chance or probability of undesirable outcomes—the more likely an undesirable outcome, the riskier the decision. It is useful, however, to define risk more precisely. This more precise definition requires a step-by-step development, which constitutes the remainder of this section.

Probability Distributions

The *probability* of an event is defined as the chance, or odds, that the event will occur. For example, a sales manager may state, "There is a 70 percent chance we will get that order from Exco Corporation and a 30 percent chance that we will not get it." If all possible events or outcomes are listed, and if a probability of occurrence is assigned to each event, then the listing is defined as a *probability distribution*. For our sales example, we could set up the following probability distribution:

Event (1)	Probability of Occurrence (2)
Receives order	0.7 = 70%
Does not receive order	0.3 = 30%
	1.0 = 100%

The possible outcomes are listed in column 1, while the probabilities of each outcome, expressed both as decimals and percentages, are given in column 2. Notice that the probabilities sum to 1.0 or 100 percent, as they must if the probability distribution is complete.

Risk in this very simple example can be read from the probability distribution as a 30 percent chance that the undesirable event (the firm does not receive the order from Exco Corporation) occurs. For most managerial decisions, however, the relative desirability of alternative events or outcomes is not so absolute as indicated here. For this reason, a more general measure of the relationship between risk and the probability distribution is required to appropriately incorporate risk into the decision process. The need for a more general measure of risk can be illustrated by considering the following situation.

Suppose a firm is considering two investments, each calling for an outlay of $1,000. Only one will be chosen. Assume also that the profits on the two projects are related to the level of general economic activity in the coming year as shown in Table 3.1, a table known as a *payoff matrix*. Here we see that both projects will provide a $500 profit in a normal economy, higher profits in a boom economy, and lower profits if a recession occurs. Notice also that the profits from Project B vary far more widely under the different states of the economy than do the profits from Project A. In a normal economy both projects return $500 in profit. Should the economy be in a recession next year, Project A will still provide a $400 profit, substantially more than the $0 profit from Project B in a recession. On the other hand, if the economy is booming next year, Project B's profit will increase to $1,000 while profit for Project A will increase only moderately to $600.

How, then, is one to evaluate these alternatives? Project A is clearly more desirable if the economy is in a recession, while Project B is superior in a boom economy. (In a normal economy the projects offer the same profit potential and we would not favor one over the other.) To answer the question we need to know how likely it is that we will have a boom, a recession, or normal economic conditions. If we have probabilities for the occurrence of these events, we can develop a probability distribution of profits for the two projects, and from these obtain measures of both the expected profits and the variability of profits. These measures enable us to evaluate the projects in terms of their expected profit and the risk that the profit will deviate from the expected value.

To continue the example, assume that economic forecasts indicate that, given current trends in economic indicators, the chances are 2 in 10 that a recession will occur, 6 in 10 that the economy will be normal, and 2 in 10 that there will be a boom. Redefining *chances* as *probability*, we find that the probability of a recession is 0.2, or 20 percent; the probability of normal economic activity is 0.6, or 60 per-

TABLE 3.1

Payoff Matrix for Projects A and B

State of the Economy	Profits	
	Project A	Project B
Recession	$400	$ 0
Normal	500	500
Boom	600	1,000

TABLE 3.2

Calculation of Expected Values

	State of the Economy (1)	Probability of This State Occurring (2)	Outcome if This State Occurs (3)	(2) × (3) (4)
Project A	Recession	0.2	$ 400	$ 80
	Normal	0.6	500	300
	Boom	0.2	600	120
		1.0	Expected Profit A	$500
Project B	Recession	0.2	$ 0	$ 0
	Normal	0.6	500	300
	Boom	0.2	1,000	200
		1.0	Expected Profit B	$500

cent; and the probability of a boom is 0.2, or 20 percent. Notice that the probabilities add up to 1.0, or 100 percent: $0.2 + 0.6 + 0.2 = 1.0$, or 100 percent. These probabilities have been added to the payoff matrix in Table 3.1 to provide the probability distributions of profit for Projects A and B shown in Table 3.2.

If we multiply each possible outcome by its probability of occurrence and then add these products, we have a weighted average of the outcomes. The weights are the probabilities of occurrence, and the weighted average is defined as the *expected outcome*. Column 4 of Table 3.2 illustrates the calculation of the expected profits for Projects A and B. We multiply each possible profit level (column 3) by its probability of occurrence (column 2) to obtain weighted values of the possible profits. When column 4 of the table is summed for each project, we obtain a weighted average of the profits under various states of the economy; this weighted average is defined as the *expected profit* from the project.[2]

The expected profit calculation can also be expressed by the equation:

$$\text{Expected profit} = E(\pi) = \sum_{i=1}^{N} \pi_i \cdot P_i. \qquad (3.1)$$

Here π_i is the profit level associated with the ith outcome. P_i is the probability that outcome i will occur, and N is the number of possible outcomes or states of nature. Thus, $E(\pi)$ is a weighted average of the possible outcomes (the π_i values), with each outcome's weight being equal to its probability of occurrence.

---

[2]The weighted average or expected outcome need not be equal to the project's outcome for a normal state of the economy, although it is in this example.

Using the data for Project A we obtain its expected profit as follows:

$$E(\pi_A) = \sum_{i=1}^{3} \pi_i \cdot P_i$$
$$= \pi_1 \cdot P_1 + \pi_2 \cdot P_2 + \pi_3 \cdot P_3$$
$$= \$400(0.2) + \$500(0.6) + \$600(0.2)$$
$$= \$500.$$

We can graph the results shown in Table 3.2 to obtain a picture of the variability of actual outcomes; this is shown as a bar chart in Figure 3.1. The height of each bar signifies the probability that a given outcome will occur. The range of probable outcomes for Project A is from \$400 to \$600, with an average, or *expected value*, of

FIGURE 3.1

Relationship between State of the Economy and Project Returns

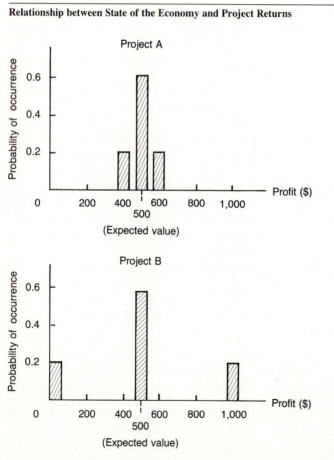

FIGURE 3.2

Probability Distributions Showing Relationship between State of the Economy and Project Returns

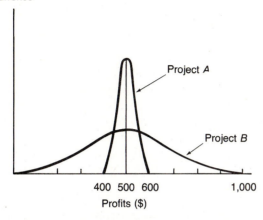

Probability of
occurrence

Project A

Project B

400 500 600   1,000

Profits ($)

Note: The assumptions regarding the probabilities of various outcomes have been changed from those in Figure 3.1. We no longer assume there is a zero probability that Project A will yield less than $400 or more than $600 and that Project B will yield less than $0 or more than $1,000. Rather, we have constructed normal distributions centered at $500 with approximately the same variability of outcome as indicated in Figure 3.1. While the probability of obtaining *exactly* $500 was 60 percent in Figure 3.1, in Figure 3.2 it is *much smaller*, because here there are an infinite number of possible outcomes, instead of just three. With continuous distributions, as in Figure 3.2, it is generally more appropriate to ask what is the cumulative probability of obtaining *at least* some specified value than to ask what the probability is of obtaining exactly that value. (Indeed, with a continuous distribution, the probability of occurrence for any single value is zero.) This cumulative probability is equal to the area under the probability distribution curve up to the point of interest. This topic is covered in more detail later in the chapter and in Appendix 3A at the end of the chapter.

$500. The expected value for Project B is also $500, but the range of possible outcomes is from $0 to $1,000.

Thus far we have assumed that only three states of the economy can exist: recession, normal, and boom. Actually, the state of the economy could range from a deep depression, as in the early 1930s, to a tremendous boom, with an unlimited number of possibilities in between. Suppose we had the time and the information to assign a probability to each possible state of the economy (with the sum of the probabilities still equaling 1.0) and to assign a monetary outcome to each project for each state of the economy. We would have a table similar to Table 3.2 except that it would have many more entries for "state of the economy," "probability," and "outcome if this state occurs." This table could be used to calculate expected values as shown above, and the probabilities and outcomes could be approximated by the continuous curves in Figure 3.2.

Figure 3.2 is a graph of the *probability distribution of returns* on Projects A and B. In general, the tighter the probability distribution, the more likely that the actual outcome will be close to the expected value, or equivalently, the less likely it is that deviations of the actual outcome from the expected value will be large. That is, the tighter the probability distribution—or alternatively stated, the more peaked the distribution—the lower the risk. Since Project A has a relatively tight probability distribution, its *actual* profit is likely to be closer to the *expected* $500 than is that of Project B.

Measuring Risk

Risk is a complex concept and a great deal of controversy has surrounded attempts to define and measure it. However, a common definition and one that is satisfactory for many purposes, is stated in terms of probability distributions such as those presented in Figure 3.2. This notion of risk is conveyed by the observation that *the tighter the probability distribution of possible outcomes, the smaller the risk of a given decision*, since there is a lower probability that the actual outcome will deviate significantly from the expected value. According to this definition, Project A is less risky than Project B.

To be most useful, our measure of risk should have some definite value—we need a *measure* of the tightness of the probability distribution. One such measure is the *standard deviation*, the symbol for which is σ, read *sigma*. The smaller the standard deviation, the tighter the probability distribution and, accordingly, the lower the riskiness of the alternative.[3] To calculate the standard deviation, we proceed as follows:

1. Calculate the expected value or mean of the distribution:

$$\text{Expected value} = \bar{\pi} = \sum_{i=1}^{n} (\pi_i P_i). \tag{3.2}$$

Here π is the profit or return associated with the ith outcome; P_i is the probability the ith outcome will occur; and $\bar{\pi}$, the expected value, is a weighted average of the various possible outcomes, each weighted by the probability of its occurrence.

2. Subtract the expected value from each possible outcome to obtain a set of deviations about the expected value:

$$\text{Deviation}_i = \pi_i - \bar{\pi}.$$

[3] Since we define risk in terms of the chance of an undesirable outcome, it would seem logical to measure risk in terms of the probability of losses, or at least of returns below the expected return, rather than by the entire distribution. Measures of below-expected returns, which are known as semivariance measures, have been developed, but they are difficult to analyze. In addition, such measures are unnecessary if the distribution of future returns is reasonably symmetric about the expected return. For many managerial problems this assumption of symmetry is reasonable, and thus we can use total variability to measure risk.

3. Square each deviation; multiply the squared deviation by the probability of occurrence for its related outcome; and sum these products. This arithmetic mean of the squared deviations is the variance of the probability distribution:

$$\text{Variance} = \sigma^2 = \sum_{i=1}^{n} (\pi_i - \bar{\pi})^2 P_i. \tag{3.3}$$

4. The standard deviation is found by obtaining the square root of the variance:

$$\text{Standard deviation} = \sigma = \sqrt{\sum_{i=1}^{n} (\pi_i - \bar{\pi})^2 P_i.} \tag{3.4}$$

The calculation of the standard deviation of profit for Project A illustrates this procedure. (The calculation of the expected profit was shown above and is therefore not repeated.)

Deviation $(\pi_i - \bar{\pi})$	Deviation^2 $(\pi_i - \bar{\pi})^2$	Deviation^2 × Probability $(\pi_i - \bar{\pi})^2 \cdot P_i$
$400 − $500 = −$100	$10,000	$10,000(0.2) = $2,000
$500 − $500 = 0	0	0(0.6) = 0
$600 − $500 = $100	$10,000	$10,000(0.2) = $2,000
		Variance = σ^2 = $4,000

$$\text{Standard deviation} = \sigma = \sqrt{\sigma^2} = \sqrt{\$4,000} = \$63.25.$$

Using the same procedure we can calculate the standard deviation of Project B's profit as $316.23. Since Project B's standard deviation is larger, it is the riskier project.

This relationship between risk and the standard deviation can be clarified by examining the characteristics of a normal distribution as shown in Figure 3.3. If a probability distribution is normal, the actual outcome will lie within ±1 standard deviation of the mean or expected value about 68 percent of the time. That is, there is a 68 percent probability that the actual outcome will lie in the range "Expected Outcome ±1σ." Similarly, the probability that the actual outcome will be within two standard deviations of the expected outcome is approximately 95 percent, and there is a better than 99 percent probability that the actual event will occur in the range of three standard deviations about the mean of the distribution. Thus, the smaller the standard deviation, the tighter the distribution about the expected value and the smaller the probability or risk of an outcome that is very far below the mean or expected value of the distribution.

FIGURE 3.3

Probability Ranges for a Normal Distribution

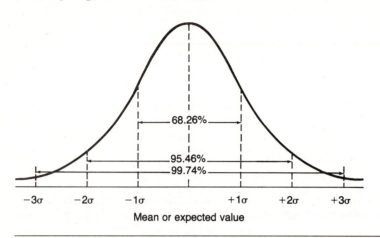

Notes:

a. The area under the normal curve equals 1.0 or 100 percent. Thus, the areas under any pair of normal curves drawn on the same scale, whether they are peaked or flat, must be equal.

b. Half the area under a normal curve is to the left of the mean, indicating that there is a 50 percent probability that the actual outcome will be less than the mean and a 50 percent probability that it will be greater than the mean.

c. Of the area under the curve, 68.26 percent is within $\pm 1\sigma$ of the mean, indicating that the odds are 68.26 percent that the actual outcome will be within the range mean -1σ to mean $+1\sigma$.

d. Procedures are available for finding the probability of other earnings ranges. These procedures are covered in Appendix A to this chapter.

e. For a normal distribution, the larger the value of σ, the greater the probability that the actual outcome will vary widely from and hence perhaps be far below the most likely outcome. Since the odds on having the actual results turn out to be bad is our definition of risk, and since σ measures these odds, we can use σ as a measure of risk.

We should note that problems can arise when the standard deviation is used as the measure of risk. Specifically, in an investment problem, if one project is larger than another—that is, if it has a larger cost and larger expected cash flows—it will normally have a larger standard deviation without necessarily being more risky. For example, if a project has expected returns of $1 million and a standard deviation of only $1,000, it is certainly less risky than a project with expected returns of $1,000 and a standard deviation of $500, the reason being that the *relative* variation for the larger project is much smaller.

One way of eliminating this problem is to calculate a measure of the relative risk involved, by dividing the standard deviation by the mean expectation, or expected value, $\bar{R}$, to obtain the *coefficient of variation*:

$$\text{Coefficient of variation} = \nu = \frac{\sigma}{\bar{R}} . \tag{3.5}$$

In general, when comparing decision alternatives whose costs and benefits are not of approximately equal size, the coefficient of variation provides better measure of relative risk than does the standard deviation.[4]

UTILITY THEORY AND RISK AVERSION

The assumption of risk aversion is basic to many decision models used in managerial economics. Because this assumption is so crucial, it is appropriate to examine attitudes toward risk and discuss why risk aversion holds in general.

In theory, we can identify three possible attitudes toward risk: a desire for risk, an aversion to risk, and an indifference to risk. A *risk seeker* is one who prefers risk. Given a choice between more and less risky investments, with identical expected monetary returns, the *risk seeker* will select the riskier investment. Faced with the same choice, the *risk averter* will select the less risky investment. The person who is *indifferent to risk* will be indifferent between two investment projects with identical expected monetary returns regardless of their relative risks. *There undoubtedly are some who prefer risk and others who are indifferent to it, but both logic and observation suggest that business managers and investors are predominantly risk averters.*

Why should risk aversion generally hold? Given two alternatives, each with the same expected dollar returns, why do most decision makers prefer the less risky one? Several theories have been proposed to answer this question, but perhaps the most logically satisfying one involves *utility theory*.

At the heart of risk aversion is the notion of *diminishing marginal utility for money*. If a person with no money receives $1,000, it can satisfy his most immediate needs. If a second $1,000 is then received, it can be used, but the second $1,000 is not quite so necessary as the first $1,000. Thus, the value, or utility, of the second, or *marginal*, $1,000 is less than the utility of the first $1,000, and so on for additional increments of money. We therefore say that the marginal utility of money is diminishing.

Figure 3.4 graphs the relationship between income, or wealth and its utility, where utility is measured in units called *utils*.

---

[4]Risk as defined above in terms of both the standard deviation and the coefficient of variation is based on the *total* variability of a project's outcomes or returns. There are situations, however, when a project's total variability overstates its risk. This is because projects whose returns are less than perfectly correlated with each other can be combined and the variability of the resulting combination, or "portfolio," will be less than the sum of the individual variabilities. Much of the recent work in finance is based on the idea that a project's risk should be measured in terms of its contribution to total return variability on a portfolio of assets. This contribution to overall variation is measured by a concept known as beta which is related to the systematic variability or covariance of one asset's return, with returns on other assets. This risk concept, like the two discussed above, is based on the variability of returns, and for our purposes it is not necessary that we examine the alternative constructs more closely. The interested reader should consult a basic finance textbook such as E. F. Brigham, *Financial Management*, 3rd ed. (Hinsdale, Ill.: The Dryden Press, 1982), Chapter 5 for a more detailed discussion of these alternative risk concepts.

FIGURE 3.4

Relationships between Money and its Utility

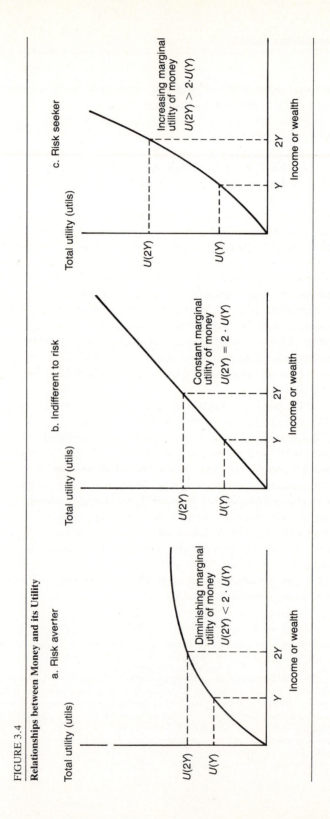

a. Risk averter

Total utility (utils)

U(2Y)

U(Y)

Diminishing marginal
utility of money
U(2Y) < 2 · U(Y)

Y   2Y

Income or wealth

b. Indifferent to risk

Total utility (utils)

U(2Y)

U(Y)

Constant marginal
utility of money
U(2Y) = 2 · U(Y)

Y   2Y

Income or wealth

c. Risk seeker

Total utility (utils)

U(2Y)

U(Y)

Increasing marginal
utility of money
U(2Y) > 2·U(Y)

Y   2Y

Income or wealth

Curve 3.4a describes the relationship between utility and income or wealth for a risk averter. Here a diminishing marginal utility of income is evident. This means that if the individual's income were to suddenly double, he or she would experience an increase in utility (happiness, or satisfaction) but the new level of total utility would not be twice the previous level. That is, in cases of diminishing marginal utility of money, there is a less than proportional relationship between total utility and money. Accordingly, the utility of a doubled income is less than twice the utility of the original income level. By way of contrast, for those who are indifferent to risk there is a strictly proportional relationship between total utility and money. Such a relationship implies a constant marginal utility of money as illustrated in Figure 3.4b. In cases of a constant marginal utility of money, the utility of a doubled income is exactly twice the utility of the original income level. And finally, for risk seekers there is a more than proportional relationship between total utility and money. In this case the marginal utility of money is increasing. As shown in Figure 3.4c, with increasing marginal utility of money, the utility of a doubled income is more than twice the utility of the original income level.

Therefore, while total utility increases with income for risk averters, risk seekers, and those who are indifferent to risk, the relationship between total utility and income is quite different for each group. These differences lead directly to differences in risk attitudes. Because individuals with a diminishing marginal utility for money will suffer more pain from a dollar lost than they will derive pleasure from a dollar gained, they will be very much opposed to risk. Thus, they will require a very high return on any investment that is subject to much risk. In Figure 3.5, for example, a gain of $2,500 from a base of $5,000 brings 2 utils of additional satisfaction; but a $2,500 loss causes a 4-util satisfaction loss. A person with this utility function and $5,000 would, therefore, be unwilling to make an investment with a 50-50 chance of winning or losing $2,500, the reason being that the 9-util expected utility of such a gamble [$E(u) = 0.5$ times the utility of $2,500 + 0.5$ times the utility of $7,500 = 0.5 \times 6 + 0.5 \times 12 = 9$] is less than the 10 units of utility obtained by forgoing the investment and keeping the $5,000 current wealth with certainty.[5]

A second example should clarify this relationship between utility and risk aversion. Assume that government bonds are riskless securities and that such bonds currently offer a 9 percent rate of return. If an individual buys a $5,000 U.S. Treasury bond and holds it for one year, he or she will end up with $5,450, a profit of $450.

Suppose there is an alternative investment opportunity that calls for the $5,000 to back a wildcat oil-drilling venture. If the drilling venture is successful, the investment will be worth $10,000 at the end of the year. If it is unsuccessful, the

[5]For a risk averter the expected utility of a gamble will always be less than the utility of the expected dollar payoff. Since an individual with a constant marginal utility for money will value a dollar gained just as highly as a dollar lost, the expected utility from a fair gamble such as the one offered here will always be exactly equal to the utility of the expected outcome. Because of this, an individual indifferent to risk can make decisions on the basis of expected monetary outcomes and need not be concerned with possible variation in the distribution of outcomes.

investors can liquidate their holdings and recover $2,500. There is a 60 percent chance that oil will be discovered, and a 40 percent chance of a dry hole or no oil. If an investor has only $5,000 to invest, should he choose the riskless government bond or the risky drilling operation?

To analyze this question let us first calculate the expected monetary values of the two investments; this is done in Table 3.3. The calculation in the table is not really necessary for the government bond; the $5,450 outcome will occur regardless of what happens in the oil field. The oil venture calculation, however, shows that the expected value of this venture—$7,000—is higher than that of the bond. Does this mean the investor should put his money in the wildcat well? Not necessarily—it depends on the investor's utility function. If an investor's marginal utility for money is sharply diminishing, then the potential loss of utility from a dry hole might not be compensated for by the potential gain in utility from a producing well. If the risk averter utility function shown in Figure 3.5 is applicable, this is precisely the case. Four utils will be lost if no oil is found, and only three will be gained if the well becomes a producer.

Let us modify the expected monetary value calculation to reflect utility considerations. Reading from Figure 3.5, we see that this particular risk averse investor will have 13 utils if he invests in the wildcat venture and oil is found and 6 utils if no oil is found. He will have 10.7 utils with certainty if he chooses the government bond. This information is used in Table 3.4 to calculate the *expected utility* for the oil investment. No calculation is needed for the government bond; its utility is 10.7 (read from Figure 3.5), regardless of the outcome of the oil venture.

FIGURE 3.5

Relationship between Money and Its Utility

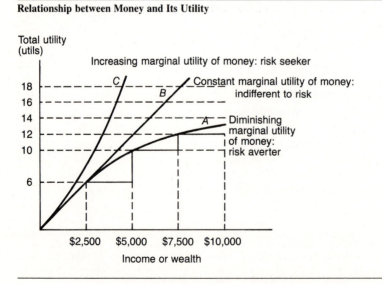

TABLE 3.3

Expected Returns from Two Projects

State of Nature	Drilling Operation			Government Bond		
	Probability (1)	Outcome (2)	(1) × (2) (3)	Probability (1)	Outcome (2)	(1) × (2) (3)
Oil	0.6	$10,000	$6,000	0.6	$5,450	$3,270
No oil	0.4	2,500	1,000	0.4	5,450	2,180
		Expected value	$7,000		Expected value	$5,450

TABLE 3.4

Expected Utility of the Oil-Drilling Project

State of Nature	Probability (1)	Monetary Outcome (2)	Associated Utility (3)	Expected Utility (Utils) (1) × (3) (4)
Oil	0.6	$10,000	13.0	7.8
No oil	0.4	2,500	6.0	2.4
				10.2

Since the expected utility from the wildcat venture is only 10.2 utils, versus 10.7 from the government bond, we see that the government bond is the preferred investment. Thus, even though the expected *monetary value* for the oil venture is higher, expected utility is greater for the bond; risk considerations dictate that the investor should buy the government bond.

ADJUSTING THE VALUATION MODEL FOR RISK

Diminishing marginal utility leads directly to risk aversion, and risk aversion is reflected in the valuation model used by investors to determine the worth of a firm. Thus, if a firm takes an action that increases its risk level, this action affects its value. To illustrate, consider the basic valuation model developed in Chapter 1:

$$V = \sum_{t=1}^{n} \frac{\pi_t}{(1 + i)^t}.$$

(3.6)

This model states that value is the discounted present worth of future profits or income. The stream of profits in the numerator, π, is really the expected value of the

profits each year. If the firm must choose between two alternative methods of operation, one with high expected profits and high risk and another with smaller expected
profits and lower risk, will the higher expected profits be sufficient to offset the
higher risk? If so, the riskier alternative is the preferred one; if not, the low-risk
procedure should be adopted.

Certainty Equivalent Adjustments

A number of methods have been proposed to account for risk in the valuation
model. One of these, the certainty equivalent approach follows directly from the
concept of utility theory developed above. Under the certainty equivalent approach,
decision makers must specify the amount of money that they would have to be as-
sured of receiving to make them indifferent between this certain sum and the expected value of a risky alternative. To illustrate, suppose you face the following
alternatives:

1. Invest $100,000. If the project is successful, you receive $1 million; if it is a
failure you receive nothing, i.e., the $100,000 is lost. If the probability of success is
0.5 or 50 percent, the expected payoff of the investment is $500,000 (= 0.5 ×
$1,000,000 + 0.5 × 0).

2. You do not make the investment, and you retain the $100,000.

If you find yourself indifferent about the two alternatives, $100,000 is your cer-
tainty equivalent for the risky $500,000 expected return. In other words, the certain
or riskless amount provides exactly the same utility as the risky alternative and,
therefore, you are indifferent between them. In this example, any certainty equivalent less than $500,000 indicates risk aversion. That is, if the maximum amount
you would be willing to invest in the first alternative is less than $500,000, you are
exhibiting risk averse behavior. In general, any risky investment with a certainty
equivalent less than the expected dollar value indicates risk aversion. A certainty
equivalent equal to the expected value indicates risk indifference. And finally a certainty equivalent greater than the expected value indicates risk preference. Therefore, an individual's attitude toward risk is directly reflected in the certainty equivalent adjustment factor, calculated as the ratio of the equivalent certain dollar sum
(i.e., the certain sum whose utility is equal to the expected utility of the risky alternative) divided by the expected dollar outcome from the risky alternative:

$$\alpha = \frac{\text{Equivalent certain sum}}{\text{Expected risky sum}}.$$

The following relationships enable one to use the certainty equivalent adjustment
factor to analyze risk attitudes:

$\alpha < 1$ implies risk aversion,

$\alpha = 1$ implies risk indifference,

and $\alpha > 1$ implies risk preference.

The certainty equivalent concept is illustrated in Figures 3.6 and 3.7. Figure 3.6 shows a series of risk–return combinations to which the decision maker is indifferent. For example, Point A represents an investment with a perceived degree of risk ν_A and expected dollar return of \$3,000. The risk–return trade-off function or indifference curve shows a person who is indifferent to a certain \$1,000, an expected \$2,000 with risk ν_B, and an expected \$3,000 with risk ν_A.

The indifference curve shown in Figure 3.6 can be used to construct a risk-aversion function such as the one illustrated in Figure 3.7. This conversion is obtained by dividing each risky return into its certainty equivalent return to obtain a certainty equivalent adjustment factor, α, for each level of risk, ν. For example, the certainty equivalent adjustment factor for risk level ν_A is:

$$\alpha_A = \frac{\$1,000}{\$3,000} = 0.33.$$

FIGURE 3.6

Certainty Equivalent Returns

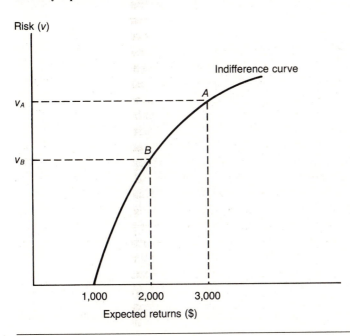

FIGURE 3.7

Hypothetical Risk-Aversion Function

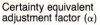

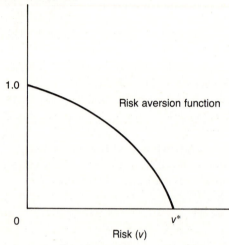

Note: As we have drawn it, the risk-aversion function assumes that $\alpha = 0$ when $\nu \geq \nu^*$. Theoretically, α would never actually reach zero; rather, it would approach zero when risk becomes quite high.

For risk level ν_B we have:

$$\alpha_B = \frac{\$1,000}{\$2,000} = 0.50.$$

Conceptually, α values could be developed for all possible levels of ν (risk). The range of α would be from 1.0 for $\nu = 0$ to a value close to 0 for large values of ν, assuming risk aversion.

Given the risk-aversion function and the degree of risk inherent in any risky return, the expected risky return could be replaced by its certainty equivalent:

$$\text{Certainty equivalent of } \pi_t = \alpha \pi_t,$$

and Equation 3.6 could then be converted to Equation 3.7, a valuation model that explicitly accounts for risk:

$$V = \sum_{t=1}^{n} \frac{\alpha \pi_t}{(1 + i)^t}.$$ **(3.7)**

Here expected future profits, π_t, are converted to their certainty equivalents, $\alpha\pi_t$, and are discounted at a risk free rate, i, to obtain the present value of a firm or project. With the valuation model in this form, one can appraise the effects of different courses of action with different risks and expected returns.

In order to use Equation 3.7 for real-world decision making, managers must obtain estimates of appropriate α's for various investment opportunities. Deriving such estimates can prove formidable, since α levels vary according to the size and riskiness of investment projects, as well as to the risk attitudes of managers and investors. In many instances, however, the record of past investments can be used as a guide to determine appropriate certainty equivalent adjustment factors.

Use of Certainty Equivalent Adjustment Factors: An Illustration

The following example illustrates how managers use certainty equivalent adjustment factors for decision making. Fitness World, Inc. (FWI) has recently opened a number of health clubs in small to medium-sized midwestern cities. These clubs have been successful in generating attractive rates of return relative to the levels of risk undertaken. FWI managers believe that three health clubs in Ames, Iowa, Bloomington, Indiana, and Columbus, Ohio, are very close to the cutoff point in terms of their acceptability; therefore, they can be used to gain insight into management's risk attitude.

In deciding whether or not to establish these clubs, labeled A, B, and C for simplicity, FWI used the information contained in Table 3.5. In the table we see that the expected profit contribution increases from Project A to B to C. The fact that FWI was only willing to invest something less than the level of expected profit contribution for each project suggests that the managers were averse to risk. Examination of the implied certainty equivalent adjustment factors for each project provides further insight into FWI management's risk aversion.

Since FWI management viewed each project as just acceptable, the required investment outlay can be viewed as the certainty equivalent of the project's expected risky return. That is, management was just willing to exchange a certain sum (the annual investment) for a distribution of risky returns (the project) with a given expected return and level of risk. Thus, dividing the investment amount by the expected risky return provides a measure of the implied certainty equivalent adjustment factor, α, for each project. As shown in Table 3.5, α for Project A is 0.87. If FWI's management focuses on the coefficient of variation, ν, for risk considerations, this means that with $\nu = 0.217$, the firm has used (either explicitly or implicitly) a certainty equivalent adjustment factor, $\alpha = 0.87$. Alternatively stated $\alpha_A = 0.87$ means that FWI viewed $0.87 as the certainty equivalent of $1 of expected return on Project A and was willing to pay that amount for each expected risky dollar. Based on the data for Projects B and C, we see that with $\nu_B = 0.257$, $\alpha_B = 0.86$ and with $\nu_C = 0.273$, $\alpha_C = 0.82$. That is, the implicit α's for Projects B

TABLE 3.5

FWI Illustration: Calculation of Certainty Equivalent Adjustment Factors

Outcome (1)	Profit Contribution (2)	Probability (3)	Expected Profit Contribution (Risky Sum) (4)	Annual Investment Cost (Certain Sum) (5)	Risk (6)
Project A					
Failure	$ 90,000	.5	$115,000	$100,000	.217
Success	140,000	.5			

$$\alpha_A = \frac{\$100,000}{\$115,000} = 0.87$$

Project B					
Failure	130,000	.5	175,000	150,000	.257
Success	220,000	.5			

$$\alpha_B = \frac{\$150,000}{\$175,000} = 0.86$$

Project C					
Failure	200,000	.5	275,000	225,000	.273
Success	350,000	.5			

$$\alpha_C = \frac{\$225,000}{\$275,000} = 0.82$$

Note: A project's profit contribution is calculated as total revenues minus total variable costs. To simplify the analysis, we assume that the annual investment cost includes the return required for the use of the funds as measured by the yield available on a riskless security. For example, the $100,000 annual investment cost for Project A is found as the actual investment cost of $88,500 times 1.13 to account for the 13% yield then available on riskless U.S. Treasury bonds.

and C provide additional measures of the certainty equivalent adjustment factors FWI assigns to various risk levels. Using these observations as well as similar ones for other accepted projects, we could construct for FWI a risk-aversion function of the type shown in Figure 3.7.

This analysis of historical investment decisions provides information that we can use to make future investment decisions. For example, if we know a potential project's required investment and risk level, we can calculate the α implied by a decision to accept the investment, and we can compare it with α's for prior projects that had similar risks. Risk averse individuals should invest in projects if calculated α's are less than or equal to those for accepted historical projects that have the same risk. Further, given an estimate of expected return and risk, the maximum amount the firm should be willing to invest in a given project can also be determined using the certainty equivalent adjustment factor. Here we can use the expected return and the α on prior projects with similar risk to calculate the maximum that the firm will invest in the project (certainty equivalent amount). Management will accept projects if the level of required investment per dollar of expected return is less than or equal to that for historical projects of similar risk.

Risk-Adjusted Discount Rates

Another way to incorporate risk in the valuation model is to adjust the discount rate, i. Like the certainty equivalent factor, risk-adjusted discount rates are based on investors' trade-off between risk and return. For example, suppose investors are willing to trade between risk and return, as shown in Figure 3.8. The curve is defined as a *market indifference curve* or a *risk–return trade-off function*. The average investor is indifferent to a riskless asset with a sure 10 percent rate of return, a moderately risky asset with a 20 percent expected return, and a very risky asset with a 30 percent expected return. As risk increases, higher expected returns on investment are required to compensate investors for the additional risk.

FIGURE 3.8

Relationship between Risk and Rate of Return

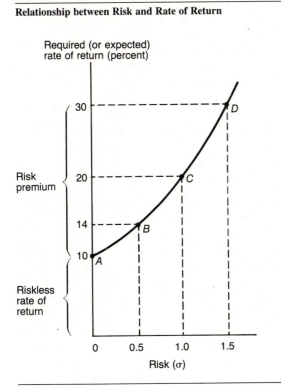

The difference between the expected rate of return on a particular risky asset and the rate of return on a riskless asset is defined as the *risk premium* on the risky asset. In the hypothetical situation depicted in Figure 3.8 the riskless rate is assumed to be 10 percent; a 4 percent risk premium is required to compensate for the level of risk indicated by $\sigma = 0.5$; and a 20 percent risk premium is attached to an investment with a risk of $\sigma = 1.5$.

Since required returns are related to the level of risk associated with a particular investment, we can modify the basic valuation model, Equation 3.6, to account for risk through an adjustment of the discount rate, i. Such a modification results in the valuation model:

$$V = \sum_{t=1}^{n} \frac{\pi_t}{(1 + k)^t} . \qquad (3.8)$$

In Equation 3.8, value is found as the present worth of expected future income or profits, π_t, discounted at a risk-adjusted rate. The risk-adjusted discount rate, k, is determined as the sum of the riskless rate of return and the risk premium required as compensation for the level of risk accepted. Assuming that decision makers use the risk–return trade-off function shown in Figure 3.8, they would evaluate a firm or project with risk level $\sigma = 0.5$ using a 14 percent discount rate, composed of a 10 percent riskless interest rate and a 4 percent risk premium. Similarly, a riskier project with $\sigma = 1.5$ would require a risk premium of 20 percent and, thus, would be evaluated using a 30 percent discount rate (30% = 10% riskless rate + 20% risk premium).

Use of Risk-Adjusted Discount Rates: An Illustration

The following example illustrates the use of risk-adjusted discount rates for managerial decision making. The Extron Typewriter Company has to decide which of two mutually exclusive computer interfaces to manufacture. These interfaces allow an electronic typewriter to be connected to a computer as an input-output device. One interface is specifically designed for Extron typewriters and cannot be used with those of other manufacturers; the other adapts to a wide variety of electronic typewriters, both Extron's and those of competitors. The expected investment outlay for design, engineering, production setup, and so on is $600,000 for each alternative. Expected cash inflows are $220,000 a year for five years if the interface can be used only with Extron typewriters (Project A) and $260,000 for five years if the interface can be used with a variety of electronic typewriters (Project B). Because of the captive market for Project A, however, the standard deviation of the expected annual returns from the project is only 1.0, while that of Project B is 1.5. In view of this risk differential, Extron's management decides that Project A should be evaluated with a 20 percent cost of capital, while the appropriate cost of capital for Project B is 30 percent. Which project should be selected?

We can calculate the risk-adjusted value for each project as follows:[6]

$$\text{Value}_A = \sum_{t=1}^{5} \frac{\$220{,}000}{(1.20)^t} - \$600{,}000$$

$$= \$220{,}000 \times \left(\sum_{t=1}^{5} \frac{1}{(1.20)^t} \right) - \$600{,}000$$

$$= \$220{,}000 \times 2.991 - \$600{,}000$$

$$= \$58{,}020$$

$$\text{Value}_B = \sum_{t=1}^{5} \frac{\$260{,}000}{(1.30)^t} - \$600{,}000$$

$$= \$260{,}000 \times \left(\sum_{t=1}^{5} \frac{1}{(1.30)^t} \right) - \$600{,}000$$

$$= \$260{,}000 \times 2.436 - \$600{,}000$$

$$= \$33{,}360$$

Because the risk-adjusted value of the safer Project A is larger than that for Project B, the firm should choose Project A. This choice maximizes the value of the firm.

---

[6] The terms

$$\sum_{t=1}^{5} \frac{1}{(1.20)^t} = 2.991$$

and

$$\sum_{t=1}^{5} \frac{1}{(1.30)^t} = 2.436$$

are defined as present value of an annuity interest factors. Appendix A at the end of the text explains how interest factors are calculated. Tables of interest factors for various interest rates and years (t values) are contained in Appendix C at the end of the text.

TECHNIQUES FOR DECISION MAKING
UNDER UNCERTAINTY

In many decision situations, the data required for incorporating risk analysis into the decision process is not readily available in a usable form. In such cases *decision trees* and *computer simulation* help one to develop and organize risk data for decision making. We shall now examine these two decision making techniques and the role that they play in decision making under conditions of uncertainty.

Decision Trees

Many important decisions are not made at one point in time but rather in stages. For example, a petroleum firm considering the possibility of expanding into agricultural chemicals might take the following steps:

1. Spend $100,000 to survey supply and demand conditions in the agricultural chemical industry.

2. If the survey results are favorable, spend $2 million on a pilot plant to investigate production methods.

3. Depending on the costs estimated from the pilot study and the demand potential from the market study, either abandon the project, build a large plant, or build a small one.

Thus, decisions are actually made in stages with subsequent decisions depending on the results of prior decisions.

The sequence of events can be mapped out to resemble the branches of a tree, hence the term *decision tree*. As an example consider Figure 3.9, which assumes that the petroleum company has completed its industry supply and demand analysis and pilot plant study, and has determined that it should develop a full-scale production facility. The firm can build a large plant or a small one. Demand expectations for the plant's products are 50 percent for high demand, 30 percent for medium demand, and 20 percent for low demand. Depending on demand, net cash flows (sales revenues minus operating costs), all discounted to the present, will range from $8.8 million to $1.4 million if a large plant is built, and from $2.6 million to $1.4 million if a small plant is built.

Since the demand probabilities are known, we can find the expected values of cash flows, which are given in column 5 of Figure 3.9. Finally, we can deduct the investment outlays from the expected net revenues to obtain the expected net present value of each decision. In the example, the expected net present value is $730,000 for the large plant and $300,000 for the small one.

Since the net present value of the large plant is higher, should the decision be to

FIGURE 3.9

Illustrative Decision Tree

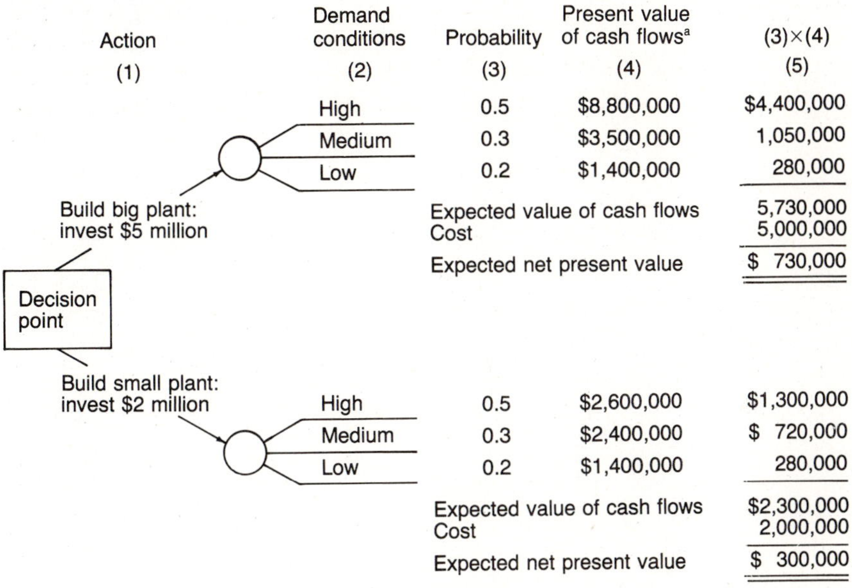

Action (1)	Demand conditions (2)	Probability (3)	Present value of cash flows[a] (4)	(3)×(4) (5)
	High	0.5	$8,800,000	$4,400,000
	Medium	0.3	$3,500,000	1,050,000
	Low	0.2	$1,400,000	280,000
Build big plant: invest $5 million			Expected value of cash flows Cost	5,730,000 5,000,000
			Expected net present value	$ 730,000
Decision point				
Build small plant: invest $2 million	High	0.5	$2,600,000	$1,300,000
	Medium	0.3	$2,400,000	$ 720,000
	Low	0.2	$1,400,000	280,000
			Expected value of cash flows Cost	$2,300,000 2,000,000
			Expected net present value	$ 300,000

[a]The figures in column 4 are the annual cash flows from operation—revenues minus cash operating costs—discounted at the firm's cost of capital.

construct it? Perhaps, but not necessarily. Notice that the range of outcomes is greater if the large plant is built, with the actual net present values (column 4, present values, in Figure 3.9 minus the investment cost) varying from $3.8 million to *minus* $3.6 million. However, a range of only $600,000 to *minus* $600,000 exists for the small plant. Since the required investment for the two plants is not the same, we must examine the coefficients of variation of the net present value possibilities in order to determine which alternative actually entails the greater risk. The coefficient of variation for the large plant's present value is 4.3, while that for the small plant is only 1.5.[7] Risk is greater for building the large plant.

The decision maker could take account of the risk differentials in a variety of ways. Utility values could be assigned to the cash flows given in column 4 of Figure 3.9, thus stating column 5 in terms of expected utility. The plant size that provided

[7]Using Equation 3.4 and the data on possible returns in Figure 3.9, the standard deviation of return for the large plant is $3.155 million, and for the smaller is $458,260. Dividing each of these standard deviations by the expected returns for their respective plant size, as in Equation 3.5, gives the coefficient of variation.

FIGURE 3.10

Decision Tree with Multiple Decision Points

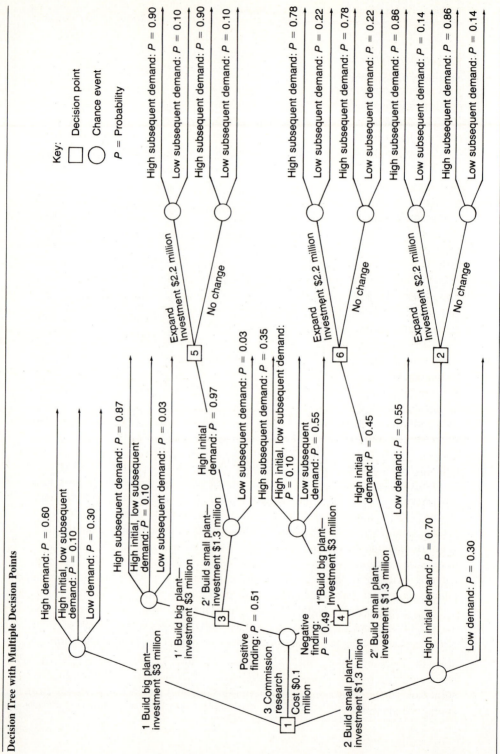

Key:

□ Decision point

○ Chance event

P = Probability

High demand: P = 0.60

High initial, low subsequent demand: P = 0.10

Low demand: P = 0.30

High subsequent demand: P = 0.87

High initial, low subsequent demand: P = 0.10

Low subsequent demand: P = 0.03

High subsequent demand: P = 0.90

Low subsequent demand: P = 0.10

High subsequent demand: P = 0.90

Low subsequent demand: P = 0.10

Expand Investment $2.2 million

No change

High initial demand: P = 0.97

Low subsequent demand: P = 0.03

High subsequent demand: P = 0.35

High initial, low subsequent demand: P = 0.10

Low subsequent demand: P = 0.55

High subsequent demand: P = 0.78

Low subsequent demand: P = 0.22

High subsequent demand: P = 0.78

Low subsequent demand: P = 0.22

High subsequent demand: P = 0.86

Low subsequent demand: P = 0.14

High subsequent demand: P = 0.86

Low subsequent demand: P = 0.14

Expand Investment $2.2 million

No change

Expand Investment $2.2 million

No change

5

6

2

1' Build big plant— investment $3 million

2' Build small plant— investment $1.3 million

1" Build big plant— Investment $3 million

2" Build small plant— investment $1.3 million

3

4

Positive finding: P = 0.51

Negative finding: P = 0.49

3 Commission research

Cost $0.1 million

1

1 Build big plant— investment $3 million

2 Build small plant— investment $1.3 million

High initial demand: P = 0.45

Low demand: P = 0.55

High initial demand: P = 0.70

Low demand: P = 0.30

the greatest expected utility could then be chosen. Alternatively, a manager could use the certainty equivalent or risk-adjusted discount rate methods in calculating the present values given in column 4. The plant that offered the larger risk-adjusted net present value would then be the optimal choice.

The decision tree illustrated in Figure 3.9 is quite simple; in actual use, the trees are frequently far more complex and involve a number of sequential decision points. An example of a more complex tree is illustrated in Figure 3.10. The numbered boxes represent *decision points*, instances when the management must choose among several alternatives; the circles represent the possible outcomes, one of which will follow the decisions. At Decision Point 1, the firm has three choices: to invest $3 million in a large plant, to invest $1.3 million in a small plant, or to spend $100,000 on market research. If the large plant is built, the firm follows the upper branch, and its position has been fixed—it can only hope that demand will be high. If it builds the small plant, it follows the lower branch. If demand is low, no further action is required; if demand is high, Decision Point 2 is reached, and the firm either must do nothing or must expand the plant at a cost of another $2.2 million. (Thus, if it obtains a large plant through expansion, the cost is $500,000 greater than if it had built the large plant in the first place.)

If the decision at Point 1 is to pay $100,000 for more information, the firm moves to the center branch. The research modifies the firm's information about potential demand. Initially, the probabilities were 70 percent for high demand and 30 percent for low demand. The research survey will show either favorable (positive) or unfavorable (negative) demand prospects. If they are positive, we assume that the probability for high final demand will be 87 percent, and that for low demand will be 13 percent; if the research yields negative results, the odds on high final demand are only 35 percent, and those for low demand are 65 percent. These results will influence the firm's decision whether to build a large plant or a small plant.

If the firm builds a large plant and demand is high, sales and profits will be large. If, however, it builds a large plant and there is little demand, sales will be low and they will incur losses. On the other hand, if it builds a small plant and demand is high, sales and profits will be lower than they could have been had a large plant been built, yet they will eliminate the chances of losses in the event of low demand. To build the large plant is therefore riskier than to build the small plant. The cost of the research is, in effect, an expenditure serving to reduce the degree of uncertainty in the decision; the research provides additional information on the probability of high versus low demand, thus reducing the level of risk.

The decision tree in Figure 3.10 is incomplete because no dollar outcomes (or utility values) are assigned to the various situations. If such values are assigned, along the lines shown in the last two columns of Figure 3.9, expected values can be obtained for each of the alternative actions along with measures of the possible variability of outcomes. These values will then help the decision maker to choose among the alternatives.

Simulation

Another technique designed to assist managers in making decisions under uncertainty is computer simulation. To illustrate the technique, let us consider the decision to build a new textile plant. The exact cost of the plant is not known. It is expected to be about $150 million. If no difficulties arise in construction, the cost can be as low as $125 million; however, an unfortunate series of events—strikes, unprojected increases in material costs, and technical problems—could result in an investment outlay as high as $225 million.

Revenues from the new facility, which will operate for many years, depend on population growth and personal income in the region, competition, developments in synthetic fabrics, research, and textile import quotas. Operating costs depend on production efficiency, materials, and labor cost trends. Because both sales revenues and operating costs are uncertain, annual profits are also uncertain.

Assuming that probability distributions can be developed for each of the major cost and revenue determinants, a computer program can be constructed to simulate what is likely to occur. In effect, the computer selects one value at random from each of the relevant distributions, combines it with values selected from the other distributions, and produces an estimated profit and net present value, or rate of return, on investment. This particular profit and rate of return occur only for the particular combination of values selected during the trial. The computer proceeds to select other sets of values and to compute other profits and rates of return for perhaps several hundred trials. A count is kept of the number of times each of the various rates of return is computed. When the computer runs are completed, the frequency with which the various rates of return occurred can be plotted as a frequency distribution.

The procedure is illustrated in Figures 3.11 and 3.12. Figure 3.11 is a flow chart outlining the simulation procedure described above; Figure 3.12 illustrates the frequency distribution of rates of return generated by such a simulation for two alternative projects, X and Y, each with an expected cost of $20 million. The expected rate of return on Investment X is 15 percent, and that of Investment Y is 20 percent. However, these are only the average rates of return generated by the computer; simulated rates ranged from -10 percent to $+45$ percent for Investment Y, and from 5 to 25 percent for Investment X. The standard deviation generated for X is only 4 percentage points; that for Y is 12 percentage points. From this we can calculate a coefficient of variation of 0.267 for Project X, and 0.60 for Project Y. On the basis of total variability, Investment Y is riskier than Investment X. The computer simulation has provided an estimate both of the expected returns on the two projects and of their relative risks. A decision about which alternative should be chosen can now be made on the basis of one of the techniques—certainty equivalent, or risk-adjusted discount rate, present value determination, or expected utility—discussed above.

One final point should be made about the use of computer simulation for risk

FIGURE 3.11

Simulation for Investment Planning

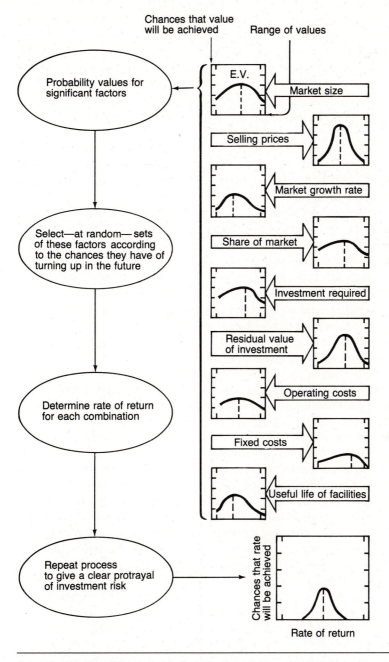

FIGURE 3.12

Expected Rates of Return on Investments *X* and *Y*

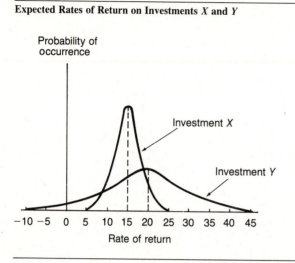

analysis. The technique requires obtaining probability distributions about a number of variables such as investment outlays, unit sales, product prices, input prices, and asset lives, all of which involve a fair amount of programming and machine-time costs. Full-scale simulation is expensive, and therefore used primarily for large and expensive projects such as major plant expansions or new-product decisions. In these cases, however, when a firm is deciding whether or not to accept a major undertaking involving an outlay of millions of dollars, computer simulation can provide valuable insights into the relative merits of alternative strategies.

It should also be noted that a somewhat less expensive simulation technique is available as an alternative method of analyzing the outcomes of various projects or strategies. Instead of using probability distributions for each of the variables in the problem, we can simulate the results by starting with best-guess estimates for each variable, and then change the values of the variables (within reasonable limits) to see the effects of such changes on the returns generated by the project. Typically, returns are highly sensitive to some variables, less so to others. Attention is then concentrated on the variables to which profitability is most sensitive. This technique, known as sensitivity analysis, is considerably less expensive than the full-scale simulation and provides similar data for decision-making purposes.

SUMMARY

Risk analysis plays an integral role in the decision process for most business problems. In this chapter we defined the concept of risk, introduced it into the valuation model for the firm, and then examined several techniques for decision making under conditions of uncertainty.

Risk in economic analysis is characterized by variability of outcomes, and it is defined in terms of probability distributions of possible results. The tighter the distribution, the lower the variability, and hence the lower the risk. The standard deviation and coefficient of variation are two frequently used measures of risk in economic analysis.

The assumption of risk aversion by investors and managers is based on utility relationships. For most individuals, marginal utility is sharply diminishing, and this leads directly to risk aversion. Investor risk aversion affects the valuation of the firm and must, therefore, be taken into account for managerial decision making. The basic valuation model can be adjusted to reflect this risk effect through the use of certainty equivalent adjustment factors and risk-adjusted discount rates.

Decision making under conditions of uncertainty is greatly facilitated by decision trees and simulation, two techniques used to structure problems and to generate data necessary for risk analysis. Decision trees map out the sequence of events in a decision problem, providing a means for examining the branching that takes place at each decision point and chance event. Simulation techniques can be used to generate frequency distributions of possible outcomes for alternative decisions and to provide inputs for expected utility, certainty equivalent, or risk-adjusted discount rate analysis.

The concepts and techniques of analysis introduced in this chapter play major roles in the analyses used in subsequent chapters. We refer to them frequently in analyzing problems in the areas of demand, production, cost, pricing, and capital budgeting.

QUESTIONS

3.1 Define the following terms using graphs to illustrate your answers where feasible:

    a. Probability distribution

    b. Expected value

    c. Standard deviation

    d. Coefficient of variation

    e. Risk

    f. Diminishing marginal utility

    g. Certainty equivalent

    h. Risk-adjusted discount rate

    i. Decision tree

    j. Simulation

3.2 The probability distribution of a less risky expected return is more peaked than that of a risky return. What shape would a graph of the probability distribution have for completely certain returns and for completely uncertain returns?

3.3 What is the main difficulty associated with making decisions on the basis of comparisons among expected monetary values of alternative courses of action?

3.4 In this chapter we have defined risk in terms of the variability of possible outcomes; that is, the standard deviation of these outcomes. In constructing this measure of risk, we have implicitly given equal weight to variations on both sides of the expected value. Can you see any problems resulting from this treatment?

3.5 Use the data in Figure 3.5 to show that for an individual with constant marginal utility of money, the expected utility of a gamble is equal to the utility of the expected dollar outcome. (Hint: Use a gamble with a 50-50 chance of a $2,500 or a $7,500 payoff.)

3.6 "On reflection, the use of the market indifference curve concept illustrated in Figure 3.8 as a basis for determining risk-adjusted discount rates is all right in theory, but cannot be applied in practice. Market estimates of investors' reactions to risk cannot be measured precisely, so it is impossible to construct a set of risk-adjusted discount rates for the different classes of investment." Comment on this statement.

3.7 What is the value of decision trees in managerial decision making?

3.8 Are the risk levels of investment alternatives irrelevant to the risk neutral investor?

PROBLEMS

3.1 Gina Davids estimates that 3 out of every 50 individuals who take her free microwave cooking course buy a new microwave oven, and 20 out of 50 buy new microwave cooking utensils (dishes, cookbooks, etc.). Davids nets $20 for each new microwave sold, and an average $3 on each sale of cooking utensils. What is Davids' expected income on each course if attendance averages 25 persons?

3.2 Paul Daniels, marketing director for Nisswa Records, Inc., has just completed an agreement to re-release a recording of Jeanne Mooty's greatest hits. (Mooty had a number of hits on the country–western charts during the late 1950s and early 1960s.) Preliminary market research indicates two feasible marketing strategies: a. concentration on developing general consumer acceptance by advertising on late-night television, or b. concentration on distributor acceptance through intensive sales calls by company representatives. Daniels has developed estimates for sales under each alternative plan and has constructed payoff matrices according to his assessment of the likelihood of product acceptance under each plan. These matrices are illustrated as follows:

Strategy 1: Consumer-Television Promotion		Strategy 2: Distributor-Oriented Promotion	
Probability	Outcome (Sales)	Probability	Outcome (Sales)
0.1	$ 250,000	0.3	$ 500,000
0.4	750,000	0.4	750,000
0.4	1,250,000	0.3	1,000,000
0.1	1,750,000		

a. Assume that the company has a 50 percent profit margin on sales; that is, profits are equal to one-half of sales revenues. Calculate the expected profits for each plan.

b. Construct a simple bar graph of the possible profit outcomes for each plan. On the basis of the appearance of the two graphs, which plan appears to be more risky?

c. Calculate the risk (standard deviation of the profit distribution) associated with each plan.

d. Assume that the management of Nisswa has a utility function like the one illustrated below. Which marketing strategy should Daniels recommend?

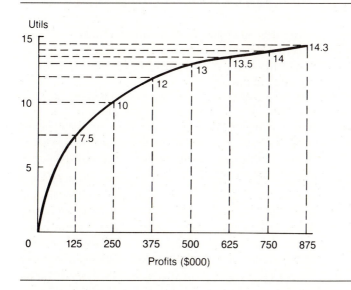

3.3 Bob Mathews is considering two alternative investments, each costing $5,000. Present values of possible outcomes and their probabilities of occurrence are:

	Investment A			Investment B		
	Outcome			Outcome		
	1	2	3	1	2	3
Net present value	$4,000	$6,000	$8,000	$3,000	$7,000	$8,000
Probability of occurrence	0.25	0.50	0.25	0.30	0.50	0.20

a. Calculate the expected present values of the two investments.

b. Calculate the standard deviation for each investment. Which alternative is riskier?

c. If Bob has a constant marginal utility of income as indicated by the utility function $U = 30 + 2X$, where X is thousands of dollars of present value, which investment should he choose? Why?

d. If Bob's utility of income is given by the function $U = 30X - X^2$ (which indicates diminishing marginal utility), which investment should he select? Why?

3.4 An investor with the utility function $U = 200I - I^2$ (I = hundreds of dollars of income) is considering the purchase of a security whose value is related to the level of interest rates. Specifically, the security will have a value of $3,000, $5,000, or $8,000 at the end of the month depending upon whether interest rates increase, remain unchanged or fall. The probabilities of these interest rate outcomes are 0.3, 0.6, and 0.1 respectively. The alternative for the investor is to purchase a T-bill with a 30-day maturity in which case the end of period value will be $4,000.

a. Is this investor risk averse? How do you know?

b. Calculate the expected dollar return from the risky investment.

c. What is the expected utility of the risky investment?

d. Which alternative will the investor choose? Why?

3.5 Hendricks Manufacturing is contemplating replacement of some production equipment with new electronically controlled machinery. While cost savings can be expected, the magnitude of such savings will be determined by the degree of utilization. Hendricks's production manager estimates:

Probability	Annual Cost Savings
.6	$5 million
.4	$3 million

During the past year, this same production manager has approved investments to replace production equipment on three different occasions. In analyzing these past investment decisions you discover the following:

Project	Certainty Equivalent	Coefficient of Variation
A	.87	.20
B	.85	.22
C	.80	.25

a. Calculate the expected return, standard deviation, and coefficient of variation for the cost savings on the new electronic machinery.

b. Given the production manager's prior decisions, calculate a range for the maximum acceptable purchase price for the new equipment, using a 5 year life and 12 percent risk-free discount rate.

3.6 Lisa's Fashion Boutiques Inc. is considering the possibility of expanding its promotional effort in one of three possible market areas. A preliminary analysis has revealed the following returns to local advertising campaigns.

	Market					
	Austin, TX		Madison, WI		Sacramento, CA	
	Pr	Revenue	Pr	Revenue	Pr	Revenue
Low Success	.4	$500,000	.4	$300,000	.2	$400,000
Medium Success	.4	600,000	.2	400,000	.4	500,000
High Success	.2	800,000	.4	500,000	.4	550,000

a. Calculate the expected revenue from each market.

b. Calculate the standard deviation for each market's returns.

c. Determine the coefficient of variation for each market.

d. On the basis of these findings can you decide in which market Lisa's should expand its promotional effort? Alternatively, can any be eliminated from consideration?

3.7 The Sport-Time Equipment Company manufactures a line of tennis rackets. Part of its production facility is to be replaced by one of two innovative pieces of equipment. The benefits (net cash flows) will be generated over the four-year useful lives of the machines and have the following expectational characteristics:

	Probability	Annual Cash Flow		Probability	Annual Cash Flow
Alternative #1	0.30	$2,900	Alternative #2	0.30	0
	0.50	3,500		0.50	4,000
	0.20	4,100		0.20	8,000

Whichever piece of equipment is chosen, the cost will be the same, $4,000.

a. What are the expected annual net cash flows from each project?

b. Given that the firm uses a discount rate of 12 percent for cash flows with a high degree of dispersion and a 10 percent rate for less risky cash flows, which machine has the highest expected net present value?

c. Suppose we know that the firm is indifferent between a "certain" 4-year annuity of $3,292 per year and the payoff of alternative #1, and would also be indifferent between a "certain" 4-year annuity of $3,300 per year and the return from alternative #2. What certainty equivalent adjustment factors do these figures indicate for each project?

d. Under these circumstances, which piece of equipment should be chosen if the firm uses an *NPV* certainty equivalent approach and an 8 percent riskless discount rate?

3.8 A severe winter storm has interrupted regular shipments of heating oil to Andrew's Manufacturing Co. While shipments are expected to resume within a week to ten days, Andrew's fuel supply is nearly depleted, and it may have to temporarily cease production. Unless Andrew's receives delivery of adequate fuel supplies within 48 hours, it will be forced to shut down, resulting in costs for cold temperature damage to plant and equipment of $10,000. Steve Johnson, Andrew's operations manager, has been able to line up two alternative short-term suppliers of heating oil. Western Oil and Fuel Co. has quoted a rate of $6,000 for on-time delivery, while Northwestern Heating Supply has quoted a rate of only $4,000. However, based upon past experience, Johnson estimates that the probability of on-time delivery by Western Oil and Fuel Co. is 0.8 while for Northwestern Heating Supply the probability is only 0.4.

a. Lay out the relevant decision tree diagram illustrating all possibilities and their relative probabilities.

b. Is it possible to make an optimal purchase decision here without knowing the firm's attitude toward risk? If so, do so. If not, why not?

c. Assume Johnson attempts to minimize expected cost. What probability of on-time arrival by Northwestern Heating Supply would make Johnson indifferent between the Western Oil and Fuel Co. and the Northwestern Heating Supply alternatives?

3.9 The Char-King Manufacturing Company has experienced a leveling off in demand for its deluxe ($250) charcoal grill. The variable cost of producing the grill is $200 a unit, irrespective of the quantity manufactured. Thus, Char-King earns a $50 profit contribution (or profit margin, as it is frequently called) on each grill sold. Sales projections for the following two years show expected sales at a constant 20,000 units a year.

The firm's management has done research on two alternative programs for improving demand and has come up with sales estimates and probability distributions for the following two years (the planning horizon):

Plan A calls for adding a built-in thermometer to the grill at a cost of $10,000 a year plus $2 for each unit manufactured. The $250 sales price would be maintained.

Plan B calls for lowering the selling price from $250 to $245 a unit and increasing the advertising expenditure by $20,000 a year.

For the first year, the following probabilities of success and failure, and corresponding expected sales changes, have been estimated:

Plan	Probability	Outcome in First Year
A	0.8 (success)	Increase 5,000 units
	0.2 (failure)	Increase 500 units
B	0.7 (success)	Increase 5,500 units
	0.3 (failure)	Increase 2,000 units

In the second year, the competition is likely to react (especially if the program is successful). The following probabilities of competitor retaliation and corresponding expected sales changes are given:

Plan	Probability	Competitor Reaction	Unit Sales Increase in Year 2 over Year 0
A	0.7 given 1st year success	Reaction	3,000
	0.3 given 1st year success	No reaction	6,500
	0.2 given 1st year failure	Reaction	0
	0.8 given 1st year failure	No reaction	400
B	0.5 given 1st year success	Reaction	2,000
	0.5 given 1st year success	No reaction	6,000
	0.1 given 1st year failure	Reaction	0
	0.9 given 1st year failure	No reaction	500

a. Construct a decision tree for the firm to use in evaluating the two programs.

b. Assuming that all costs and revenues for a year are incurred at the end of the year for which they apply, compute the *NPV* of the incremental profit contribution at each branch terminal for each project using a discount rate of 10 percent. Next, find the expected *NPV* of each project as a weighted average of these terminal *NPV*s.

c. Which project appears most risky? Least risky? (Answer this question with the aid of graphs of the *NPV* distributions for all terminal branches. Do not calculate standard deviations.)

d. Which project, if any, should Char-King select? Why?

SELECTED REFERENCES

Bierman, Harold, Jr. *Strategic Financial Planning*. New York: Free Press, 1980.

Brown, Rex. "Do Managers Find Decision Theory Useful?" *Harvard Business Review* 48 (May–June 1970): 78–89.

Crum, Roy L., and Derkinderen, Frans G. J. (eds.). *Capital Budgeting Under Conditions of Uncertainty*. Boston: Martinus Nijhoff Publishers, 1981.

Durand, David. "Comprehensiveness in Capital Budgeting." *Financial Management* 10 (Winter 1981): 7–13.

Green, P. E. "Bayesian Decision Theory in Pricing Strategy." *Journal of Marketing* 27 (January 1963): 5–14.

Grether, David M. "Recent Psychological Studies of Behavior Under Uncertainty." *American Economic Review* 68 (May 1978): 70–74.

Hull, J., Moore, P. G., and Thomas, H. "Utility and Its Measurement." *Journal of the Royal Statistical Society* (1973): 136, Part 2, pp. 226–247.

Kihlstrom, Richard E., and Mirman, Leonard J. "Constant, Increasing and Decreasing Risk Aversion with Many Commodities." *Review of Economic Studies* 48 (April 1981): 271–280.

Magee, John F. "How to Use Decision Trees in Capital Budgeting." *Harvard Business Review* 42 (September–October 1964): 79–95.

Morgan, James N. "Multiple Motives, Group Decisions, Uncertainty, Ignorance, and Confusion: A Realistic Economics of the Consumer Requires Some Psychology." *American Economic Review* 68 (May 1978): 58–63.

Pappas, James L., and Huber, George P. "Probabilistic Short-Term Financial Planning." *Financial Management* 2 (Autumn 1973): 36–44.

Singhvi, Surendra S. *Planning for Capital Investments*. Oxford, Ohio: Planning Executives Institute, 1979.

APPENDIX 3A

PROBABILITY AS THE AREA UNDER THE NORMAL CURVE

The probability concepts introduced in Chapter 3 related risk to the variability of outcome and used this relationship to develop an approach to decision making under conditions of uncertainty. Often, important insight about the nature of risks associated with particular activities or courses of action can be gained through additional analysis of probability distributions. In this appendix we examine the application of probability theory to decision analysis under uncertainty in somewhat greater depth.

In the chapter we saw that probability distributions can be viewed in either of two ways: 1. as a series of *discrete values* represented by a bar chart, such as Figure 3.1, or 2. as a *continuous function* represented by a smooth curve, such as that in

FIGURE 3A.1

Continuous Probability Distribution

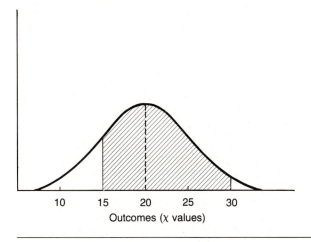

Outcomes (χ values)

Figure 3.2. Actually, there is an important difference in the way these two graphs are interpreted: The probabilities associated with the outcomes in Figure 3.1 are given by the *height* of each bar, while in Figure 3.2 the probabilities must be found by calculating the *area* under the curve between points of interest. Suppose, for example, that we have the continuous probability distribution shown in Figure 3A.1. This is a normal curve with a mean of 20 and a standard deviation of 5; x could be dollars of sales, profits, or costs; units of output; percentage rates of return; or any other units. If we want to know the probability that an outcome will fall between 15 and 30, we must calculate the area beneath the curve between these points, or the shaded area in the diagram.

   The area under the curve between 15 and 30 can be determined by integrating the curve over this interval, or, since the distribution is normal, by reference to statistical tables of the area under the normal curve, such as Table 3A.1 or Appendix D to this book.[1] To use these tables, it is necessary only to know the mean and standard deviation of the distribution.[2]

---

[1]The equation for the normal curve is tedious to integrate, which makes the use of tables much more convenient. The equation for the normal curve is

$$f(x) = \frac{1}{\sqrt{2\pi\sigma^2}} e^{-(x-\mu)^2/2\sigma^2},$$

where π and e are mathematical constants; μ (read mu) and σ denote the mean and standard deviation of the probability distribution, and x is any possible outcome.

[2]The procedures for calculating means and standard deviations are illustrated in Chapter 3.

TABLE 3A.1

Area under the Normal Curve

z^a	Area from the Mean to the Point of Interest	Ordinate
0.0	0.0000	0.3989
0.5	0.1915	0.3521
1.0	0.3413	0.2420
1.5	0.4332	0.1295
2.0	0.4773	0.0540
2.5	0.4938	0.0175
3.0	0.4987	0.0044

[a] z is the number of standard deviations from the mean. Some area tables are set up to indicate the area to the left or right of the point of interest; in this book we indicate the area between the mean and the point of interest.

The distribution to be investigated must first be standardized by using the following formula:

$$z = \frac{x - \mu}{\sigma}, \qquad \qquad \textbf{(3A.1)}$$

where z is the standardized variable, or the number of standard deviations from the mean,[3] x is the outcome of interest, and μ and σ are the mean and standard deviation of the distribution, respectively. For our example, where we are interested in the probability that an outcome will fall between 15 and 30, we first normalize these points of interest using Equation 3A.1:

$$z_1 = \frac{15 - 20}{5} = -1.0; \qquad z_2 = \frac{30 - 20}{5} = 2.0.$$

The areas associated with these z values are found in Table 3A.1 to be 0.3413 and 0.4773.[4] This means that the probability is 0.3413 that the actual outcome will fall between 15 and 20, and 0.4773 that it will fall between 20 and 30. Summing these probabilities shows that the probability of an outcome falling between 15 and 30 is 0.8186, or 81.86 percent.

Suppose we had been interested in determining the probability that the actual outcome would be greater than 15. Here we would first note that the probability is

[3]Note that if the point of interest is 1σ away from the mean, then $x - \mu = \sigma$, so $z = \sigma/\sigma = 1.0$. Thus, when $z = 1.0$, the point of interest is 1σ away from the mean; when $z = 2$, the value is 2σ, and so forth.

[4]Note that the negative sign on z_1 is ignored, since the normal curve is symmetrical around the mean; the minus sign merely indicates that the point lies to the left of the mean.

0.3413 that the outcome will be between 15 and 20, then observe that the probability is 0.5000 of an outcome greater than the mean, 20. Thus the probability is 0.3413 + 0.5000 = 0.8413, or 84.13 percent, that the outcome will exceed 15.

Some interesting properties of normal probability distributions can be seen by examining Table 3A.1 and Figure 3A.2, which is a graph of the normal curve. For any normal distribution, the probability of an outcome falling within plus or minus one standard deviation from the mean is 0.6826, or 68.26 percent (0.3413 × 2.0). If we take the range within two standards of the mean, the probability of an occurrence within this range is 95.46 percent, and 99.74 percent of all outcomes will fall within three standard deviations of the mean. Although the distribution theoretically runs from minus infinity to plus infinity, the probability of occurrences beyond three standard deviations is very near zero.

ILLUSTRATING THE USE OF PROBABILITY CONCEPTS

The concepts discussed both in the chapter and in the preceding section can be clarified by a numerical example. Assume a firm is considering two alternative promotions for its product and that it can estimate the sales results from each promotion under a variety of market responses. Assume further that the probability of occurrence of these market responses can be assigned on the basis of prior experiences. With this information we construct Table 3A.2.

The expected sales revenues of Promotions *A* and *B* are calculated by Equation 3A.2:

FIGURE 3A.2

The Normal Curve

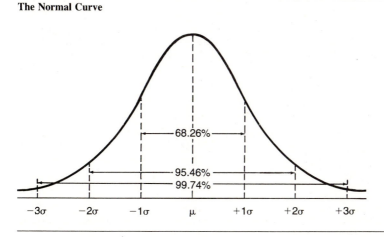

$$\bar{R} = \sum_{i=1}^{n} R_i P_i, \qquad\qquad\qquad (3A.2)$$

and the standard deviations of their respective returns are found by Equation 3A.3:

$$\sigma = \sqrt{\sum_{i=1}^{n} (R_i - \bar{R})^2 P_i}. \qquad\qquad\qquad (3A.3)$$

If we assume that the sales revenues from Promotions A and B are normally distributed, and if we know the mean and the standard deviation as calculated in Table 3A.2, we can graph probability distributions for Promotions A and B; these distributions are shown in Figure 3A.3.[5] The expected value of each promotion's sales revenues is \$500; however, the flatter graph of B indicates that this is the riskier promotion.

Suppose we want to determine the probabilities that the actual sales revenues of Promotions A and B will lie in the interval between \$450 and \$575. Using Equation 3A.1 and Figure 3A.3, we can calculate the respective probability distributions. The first step is to calculate the z values of the interval limits for the two promotions. For Promotion A:

[5]Normal probability distributions can be constructed, once the mean and standard deviation are known, using a table of *ordinates* of the normal curve. (See column 3 of Table 3A.1.) This table is similar to the table of areas used above, except that the ordinate tables give relative *heights* of the probability curve $f(x)$ at various z values rather than areas beneath the curve. Figure 3A.3 was constructed by plotting points at various z values according to the following formula:

$$f(x) = \frac{1}{\sigma} \times \text{Ordinate for } z \text{ value},$$

where the ordinate value is read from a table of ordinates.

For example, the points corresponding to the mean and $+1$ standard deviation for Promotions A and B were calculated as follows:

	z	Ordinate at z	$1/\sigma$	$f(x)$ $(3) \times (4)$
(1)	*(2)*	*(3)*	*(4)*	*(5)*
Promotion A				
Mean = 500.00	0	0.3989	1/70.71	0.0056
$+ 1\sigma = 570.71$	1	0.2420	1/70.71	0.0034
$+ 2\sigma = 641.42$	2	0.0540	1/70.71	0.0008
Promotion B				
Mean = 500.00	0	0.3989	1/141.42	0.0028
$+ 1\sigma = 641.42$	1	0.2420	1/141.42	0.0017
$+ 2\sigma = 782.84$	2	0.0540	1/141.42	0.0004

Column 5 gives the relative heights of the two distributions. Thus, if we decide (for pictorial convenience) to let the curve for Promotion B be 2.8 inches high at the mean, then the curve should be 1.7 inches high at $\mu \pm 1\sigma$, and the curve for Promotion A should be 5.6 inches at the mean and 3.4 inches at $\mu \pm 1\sigma$. Other points in Figure 3A.3 were determined in a similar manner.

TABLE 3A.2

Means and Standard Deviations of Promotions A and B

Market Response Level	Probability of Its Occurring, P_i	Return R_i		$R_i P_i$
Promotion A				
Poor	0.25	$400		$100
Good	0.50	500		250
Very Good	0.25	600		150
	1.00		Expected value =	$500

Standard deviation = σ_A = $70.71.

Promotion B				
Poor	0.25	$300		$ 75
Good	0.50	500		250
Very Good	0.25	700		175
	1.00		Expected value =	$500

Standard deviation = σ_B = $141.42.

FIGURE 3A.3

Probability Distributions for Promotions A and B

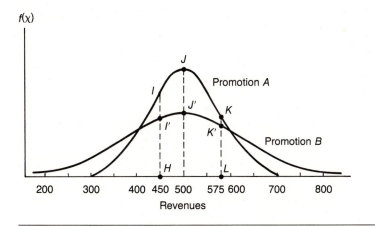

$$\text{Lower } z_1 = \frac{\$450 - \$500}{\$70.71} = -0.71.$$

$$\text{Upper } z_2 = \frac{\$575 - \$500}{\$70.71} = 1.06.$$

For Promotion B:

$$\text{Lower } z_1 = \frac{\$450 - \$500}{\$141.42} = -0.35.$$

$$\text{Upper } z_2 = \frac{\$575 - \$500}{\$141.42} = 0.53.$$

In Appendix D at the end of the book, which contains a more complete table of z values, we find the areas under a normal curve for each of these four z values:

	z Value	Area
Promotion A		
Lower z:	-0.71	0.2611
Upper z:	1.06	0.3554
	Total area =	0.6165 or 61.65%
Promotion B		
Lower z:	-0.35	0.1368
Upper z:	0.53	0.2019
	Total area =	0.3387 or 33.87%

Thus, there is about a 62 percent chance that the actual sales revenues will lie in the interval between $450 and $575 for Promotion A and about a 34 percent probability that B's sales will fall in this interval.

Now look back at Figure 3A.3 and observe the two areas that were just calculated. For Promotion A, the area bounded by $HIJKL$ represents about 62 percent of the area under A's curve. For Promotion B, that area bounded by $HI'J'K'L$ includes about 34 percent of the total area.

CUMULATIVE PROBABILITY

Suppose we ask these questions: What is the probability that the sales generated by Promotion A will be at least $100? $150? $200? and so on. Obviously, there is a higher probability of their being at least $100 rather than $150, $150 rather than $200, and so on. In general, the most convenient way of expressing the answer to such "at least" questions is through the use of *cumulative probability distributions*. These distributions for Promotions A and B are calculated in Table 3A.3 and plotted in Figure 3A.4.

TABLE 3A.3

Cumulative Probability Distributions for Promotions *A* and *B*

Return	z Value	Cumulative Probability	Return	z Value	Cumulative Probability
Promotion *A*			**Promotion *B***		
$300	−2.83	0.9977[a]	$200	−2.12	0.9830[a]
400	−1.41	0.9207	300	−1.41	0.9207
450	−0.71	0.7611	400	−0.71	0.7611
500	0.00	0.5000[b]	450	−0.35	0.6368
575	1.06	0.1446[c]	500	0.00	0.5000[b]
600	1.41	0.0793	575	0.53	0.2981[c]
700	2.83	0.0023	600	0.71	0.2389
			700	1.41	0.0793
			800	2.12	0.0170

[a]0.5000 plus the area between the mean and the point of interest; for example, for Promotion *A*, 0.5000 + 0.4977 = 0.9977 = 99.77% for *z* = −2.83.

[b]The mean has a cumulative probability of 0.5000 = 50%.

[c]0.5000 less area between the mean and the point of interest; for example, for Promotion *A*, 0.5000 − 0.3554 = 0.1446 = 14.46% for *z* = 1.06.

FIGURE 3A.4

Cumulative Probability Distributions for Promotions *A* and *B*

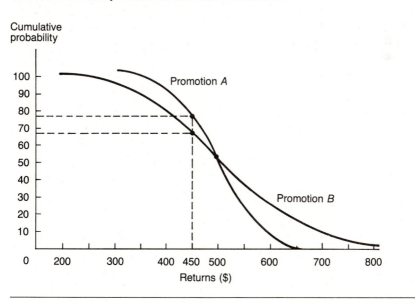

Suppose Promotions A and B each cost $450. Then, if each promotion results in at least $450 in sales revenue, they will both break even. What is the probability of breaking even on each promotion? From Figure 3A.4 we see that the probability is 76 percent that Promotion A will break even, while the break-even probability is only 66 percent for the riskier Promotion B. However, there is virtually no chance (less than ¼ percent) that A will yield more than $700 in added sales revenue, while B has almost an 8 percent chance of generating $700 or more.

SUMMARY

In this appendix we have reviewed the basics of probability theory and demonstrated how it can be used in a variety of risk analyses. Relatively simple probability calculations can provide substantial information about the risk of alternative courses of action, as illustrated in the standardized normal distribution.

PROBLEM

3A.1 Hastings Realty is considering a boost in advertising in order to reduce a large inventory of unsold homes. The firm's management plans to make its media decision using the following data on the expected success of television versus newspaper promotions:

	Market Response	Probability of Occurring, P_i	Return, R_i (Commission Revenues)
Television	Poor	0.25	$ 2,000
	Good	0.50	6,000
	Very Good	0.25	10,000
Newspaper	Poor	0.25	4,000
	Good	0.50	6,000
	Very Good	0.25	8,000

For simplicity, assume that the returns from each promotion are normally distributed.

    a. Calculate the expected return, standard deviation, and coefficient of variation for each promotion.

    b. If the television promotion costs $4,000 while the newspaper promotion costs $3,000, what is the probability each will generate a profit?

ALTERNATIVE DECISION RULES

The decision criterion stressed throughout this book is maximization of value. Typically, value maximization is obtained through use of risk-adjusted valuation models as described in this chapter. Under certain circumstances, especially in situations where the environment is viewed as being malevolent rather than neutral and where probabilities of occurrence for states of nature are difficult to assign, other decision criteria may be appropriate. These rules are perhaps most relevant in oligopoly situations, where firms can be expected to react to the actions taken by one of their competitors. A number of criteria for dealing with such cases have been advanced in the literature, and several are discussed in this appendix.

To simplify the analysis, the oil venture versus government bond example developed in this chapter is re-examined. The payoff matrix for that example is reproduced in Table 3B.1.

MAXIMIN DECISION RULE

One decision criterion widely discussed in the literature on decision making under uncertainty is the *maximin* criterion. This criterion states that the decision maker should select the alternative that provides the best of the worst possible outcomes. This is done by finding the worst possible, or minimum, outcome for each alternative and then choosing the alternative whose worst outcome provides the highest, or maximum, payoff. Hence, this criterion instructs one to maximize the minimum possible outcome.

In our example the worst possible outcome from investing in the oil well venture is the $2,500 payoff that will result if the well turns out to be a dry hole. The government bond provides a payoff of $5,450 under either state of nature; therefore, $5,450 is the worst outcome possible with an investment in the bond. The maximin criterion requires us to select the government bond, since its minimum possible outcome is greater than the $2,500 minimum payoff for the oil venture.

TABLE 3B.1

Payoff Matrix

Alternatives	States of Nature	
	Oil	No Oil
Invest in government bonds	$ 5,450	$5,450
Invest in oil venture	$10,000	$2,500

Although this decision criterion suffers from the obvious shortcoming of examining only the most pessimistic outcome for each alternative, we should not dismiss it immediately as being too naïve and unsophisticated for use in some decision situations. The maximin criterion implicitly assumes a *very* strong aversion to risk, and we might therefore associate its use with decisions involving the possibility of a catastrophic outcome. In other words, at times when the alternative decisions available to the decision maker involve outcomes for various states of nature that endanger the survival of the organization, the maximin criterion may be an appropriate technique for decision making. Similarly, if the state of nature that prevails is dependent upon the course of action taken by the decision maker, the maximin decision criterion might be most appropriate. This might be the case, for example, if a gasoline station manager considers a price reduction where the possible states of nature are (1) the station on the opposite corner reduces price, or (2) the competing station retains the current price. One might well expect that a decision by the station manager to reduce prices would cause the competitor to follow suit, resulting in the worst possible outcome for that decision alternative.

MINIMAX REGRET DECISION RULE

A second decision criterion that we might examine uses the relative "loss" of a decision rather than its absolute outcome for decision making. This decision rule, known as the *minimax regret* criterion, states that the decision maker should attempt to minimize the regret associated with the opportunity cost of a wrong decision *after the fact*. Alternatively stated, this criterion instructs one to minimize the difference between the possible outcomes of the chosen alternative and the best possible outcome for each state of nature.

In order to clarify this technique, we need to examine the concept of an opportunity loss or "regret" in greater detail. An *opportunity loss* can be defined as the difference between the payoff obtained from any particular alternative and the highest possible payoff for the resulting state of nature. It results from the fact that the return we actually receive using any decision criterion under conditions of uncertainty will frequently be lower than the maximum return obtainable if we had perfect knowledge of the outcomes beforehand.

Table 3B.2 is the opportunity loss, or regret, matrix associated with the investment problem we have been examining. It was constructed by finding the maximum payoff for each state of nature in Table 3B.1 and then subtracting the payoff associated with each alternative from that figure. The $4,550 in the upper left-hand box of Table 3B.2, for example, was obtained by subtracting the $5,450 outcome for an investment in the government bonds from the $10,000 payoff from the producing oil well. Notice that the opportunity loss is always a positive figure (or zero), since we are subtracting in each case from the largest payoff for each state of nature.

TABLE 3B.2

Opportunity Loss or "Regret" Matrix

| | States of Nature | |
Alternatives	Oil	No Oil
Invest in government bonds	$4,550	0
Invest in oil venture	0	$2,950

The minimax regret criterion requires the decision maker to choose the invest-ment in the oil drilling venture, since this decision minimizes the maximum regret, or opportunity loss, he suffers. The maximum regret in this case is limited to the $2,950 loss that results if the oil venture is unsuccessful. Had our investor put the money in the government bond, and had the drilling venture been successful, the op-portunity loss would have been $4,550, or $1,600 more than the maximum regret associated with the investment in the oil venture.

AN ALTERNATIVE USE OF THE OPPORTUNITY-LOSS CONCEPT

This opportunity-loss concept can be used in yet another way in risk analysis. We have defined an opportunity loss as a cost associated with uncertainty. Therefore, the *expected opportunity loss* associated with a decision provides a measure of the expected monetary gain which would result from the removal of all uncertainty about the occurrence of future events. It represents the difference between the high-est expected payoff available from one of the decision alternatives and the expected payoff associated with choosing the correct alternative under each state of nature. Using the concept of an expected opportunity loss, we can determine in many cases whether additional information about the alternatives should be obtained before making a final decision.

Let us again examine our investment problem to illustrate this use of the oppor-tunity loss. On the basis of the data in Table 3B.2 we can calculate the expected opportunity loss of each alternative as shown in Table 3B.3.

The minimum expected opportunity loss in this case is $1,180, an amount greater than 20 percent of the initial investment.[1] The decision maker might feel that with an expected opportunity loss of this magnitude, he should spend more money

---

[1] Notice that this $1,180 is the *minimum* possible expected opportunity loss, and it results if the investor puts the money in the oil well. Use of the minimax regret criterion and investment in the bonds results in the larger expected oppor-tunity loss of $2,730. Similarly, it is the difference between the expected return from a correct decision—regardless of the state of nature—and the highest expected return from a single alternative—again the oil venture.

TABLE 3B.3

Calculation of Expected Opportunity Losses

From the Loss Matrix

State of Nature	Oil Venture			Government Bonds		
	Probability of This State of Nature (1)	Opportunity Loss of This State of Nature (2)	Expected Opportunity Loss (1) × (2) (3)	Probability of This State of Nature (1)	Opportunity Loss of This State of Nature (2)	Expected Opportunity Loss (1) × (2) (3)
Oil	0.6	0	0	0.6	$4,550	$2,730
No oil	0.4	$2,950	$1,180	0.4	0	0
			$1,180			$2,730

Minimum Expected Opportunity Loss = $1,180 = Cost of Uncertainty

From the Payoff Matrix

State of Nature	Drilling Operation			Government Bond		
	Probability (1)	Outcome (2)	(1) × (2) (3)	Probability (1)	Outcome (2)	(1) × (2) (3)
Oil	0.6	$10,000	$6,000	0.6	$5,450	$3,270
No oil	0.4	2,500	1,000	0.4	5,450	2,180
		Expected value	$7,000		Expected value	$5,450

Expected Value of a "Correct" Decision after the Fact = $10,000 × 0.6 + $5,450 × 0.4 = $8,180.

Cost of Uncertainty = Expected Value of a "Correct" Decision − Expected Value of the Best Alternative = $8,180 − $7,000 = $1,180.

to reduce the uncertainty in the original decision problem before making a final selection. In this example, our investor might hire a geologist to conduct additional tests of the rock formations or perhaps to make some seismic recordings in the area where the well is to be drilled.

We must emphasize that additional expenditures on information gathering will not guarantee that the costs associated with uncertainty will be reduced. (The geologist might make an examination of the area and be unable to change the predicted 60 percent odds that oil will be discovered.) The opportunity-loss concept merely informs the decision maker of the *possible* opportunity for reducing the cost of imperfect knowledge. We do, however, often see firms engaging in activities aimed at reducing the uncertainty of payoff for various alternatives before making an irrevocable decision. For example, a food-manufacturing company will employ extensive marketing tests in selected areas to gain better estimates of sales potential before going ahead with large-scale production of a new product. Similarly, an automobile manufacturer frequently installs new equipment in a limited number of models to ascertain reliability and customer reaction before including the equipment in all models.

PROBLEMS

3B.1 Indicate whether each of the following statements is true or false and explain why.

I. The "cost of uncertainty" is:

    a. The cost of removing uncertainty with respect to which state of nature will occur.

    b. The minimum expected opportunity loss.

    c. The maximum value to a risk averter of completely resolving uncertainty as to which state of nature will occur.

    d. The expected gain (i.e., increase in return or decrease in cost) from completely resolving uncertainty about which state of nature will occur.

II. Given the payoff matrix

States of Nature

		1	2
	A	50	60
Alternatives	B	70	35

where the elements are dollars of return and the probabilities of the states of nature are 0.4 and 0.6 respectively,

a. Alternative A will be chosen using a maximin decision criterion.

b. Alternative B will be chosen using a minimax regret decision criterion.

c. The cost of uncertainty is $15.

d. A risk indifferent individual would pay no more than the cost of uncertainty to completely resolve uncertainty about whether state of nature 1 or 2 will occur.

3B.2 The manager of Moss Corporation of America is faced with a very uncertain labor market for next summer's moss harvest. He has the opportunity to contract now for a harvest crew at a cost of $20,000 for the season. Alternatively he can wait until summer and employ a crew at the then current market rate. If the economy is in a decline at that time the crew will cost $15,000, but if the economy hasn't slackened appreciably, the cost will be $23,000.

    a. Assuming no risk aversion, at what probability of a decline would the manager contract now for a harvest crew?

    b. If the probability of a decline is 0.8, what would the manager pay for an option to hire a crew next summer at $20,000?

3B.3 The buyer for Birch Lake Sporting Goods is currently faced with the problem of ordering swimsuits for the coming season. Swimsuits must be ordered at this time, and reorders are not possible because of the long delivery lead time. The buyer predicts that sales will be 1,000 suits if the spring and summer period is warmer than normal, 800 suits for a normal season, and only 500 suits if the weather is cool and damp. Probabilities for these outcomes based on long-range weather forecasts are 0.2, 0.7, and 0.1 respectively. Swimsuits cost $25 and sell for $60. Because Birch Lake sells in a very fashion-conscious market, unsold suits cannot be held for the next year. They are therefore sold at the end of the season for $10.

    a. Assume there are no other costs associated with swimwear sales, and construct a payoff matrix that depicts the buyer's decision problem. Assume also that the buyer will purchase 500, 800, or 1,000 suits.

    b. Using a minimax regret criterion, what quantity of suits will the buyer order?

    c. What is the cost of uncertainty in this problem?

    d. Of what use is knowledge of the cost of uncertainty?

3B.4 Assume you face the following investment alternatives. You can acquire shares of common stock in Reichelt Mortgage Guarantee Corporation, or you can put your money in U.S. treasury bills. The return over your planned holding period will be $40,000 if you purchase the treasury bills. If you buy the stock of Reichelt Mortgage Guarantee Corporation, you will receive a return of $100,000 if a contemplated merger of Reichelt Mortgage Guarantee Corporation and Mortgage Insurance Corporation of America takes place. If the merger fails, you will lose $50,000.

    a. Construct the payoff matrix for this problem.

    b. Which choice would you make using a maximin decision criterion? A minimax regret criterion?

c. Under what conditions would each of the decision criteria specified in Part b be appropriate?

d. What is the "cost of uncertainty" in this problem if you place a 70 percent probability on the merger being completed?

e. Explain what the cost of uncertainty is and how you might attempt to mitigate its impact.

3B.5 The city clerk of a midwestern city is faced with the following problem. Tomorrow is the last day that the ballot for the upcoming election can be submitted to the printing contractor if it is to be completed in time for the election. The city clerk is uncertain, however, whether an industrial revenue bond referendum will appear on the ballot. Currently the issue has been postponed. However, the city council may well pass a resolution next Tuesday requiring the inclusion of the issue on the ballot. The costs associated with various courses of actions and events are as follows. If the ballot is sent to the printer without the referendum and the city council does not act, the cost will be $50,000. If the council should act to put the issue on the ballot, however, the cost will increase to $90,000. If, on the other hand, the city clerk sends the ballot to the printer with the referendum question on it, the cost will be $60,000 if the council acts to include the question on the final ballot and $75,000 if it fails to act and the referendum must be removed.

a. Draw a decision tree that describes the decision problem faced by the city clerk. Label the tree as completely as possible.

b. In which form should the city clerk send the ballot to the printer if the probability for positive city council action is believed to be 0.6? (Assume the decision is made on the basis of minimizing expected costs.)

c. At what probability that the referendum will ultimately be included on the ballot would the city clerk be indifferent as to the form in which the ballot is sent to the printers?

d. What decision would the city clerk make using a minimax regret criterion?

e. What is the cost of uncertainty? Of what use is knowledge of this cost to the city clerk? Assume the conditions of Part b above.

CHAPTER 4
DEMAND THEORY

In many respects the most important determinant of a firm's profitability is the demand for its products. No matter how efficient its production processes and regardless of the astuteness of its financial manager, personnel director, or other officers, the firm cannot operate profitably unless a demand for its products exists or can be created, or unless it can find a new set of products for which a demand exists.

Because of the critical role of demand as a determinant of profitability, estimates of expected future demand constitute a key element in all planning activities. Production decisions are profoundly influenced by the firm's underlying demand function. For example, if demand is relatively stable, then long, continuous production runs may be scheduled; if demand fluctuates, either flexible production processes must be employed or sizable inventories must be carried. Demand conditions in the product market also affect the firm's labor and capital requirements. If product demand is strong and growing, the financial manager must arrange to finance the firm's growing capital requirements, and the personnel director must arrange to recruit and train a sufficiently large work force to produce and sell the firm's products.

The demand function also interacts with the set of possible production technologies to determine the market structure of various industries and, hence, the level of competition in the economy. Where these demand and production factors would lead to monopoly or oligopoly, direct regulation or antitrust actions may be required to prevent exploitation. In Chapters 10, 11, and 12—where market structure, pricing, and antitrust policy are discussed—the importance of demand as a determinant of public policy will become quite apparent.

Demand is a complex subject, but it must be thoroughly understood because it helps managers to achieve their goals. Accordingly, in this chapter we examine the theory of demand, emphasizing the major determinants of demand for goods and services, the methods of analyzing the strength of demand for a product, and the effect of changing conditions on that demand. In the following chapter we use the theoretical relationships developed here to formulate models that can be used to actually estimate demand functions.

THE BASIS FOR DEMAND

The term *demand* refers to the number of units of a particular good or service that customers are willing to purchase during a specified period and under a given set of conditions. The time period might be a year, and the conditions that must be specified would include the price of the good in question, prices and availability of competitive goods, expectations of price changes, consumer incomes, consumer tastes and preferences, advertising expenditures, and so on. The amount of the product that consumers wish to purchase—the *demand* for the product—is dependent on all these factors.

For managerial decision making, the primary focus is on market demand. Market demand, however, is merely the aggregate of individual, or personal, demand, and much insight into market demand relationships is gained by understanding the nature of individual demand.

At the level of the individual, demand is determined by two factors: (1) the value associated with acquiring and using the good or service, and (2) the ability to acquire. Both are required for effective individual demand. Desire without purchasing power may lead to want, but not to demand.

There are two basic models of individual demand. One, known as the theory of consumer behavior, relates to the demand for personal consumption products. This model is appropriate for analyzing individual demand for goods and services that directly satisfy consumer wants. In this model the value or worth of a good or service—its *utility*—is the prime determinant of individual demand. Individuals are viewed as attempting to maximize the total utility provided by the goods and services they acquire and consume. This optimization process requires them to examine such relationships as the marginal utility of acquiring additional units of a product and the relative value of acquiring one product as opposed to another. Characteristics of both the product and the individual are important determinants of personal demand for consumer products. More will be said on this issue following an introduction to the second model of individual demand.

Many goods and services are acquired not for their direct consumption value but rather because they are important inputs in the manufacture and distribution of other products. The demand for production workers, salespersons, managers, office business machines, production equipment, and so on are all examples of goods and services whose individual demand is not directly related to final personal consumption but rather is derived indirectly from it. For products whose demand is derived rather than direct, the theory of the firm provides the basis for analyzing individual demand. That is, demand for those goods stems from the value they provide to the firm—value in terms of their impact on the maximization of value objective of the firm. As with all managerial decisions, the key components in this demand determination are the marginal benefits and marginal costs associated with employing the good or service.

Regardless of whether a good or service is in demand at the individual level as a final consumption product (direct demand) or as a factor in providing other goods and services (derived demand), the fundamentals of economic analysis provide a basis for investigating the characteristics of that demand. In both situations individual demand arises from an attempt to maximize an objective. (For final consumption products it is utility maximization as developed by the theory of consumer behavior.) For goods and services used in the production of other products, the theory of the firm provides the framework for the optimization problem. Since both demand models are based on optimization (only the nature of the objective differs), it should come as no surprise that while the specific product and individual characteristics affecting demand may differ, the fundamental relationships are essentially the same. This means that the principles of managerial economics, and particularly the principles of optimal resource use (developed for the firm in Chapter 6), provide a basis for understanding individual demand by both firms and final consumers. With this brief introduction to individual demand we now turn attention to the market demand relationship.

THE MARKET DEMAND FUNCTION

Although an understanding of individual demand provides important insight into the characteristics of demand and enables one to more thoroughly analyze important demand relationships, it is the aggregate of individual demand that a firm faces in the market. The market demand function for a product is a statement of the relationship between the quantity demanded and all the factors that affect this quantity. Written in general functional form, the demand function may be expressed as:

Quantity of $= Q_x = f$ (price of X, prices of competitive goods,   **(4.1)**
Product X expectations of price changes, consumer in-
Demanded   comes, tastes and preferences, advertising
                          expenditures, and so on).

The generalized demand function expressed in Equation 4.1 is really just a listing of the variables that influence demand; for use in managerial decision making, the demand function must be made explicit. That is, the relationship between quantity demanded and each of the demand determining variables must be specified. To illustrate what is involved, let us assume that we are analyzing the demand for automobiles, and the demand function has been specified as follows:

$$Q = a_1 P + a_2 Y + a_3 Pop + a_4 C + a_5 A. \qquad \textbf{(4.2)}$$

This equation states that the number of automobiles demanded during a given year, Q, is a linear function of the average price of cars, P; average per capita disposable income, Y; population, Pop; an index of credit availability, C; and advertising expenditures, A. The terms $a_1, a_2, \ldots, a_5$ are called the *parameters* of the demand function. We shall examine procedures for estimating their values, together with indicators of how confident we are in these estimates in the following chapter. For now, we shall simply assume that we know the parameters and that the demand function does accurately predict the quantity of the product demanded.[1]

Substituting a set of assumed parameter values into Equation 4.2, we obtain:

$$Q = -3,000P + 1,000Y + 0.05Pop + 1,500,000C + 0.05A. \qquad \textbf{(4.3)}$$

Equation 4.3 indicates that automobile demand falls by 3,000 units for each $1 increase in the average price charged; it increases by 1,000 units for each $1 increase in per capita disposable income; it increases by 0.05 units for each additional person in the population; it increases by 1.5 million units if the index of credit availability increases 1 unit; and it increases by 0.05 units for each $1 spent on advertising.

If we multiply each parameter in Equation 4.3 by the value of its respective variable and then sum these products, we will have the estimated demand for automobiles during the coming year. Table 4.1 illustrates this process, showing that the estimated demand for autos, assuming the stated values of the independent variables, will be approximately 10.5 million units.

---

[1] If all the variables that influence demand are not included in the demand function, or if the parameters are not correctly specified, the equation will not predict demand accurately, sales forecasts will be in error, and incorrect expansion and operating decisions will be made. Obviously, the more accurate the firm's demand estimates, the lower its risk. Thus, a close relationship exists between risk and the ability to estimate accurately the demand function. These points are elaborated on in Chapter 5, where techniques for estimating demand functions are developed.

TABLE 4.1

Estimating Industry Demand for Automobiles Using a Hypothetical Demand Function

Independent Variable (1)	Estimated Value of the Independent Variable for Coming Year (2)	Parameter (3)	Estimated Total Demand (2) × (3) (4)
Average price	$9,000	−3,000	−27,000,000
Disposable income	$17,000	1,000	17,000,000
Population	220,000,000	0.05	11,000,000
Index of credit terms	3.00	1,500,000	4,500,000
Advertising expenditures	$100,000,000	0.05	5,000,000
		Total demand	10,500,000

Industry Demand versus Firm Demand

Demand functions can be specified either for an entire industry or for an individual firm. Somewhat different independent variables would typically be used in industry, as compared to firm, demand equations; most importantly the variables representing competitors' actions would be stressed in firm demand functions. For example, a firm's demand function would include the competitor's price and the competitors' advertising expenditures. Demand for the firm's product would be negatively related to its own price, but positively related to the price charged by competing firms. Similarly, demand for its products would increase with its own advertising expenditures, but could increase or decrease with additional advertising by other firms.

Moreover, the parameters for specific variables would differ in the two functions. To illustrate, population would influence the demand for Ford's automobiles and for all producers' autos, but the parameter value in Ford's demand function would be smaller than that in the industry demand function. Only if Ford had 100 percent of the market—that is, if Ford *were* the industry—would the parameters for the firm and the industry be identical.

Since firm and industry demand functions differ, different models, or equations, must be estimated for analyzing the two levels of demand. This matter need not concern us in the present chapter, however, because the demand relationships developed here are applicable to both firm and industry demand functions.

THE DEMAND CURVE

The *demand function* specifies the relationship between quantity demanded and *all* the variables that determine demand. The *demand curve* is that part of the demand function that expresses the relation between the price charged for a product and the quantity demanded, *holding constant the effects of all other independent variables.* Frequently, a demand curve is shown in the form of a graph, and all independent variables in the demand function, except the price of the product, are assumed to be fixed. In the automobile demand function given in Equation 4.3 and Table 4.1, for example, we could hold constant income, population, credit policies, and advertising expenditures, to examine the relationship between price and quantity demanded.

To illustrate the process, consider the relationship depicted in Equation 4.3 and Table 4.1. Assuming that income, population, credit conditions, and advertising expenditures are all held constant at their Table 4.1 values, we can express the relationship between changes in price and changes in quantity demanded as:

$$Q = -3,000\,(P) + 1,000\,(17,000) + 0.05\,(220,000,000) \qquad \textbf{(4.4)}$$
$$+\ 1,500,000\,(3) + 0.05\,(100,000,000)$$
$$=\ -3,000P + 17,000,000 + 11,000,000 + 4,500,000 + 5,000,000$$
$$=\ 37,500,000 - 3,000P.$$

Equation 4.4, which represents the demand curve for automobiles—given the specified values of all of the other variables in the demand function for automobiles—is presented graphically in Figure 4.1. As is typical for most products, we see that a reduction in price increases the quantity demanded, and, conversely, an increase in price decreases the quantity demanded.

Relationship Between Demand Function and Demand Curve

The interrelationship between the demand function and the demand curve can be demonstrated graphically. Figure 4.2 shows three demand curves for automobiles: D_1, D_2, and D_3. Each curve is constructed in a manner similar to Figure 4.1, and each represents the relationship between price and quantity, holding constant the values of all the other variables in the demand function. If D_1 is the appropriate curve, then 10.5 million automobiles can be sold if the average price is $9,000, while only 7.5 million autos will be demanded if the average price is raised to $10,000. Changes such as these are defined as *movements along a demand curve.*

A *demand curve shift*—a shift from one demand curve to another—indicates a change in one or more of the nonprice variables in the product's demand function. For example, a shift from D_1 to D_2 might be caused by a decrease in incomes or advertising expenditures, by more restrictive credit terms, or by a combination of these and other changes.

Consider the effect of shifts in the demand curve from D_1 to D_2 to D_3. At an average price of $9,000 per car, the demand for autos falls from 10.5 million to 8 million to 6 million. Alternatively, if the number of units is fixed at a constant amount, say 8 million, these cars could be sold only at successively lower prices,

FIGURE 4.1

A Hypothetical Automobile Demand Curve

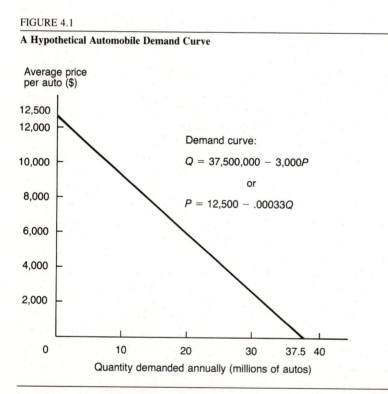

Note: The dependent variable (quantity demanded) is plotted on the horizontal axis and the independent variable (price) on the vertical axis. Ordinarily, we would expect to see the dependent variable on the vertical scale and the independent variable on the horizontal scale. This point can be confusing, because it is easy to write a demand equation as in Equation 4.4, then *incorrectly* graph it by treating the 37,500,000 as the *Y*-axis intercept instead of the *X*-axis intercept, and similarly misspecify the slope of the curve.

The practice of plotting price on the vertical axis and quantity on the horizontal axis originated many years ago with the theory of competitive markets. Here firms have no control over price, but they can control output, and output in turn determines market price. Hence, in the original model, price was the dependent variable and quantity (supplied, not demanded) was the independent variable. For that reason, price/quantity graphs appear as they do.

FIGURE 4.2

Hypothetical Automobile Demand Curves

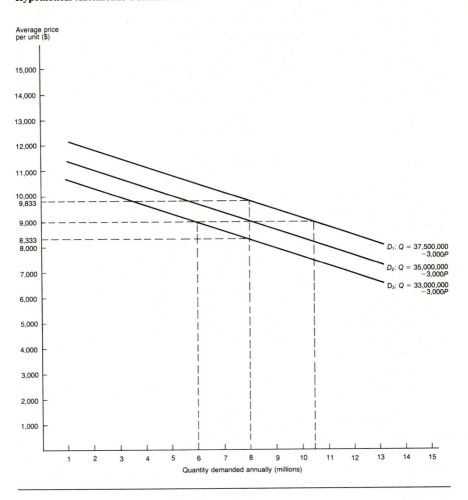

ranging from $9,833 to $8,333 as the demand curve shifts from D_1 to D_3. The result of the shift is a lower level of demand at each sales price; the cause of the shift could be lower disposable incomes, tighter credit, a less aggressive advertising campaign, or a combination of these and other factors.[2]

---

[2] If we were considering the demand curve for a *firm*, rather than for an *industry*, this shift might also occur because of competitors' price cuts, more aggressive promotional activities, and so on.

Demand Relationships and Managerial Decisions

A firm must have reasonably good information about its demand function to make effective long-run planning decisions and short-run operating decisions. For example, one must know the effect of changing prices on demand to establish or alter price policy. Similarly, one must know the effects of credit terms on demand to appraise the desirability of a new credit program. In long-run planning, good estimates of the sensitivity of demand to both population and income changes enable a firm to predict future growth potential and, thus, to establish effective long-range programs.

MEASURING RESPONSIVENESS: ELASTICITY

The firm must know how sensitive demand is to changes in the demand determining variables in its demand function. Some variables like price and advertising can be controlled by the firm, and it is obviously essential to know the effects of altering them if one wants to make good price and advertising decisions. Although other variables are outside the control of the firm—consumer incomes and competitors' prices, for example—the effect of changes in these variables must also be known if the firm is to respond effectively to changes in the economic environment within which it operates. Indeed, anticipating the values of variables outside the firm's control and estimating the response of demand to changes in these variables are major elements in demand analysis.

One measure of responsiveness frequently employed in demand analysis is *elasticity*, defined as *the percentage change in quantity demanded resulting from a 1 percent change in the value of one of the demand determining variables*. The equation for calculating elasticity is:

$$\text{Elasticity} = \frac{\text{Percentage Change in } Q}{\text{Percentage Change in } X} = \frac{\Delta Q/Q}{\Delta X/X} \tag{4.5}$$

$$= \frac{\Delta Q}{\Delta X} \cdot \frac{X}{Q} \, .$$

For demand elasticity, Q is quantity demanded, X is any variable in the demand function, and Δ designates the amount of change in the variable. There is thus an elasticity for each independent variable in a demand function.

Point Elasticity and Arc Elasticity

Elasticity can be measured as point elasticity and arc elasticity. The elasticities of a demand function generally vary at different points on the function. *Point elasticity* measures the elasticity at a given point; *arc elasticity* measures the average elasticity over some range of the function.

Note that the first term in Equation 4.5, $\Delta Q/\Delta X$, is an approximate measure of the marginal relationship between X and Q. This term, when multiplied by the second term in the equation, X/Q, equals elasticity. At the limit, where ΔX is very small, $\Delta Q/\Delta X = \partial Q/\partial X$ (the partial derivative of the function taken with respect to X). This precise marginal relationship at a specific point on the function is used in the equation for point elasticity.[3] Thus, using the Greek letter ε (epsilon) as the symbol for point elasticity, we have:

$$\text{Point elasticity} = \varepsilon_x = \frac{\partial Q}{\partial X} \cdot \frac{X}{Q} . \qquad (4.6)$$

In other words, point elasticity is determined by multiplying the partial derivative of the demand function, at a given point, by the ratio X/Q at that point.

An example using the demand relationship described by Equation 4.3 and the variable values given in Table 4.1 will illustrate the construction of a point elasticity estimate. Assume that we are interested in analyzing the responsiveness of automobile demand to changes in advertising expenditures. The point advertising elasticity at the 10.5 million unit demand level shown in Table 4.1 is calculated as:

$$\text{Point advertising elasticity} = \varepsilon_A = \frac{\partial Q}{\partial A} \cdot \frac{A}{Q} .$$

Since the partial derivative of the demand function, Equation 4.3, taken with respect to the advertising variable ($\partial Q/\partial A$) is 0.05, and advertising expenditures at the 10.5 million unit demand level are $100 million:

$$\varepsilon_A = 0.05 \cdot \frac{100,000,000}{10,500,000}$$

$$\approx 0.48.$$

Thus, a 1 percent change in advertising expenditures results in approximately a 0.48 percent change in the number of automobiles demanded. The elasticity is positive, indicating a direct relationship between advertising outlays and automobile demand; that is, an increase in advertising expenditures leads to an increase in demand, and, conversely, a decrease in advertising expenditures leads to a decrease in demand.

For many business decisions, managers are concerned with the impact of substantial changes in a demand determining factor, such as advertising, rather than

---

[3] Since we are concerned with the response of quantity demanded to changes in one independent variable, X, *holding all other variables constant*, we use the partial derivative $\partial Q/\partial X$.

with the impact of a unitary change. In these instances the point-elasticity concept suffers a significant shortcoming. To see the nature of the problem, consider the calculation of the advertising elasticity of demand for automobiles when advertising changes from $100 million to $50 million. Assume for this example that all the other demand influencing variables retain their Table 4.1 values. With advertising at $100 million, demand is 10.5 million units. Changing advertising to $50 million results in a 2.5 million-unit decline in automobile demand ($-$50 million $\times$ 0.05 = 2.5 million), so total demand at that level is 8 million units.[4] Using Equation 4.5 to calculate the point price elasticity for the change from $100 million in advertising to $50 million, we find that:

$$\text{Advertising elasticity} = \frac{-2.5 \text{ million}}{-50 \text{ million}} \cdot \frac{100 \text{ million}}{10.5 \text{ million}} = 0.48.$$

The advertising elasticity is 0.48, just as we found above using the point elasticity equation. Consider, however, the indicated elasticity if we move in the opposite direction; that is, the advertising elasticity associated with increasing advertising from $50 million to $100 million. The indicated elasticity is:

$$\text{Advertising elasticity} = \frac{+2.5 \text{ million}}{+50 \text{ million}} \cdot \frac{50 \text{ million}}{8 \text{ million}} = 0.31.$$

We see that the indicated elasticity is quite different. The problem stems from the fact that elasticity relationships are typically not constant but change with different values of the variables. The advertising elasticity of 0.31 is the point elasticity where advertising is $50 million and the quantity demanded is 8 million. (This can be verified by calculating the point advertising elasticity at the $50 million level, as was done above at the $100 million level.) To overcome this problem of changing elasticities, an arc elasticity equation has been formulated to calculate an average elasticity for incremental as opposed to marginal (unitary) changes. The arc elasticity equation is:

$$\text{Arc elasticity} = E = \frac{\dfrac{\text{Change in } Q}{\text{Average } Q}}{\dfrac{\text{Change in } X}{\text{Average } X}} = \frac{\dfrac{Q_2 - Q_1}{(Q_2 + Q_1)/2}}{\dfrac{X_2 - X_1}{(X_2 + X_1)/2}} \qquad (4.7)$$

$$= \frac{\dfrac{\Delta Q}{(Q_2 + Q_1)/2}}{\dfrac{\Delta X}{(X_2 + X_1)/2}} = \frac{\Delta Q}{\Delta X} \cdot \frac{X_2 + X_1}{Q_2 + Q_1}.$$

---

[4]This change in demand can be illustrated graphically using Figure 4.2. Assuming population, income, credit availability, and all other factors that influence the level of automobile sales, *except advertising*, remain unchanged from

Again we divide the percentage change in quantity demanded by the percentage change in a demand determining variable, but here the bases used to calculate the percentage changes are averages of the two data points rather than the initially observed value. Use of the arc elasticity equation eliminates the problem of the elasticity measure being dependent upon which end of the range is viewed as the initial point and results in a more accurate measure of the average relative relationship between the two variables over the range indicated by the data. The arc advertising elasticity over the $50 million to $100 million range can be calculated as:

$$\text{Arc advertising elasticity} = \frac{\Delta Q}{\Delta A} \cdot \frac{A_2 + A_1}{Q_2 + Q_1}$$

$$= \frac{-2,500,000}{-50,000,000} \left(\frac{50,000,000 + 100,000,000}{8,000,000 + 10,500,000} \right)$$

$$= \frac{-2,500,000}{-50,000,000} \cdot \frac{150,000,000}{18,500,000} \approx 0.41.$$

Thus, on average a 1 percent change in the level of advertising expenditures in the range of $50 million to $100 million will result in a 0.41 percent change in automobile demand.

We can recapitulate by noting that point elasticity is a marginal concept. It measures the elasticity at a specific point on a function. Proper use of point elasticity is limited to analysis of very small (unitary) changes in variables. Arc elasticity is a better concept for measuring the average elasticity over an extended range. It is the appropriate tool for incremental analysis.

The concept of elasticity is quite general—it involves simply the percentage change in one variable associated with a given percentage change in another variable. In addition to use in demand analysis, the concept is used in finance, where the impact of changes in sales on earnings under different production setups (operating leverage) and different financial structures (financial leverage) is measured by an elasticity factor. Elasticities are also used to compare the effects of output changes on costs. However, the concept is most frequently used in demand analysis, and several specific demand elasticities are particularly useful in managerial decision making.

PRICE ELASTICITY OF DEMAND

Probably the most widely used elasticity measure is the *price elasticity of demand*, which provides a measure of the responsiveness of the quantity demanded to

---

their Table 4.1 values, the shift from demand curve D_1 to demand curve D_2 reflects the impact of reducing advertising to $50 million. At a $9,000 price, automobile demand along demand schedule D_2 is 8 million units.

changes in the price of the product, holding constant the values of all other variables in the demand function.

Using the formula for point elasticity, price elasticity of demand is found as:

$$\text{Point price elasticity} = \varepsilon_p = \frac{\partial Q}{\partial P} \cdot \frac{P}{Q} , \qquad (4.8)$$

where $\partial Q/\partial P$ is the partial derivative of the demand function with respect to price, and P and Q are the price and quantity at a point on the demand curve.

The concept of point price elasticity can be illustrated by referring to Equation 4.3, which was used to construct demand curve D_1 in Figure 4.2.

$$Q = -3,000P + 1,000Y + 0.05Pop + 1,500,000C + 0.05A. \qquad (4.3)$$

The partial derivative with respect to price is:

$$\frac{\partial Q}{\partial P} = -3,000, \text{ a constant.}$$

Now let us calculate ε_p at two points on the demand curve: (1) where $P_1 = \$9,000$ and $Q_1 = 10,500,000$, and (2) where $P_2 = \$9,500$ and $Q_2 = 9,000,000$:

$$(1)\ \varepsilon_{p1} = (-3,000) \frac{9,000}{10,500,000} = -2.57,$$

$$(2)\ \varepsilon_{p2} = (-3,000) \frac{9,500}{9,000,000} = -3.17.$$

Thus, on demand curve D_1 a 1 percent increase in price from the \$9,000 level results in a 2.57 percent reduction in the quantity demanded; but at a \$9,500 price a 1 percent increase results in a 3.17 percent reduction in demand. This example illustrates that price elasticity can vary along a demand curve, with ε_p increasing in absolute value at higher prices and lower quantities.[5]

Note also that the price elasticities are negative. This follows from the fact that the quantity demanded for most goods and services is inversely related to price. Thus, in the example, at a \$9,000 price, a 1 percent *increase* (*decrease*) in price leads to a 2.57 percent *decrease* (*increase*) in the quantity demanded.[6]

---

[5] As we will show in a later section, price elasticity always varies along a linear demand curve. It can, however, under certain conditions, be constant along a curvilinear demand curve.

[6] In some texts the equation for price elasticity is multiplied by -1 to change price elasticities to positive numbers. We do not follow this convention, although it creates no problem so long as one remembers the inverse relationship between price and quantity. We alert the reader to this possible construction because price elasticities are sometimes reported as positive numbers.

Using the arc elasticity concept, the equation for price elasticity is:

$$\text{Arc price elasticity} = E_p = \frac{(Q_2 - Q_1)/(Q_2 + Q_1)}{(P_2 - P_1)/(P_2 + P_1)}$$

$$= \frac{Q_2 - Q_1}{P_2 - P_1} \cdot \frac{P_2 + P_1}{Q_2 + Q_1}.$$

This form is especially useful for analyzing the average sensitivity of demand to price changes over an extended range. For example, the average price elasticity from \$9,000 to \$9,500 is:

$$E_p = \frac{9,000,000 - 10,500,000}{9,500 - 9,000} \cdot \frac{9,500 + 9,000}{9,000,000 + 10,500,000}$$

$$= \frac{-1,500,000}{500} \cdot \frac{18,500}{19,500,000} = -2.85.$$

This means that on average, a 1 percent change in price leads to a 2.85 percent change in quantity demanded when price is between \$9,000 and \$9,500.

Relationship between Price Elasticity and Revenue

One of the most important aspects of the price elasticity concept lies in the fact that it provides a useful summary measure of the effect of a price change on revenues. Depending on the degree of price elasticity, a given change in price will increase, decrease, or leave total revenue unchanged. If we have a good estimate of price elasticity, we can estimate quite accurately the new total revenue that will follow a price change.

Elastic, Unitary, and Inelastic Demand. For decision-making purposes, three specific ranges of price elasticity have been identified. Using $|\varepsilon_p|$ to denote the absolute value of the price elasticity, the three ranges can be denoted as:

(1) $|\varepsilon_p| > 1.0$, defined as elastic demand.
Example: $\varepsilon_p = -3.2$ and $|\varepsilon_p| = 3.2$
(2) $|\varepsilon_p| = 1.0$, defined as unitary elasticity.
Example: $\varepsilon_p = -1.0$ and $|\varepsilon_p| = 1.0$
(3) $|\varepsilon_p| < 1.0$, defined as inelastic demand.
Example: $\varepsilon_p = -0.5$ and $|\varepsilon_p| = 0.5$

If demand is *elastic* (that is, $|\varepsilon_p| > 1$), the relative change in quantity is larger

than that of price, so a given percentage increase in price causes quantity to decrease by a larger percentage, decreasing total revenue. Thus, if demand is elastic, a
price increase will lower total revenue, and a decrease in price will raise total revenue. Now consider *unitary elasticity*, the situation where the percentage change in
quantity divided by the percentage change in price equals -1. Since price and quantity are inversely related, a price elasticity of -1 means that the effect of a price
change is *exactly* offset by the change in quantity demanded, with the result that
total revenue, the product of price times quantity, *remains* constant. Finally, if demand is inelastic, a price increase will produce a less than proportionate decline in
the quantity demanded, so total revenues will rise. These relationships are summarized below:

(1) Elastic demand: $|\varepsilon_p| > 1.0$. Total revenue declines with price increases; rises
with price decreases.

(2) Unitary elasticity: $|\varepsilon_p| = 1.0$. Total revenue is unaffected by changes in price.

(3) Inelastic demand: $|\varepsilon_p| < 1.0$. Total revenue rises with price increases; declines
with price decreases.

The Limiting Cases. Price elasticity can range from between 0 (completely inelastic) to $-\infty$ (perfectly elastic). To illustrate, consider first the case where the quantity
demanded is independent of price, so that some fixed amount, Q^*, will be demanded regardless of price. The demand curve of such a good is shown in Figure
4.3. Price elasticity is defined (using the point elasticity definition) as the partial
derivative of the demand function taken with respect to price, $\partial Q/\partial P$, multiplied by
the ratio P/Q. That is:

$$\varepsilon_p = \frac{\partial Q}{\partial P} \cdot \frac{P}{Q} . \tag{4.8}$$

Since demand as illustrated in Figure 4.3 remains constant regardless of price, the
partial derivative $\partial Q/\partial P$ is equal to zero; hence, price elasticity for the product will
be equal to zero.[7]

   The other limiting case, that of infinite elasticity where $\varepsilon_p = -\infty$, is shown in
Figure 4.4. The slope of the properly oriented demand curve, $\partial Q/\partial P$, is $-\infty$, so the
value of ε_p in Equation 4.8 must be $-\infty$ regardless of the P/Q ratio.

---

[7] This can be confusing if one does not remember that the axes of Figure 4.3 are reversed in the sense that the dependent
variable, Q, is plotted on the X axis. One must remember that $Q = Q^* = $ a constant. In other words, $Q = Q^* + 0 \cdot P$,
so $\partial Q/\partial P$ is zero or, alternatively, the slope of the demand curve properly oriented is zero. The reversal of the axis
results in a demand curve whose slope is the inverse of the true marginal relationship between quantity and price. Thus,
the slope in Figure 4.3 is $\partial P/\partial Q = \infty$, which is 1 divided by the marginal relationship expressed by $\partial Q/\partial Q = 0$; that is,
the slope in Figure 4.3 equals $1/0 = \infty$.

FIGURE 4.3

Completely Inelastic Demand Curve: $\varepsilon_p = 0$

Price per unit ($)

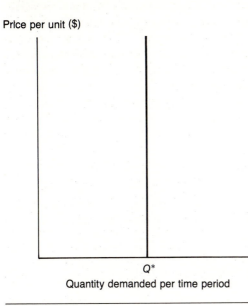

Q^*

Quantity demanded per time period

FIGURE 4.4

Perfectly Elastic Demand Curve: $\varepsilon_p = -\infty$

Price per unit ($)

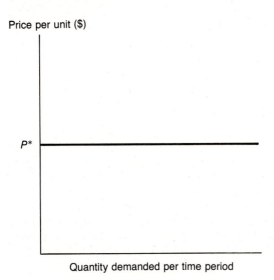

P^*

Quantity demanded per time period

The economic as well as the mathematical properties of these limiting cases should be understood. A firm faced with the vertical, perfectly inelastic demand curve could charge any price and still sell Q^* units. Thus, it could exploit its market and, theoretically, appropriate all of its customers' incomes or wealth. Conversely, a firm facing a horizontal, perfectly elastic demand curve can sell an unlimited amount of output at the price P^*, but would lose all of its demand if it raised the price by even a small amount. Neither condition holds in the real world, but monopolistic firms selling necessities (for example, water companies) have relatively inelastic demand curves, while firms in highly competitive industries (for example, grain production) face highly elastic demand curves.

Varying Elasticity at Different Points on a Demand Curve

All linear demand curves, except perfectly elastic or perfectly inelastic ones, are subject to varying elasticities at different points on the curve. In other words, any given linear demand curve will be price elastic at some output levels but inelastic at others. To see this, recall again the definition of point price elasticity:

$$\varepsilon_p = \frac{\partial Q}{\partial P} \cdot \frac{P}{Q} . \tag{4.8}$$

The slope of a linear demand curve, $\partial P/\partial Q$, is constant, and thus so is its reciprocal, $1/(\partial P/\partial Q) = \partial Q/\partial P$. However, the ratio P/Q varies from 0 at the point where the demand curve intersects the horizontal axis (where price = 0) to $+\infty$ at the vertical (price) axis intercept (where quantity = 0). Since we are multiplying a negative constant by a ratio which varies between 0 and $+\infty$, the price elasticity of a linear curve must range from 0 to $-\infty$.

Figure 4.5 illustrates this relationship. As the demand curve approaches the vertical axis, the ratio P/Q approaches infinity, and ε_p approaches minus infinity. As the demand curve approaches the horizontal axis, the ratio P/Q approaches 0, causing ε_p also to approach 0. At the midpoint of the demand curve $(\partial Q/\partial P)\,(P/Q) = -1.0$; this is the point of unitary elasticity.

Relationships among Price Elasticity and Average, Marginal, and Total Revenue

We can further clarify the relationship between price elasticity and total revenue developed above, and we can emphasize its importance in demand analysis by examining Figure 4.6 and Table 4.2. Figure 4.6(a) reproduces the demand curve shown in Figure 4.5, but adds the associated marginal revenue curve. The demand curve shown in Figure 4.6 is of the general linear form

$$P = a - bQ, \tag{4.9}$$

FIGURE 4.5

Elasticities along a Linear Demand Curve

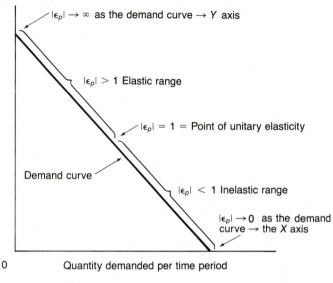

Price per unit ($)

$|\epsilon_p| \to \infty$ as the demand curve $\to Y$ axis

$|\epsilon_p| > 1$ Elastic range

$|\epsilon_p| = 1 =$ Point of unitary elasticity

Demand curve

$|\epsilon_p| < 1$ Inelastic range

$|\epsilon_p| \to 0$ as the demand curve $\to$ the X axis

0   Quantity demanded per time period

where a is the intercept and b is the slope coefficient. It follows that total revenue (*TR*) can be expressed as:

$$TR = P \cdot Q,$$

$$= (a - bQ) \cdot Q,$$

$$= aQ - bQ^2,$$

and marginal revenue (*MR*) can be found by differentiating total revenue with respect to quantity:

$$MR = \frac{dTR}{dQ} = a - 2bQ. \qquad (4.10)$$

The relationship between demand (average revenue) and marginal revenue becomes clear when one compares Equations 4.9 and 4.10. Each equation has the same intercept a. This means that both curves begin at the same point along the vertical price axis. However, the marginal revenue curve has twice the negative slope of the demand curve. This means that the marginal revenue curve will intersect the horizontal axis at $1/2\ Q_x$, given that the demand curve intersects at Q_x. From Figure 4.6(a)

FIGURE 4.6

Relationships among Price Elasticity and Marginal, Average, and Total Revenue: (a) Demand (Average Revenue) and Marginal Revenue Curves, (b) Total Revenue

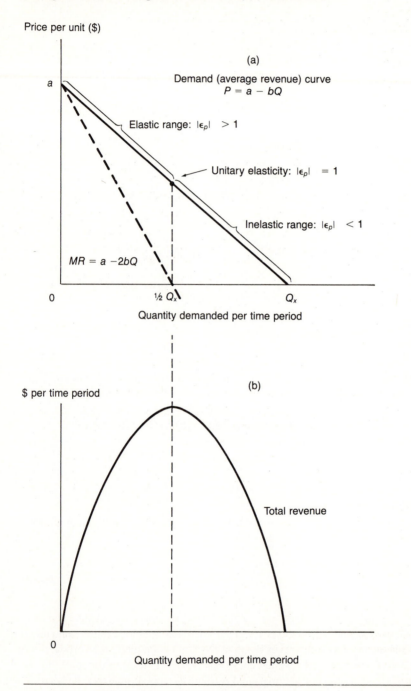

Price per unit ($)

(a)

Demand (average revenue) curve
$P = a - bQ$

a

Elastic range: $|\epsilon_p| > 1$

Unitary elasticity: $|\epsilon_p| = 1$

Inelastic range: $|\epsilon_p| < 1$

$MR = a - 2bQ$

0   ½ Q_x Q_x

Quantity demanded per time period

$ per time period

(b)

Total revenue

0

Quantity demanded per time period

TABLE 4.2

Elasticity and Revenue Relationships

Price P	Quantity Q	Total Revenue $TR = P \cdot Q$	Marginal Revenue $MR = \Delta TR$	Elasticity[a] E_p
100	1	100		
			80	−6.33
90	2	180		
			60	−3.40
80	3	240		
			40	−2.14
70	4	280		
			20	−1.44
60	5	300		
			0	−1.00
50	6	300		
			−20	−0.69
40	7	280		
			−40	−0.47
30	8	240		
			−60	−0.29
20	9	180		
			−80	−0.16
10	10	100		

[a]Since the price and quantity data in the table are discrete numbers, the price elasticities have been calculated using the arc elasticity equation:

$$E_p = \frac{Q_2 - Q_1}{P_2 - P_1} \cdot \frac{P_2 + P_1}{Q_2 + Q_1} .$$

we can also see that marginal revenue is positive in the range where demand is price elastic, zero where $\varepsilon_p = -1$, and negative in the inelastic range. Thus, there is an obvious relationship between price elasticity and both average and marginal revenue.

As shown in Figure 4.6(b), price elasticity is also closely related to total revenue. Total revenue increases with price reductions in the elastic range (where $MR > 0$) because the increase in quantity demanded at the new lower price more than offsets the lower revenue per unit received at that reduced price. Total revenue peaks at the point of unitary elasticity (where $MR = 0$), since the increase in quantity associated with the price reduction exactly offsets the lower revenue per unit. Finally, total revenue declines when price is reduced in the inelastic range (where $MR < 0$), because the quantity demanded continues to increase with reductions in price, but the relative increase in quantity is less than the percentage decrease in price, and thus it is not large enough to offset the reduction in revenue per unit sold.[8]

[8]A completely general formula relating marginal revenue to price elasticity is:

$$MR = P \left(1 + \frac{1}{\varepsilon_p} \right). \tag{4.11}$$

This equation follows directly from the definitions of marginal revenue and price elasticity. Recall that marginal revenue is the derivative of the total revenue function. That is, $MR = dTR/dQ$. Since total revenue equals price times quantity ($TR = P \cdot Q$), marginal revenue is found by taking the derivative of the function $P \cdot Q$ with respect to Q:

$$MR = \frac{d(P \cdot Q)}{dQ}. \tag{4.12}$$

The numerical example in Table 4.2 illustrates these relationships. It can be seen that for one to five units of output demand is elastic, $|\varepsilon_p| > 1$, and a reduction in price leads to an increase in total revenue. For example, decreasing price from $80 to $70 results in output increasing from three units to four units. Marginal revenue is positive over this range of output, and total revenue increases from $240 to $280. For output above six units (price below $50) demand is inelastic, $|\varepsilon_p| < 1$. Here price reductions result in less total revenue, because the increase in quantity demanded is not large enough to offset the lower price per unit. With total revenue decreasing as output expands, marginal revenue must be negative. For example, reducing price from $30 to $20 results in revenue declining from $240 to $180 though output increased from eight to nine units. Marginal revenue is $-$60$.

Because price and quantity are interdependent in the typical demand situation, the rule for differentiating a product (see Chapter 2) must be employed in taking the derivative of Equation 4.12:

$$MR = \frac{dTR}{dQ} = \frac{dP \cdot Q}{dQ} = P \cdot \frac{dQ}{dQ} + Q \cdot \frac{dP}{dQ} \tag{4.13}$$

$$= P \cdot 1 + Q \cdot \frac{dP}{dQ}$$

$$= P + Q \cdot \frac{dP}{dQ} \, .$$

Equation 4.13 is a completely general specification of marginal revenue which can be rewritten as:

$$MR = P \left(1 + \frac{Q}{P} \cdot \frac{dP}{dQ} \right) . \tag{4.13A}$$

(That Equations 4.13 and 4.13A are in fact identical can be easily seen by expanding Equation 4.13A by multiplying the terms within the parentheses by the factor P.)

Note now that the term $Q/P \cdot dP/dQ$ in Equation 4.13A is the reciprocal of the definition for point price elasticity $(\varepsilon_p = dQ/dP \cdot P/Q)$:

$$\frac{Q}{P} \cdot \frac{dP}{dQ} = \frac{1}{\frac{dQ}{dP} \cdot \frac{P}{Q}} = \frac{1}{\varepsilon_p}$$

Thus, Equation 4.13A can be rewritten as Equation 4.11:

$$MR = P \left(1 + \frac{1}{\varepsilon_p} \right) . \tag{4.11}$$

The reader (recalling that price elasticities are negative numbers) should be able to confirm, using Equation 4.11, the important relationships among marginal revenue and elastic ($|\varepsilon_p| > 1.0$), inelastic ($|\varepsilon_p| < 1.0$), and unit elastic ($|\varepsilon_p| = 1.0$) demand.

Determinants of Price Elasticity

Industry Demand. Why is the price elasticity of demand high for one product and low for another? In general, there are three major causes for differential price elasticities: (1) The extent to which a good is considered to be a necessity, (2) the availability of substitute goods which satisfy a given need, and (3) the proportion of income spent on the product. A relatively constant quantity of such necessities as salt and electricity for residential lighting purposes will be purchased almost irrespective of price, at least within the price ranges customarily encountered. For these goods there are no close substitutes. Other goods—grapes, for example—while desirable, face considerably more competition, and the demand for them will depend more on price.

Similarly, the demand for high-priced goods that account for a large portion of purchasers' incomes will be relatively more sensitive to price. Demand for less expensive products, on the other hand, will not be so sensitive to price—the small percentage of income spent on these goods means that it simply will not be worthwhile to waste time and effort worrying about their prices. Accordingly, the elasticity of demand will typically be higher for major items than for minor ones. Thus, the price elasticity of demand for automobiles is higher than that for automobile tires.

Firm Demand. Are the price elasticities of an individual firm's demand curve the same as its respective industry demand curve? In general, the answer is an emphatic no. The reason for this is discussed in detail in Chapter 10, which deals with market structure, but an intuitive explanation can be given here.

In pure monopoly the firm's demand curve is also the industry's demand curve, so obviously the firm's elasticity at any output is the same as that of the industry. Consider the other extreme—pure competition, as approximated by wheat farming. The industry demand curve for wheat is downward sloping: the lower its price, the greater the quantity of wheat that will be demanded. However, the demand curve facing any individual wheat farmer is horizontal. A farmer can sell any amount of wheat at the going price, but if he raises the price the smallest fraction of a cent he can sell nothing. The wheat farmer's demand curve—or that of any firm operating under pure competition—is therefore perfectly elastic. Figure 4.4 illustrated such a demand curve.

Uses of Price Elasticity

Price elasticity is useful for a number of purposes. First, firms need to be aware of the elasticity of their own demand curves when they price their products. For example, a profit-maximizing firm would never choose to lower its prices in the inelastic range of its demand curve—such a price decrease would decrease total revenue and at the same time increase costs, since output would be rising. The result would be a dramatic decrease in profits. Even over the range where demand is elastic, a firm will not necessarily find it profitable to cut price; the profitability of such an action depends on whether the marginal revenues generated by the price reduction exceed the marginal cost of the added production. Price elasticities can be used to answer such questions as these:

1. What will be the impact on sales of a 5 percent price increase?

2. How great a price reduction is necessary to increase sales by 20 percent?

The energy crisis that developed following the 1973–74 Arab oil embargo illustrates the importance of price elasticity. First, electric utility companies were forced to raise prices dramatically because of rapid increases in fuel costs. The question immediately arose: How much of a cutback in quantity demanded and, hence, reduction in future capacity needs would these price increases cause, that is, what is the price elasticity of electricity? In view of the long lead times required to build electric generating capacity and the major economic dislocations that arise from power outages, this was a most critical question for both the consumers and producers of electricity.

Similarly, price elasticity has played a major role in the debate on a national petroleum policy since that same period. Some industry and government economists believed that the price elasticities for petroleum products were sufficiently large that the rather substantial oil price increases which occurred in late 1973 and early 1974 would reduce the quantity demanded sufficiently to remove the imbalance between supply and demand. Others argued that the price elasticities were so low that only unconscionable price increases could reduce the quantity demanded sufficiently to overcome the supply shortfall, and therefore a rationing system was needed as a replacement for market allocation of petroleum products. These same issues have been a focal point of the controversy concerning deregulation of natural gas prices in the U.S.[9] These strongly interrelated energy issues continue to have important implications for all sectors of the economy, and price elasticity analysis is playing an increasingly important role in the search for solutions.

Yet another current example of the importance of price elasticity in managerial decision making relates to the widespread discounting or reduced fares introduced in the airline industry following deregulation by the Civil Aeronautics Board. Many of the discounts were in the range of 30 to 40 percent off the standard fare. The question of whether the reduced fares would attract enough additional travelers to

---

[9] In the debate on energy policy the relationship between price and quantity supplied—the price elasticity of supply—is also an important component for determining an appropriate policy. As with most economic issues, both sides of the marketplace (demand and supply) must be analyzed to arrive at a rational decision.

offset the lower revenues per passenger was directly related to the question of the price elasticity of demand for air travel.

Additional uses of price elasticity are examined in later chapters. We now shift to an introduction of several other key demand relationships.

INCOME ELASTICITY OF DEMAND

For many goods, income is a major determinant of demand; it is frequently as important as price, advertising expenditures, credit terms, or any other variable in the demand function. This is particularly true of luxury items such as foreign sports cars, country club memberships, art treasures, and the like. On the other hand, the demand for such basic commodities as salt, bread, and milk is not very responsive to income changes. These goods are bought in fairly constant amounts regardless of changes in income.[10]

The income elasticity of demand provides a measure of the responsiveness of quantity demanded to changes in income, holding constant the impact of all other variables which influence demand. Using the calculus equation for point elasticity, and letting I represent income, point income elasticity is defined as:

$$\varepsilon_I = \frac{\partial Q}{\partial I} \cdot \frac{I}{Q} . \tag{4.14}$$

Income and the quantity purchased typically move in the same direction. That is, income and sales are directly rather than inversely related, so $\partial Q/\partial I$ and hence ε_I are positive. For a limited number of products, termed *inferior goods*, this does not hold. For such products as beans and potatoes, for example, demand declines as income increases, because consumers replace them with more expensive alternatives. More typical products, whose demand is positively related to income, are defined as *normal* or *superior goods*.

To examine income elasticity over a range of income rather than at a single point, we use the arc elasticity relationship:

$$E_I = \frac{(Q_2 - Q_1)/(Q_2 + Q_1)}{(I_2 - I_1)/(I_2 + I_1)} . \tag{4.15}$$

Again, this provides a measure of the average relative responsiveness of demand for the product to a change in income in the range from I_1 to I_2.

---

[10] Income can be measured in many ways—for example, on a per capita, per household, or aggregate basis. Gross national product, national income, personal income, and disposable personal income have all been used as income measures in demand studies.

For most products income elasticity is positive, indicating that as the economy expands and national income increases, demand for the product will also rise. However, the actual size of the elasticity coefficient is also important. Suppose, for example, that ε_I for a particular product is 0.3. This means that a 1 percent increase in income will cause demand for this product to increase by only $\frac{3}{10}$ of 1 percent—the product would thus not be maintaining its relative importance in the economy. Another product might have an income elasticity of 2.5; for this product, demand will increase 2½ times as fast as income. *We see, then, that if ε_I < 1.0 for a particular good, producers of the good will not share proportionately in increases in national income. On the other hand, if ε_I > 1.0, the industry will gain more than a proportionate share of increases in income.*

These relationships have important policy implications for both firms and governmental agencies. Firms whose demand functions have high income elasticities will have good growth opportunities in an expanding economy, so forecasts of aggregate economic activity will figure importantly in their plans. Companies faced with low income elasticities, on the other hand, are not so sensitive to the level of business activity. This may be good in that such a business is harmed relatively little by economic downturns, but since the company cannot expect to share fully in a growing economy, it may seek entry into industries that provide better growth opportunities.

Income elasticity can also play an important role in the marketing activities of a firm. If per capita or household income is found to be an important determinant of the demand for a particular product, this can affect the location and nature of sales outlets. It can also have an impact on advertising and other promotional activities. For example, many firms providing products or services with high income elasticities direct significant promotional efforts at young professionals in such areas as business, law, and medicine, primarily because of the potential for substantially increased future business from them as their incomes increase.

At the national level the question of income elasticity has figured importantly in several key areas. Agriculture, for example, has had problems for many years partly because the income elasticity of many food products is less than 1.0. This fact has made it difficult for farmers' incomes to keep up with those of urban workers, a problem that, in turn, has caused much concern in Washington, D.C., and national capitals throughout the world.

A somewhat similar problem arises in housing. Congress and all presidents since the end of World War II have stated that improving the United States housing stock is a primary national goal. If, on the one hand, the income elasticity for housing is high, something in excess of 1.0, an improvement of the housing stock will be a natural by-product of a prosperous economy. On the other hand, if housing income elasticity is low, a relatively small percentage of additional income will be spent on houses; as a result, the housing stock will not improve much even if the economy is booming and incomes are increasing. In this case direct governmental actions such as public housing or rent and interest subsidies are necessary to bring the housing stock up to the prescribed level. In any event, not only has the income elasticity of housing been an important issue in debates on national housing policy, but these very debates have also stimulated a great deal of research into the theory and measurement of income elasticities.

CROSS-PRICE ELASTICITY OF DEMAND

The demand for many goods is influenced by the prices of other goods. For example, the demand for beef is related to the price of a close substitute, pork. As the price of pork increases, so does the demand for beef; consumers substitute beef for the now relatively more expensive pork.

This direct relationship between the price of one good and the quantity of a second good purchased holds for all *substitute* products. Other goods—for example, stereo record players and stereo records, or cameras and film—exhibit a completely different relationship. Here, price increases in one product typically lead to a reduction in demand for the other. Goods that are inversely related in this manner are known as *complements*; they are used together rather than in place of each other.

The concept of cross-price elasticity is utilized to examine the responsiveness of demand for one product to changes in the price of another. Point cross-price elasticity is given by the equation

$$\varepsilon_{PX} = \frac{\partial Q_Y}{\partial P_X} \cdot \frac{P_X}{Q_Y}, \qquad (4.16)$$

where Y and X are two different goods. The arc cross-price elasticity relationship is constructed in the same manner as was previously described for price and income elasticities.

The cross-price elasticity for substitutes is always positive—the price of one good and the demand for the other always move in the same direction. Cross-price elasticity is negative for complements—price and quantity move in opposite directions. Finally, cross-price elasticity is zero, or nearly zero, for unrelated goods; variations in the price of one good have no effect on demand for the second.

We can illustrate the concept of cross-price elasticity by considering the following unspecified demand function for Product Y:

$$Q_Y = f(P_W, P_X, P_Y, P_Z, I).$$

Here Q_Y is the quantity of Y demanded; P_W, P_X, P_Y, and P_Z are the prices of goods W, X, Y, and Z; and I is disposable income. For simplicity, assume that these are the only variables that affect Q_Y, and that the parameters of the demand equation have been estimated, using techniques developed in the next chapter, as follows:

$$Q_Y = 5,000 - 0.3P_W + 0.2P_X - 0.5P_Y + 0.000001P_Z + 0.0037I.$$

The partial derivatives of Q_Y with respect to the prices of the other goods are:

$$\frac{\partial Q_Y}{\partial P_W} = -0.3$$

$$\frac{\partial Q_Y}{\partial P_X} = +0.2$$

$$\frac{\partial Q_Y}{\partial P_Z} = 0.000001 \approx 0.$$

Since both P and Q are always positive, the ratios P_W/Q_Y, P_X/Q_Y, and P_Z/Q_Y are also positive. Therefore, the signs of the three cross-price elasticities in the example are determined by their partial derivatives:

$\varepsilon_{PW} = (-0.3)(P_W/Q_Y) < 0$. Accordingly, W and Y are complements.

$\varepsilon_{PX} = (0.2)(P_X/Q_Y) > 0$. Accordingly, X and Y are substitutes.

$\varepsilon_{PZ} = (0.000001)(P_Z/Q_Y) \approx 0$, so long as the ratio P_Z/Q_Y is not extremely large. Accordingly, Z and Y are independent.

The concept of cross-price elasticity is used for two main purposes. First, it is obviously important for the firm to be aware of how the demand for its product is likely to respond to changes in the prices of other goods; this information is necessary for formulating the firm's own pricing strategy and for analyzing the risk associated with various products. This is particularly important for firms with extensive product lines, where significant substitution or complementary interrelationships exist between the various products. Second, cross-price elasticity is used in industrial organization to measure the interrelationships among industries. To illustrate, one firm may appear to completely dominate a particular market—it is the only supplier of a particular product in the market. If, however, the cross-price elasticity between this firm's product and products in related industries is large and positive, the firm, even though it may be a monopolist in a narrow sense, will not be able to raise its prices without losing sales to other firms in related industries.[11] The importance of the cross-price elasticity of demand concept is explored further in Chapter 10, where market structures are examined, and in Chapter 11, where its role in multiple product pricing is analyzed.

---

[11] This argument has been raised in connection with antitrust actions. In banking, for example, even though relatively few banks may exist in a given market, banks compete with savings and loan associations, credit unions, commercial finance companies, and the like. The extent of this competition has been gauged in terms of cross-elasticities of demand between various banking services and competing institutions.

OTHER DEMAND ELASTICITIES

The elasticity concept is simply a way of measuring the effect of a change in an independent variable on the dependent variable in any functional relationship. The dependent variable in this chapter is the demand for a product, and the demand elasticity of any variable in the demand function may be calculated. We have emphasized the three most common demand elasticities—price elasticity, income elasticity, and cross-price elasticity—but examples of other demand elasticities will reinforce the generality of the concept.

In the housing market mortgage interest rates are an important determinant of demand; accordingly, the interest rate elasticity has been used in analyzing and forecasting the demand for housing construction. Studies indicate that the interest rate elasticity of residential housing demand is about −0.15. This indicates that a 10 percent rise in interest rates decreases by 1.5 percent the demand for housing, provided all the other variables remain unchanged.[12] If Federal Reserve policy is expected to cause interest rates to rise from 10 to 12 percent, a 20 percent increase, we can project a 3 percent decrease ($-0.15 \times 20 = -3$) in housing demand as the result of this change in interest rates.

Public utilities calculate the weather elasticity of demand for their services. They measure weather using degree days as an indicator of average temperatures. This elasticity factor is used, in conjunction with weather forecasts, to anticipate service demand and peak-load conditions.

We return to the topic of elasticities in the following chapter, where we examine empirical techniques used in estimating demand. First, however, we must consider some additional demand concepts useful for managerial decision making.

TIME IMPACT ON ELASTICITY

Time is an important factor in demand analysis. One of the important time characteristics of demand relates to the lack of instantaneous response in the marketplace.

Consumers often react slowly to changes in prices and other conditions in the marketplace. To illustrate this delayed or lagged effect consider the demand for electric power. Suppose an electric utility raises its rates by 30 percent. What effect will this have on the quantity of electric power demanded? In the very short run the effect will be slight. Customers may be more careful to turn off unneeded lights, but total demand, which is highly dependent on the appliances owned by the utility's residential customers and the equipment operated by their industrial and commer-

---

[12] Actually, this elasticity coefficient varies over time as other conditions in the economy change. Other things are held constant when measuring elasticity, but in the real world other things are *not* typically constant over time.

cial customers, will probably not be greatly affected. Prices will go up and quantity demanded will not fall very much, so total revenue will increase substantially. In other words, the short-run demand for electric power is relatively *inelastic*.

Over the longer run, however, the increase in power rates has more substantial effects. Residential users will reduce their purchases of air conditioners, electric heating units, and other appliances, and those appliances that are purchased will be more energy-efficient. These actions will reduce the demand for power. Similarly, industrial users will tend to switch to other energy sources, will employ less energy-intensive production methods, or will relocate in areas where electric costs are lower. Thus, the ultimate effect of the price increase on demand may be substantial, but it will take a number of years before the full impact is felt. This phenomenon of long-run elasticity exceeding short-run elasticity is typical for most demand determining factors.

PRICE ELASTICITY FOR DERIVED DEMAND PRODUCTS

The demand functions of some goods contain as one of the independent variables the demand for a second product. This relationship indicates that the quantity of the good purchased is derived from the demand for the other good, so we use the term *derived demand* to denote this kind of relationship. The demand for mortgage money is an example. The quantity of mortgage credit demanded is not determined autonomously or directly; rather, it is derived from the more fundamental demand for housing. Similarly, the demand for air transportation to major resort areas is not a direct demand but rather is derived from the demand for recreation. Although the demand for consumer goods (or final products) may or may not be derived, the demand for all producers' goods (those products used in the manufacture of goods for final consumption) is derived; the aggregate demand for consumption goods determines in large part the demand for the capital equipment, materials, labor, and energy used to manufacture them. For example, the demands for steel, aluminum, and plastics are all derived demands, as are the demands for machine tools and labor. None of these producers' goods is demanded because of its direct value to consumers but rather because of the role its derived demand plays in the production of goods and services.

As one would expect, the demand for producers' goods is related to the demand for the final products they are used to make; therefore, an examination of the final product's demand is an important part of the demand analysis for the intermediate, or producers' goods. This relationship is not always a direct one. For example, the demand for intermediate goods is typically less price elastic than is the demand for the resulting final product. This is because the intermediate good represents only one input in the production process; and unless its cost represents a major part of the total cost of the final product, any given percentage price change for the intermediate good will result in a smaller percentage change in the cost (and price) of the final product.

This relationship can be illustrated by looking at the demand for a specially formulated epoxy paint used in the finish of a sailboat. The total cost to manufacture the boat is $5,000, and $100 of this is the cost of the paint. Assume the price of the paint is doubled (a 100 percent increase) so that it now requires $200 of this input for each sailboat produced. In this situation the total cost of the final product—and presumably its price—will increase by only 2 percent ($100/5,000 = 0.02$). If the price elasticity of demand for the sailboat is -3.0, this 2 percent increase in its price would result in a 6 percent reduction in final demand. Assuming the amount of the epoxy paint required to finish each boat was fixed and that no good substitutes were available so that it continued to be used in the manufacturing process, the 100 percent increase in the price of the paint would result in only a 6 percent reduction in its demand. That implies a price elasticity of -0.06 percent ($-6/100 = -0.06 = \varepsilon_p$). In other words, a 1 percent increase in the price of the paint would cause demand for it to decline by only six-hundredths of 1 percent. The demand for the epoxy paint is extremely price inelastic even though the demand for the final product is quite elastic.

SUMMARY

The demand for a firm's products is a critical determinant of its profitability, and demand forecasts enter as key elements in virtually all managerial planning. To make a reliable demand forecast, one must have a thorough understanding of certain concepts and relationships. These concepts were introduced in this chapter; and they are used extensively in the following one, where we consider ways of actually estimating demand functions.

Several general points were noted. First, product demand is usually a function of several variables, such as price, income, and advertising expenditures. The explicit statement of these relationships is the *demand function*. The partial relationship between *the quantity demanded* and price is expressed by the *demand curve*. *Shifts in the demand curve* represent changes in variables other than price in the demand function; *movements along a demand curve* imply that factors other than price in the demand function are held constant.

A key concept introduced in the chapter is *elasticity*, the percentage change in quantity demanded associated with a percentage change in one of the determinants of demand. *Price* elasticity, ε_p and E_p, denoting *point* and *arc* elasticity respectively, relates changes in the quantity demanded to changes in the product's own price. If $|\varepsilon_p| > 1.0$, this is defined as *elastic* demand, and a price reduction leads to an increase in total revenue. If $|\varepsilon_p| < 1.0$, we have *inelastic* demand, and a price reduction decreases total revenue. If $|\varepsilon_p| = 1.0$, demand is unitary elastic and price and quantity changes exactly offset each other, resulting in no change in total revenue.

Income elasticity, ε_I or E_I, relates demand to a measure of income. Ordinarily, ε_I is positive, signifying that higher incomes cause greater demand, but the size of the elasticity coefficient is also important. If $\varepsilon_I > 1.0$, demand increases more than in proportion to income increases; if $\varepsilon_I < 1.0$, the converse holds. This has important implications for the growth and variability of a product's demand.

Cross-price elasticity, ε_{PX} or E_{PX}, relates the demand for Product Y to the price of Product X. If $\varepsilon_{PX} > 0$, an increase in P_X causes an increase in Q_Y, and the goods are *substitutes*. If $\varepsilon_{PX} < 0$, the goods are *complements*; if $\varepsilon_{PX} \approx 0$, the goods are *independent*.

Other kinds of elasticity may be calculated and used in demand analysis: Interest rate elasticity and advertising elasticity are two examples.

Another important point in demand analysis concerns the concept of *derived demand*—the demand for one product may be derived from a more fundamental demand for another. It was shown that the demand for capital goods is derived from the demand for consumer products.

Time has an impact on demand relationships in numerous ways. The frictions in the marketplace typically cause short-run demand impacts to be smaller than the impact over an extended period where the full influence of a change has run its course.

All the concepts developed in this chapter are used in the following chapter, where we discuss techniques for empirically measuring demand.

QUESTIONS

4.1 Explain the rationale for each of the demand variables in Equation 4.1.

4.2 Distinguish between a demand function and a demand curve. What is the difference between a change in the quantity demanded and a shift in the demand curve?

4.3 What is the relationship between a demand function and a total revenue function? Explain how one would construct the total revenue function corresponding to a given demand function.

4.4 Define each of the following terms giving both a verbal explanation and the equation.
   a. Point elasticity
   b. Arc elasticity
   c. Price elasticity
   d. Cross-price elasticity
   e. Income elasticity

4.5 What is likely to be the sign of the cross-price elasticities of demand between
  a. Movie cameras and video discs? Why?
  b. Movie cameras and film? Why?
  c. Movie cameras and milk? Why?

4.6 What relationship do you think would exist between the shape of a firm's demand curve and the degree of competition existing in its industry (that is, whether the industry is highly competitive or is monopolistic)?

4.7 How could the cross-price elasticity concept be used in an analysis of the degree of competition in the industry?

4.8 Do you think that the price elasticity of demand would be greater if computed for an industry or for one firm in the industry? Why?

PROBLEMS

4.1 KRMY-TV is currently contemplating a T-shirt advertising promotion. Limited sales data from a few T-shirt shops marketing a prototype of the KRMY design indicate that

$$Q = 1500 - 200\,P,$$

where Q is T-shirt sales and P is price.
  a. How many T-shirts could KRMY sell at $5 each?
  b. What price would KRMY have to charge to sell 1,000 T-shirts?
  c. At what price would T-shirt sales equal zero?
  d. How many T-shirts could be given away?
  e. Plot the demand, marginal revenue, and total revenue curves.
  f. Calculate the point price elasticity of demand at a price of $3.
  g. At what price would the point price elasticity of demand be -1?

4.2 Published reports concerning ticket sales for closed circuit television viewing of two recent world middleweight championship fights provide an interesting basis for a case study in price elasticities for leisure-time products. The initial bout between two world-renowned middleweight boxers brought a capacity crowd to the 18,000-seat capital center in Landover, Maryland. The overwhelming success of the first fight prompted promoters to increase average ticket prices for the rematch from $25 to $50. Only 6,000 tickets were sold for the second fight.
  a. What key assumptions must be met in order to use the above information to specify a demand relation?
  b. Given that these assumptions are met, specify a demand relation and use this relation to find the revenue maximizing ticket price. Assume a linear form for the demand relation.

c. Again presuming that the required assumptions are met, calculate the arc price elasticity of demand over the price range from $25 to $50.

4.3 There is a major controversy in the U.S. concerning the dairy product price support program. At the current "supported" price, the quantity of the product supplied by dairy farmers far exceeds the quantity demanded by consumers. The result is that the U.S. government has bought and is storing large quantities of dairy products.

　　a. Dairy industry proponents argue that although there is a surplus of supply at this time, price supports are needed to prevent a catastrophic price decline. They claim that only very large price reductions would work to increase consumer demand and thereby remove the surplus. What is the implicit statement about the price elasticity of demand for dairy products in this argument?

　　b. Assume the price elasticity of demand for dairy products is -1.35. How large must the price reduction be to increase consumer demand by 9 percent?

　　c. Assuming that at current prices there is a 9 percent excess of supply over consumer demand, would you expect a price reduction of the magnitude found in Part b (above) to be required to balance supply and demand? Why or why not?

　　d. Assuming the dairy product price support program is reduced or canceled, what impact would you expect on the demand for other foods? Explain how demand relationships affect your answer to this question.

4.4 Walt Francis, owner of Walt's Sporting Goods, has just received a proposal from his marketing manager calling for a price reduction on fishing rods. The marketing manager assures Walt that such a price reduction will increase output, revenue, and profits.

　　a. If trade publications estimate the price elasticity of demand for fishing rods at -1.2, is a price reduction likely to increase unit sales? Revenues?

　　b. If purchase costs per fishing rod are $3, would you recommend a price reduction if the current price is $18? Explain.

4.5 ALH Computer Games Co. sells computer game programs. During 1982, ALH sold 10,000 Sac-Man games per month at a price of $60. In January 1983 a competitor cut the price on a similar game from $65 to $55. The following month ALH sold only 8,000 Sac-Man games.

　　a. Determine the arc cross-price elasticity of demand between ALH's and its competitor's games. (Assume that ALH's price is held constant.)

　　b. Assume that the price elasticity for ALH Sac-Man games is -2.0. Assume also that its competitor keeps the price of its game at $55. What price cut must be made by ALH to increase its sales volume back to 10,000 games per month?

4.6 The demand for cable television service in a Midwest market is characterized by the following elasticities: price elasticity $= -.9$; cross-price elasticity with "Home Movies" $= -.75$; income elasticity $= +0.80$.

Indicate whether each of the following statements is true or false, and explain why.

a. If the cable television company wants to increase the number of customers it serves, it should reduce price.

b. Reducing price will increase the number of customers for cable television and the revenues generated.

c. "Home Movies" is a complementary good to cable television service.

d. "Home Movies" is a substitute good to cable television service.

e. Reducing the price of "Home Movies" would increase the number of customers acquiring cable television service.

f. Reducing the price of "Home Movies" would reduce the revenues from cable television service.

g. Cable television is an inferior good.

h. A 10 percent increase in income will result in an 80 percent increase in demand for cable television service.

4.7 Bill's Poster Shops, Inc., has completed an analysis of weekly demand for its posters in three San Francisco-area outlets. Bill's study revealed:

$$Qx = 56,000 - 2,000Px + 5,000 \, Pop + 1,000 \, Py,$$

where Qx = annual poster demand, Px = poster price in dollars, Pop = high school and college student population within a four mile radius (in thousands), and Py = a price index of competitor poster prices in dollars. During this period a typical outlet had Px = \$5, Pop = 10,000, and Py = \$4.

a. What is the demand curve faced by the average Bill's outlet?

b. What is the current point price elasticity for Bill's posters?

c. What is the cross-price elasticity of demand faced by a typical Bill's outlet?

4.8 Mary Lee's "Old Fashioned" Ice Cream Shops have enjoyed explosive growth in northeastern states within recent years. A move to extend Mary Lee's market to midwestern states is currently being contemplated. Mary Lee's has retained an independent management consulting firm to analyze demand for its products. This analysis of Mary Lee's outlets in 16 regional markets found the following:

$$Q = 14.6 - 2.5 \, P + 12.5 \, I + 5 \, W - .5 \, \bar{A} + 5 \, A - .25 \, A^2,$$

where

Q = Number of customers served (in hundreds)

P = Average price paid by each customer (in dollars)

I = Disposable income in relevant market (in millions of dollars)

$W =$ Weather measured by average temperature

$\tilde{A} =$ Competitor advertising expenditures (in thousands of dollars)

$A =$ Mary Lee's "own" advertising (in thousands of dollars).

Columbus, Ohio, was a typical (average) market included in the empirical analysis. During 1983 in Columbus $P = \$4$, $I = \$180,000,000$, $W = 54°$, $\tilde{A} = \$64,000$, $A = \$6,000$.

Calculate and interpret the relevant point elasticity with respect to:

a. Own price

b. Income

c. Weather

d. Competitor advertising

e. Own advertising.

SELECTED REFERENCES

Bernardo, John J. "A Programming Approach to Measure Attribute Utilities." *Journal of Economics and Business* 33 (Spring/Summer 1981): 239–245.

Clarke, Edward H. *Demand Revelation and the Provision of Public Goods*. Cambridge, Mass.: Harper & Row, Ballinger, 1980.

Clarkson, Geoffrey P. *The Theory of Consumer Demand: A Critical Appraisal*. Englewood Cliffs, N.J.: Prentice-Hall, 1963.

Friedman, Milton. *A Theory of the Consumption Function*. Princeton: Princeton University Press, 1957.

Henderson, James M., and Quandt, Richard E. *Microeconomic Theory*, 2d ed., Chapter 2. New York: McGraw-Hill, 1971.

Hicks, John R. *A Revision of Demand Theory*. London: Oxford University Press, 1959.

Knight, Frank H. "Realism and Relevance in the Theory of Demand." *Journal of Political Economy* 50 (1944): 289–318.

Lancaster, Kelvin J. *Consumer Demand: A New Approach*. New York: Columbia University Press, 1971.

Lancaster, Kelvin J. "A New Approach to Consumer Theory." *Journal of Political Economy* 74 (February 1966): 132–157.

Landsburg, Steven E. "Taste Change in the United Kingdom, 1900–1955." *Journal of Political Economy* 89 (February 1981): 92–104.

Morgan, James N. "Multiple Motives, Group Decisions, Uncertainty, Ignorance and Confusion: A Realistic Economics of the Consumer Requires Some Psychology." *American Economic Review* 68 (May 1978): 58–63.

Pollak, Robert A. "Endogenous Tastes in Demand and Welfare Analysis." *American Economic Review* 68 (May 1978): 374–379.

CHAPTER 5
DEMAND ESTIMATION

In Chapter 4 we introduced several concepts useful in demand analysis and indicated the key role that product demand plays in most business decisions. To use these important demand relationships in decision analysis, one must be able to empirically estimate the structural form and parameters of the demand function. In this chapter we consider procedures used in this estimation.

In some cases it is relatively easy to obtain accurate estimates of demand relationships, especially those necessary for short-run demand or sales forecasting. In other situations it is exceedingly difficult to obtain even the information needed to make short-run demand forecasts, and still more difficult to make long-run forecasts, or to determine how changes in specific demand variables—price, advertising expenditures, credit terms, prices of competing products, and so on—will affect demand. These demand relationships are sufficiently important that we should devote time and effort to try to estimate them.

We explore the three primary methods used to estimate the parameters (coefficients) of the demand function: the interview (or survey) method, market experimentation, and regression analysis. The first two techniques are covered extensively in marketing courses, so we will only introduce them and show how they are used to supplement regression analysis. Regression analysis, on the other hand, is examined in detail for two reasons. First, in many instances regression analysis is the best, or perhaps even the only, means of estimating the demand equation. Second, the technique of regression analysis is probably the single most important estimating technique used in managerial economics, and perhaps in all aspects of business administration. In addition to its use in demand analysis, regression is used, for example, to study production and cost functions and cost of capital relationships. Accordingly, in this chapter we examine in some detail the technique of regression analysis in connection with demand. In later chapters we shall draw on this tool extensively.

THE IDENTIFICATION PROBLEM

One reason that it is difficult to obtain accurate estimates of demand relationships is the close interrelationships among most economic variables. To see why this poses a difficulty, consider the problem of estimating the demand curve for Product X. If we have data on the price charged and the quantity purchased at several points in time, a logical first step might be to plot this information as is shown in Figure 5.1. Can the line AB be interpreted as a demand curve and points 1, 2, and 3 as various price/quantity demanded combinations on the demand curve? The curve connecting the points is negatively sloped, indicating the typical inverse relationship between the price charged for a product and the quantity demanded, and each data point does represent the quantity of X purchased at a particular price. Nevertheless, the available data is insufficient to allow us to conclude that AB is in fact the demand curve for X.

Let us see why this is so. For each of several points in time we have the price charged for X and the quantity purchased. But this will not necessarily trace out a demand curve. In the previous chapter we stated that the demand curve shows the relationship between the price charged for a good and the quantity demanded, *holding constant the effect of all other variables in the demand function*. Thus, in order to plot the demand curve, we must obtain data on the price/quantity relationship, keeping constant the effects of all factors in the demand function other than price.

The price/quantity data used to construct Figure 5.1 are insufficient to develop a demand curve since the effects of all other demand-related variables may or may not have been eliminated. The line AB might be a demand curve, but then again, it might not be. To see this, consider Figure 5.2, where the price/quantity data are again plotted, along with the hypothesized true supply and demand curves for Product X.[1] There we see that the data points indicate nothing more than the simul-

---

[1] Supply curves indicate the relationship between the quantity of a product that producers will make available for sale and the price they receive, holding constant the effect of all other factors in the firms' supply functions.

FIGURE 5.1

Price/Quantity Plot

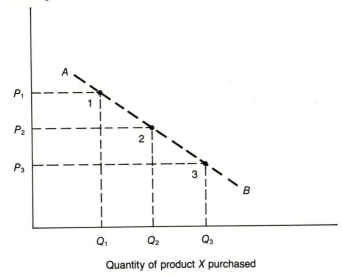

Price charged

A

P_1

1

P_2

2

P_3

3

B

Q_1 Q_2 Q_3

Quantity of product X purchased

FIGURE 5.2

Supply and Demand Curves

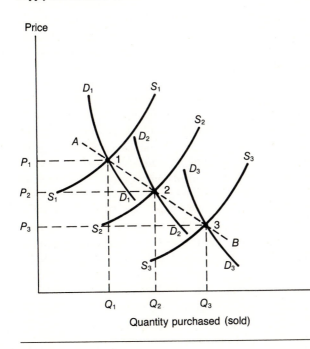

Price

D_1 S_1

S_2

D_2

S_3

A

P_1 1

D_3

P_2 S_1 D_1 2

P_3 S_2 D_2 3

B

S_3 D_3

Q_1 Q_2 Q_3

Quantity purchased (sold)

taneous solution of supply and demand relationships at three points in time. That is, the price/quantity data that we observe are the result of the interplay between the quantity of X supplied by producers and the quantity demanded by consumers. The intersection of the supply and demand curves at each point in time results in the observed price/quantity points, but the line AB is *not* a demand curve.

In Figure 5.2 we see that nonprice variables in both the supply and demand functions have changed between the data points. Suppose, for example, that new and more efficient facilities for producing X are completed between observation dates, and as a result the quantity supplied at any given price is larger. This causes a shift of the supply curve from S_1 to S_2 to S_3. Similarly, the price of a complementary product may have fallen or consumer incomes may have risen, so at any given price larger quantities of X are demanded in the later periods. This second phenomenon results in a shift of the demand curve from D_1 to D_2 to D_3.

Now observe what has occurred. Both the supply curve and the demand curve have shifted over time. This has resulted in a declining price and an increasing quantity purchased. The three intersection points of the supply and the demand curves in Figure 5.2—points 1, 2, and 3—are the same points plotted in Figure 5.1. But these are not three points on a single demand curve for Product X. Each point is on a *different* demand curve—one that is shifting over time—so connecting them does not trace out the product demand curve.

Observe the effect of erroneously interpreting the line AB (which connects the points 1, 2, and 3) as a demand curve. If a firm makes this mistake, it might assume that a reduction in price from P_1 to P_2 increases the quantity demanded from Q_1 to Q_2. An expansion of this magnitude may well justify the price reduction. Such a price cut, however, will result in a much smaller increase in the quantity demanded—the true demand curve is much less elastic than is the line AB—so a price reduction is much less desirable than it first appeared.

Given the interrelationship between demand and supply curves, can data on prices and quantities purchased ever be used to estimate a demand curve? They can, but only under two sets of conditions: (1) the demand curve has *not* shifted, but the supply curve *has* shifted; or (2) we have enough information to determine just how each curve has shifted between data observations. For example, if a technological breakthrough occurs in the manufacture of a product so that costs in the industry fall markedly within a short period during which demand conditions are stable (as happened in the electronics industry with the manufacture of hand-held calculators and digital watches), the situation depicted in Figure 5.3 may arise. The demand curve, which initially was unknown, is assumed to be stable. The supply curve shifts from S_1 to S_2 to S_3. Each price/quantity point represents the intersection of the supply and the demand curves. Since the demand determining factors other than price are assumed to be stable, points 1, 2, and 3 must all be on the same demand curve, so the demand curve DD can be estimated by connecting the three points.

It is clear from this example that the problem of simultaneous relationships in demand analysis can be overcome only if one has enough information to *identify* the

FIGURE 5.3

Shifting Supply Curve Tracing Out Stable Demand Curve

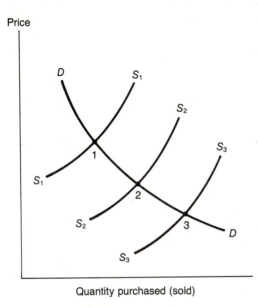

Price

Quantity purchased (sold)

interrelated functions so that shifts in one curve can be distinguished from shifts in the other. For this reason, the problem of estimating one function when simultaneous relationships exist is known as the *identification problem*. To separate shifts in demand from changes in supply, we must have more information than just the price/quantity data; information about which curve is shifting, and to what extent it is shifting, is necessary to identify and estimate the demand relationship. Frequently this information is unavailable. In these cases, statistical techniques of demand estimation, such as regression analysis, cannot provide estimates of the demand function parameters. When the identification problem cannot be solved, such techniques as consumer interviews and market experiments can sometimes be used to obtain information about important demand function relationships. These techniques are also useful for providing data for use in statistical demand analysis when the identification problem can be resolved.

CONSUMER INTERVIEWS

The consumer interview, or survey procedure, requires the questioning of a firm's customers or potential customers in an attempt to estimate the relationship between the demand for its products and a variety of variables perceived to be important for the marketing and profit planning functions. The technique can be applied naïvely by simply stopping shoppers and asking questions about the quantity of the product they would purchase at different prices. At the other extreme, to elicit the desired information, trained interviewers may present sophisticated questions to a carefully selected sample.

Theoretically, consumer surveys can provide excellent information on a number of important demand relationships. The firm might question each of its customers (or take a statistical sample if the number of customers is large) about projected purchases under a variety of different conditions relating to price, advertising expenditures, prices of substitutes and complements, income, and any number of other variables in the demand function. Then, by aggregating data, the firm could forecast its total demand and estimate some of the important parameters in the demand function for its product.

Unfortunately, this procedure does not necessarily work smoothly in actual practice. The quantity and quality of information obtainable by this technique is likely to be limited. Consumers are often unable, and in many cases unwilling, to provide accurate answers to hypothetical questions about how they would react to changes in the key demand variables.

Consider the problem of attempting to determine the effect of just two variables, price and advertising expenditures, on the demand for automobiles. If an interviewer asked how you would react to a 1, 2, or 3 percent increase (or decrease) in the price of a specific model of car, could you respond accurately? What if the question relates to the effect of shifting the emphasis in the firm's advertising campaign from fuel efficiency to safety or to changing the advertising media? Could you tell how this action would affect your demand for the car? Because most people are unable to answer such questions—even for major items such as automobiles, appliances, and housing—it is obviously difficult to use such a technique to estimate the demand relationships for most consumer goods.

We do not wish to imply that consumer survey techniques have no merit in demand analysis. Using subtle inquiries, a trained interviewer can extract a good deal of useful information from consumers. For example, an interviewer might ask questions about the relative prices of several competing goods and learn that most people are unaware of existing price differentials. This is a good indication that demand is not highly responsive to price changes, so a producer would not attempt to increase demand by reducing price—consumers would probably not even notice the reduction. Similar questions can be used to determine whether consumers are aware of advertising programs and to what extent they are aware, what their reaction is to the ads, and so on. Thus, some useful information is obtainable by surveys, and the quality of the results is adequate for some decision purposes.

Also, for certain kinds of demand information there is no substitute for the consumer interview. For example, in short-term demand or sales forecasting, consumer attitudes and expectations about future business conditions frequently make the difference between an accurate estimate and one that misses by a wide margin. Such subjective information can typically be obtained only through interview methods.[2]

MARKET STUDIES AND EXPERIMENTATION

An alternative technique for obtaining useful information about a product's demand function involves market experiments. One market experiment technique entails examining consumer behavior in actual markets. The firm locates one or more markets with specific characteristics, then varies prices, packaging, advertising, and other controllable variables in the demand function, with the variations occurring either over time or between markets. For example, Del Monte Corporation may have determined that uncontrollable consumer characteristics are quite similar in Denver and Salt Lake City. Del Monte could raise the price of sliced pineapple in Salt Lake City vis-à-vis that in Denver, then compare pineapple sales in the two markets. Alternatively, Del Monte could make a series of weekly or monthly price changes in one market, then determine how these changes affected demand. With several segregated markets, the firm may also be able to use census or survey data to determine how such demographic characteristics as income, family size, educational level, and ethnic background affect demand. Market experiments have several serious shortcomings. They are expensive and are therefore usually undertaken on a scale too small to allow high levels of confidence in the results. Related to this problem is the one of short-run versus long-run effects. Market experiments are seldom run for sufficiently long periods to indicate the long-run effects of various price, advertising, or packaging strategies. The experimenter is thus forced to examine short-run data and attempt to extend it to a longer period.

Difficulties associated with the uncontrolled parts of the market experiment also reduce its value as an estimating tool. A change in economic conditions during the experiment is likely to invalidate the results, especially if the experiment includes the use of several separated markets; a local strike or layoffs by a major employer in one of the market areas, a severe snowstorm, or the like might well ruin the experiment. Likewise, a change in a competing product's promotion, price, or packaging might distort the results. There is also the danger that customers lost during the experiment as a result of price manipulations cannot be regained when the experiment ends.

A second market experimentation procedure utilizes a controlled laboratory ex-

---

[2]The use of interview or survey techniques for sales forecasting is covered more extensively in Appendix B at the end of the book.

periment wherein consumers are given funds with which to shop in a simulated store. By varying prices, product packaging, displays, and other factors, the experimenter can often learn a great deal about consumer behavior. The laboratory experiment, while providing similar information as field experiments, has an advantage because of lower cost and greater control of extraneous factors.

The consumer clinic or laboratory experiment technique is not without shortcomings, however. The primary difficulty is that the subjects invariably know that they are part of an experiment, and this knowledge may well distort their shopping habits. They may, for example, exhibit considerably more price consciousness than is typical in their everyday shopping. Moreover, the high cost of such experiments necessarily limits the sample size, which makes inference from the sample to the general population tenuous at best.

Demand for Oranges: An Illustrative Market Experiment

During 1962 researchers from the University of Florida conducted a market experiment in Grand Rapids, Michigan, to examine the competition between California and Florida Valencia oranges. The experiment was designed to provide estimates of the price elasticities of demand for the various oranges included in the study, as well as to measure the cross-price elasticities of demand among varieties of oranges.[3]

The researchers chose Grand Rapids because its size, economic base, and demographic characteristics are representative of the Midwest market for oranges. Nine supermarkets located throughout the city cooperated in the experiment, which consisted of varying the prices charged for Florida and California Valencia oranges daily for 31 days and recording the quantities of each variety sold. The price variations for each variety of orange covered a range of 32¢ a dozen (±16¢ around the price per dozen that existed in the market at the time the study began). More than 9,250 dozen oranges were sold during the experiment.

The price and quantity data obtained in this study enabled the researchers to examine the relationship between sales of each variety of orange and its price, as well as the relationship between sales and the price charged for competing varieties. The results of the study are summarized in Table 5.1, where the elasticities of these price variables are reported. The numbers along the diagonal represent the price elasticities of the three varieties of oranges, while the off-diagonal figures estimate the cross-price elasticities of demand.

The price elasticity for all three varieties was quite large. The −3.07 price elas-

[3]This section is adapted from Marshall B. Godwin, W. Fred Chapman, Jr., and William T. Hanley, *Competition between Florida and California Valencia Oranges in the Fruit Market*, Bulletin 704, December 1965, Agricultural Experiment Stations, Institute of Food and Agricultural Services, University of Florida, Gainesville, Florida, in cooperation with the U.S. Department of Agriculture, Florida Citrus Commission.

TABLE 5.1

Demand Relationships for California and Florida Valencia Oranges

A 1 Percent Change in the Price of	Percentage Change in the Sales of		
	Florida Indian River	Florida Interior	California
Florida Indian River	−3.07	+1.56	+0.01
Florida Interior	+1.16	−3.01	+0.14
California	+0.18	+0.09	−2.76

ticity for Florida Indian River oranges means that a 1 percent decrease in their price resulted in a 3.07 percent increase in their sales. The other Florida oranges had a similar price elasticity, while the price elasticity of the California oranges was somewhat lower, indicating that demand for California oranges is less responsive to price changes than is demand for the Florida varieties.

The cross-price elasticities of demand reveal some interesting demand relationships among these three varieties of oranges. First, note that cross-price elasticities of demand between the two Florida varieties are positive and relatively large. This indicates that consumers view these two varieties as close substitutes and therefore switch readily between them when price differentials exist. The cross-price elasticities of demand between the Florida and California oranges, on the other hand, are all very small, indicating that consumers do not view them as close substitutes. That is, the market for California oranges in Grand Rapids is quite distinct from the market for Florida varieties.

This market study provided estimates of two important demand relationships, the price elasticity of demand for Florida and California oranges and their cross-price elasticities of demand. The researchers were able to identify and measure these relationships because the 31-day study period was brief enough to prevent changes in incomes, tastes, population, and other variables that would influence the demand for oranges; and they were able to insure that adequate supply quantities of the various Valencia oranges were available to consumers at each experimental price.

Summary on Market Experiments

The market experiment demand estimation technique can provide valuable demand information, as was indicated by the example of Florida and California oranges. The rather sizable drawbacks associated with the cost and uncontrollable factors of such experiments, however, tend to limit their use to those situations where the information needed for statistical demand estimation cannot be obtained from historical records. Frequently a market experiment is used as a means of developing some of the data required for a statistical analysis of demand relationships.

REGRESSION ANALYSIS

The statistical method most frequently employed in demand estimation is *regression analysis*. There are limitations to this technique, but regression analysis can often provide good estimates of demand functions at relatively small cost.

Specifying the Variables

The first step in regression analysis is to specify the variables that are expected to influence demand. Product demand, measured in physical units, is the dependent variable. The list of independent variables, or those which influence demand, always includes the price of the product and generally includes such factors as the prices of complementary and competitive products, advertising expenditures, consumer incomes, and population of the consuming group. Demand functions for expensive durable goods, such as automobiles and houses, include interest rates and other credit terms; those for ski equipment, beverages, or air-conditioners include weather conditions. Demand determinants for capital goods, such as industrial machinery, include corporate profitability, output to capacity ratios, and wage rate trends.

Obtaining Data on the Variables

The second step in regression analysis is to obtain accurate estimates of the variables: measures of price, credit terms, output/capacity ratios, advertising expenditures, incomes, and the like. Obtaining estimates of these variables is not always easy, especially if the study involves data for past years. Further, some key variables, such as consumer attitudes toward quality and their expectations about future business conditions—which are quite important in demand functions for many consumer goods—may have to be obtained by survey (questionnaire and interview) techniques, which introduces an element of subjectivity into the data, or by market or laboratory experiments, which may produce biased data.

Specifying the Form of the Equation

Linear Functions. Once the variables have been specified and the data gathered, the next step is to specify the form of the equation or the manner in which the independent variables are assumed to interact to determine the level of demand. The most common specification is a linear relationship such as the following:

$$Q = a + bP + cA + dY. \tag{5.1}$$

Here Q represents the quantity of a particular product demanded, P is the price charged, A represents advertising expenditures, and Y is per capita disposable income. The quantity demanded is assumed to change linearly with changes in each of the independent variables. For example, if $b = -1.5$, demand will decline by 1½ units for each 1-unit increase in the price of the product. The demand curve for a demand function such as that shown in Equation 5.1 is linear; that is, it is a straight line.

Linear demand functions have great appeal in empirical work for two reasons. First, experience has shown that many demand relationships are in fact approximately linear over the range for which data are typically encountered. Second, a convenient statistical technique, the method of least squares, can be used to estimate the parameters a, b, c, and d, the regression coefficients, for linear equations. More will be said about least squares below, but first it is useful to examine other forms of demand functions.

Power Functions. The second most commonly specified demand relationship is the multiplicative form:

$$Q = aP^bA^cY^d. \tag{5.2}$$

This equation is popular primarily because of two features. First, the multiplicative equation is frequently the most logical form of the demand function. It is often the one with the most intuitive appeal, assuming as it does that the marginal effects of each independent variable on demand are not constant but, rather, depend on the value of the variable as well as on the value of all other variables in the demand function. This can be easily seen by considering the partial derivative of Equation 5.2 with respect to income, $\partial Q/\partial Y = adP^bA^cY^{d-1}$, which includes all the variables in the original demand function. Thus, the marginal effect of a change in per capita disposable income on the product demand specified in Equation 5.2 depends on the level of income, as well as on advertising expenditures and the price charged for the product.

This changing marginal relationship is often far more realistic than the implicit assumption in a linear model, namely, that the marginal relation is constant. For example, as incomes increase from a low level to a higher level, the demand for sirloin steak might increase continuously. However, it is unlikely that the increase in demand will be linear. Instead, it will probably be more rapid at lower income levels, then gradually taper off at higher levels. A similar relationship probably holds for advertising expenditures. At low to moderate levels of spending the marginal impact on sales of an additional dollar of advertising is likely to be quite large. With very high spending levels, however, there may well be a saturation effect and a resultant decrease in the marginal effect on demand of each added advertising dollar. In such situations, use of a nonlinear demand function, such as a power function, is indicated.

The second reason for the popularity of the multiplicative demand function is that Equation 5.2 is an algebraic form that can be transformed into a linear relationship using logarithms, and then estimated by the least squares regression technique. Thus, Equation 5.2 is equivalent to:

$$\log Q = \log a + b \cdot \log P + c \cdot \log A + d \cdot \log Y. \qquad (5.3)$$

Equation 5.2 is linear in logarithms, and when it is written in the form of Equation 5.3 the coefficients of the equation ($\log a$, b, c, and d) can be estimated by least squares regression analysis.

An interesting and useful feature of a multiplicative relationship, such as the one specified in Equation 5.2, is that demand functions of this form have constant elasticities over the full range of data examined. Further, these elasticities are given by the coefficients estimated in the regression analysis. For example, consider the price elasticity of demand for the product whose demand function is represented by Equation 5.2. It was shown in Chapter 4 that point price elasticity is obtained by taking the partial derivative of the demand function with respect to price, then multiplying that partial derivative by the ratio of price to quantity demanded:

$$\varepsilon_p = \frac{\partial Q}{\partial P} \cdot \frac{P}{Q}. \qquad (5.4)$$

Differentiating Equation 5.2 with respect to price, we obtain:

$$\frac{\partial Q}{\partial P} = abP^{b-1}A^cY^d. \qquad (5.5)$$

Therefore,

$$\varepsilon_p = abP^{b-1}A^cY^d \cdot \frac{P}{Q}. \qquad (5.6)$$

Substituting Equation 5.2 for Q in Equation 5.6 gives:

$$\varepsilon_p = abP^{b-1}A^cY^d \cdot \frac{P}{aP^bA^cY^d}. \qquad (5.7)$$

Combining terms and canceling where possible in Equation 5.7, we obtain:

$$\varepsilon_p = \frac{abP^{b-1}A^cY^d}{1} \cdot \frac{P}{aP^bA^cY^d}$$

$$= \frac{abP^bA^cY^d}{P} \cdot \frac{P}{aP^bA^cY^d}$$

$$= b.$$

Thus, the price elasticity of demand is equal to the exponent of price in the multiplicative demand function given as Equation 5.2. Since the elasticity is simply equal to b, it is not a function of the price/quantity ratio and hence is constant. This constant elasticity relationship holds for *all* the variables in any multiplicative demand relationship.

Constant elasticities, where they occur, are useful properties in demand equations. As an example, if the income elasticity of demand for housing is constant, then increases in income can be expected to produce proportionate changes in the demand for housing over wide ranges of income. If this feature does not hold—and recall from the discussion of Figure 4.5 that the elasticity of linear demand curves *always* changes over the range of the curve—decision makers concerned with housing demand have to worry about differing elasticities at different income levels. Thus, while we cannot force a demand curve into the multiplicative form of Equation 5.2, if it is in fact of this kind it will also have the useful property of constant elasticities.

Choosing the Form of the Equation. The algebraic form of the demand function—linear, multiplicative, or other forms—should always be chosen to reflect the true relationships between variables in the system being studied. That is, care should be taken to insure that the structural form chosen for an empirical demand function is consistent with the underlying theory of demand. In practice, however, there is often no a priori basis for specifying the form of the relationship. In such cases several theoretically appropriate forms may be tested, and the one that best fits the data should be selected as being most likely to reflect the true relationship. Methods of fitting regression equations are described in the following section.

Estimating the Regression Parameters

Regression equations are typically fitted—that is, the coefficients a, b, c, and d of Equation 5.1 or 5.2 are estimated—by the method of least squares. Using a very simple two-variable case, we can demonstrate the method as follows. Assume that data on XYZ Corporation's sales of Product Y and the advertising expenditures on

TABLE 5.2

Sales and Advertising Data for XYZ Corporation

	1977	1978	1979	1980	1981	1982	1983	Mean
Sales (thousands of units)	37	48	45	36	25	55	63	$\bar{Y} = 44$
Advertising expenditures (millions of dollars)	$4.5	$6.5	$3.5	$3.0	$2.5	$8.5	$7.5	$\bar{A} = \$5.1$

FIGURE 5.4

Relationship between Sales and Advertising Expenditures for XYZ Corporation

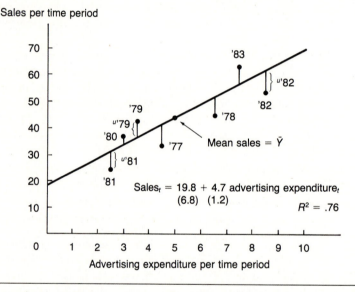

this product have been collected over the past seven years. (The data are given in
Table 5.2.) If a linear relationship between sales of Y and advertising expenditures,
A, is hypothesized, the regression equation would take the following form:

$$\text{Sales } Y = a + bA. \tag{5.8}$$

The method of least squares is then applied to select the values of a and b that
best fit the data in Table 5.2 to the regression equation. The procedure is presented
graphically in Figure 5.4. Here each point represents the advertising expenditure
and sales of Y in a given year. In terms of Equation 5.8, each point can be specified
by the relationship:

$$\text{Sales}_t = Y_t = a + bA_t + u_t, \tag{5.9}$$

where u is a residual term that includes the effects of all determinants of sales that have been omitted from the regression equation, as well as a stochastic or random element, and t is used to denote the year of the observation.[4] Notice that in this regression equation, a is the intercept of the regression line with the sales axis, b is the slope of the line, and u_t is the error term or residual which measures the vertical deviation of each tth data point from the fitted regression line. The sum of the squares of these error terms is minimized by the choice of a and b through the least squares technique.[5]

The least squares process for fitting a regression equation is nothing more than an application of the optimization procedure developed in Chapter 2 to the problem of minimizing the sum of the squared deviations from the fitted line. We can demonstrate this by continuing with the sales/advertising example for XYZ Corporation. Solving Equation 5.9 for the error term, u_t, results in:

$$u_t = Y_t - a - bA_t.$$

Thus, the expression for the sum of the squared error terms is:

$$\sum_{t=1977}^{1983} u_t^2 = \sum_{t=1977}^{1983} (Y_t - a - bA_t)^2. \tag{5.10}$$

The least squares regression technique is a procedure for minimizing Equation 5.10 by choice of the two decision variables a and b, the coefficients of the regression equation. Such minimization is accomplished by differentiating Equation 5.10 with respect to a and b, setting the partial derivatives equal to zero, and solving the resulting two-equation system for a and b:

$$\frac{\partial \sum_{t=1977}^{1983} u_t^2}{\partial a} = -2 \sum_{t=1977}^{1983} (Y_t - a - bA_t) = 0. \tag{5.11}$$

$$\frac{\partial \sum_{t=1977}^{1983} u_t^2}{\partial b} = -2 \sum_{t=1977}^{1983} A_t(Y_t - a - bA_t) = 0. \tag{5.12}$$

---

[4]One point that should be noted deals with the subscript t used to identify the year of each observation. When time series data are being examined, as they are in our example, the term t is used for the subscript. However, if cross-sectional data are being examined—for example, if we are examining the sales of Product Y during a given year in different markets where advertising expenditures had varied—we would designate the various markets with the subscript i. In other words, in time series work the subscript t is typically employed; while in cross-sectional work i is used.

[5]The error terms are squared because the deviations are both positive and negative and, hence, many different lines can be fitted that will result in the sum of the actual deviations being zero. That is, the *sum* of the deviations can be zero even

Equations 5.11 and 5.12 are called the *normal equations*, and when solved for *a* and *b* they result in:

$$b = \frac{\displaystyle\sum_{t\,=\,1977}^{1983} (A_t - \bar{A})(Y_t - \bar{Y})}{\displaystyle\sum_{t\,=\,1977}^{1983} (A_t - \bar{A})^2} \qquad (5.13)$$

and

$$a = \bar{Y} - b\bar{A}, \qquad (5.14)$$

where $\bar{A}$ and $\bar{Y}$ are the mean values for the advertising and sales observations respectively. Inserting the data from Table 5.2 into Equations 5.13 and 5.14 results in estimates of 19.8 for *a* and 4.7 for *b*, so the sales/advertising regression for XYZ Corporation is estimated to be:

$$\text{Sales}_t = Y_t = 19.8 + 4.7A_t.$$

Notice that we have dropped the error term, u_t, at this point since its expected value is always zero.

While the relationships developed above are important for understanding regression analysis, it is seldom necessary to actually perform the calculations, since virtually all computers and many calculators are equipped with "canned" regression programs, and all one need do is input data similar to those given in Table 5.2 to obtain the coefficients of the equation. In fact, if the problem is small enough for the equation to be conveniently fitted by hand (or with a desk calculator), a freehand graphic fit is generally accurate enough, and the least squares estimating technique is unnecessary. However, if many data points are involved, or if two or more independent variables are included in the equation, then computer solutions are the only practical means of implementing the least squares technique. Accordingly, we shall concentrate on setting up regression problems for computer solution and interpreting the output, rather than dwelling on the mathematical process itself.

Interpreting the Regression Equation

Once we have estimates of the regression equation, how do we interpret the values of the coefficients? First, *a*, the intercept term, frequently has no economic mean-

---

though substantial positive and negative deviations exist. By squaring the deviations we are summing a set of positive numbers, and the line which minimizes this sum most accurately depicts the relationship between the dependent and the independent variables.

ing. Caution must always be exercised when interpreting points outside the range of the observed data, and typically the intercept lies far outside this range. In our present example the intercept cannot be interpreted as the expected level of sales if advertising is completely eliminated. It *might* be true that the level of sales with zero advertising would equal the intercept term, *a*, but since the current example includes no observations of sales at zero advertising expenditures, we cannot safely assume that 19,800 units can be sold with no advertising. Similarly, it would be hazardous to extend the sales/advertising curve very far upward from the range of observed values. For example, we could not extrapolate the sales curve out to advertising expenditures of $15 or $20 million and have much confidence in the predicted level of sales (recall the discussion above about the possible saturation of advertising's impact on demand). In summary, it is very important that we restrict our interpretation of regression relationships to within the range of data observations.

The slope coefficient, *b*, gives us an estimate of the change in sales associated with a 1-unit change in advertising expenditures. Since advertising expenditures were measured in millions of dollars for the regression estimation, while sales were in thousands of units, a $1-million increase in advertising will lead to a 4,700-unit expected increase in sales; a $2-million advertising increase to 9,400 additional units sold; and so on. Again, caution must be used when extending the analysis beyond the range of observed values in the data used to estimate the regression coefficients.

The results of this simple two-variable regression model can easily be extended to multiple variable models. To illustrate the extension, suppose that we also have information on the average price, *P*, charged for Product *Y* in each of the seven years. This new information can be added to the linear model given in Equation 5.9, resulting in the following regression equation:

$$\text{Sales } Y_t = a + bA_t + cP_t + u_t. \tag{5.15}$$

Again, computer programs using the method of least squares can be used to fit the data to the model and to estimate the parameters *a*, *b*, and *c*. When this is done, we interpret the coefficients as follows: *a* is again an intercept term that may or may not have economic significance depending upon the range of sample values; *b* is the expected change in sales related to a 1-unit change in advertising expenditure, *holding constant the price of* Y; and *c* is the expected change in sales related to a 1-unit change in price, *holding constant advertising expenditures*. The coefficients of a multiple regression model are, therefore, equivalent to the partial derivatives of the function:

$$\frac{\partial \text{ sales } Y}{\partial \text{ advertising}} = b, \text{ and } \frac{\partial \text{ sales } Y}{\partial \text{ price}} = c.$$

Graphic representations of multiple regression models are not generally feasible, but Figure 5.4 can be used to gain insights into the process. Note that actual sales in 1982 were well below the value predicted by the regression line, so u_{82} was large and negative. Similarly, note that actual sales exceeded the predicted level in 1979, so u_{79} was large and positive. Now suppose that our new information on prices reveals that the average price of Y was relatively low in 1979 but high in 1982. Further, high prices prevailed in 1981, 1977, and 1978, while prices were low in 1980 and 1983 as well as in 1979. Thus, the price data seem to explain the deviations in the graph. Accordingly, we would expect that when the price data are added to the regression equation, the error terms, u_t, will be reduced; that is, the average absolute value of u in Equation 5.15 should be less than that of u in Equation 5.9, since more of the variation in sales can be explained by variables included in the model and, therefore, less need be absorbed by the error terms. Given that the sum of the squared error terms will be lower, Equation 5.15 is said to provide a better fit or explanation of the observed data.

REGRESSION STATISTICS [6]

When we use the least squares technique for estimating the parameters of a demand model, several available statistics greatly increase the value of the results for decision making purposes. These statistics, which are included in the regular output of most computer regression routines, are described below.

Measures of Overall Explanatory Power

Coefficient of Determination. The coefficient of determination, typically indicated by the symbol R^2, is the statistic that indicates how well the entire regression model explains changes in the value of the dependent variable.[7] It is defined as *the proportion of the total variation in the dependent variable that is explained by the full set of independent variables included in the model*. Accordingly, R^2 can take on values ranging from 0, indicating that the model provides no explanation of the variation in the dependent variable, to 1.0, indicating that all the variation has been explained by the independent variables. The coefficient of determination for the regression model illustrated in Figure 5.4 was 0.76, indicating that 76 percent of the total variation in XYZ Corporation's sales of Product Y are explained by variation in advertising expenditures. If the coefficient of determination is high, the deviations about

---

[6] This section may be omitted without loss of continuity. The statistics given here are developed more fully in statistics texts.

[7] In simple regression—that is, regression models with only one independent variable—the *correlation coefficient*, r, measures the goodness of fit. In multiple regression, R, the coefficient of multiple correlation, is used similarly. The square of the coefficient of multiple correlation R^2, is defined as the coefficient of determination.

a regression line, such as that shown in Figure 5.4, will be small—the actual observations will be close to the regression line and the values of u_t will be small.

This relationship can be clarified somewhat by examining the algebraic formulation of R^2. The total variation in Y, the dependent variable in a regression model, can be measured by summing the squares of the deviations about the mean of that variable:

$$\text{Total Variation in } Y = \sum_{t=1}^{n} (Y_t - \bar{Y})^2. \tag{5.16}$$

The deviations of each observed value, Y_t, from the mean value, $\bar{Y}$, are squared; then these squared deviations are summed to arrive at a measure of the total variation in Y. If Y were a constant, Y_t would equal $\bar{Y}$ for all observations, and there would be no variance in Y. In this case Equation 5.16 would equal 0. The greater the variability in Y, the larger the value of Equation 5.16.

Regression analysis breaks this total variation in the dependent variable into two parts: the variation explained by changes in the independent variables and the variation that cannot be explained by the regression model. This breakdown is illustrated in Figure 5.5. The total variation at a given data observation is seen to be $Y_t - \bar{Y}$. The predicted value of Y at each data point, $\hat{Y}_t$, can be calculated as:

$$\hat{Y}_t = a + bX_t. \tag{5.17}$$

Using $\hat{Y}_t$ as derived in Equation 5.17, we define the value $\hat{Y}_t - \bar{Y}$ as the explained variation at point t, and the total variation explained by the regression equation is:

$$\text{Total Explained Variation} = \sum_{t=1}^{n} (\hat{Y}_t - \bar{Y})^2. \tag{5.18}$$

The unexplained variation is simply the sum of the squared deviations about the regression line:

$$\text{Total Unexplained Variation} = \sum_{t=1}^{n} (Y_t - \hat{Y}_t)^2 = \sum_{t=1}^{n} u_t^2. \tag{5.19}$$

The total variation must equal the sum of the total explained and unexplained variations, so we can write:

$$\text{Equation 5.16} = \text{Equation 5.18} + \text{Equation 5.19,}$$

FIGURE 5.5

Explained and Unexplained Variation of the Dependent Variable in a Regression Model

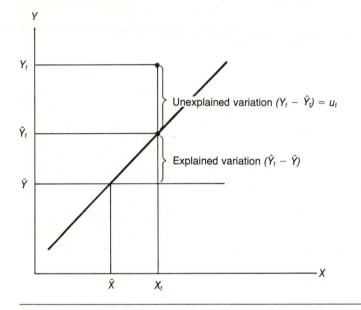

or

$$\sum (Y_t - \bar{Y})^2 = \sum (\hat{Y}_t - \bar{Y})^2 + \sum u_t^2.$$

The coefficient of determination, R^2, is defined as the proportion of the total variation, which is explained by the regression model. Thus:

$$R^2 = \frac{\sum (\hat{Y}_t - \bar{Y})^2}{\sum (Y_t - \bar{Y})^2}. \qquad (5.20)$$

An R^2 of 1.0 indicates that all the variation has been explained. In this case, $\Sigma(\hat{Y}_t - \bar{Y})^2$ must exactly equal $\Sigma(Y_t - \bar{Y})^2$ or, alternatively stated, each predicted value for the dependent variable must exactly equal the corresponding observed value; that is, $\hat{Y}_t = Y_t$ for all t observations. Each data point will lie on the regression curve, and all residuals or error terms will be zero; that is, $u_t = 0$, for all t's.

As the size of the deviations about the regression curve increases, the coefficient of determination will fall. At the extreme, the sum of the squared error terms will be equal to the total variations in the dependent variable, and R^2 will equal zero. In this case, the regression equation has been totally unable to explain variation in the dependent variable.

In an actual regression study the coefficient of determination will seldom be equal to either 0 or 1.0. For work in empirical demand estimation, values of R^2 of about 0.80, indicating that about 80 percent of the variation in demand has been explained, are quite acceptable. For some types of goods R^2's as high as 0.90 to 0.95 are obtainable; for others we must be satisfied with considerably less explanation of variations in demand.

Generally speaking, analyzing demand for a given firm or industry over time—time series analysis—will lead to higher levels for R^2 than will similar analyses across firms, or industries, at a given point in time–cross-sectional analysis. This is because most economic phenomena are closely related to the overall level of economic activity and thus have an important trend element, whereas such exogenous factors are held constant in cross section analyses. Therefore, in judging whether or not R^2 is sufficiently high, one must consider the type of analysis conducted and the anticipated use of statistical results. A low coefficient of determination indicates that the model is inadequate for explaining the demand for the product. The most general cause for this problem is the omission of some important variable or variables from the model.

Corrected Coefficient of Determination, $\bar{R}^2$. As stated above, an R^2 of 1.0 will result when each data point lies exactly on the regression curve. While one might think that any regression model with an $R^2 = 1$ would prove highly reliable as a forecasting device, this is not always the case. The coefficient of determination for any regression equation can be made artificially high if too small a sample is used to estimate the model's coefficients. At the extreme, R^2 will always equal 1.0 when the number of data observations is equal to the number of estimated coefficients because then each data point (observation) can be placed exactly on the regression function.

To conduct meaningful regression analysis the data sample used to estimate the coefficients of the regression equation must be sufficiently large to accurately reflect the important characteristics of the true relationship. This suggests that we need a substantial number of data observations to adequately fit a regression model. More precisely, what is needed is a substantial number of degrees of freedom (*df*). *Degrees of freedom* is defined as the number of data observations beyond the minimum necessary to calculate a given regression coefficient or statistic. For example, to calculate an intercept term we need at least one observation; to calculate an intercept term plus one slope coefficient we need at least two observations, and so on. Since a regression's R^2 always approaches 1.0 as the *df* approaches zero, statisticians have developed a method for correcting R^2 to account for the number of degrees of freedom. The corrected coefficient of determination, denoted by the symbol $\bar{R}^2$, is given by

$$\bar{R}^2 = R^2 - \left(\frac{k-1}{n-k} \right)(1 - R^2), \tag{5.21}$$

where n is the number of observations (data points) and k is the number of estimated coefficients (intercept plus the number of slope coefficients). From Equation 5.21 it is obvious that the adjustment to R^2 will be large when n, the sample size, is small relative to k, the number of coefficients being estimated, and the adjustment to R^2 will be small when n is large relative to k. Our confidence in the reliability of a given regression model will be high when both R^2 and degrees of freedom are substantial.

F-Statistic. Another useful statistic for measuring the overall explanatory power of the regression equation is the F-statistic. As with the coefficient of determination, R^2, and corrected coefficient of determination, $\bar{R}^2$, the F-statistic relates to the relationship between the explained and unexplained variation in the dependent variable. Whereas R^2 and $\bar{R}^2$ provide evidence on whether the proportion of explained variation is high or low, the F-statistic provides evidence on whether or not a statistically significant proportion of the total variation in the dependent variable has been explained. Like $\bar{R}^2$, the F-statistic is adjusted for degrees of freedom and is defined as:

$$F = \frac{\text{Total explained variation}/(k - 1)}{\text{Total unexplained variation}/(n - k)} .$$

The F-statistic can be calculated in terms of the coefficient of determination as:

$$F = \frac{R^2/(k - 1)}{(1 - R^2)/(n - k)} . \tag{5.22}$$

The F-statistic is used to test whether a significant proportion of the total variation in the dependent variable has been explained by the estimated regression equation. The hypothesis actually tested is that the dependent variable is statistically *unrelated* to all of the independent variables included in the model. If this hypothesis cannot be rejected, the total explained variation in the regression (and hence also $\bar{R}^2$) will be quite small. At the extreme, the F-statistic will take on a value of zero when the regression equation taken as a whole provides absolutely no explanation of the variation in the dependent variable (that is, if $\bar{R}^2 = 0$, then $F = 0$). As the F-statistic increases from zero, the hypothesis that the dependent variable is not statistically related to one or more of the independent variables in the regression equation becomes easier to reject. At some point the F-statistic will become sufficiently large to enable one to reject the independence hypothesis and substitute an assumption that at least some of the variables in the regression model are significant factors in explaining the variation in the dependent variable.

The F-test is the procedure used to determine whether the F-statistic associated with a specific regression equation is large enough to enable one to reject the hypothesis that the regression model does not significantly explain the variation in the dependent variable. Performing this test involves comparing the F-statistic for a regression equation with a critical value from a table of the F-distribution. If the F-statistic for the regression *exceeds* the critical value in the F-distribution table, one can reject the hypothesis of independence between the dependent variable and the set of independent variables in the regression. One can then conclude that the regression equation, taken as a whole, does significantly explain the variation in the dependent variable.

Tables of critical values of the F-distribution are constructed for various levels of statistical significance. The F-tables in Appendix D at the end of this text, for example, provide critical F-values at the 10 percent, 5 percent, and 1 percent significance levels; if a regression equation's F-statistic exceeds the F-value in the table, we can be 90, 95, or 99 percent certain that the model significantly explains the variance of the dependent variable. These 90, 95, and 99 percent confidence levels are "popular" levels for hypothesis rejection, because they imply that a true hypothesis will be rejected only one out of ten, one out of twenty, or one out of one hundred times, respectively. Such error rates are quite small and typically quite acceptable.

Critical values in an F-distribution depend upon two degrees-of-freedom characteristics of the F-statistic, one related to the numerator and one associated with the denominator. In the numerator the degrees of freedom equal the number of independent variables in the regression equation $(k - 1)$. The degrees of freedom for the denominator of the F-statistic are equal to the number of data observations minus the number of estimated coefficients $(n - k)$. Thus, the critical value of F can be denoted as $F_{f1, f2}$, where $f1$, the degrees of freedom for the numerator, equals $k - 1$; and $f2$, the degrees of freedom for the denominator, equals $n - k$.

Examination of the following example should clarify the use of the F-statistic. Assume that a regression analysis has been completed with the following results:

$F = 6.89$.

k = number of estimated coefficients (including intercept) = 6.

n = number of data observations = 20.

The relevant critical F-value would be denoted as $F_{5, 14}$ since $f1 = k - 1 = 5$ and $f2 = n - k = 14$. The table of F-values in Appendix D indicates the critical F-values:

$F_{5, 14} = 2.31$ for the 10 percent significance (90 percent confidence) level.

$F_{5, 14} = 2.96$ for the 5 percent significance (95 percent confidence) level.

$F_{5, 14} = 4.69$ for the 1 percent significance (99 percent confidence) level.

Since the F-statistic for the sample regression $(F = 6.89)$ is larger than the critical F-value for the 1 percent significance level $(F_{5, 14} = 4.69$ at the 1 percent significance level), we can reject the hypothesis of independence between the dependent and independent variables and conclude that the regression model explains a statistically significant proportion of the total variation in the dependent variable. (Since the F-statistic for the regression exceeds the critical F-value for the 1 percent significance level, there is less than a 1 percent probability that we are wrong in rejecting the independence hypothesis in favor of an assumption that the regression does provide a significant explanation of the variation in the dependent variable.)

Standard Error of the Estimate. Yet another measure useful for examining the accuracy of the regression model as a whole is the standard error of the estimate. This statistic provides a means of estimating a confidence interval for predicting values of the dependent variable, *given* values for the independent variables. That is, the standard error of the estimate is used to determine a range within which we can predict the dependent variable with varying degrees of statistical confidence. Thus, although our best estimate of the tth value for the dependent variable is $\hat{Y}_t$, the value predicted by the regression equation, we can use the standard error of the estimate to determine just how accurate a prediction $\hat{Y}_t$ is likely to be.

If we can assume that the error terms are normally distributed about the regression equation, there is a 95 percent probability that future observations of the dependent variable will lie within the range $\hat{Y}_t \pm 1.96$ standard errors of the estimate. The probability that some future observation of Y_t will lie within 2.576 standard errors of its predicted value increases to 99 percent.[8] It is clear, then, that greater predictive accuracy is associated with smaller standard errors of the estimate.

This concept is illustrated graphically in Figure 5.6. Here we see the scatter of points between X and Y, the least squares regression line, and the upper and lower 95 percent confidence limits. Ninety-five percent of all actual data observations will lie within ± 1.96 standard errors of the regression line. Thus, given the value of X, we can use the interval between the upper and the lower confidence bounds to predict the value of Y with a 95 percent probability that the actual outcome (Y value) will lie within that confidence interval. Notice that the confidence bounds are closest to the regression line in the vicinity of the mean values of X and Y—that is, at the center of the scatter diagram—then they diverge from the regression line toward the extremes of the observed points. This underscores a point made earlier: that not too much confidence can be put in the predictive value of a regression equation beyond the range of observed values.

Measures of Individual Variable Explanatory Power

T-statistic. Just as the standard error of the estimate indicates the precision with which the regression model can be expected to predict the dependent variable, the

---

[8] The standard error is, in effect, equivalent to a standard deviation; it is the standard deviation of the dependent variable about the regression line. We should note that the standard error of the estimate provides only an approximation to the true distribution of errors, and in actuality the confidence band widens as observations deviate from the mean values, as is shown in Figure 5.6.

FIGURE 5.6

Illustration of the Use of the Standard Error of the Estimate to Define Confidence Intervals

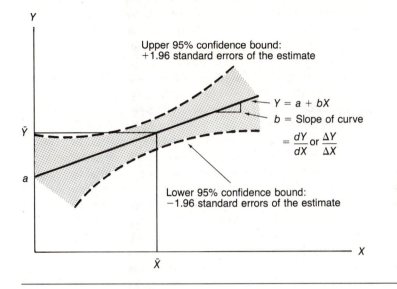

standard error of the coefficient provides a measure of the confidence we can place in the estimated regression parameter for each independent variable. When the standard error of a given estimated coefficient is relatively small, a strong relationship between X and Y is suggested, and we can assume with a high level of confidence that the estimated coefficient accurately describes the relationship between X and Y. On the other hand, when the standard error of a coefficient is relatively large, the underlying relationship between X and Y is typically weak, and we would not place as much confidence in the coefficient estimate.

A wide variety of tests can be conducted based upon the size of a given estimated coefficient and its standard error. These tests are known as t-tests. Generally speaking, a t-test is performed to test whether the estimated coefficient $\hat{b}$ is significantly different from some hypothesized value, b^*. The t-statistic is given by:[9]

$$t = \frac{\hat{b} - b^*}{\text{Standard error of } (\hat{b} - b^*)} \; . \tag{5.23}$$

---

[9] The standard error of $(\hat{b} - b^*)$, typically denoted as $\sigma_{(\hat{b} - b^*)}$, is calculated as:

$$\sigma_{(\hat{b} - b^*)} = \sqrt{\sigma_{\hat{b}}^2 + \sigma_{b^*}^2 - 2\sigma_{\hat{b}, b^*}} \; .$$

Here $\sigma_{\hat{b}}$ and σ_{b^*} are the standard errors of $\hat{b}$ and b^* respectively, and $\sigma_{\hat{b}, b^*}$ is the covariance of $\hat{b}$ and b^*. All of these regression statistics are typically provided as output of computerized regression analysis programs. It should be noted that when b^* is a known constant rather than an estimated value, the standard error of b^* and covariance between $\hat{b}$ and

Thus, the t-statistic is a measure of the number of standard errors between $\hat{b}$ and the hypothesized value b^*. A t-test consists of comparing the calculated t-statistic with an appropriate critical t-value. If the sample used to estimate the regression parameters is large (for example, $d.f. = n - k > 30$), the t-statistic follows a normal distribution, and the properties of a normal distribution can be used to determine critical t-values and to make confidence statements concerning the relationship between $\hat{b}$ and b^*. For small sample sizes (for example, $d.f. < 30$), the t-distribution deviates from a normal distribution, and a t-table such as that provided in Appendix D at the end of this text should be used for finding critical t-values.

There are two general types of hypothesis tests commonly undertaken using the t-statistic. Most common are simple tests of the size or magnitude of a given coefficient estimate. Should we want to know if a given variable, X, has an effect on Y, it is appropriate to test the null hypothesis that $\hat{b}$ is equal to zero. That is, we test to determine whether X is *unrelated* to Y. If we can reject this hypothesis, we can infer that Y does indeed appear to be affected by X. If, however, we cannot reject the hypothesis that $\hat{b}$ is equal to zero, then we have no statistical evidence that Y is affected by X. *Tests of the impact or effect of* X *on* Y *are "two-tail"* t-*tests.*

Many managerial questions go beyond the simple matter of whether or not X influences Y. In some instances, it is interesting to determine whether a given variable, X, has a positive or a negative effect on Y, or whether the effect of variable X_1 is greater or smaller than the effect of variable X_2. *Tests of direction (positive or negative) or comparative magnitude are "one-tail"* t-*tests.*

To better understand the difference between one- and two-tail t-tests it will be useful to consider the nature of the t-distribution. The t-statistic has what statisticians call an approximately normal distribution. That is, for large sample sizes the t-statistic, as given by Equation 5.23, is normally distributed. From the t-distribution shown in Figure 5.7 we see that 90 percent of the total area beneath the bell-shaped curve is between $t = -1.645$ and $t = +1.645$, and 95 percent of this total area is between $t = -1.96$ and $t = +1.96$. Therefore, the probability of a t-value greater than $+1.645$ is only 5 percent, which is equal to the area in the one tail of the distribution beyond $t = +1.645$. A t-value greater than $+1.96$ has a probability of only 2.5 percent, again equal to the area in the t-distribution above a t of $+1.96$. The probability that the t-statistic will be *either* larger than $+1.645$ *or* smaller than -1.645 is 10 percent, equal to the combined areas in the *two* tails of the t-distribution outside $t = \pm1.645$. Similarly, the probability of a t-statistic with an absolute value greater than 1.96 (i.e., larger than $+1.96$ or smaller than -1.96) is 5 percent, equal to the combined areas in the two tails beyond $t = \pm1.96$. The difference between one- and two-tail tests relates to the "tails" of the t-distribution. In a two-tail t-test we reject the null hypothesis with a finding that the t-statistic is not in the *region around zero*. That is, we want a t-statistic that is in *either* tail of the

---

b^* are both zero so the standard error of $(\hat{b}-b^*)$ in this instance reduces to just the standard error of $\hat{b}$, and the t-statistic is given by the expression $t = \hat{b}-b^*/\sigma_{\hat{b}}$.

FIGURE 5.7

The _T_-Distribution

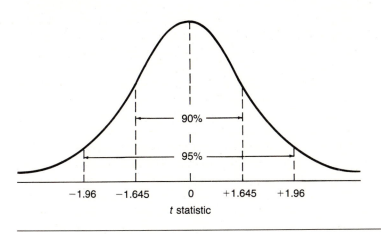

t statistic

distribution. In a one-tail t-test we reject the null hypothesis with a finding that the t-statistic is in one specified tail of the distribution.

The use of both one- and two-tail t-tests for hypothesis testing can be further examined by reconsidering Equation 5.15.

$$\text{Sales } Y_t = a + b A_t + c P_t + u_t, \qquad (5.15)$$

where Y_t is sales, A_t is advertising, and P_t is the average price of Y_t. Questions a manager might ask could lead to some of the following t-tests: [10]

Question	Hypothesis	t-Test
1. Does advertising affect sales?	1. Sales are unaffected by advertising, i.e., $H_0:b^* = 0$.	$t = \left\| \dfrac{\hat{b} - 0}{\sigma_{\hat{b}}} \right\| > t^*\text{(two-tail)}$
2. Does advertising increase sales?	2. The true parameter relating sales to advertising is negative, i.e., $H_0:b^* < 0$.	$t = \dfrac{\hat{b} - 0}{\sigma_{\hat{b}}} > t^*\text{(one-tail)}$
3. Is the effect of advertising on sales greater than the price effect?	3. The effect of price on sales is greater than the effect of advertising, i.e., $H_0:b^* - c^* < 0$.	$t = \dfrac{\hat{b} - \hat{c}}{\sigma_{(b^* - c^*)}} > t^*\text{(one-tail)}$

[10] Note that two-tail t-tests are conducted in terms of absolute values, since either positive or negative t-values can lead to rejection of the null hypothesis.

Note that each question cannot be answered directly, rather by rejecting the alternate case or hypothesis we can answer each question by inference. For example, we cannot *prove* that advertising has an impact on sales. However, if we can reject as unlikely the hypothesis that there is no effect, we can *infer* that there is reasonable evidence to suggest that advertising does have an effect on sales. The first of the *t*-tests is a two-tail test because we can reject the null hypothesis, that the true value for *b* is zero, with a *t*-statistic that is either large and positive or very small (large negative number). That is, the true value could be either positive or negative, resulting in a positive or negative *t*-statistic, and we would reject the hypothesis that it was zero. The second and third *t*-tests are one-tail tests since rejection of the null hypothesis requires a large *positive t* in each case.

It is interesting to note that one-tail tests result in higher confidence levels. For example, with an estimated $t = -1.70$ for $\hat{b}$ we can reject the two-tail hypothesis $b^* = 0$ with 90 percent confidence ($|t| > 1.645$), but can reject the one-tail hypothesis that $b^* > 0$ with 95 percent confidence ($t < -1.645$). Similarly, with an estimated $t = +1.96$ for $\hat{b}$ we can reject the two-tail hypothesis that $b^* = 0$ with 95 percent confidence, but can reject the one-tail hypothesis that $b^* < 0$ with 97.5 percent confidence. We must remember, however, that the choice between making one- or two-tail hypothesis tests is never made on the basis of which type of test can most easily yield statistically significant results, but depends instead on the type of economic question being analyzed.

Multicollinearity Problems in Regression Analysis

We have seen the usefulness of the coefficient of determination, R^2, and the standard errors of the slope coefficients, but additional information may be gained by comparing these statistics. Suppose that the coefficient of determination for a regression model is large, near 1.0, indicating that the model as a whole explains most of the variation in the dependent variable. However, assume also that the standard errors of the coefficients for the various independent variables are also quite large in relation to the size of the coefficients, so that little confidence can be placed in the estimated relationship between any single independent variable and the dependent variable. This condition indicates that, while the regression model demonstrates a significant relationship between the dependent variable and the independent variables as a group, the technique has been unable to separate the specific relationships between each independent variable and the dependent variable. This is the problem of simultaneous relationships, or multicollinearity, among the independent variables. It means simply that the independent variables are not really independent of one another, but rather have values that are jointly or simultaneously determined.

Home ownership and family income provide an example of this type of difficulty. A firm might believe that whether a given family will buy its product is dependent upon, among other things, the family's income and whether the family owns its home or rents. Because families who own their homes tend to have relatively high incomes, these two variables are highly correlated.

This problem can be troublesome in regression analysis, at the extreme resulting in arbitrary values being assigned for the coefficients of the mutually correlated variables. For example, if two independent variables move up and down together, the least squares regression technique *can* assign one variable an arbitrarily high coefficient and the other an arbitrarily low coefficient, with the two largely offsetting each other. In such a case neither coefficient would have any correspondence to the true relationships of the system being investigated. When this problem occurs, it is sometimes best to remove all but one of the correlated independent variables from the model before the parameters are estimated using a single equation regression model.[11] Even then, the resulting regression coefficient assigned to the remaining variable can be used only for forecasting purposes rather than for explaining demand relationships. That is, the coefficient of the remaining variable indicates the joint effect on demand, both of it and of the removed correlated variable. Thus, the model is still unable to separate the effects of the two mutually correlated variables. The coefficient is not arbitrarily assigned in this case, however, and so long as the relationship between the correlated independent variables does not change, it can be used for predictive purposes.

Other Problems in Regression Analysis

In addition to the assumption of independence among the independent variables, or the problem of multicollinearity, least squares regression analysis requires four assumptions about the error terms, u_t, or the residuals, as they are commonly called:

1. Residuals are assumed to be randomly distributed.

2. Residuals are assumed to follow a normal distribution.

3. Residuals are assumed to have an expected value of zero.

4. Residuals are assumed to have a constant variance.

A violation of any one of these assumptions reduces the validity of the least ordinary squares technique for estimating demand relationships.

The residuals are typically calculated and printed as part of the output by most computer programs for regression analysis, and one can examine the residuals in a number of ways to determine if any of the assumptions have been violated. For most cases a graphic method is quite revealing and easy to use. Three basic graphs of the residuals will indicate most violations of the basic assumptions.

---

[11] For a discussion of demand estimation using simultaneous equation models, see Chapter 12 of W. J. Baumol, *Economic Theory and Operations Analysis*, 3rd ed. (Englewood Cliffs, N.J.: Prentice-Hall, 1972).

FIGURE 5.8

A Frequency Distribution of the Residuals

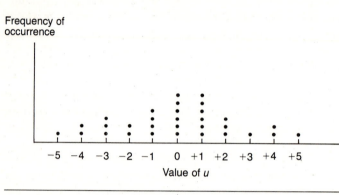

Frequency of
occurrence

FIGURE 5.9

Sequence Plot of the Residuals

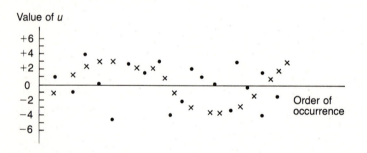

Value of u

Frequency Distribution. Plotting the residuals on a linear scale, as in Figure 5.8, provides a frequency distribution of the residuals. This distribution can be examined to determine whether the residuals appear to be normally distributed and whether the mean of the residuals is equal to zero. In most cases the frequency plots will not form a perfect bell-shaped (normal) curve, but any serious deviation from this shape will be readily indicated.

Sequence Plot. A plot of the residuals in order of occurrence provides another useful means of detecting violations of the regression assumptions. This plot is most beneficial for time series models, where the sequence of the data has an economic interpretation. In plotting the residuals over time (or, more generally, in their order of occurrence), we expect them to be randomly distributed about a mean of zero, as in Figure 5.9. Reviewing the complete graph of the residuals plotted in sequence, we hope to see a horizontal band centered about the value zero, as is true of the dots in Figure 5.9. Within that band there should be no systematic patterns, indicating that the residuals are not occurring randomly, as is true of the x's in the figure; that is, any repetitive sequence in this plot, such as the x's, indicates that the residuals are not independent of one another but rather are serially correlated.

The problem of serial correlation (or autocorrelation, as it is called in time series regression) occurs frequently and is not always easily detected by the graphic technique discussed here. For this reason the Durbin-Watson statistic is often calculated and used to measure the extent of serial correlation in the residuals.[12] A value of approximately 2 for the Durbin-Watson statistic indicates the absence of serial correlation; deviations from this value indicate that the residuals are not randomly distributed.

When serial correlation exists, it can be removed by making a transformation of the data. Taking first differences is one such transformation. For example, in demand analysis, serial correlation of the residuals is often caused by slowly changing variables such as consumer tastes or the development of new competing or complementary products that are difficult if not impossible to measure and, hence, cannot be included in the statistical analysis. Specification of the demand model in terms of first differences—that is, in terms of the change in each variable from one period to the next—however, frequently overcomes this problem. Thus, in demand studies one often encounters regression models of the form:[13]

$$\Delta \text{ demand} = f(\Delta \text{ price}, \Delta \text{ income}, \Delta \text{ advertising, and so on}).$$

[12] The Durbin-Watson statistic, d, is calculated by the equation:

$$d = \frac{\sum\limits_{i=1}^{N} (u_i - u_{i-1})^2}{\sum\limits_{i=1}^{N} u_i^2}. \tag{5.24}$$

Essentially, the sum of the squared first differences of the residuals, $(u_i - u_{i-1})^2$, is divided by the sum of the squared residuals. Equation 5.24 can be rewritten as:

$$d = \frac{2\sum\limits_{i=1}^{N} u_i^2 - 2\sum\limits_{i=1}^{N} u_i u_{i-1}}{\sum\limits_{i=1}^{N} u_i^2} = 2(1 - \rho), \tag{5.25}$$

where ρ is the correlation coefficient between successive residuals. Thus, if $\rho = 0$, indicating that the residuals are serially independent, d will equal 2. As ρ approaches $+1$, indicating positive serial correlation, d will fall toward 0; and if ρ is negative, indicating negative serial correlation, d will increase, with an upper limit of $+4$ being associated with perfect negative serial correlation ($\rho = -1$).

[13] The use of first difference equations, while very popular, is not a panacea for serial correlation problems. See Chapter 7 in J. Johnston, *Econometric Methods* (New York: McGraw-Hill, 1960) for a more complete discussion of the problem.

FIGURE 5.10

Hypothetical Residual Patterns

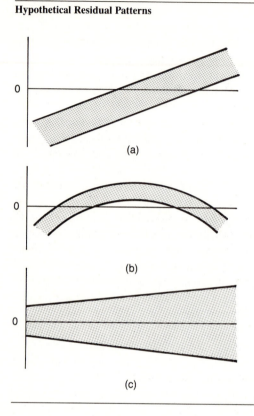

(a)

(b)

(c)

Returning to the sequence plot of the residuals, three general patterns indicate violation of one or more of the regression assumptions. These three patterns are illustrated in Figure 5.10(a), (b), and (c). The pattern shown in Figure 5.10(a) occurs
frequently in time series regression where a trend variable has not been included in
the model. In other words, the demand function is slowly changing over time (due
perhaps to changing tastes, styles of living, and other factors); the model can be
improved by explicitly accounting for this trend by including time as one of the
variables explaining demand for the product. Sometimes the trend effect is not constant over time but rather indicates an increasing or a decreasing rate of change.
When this is the case, a sequence plot of the residuals might appear as in Figure
5.10(b). Inclusion of time variables in quadratic terms will correct this problem.

 A sequence plot such as that illustrated in Figure 5.10(c) indicates a somewhat
more serious problem. There, the plotted points indicate that the variance of the
residuals about their expected value is not constant over the range of observation.
This will invalidate many of the statistics used to determine the usefulness of the

regression coefficients. A weighted least squares regression analysis can be used to correct for this difficulty.[14]

Plots against the Regression Variables. The third useful kind of plot of the residuals is against the variables of the regression model. In each case the desired pattern would appear as in Figure 5.9, a horizontal band centered on zero and with a constant dispersion, or variance.

Plots similar to those in Figure 5.10 all indicate difficulties of one form or another. A band that is positively (or negatively) sloped, as in Figure 5.10(a), indicates an error in the regression calculations when the residuals have been plotted against one of the independent variables in the model. Essentially, the linear effect of that variable has not been properly accounted for. If such a pattern appears in a plot of the residuals against the dependent variable, it indicates either an error in calculation as described above or else a misspecification of the regression model, such as omitting a key variable from the analysis or suppressing the intercept term in the regression model.

The curved band in Figure 5.10(b) again indicates the need for power terms in the equation. That pattern for residuals plotted against an independent variable indicates the need for a quadratic term in that same variable. If the plot is against the dependent variable, the indicated problem is also probably the absence of a higher order term; that is, $Y = a + bX - cX^2$, in the model.

A megaphone plot similar to Figure 5.10(c) in all cases indicates that the variance of the residuals is not constant. The corrective action in this case is either to use a weighted least squares regression technique or to make a transformation of the dependent variable (such as changing to the logarithm of the data or using a ratio) prior to estimating the regression parameters.

FROZEN FRUIT PIE DEMAND: AN ILLUSTRATIVE REGRESSION ANALYSIS PROBLEM

In late 1982 Wisco Foods, Inc., a regional processor located in the upper Midwest, undertook an empirical estimation of the demand relationships for its frozen fruit pies. The firm was attempting to formulate its pricing and promotional plans for the following year, and management was interested in learning how certain decisions would affect sales of the frozen pies.

An analysis of earlier demand studies for its other prepared foods led Wisco

---

[14] A discussion of the weighted least squares technique is outside the scope of materials that can be covered in a single course on managerial economics. The interested reader is referred to N. R. Draper and H. Smith, *Applied Regression Analysis* (New York: Wiley, 1966), pp. 77–81.

to a hypothesis that demand for the fruit pies was a linear function of the price charged, advertising and promotional activities, the price of a competing brand of frozen pies, per capita income, and population in the market area. It was decided that a trend term should also be included in the hypothesized demand function to account both for the continuing shift to prepared foods and for the growth in sales resulting from increased consumer awareness of the product.

Wisco had been processing these frozen pies for about three years, and its market research department had two years of quarterly data for six regions on sales quantities, on the retail price charged for its pies, on local advertising and promotional expenditures, and on the price charged for the major competing brand of frozen pies. Statistical data published by *Sales Management* magazine on population and disposable incomes in each of the six locations was also available for the analysis; it was thus possible to include all the hypothesized demand determinants in the empirical estimation.

The following regression equation was fitted to the data:

$$Q_{it} = a + bP_{it} + cA_{it} + dPX_{it} + eY_{it} + fPop_{it} + gT_{it} + u_{it}. \tag{5.26}$$

Here, Q is the quantity of pies sold during the tth quarter; P is the retail price in cents of Wisco's frozen pies; A represents the dollars spent for advertising and promotional activities; PX is the price, measured in cents, charged for competing pies; Y is dollars of per capita disposable income; Pop is the population of the market area; and T is the trend factor. The subscript i indicates the regional market from which the observation was taken, while the subscript t represents the quarter during which the observation occurred.

Least squares estimation of the regression equation on the basis of the 48 data observations (8 quarters of data for each of the 6 areas) resulted in the estimated regression parameters and statistics given in Table 5.3.

The terms in parentheses are the standard errors of the coefficients. An analysis of the error terms, or residuals, indicated that all the required assumptions regarding their distribution were met; hence the least squares regression procedure is a valid technique for estimating the parameters of this demand function.

TABLE 5.3

Estimated Demand Function for Frozen Pies

$$Q = -500 - 275P_{it} + 5A_{it} + 150PX_{it} + 7.25Y_{it} + 0.25Pop_{it} + 875T. \tag{5.27}$$
$$\quad\ (52)\quad (1.1)\quad (66)\qquad (3.2)\qquad (0.09)\qquad (230)$$

Coefficient of determination $= R^2 = 0.92$.

Corrected coefficient of determination $= \bar{R}^2 = 0.91$

$F = 78.6$

Standard error of the estimate $= 775$.

The coefficients of the regression equation can be interpreted as follows: The intercept term, -500, has no economic meaning in this instance—it lies far outside the range of observed data and obviously cannot be interpreted as the demand for Wisco's frozen fruit pies when all the independent variables take on zero values. The coefficient of each independent variable indicates the marginal relationship between that variable and sales of the pies, holding constant the effect of all the other variables in the demand function. For example, -275, the coefficient of P, the price charged for Wisco's pies, indicates that when we hold constant the effects of all other demand variables, each 1¢ increase in price will cause quarterly sales to decline by 275 pies. Similarly, the coefficient of A, the advertising and promotional variable, indicates that for each dollar spent on advertising during the quarter, 5 additional pies will be sold, and the coefficient of the disposable income variable, $+7.25$, indicates that an added dollar of disposable per capita income leads on the average to an increase of 7.25 pies demanded quarterly.

The coefficient of determination ($R^2 = 0.92$) indicates that 92 percent of the total variation in pie sales has been explained by the regression model, a very satisfactory level of explanation for the model as a whole. The corrected coefficient of determination is also high ($\bar{R}^2 = 0.91$), indicating only a minor adjustment to R^2 given the large sample size relative to the number of estimated coefficients included in the analysis. Furthermore, the F-statistic for the regression is 78.6, which is much larger than the critical F-value ($F_{6,40} = 3.29$ at the 1 percent significance level), indicating that the regression equation provides a statistically significant explanation of variation in sales of Wisco's frozen fruit pies.[15] Also, each parameter estimate (the coefficients associated with each independent variable) is over twice as large as its standard error, which means that the estimates are all statistically different from zero. That is, we can reject at the 95 percent confidence level the hypothesis that any of the independent variables is unrelated to the demand for Wisco's frozen fruit pies. Note further that the standard errors of the two key controllable decision variables, price and advertising, are very small in relation to their respective coefficients. This means that the regression coefficients for these two variables are probably very good estimates of the true relationship between them and the demand for Wisco's pies, so they can be used with a great deal of confidence for decision-making purposes.

The standard error of the estimate provides a measure of the confidence interval within which quarterly sales of Wisco's pies can be forecast. For example, assume that Wisco wishes to project next quarter's sales in Market Area B. It has set the price of its pies at $1.50 (or 150 cents) and promotional expenditures at $1,000. The prices of the competing pies are expected to remain at their current level of

---

[15] Here the degrees of freedom for the critical F-value are $k - 1 = 6$ and $n - k = 41$. Note that Appendix D at the back of the book includes a value for $F_{6,40}$ but not for $f_{6,41}$. To find $F_{6,41}$ we can interpolate. However, this process is quite tedious and can be avoided if we note that critical F-values decline as we proceed down each column. This means that if our calculated F-value exceeds the next *highest* available F-value ($F_{6,40}$) it will surely exceed the critical F-value of interest ($F_{6,41} = 3.27$).

$1.40; population in the market area is 50,000; per capita disposable income is
$5,000; and the quarter being forecast is the ninth quarter in the model. Inserting
these values into the demand equation results in an estimated demand of 40,875
pies:

$$Q = -500 - 275(150) + 5(1,000) + 150(140) + 7.25(5,000)$$
$$+ 0.25(50,000) + 875(9) = 40,875.$$

While 40,875 is the best point estimate of demand, the standard error of the estimate allows us to construct a confidence interval for sales projection. For example,
sales can be projected to fall within an interval of ± 1.96 standard errors of the estimate about the expected sales level, with a confidence level of 95 percent. The standard error of the estimate for Wisco's pies is 775. Thus, an interval of $\pm 1,519$ pies
about the expected sales of 40,875 pies represents the 95 percent confidence interval. This means that one can predict with a 95 percent probability of being correct
that the sales of Wisco's pies during the next quarter in Market Area B will lie in the
range of 39,356 to 42,394 pies. Wisco could use Equation 5.23 to forecast sales in
each of the six areas, then sum these area forecasts to obtain the estimated demand
for the product line as a whole.

SUMMARY

In this chapter we examined a variety of techniques for empirically analyzing demand relationships. At the outset we described the identification problem and demonstrated that it can be a serious obstruction to statistical demand estimation. The
identification problem results from the close interrelationships between many economic variables, and it can be overcome only if one has enough a priori information
to identify and separate the individual relations so that shifts in a function can be
distinguished from movements along the function.

Next, we considered the use of consumer interview and market experiment
techniques for demand estimation in the situations where the data necessary for statistical analysis are not available. These techniques can provide valuable information about some important demand relationships. However, because of the high
costs and severe limits on the information that can be obtained from them, statistical
demand estimation is typically employed for empirical demand studies.

Because least squares regression analysis is by far the most widely used statistical estimating procedure in demand analysis, this technique was examined in some
detail. The emphasis was on the specification of the regression model and the interpretation and use of the estimated parameters and associated regression statistics.
Several problems that are frequently encountered in regression analysis were also
examined. The chapter concluded with an example of the use of a regression model
for empirically estimating a product's demand function.

The regression techniques introduced in this chapter are also widely used in empirical cost estimation. We shall therefore refer back to this material when cost studies are considered in Chapter 7.

QUESTIONS

5.1 What is the identification problem? Could it present a problem for statistical estimation of the demand/advertising relationship for a product? Would you expect this problem to be common for many products?

5.2 Why might a firm's customers be unwilling or unable to supply accurate information about their demand for its products?

5.3 What are some possible advantages that might cause a firm to give demand-related information to the suppliers of materials it uses?

5.4 In the market study of the demand for oranges cited in the chapter, why do you suppose a lower cross-price elasticity existed between California oranges and Florida oranges than between varieties of Florida oranges? Can these cross-price elasticity relationships have anything to do with the lower price elasticity observed for California oranges?

PROBLEMS

5.1 You are given the following information:

	1977	1978	1979	1980	1981	1982	1983
Price	8.8	8.0	7.5	6.9	6.2	5.6	5.0
Quantity sold (000)	3.6	5.5	7.5	8.0	11.2	13.0	15.0

The quantity supplied is approximated by the following equation:

$$Q_s = -40{,}000 + 5{,}000P + 5{,}000T.$$

$T = 0.0$ in 1977 and increases by 1.0 each year.

a. Plot the supply curves. (*Hint*: You are to determine a *series* of curves, one for each year. Determine the Y intercept first, letting $T = 0$ and $Q_s = 0$ for year 1977, and so on.)

b. Now plot the price/quantity data given above. Use the same graph as in Part a.

c. Determine a linear approximation to the demand curve. What assumptions do you need in order to make this determination, other than the assumption of linearity?

d. What is the relationship of this problem to the identification problem?

5.2 Calculate the point price, advertising, income, and cross-price-elasticity for Wisco Foods' frozen fruit pies in the territory for which demand was forecasted in the regression example in the chapter. Interpret each elasticity and comment on its use in Wisco's planning activities.

5.3 In 1971 the management of California Copy Machines, a major distributor of office supplies and equipment, established a service plan for its most popular copy machine. Any customer who purchased a machine could buy either a one-year or a two-year complete service contract, covering both labor and parts, to take effect at the end of the normal factory warranty period.

In early 1983 the marketing manager decided to evaluate sales of the contracts with respect to the sales volume during the preceding twelve years. The following data are available for analysis:

Year	Advertising A	Premium for 1-Year Contract, P_x	Premium for 2-Year Contract, P_Q	Number of 2-Year Contracts Purchased, Q
1971	$60,000	$25	$60	5,000
1972	60,000	25	65	4,900
1973	65,000	30	65	5,000
1974	65,000	35	65	5,100
1975	65,000	25	60	5,000
1976	65,000	30	60	5,100
1977	60,000	30	60	5,000
1978	65,000	30	70	5,100
1979	65,000	25	70	4,900
1980	65,000	25	75	4,800
1981	75,000	30	75	5,000
1982	80,000	30	75	5,100

You are to prepare data that will aid the sales manager in his analysis, then interpret the economic significance of the data. Remember that in order to determine the required elasticities, you should only use years when all other factors are held constant. Note also that by using only consecutive years, changes in factors that are not explicitly accounted for in the data are less likely to affect the estimated elasticities. You are also to calculate averages of the elasticities for individual years.

a. What is the arc price elasticity of demand for the two-year contract?

b. What is the arc advertising elasticity of demand for the two-year contract?

c. What is the arc cross-price elasticity of demand between the one-year contract and the two-year contract? Are the one-year and two-year contracts close substitutes?

d. On the basis of a linear regression model, the demand function for the two-year service contract is estimated to be:

$$Q = 4{,}589 + 0.010A + 16.403P_x - 10.829P_Q.$$

(i) Calculate the point price, advertising, and cross-price elasticities for 1979 and 1982, using the regression equation.

(ii) Compare the results in Part d(i) to the results in Parts a, b, and c. Which elasticity figures do you feel provide better estimates of the true relationships? Why?

(iii) The following standard errors of the coefficients apply: $(A) = 0.004$, $(P_x) = 5.357$, and $(P_Q) = 3.778$. For each independent variable, determine whether you can reject at a 95 percent confidence level the hypothesis that no relationship exists between the independent variables and the dependent variable (Q).

(iv) The coefficient of determination, R^2, is 0.750. What proportion of the total variation in the dependent variable (Q) is explained by the full set of independent variables included in the model? What other independent variables might be added to the equation to obtain a better explanation of the variation in the dependent variable (Q)?

e. On the basis of a multiplicative demand relationship, the demand function for the two-year service contract is estimated as follows:

$$Q = 1{,}500A^{0.134} \, P_x^{0.097} \, P_Q^{-0.144}.$$

(i) Calculate the point price, advertising, and cross-price elasticities for the years 1979 and 1982. Compare the new elasticities with the results in Part d(i) as well as with those found in Parts a, b, and c. What distinction can you make between these elasticities and those estimated in Part d(i)?

(ii) The standard errors of the exponents [16] in the multiplicative demand function are as follows:

$$(b) = 0.047, \ (c) = 0.031, \text{ and } (d) = 0.041.$$

Can you reject at a 95 percent confidence level the hypothesis that no relationship exists between the independent variables and the dependent variable?

---

[16] The exponents are the coefficients in the linear equation $\log Q = \log a + b \log A + c \log P_x + d \log P_Q$.

(iii) The coefficient of determination of the multiplicative demand equation, R^2, equals 0.761. Compare this R^2 with that for the linear model.

5.4 EMH Corporation distributes farm machinery. Recently EMH hired a consultant to estimate the demand function for one of the lines it carries. Using regression analysis, the consultant estimated the function:

$$Q_x = -12,400 - 0.9P_x + 50A + 300S - 35i + 0.5P_y$$
$$\quad\quad (10,000) \quad (0.33) \quad (21) \quad (66) \quad (8.1) \quad (0.19)$$

$$R^2 = .85, \text{ Standard Error of the Estimate} = 27.$$

Here Q_x is the quantity demanded (measured in units), EMH P_x is the price in dollars of the unit, A is hundreds of dollars of advertising by EMH, S is a service quality variable measured by the amount EMH spends for service department staff (measured in thousands of dollars); i is the prime rate of interest measured in percents; and P_y is the price in dollars of a competing line of equipment. The standard errors of the coefficients are shown in the parentheses.

a. What percentage of the variability in demand has this empirical equation *not* been able to explain or account for?

b. Assuming the number of observations is large enough so that one can use a normal distribution to estimate probabilities for the parameter estimates, what is the probability that the parameter relating service and demand is at least $+100$?

c. EMH has determined that currently, $P_x = \$2,200$, $A = \$20,000$, $S = \$15,000$, $i = .15$, and $P_y = \$2,500$. What is the *demand curve* facing EMH?

d. Assuming EMH changes price to $2,400 (but all else remains unchanged from Part c), what is the 95 percent confidence level forecast range for demand?

e. EMH is considering spending an added $5,000 on advertising. What would this expenditure do to the demand curve facing EMH?

f. Would the $5,000 in Part e be better spent if used to expand the service department staff? Explain briefly.

5.5 Advanced Technology Corporation manufactures a business computer system which it is attempting to market for personal use in the home. Advanced hired a market research firm to analyze the demand potential for this market and received the following results. Using historical data on sales of similar products and consumer surveys, the research firm estimated the demand function

$$Q = -85,000 + 1500I - 10P + 24A - .01A^2 + 2P_Y$$
$$\quad\quad (50,000) \quad (500) \quad (2.9) \quad (9) \quad (.004) \quad (1.2)$$

Here, Q = units demanded annually; I = average disposable family income measured in hundreds of dollars; P = price of the Advanced computer system; A = hundreds of dollars of advertising by Advanced; and P_Y = the price of a line of competing computers. The coefficient of determination for the regression was $R^2 = 0.8$, the standard error of the estimate was 1,100, and the standard errors of the co-efficients are shown in parentheses below the equation.

Advanced believes that the current values of the non-controllable variables in the demand function are:

$$I = \$6,000 \text{ and } P_Y = \$600.$$

a. If Advanced determines that it will set a $950 price on its computer, what is the optimal advertising expenditure assuming Advanced's objective is maximization of sales revenue?

b. What is the demand curve facing Advanced assuming the firm sets advertising at the level determined above?

c. Do you believe that the planned $950 price is optimal? Why?

d. What is Advanced's total revenue function for this product?

e. Determine the marginal revenue curve for the product.

f. How would you evaluate the growth potential for this product? Explain your answer.

g. Using the variable values given in the problem (including Part a), estimate the sales demand for the computer. Indicate the 99 percent confidence interval for your estimate. Assume n equals 66.

h. Calculate the cross-price elasticity with product Y. Would you be concerned about the possibility of a price change in product Y? Why?

5.6 Johnson and Anderson Manufacturing Company produces insulated blankets designed to reduce heat loss by residential hot water heaters. JAMCO currently markets its products through independent hardware stores and is considering various means of increasing sales. A JAMCO study of 1980 sales in 23 markets revealed (standard errors in parentheses):

$$Q = 0.5 - 1.5P + 3.0A + 0.25I + 7.0N$$
$$(1.2) \quad (0.5) \quad (0.5) \quad (0.3) \quad (2.7)$$

$$R^2 = .48, \text{ Standard Error of the Estimate} = 0.5.$$

Q = Blankets sold (in hundreds).

P = Blanket price (in dollars).

A = Advertising expenditures (in thousands of dollars).

I = Disposable income per household (in thousands of dollars).

N = Number of retail outlets.

a. Fully evaluate and interpret these results on an overall basis. Include in your analysis a discussion of:

(i) R^2

(ii) $\bar{R}^2$

(iii) F-Statistic

(iv) Standard Error of the Estimate.

b. Does the quantity sold depend upon the number of retail outlets in a market?

c. Des Moines, Iowa, was a typical market for JAMCO products. During 1980 in Des Moines $P = \$20$, $A = \$1,000$, $I = \$20,000$, $N = 4$. Calculate and interpret the relevant point income elasticity of demand.

5.7 Kitchen Tile, Inc., is a rapidly growing chain of ceramic tile outlets that cater to the do-it-yourself home remodeling market. In 1979, 33 stores were operated in small-to-medium-sized metropolitan markets. An in-house study of sales by these outlets revealed (standard errors in parentheses):

$$Q = 5.0 - 5.0P + 1.5A + 0.5I + 0.2HF$$
$$\quad\;\; (6.5)\;\; (1.81)\;\; (1.14)\;\; (0.15)\;\;\;\; (0.10)$$

$$R^2 = .86, \text{ Standard Error of the Estimate} = 6.$$

Q = Tile sales (in thousand of cases).

P = Tile price (per case).

A = Advertising expenditures (in thousands of dollars).

I = Disposable income per household (in thousands of dollars).

HF = Household formations (in hundreds).

a. Fully evaluate and interpret these empirical results on an overall basis.

b. Is quantity demanded sensitive to "own" price?

c. Austin, Texas, was a typical market covered by this analysis. During 1979 in the Austin market $P = \$5$, $A = \$40,000$, $I = \$20,000$ and $HF = 5,000$. Calculate and interpret the relevant point elasticity for advertising.

d. What is the probability that the Austin store made a profit during 1979 if total costs were $312,600?

5.8 U-Pumpit, Inc., a national chain of self-service gas stations, has asked you to conduct a study of the demand for gasoline. You do so by analyzing the most recent data available for this highly competitive market. Your statistical study covering 40 quarters over the 1969 to 1978 period revealed:

$$\ln Q = 2.01 - 0.53 \ln P + 1.65 \ln I + 3.25 \ln T - 0.25 \ln PT$$
$$\quad\;\; (1.65)\;\; (0.10)\qquad\; (0.95)\qquad\; (1.85)\qquad\; (0.19)$$

$$R^2 = .97, \text{ Standard Error of the Estimate} = 0.693$$

(or in terms of Q, S.E.E. $= 2$), $\sigma_{b_I, b_T} = .3$, $\sigma_{b_I, b_{RT}} = .65$, $\sigma_{b_P, b_{PT}} = .014$.

$ln\ x$ = indicates the natural logarithm of the variable x.

Q = quarterly demand for gasoline in billions of gallons.

P = average price in cents per gallon.

I = quarterly disposable income in billions of dollars.

T = average temperature in degrees.

PT = a public transportation index of available seat miles per capita.

a. Fully evaluate and interpret the empirical results reported above on an overall basis. Include in your analysis a discussion of:
    (i) R^2
    (ii) $\bar{R}^2$
    (iii) F-Statistic
    (iv) Standard Error of the Estimate.
b. Is the quantity demanded sensitive to "own" price?
c. Will a recession hurt demand?
d. Will cold weather help demand?
e. Note that each coefficient is an elasticity estimate. Based upon these estimates, do price increases have a bigger effect than increases in the availability of public transportation?
f. Calculate and interpret the elasticity of demand with respect to:
    (i) "own price"
    (ii) income
    (iii) public transportation availability.

SELECTED REFERENCES

Atkinson, L. Jay. "Factors Affecting the Purchase Value of New Houses." *Survey of Current Business* (August 1966): 20–34.

Carlson, Rodney L. "Seemingly Unrelated Regression and the Demand for Automobiles of Different Sizes, 1965–1975: A Disaggregate Approach." *Journal of Business* 51 (April 1978): 243–262.

Clark, Kim B., and Freeman, Richard B. "How Elastic Is the Demand for Labor?" *Review of Economics and Statistics* 62 (November 1980): 509–520.

Crafton, Steven M., and Hoffer, George E. "Estimating a Transaction Price for New Automobiles." *Journal of Business* 54 (October 1981): 611–621.

Freedman, David. "Some Pitfalls in Large Econometric Models: a Case Study." *Journal of Business* 54 (July 1981): 479–500.

Halvorsen, Robert. "Residential Demand for Electric Energy." *Review of Economics and Statistics* 57 (February 1975): 12–18.

Hammond, J. D.; Houston, D. B.; and Melander, E. R. "Determinants of Household Life Insurance Premium Expenditures." *Journal of Risk and Insurance* 34 (September 1967): 397–408.

Manning, Willard G., and Phelps, Charles E. "The Demand for Dental Care." *Bell Journal of Economics* 10 (Autumn 1979): 503–525.

Mark, John; Brown, Frank; and Person, B. J. "Consumer Demand Theory, Goods and Characteristics: Breathing Empirical Content into the Lancastrian Approach." *Managerial and Decision Economics* 2 (March 1981): 32–39.

Nevin, John R. "Laboratory Experiments for Establishing Consumer Demand: A Validation Study." *Journal of Marketing Research* 11 (August 1974): 261–268.

Ramsey, J.; Rache, R.; and Allen B. "An Analysis of the Private and Commercial Demand for Gasoline." *Review of Economics and Statistics* 57 (November 1975): 502–507.

Working, E. J. "What Do Statistical 'Demand Curves' Show?" *Quarterly Journal of Economics* 41 (February 1927): 212–235.

CHAPTER 6

PRODUCTION

Given the demand for its product, how does a firm determine the optimal level of output? Given several alternative production methods, which one should the firm choose? If the firm undertakes an expansion program to increase productive capacity, will the cost per unit be higher or lower after the expansion? These questions are critically important to the firm, and answers, or at least insights useful in analyzing the questions, are provided by the study of production.

Production is concerned with the way in which resources (inputs) are employed to produce a firm's products (outputs). The concept of production is quite broad and encompasses both the manufacture of physical goods and the provision of services. In both cases, production theory focuses on the efficient use of inputs to create outputs. In other words, production analysis examines the technical and economic characteristics of systems used to provide goods and services, with the aim of determining the optimal manner of combining inputs so as to minimize costs.

It is worth emphasizing that the term *production* refers to more than the physical transformation of resources. Production involves all the activities associated with providing goods and services. Thus, the hiring of workers (from unskilled labor to top management), personnel training, and the organizational structure used to maximize productivity are all part of the production process. The acquisition of capital resources and their efficient employment are also parts of production, as are the design and use of appropriate accounting control systems.

Thus, in addition to providing an important foundation for the understanding of costs and cost/output relationships, production theory enhances one's comprehension of the integrated nature of the firm. Perhaps no other single topic in managerial economics so clearly lays out the interrelationships among the various factors employed by the firm and among the functional components (for example, the output/revenue and output/cost components) in our valuation model of the firm.

PRODUCTION FUNCTION

A production function relates inputs to outputs. It specifies the maximum possible output that can be produced for a given amount of inputs or, alternatively, the minimum quantity of inputs necessary to produce a given level of output. Production functions are determined by the technology available to the firm. That is, the input/output relationship for any production system is a function of the technological level of the plant, equipment, labor, materials, and so on employed by the firm. Any improvement in technology, such as the addition of a process control computer which permits a manufacturing company to produce a given quantity of output with fewer raw materials and less energy and labor, or a training program which increases the productivity of labor, results in a new production function.

The basic properties of production functions can be illustrated by examining a simple two-input, one-output system. Consider a production process in which various quantities of two inputs, X and Y, can be used to produce a product, Q. The inputs X and Y might represent resources such as labor and capital or energy and raw materials. The product Q could be a physical item such as television sets, cargo ships, or breakfast cereal, but it could also be a service such as medical care, education, or banking services.

The production function for this system can be written as the following general relationship:

$$Q = f(X, Y). \tag{6.1}$$

Table 6.1 is a tabular representation of such a two-input, single-output production system. Each element in the table shows the maximum quantity of Q that can be produced with a specific combination of X and Y. The table shows, for example, that 2 units of X and 3 units of Y can be combined to produce 49 units of output; 5 units of X coupled with 5 units of Y results in 92 units of output; 4 units of X and 10 units of Y produce 101 units of Q; and so on. The units of input could represent

TABLE 6.1

Representative Production Table

Units of Y Employed	Output Quantity									
10	52	71	87	101	113	122	127	129	130	131
9	56	74	89	102	111	120	125	127	128	129
8	59	75	91	99	108	117	122	124	125	126
7	61	77	87	96	104	112	117	120	121	122
6	62	72	82	91	99	107	111	114	116	117
5	55	66	75	84	92	99	104	107	109	110
4	47	58	68	77	85	91	97	100	102	103
3	35	49	59	68	76	83	89	91	90	89
2	15	31	48	59	68	72	73	72	70	67
1	5	12	35	48	56	55	53	50	46	40
	1	2	3	4	5	6	7	8	9	10

Units of X Employed

hours of labor, *dollars* of capital, *cubic feet* of natural gas, *tons* of raw materials, and so on. Similarly, units of Q could be *numbers* of television sets or cargo ships, *boxes* of cereal, *patient days* of hospital care, customer *transactions* of a banking facility, and so on.

The production relationships in Table 6.1 can also be displayed graphically as in Figure 6.1. There the height of the bars associated with each input combination indicates the output produced. The tops of the output bars map the production surface for the system.

The discrete production data shown in Table 6.1 and Figure 6.1 can be generalized by assuming that the underlying production function is continuous. This generalization will aid us in our examination of production concepts.

A continuous production function means the inputs can be varied in a continuous fashion rather than incrementally, as in the preceding example. For a continuous production function, all possible combinations of the inputs can be represented by the graph of the input surface, as shown in Figure 6.2. Each point in the XY plane represents a combination of Inputs X and Y that will result in some level of output, Q, determined by the relationship expressed in Equation 6.1.

The three-dimensional diagram in Figure 6.3 is a graphic illustration of a continuous production function for a two-input, single-output system. Following the X axis outward indicates that increasing amounts of Input X are being used; going out the Y axis represents an increasing usage of Y; and moving up the Q axis means that larger amounts of output are being produced. The maximum amount of Q that can be produced with each combination of Inputs X and Y is represented by the height of the production surface erected above the input plane. Q^*, for example, is the max-

FIGURE 6.1

Representative Production Surface

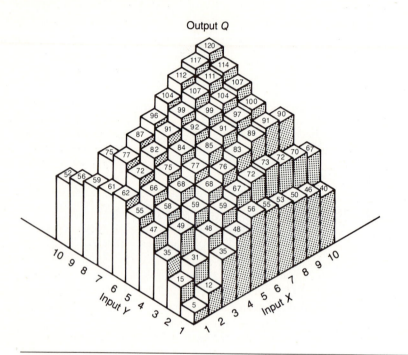

FIGURE 6.2

Input Surface for the Production Function: $Q = f(X, Y)$

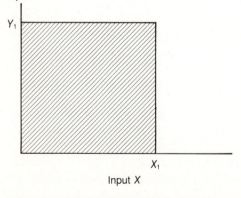

FIGURE 6.3

Production Surface

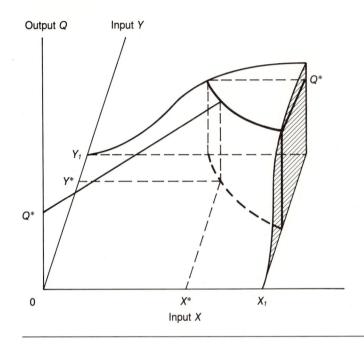

imum amount of Q that can be produced using the combination X^*, Y^* of the inputs.

In studying production functions, there are two types of relationships between inputs and outputs that are of interest for managerial decision making. One is the relationship between output and variation in all the inputs taken together. This type of production relationship is known as the *returns to scale characteristic* of a production system. Returns to scale play an important role in managerial decisions. They affect the optimal scale of a firm or its production facilities. They also affect the nature of competition in an industry and thus are factors in determining the profitability of investment in a particular economic sector.

The second important relationship in a production system is that between output and variation in only one of the inputs employed. The terms *factor productivity* and *returns to a factor* are used to denote this relationship between the quantity of an individual input (or factor of production) employed and the output produced. Factor productivity is the key to determining the optimal combination, or proportions of inputs, that should be used to produce a product. That is, factor productivity provides the basis for efficient resource employment in a production system. Because an understanding of factor productivity will aid in our comprehension of returns to scale, we examine this relationship first.

TABLE 6.2

Total Product, Marginal Product, and Average Product of Factor X, Holding $Y = 2$

Input Quantity (X)	Total Product of the Input (Q)	Marginal Product of the Input $MP_X = \Delta Q/\Delta X$	Average Product of the Input $AP_X = Q/X$
1	15	+15	15.0
2	31	+16	15.5
3	48	+17	16.0
4	59	+11	14.7
5	68	+ 9	13.6
6	72	+ 4	12.0
7	73	+ 1	10.4
8	72	− 1	9.0
9	70	− 2	7.8
10	67	− 3	6.7

TOTAL, AVERAGE, AND MARGINAL PRODUCT

We have noted that the economic concept known as factor productivity or returns to a factor is important in the process of determining optimal input combinations for a production system. Because the process of optimization entails an analysis of the relationship between the total and marginal values of a function, it will prove useful to introduce the concepts of total, average, and marginal products for the resources employed in a production system.

The term *total product* is used to denote the total output from a production system. It is in fact synonymous with Q in Equation 6.1. Total product is a measure of the total output or product that results from employing a specific quantity of resources in a production system.

The concept of the total product is used to describe the relationship between output and variation in only one input in a production function. For example, suppose that Table 6.1 represents a production system in which Y is a capital resource and X represents a labor input. If a firm is operating with a given level of capital (say, $Y = 2$), then the relevant production function for the firm in the short run is represented by the row in Table 6.1 corresponding to that level of fixed capital.[1] Operating with 2 units of capital, the output (total product) from the system will depend upon the quantity of labor (X) employed. This total product of X can be read from the $Y = 2$ row in Table 6.1. It is also shown in column 2 of Table 6.2 and is illustrated graphically in Figure 6.4(a).

---

[1] In economic terminology the *short run* corresponds to a period of time during which at least one resource in a production system is fixed; that is, the quantity of that resource is constant regardless of the quantity of output produced. This concept is elaborated on in Chapter 7.

FIGURE 6.4

Total, Average, and Marginal Product for Input X: Given $Y = 2$

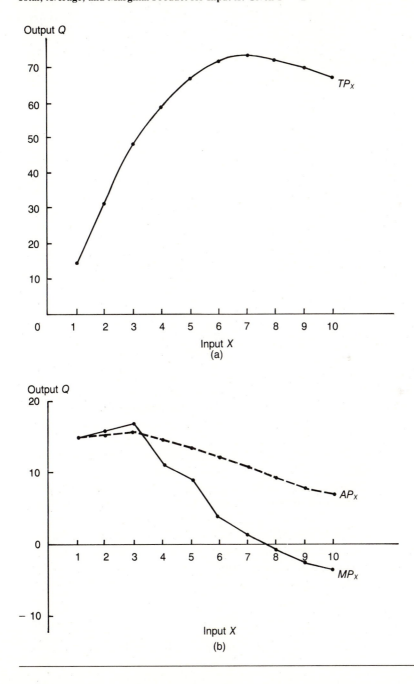

FIGURE 6.5

Total Product Curves for X and Y

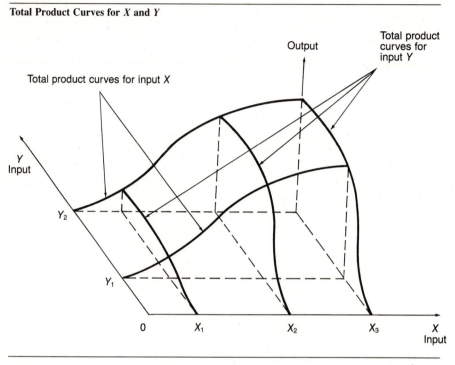

More generally, the total product of a production factor can be expressed as a function relating output to the quantity of the resource employed. Continuing the example, the total product of X is given by the production function:

$$Q = f(X|Y = 2).$$

This equation relates the output quantity Q (the total product of X) to the quantity of Input X employed, fixing the quantity of Y used at 2 units. One would of course obtain other total product functions for X if the factor Y were fixed at levels other than 2 units.

Figure 6.5 illustrates the more general concept of the total product of an input as the schedule of output obtained as that input increases, *holding constant the amounts of the other inputs employed*. (In Figure 6.5 we are once again assuming a continuous production function where inputs can be varied in a continuous fashion rather than discretely, as in the preceding example.) Now suppose we fix, or hold constant, the amount of Input Y at the level Y_1. The total product curve of Input X, holding Input Y constant at Y_1, originates at Y_1 and rises along the production surface as the use of Input X is increased. Four other total product curves are shown in the figure: another for X, holding Y constant at Y_2, and three for Input Y, holding X fixed at X_1, X_2, and X_3, respectively.

Total product curves from Figure 6.5 can also be drawn in two-dimensional space. A total product curve for Input X, holding Y constant at Y_1, is shown in Figure 6.6(a). This curve is developed directly from Figure 6.5, and a series of such curves can be drawn for various levels of Y. Similarly, total product curves can be drawn for Input Y, holding X constant at various levels.

Given the total product function for an input, the marginal and average products can easily be derived. First, recognize that *the marginal product of a factor*, MP_X, *is the change in output associated with a unit change in the factor*, *holding other inputs constant*. Accordingly, for a discrete total product function (such as is shown in Table 6.2 and Figure 6.4), the marginal product is expressed by the relationship:

$$MP_X = \frac{\Delta Q}{\Delta X},$$

where ΔQ is the change in output resulting from a change of ΔX units in the variable input factor. Again this expression assumes that the quantity of the other input, Y, remains unchanged.

If an input can be varied continuously rather than incrementally, then the marginal product is found by taking the partial derivative of the production function with respect to that variable.[2] Thus, for the production function defined by Equation 6.1, the marginal product of Input X is given by:

$$MP_X = \frac{\partial Q}{\partial X}.$$

A factor's *average product* is the total product divided by the units of the input employed, or:

$$AP_X = \frac{Q}{X}.$$

The average product for X, given $Y = 2$ units, in the discrete production example is shown in column 4 of Table 6.2.

For a continuous total product function, as illustrated in Figure 6.6(a), the marginal product is equal to the slope of the total product curve, while the average product is equal to the slope of a line drawn from the origin to a point on the total product curve. The average and marginal products for Input X can be determined in this

---

[2] Recall that a partial derivative of a function measures the change in the function as one variable changes value, holding constant the values of all other variables.

FIGURE 6.6

Total, Marginal, and Average Product Curves: (a) Total Product Curve for X, Holding $Y = Y_1$; (b) Marginal Product Curve for X, Holding $Y = Y_1$

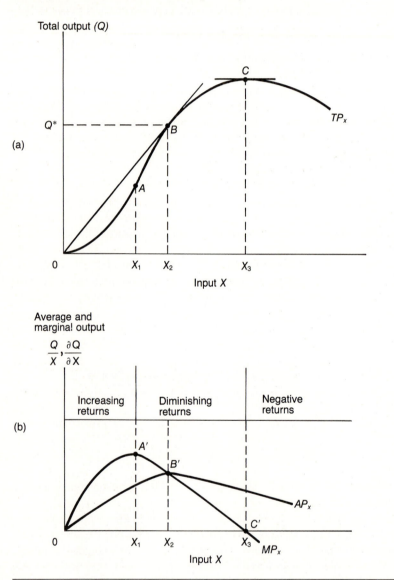

manner, and these points are plotted to form the average and marginal product curves shown in Figure 6.6(b).

Three points of interest, A, B and C, may be identified on the total product curve in Figure 6.6(a), and each has a corresponding location on the average or marginal curves. Point A is the inflection point of the total product curve. The marginal product of X (the slope of the total product curve) increases until this point is reached, after which it begins to decrease. This phenomenon can be seen in Figure 6.6(b), as MP_X is at a maximum at A'.

The second point on the total product curve, B, indicates the output at which the average and the marginal products are equal. The slope of a line from the origin to any point on the total product curve measures the average product of X at that point, while the marginal product is equal to the slope of the total product curve. At Point B, where X_2 units of Input X are employed, such a line from the origin is tangent to the total product curve, so $MP_X = AP_X$. Note also that the slopes of successive lines drawn from the origin to the total product curve increase until Point B, after which their slopes decline. Thus, the average product curve rises until it reaches B, then declines; this feature is also shown in Figure 6.6(b) as Point B'. Here we see again that $MP_X = AP_X$, and that AP_X is at a maximum.

The third point, C, indicates where the slope of the total product curve is zero and the curve is at a maximum. Beyond C the marginal product of X is negative, indicating that an increase in the usage of Input X results in a *reduction* of total product. The corresponding point in Figure 6.6(b) is C', the point where the marginal product curve intersects the X axis.

THE LAW OF DIMINISHING RETURNS TO A FACTOR

The total and the marginal product curves in Figure 6.6 demonstrate the property known as the law of diminishing returns. This law states that as the quantity of a variable input increases, with the quantities of all other factors being held constant, resulting *increases* in output eventually diminish. Alternatively stated, the law of diminishing returns states that the marginal product of the variable factor must eventually decline if enough of it is combined with some fixed quantity of one or more other factors in a production system.[3]

The law of diminishing returns is not a law that can be derived deductively. Rather, it is a generalization of an empirical relationship that has been observed to be true in every known production system. The basis for this relationship is easily demonstrated for the labor input in a production process where a fixed amount of capital is employed.

---

[3]Because the law of diminishing returns deals specifically with the *marginal* product of an input factor, it is sometimes called the law of diminishing *marginal* returns to emphasize the point.

Consider a factory with an assembly line for the production of automobiles. If one employee is put to work manufacturing automobiles, that individual must perform each of the activities necessary to construct a car. Output from such a combination of labor and capital is likely to be quite small. (In fact, it may be less than could be achieved with a smaller amount of capital because of the inefficiency of having one employee accompany the car down the assembly line rather than building the car at a single station.)

As additional units of labor are added to this production system—holding constant the capital input—output is likely to expand rapidly. The intensity with which the capital resource is used increases with the additional labor input, and an increasingly efficient input combination results. The improvement in capital utilization resulting from the increased labor employment could result in the marginal product (increase in output) of each successive employee actually increasing over some range of labor additions. This increasing marginal productivity might result from each unit of labor using a more manageable quantity of capital than is possible with less total labor input (for example, working at a single assembly station). The specialization of activity that could accompany increased labor employment is another factor that might lead to an increasing marginal product for labor as successive units are employed.

An illustration of a production situation where the marginal product of an input increases over some range was presented in Table 6.2. There, the first unit of labor (Input X) resulted in 15 units of production. With 2 units of labor 31 units were produced—the marginal product of the second unit of labor (16) exceeded that of the first (15). Similarly, addition of another unit of labor resulted in output increasing to 48 units, indicating a marginal product of 17 for the third unit of labor.

Eventually, enough labor will be combined with the fixed capital input that the benefits of further labor additions will not be as large as the benefits achieved earlier. When this occurs, the rate of increase in output per additional unit of labor (the marginal product of labor) will drop. Although total output will continue to increase as added units of labor are employed (the marginal product of labor is positive), the rate of increase in output will decline (the marginal product will decrease). This diminishing marginal productivity is exhibited by the fourth, fifth, sixth, and seventh units of Input X in Table 6.2.

Finally, a point may be reached where the quantity of the variable input factor is so large that total output actually begins to decline with additional employment of that factor. In the automobile assembly example this would occur when the labor force became so large that employees were getting in each other's way and hindering the manufacturing process. This happened in Table 6.2 when more than 7 units of Input X were combined with 2 units of Input Y. The 8th unit of X resulted in a 1-unit reduction in total output (its marginal product was −1), while units 9 and 10 caused output to fall by 2 and 3 units respectively.

In Figure 6.6(b) the regions where the variable input factor X exhibited increasing, diminishing, and negative returns have been labeled. While the information provided by these return or productivity relationships is insufficient to enable one to determine the optimal quantities of the inputs to use in a production system, it does enable one to eliminate a set of input combinations that would be irrational under realistic economic conditions.[4]

This concept of irrational stages of production, as well as the underlying factor, productivity relationships, can be more fully explored using isoquant analysis, which explicitly recognizes the potential variability of both factors in a two-input, one-output production system. This technique is introduced in the following section where it is used to examine the role of input substitutability in determining optimal input combinations.

PRODUCTION ISOQUANTS

Although one can examine the properties of production functions graphically using three-dimensional production surfaces like the one shown in Figure 6.3, a two-dimensional representation using isoquants is often equally instructive and simpler to use. The term *isoquant*—derived from *iso*, meaning equal, and *quant*, meaning quantity—denotes a curve that represents all the different combinations of inputs which, when combined efficiently, produce a specified quantity of output.[5] For example, we see in Table 6.1 that 91 units of output can be produced by four input combinations: $X = 3$, $Y = 8$; $X = 4$, $Y = 6$; $X = 6$, $Y = 4$; and $X = 8$, $Y = 3$. Therefore, those four input combinations would all lie on the $Q = 91$ isoquant. Similarly, the combinations $X = 6$, $Y = 10$; $X = 7$, $Y = 8$; $X = 10$, $Y = 7$ all result in 122 units of production and, hence, lie on the $Q = 122$ isoquant.

These two isoquants are illustrated in Figure 6.7. Each point on the $Q = 91$ isoquant indicates a different combination of X and Y that can be used to produce 91 units of output. For example, 91 units can be produced with 3 units of X and 8 units of Y, with 4 units of X and 6 units of Y, or with any other combination of X and Y on the isoquant $Q = 91$. A similar interpretation can be given the isoquant for $Q = 122$ units of output.

The isoquants for the continuous production function displayed in Figure 6.3 can be located by passing a series of planes through the production surface, horizontal to the XY plane, at various heights. Each plane represents a different level of

---

[4] The determination of optimal input combinations must be deferred until later in this chapter, when the role of revenues and costs is introduced into the production analysis.

[5] Efficiency in this case refers to *technological efficiency*. Thus, if 2 units of X and 3 units of Y can be combined to produce 49 units of output but can also be combined less efficiently to produce only 45 units of output, the $X = 2$, $Y = 3$ input combination will lie only on the $Q = 49$ isoquant. The $X = 2$, $Y = 3$ combination resulting in $Q = 45$ is not technologically efficient since this same input combination can produce a larger output quantity; hence, such a combination would not appear in a production function (and therefore not on the $Q = 45$ isoquant). Production theory assumes that only the most productive techniques are used in converting resources to products.

FIGURE 6.7

Representative Isoquants from Table 6.1

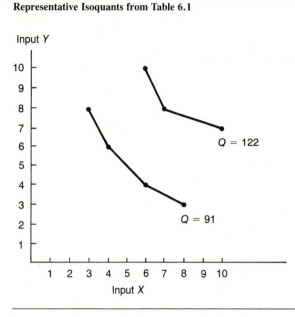

output.[6] Two such planes have been passed through the production surface shown in Figure 6.8 at heights Q_1 and Q_2. Every point on the production surface with a height of Q_1 above the input plane—that is, all points along curve Q_1—represent an equal quantity, or isoquant, of Q_1 units of output. The curve Q_2 maps out the locus of all input combinations that result in Q_2 units of production.

These isoquant curves can be transferred to the input surface, as indicated by the dashed curves Q'_1 and Q'_2 in Figure 6.8, then further transferred to the two-dimensional graph shown in Figure 6.9. These latter curves represent the standard form of an isoquant.

Substituting Input Factors

The shapes of the isoquants reveal a great deal about the substitutability of the input factors; that is, the ability to substitute one input for another in the production process. This point is illustrated in Figure 6.10(a), (b), and (c).

In some production systems certain inputs can be easily substituted for one another. In the production of electricity, for example, the fuels used to power the generators might represent readily substitutable inputs. Figure 6.10(a) shows isoquants

---

[6] Those familiar with topographic maps can see this relationship by visualizing the production surface as a mountain and the isoquant as a contour line, or isoelevation line, connecting all points of equal altitude.

FIGURE 6.8

Isoquant Determination

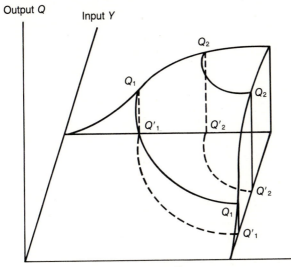

FIGURE 6.9

Production Isoquants

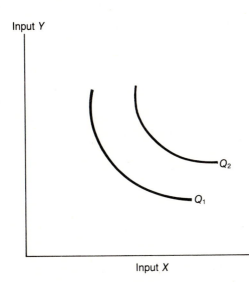

FIGURE 6.10

Isoquants for Inputs with Varying Degrees of Substitutability: (a) Electric Power Generation; (b) Bicycle Production; (c) Dresses

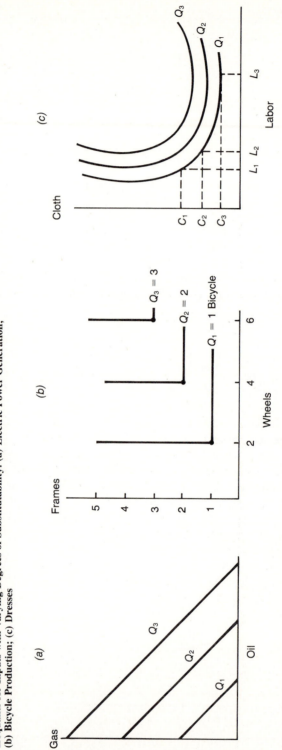

for such an electric power generation system. The technology, a power plant with a bank of boilers equipped to burn either oil or gas, is given; various amounts of electric power can be produced by burning gas only, oil only, or varying amounts of each. Gas and oil are perfect substitutes here, and the isoquants are straight lines. Other examples of readily substitutable inputs include fish meal and soybeans to provide protein in a feed mix; energy and time in a drying process; United Parcel Service and the U.S. Postal Service for delivery of packages. In each of these cases one would expect to find linear production isoquants.

At the other extreme of input substitutability are production systems where inputs are perfect complements for each other. In these situations exact amounts of each input are required to produce a given quantity of output. Figure 6.10(b), illustrating the isoquants for bicycles, represents this case of complete nonsubstitutability. Exactly two wheels and one frame are required to produce a bicycle, and in no way can wheels be substituted for frames, or vice versa. Pants and coats for suits, engines and bodies for trucks, barbers and shears for haircuts, and chemicals in compounds for prescription drugs are further examples of complementary inputs. Production isoquants in the case of complementary inputs take the shape of right angles as indicated in Figure 6.10(b).

Figure 6.10(c) shows an intermediate situation, that of a production process where inputs can be substituted for each other, but the substitutability is not perfect. A dress can be made with a relatively small amount of labor (L_1) and a large amount of cloth (C_1). The same dress can also be made with less cloth (C_2) if more labor (L_2) is used because the worker can cut the material more carefully and reduce waste. Finally, the dress can be made with still less cloth (C_3), but the worker must be so extremely painstaking that the labor input requirement increases to L_3. Note that while a relatively small addition of labor, from L_1 to L_2, allows the input of cloth to be reduced from C_1 to C_2, a very large increase in labor, from L_2 to L_3, is required to obtain a similar reduction in cloth from C_2 to C_3. The substitutability of labor for cloth diminishes from L_1 to L_2 to L_3. (The substitutability of cloth for labor in the manufacture of dresses also diminishes, as can be seen by considering the quantity of cloth that must be added to replace each unit of reduced labor in moving from L_3 to L_1.)

Most labor–capital substitutions in production systems exhibit this diminishing substitutability. Energy and insulation used in providing heating services also exhibit diminishing substitutability, as do doctors and medical technicians in providing health care services.

MARGINAL RATE OF TECHNICAL SUBSTITUTION

The slope of the isoquant provides the key to the substitutability of input factors. In Figure 6.10(c), the slope of the isoquant is simply the change in Input Y (cloth) divided by the change in Input X (labor). This relationship, known as the *marginal rate of technical substitution* (*MRTS*) *of factor inputs*,[7] provides a measure of the amount of one input factor that must be substituted for one unit of the other input factor if output is to remain unchanged. This can be stated algebraically:

$$MRTS = \frac{\Delta Y}{\Delta X} = \text{Slope of an Isoquant.} \tag{6.2}$$

The marginal rate of technical substitution is usually not constant, but diminishes as the amount of substitution increases. In Figure 6.10(c), for example, as more and more labor is substituted for cloth, the increment of labor necessary to replace cloth is increasing. Finally, at the extremes, the isoquant may even become positively sloped, indicating that there is a limit to the range over which the input factors may be substituted for each other while the level of production is held constant.[8]

The input substitution relationship indicated by the slope of a production iso-quant follows directly from the concept of diminishing marginal productivity introduced above in the section entitled "The Law of Diminishing Returns to a Factor." To see this, note that the marginal rate of technical substitution is equal to minus one times the ratio of the marginal products of the input factors. Since output is held constant along an isoquant, if Input Y is reduced, causing output to decline, Input X must be increased sufficiently to return output to the original level. The loss in output resulting from a small reduction in Y is equal to the marginal product of Y, MP_Y, multiplied by the change in Y, ΔY. That is:

$$\Delta Q = MP_Y \cdot \Delta Y. \tag{6.3}$$

Similarly, the change in Q associated with the increased use of Input X is given by the expression:

$$\Delta Q = MP_X \cdot \Delta X. \tag{6.4}$$

For substitution of X for Y along an isoquant, the absolute value of ΔQ in Equations 6.3 and 6.4 must be the same. That is, the change in output associated with the reduction in Input Y must be exactly offset by the change in output resulting from the increase in Input X if we are to remain on the same isoquant. Therefore, ΔQ in Equations 6.3 and 6.4 must be equal in size and have the opposite signs. From this it follows that:

$$-MP_Y \cdot \Delta Y = MP_X \cdot \Delta X. \tag{6.5}$$

[7] This term is often shortened to just the *marginal rate of substitution*.

[8] The classic example of this case is the use of land and labor to produce a given output of wheat. As labor is substituted for land, at some point the farmers trample the wheat. As more labor is added, more land must also be added, if wheat output is to be maintained. The new workers must have some place to stand.

Transposing the variables in Equation 6.5 produces the relationship:

$$MRTS = -\frac{MP_X}{MP_Y} = \frac{\Delta Y}{\Delta X} = \text{Slope of an Isoquant.}^9 \qquad \textbf{(6.6)}$$

Thus, the slope of a production isoquant, shown in Equation 6.2 to be equal to $\Delta Y/\Delta X$, is determined by the ratio of the marginal products of the inputs. Looking at Figure 6.10(c) we can see that the isoquant Q has a very steep negative slope at the point L_1C_1. This means that when cloth is relatively abundant, the marginal product of labor is high as compared with the marginal product of cloth. On the other hand, when labor is relatively abundant at, say, point L_3C_3, the marginal product of labor is low relative to the marginal product of cloth.

Equation 6.6 provides a basis for examining the concept of irrational input combinations. It is irrational for a firm to combine resources in such a way that the marginal product of any input is negative, since this implies that output could be increased by using less of that resource.[10] Note from Equation 6.6 that if the inputs X and Y are combined in proportions such that the marginal product of either factor is negative, then the slope of the production isoquant will be positive. That is, in order for a production isoquant to be positively sloped, one of the input factors must have a negative marginal product. From this it follows that input combinations lying along a positively sloped portion of a production isoquant are irrational and would be avoided by the firm.

In Figure 6.11 the rational limits of input substitution are indicated by the points where the isoquants become positively sloped. The limits to the range of sub-stitutability of X for Y are indicated by the tangencies between the isoquants and a set of lines drawn perpendicular to the Y axis. Similarly, the limits of substitutability

---

[9]This result can also be demonstrated by noting that along any isoquant the total differential of the production function must be zero. (Output is fixed along an isoquant.) Thus for the production function given by Equation 6.1, setting the total differential equal to zero gives:

$$\frac{\partial Q}{\partial X} dX + \frac{\partial Q}{\partial Y} dY = 0$$

and, rearranging terms:

$$(-)\frac{\partial Q/\partial X}{\partial Q/\partial Y} = \frac{dY}{dX}.$$

Or, since $\partial Q/\partial X = MP_X$ and $\partial Q/\partial Y = MP_Y$,

$$(-)\frac{MP_X}{MP_Y} = \frac{dY}{dX} = \text{Slope of the Isoquant.}$$

[10]This is technically correct only if the resource has a nonnegative cost. Thus, for example, a firm might employ additional workers even though the marginal product of labor was negative if it received a government subsidy for that employment which more than offset the cost of the output reduction.

FIGURE 6.11

Maximum Variable Proportions for Inputs X and Y

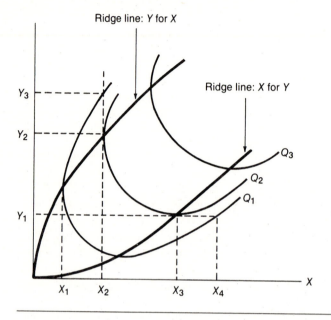

of Y for X are shown by the tangencies of lines perpendicular to the X axis. The maximum and the minimum proportions of Y and X that would be combined to produce each level of output are determined by the tangencies of these lines with the production isoquants.

It is irrational for a firm to use any input combination outside these tangencies, or *ridge lines*, as they are called. The reason such combinations are irrational lies in the fact that the marginal product (the change in output resulting from an incremental increase in an input factor) of the relatively more abundant input is negative outside the ridge lines. This means that addition of the last unit of the excessive input factor actually reduces the output of the production system. Obviously, if the input factor has a positive cost, it would be irrational for a firm to buy and employ additional units that caused production to decrease. To illustrate, suppose a firm is currently operating with a fixed quantity of Input Y equal to Y_1 units, as shown in Figure 6.11. In such a situation the firm would never employ more than X_3 units of Input X because employment of additional units of X results in successively lower output quantities being produced. For example, if the firm combines Y_1 and X_4, output is equal to Q_1 units. By reducing usage of X from X_4 to X_3, output can be increased from Q_1 to Q_2.

A similar relationship is shown for Input Y. We see that in the area above the upper ridge line the relative amount of Y is excessive. In this area it is possible to increase production (move to a higher isoquant) by reducing the amount of Y employed. For example, the input combination X_2Y_3 results in Q_1 units of output. However, by reducing to Y_2 the amount of Y employed while holding X constant at X_2, the firm produces a higher level of output, Q_2. This means that the marginal product of Y is negative, since reducing its usage increases production. Thus, in the area above the upper ridge line Input Y is excessive relative to Input X, and here Y's marginal product is negative. For combinations below the lower ridge line Input X is excessive relative to the amount of Input Y employed, and here X's marginal product is negative. Only for input combinations lying between the ridge lines will *both* inputs have positive marginal products, and it is here (along the negatively sloped portion of the isoquant) that we must look for optimal input combinations.

THE ROLE OF REVENUE AND COST IN PRODUCTION

To answer the question of what constitutes an optimal input combination in a production system we must move beyond technological relationships and introduce revenues and costs. In an advanced economy productive activity results in goods that are sold rather than *consumed* by the producer, so we must be concerned with returns to the owners of the various input factors—labor, materials, and capital—that result from those sales. Therefore, to gain an understanding of how the factors of production should be combined for maximum efficiency, it is necessary that we shift from an analysis of *physical* productivity of inputs to an examination of their *economic* productivity, or revenue-generating capability. The conversion from physical to economic relationships is accomplished by multiplying the marginal product of the input factors by the marginal revenue resulting from the sale of the goods or services produced, to obtain a quantity known as the *marginal revenue product* of the input:

$$\text{Marginal Revenue Product of Input } X = MRP_x$$
$$= (\text{Marginal Product}_x) \cdot (\text{Marginal Revenue}_Q).$$

The marginal revenue product is the value of a marginal unit of a particular input factor when used in the production of a specific product. For example, if the addition of one more laborer to a work force would result in the production of two incremental units of a product that can be sold for $5 per unit, the marginal product of labor is 2, and its marginal revenue product is $10 ($2 \times \$5$). Table 6.3 illustrates the marginal revenue product concept for a simple one-factor production system. The marginal revenue product values shown in column 4 of that table assume each unit

TABLE 6.3

Marginal Revenue Product for a Single Input

Units of Input (X)	Total Product of X (Q)	Marginal Product of X (ΔQ)	Marginal Revenue Product of X ($MP_X \times \$5$)
1	3	3	$15
2	7	4	$20
3	10	3	$15
4	12	2	$10
5	13	1	$5

of output can be sold for $5. Thus, the marginal revenue product of the first unit of X employed equals the 3 units of output produced times the $5 revenue received per unit, or $MRP_{X=1} = \$15$. The second unit of X adds 4 units of production (that is, $MP_{X=2} = 4$); hence, the MRP of the second unit of X is $20 (4 · $5). The marginal revenue products of the other quantities of X are all determined in this manner.

Optimal Level of a Single Input

To see how the economic productivity of an input, as defined by its marginal revenue product, is related to the use of the factor for productive purposes, one need only consider the simple question: If the price of input X in the production system depicted in Table 6.3 is $12, how many units of X would a firm use? Clearly the answer is that 3 units of X would be employed, because the value of adding each of these units as measured by their marginal revenue products exceeds the related cost. The fourth unit of X would not be used, because the value of the marginal product produced by the fourth unit of X ($10) is less than the cost of that factor ($12).

The relationship between resource productivity as measured by the marginal revenue product and optimal employment or factor use can be generalized by referring to the basic marginal principles of profit maximization developed in Chapter 2. Recall that so long as marginal revenue exceeds marginal cost, profits must increase. In the context of production decisions this means that if the marginal revenue product of an input—that is, the marginal revenue generated by its employment in a production system—exceeds its marginal cost, then profits are increased as input employment increases. Similarly, when the marginal revenue product is less than the cost of the factor, marginal profit is negative, so the firm would reduce employment of that factor.

This concept of optimal resource use can be clarified by examining a very simple production system in which a single variable input, L, is used to produce a single product, Q. Profit maximization requires that production be at a level such that marginal revenue equals marginal cost. Since the only variable factor in the system is Input L, the marginal cost of production can be expressed as:

$$MC_Q = \frac{\Delta Cost}{\Delta Quantity} \tag{6.7}$$

$$= \frac{P_L}{MP_L} \, .$$

That is, dividing P_L, the price of a marginal unit of L, by MP_L, the number of units of output gained by the employment of an added unit of L, provides a measure of the marginal cost of producing each additional unit of the product.

Since marginal revenue must equal marginal cost at the profit maximizing output level, MR_Q can be substituted for MC_Q in Equation 6.7, resulting in the expression,

$$MR_Q = \frac{P_L}{MP_L} \, . \tag{6.8}$$

Equation 6.8 must hold for profit maximization since it was demonstrated immediately above that the right-hand side of Equation 6.8 is just another expression for marginal cost. Solving Equation 6.8 for P_L results in:

$$P_L = MR_Q \cdot MP_L,$$

or, since $MR_Q \cdot MP_L$ is defined as the marginal revenue product of L:

$$P_L = MRP_L. \tag{6.9}$$

Equation 6.9 states the general result that a profit maximizing firm will always employ an input up to the point where its marginal revenue product is equal to its cost. If the marginal revenue product exceeds the cost of the input, profits are increased by employing additional units of the factor. Similarly, when the resource's price is greater than its marginal revenue product, profit is increased by using less of the factor. Only at the level of usage where $MRP = P$ are profits maximized.

It follows from the above analysis that the demand curve for a factor of production is defined by its MRP. Figure 6.12 illustrates this point. There the marginal revenue product for an input, L, is shown along with its market price, P^*_L. Over the range 0 to L^*, expanding usage of L will increase total profits, since the marginal revenue product gained from employing each unit of L exceeds its price. Beyond L^*, increased usage of L will reduce profits, since the benefits gained (MRP_L) are less than the costs incurred (P_L). Only at L^*, where $P^*_L = MRP_L$, will total profits

FIGURE 6.12

The MRP Curve is an Input Demand Curve

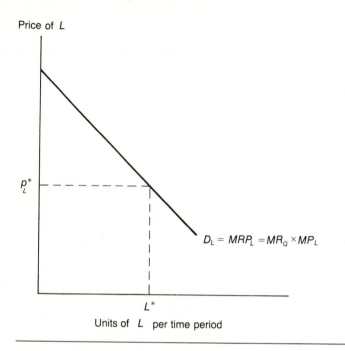

Price of L

p^*_L

$D_L = MRP_L = MR_Q \times MP_L$

L^*

Units of L per time period

be maximized. Of course, if P^*_L were higher the quantity of L demanded would be reduced. Similarly, if P^*_L were lower the quantity of L purchased would be greater.

Optimal Combination of Multiple Inputs

The results of the preceding section can be extended to production systems employing several input factors. Although there are several possible approaches to this extension, one of the simplest involves combining technological and market relationships through the use of isoquant and isocost curves. That is, the optimal input proportions can be found graphically for a two-input, single-output system by adding an "isocost curve" (a line of constant costs) to the diagram of production isoquants. Each point on an isocost curve represents some combination of inputs, say X and Y, whose cost is equal to a constant expenditure. Isocost curves, which are illustrated in Figure 6.13, are constructed in the following manner: Let $P_x = \$500$ and $P_y = \$250$; these are the prices of X and Y. For a given expenditure, say, $E_1 = \$1,000$, the firm can purchase 4 units of Y ($\$1,000/\$250 = 4$ units) and no units of X, or 2 units of X ($\$1,000/\$500 = 2$ units) but none of Y. These two quantities represent the X and Y intercepts of an isocost curve, and a straight line connecting them provides the locus of all combinations of X and Y that can be purchased for $1,000.

The equation for an isocost curve is merely a statement of the various combinations of the inputs that can be purchased for a given expenditure. For example, the various combinations of X and Y that can be purchased for a fixed expenditure, E, are given by the expression:

$$E = P_X \cdot X + P_Y \cdot Y.$$

Solving this expression for Y so that it can be graphed, as in Figure 6.13, results in:

$$Y = \frac{E}{P_Y} - \frac{P_X}{P_Y} X. \qquad (6.10)$$

Note that the first term in Equation 6.10 is the Y-axis intercept of the isocost curve. It indicates the quantity of Input Y that can be purchased with a given budget or expenditure limit, *assuming zero units of Input* X *are bought*. The slope of an isocost curve dY/dX is equal to $-P_X/P_Y$ and, therefore, is a measure of the relative prices of the inputs. From this, it follows that a change in the expenditure level, E, leads to a parallel shift of an isocost curve, while changes in the prices of the inputs result in changes in the slope of the curve.

FIGURE 6.13

Isocost Curves

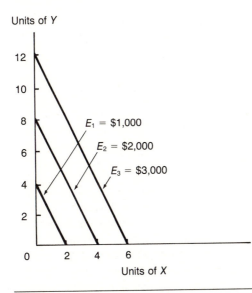

Units of Y

$E_1 = \$1,000$

$E_2 = \$2,000$

$E_3 = \$3,000$

Units of X

FIGURE 6.14

Optimal Input Combination

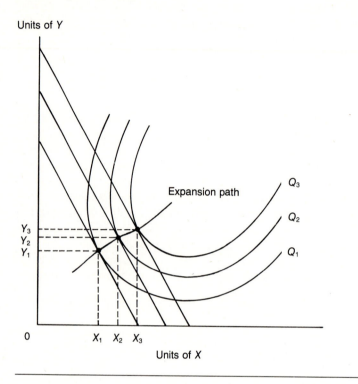

Units of Y

Expansion path

Q_3

Q_2

Q_1

Y_3
Y_2
Y_1

0   X_1 X_2 X_3

Units of X

Extending the example introduced above and illustrated in Figure 6.13 will clarify these relationships. With a $1,000 expenditure level, the Y-axis intercept of the isocost curve has already been shown to be 4 units. The slope of the isocost curve is determined by the relative prices. Thus, in Figure 6.13 the slope of the isocost curves is given by the expression:

$$\text{Slope} = -\frac{P_X}{P_Y} = -\frac{\$500}{\$250} = -2.$$

Suppose a firm has only $1,000 to spend on inputs for the production of Q. Combining a set of production isoquants with the isocost curve, E_1, of Figure 6.13 to form Figure 6.14, we find that the optimal input combination occurs at Point A, the point of tangency between the isocost curve and a production isoquant. At that point, X and Y are combined in proportions that maximize the output attainable for expenditure E_1. No other combination of X and Y that can be purchased for $1,000 will produce as much output. Alternatively stated, the combination X_1Y_1 is the least-cost input combination that can be used to produce output Q_1. Similarly, X_2Y_2 is the least-cost input combination for producing Q_2, X_3Y_3 is the least-cost input combination for producing Q_3, and so on. All other possible combinations for producing Q_1, Q_2, and Q_3 are intersected by higher isocost curves. The line connecting points of tangency between isoquant and isocost curves (such as A, B, and C) constitutes what economists call an expansion path since it depicts optimal input combinations as the scale of production expands.

The fact that optimal input combinations occur at a point of tangency between a production isoquant and an isocost curve leads to a very important economic principle. The slope of an isocost curve was shown above to be equal to $-P_X/P_Y$. Recall that the slope of an isoquant curve is equal to the marginal rate of technical substitution of one input factor for the other when production is held constant at some level. The marginal rate of technical substitution was shown in Equation 6.6 to be given by the ratio of the marginal products of the input factors. That is, the slope of a production isoquant equals $-MP_X/MP_Y$.

At the point where inputs are combined optimally, there is a tangency between the isocost and the isoquant curves, and, hence, their slopes are equal. Therefore, for optimal input combinations the ratio of the prices of the inputs must be equal to the ratio of their marginal products, as is shown in Equation 6.11:

$$-\frac{P_X}{P_Y} = -\frac{MP_X}{MP_Y}. \qquad (6.11)$$

Or, alternatively, the ratios of marginal product to price must be equal for each input:

$$\frac{MP_X}{P_X} = \frac{MP_Y}{P_Y}. \qquad (6.12)$$

The economic principle for least-cost combinations of inputs, as given in Equation 6.12, implies that the optimal proportions are such that an additional dollar spent on a given input adds as much to total output as would a dollar spent on any other input. Any combination violating this rule is suboptimal in the sense that a change of inputs could result in the same quantity of output being produced for a lower cost.[11] Consider the case of a firm combining X and Y in such a way that the marginal product of X equals 10, while that of Y equals 9. Assuming that X costs $2 a unit and Y costs $3, the marginal product per dollar spent is found to be:

$$\frac{MP_X}{P_X} = \frac{10}{2} = 5 \text{ and } \frac{MP_Y}{P_Y} = \frac{9}{3} = 3.$$

---

[11] The optimal input relationship shown in Equations 6.11 and 6.12 can also be derived using the Lagrangian technique to solve either a production maximization problem subject to a budget constraint or a cost minimization problem subject to an output requirement. Both approaches are developed in the Appendix to this chapter.

This combination violates the optimal proportions rule: The ratios of the marginal products to prices are not equal. In this situation the firm can reduce its use of Y by 1 unit, reducing total output by 9 units and total costs by \$3. Then, by employing an additional nine-tenths of 1 unit of X at a cost of \$1.80, the 9 units of lost production may be regained. The result is production of the 9 units of output at a total cost which is less than in the original situation—the \$3 saved on Y is offset by only an additional \$1.80 spent on X for a net cost reduction of \$1.20.[12]

Optimal Level of Multiple Inputs

Combining a production system's inputs in proportions that meet the conditions of Equation 6.12 insures that *any* output quantity will be produced at minimum cost. That is, cost minimization requires only that the ratios of marginal product to price be equal for each input, i.e., that inputs be combined in optimal proportions. Profit maximization, however, requires that a firm employ optimal input proportions *and* produce an optimal quantity of output. Thus, *cost minimization (optimal input proportions) is a necessary but not sufficient condition for profit maximization.*

At the optimal (profit maximizing) output level, meeting the conditions of Equation 6.12 is equivalent to employing each input up to the point where its marginal revenue product is equal to its price—the optimality condition developed in Equation 6.9. To see this, note that by the same reasoning that led to the development of Equation 6.7, the inverse of the ratios expressed in Equation 6.12 must necessarily measure the marginal cost of producing goods at any output level. That is, dividing the price of an input by the marginal product of that input is by definition the marginal cost $(MC = \Delta \text{cost}/\Delta \text{output})$ of producing the output that results from use of an additional unit of the input.

$$\frac{P_X}{MP_X} = \frac{P_Y}{MP_Y} = MC_Q. \tag{6.13}$$

Now since marginal cost will equal marginal revenue at the optimal output level, Equation 6.13 can be written as the following system of equations:

$$\frac{P_X}{MP_X} = MR_Q,$$

and

$$\frac{P_Y}{MP_Y} = MR_Q.$$

[12] This new input combination may still be suboptimal; that is, the example merely indicates that an alternative combination of inputs can lower production costs. It would be necessary to examine the new marginal product/price ratios for an input combination of 10.9 units of X and 8 units of Y to determine if further savings are possible.

Rearranging produces:

$$P_X = MP_X \cdot MR_Q = MRP_X \qquad\qquad (6.14)$$

and

$$P_Y = MP_Y \cdot MR_Q = MRP_Y. \qquad\qquad (6.15)$$

Thus, a firm's profits will be maximized when price equals marginal revenue product for each input. The difference between cost minimization and profit maximization is that cost minimization (optimal input proportions) requires considering only the supply-related factors of input prices and marginal productivity, whereas profit maximization requires consideration of these supply-related factors *and* the demand-related marginal revenue of output. When a firm employs each input in a production system so that its MRP = Price, it insures that inputs are being combined in optimal proportions *and* that the total level of resource employment is optimal.

RETURNS TO SCALE

Thus far our discussion of production has focused on the productivity of an individual input. A closely related topic is the question of how a proportionate increase in *all* the inputs will affect total production. This is the question of *returns to scale*, and there are three possible situations. First, if the proportional increase in all inputs is equal to the proportional increase in output, *returns to scale are constant*. For example, if a simultaneous doubling of all inputs leads to a doubling of output, then returns to scale are constant. Second, the proportional increase in output may be larger than that of the inputs, which is termed *increasing returns to scale*. Third, if output increases less than proportionally with input increases, we have *decreasing returns to scale*.

The returns to scale concept can be clarified by reexamining the production data in Table 6.1. Assume the production system represented by that data is currently operating with 1 unit of Input X and 3 units of Input Y. Production from such an input combination would be 35 units. Suppose we are interested in determining the effect on the quantity of output produced of a 100 percent increase in the quantity of the two input factors used in the production process. Doubling X and Y results in an input combination where $X = 2$ and $Y = 6$. Output from this input combination would be 72 units. A 100 percent increase in both X and Y increases output by 37 units (72 − 35), a 106 percent increase (37/35 = 1.06). Thus, output increases more than proportionately to the increase in the productive factors. The production system exhibits increasing returns to scale over this range of input use.

The returns to scale of a production system can vary over different levels of input use. Consider, for example, the effect of a 50 percent increase in X and Y from

FIGURE 6.15

Returns to Scale

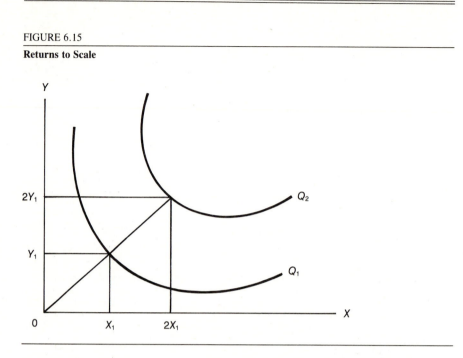

the combination $X = 2$, $Y = 6$. Increasing X by 50 percent results in an employ-ment of 3 units of that factor ($2 \times 1.5 = 3$), while a 50 percent increase in Y leads to 9 units ($6 \times 1.5 = 9$) of that input being used. The new input combination results in 89 units of production, and we see that a 50 percent increase in input factors produces only a 24 percent [$(89 - 72)/72 = 0.24$] increase in output. Since the output increase is less than proportionate to the increase in inputs, the production system exhibits decreasing returns to scale over this range of input use.

Isoquant analysis can be used to examine returns to scale for a two-input, single-output production system. Consider in Figure 6.15 the production of Q_1 units of output using the input combination of X_1Y_1. Doubling both inputs shifts production to Q_2. If Q_2 is precisely twice as large as Q_1, the system is said to exhibit constant returns to scale over the range X_1Y_1 to X_2Y_2. If Q_2 is greater than twice Q_1, returns to scale are increasing, and if Q_2 is less than double Q_1, the system exhibits decreasing returns to scale.

The returns to scale implicit in a given production function can also be exam-ined in terms of two- and three-dimensional graphs such as those drawn in Figures 6.16 through 6.19. In these graphs the slope of a curve drawn from the origin up the production surface indicates whether returns to scale are constant, increasing, or decreasing.[13] In the production system illustrated in Figure 6.16(a), for example, a

---

[13]Both inputs X and Y can be plotted on the horizontal axis of the (b) portions of Figures 6.16 to 6.21, since they are being used in constant proportions to one another. What is actually being plotted on the horizontal axis is the number of units of some fixed input combination.

FIGURE 6.16

Constant Returns to Scale

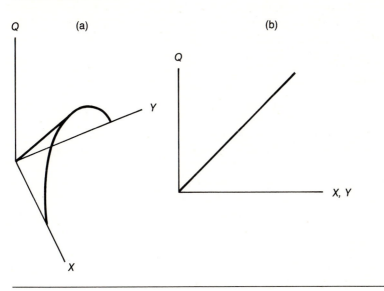

FIGURE 6.17

Increasing Returns to Scale

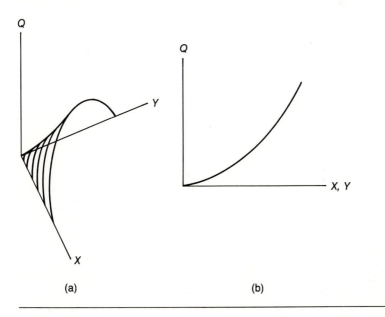

curve drawn from the origin will have a constant slope, indicating that returns to scale are constant. Accordingly, the outputs for given (optimal) combinations of X and Y shown in Figure 6.16(b) are increasing exactly proportionally to increases in X and Y. In Figure 6.17, the backbone curve from the origin exhibits a constantly increasing slope, indicating increasing returns to scale. The situation is reversed in Figure 6.18, where the production surface is increasing at a decreasing rate, indicating that decreasing returns to scale are present.

A more general specification is for a production function to have first increasing, then decreasing, returns to scale, as is shown in Figure 6.19. The region of increasing returns is attributable to specialization—as output increases, specialized labor can be used and efficient, large-scale machinery can be employed in the production process. Beyond some scale of operations, however, not only are further gains from specialization limited but also problems of coordination may begin to increase costs substantially. When coordination expenses more than offset additional benefits of specialization, decreasing returns to scale set in.

Output Elasticity and Returns to Scale

Whereas graphic representations of returns to scale such as those provided in Figures 6.16, 6.17, and 6.18 are intuitively appealing, returns to scale can be more accurately determined for production functions through an analysis of output elasticities. *Output elasticity, ε_Q, is defined as the percentage change in output associated with a one percent change in all inputs.* Letting X represent the entire set of input factors,

$$\varepsilon_Q = \frac{\text{Percentage change in Output } (Q)}{\text{Percentage change in all Inputs } (X)}$$

$$= \frac{\partial Q}{\partial X} \cdot \frac{X}{Q}$$

If we remember that X refers to a complete set of input factors, i.e., X = capital + labor + energy, etc., then it becomes clear that:

If	then	returns to scale are
Percentage change in Q > Percentage change in X	$\varepsilon_Q > 1$	increasing
Percentage change in Q = Percentage change in X	$\varepsilon_Q = 1$	constant
Percentage change in Q < Percentage change in X	$\varepsilon_Q < 1$	diminishing

Output elasticity and returns to scale can also be analyzed by examining the relationship between increases in the inputs and the quantity of output produced. Assume that all inputs in the unspecified production function $Q = f(X, Y, Z)$ are multiplied by the constant k. That is, all inputs are increased proportionately by the

FIGURE 6.18

Decreasing Returns to Scale

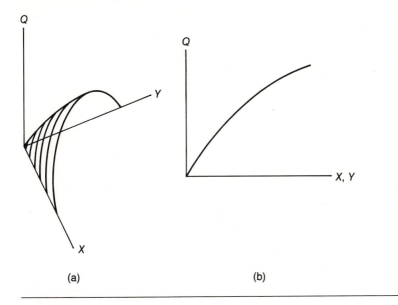

(a)   (b)

FIGURE 6.19

Variable Returns to Scale

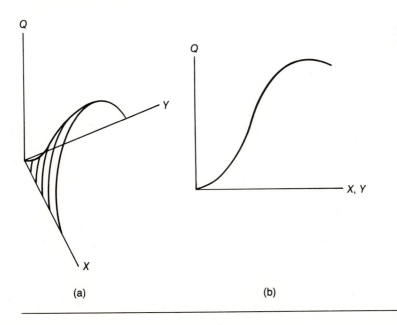

(a)   (b)

factor k ($k = 1.01$ for a 1 percent increase, $k = 1.02$ for a 2 percent increase, and so on). Then the production function can be rewritten as

$$hQ = f(kX, \; kY, \; kZ). \tag{6.16}$$

Here h is the proportional increase in Q resulting from a k-fold increase in each input factor. From Equation 6.16 it is evident that the following relationships hold: [14]

If $h < k$, then the percentage change in Q is less than the percentage change in the inputs, and the production function exhibits decreasing returns to scale.

If $h = k$, then the percentage change in Q equals the percentage change in the inputs, and the production function exhibits constant returns to scale.

If $h > k$, then the percentage change in Q is greater than the percentage change in the inputs, and the production function exhibits increasing returns to scale.

To illustrate, consider the production function $Q = 2X + 3Y + 1.5Z$. We can examine the returns to scale for this function by determining how increasing all inputs by 2 percent affects output. Initially, let $X = 1$, $Y = 2$, and $Z = 2$, so output is found to be:

$$Q_1 = 2(1) + 3(2) + 1.5(2)$$

$$= 2 + 6 + 3 = 11 \text{ units.}$$

Increasing all inputs by 2 percent (letting $k = 1.02$) leads to the input quantities $X = 1.02$, $Y = 2.04$, and $Z = 2.04$, and:

$$Q_2 = 2(1.02) + 3(2.04) + 1.5(2.04)$$

$$= 2.04 + 6.12 + 3.06 = 11.22 \text{ units.}$$

Since $k = 1.02$ and $h = Q_2/Q_1 = 11.22/11 = 1.02$, $k = h$, a k-fold increase in all inputs leads to a k-fold increase in output, and the system exhibits constant returns to scale.

EMPIRICAL PRODUCTION FUNCTIONS

From a theoretical standpoint, the most appealing form of a production function might be a cubic, such as the equation:

---

[14]For certain production functions called homogenous production functions, when each input factor is multiplied by a constant k, the constant can be completely factored out of the expression. In this case we obtain an expression of the

$$Q = a + bXY + cX^2Y + dXY^2 - eX^3Y - fXY^3. \qquad (6.17)$$

This form, graphed in Figure 6.19, is general in that it exhibits stages of first increasing and then decreasing returns to scale. Similarly, the marginal products of the input factors also exhibit this pattern of first increasing and then decreasing returns, as was illustrated in Figure 6.6.[15]

Given enough input/output observations, either over time for a single firm or at a point in time for a number of firms in an industry, regression techniques can be used to estimate the parameters of the production function. Frequently, however, the data observations do not exhibit enough dispersion to indicate the full range of increasing and then decreasing returns. In these cases simpler functional specifications can be used to estimate the production function within the range of data available. In other words, the generality of a cubic function may be unnecessary, and an alternative model specification can be used for empirical estimation. The power function described below is one approximation for production functions that has proven extremely useful in empirical studies.

Power Functions

One function commonly employed in production studies is the power function, which indicates a multiplicative relationship between the various inputs and takes the form:

$$Q = aX^bY^c. \qquad (6.18)$$

Power functions have several properties useful in empirical research. First, power functions allow the marginal productivity of a given input to depend upon the levels of all inputs employed, a condition that often holds in actual production systems. Second, they are linear in logarithms and thus can be easily analyzed using linear regression analysis. That is, Equation 6.18 is equivalent to:

$$\log Q = \log a + b \log X + c \log Y. \qquad (6.19)$$

The least squares technique can be used to estimate the coefficients of Equation 6.19 and thereby the parameters of Equation 6.18.

Third, power functions facilitate returns to scale estimation. Returns to scale are easily calculated by summing the exponents of the power function (or alter-

---

form $hQ = k^n f(X,Y,Z)$. Here the exponent n provides the key to the returns-to-scale question. If $n = 1$, then $h = k$ and the function has constant returns to scale. However, if $n > 1$, then $h > k$, and increasing returns to scale are present, while $n < 1$ indicates $h < k$ and decreasing returns to scale.

[15]This can be seen by noting the partial derivatives, for example, $\partial Q/\partial X = bY + 2cXY + dY^2 - 3eX^2Y$, which first increases and then decreases as X increases, assuming $c > e$.

nately by summing the loglinear coefficient estimates). If the sum of the exponents is less than one, diminishing returns are indicated. A sum greater than one indicates increasing returns. Finally, if the sum of the exponents is exactly one, returns to scale are constant and the powerful tool of linear programming, described in Chapter 9, can be used to determine the optimal input/output relationships for the firm.

Power functions have been employed in a large number of empirical production studies, particularly since Charles W. Cobb and Paul H. Douglas's pioneering work in the late 1920s. The impact of this work was so great that power production functions are now frequently referred to as Cobb–Douglas production functions.

Selection of a Functional Form for Empirical Studies

Many other alternative functional forms are available for empirical production study. As with empirical demand estimation, the primary determinant of the form of function to use in the empirical model should depend on the relationship hypothesized by the researcher. Selection of the functional form on this basis is difficult, however, and in many instances several alternative model specifications must be fitted to the data to determine which form seems most representative of actual conditions.

SUMMARY

In this chapter we learned that a firm's production function is determined by the technological level of the plant and equipment it employs. It relates inputs to outputs, showing the maximum product obtainable from a given set of inputs.

Several important properties of production systems were examined, including the substitutability of inputs—a characteristic expressed by the marginal rate of substitution—and diminishing returns to factor inputs. The production function was also used to demonstrate that only those input combinations where the marginal products of all input factors are positive need be analyzed to determine the optimal input proportions.

Adding prices to the analysis enabled us to specify the necessary conditions for optimality in input combination. The least-cost combination of inputs requires input proportions such that an additional dollar's worth of each input adds as much to total output as does a dollar's worth of any other input. Algebraically, this relationship is given by the expression:

$$\frac{MP_X}{P_X} = \frac{MP_Y}{P_Y} .$$

It was also demonstrated that employment of resources up to the point where the marginal revenue products equaled price resulted not only in least-cost-input combinations but also in profit maximizing activity levels. Algebraically this relationship is given by the expressions:

$$MRP_X = P_X,$$

and

$$MRP_Y = P_Y.$$

The question of returns to scale was also examined, and several methods of measuring this property were illustrated. Returns to scale in production plays a major role in determining market structures, a topic examined in Chapters 10 and 12.

Empirical estimation of production functions frequently makes use of the statistical methods of regression analysis. While theoretical considerations indicate that cubic equations, with their greater generality, might be preferred for estimation purposes, it was shown that simpler functional forms are often quite adequate for estimation of demand relationships over the range of data available. In fact, the power function, or the Cobb–Douglas production function, is by far the most frequently encountered form in empirical work.

QUESTIONS

6.1 Using the total product curve illustrated below:

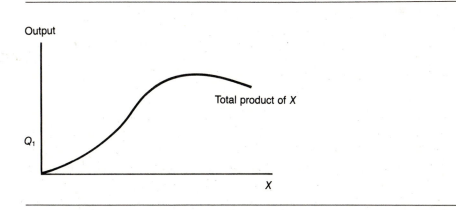

a. Describe both geometrically and verbally the marginal product and the average product associated with Output Q_1.
b. At what points along the curve will the marginal and the average products be maximized?

c. How could you use the related marginal product curve to delineate the maximum quantity of input for Factor X that is not irrational, holding constant the amounts of all other inputs? Illustrate graphically.

6.2 Given the isoquant diagram illustrated below (in which C^* and L^* indicate the optimal combination for producing Output Q^* as determined by a tangency between an isocost curve and an isoquant curve):

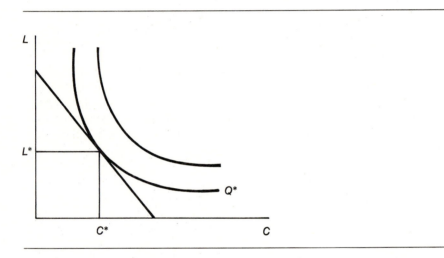

a. What would be the effect of an increase in the relative productivity of labor, L, in this production system on the isocost and the isoquant curves and on the optimal input combination?

b. What would be the effect of a technological change that increased the productivity of capital, C, on the curves and on the combination referred to in Part a?

c. What would be the effect of a change that proportionally increases the effectiveness of both capital and labor simultaneously?

6.3 Using a diagram of isoquant and isocost curves like those shown in Question 6.2, demonstrate that *both* relative input prices and factor productivity play roles in determining optimal input combinations.

6.4 Is the use of least-cost input combinations a necessary condition for profit maximization? Is it a sufficient condition? Explain.

6.5 A labor economist discussing productivity once argued: "If you worked 2,000 hours last year at a $3.50 per hour wage rate and produced 10,000 widgets, your output per hour was five widgets—total output divided by total hours worked. If you are averaging six widgets an hour this year, your productivity (output per hour) has increased 20 percent. Assuming a widget sells for $2, the same as last year, and you still get paid $3.50 per hour, your employer's labor cost per widget has gone down from 70¢ to 58¢. He gets added profits on each widget, so he can afford to share his extra profits with his workers."

a. Under what circumstances would this reasoning be correct?

b. Assume that last year the firm employed $30,000 in capital equipment per employee and also spent $1 per unit on materials used in the production of widgets. This year the firm has expanded its investment in capital equipment per employee to $40,000 and is now paying $1.083 for materials going into a widget because the supplier of those materials is doing more finishing work, reducing the labor effort necessary to assemble a widget. Does the labor economist's argument hold in this case if one assumes that capital investment has a 10 percent cost? Explain why or why not, and use the data provided to prove your point.

6.6 In our analysis of production relationships, we developed the requirement that marginal product-to-price ratios must be equal for all inputs in efficient input combinations. Although this is a necessary condition for the optimal employment of input factors, it is not sufficient for determination of the most profitable quantity of a resource to use in a production system.

a. Explain the above statement. (That is, explain why the MP/P relationship is deficient as a mechanism for determining optimal resource employment levels.)

b. Develop the appropriate relationship for determining the quantities of all inputs to employ in a production system, and explain its rationale.

6.7 Suppose labor, capital, and energy inputs must be combined in fixed proportions. Does this mean returns to scale will be constant?

PROBLEMS

6.1 The following production table provides estimates of the maximum amounts of output possible with different combinations of two input factors, X and Y. (Assume that these are just illustrative points on a spectrum of continuous input combinations.)

Units of Y Used	Estimated Output per Day				
5	316	448	548	632	705
4	282	400	490	564	632
3	245	346	423	490	548
2	200	282	346	400	448
1	141	200	245	282	316
	1	2	3	4	5
			Units of X Used		

a. Do the two inputs exhibit the characteristic of constant, increasing, or decreasing marginal rates of technical substitution? How do you know?

b. Assuming output sells for 25¢ per unit, complete the following tables:

		X Fixed at 2 Units		
Units of Y Used	Total Product of Y	Marginal Product of Y	Average Product of Y	Marginal Revenue Product of Y
1				
2				
3				
4				
5				

		Y Fixed at 3 Units		
Units of X Used	Total Product of X	Marginal Product of X	Average Product of X	Marginal Revenue Product of X
1				
2				
3				
4				
5				

c. Assume that the quantity of X is fixed at two units. If the output of this production system sells for 25¢ and the cost of Y is $15 a day, how many units of Y will be employed?

d. Assume that the company is currently producing 400 units of output per day, using four units of X and two units of Y. The daily cost per unit of X is $15 and that of Y is also $15. Would you recommend a change in the present input combination? Why or why not?

e. What is the nature of the returns to scale for this production system if the optimal input combination requires that $X = Y$?

6.2 Determine whether the following production functions exhibit constant, increasing, or decreasing returns to scale:

    a. $Q = 0.5X + 60Y + 7Z$

    b. $Q = 2L + 400$

    c. $Q = 43L + 22K + 0.5LK.$

6.3 Determine the returns to scale for the following production functions:

a. $Q = 6K^{0.6}L^{0.2}M^{0.3}$.
b. $Q = L^{1/4}K^{3/4}$.
c. $Q = 0.5X^{0.4}Y^{0.6}Z^{0.5}$.
d. $Q = 4M^2 + 8MN + L^2$.
e. $Q = \sqrt{2M_1^2 + 0.1M_2^2 + 10M_3^2}$.

6.4 Fast Stop, a convenience store firm, is examining a solar heating system for one of its stores. The proposed system is composed of 4,200 square feet of solar panels and 20,000 cubic feet of a storage medium. The solar company that has designed the system estimates that if the solar panels were increased in the system there would be an annual heat gain of 8,000 btu's for each additional square foot of panel installed. They also estimate a 4,000-btu annual gain for each additional cubic foot of storage.

   a. What is the marginal rate of technical substitution between solar panels and storage in this system?

   b. Assuming it would cost $50 (annually) per square foot to expand the solar panels and $25 (annually) per cubic foot to expand the storage medium, is the original design optimal with respect to a cost minimization objective assuming its scale is correct? Explain.

   c. The alternative fuel used by Fast Stop for heating its store is natural gas. What must the cost of the natural gas required to provide one btu of heat be if the scale of the solar system described above is optimal? Explain.

6.5 Elwell Oil, Ltd., has designed a pipeline that provides a throughput of 80,000 barrels of oil per 24-hour period. If the diameter of the pipeline were increased by 2 inches, throughput would increase 10,000 barrels per day. Alternatively, throughput could be increased by 12,000 barrels per day if the original pipe diameter were used with pumps that were 200 horsepower larger.

   a. Estimate the marginal rate of technical substitution between pump horsepower and pipe diameter.

   b. Assuming the cost of additional pump size is $500 per horsepower and the cost of larger-diameter pipe is $100,000 per inch, does the original design exhibit the property required for optimal input combinations? If so, why? If not, why not?

6.6 Credit Score, Inc., is a company that provides credit-checking services to retailers in a major midwestern city. Credit Score provides its service using two resources, labor and a time-shared computer. Credit Score employs relatively skilled labor that costs $20 per hour including all fringe benefits. The time-shared computer costs $200 for each hour it is used. Credit Score receives $10 for each credit check it performs.

Credit Score is currently operating at capacity and finds it can't provide enough service to satisfy the demands of its clients. Additional credit checks can be done if more labor or more computer time is employed. An additional hour of labor would result in two additional credit checks being completed. Another hour of computer time would increase output by 20 credit checks.

a. What are the marginal products of labor and the computer in this production system?

b. What is the marginal rate of technical substitution between labor and the computer?

c. What are the marginal revenue products of labor and computer hours?

d. Would it be profitable for Credit Score to expand its service? Explain.

6.7 A recent government study of small independent oil companies estimated the following production function:

$$\ln Q = 1.39 + 2.0 \ln K + 0.5 \ln L + 4.0 \ln E,$$

which converts to:

$Q = 4K^{2.0}L^{0.5}E^{4.0}$

$\ln$ = the natural logarithm

Q = oil output in barrels

K = capital in hundred-thousands of dollars

L = labor in thousands of worker hours

E = energy (oil) input in millions of barrels per year.

During the period covered by this analysis the competitive price of oil was $40 per barrel, and a representative firm had capital of $125,000,000, and an oil input of 200,000 barrels.

a. Calculate the optimal employment level for a typical firm given a competitive wage of $12.50 per hour.

b. Calculate the employment effect of an increase in oil prices to $50 per barrel, holding all else constant.

c. Determine the maximum cost of capital that will permit this new higher level of employment (from Part b) to be maintained.

6.8 Joe Maguire, production manager for the Hamshire, Texas, operations of Harvestone Cooperatives, has authorized an engineering analysis of the planting, cultivation, and harvesting (PCH) division in order to learn whether or not additional increases in operating efficiency might be possible. In this analysis a production function for the PCH division was estimated where:

$$Q = 600L^{0.1}K^{0.1}N^{0.8}$$

and

Q = Output (in hundreds of bushels),

L = Labor input (in worker years),

K = Capital investment input (in dollars),

N = Land input (in sections, where 1 section = 640 acres).

a. If input prices for labor, capital, and land can be written as P_L, P_K, and P_N, respectively, what relative proportions of L, K, and N should be employed?

b. During the coming period PCH plans to work 24 sections and employ 10 workers. Workers earn \$19,200 per year, and land is leased at an annual rate of \$100 per acre. If PCH has a required rate of return of 24 percent, what level of capital investment (in machinery, buildings, etc.) could be justified? (Assume employment levels for L and N are optimal, given the price of the output.)

6.9 Copper International Corporation (CIC) has just completed extensive testing to establish the total mineral reserves in a recent copper discovery. Based on these tests and careful analysis of the market for the minerals contained in the ore body, the project manager has put together a preliminary report on the capital investment the CIC will need in order to efficiently mine and process the minerals. The key factors in the report are as follows:

1. The production function is of a Cobb–Douglas type and can be expressed as $Q = 0.2L^{0.5}K^{0.5}$, where Q equals annual tons of production, L equals the number of employees, and K equals the dollar amount of capital invested.

2. The ore body is extremely large and will be mined for 100 years or more. (Note that this assumption allows one to focus on annual returns to capital without concern for the termination of the project's cash flows.)

3. The annual cost of each employee is \$20,000, and CIC requires a 26 percent annual return on capital for investments of this type.

4. The expected price of the final product is given by the equation $P = 900 - 0.00005Q$.

a. Calculate the marginal physical product for both labor and capital, and use these expressions to determine the returns to each factor.

b. Use the marginal physical product expressions from Part a to calculate optimal input proportions. Show L in terms of K, and K in terms of L.

c. Calculate the marginal revenue product for both labor and capital. Write these expressions in terms of L and K. (Note: You will have to substitute $0.2L^{0.5}K^{0.5}$ for Q.)

d. Determine optimal employment levels for L and K.

e. CIC's announcement that it planned to develop the ore body was greeted by a gubernatorial statement that the mining of that ore should provide benefits to all the citizens of the state through both employment opportunities and added tax revenues generated by an extraction or severance tax that was proposed in legislation the governor sent to the state legislature. Legislative debate on the proposed severance tax has centered on the question of its impact on employment opportunities. Opponents of the tax argue that its imposition would have a negative impact on the amount of employment generated by the project.

(i) Develop a rational economic argument in support of the position that a severance tax is likely to reduce the employment opportunities related to mineral extraction.

(ii) Assuming the proposed tax amounted to $100 per unit of final product from CIC's operation, estimate its potential impact on total employment for the project.

CASE 6.1

PRODUCTIVITY IN EDUCATION: ISSUES IN DEFINING AND MEASURING OUTPUT [16]

"I can't think of any other industry where the more experienced are less productive for more money," says Rexford Moon, vice-president of the Academy for Educational Development, Inc. Behind his statement lies the academic tradition that apportions the least teaching to the most prestigious professors.

The average class load has been decreasing over the past 15 years, making teaching "not a bad calling," says one professor. Joseph Garbarino, a Berkeley professor, says: "The way to get somebody you really want when you can't match salaries elsewhere is to offer him a reduced teaching load." The American Association of University Professors recommends 6 hours per week for professors in universities, 9 hours in colleges, and 12 in community colleges. But some teachers may carry as few as 4 hours.

Educators, however, are quick to explain that class load and work load are not synonymous. Columbia Professor Walter Metzger says that a Nobel laureate earning $30,000, who works full-time with eight graduate students who pay a total of only $24,000 in tuition, "may not do much for the finances of the university, but does an immeasurable service for the nation." And, of course, he brings research and consulting contracts to the university. Princeton's Provost William Bowen maintains that "those that do get paid the most, work the hardest—nights and weekends, too, like young pediatricians."

In a typical day recently, an associate professor of economics at Princeton reviewed a book, composed two PhD examinations, worked with students on a computer game, participated in examinations for masters' candidates, attended three committee meetings, and counseled a student who was failing. Along the way, he missed his lunch, and after dinner returned to the campus to work out a new program for the computer game.

---

[16] This material on productivity in education constitutes a small part of a *BusinessWeek* article on the unionization of college faculties. The reader is referred to the original article for a fuller statement of the relationship between productivity and unionization. See "Unions Woo the College Faculties," *BusinessWeek*, May 1, 1971, pp. 69–74. Reprinted from the May 1, 1971 issue of *BusinessWeek* by special permission. Copyright 1971 by McGraw-Hill, Inc., New York, N.Y. 10020. All rights reserved.

His class load: six hours a week. The emphasis on faculty-guided, independent student work also obscures the amount of time teachers really spend with students, and the American Council for Education's Logan Wilson says that "most aspects of professorial work don't lend themselves to a quantitative evaluation—there is no per unit cost as in an industrial model."

Nevertheless, Michigan and New York have set a regulated number of "student contact hours"—time spent in classroom and counseling. California has done the same thing by simply adding more students but not more faculty. Kerry Smith, chief executive officer of the American Association for Higher Education, predicts that this is doomed to fail because it is "artificial and arbitrary."

Allan Ostar, executive director of the American Association of State Colleges and Universities, feels that collective bargaining may promote "productivity clauses like those in industrial unions." Bargainers would obtain a trade-off: higher salaries for more work by professors.

Case Questions

a. How would you define productivity for university faculty members?

b. Do you agree with Wilson's statement that most aspects of professorial work don't lend themselves to a quantitative evaluation? How might you go about measuring such productivity?

c. Do you agree with Moon's opening statement? Think of this question in terms of your answers to Parts a and b. Are they consistent with your answer to this question?

d. Would productivity clauses for professors as described make sense economically? What problems do you see in implementing such clauses in actual practice?

e. Reconsider Parts a through d above for other service industry occupations (for example, doctors, lawyers, and legislators).

SELECTED REFERENCES

Christensen, Laurits R.; Jorgenson, Dale W.; and Lau, Lawrence J. "Transcendental Logarithmic Production Frontiers." *Review of Economics and Statistics* 55 (February 1973): 28–45.

Comitini, Salvatore, and Huang, David S. "A Study of Production and Factor Shares in the Halibut Fishing Industry." *Journal of Political Economy* 75 (1967): 366–372.

Douglas, Paul H. "Are There Laws of Production?" *American Economic Review* 38 (March 1948): 1–41.

Griliches, Zvi. "R&D and the Productivity Slowdown." *American Economic Review* 70 (May 1980): 343–348.

Johnston, J. "An Economic Study of the Production Decision." *Quarterly Journal of Economics* 75 (1961): 234–261.

Kendrick, John W., and Vaccara, Beatrice N., eds. *New Developments in Productivity Measurement and Analysis.* Chicago: University of Chicago Press, 1980.

Nadiri, M. Ishaq, and Schankerman, M. A. "Technical Change, Returns to Scale, and the Productivity Slowdown." *American Economic Review* 71 (May 1981): 314–319.

Rees, Albert. "Improving Productivity Measurement." *American Economic Review* 70 (May 1980): 340–342.

Scherer, F. M.; Beckenstein, Alan; Kaufer, Erich; Murphy, R. Dennis; and Bougeon-Maassen, Francine. *The Economics of Multi-Plant Operation.* Cambridge: Harvard University Press, 1975.

Walters, A. A. "Production and Cost Functions: An Econometric Survey." *Econometrica* 31 (January–April 1963): 1–66.

APPENDIX 6A

A CONSTRAINED OPTIMIZATION APPROACH TO DEVELOPING THE OPTIMAL INPUT COMBINATION RELATIONSHIPS

It was noted in Chapter 6 that the determination of optimal input proportions could be viewed either as a problem of maximizing output for a given expenditure level or, alternatively, as a problem of minimizing the cost of producing a specified level of output. In this appendix, we show how the Lagrangian technique for constrained optimization can be used to develop the optimal input proportion rule.

CONSTRAINED PRODUCTION MAXIMIZATION

Consider the problem of maximizing output from a production system described by the general equation:

$$Q = f(X, Y) \tag{6A.1}$$

subject to a budget constraint. The expenditure limitation can be expressed as:

$$E^* = P_X \cdot X + P_Y \cdot Y, \tag{6A.2}$$

which states that the total expenditure on inputs, E^*, is equal to the price of Input X, P_X, times the quantity of X employed, plus the price of Y, P_Y, times the quantity of that resource used in the production system. Equation 6A.2 can be rewritten in the form of a Lagrangian constraint, as developed in Chapter 2, as:

$$0 = E^* - P_X \cdot X - P_Y \cdot Y. \tag{6A.3}$$

The Lagrangian function for the maximization of the production function, Equation 6A.1, subject to the budget constraint expressed by Equation 6A.3 can then be written as:

$$\text{Max } L_Q = f(X, Y) + \lambda(E^* - P_X \cdot X - P_Y \cdot Y). \qquad \textbf{(6A.4)}$$

Maximization of the constrained production function is accomplished by setting the partial derivatives of the Lagrangian expression taken with respect to X, Y, and λ equal to zero, and then solving the resultant system of equations. The partials of Equation 6A.4 are:

$$\frac{\partial L_Q}{\partial X} = \frac{\partial f(X, Y)}{\partial X} - \lambda P_X = 0, \qquad \textbf{(6A.5)}$$

$$\frac{\partial L_Q}{\partial Y} = \frac{\partial f(X, Y)}{\partial Y} - \lambda P_Y = 0, \qquad \textbf{(6A.6)}$$

and

$$\frac{\partial L_Q}{\partial \lambda} = E^* - P_X \cdot X - P_Y \cdot Y = 0. \qquad \textbf{(6A.7)}$$

Equating these three partial derivatives to zero results in a set of conditions that must be met for output maximization subject to the budget limit.

Note that the first terms in Equations 6A.5 and 6A.6 are the marginal products of X and Y respectively. That is, $\partial f(X, Y)/\partial X$ is $\partial Q/\partial X$, which by definition is the marginal product of X; and the same is true for $\partial f(X, Y)/\partial Y$. Thus, those two expressions can be rewritten as:

$$MP_X - \lambda P_X = 0$$

and

$$MP_Y - \lambda P_Y = 0,$$

or, alternatively, as:

$$MP_X = \lambda P_X \qquad \textbf{(6A.8)}$$

and

$$MP_Y = \lambda P_Y. \qquad \textbf{(6A.9)}$$

Now, the conditions required for constrained output maximization, expressed by Equations 6A.8 and 6A.9, are also expressed by the ratio of equations. Thus:

$$\frac{MP_X}{MP_Y} = \frac{\lambda P_X}{\lambda P_Y} \, . \qquad\qquad \textbf{(6A.10)}$$

Cancelling the lambdas in Equation 6A.10 results in the optimality conditions developed in the chapter:

$$\frac{MP_X}{MP_Y} = \frac{P_X}{P_Y} \, . \qquad\qquad \textbf{(6A.11)}$$

For maximum production, given a fixed expenditure level, the input factors must be combined in such a way that the ratio of their marginal products is equal to the ratio of their prices. Alternatively, transposing in Equation 6A.11 to derive the expression:

$$\frac{MP_X}{P_X} = \frac{MP_Y}{P_Y} \, ,$$

we see that optimal input proportions require that the ratio of marginal product to price for all input factors must be equal.

CONSTRAINED COST MINIMIZATION

The relationship developed above is also derivable from the problem of minimizing the cost of producing a given quantity of output. In this case the constrained optimization problem is developed as follows. The constraint states that some level of output, Q^*, must be produced from the production system described by the function $Q = f(XY)$. Written in the standard Lagrangian format the constraint is $0 = Q^* - f(X, Y)$. The cost, or expenditure, function is given as $E = P_X \cdot X + P_Y \cdot Y$. The Lagrangian function for the constrained cost minimization problem, then, is:

$$L_E = P_X \cdot X + P_Y \cdot Y + \lambda[Q^* - f(X, Y)]. \qquad \textbf{(6A.12)}$$

Again, as shown above, the conditions for constrained cost minimization are provided by the partial derivatives of Equation 6A.12:

$$\frac{\partial L_E}{\partial X} = P_X - \lambda \frac{\partial (fX, Y)}{\partial X} = 0, \qquad\qquad \textbf{(6A.13)}$$

$$\frac{\partial L_E}{\partial Y} = P_Y - \lambda \frac{\partial (fX, Y)}{\partial Y} = 0, \quad \text{(6A.14)}$$

and

$$\frac{\partial L_E}{\partial \lambda} = Q* - f(X, Y) = 0. \quad \text{(6A.15)}$$

Notice that the last terms on the left-hand side in Equations 6A.13 and 6A.14 are the marginal products of X and Y respectively, so those expressions can be rewritten as:

$$P_X - \lambda MP_X = 0$$

and

$$P_Y - \lambda MP_Y = 0,$$

or, alternatively, as:

$$P_X = \lambda MP_X \quad \text{(6A.16)}$$

and

$$P_Y = \lambda MP_Y. \quad \text{(6A.17)}$$

Taking the ratio of Equation 6A.16 to Equation 6A.17 and cancelling the lambdas again produces the basic input optimality relationship:

$$\frac{P_X}{P_Y} = \frac{MP_X}{MP_Y}.$$

PROBLEM

6A.1 Assume a firm produces its product in a system described in the following production function and price data:

$$Q = 3X + 5Y + XY$$

$$P_x = \$3$$

$$P_y = \$6.$$

Here, X and Y are two variable input factors employed in the production of Q.

    a. What are the optimal input proportions for X and Y in this production system? Is this combination constant irrespective of the output level?

    b. It is possible to express the cost function associated with the use of X and Y in the production of Q as: Cost $= P_x \cdot X + P_y \cdot Y$, or Cost $= \$3X + \$6Y$. Use the Lagrangian technique to determine the maximum output the firm can produce operating under a \$1,000 budget constraint for X and Y. Show that the inputs used to produce that output meet the optimality conditions derived in Part a.

    c. What is the additional output that could be obtained from a marginal increase in the budget?

    d. Assume that the firm is interested in minimizing the cost of producing 14,777 units of output. Use the Lagrangian method to determine what optimal quantities of X and Y to employ. What will the cost of producing that output be? How would you interpret λ, the Lagrangian multiplier, in this problem?

CHAPTER 7
COST THEORY

Cost analysis plays a central role in managerial economics because every managerial decision requires a comparison between costs and benefits. For example, a decision to expand output requires that the increased revenues derived from added sales be compared with the higher production costs incurred. Likewise, a decision to expand capital assets requires a comparison between the revenues expected from the investment and the cost of funds to acquire the new assets. The expected benefits of an advertising program must be compared with the costs of the program. A decision to pave the employees' parking lot or refurbish the company lunchroom requires a comparison between the cost of the projects and the estimated benefits expected to result from improved morale and productivity. In each case, appropriate decision analysis requires that the benefits resulting from the decision be compared to the costs of the action.

In this chapter we examine a number of cost concepts, including alternative (or opportunity) costs, explicit versus implicit costs, marginal costs, incremental costs, and sunk costs. Further, we relate production costs to production functions, and develop long-run and short-run cost functions suitable for empirical measurement.

The materials in this chapter are useful for managerial decisions; they also help one to understand how various industry structures develop and to see some of the implications of public policy designed to alter the structure of industry.

RELEVANT COST CONCEPT

The term *cost* can be defined in a number of ways, and the correct definition varies from situation to situation, depending upon how the cost figure is to be used. Cost generally refers to the price that must be paid for an item. If we buy a product for cash and use it immediately, no problems arise in defining and measuring its cost. However, if the item is purchased, stored for a time, and then used, complications will arise. The problem is even more acute if the item is a long-lived asset that will be used at varying rates for some indeterminate period. What then is the cost of using the asset during any given period?

The cost figure that should be used in a specific application is defined as the *relevant cost*. When calculating costs for use in completing a firm's income tax returns, accountants are required by law to list the actual dollar amounts spent to purchase the labor, raw materials, and capital equipment used in production.[1] Thus, for tax purposes actual historical dollar outlays are the relevant costs. This is also true for Securities and Exchange Commission reports and for reports of profits to stockholders.

For managerial decisions, however, historical costs may not be appropriate; generally, current and projected future costs are more relevant than historical outlays. For example, consider a construction firm that has an inventory of 1,000 tons of steel purchased at a price of $250 a ton. Steel prices now double to $500 a ton. If the firm is asked to bid on a project, what cost should it assign to the steel used in the job—the $250 historical cost or the $500 current cost? The answer is the current cost. The firm must pay $500 to replace the steel it uses, and it can sell the steel for $500 if it elects not to use it on the proposed job. Therefore, $500 is the *relevant cost* of steel for purposes of bidding on the job. Note, however, that the cost of steel for tax purposes is still the $250 historical cost.

Similarly, if a firm owns a piece of equipment that has been fully depreciated—that is, its accounting book value is zero—it cannot assume that the cost of using the machine is zero. If the machine could be sold for $1,000 now, but its market value is expected to be only $200 one year from now, the relevant cost of using the machine for one additional year is $800.[2] Again, there is little relationship between

---

[1] The tax authorities also prescribe guidelines for estimating the depreciable life of capital equipment and methods for calculating depreciation.

[2] This statement contains a slight oversimplification. Actually, the cost of using the machine for one year is the current value minus the discounted present value of its value one year hence. This adjustment is necessary to account for the fact that dollars received in the future have a lower *present* worth than dollars received today.

the $800 true cost of using the machine and the zero cost that would be reported on the firm's income statement.

OPPORTUNITY COSTS

The preceding discussion of relevant costs is based upon an alternative-use concept. Economic resources have value because they can be used to produce goods and services for consumption. When a firm uses a resource for producing a particular product, it bids against alternative users. Thus, the firm must offer a price at least as great as the resource's value in an alternative use. The cost of aluminum used in the manufacture of airplanes, for example, is determined by its value in alternative uses. An airplane manufacturer must pay a price equal to this value or the aluminum will be used to produce alternative goods, such as cookware, automobiles, building materials, and so on.[3] Similarly, if a firm owns capital equipment that can be used to produce either Product A or Product B, the relevant cost of producing A includes the profit of the alternative Product B that cannot be produced because the equipment is tied up manufacturing Product A.

The opportunity cost concept, then, reflects the fact that all decisions are based on choices between alternative actions. The cost of a resource is determined by its value in its best alternative use.

EXPLICIT AND IMPLICIT COSTS

Typically, the costs of using resources in production involve both out-of-pocket or *explicit costs* plus other non-cash costs called *implicit costs*. Wages paid, utility expenses, payment for raw materials, interest paid to the holders of the firm's bonds, and rent on a building are all examples of explicit expenses. The implicit costs associated with any decision are much more difficult to compute. These costs do not involve cash expenditures and are therefore often overlooked in decision analysis. The rent a farmer could receive on buildings and fields if he did not use them is an implicit cost of his own farming activities, as is the salary he can receive by working for someone else instead of operating his own farming enterprise.

An example should clarify these cost distinctions. Consider the costs associated with the purchase and operation of a Mother Baker's Pie Shop. The franchise can be bought for $25,000; and an additional $25,000 working capital is needed for operating purposes. Jones has personal savings of $50,000 that he can invest in such an enterprise; Smith, another possible franchisee, must borrow the entire $50,000 at a

---

[3]The value of aluminum must be sufficient to attract the labor and capital required to produce aluminum. In othe words, the alternative-use concept also applies in determining the total amount of aluminum that will be produced.

cost of 15 percent, or $7,500 a year. Assume that operating costs are the same no matter who owns the shop, and that Smith and Jones are equally competent to manage it. Does Smith's $7,500 annual interest expense mean that her costs of operating the shop are greater than those of Jones? For managerial decision purposes the answer is no. Even though Smith has higher explicit costs because of the interest on the loan, the true financing cost, implicit as well as explicit, might well be the same for both individuals. Jones has an implicit cost equal to the amount he can earn on his $50,000 in some alternative use. If he can obtain a 15 percent return by investing in other assets of equal risk, then Jones's opportunity cost of putting his own $50,000 in the pie shop is $7,500 a year. In this case, Smith and Jones each have a financing cost of $7,500 a year, with Smith's cost being explicit and Jones's implicit.

Can we then say that the total cost of operating the shop will be identical for both individuals? Not necessarily. Just as the implicit cost of Jones's capital must be included in the analysis, so, too, must be the implicit cost of management. If Jones is a journeyman baker earning $18,000 a year and Smith is a master baker earning $25,000 annually, the implicit cost of management will not be equal for the two. The implicit management expense for Smith is equal to her value in her best alternative use, the $25,000 she would earn as a master baker. Jones, on the other hand, has an opportunity cost of only $18,000. Thus, Smith's relevant total costs of owning and operating the shop will be $7,000 greater than those of Jones.

INCREMENTAL AND SUNK COSTS IN DECISION ANALYSIS

The relevant-cost concept also entails the idea of incremental cost. This means that for any decision the relevant costs are limited to those that are affected by the decision. This definition of *incremental costs* as costs that vary with the decision is very much like the marginal concept, which was introduced as a key component in the optimization process. One must take care to recognize, however, that these two, while related, have significant differences. The primary distinction is that marginal costs are always defined in terms of changes in output.[4] The incremental-cost concept is considerably broader, encompassing not only the marginal-cost concept but also cost variations that arise from any aspect of the decision problem. For example, we can speak of the incremental costs of introducing a new product line or changing the production system used to produce the current product(s) of a firm.

The incremental-cost concept, although inherently simple, is sometimes violated in practice. For example, a firm may refuse to sell excess computer time for $500 an hour because it calculates its cost as $550 an hour, determined by adding a standard overhead charge of $250 an hour to a marginal operating cost of $300 an hour. If the "overhead" costs are fixed, the relevant incremental cost of computer

---

[4]More precisely, marginal costs are cost changes associated with *unitary* changes in output. The incremental-cost concept is employed when output decisions involve multiple-unit increases in production.

usage is only $300, and the firm is forgoing a $200 per hour contribution to profit by not selling its excess time. Adding a standard allocated charge for fixed costs and overhead that are not affected by a decision entails the risk of rejecting profitable opportunities or choosing a less satisfactory alternative.

Care must also be exercised to insure against incorrectly assigning a low incremental cost to a decision when in fact a higher cost prevails. This frequently happens to firms faced with temporary reductions in demand and a resulting excess production capacity. Such firms often accept contracts with prices that are sufficient to cover operating expenses, but do not fully cover all overhead and provide a normal profit margin. The firm accepts on the grounds that the contract price appears to exceed incremental costs and thus provides a contribution to total overhead and profit. After accepting, other business picks up. Soon the firm is faced with turning away more profitable business or incurring higher production costs, perhaps increasing fixed costs. In this situation the true incremental costs include the increased production costs of other business or perhaps the forgone profit of business that must be turned down due to capacity constraints. It is important to remember that incremental costs include *all* costs that are affected by the decision. This means that future costs as well as current costs must be considered and opportunity costs cannot be ignored.

Inherent in the incremental-cost concept is the principle that any cost which is not affected by the decision is an irrelevant cost for purposes of that decision. Costs which are invariant across the alternatives are labeled *sunk costs*, as they play no role in determining the optimal course of action. For example, if a firm has unused warehouse space that will otherwise stand idle, the cost of storing a new product in it will be zero, and zero is the incremental storage cost that should be considered in deciding whether to produce the new product. Similarly, a firm may have spent $5,000 on an option which permits it to purchase land for a new factory at a price of $100,000. Later it may be offered another equally usable site for $98,000. The $5,000 is a sunk cost which will not be affected by the decision as to which piece of property is acquired, and it should not enter into the analysis of the decision.

To understand this, consider the alternatives available at the time the firm is faced with the options to purchase the original property or to acquire the second property. If the firm proceeds with the purchase of the first property, it will have to pay a price of $100,000. The newly-offered property will require an expenditure of $98,000. These are the relevant costs for the decision, and, obviously, purchase of the $98,000 property results in a $2,000 savings as compared to the original property. The $5,000 paid for the original option is an expense which will not be affected by the decision at this time. It is a sunk cost which is invariant regardless of which property is actually acquired.

Because of the frequency with which sunk costs are incorrectly treated in managerial decision making, another example should prove worthwhile. Assume that a firm is offered a contract for $10,000 to construct the heating and air-conditioning ducts in a new building. The labor and other operating expenses for the job are estimated to be $7,000. The firm has all the materials required to complete the work in its inventory. Assume that the materials (primarily sheet metal) originally cost the firm $4,000 but that price declines have resulted in a current market value of $2,500. The market for sheet metal is not likely to change in the near future, so no gains are expected from holding the materials in inventory. Should the firm accept the contract?

Correct analysis of this contract proposal requires that one recognize that the $4,000 original cost for the materials in inventory is a sunk cost; it will not be affected by the decision. The firm has suffered a $1,500 loss in inventory value regardless of whether or not it accepts the contract. The relevant materials cost is the current market value of the sheet metal ($2,500). Including this cost in the analysis leads one to the correct decision, which is to accept the contract since it results in a $500 gain for the firm.

In managerial decision making, care must be exercised to insure that only costs that are actually affected by the decision are included in the analysis. The incremental costs associated with a given course of action can include both implicit and explicit costs. If a decision entails long-run commitments, any future costs stemming from those commitments must be accounted for. Any cost that is not affected by the decision alternatives available to a manager is a sunk cost and is irrelevant for purposes of that decision.

SHORT-RUN AND LONG-RUN COSTS

Proper use of the relevant-cost concept for output and pricing decisions requires an understanding of the relationship between a firm's cost and output, or its *cost function*. Cost functions are dependent (1) on the firm's production function and (2) on the market-supply function for its inputs. The production function specifies the technical relationship between combinations of inputs and the level of output, and this factor, combined with the prices of inputs, determines the cost function. Two basic cost functions are used in managerial decision making: short-run cost functions, used in most day-to-day operating decisions, and long-run cost functions, typically used for long-range planning.

How does one distinguish the short run from the long run? The short run is defined as a period during which some inputs of a firm are fixed. In the long run the firm can increase, decrease, or otherwise alter *all* factors of production without restriction. Thus, in the short-run period the firm's decisions are constrained by prior capital expenditures and other commitments; in the long run no such restrictions exist. For a public accounting firm operating out of a rented office, this period of constraint might be as short as several weeks, the time remaining on the office lease. A steel company, on the other hand, has a substantial investment in long-lived fixed assets, and until existing assets wear out and are replaced, its production and cost functions will be constrained.

In addition to the economic life of a firm's assets, their degree of specialization will also affect the period during which decisions are constrained. Consider, for example, a drugstore's purchase of an automobile for making deliveries. If the car is a standard model without modifications, it is essentially an unspecialized input factor; the car has a resale market consisting of the used-car market in general, and the pharmacy can sell it readily without an undue price reduction. If, however, the pharmacy has modified the car by adding refrigeration equipment for transporting perishable drugs, the car is a more specialized resource and its resale market is limited to those individuals and firms who need a vehicle containing refrigeration equipment. In this case, the market price of the car might not equal its value in use to the pharmacy; hence, the short run is extended. We see, then, that at one extreme a firm operating with perfectly unspecialized factors has a very brief short run; it can adjust to changes almost immediately by disposing of or purchasing assets in well-established markets. At the other extreme, when a firm employs highly-specialized factors, no ready market exists; and the firm's short run extends for the entire economic life of the resources it currently owns.

The length of time required to order, receive, and install new assets also influences the duration of the short run. Electric utilities, for example, frequently require eight or more years to bring new generating plants on line, and this obviously extends their short-run time horizon.

In summary, the long run is a period of sufficient length to permit a company to change its productive facilities completely by adding, subtracting, or modifying assets. The short run is the period during which at least some of the firm's productive inputs cannot be altered.[5] From this it is easy to see why long-run cost curves are often called *planning curves* and short-run curves *operating curves*. In the long run, plant and equipment are variable, so management can plan the most efficient physical plant, given an estimate of the firm's demand function. Once the optimal plant has been determined and the resulting investment in equipment has been made, operating decisions will be constrained by these prior decisions.

Fixed and Variable Costs

Costs that are invariant with respect to output are defined as *fixed costs*. Included are interest on borrowed capital, rental expense on leased plant and equipment, depreciation charges associated with the passage of time, property taxes, and salaries of employees who cannot be laid off during periods of reduced activity. Since all costs are variable in the long run, the fixed-cost concept is limited to short-run analysis.

Variable costs vary with changes in output; they are a function of the output level. Included are such costs as raw materials expense, depreciation associated

---

[5] Within any firm, the long and short runs will vary for different decisions. If one division rents most of its equipment and deals with readily available and standardized inputs, its short run will be considerably shorter than that of another division that requires long-lived, nonstandardized facilities.

with the use of equipment, the variable portion of utility charges, some labor costs, sales commissions, and the costs of all other inputs that vary with output.[6] In the long run, all costs are variable.

SHORT-RUN COST CURVES

Both fixed and variable costs affect the short-run costs of a firm. An illustrative short-run total cost curve is shown in Figure 7.1(a). As is apparent from the figure, total cost at each output level is the sum of total fixed costs (a constant) and total variable costs. Short-run total cost curves are constructed to reflect optimal, or least cost, input combinations for producing output *given a specific plant size*. For a currently existing plant, the short-run cost curve illustrates the minimum costs required to produce at various output levels and, therefore, can be used to guide the current operating decisions of the firm.

Since unit costs, either average or marginal, are used for most operating decision making purposes, it is useful to examine these costs briefly. Using TC to represent total cost, TFC for total fixed cost, TVC for total variable cost, and Q for the quantity of output produced, various unit costs are calculated as follows:

$$\text{Average Fixed Cost} = AFC = \frac{TFC}{Q}$$

$$\text{Average Variable Cost} = AVC = \frac{TVC}{Q}$$

$$\text{Average Total Cost} = ATC = \frac{TC}{Q} = AFC + AVC$$

$$\text{Marginal Cost}^{7} = MC = \frac{\Delta TC}{\Delta Q} = \frac{dTC}{dQ}.$$

[6] Such a sharp distinction between fixed and variable costs is not always realistic. The president's salary may be fixed for most purposes, but if the firm went into a really severe depression, this so-called fixed cost could certainly be reduced. Similarly, foremen's wages might be fixed within a certain range of outputs, but below a lower limit foremen might be laid off, while above the upper limit additional foremen would be hired. Also, the longer the duration of abnormal demand, the greater the likelihood that some fixed costs will actually be varied.

This recognition that certain costs are fixed only if output stays within prescribed limits, and that other costs can and will be varied if changed conditions are expected to persist, led to the development of the *semivariable-cost* concept. In incremental-cost analysis, it is essential that one consider the possibility of semivariable costs, which are fixed if incremental output does not exceed certain limits, but are variable outside these bounds.

[7] One frequently finds the term *incremental cost* used interchangeably with marginal cost when output changes are measured in discrete units, that is, when dealing with the relationship $\Delta TC/\Delta Q$. Actually, the term *incremental cost* is much broader than this. It refers to a change in total cost from any source—output related or not—and typically has no per-

FIGURE 7.1

Short-Run Cost Curves

$ per time period

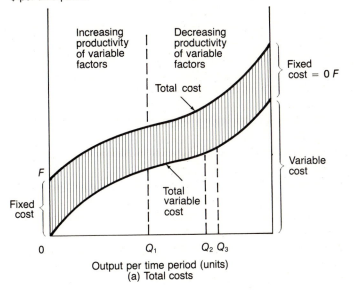

Output per time period (units)
(a) Total costs

$ per time period

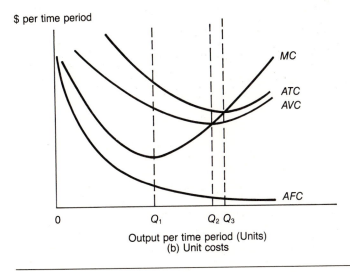

Output per time period (Units)
(b) Unit costs

The unit cost curves corresponding to the total cost curve shown in Figure 7.1(a) are shown in Figure 7.1(b). Several important short-run cost relationships may be noted. First, the shape of the total cost curve is determined entirely by the total variable cost curve. That is, the slope of the total cost curve at each output level is identical to the slope of the total variable cost curve; fixed costs merely shift the total cost curve to a higher level. This means that marginal costs are totally independent of fixed cost. Marginal cost is the change in cost associated with a *change* in output, and because fixed costs are invariant with respect to output, fixed costs can in no way affect marginal cost.

Second, the shape of the total variable cost curve, and hence the total cost curve, is largely determined by the productivity of the variable input factors employed. Note that the variable cost curve in Figure 7.1 increases first at a decreasing rate, up to output level Q_1, and then at an increasing rate. Assuming constant input factor prices, this implies that the marginal productivity of the variable production inputs is first increasing, then decreasing. In other words, the variable input factors exhibit increasing returns in the range of 0 to Q_1 units and diminishing returns thereafter. This relationship is not unexpected. A firm's fixed factors, its plant and equipment, are designed to operate at some specific production level. Operating below that output level requires input combinations in which the fixed factors are underutilized. In this output range, production can be increased more than proportionately to increases in variable inputs. At higher than planned output levels, however, the fixed factors are being more intensively utilized, the law of diminishing returns takes over, and a given percentage increase in the variable inputs will result in a smaller relative increase in output.

This relationship between short-run costs and the productivity of the variable input factors is also revealed by the unit cost curves. Marginal cost declines initially, over the range of increasing productivity, and rises thereafter. This imparts the familiar U shape to the average variable cost curve and the average total cost curve. Notice also that the marginal cost curve first declines rapidly in relation to the average variable cost curve and the average total cost curve, then turns up and intersects each of these curves at its respective minimum point.[8]

LONG-RUN COST CURVES

In the long run the firm has no fixed commitments and, accordingly, all long-run costs are variable. Additionally, just as short-run cost curves assume optimal, or

---

unit dimension. If the incremental cost is output related, then it refers to the total dollar cost difference associated with the change in output; that is, ΔTC = Incremental Cost. The incremental-cost concept is examined in greater detail in Chapter 11.

[8]The relationships among total, average, and marginal curves were discussed in Chapter 2, where we explained why the marginal cost curve intersects the average variable cost curve and the average total cost curve at their minimum points.

FIGURE 7.2

Total Cost Function for a Production System Exhibiting *Constant* Returns to Scale

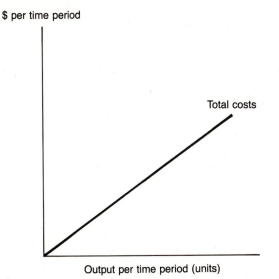

least-cost, input combinations for producing any level of output, *given a specific scale of plant*, long-run cost curves are constructed on the assumption that an optimal plant, *given existing technology*, is used to produce any given output level.[9]

Long-run cost curves reveal both the nature of returns to scale and optimal, or at least preferred, plant sizes. Thus, long-run cost curves are used to guide a firm's planning decisions.

Long-Run Total Costs

If the prices of a firm's inputs are not affected by the amount of the resource purchased, a *direct* relationship exists between cost and production. Consider a production function that exhibits constant returns to scale, as was illustrated in Figure 6.16. Such a production function is linear, and a doubling of inputs leads to a doubling of output. With constant input prices, a doubling of inputs doubles their total cost, producing a linear total cost function, as is illustrated in Figure 7.2.

If a firm's production function is subject to decreasing returns to scale, as was

---

[9] *Existing technology* refers to the state of knowledge and abilities in the industry. If technological improvements occur, as in the development of more efficient smelting processes in a foundry, the old production and cost functions no longer exist—they are replaced by new functions which can be quite different from the old ones.

FIGURE 7.3

Total Cost Function for a Production System Exhibiting *Decreasing* Returns to Scale

$ per time period

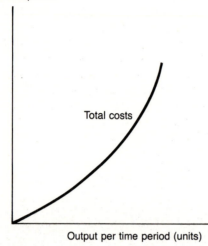

Total costs

Output per time period (units)

illustrated in Figure 6.18, inputs must more than double in order to double output. Again, assuming constant input prices, the cost function associated with a production system of this kind will rise at an increasing rate, as is shown in Figure 7.3.

A production function exhibiting first increasing and then decreasing returns to scale was shown in Figure 6.19. This production function is shown again along with its implied cubic cost function in Figure 7.4. Here costs increase less than proportionately with output over the range where returns to scale are increasing, but more than proportionately after decreasing returns set in.

All the direct relationships between production and cost functions described above are based on constant input prices. If input prices are a function of output, owing to such factors as discounts for volume purchases or, alternatively, to higher prices with greater usage because of a limited supply of inputs, the cost function will reflect this fact. For example, the cost function of a firm with constant returns to scale, but whose input prices increase with quantity purchased, will take the shape shown in Figure 7.3. Costs will rise more than proportionately as output increases. Quantity discounts, on the other hand, will produce a cost function that increases at a decreasing rate, as in the increasing returns section of Figure 7.4.

We see, then, that while cost and production are related, the nature of input prices must be examined before we attempt to relate a cost function to the underlying production function. Input prices and productivity jointly determine the total cost function.

FIGURE 7.4

Total Cost Function for a Production System Exhibiting *Increasing* Then *Decreasing* Returns to Scale

$ per time period

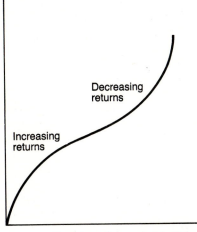
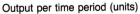

Output per time period (units)

Output per
time period (units)

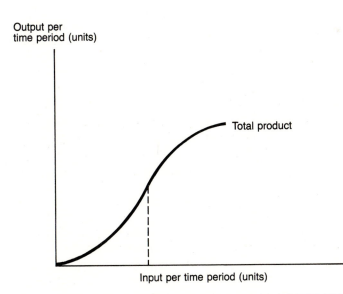

Input per time period (units)

Returns to Scale

Many factors combine to produce this pattern of first increasing, then decreasing returns to scale.[10] Economies of scale, which cause long-run average costs to decline, result from both production and market relationships. Specialization in the use of labor is one important factor that results in economies of scale. In the small firm workers will probably have several jobs, and their proficiency at any of them is likely to be less than that of employees who specialize in a single task. Thus, labor productivity is frequently greater in the large firm, where individuals can be hired to perform specialized tasks. This reduces the unit cost of production for larger scales of operation.

Technological factors also lead to economies of scale. As with labor, large-scale operations typically permit the use of highly specialized equipment, as opposed to the more versatile but less efficient machines used in smaller firms. Also, the productivity of equipment frequently increases with size much faster than does its cost. For example, a 500,000-kilowatt electricity generator costs considerably less than twice as much as a 250,000-kilowatt generator, and it also requires less than twice the fuel and labor inputs when operated at capacity.

The existence of quantity discounts also leads to economies through large-scale purchasing of raw materials, supplies, and other inputs. These economies extend to the cost of capital, as large firms typically have greater access to capital markets and can acquire funds at lower rates. These factors and many more lead to increasing returns to scale and thus to decreasing average costs. At some output level economies of scale typically no longer hold, and average costs level out or begin to rise. Increasing average costs at high output levels are often attributed to limitations in the ability of management to coordinate an organization after it reaches a very large size. This means both that staffs tend to grow more than proportionately with output, causing unit costs to rise, and that managements become less efficient as size increases, again raising the cost of producing a product. While the existence of such diseconomies of scale is disputed by some researchers, the evidence indicates that diseconomies may be significant in certain industries. Additional discussion of the role of scale economies is included in the following chapter, where empirical cost relationships are analyzed.

Cost Elasticities. While Figures 7.2, 7.3, and 7.4 are useful for illustrating the total cost and output relation to returns to scale, it is often easier to calculate returns to scale for a given production system by considering cost elasticities. *Cost elasticity, ε_c, measures the percentage change in total costs associated with a one percent change in output.*

Algebraically the elasticity of cost with respect to output is:

---

[10]The terms *economies of scale* and *increasing returns to scale* are used interchangeably.

$$\varepsilon_C = \frac{\text{Percentage Change in Cost } (C)}{\text{Percentage Change in Output } (Q)}$$

$$= \frac{\partial C}{\partial Q} \cdot \frac{Q}{C} \, .$$

Cost elasticity is related to returns to scale as follows:

If	then	returns to scale are
Percentage Change in C < Percentage Change in Q	$\varepsilon_C < 1$	Increasing
Percentage Change in C = Percentage Change in Q	$\varepsilon_C = 1$	Constant
Percentage Change in C > Percentage Change in Q	$\varepsilon_C > 1$	Decreasing

With a cost elasticity of less than one ($\varepsilon_C < 1$), costs increase at a slower rate than output. Given constant input prices this would imply a higher output-to-input ratio and increasing returns to scale. If $\varepsilon_C = 1$, then output and costs increase proportionately, and constant returns to scale are implied. And finally, if $\varepsilon_C > 1$, then for any increase in output, costs increase by a greater relative amount, implying decreasing returns to scale.[11]

Long-Run Average Costs

Additional insight into both scale economies and the relationship between long-run and short-run costs can be obtained by examining long-run average cost (LRAC) curves. Since short-run cost curves relate costs and output for a specific scale of plant and long-run cost curves identify optimal scales of plant for each production level, LRAC curves can be thought of as an envelope of the short-run average cost curves (SRAC). This concept is illustrated in Figure 7.5, where four short-run average cost curves representing four different scales of plant are shown. The four plants each have a range of output for which they are most efficient. Plant A, for example, provides the least-cost production system for output in the range 0 to Q_1 units; Plant B provides the least-cost system for output in the range Q_1 to Q_2; Plant C is most efficient for output quantities Q_2 to Q_3; Plant D provides the least-cost production process for output above Q_3.

The solid portion of each curve in Figure 7.5 indicates the minimum long-run average cost for producing each level of output, assuming only four possible scales

---

[11] To prevent confusion concerning the relationship between cost elasticity and returns to scale we remind the reader that there is an *inverse* relationship between costs and scale economies and a *direct* relationship between resource usage and scale economies. Thus, while $\varepsilon_C < 1$ implies increasing returns to scale, recall from Chapter 6 that an output elasticity *greater* than one ($\varepsilon_X > 1$) also implies increasing returns to scale. Similarly, decreasing returns to scale are implied by $\varepsilon_C > 1$ and by $\varepsilon_X < 1$.

of plant. We can generalize this by assuming that plants of many sizes, each one only slightly larger than the preceding one, are possible. As shown in Figure 7.6, the long-run average cost curve is then constructed so that it is tangent to each short-run average cost curve. At each tangency, the related scale of the plant is optimal; no other plant will produce that particular level of output at so low a total cost. The cost systems illustrated in Figures 7.5 and 7.6 display first increasing, then decreasing returns to scale. Over the range of output produced by Plants A, B, and C in Figure 7.5, average costs are declining; these declining costs mean that total costs are increasing less than proportionately with output. Since Plant D's minimum cost is greater than that for Plant C, the system exhibits decreasing returns to scale at this higher output level.

Production systems that reflect first increasing, then constant, then diminishing returns to scale result in U-shaped long-run average cost curves such as that illustrated in Figure 7.6. Notice that with a U-shaped long-run average cost curve, the most efficient plant for each output level will typically not be operating where its short-run average costs are minimized, as can be seen by referring to Figure 7.5. Plant A's short-run average cost curve is minimized at Point M, but at that output Plant B is more efficient; that is, B's short-run average costs are lower. In general,

FIGURE 7.5

Short-Run Cost Curves for Four Scales of Plant

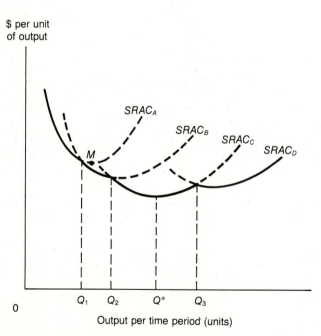

FIGURE 7.6

Long-Run Average Cost Curve as the Envelope of Short-Run Average Cost Curves

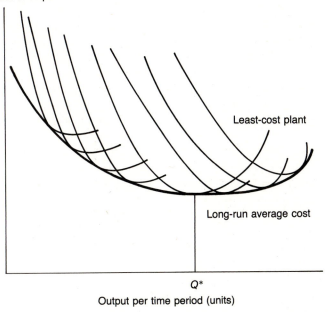

$ per unit of output

Least-cost plant

Long-run average cost

Q^*

Output per time period (units)

where increasing returns to scale exist, the least-cost plant for an output level will operate at less than full capacity.[12] Only for that single output level at which long-run average cost is minimized, Output Q^* in Figures 7.5 and 7.6, will the optimal plant be operating at the minimum point on its short-run average cost curve. At all outputs in the range where decreasing returns to scale exist—that is, at any output greater than Q^*—the most efficient plant will be operating at an output slightly greater than its capacity.

Minimum Efficient Scale

The shape of long-run average cost curves is important not only because of its implications for plant scale decisions, but also because it affects the potential level of competition that will emerge in an industry. While U-shaped cost relationships are

---

[12] We define *capacity* not as a physical limitation on output but rather as the point where short-run average costs are minimized. We should note that businessmen and business writers use the term in many different ways, so its economic interpretation is not always obvious.

quite common, they are not universal. In some industries, first increasing, then constant returns to scale are encountered. In such industries, an L-shaped long-run average cost curve emerges, and larger plants are at no relative cost disadvantage vis-a-vis smaller plants. Typically, competition will tend to be more vigorous within industries with U-shaped long-run average cost curves than where L-shaped or downward sloping long-run average cost curves exist. Insight in this area is gained by examining the concept of the minimum efficient scale (MES) of plant. *MES is defined as the output level where long-run average costs are first minimized*. Thus, MES will be found at the minimum point on a U-shaped long-run average cost curve (output Q^* in Figures 7.5 and 7.6), and at the corner of an L-shaped long-run average cost curve.

Generally speaking, competition will tend to be most vigorous within industries where MES is small relative to total industry demand because of correspondingly minor barriers to entry such as those relating to capital investment and skilled labor requirements. Competition can be less vigorous when MES is substantial because barriers to entry tend to be correspondingly substantial, limiting the number of potential competitors. In considering the competitive impact of a given MES level, we must always consider the overall size of the industry. Some industries are large enough that substantial numbers of very large and efficient competitors can be present. In such instances, even though MES is large in an absolute sense, it can be quite small in a relative sense, and vigorous competition can still be possible. Furthermore, when the cost disadvantage of operating less than MES-size plants is relatively small, there will seldom be any anticompetitive consequences. In other words, the barriers to entry effects of MES depend upon the size of the MES plant relative to total industry demand as well as the slope of the long-run average cost curve at points of less than MES-size operations.

FIRM SIZE AND PLANT SIZE

Production and cost functions exist both at the level of the individual plant and, for multiplant firms, at the level of the entire firm. The cost function of a multiplant (or multiproduct) firm can be simply the sum of the cost functions of the individual plants, or it can be greater or smaller than this figure. To illustrate, suppose that the situation as shown in Figure 7.6 holds; that is, there is a U-shaped long-run average cost curve at the plant level. If demand is sufficiently large, the firm will employ N plants, each of the optimal size and each producing Q^* units of input.

In this case what will be the shape of the firm's long-run average cost curve? Figure 7.7 shows three possibilities. First, the long-run average cost will be constant, as in (a), if there are no economies or diseconomies of combining plants. Second, costs might decline throughout the entire range of output, as in (b), if multiplant firms are more efficient than single-plant firms. Such cases, where they ex-

FIGURE 7.7

Three Possible Long-Run Average Cost Curves for a Multiplant Firm

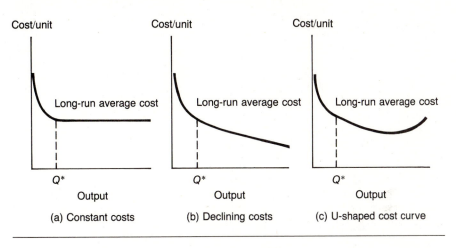

(a) Constant costs (b) Declining costs (c) U-shaped cost curve

ist, are caused by economies of multiplant operation. For example, all the plants may use a central billing service; purchasing economies may be obtained; centralized staffs of various types may serve all plants; and so on. The third possibility, shown in (c), is that costs will first decline (beyond $Q*$, the output of the most efficient plant), and then rise. Here economies of scale for multiplant costs dominate initially, but later the cost of coordinating many operating units more than offsets these multiplant cost advantages.

All three kinds of long-run cost curves have been found in the United States economy, with different ones holding in different industries. Chapter 8 on empirical cost analysis includes additional discussion of this point, as do the chapters on market structure and market efficiency.

Plant Size and Flexibility

Is the plant that can produce a given output at the lowest possible cost necessarily the optimal plant for producing that expected level of output? The answer is an unequivocal no. Consider the following situation. Although actual demand for a product is uncertain, it is expected to be 5,000 units a year. Two possible probability distributions for this demand are given in Figure 7.8. Distribution L exhibits a low degree of variability in demand, while Distribution H indicates substantially higher variation in possible demand levels.

Now suppose two plants can be employed to produce the required output. Plant A is quite specialized and is geared to produce a specified output at a low cost per

FIGURE 7.8

Probability Distributions of Demand

Probability

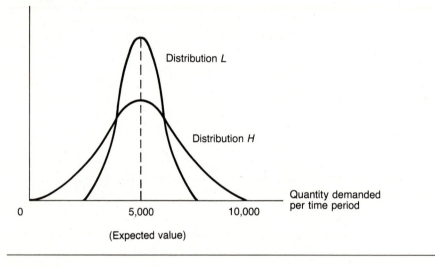

(Expected value)

FIGURE 7.9

Alternative Plants for Production of Expected 5,000 Units of Output

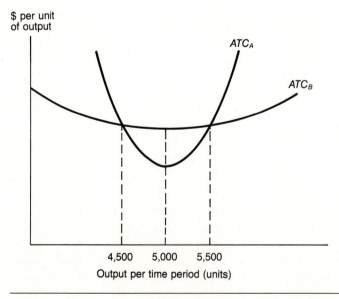

unit. If, however, more or less than the specified output is produced—in this case 5,000 units—unit production costs rise rapidly. Plant *B*, on the other hand, is more flexible. Output can be expanded or contracted without excessive cost penalties, but unit costs are not so low as those of Plant *A* at the optimal output level. These two cases are shown in Figure 7.9.

Plant *A* is more efficient than Plant *B* between 4,500 and 5,500 units of output, but outside this range *B* has lower costs. Which plant should be selected? The answer depends on the relative cost differentials at different output levels and the probability distribution for demand. The firm should select the plant on the basis of the expected average total cost and the variability of that cost.[13] In the example, if the demand probability distribution with the low variation—Distribution *L*—is correct, the more specialized facility will be optimal. If probability Distribution *H* more correctly describes the demand situation, the lower minimum cost of the more specialized facilities will be more than offset by the possibility of very high costs of producing outside the 4,500 to 5,500 unit range; and Plant *B* could have lower expected costs or a more attractive combination of expected costs and potential variation of cost.

BREAKEVEN ANALYSIS

Breakeven analysis, or profit contribution analysis as it is often called, is an important analytical technique used to study the relationships among costs, revenues, and profits. The nature of breakeven analysis is depicted in Figure 7.10, a basic breakeven chart, composed of a firm's total cost and total revenue curves. The volume of output is measured on the horizontal axis, and revenue and cost are shown on the vertical axis. Since fixed costs are constant regardless of the output produced, they are indicated by a horizontal line. Variable costs at each output level are measured by the distance between the total cost curve and the constant fixed costs. The total revenue curve indicates the price/demand relationship for the firm's product, and profits (or losses) at each output are shown by the distance between the total revenue curve and the total cost curve.

Although Figure 7.10 is called a breakeven chart and can be used to determine the output quantity at which the firm begins to earn positive profits, its analytical

---

[13] The expected average total cost is defined as follows:

$$E(ATC) = \sum_{i=1}^{N} P_i ATC_i.$$

Here $E(ATC)$ is the expected ATC; P_i is the probability of the ith output; ATC_i is the ATC associated with the ith output level; and N is the number of possible output levels. As explained in Chapter 3, the expected costs must be analyzed in the context of their potential variability in order to properly incorporate risk into the decision process.

FIGURE 7.10

A Breakeven Chart

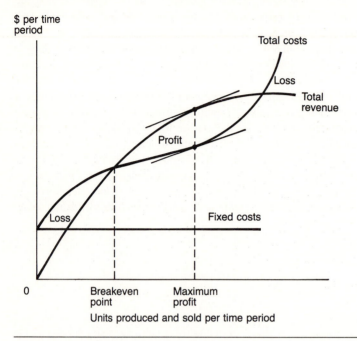

$ per time
period

Note: The slope of a line from the origin to a point on the total revenue line measures price—Total Revenue/Units Sold
= Price; the slope of a line from the origin to the total cost curve measures average cost per unit. It can be seen that the
angle of the line to the revenue curve declines as we move toward higher sales, which means the price is falling.

The slopes of the total cost and the total income lines measure marginal cost, *MC*, and marginal revenue, *MR*,
respectively. At the point where the slopes of the two total curves are equal, *MR = MC*, and profits are at a maximum.

value goes well beyond indicating the breakeven output level. The chart illustrates
the relationship between revenues and costs at all levels of output and can therefore
be used to analyze what happens to profits as volume varies.

Linear Breakeven Analysis

In practical applications of breakeven analysis, linear (straight-line) relationships
are generally assumed in order to simplify the analysis. Nonlinear breakeven analysis is intellectually appealing for two reasons: (1) It seems reasonable to expect that
in many cases increased sales can be achieved only if prices are reduced; and
(2) our analysis of cost functions suggests that the average variable cost falls over
some range of output and then begins to rise. Nevertheless, as our examples show,
linear analysis is appropriate for many uses.

Breakeven charts allow one to focus on key profit elements such as sales, fixed costs, and variable costs. In addition, even though linear breakeven charts are drawn extending from zero output to very high output quantities, no one who uses them would ordinarily be interested in, or even consider, the high and the low extremes. In other words, users of breakeven charts are really interested in only a relevant range of output, and within this range linear functions are probably reasonably accurate.

Figure 7.11 shows a typical linear breakeven chart. Fixed costs of $60,000 are represented by a horizontal line. Variable costs are assumed to be $1.80 per unit, so total costs rise by $1.80, the variable cost per unit, for each additional unit of output produced. The product is assumed to be sold for $3 per unit, so total revenue is a straight line through the origin. The slope of the total revenue line is steeper than that of the total cost line; this follows from the fact that the firm receives $3 in revenue for every unit produced and sold, but spends only $1.80 on labor, materials, and other variable input factors.

Up to the breakeven point, found at the intersection of the total revenue line and

FIGURE 7.11

A Linear Breakeven Chart

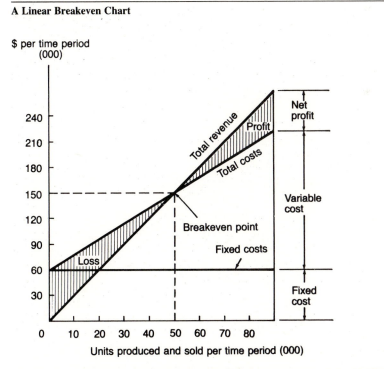

the total cost line, the firm suffers losses. After that point, it begins to make profits. Figure 7.11 indicates a breakeven point at a sales and cost level of $150,000, which occurs at a production level of 50,000 units.

Algebraic Breakeven Analysis

Although breakeven charts provide a useful means of illustrating profit/output relationships, algebraic techniques are typically a more efficient means for analyzing decision problems. The algebraic technique for solving a breakeven problem can be illustrated using the cost and revenue relationships shown in Figure 7.11. First, let:

$$P = \text{Price per Unit Sold,}$$

$$Q = \text{Quantity Produced and Sold,}$$

$$PFC = \text{Total Fixed Costs, and}$$

$$AVC = \text{Average Variable Cost.}$$

The breakeven quantity, defined as that volume of output at which total revenue $(P \cdot Q)$ is exactly equal to total costs $(TFC + AVC \cdot Q)$, is found as follows:

$$P \cdot Q = TFC + AVC \cdot Q \tag{7.1}$$

$$(P - AVC)Q = TFC$$

$$Q = \frac{TFC}{P - AVC} .$$

In the example illustrated in Figure 7.11, $P = \$3$, $AVC = \$1.80$, and $TFC = \$60,000$. The breakeven quantity is found as follows:

$$Q = \frac{\$60,000}{\$3 - \$1.80}$$

$$= 50,000 \text{ units.}$$

Example of Breakeven Analysis

The textbook publishing business provides a good example of the effective use of breakeven analysis for new product decisions. To illustrate, consider the following hypothetical example of the analysis for a college textbook:

Fixed Costs

Copy editing and other editorial costs	$ 6,000
Illustrations	16,000
Typesetting	28,000
Total fixed costs	$50,000

Variable Costs per Copy

Printing, binding, and paper	$3.20
Bookstore discounts	4.80
Commissions	.50
Author's royalties	3.20
General and administrative costs	2.30
Total variable costs per copy	$14.00

List Price per Copy	$24.00

The fixed costs can be estimated quite accurately; the variable costs, which are linear and which for the most part are set by contracts, can also be estimated with little error. The list price is variable, but competition keeps prices within a sufficiently narrow range to make a linear total revenue curve reasonable. Applying the formula of Equation 7.1, we find the breakeven sales volume to be 5,000 units:

$$Q = \frac{\$50,000}{\$24 - \$14}$$

$$= 5,000 \text{ units.}$$

Publishers can estimate the size of the total market for a given book, the competition, and other factors. With these data as a base, they can estimate the possibilities that a given book will reach or exceed the breakeven point. If the estimate is that it will do neither, the publisher may consider cutting production costs by reducing the number of illustrations, doing only light copy editing, using a lower grade of paper, negotiating with the author to reduce the royalty rate, and so on. In the publishing business—and also for new product decisions in many other industries—linear breakeven analysis has proved to be a useful tool.

Breakeven Analysis and Operating Leverage

Breakeven analysis is also a useful tool for analyzing the financial characteristics of alternative production systems. Here the analysis focuses on how total costs and profits vary with output as the firm operates in a more mechanized or automated manner and thus substitutes fixed costs for variable costs.

Operating leverage reflects the extent to which fixed production facilities, as opposed to variable production facilities, are used in operations. The relationship between operating leverage and profit variation is clearly indicated in Figure 7.12, in which three firms, *A*, *B*, and *C*, with differing degrees of leverage, are contrasted. The fixed costs of operations in Firm *B* are considered typical. It uses equipment, with which one operator can turn out a few or many units at the same labor cost, to about the same extent as the average firm in the industry. Firm *A* uses less capital equipment in its production process and has lower fixed costs, but note the steeper rate of increase in variable costs of *A* over *B*. Firm *A* breaks even at a lower level of operations than does Firm *B*. For example, at a production level of 40,000 units, *B* is losing $8,000, but *A* breaks even.

Firm *C* has the highest fixed costs. It is highly automated, using expensive, high-speed machines that require very little labor per unit produced. With such an operation, its variable costs rise slowly. Because of the high overhead resulting from charges associated with the expensive machinery, *C*'s breakeven point is higher than that of either *A* or *B*. Once Firm *C* reaches its breakeven point, however, its profits rise faster than do those of the other two firms.

Degree of Operating Leverage

Operating leverage can be defined more precisely in terms of how a given change in volume affects profits. For this purpose we use the degree of operating leverage concept. *The degree of operating leverage is defined as the percentage change in profit that results from a one percent change in units sold.* Algebraically, this may be expressed as:

$$\text{Degree of operating leverage} = \frac{\text{Percentage Change in Profit}}{\text{Percentage Change in Sales}}.$$

The degree of operating leverage is an elasticity concept, so we could call this measure the *operating leverage elasticity of profits*. When based upon linear cost and revenue curves, this elasticity measure will vary depending on the particular part of the breakeven graph that is being considered. For example, the degree of operating leverage is always greatest close to the breakeven point, where a very small change in volume can produce a very large percentage increase in profits, simply because the base profits are close to zero near the breakeven point.

For Firm *B* in Figure 7.12, the degree of operating leverage at 100,000 units of output is 2.0, calculated as follows: [14]

---

[14] To show the calculation, we arbitrarily assume that the change in Q (ΔQ) = 2,000. If we assume any other ΔQ—for example, ΔQ = 1,000 or ΔQ = 4,000—the degree of operating leverage will still turn out to be 2.0, because we are using linear cost and revenue curves. But if we choose a base different from 100,000 units, we will find the degree of leverage different from 2.0.

FIGURE 7.12

Breakeven and Operating Leverage

Firm A

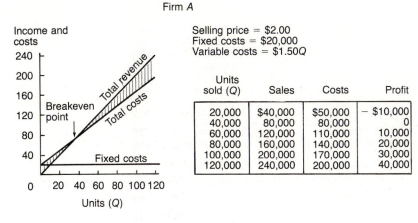

Selling price = $2.00
Fixed costs = $20,000
Variable costs = $1.50Q

Units sold (Q)	Sales	Costs	Profit
20,000	$40,000	$50,000	– $10,000
40,000	80,000	80,000	0
60,000	120,000	110,000	10,000
80,000	160,000	140,000	20,000
100,000	200,000	170,000	30,000
120,000	240,000	200,000	40,000

Firm B

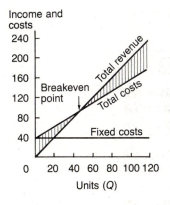

Selling price = $2.00
Fixed costs = $40,000
Variable costs = $1.20Q

Units sold (Q)	Sales	Costs	Profit
20,000	$40,000	$64,000	– $24,000
40,000	80,000	88,000	– 8,000
60,000	120,000	112,000	8,000
80,000	160,000	136,000	24,000
100,000	200,000	160,000	40,000
120,000	240,000	184,000	56,000

Firm C

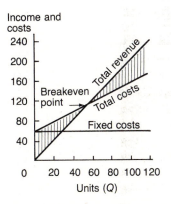

Selling price = $2.00
Fixed costs = $60,000
Variable costs = $1.00Q

Units sold (Q)	Sales	Costs	Profit
20,000	$40,000	$80,000	– $40,000
40,000	80,000	100,000	– 20,000
60,000	120,000	120,000	0
80,000	160,000	140,000	20,000
100,000	200,000	160,000	40,000
120,000	240,000	180,000	60,000

$$DOL_B = \frac{\Delta\pi/\pi}{\Delta Q/Q} \qquad\qquad (7.2)$$

$$= \frac{(\$41,600 - \$40,000)/\$40,000}{(102,000 - 100,000)/100,000} = \frac{1,600/40,000}{2,000/100,000}$$

$$= \frac{4\%}{2\%} = 2.0.$$

Here π is profit and Q is the quantity of output in units.

For linear relationships, a formula has been developed to aid in calculating the degree of operating leverage at any level of Output Q:[15]

$$\text{Degree of operating leverage at point } Q = \frac{Q(P - AVC)}{Q(P - AVC) - TFC}. \qquad (7.3)$$

Here P is the price per unit, AVC is the variable cost per unit, and TFC is total fixed costs. Using Equation 7.3 we find Firm B's degree of operating leverage at 100,000 units of output to be:

$$DOL_B \text{ at } 100,000 \text{ units} = \frac{100,000(\$2.00 - \$1.20)}{100,000(\$2.00 - \$1.20) - \$40,000}$$

$$= \frac{\$80,000}{\$40,000} = 2.0.$$

Equations 7.2 or 7.3 can also be applied to Firms A and C. When this is done, we find A's degree of operating leverage at 100,000 units to be 1.67; C's is 2.5. Thus, with a 10 percent increase in volume, C—the firm with the most operating leverage—will experience a profit increase of 25 percent. For the same 10 percent volume gain A, the firm with the least leverage, will have only a 16.7 percent profit gain.

The calculation of the degree of operating leverage shows algebraically the

---

[15] Equation 7.3 is developed as follows: The change in output is defined as ΔQ. Fixed costs are constant, so the change in profit is $\Delta Q(P - AVC)$, where P = Price per Unit and AVC = Average Variable Cost.

The initial profit is $Q(P - AVC) - TFC$, so the percentage change in profit is:

$$\frac{\Delta Q(P - AVC)}{Q(P - AVC) - TFC}.$$

The percentage change in output is $\Delta Q/Q$, so the ratio of the change in profits to the change in output is:

$$\frac{\Delta Q(P - AVC)/[Q(P - AVC) - TFC]}{\Delta Q/Q} = \frac{\Delta Q(P - AVC)}{Q(P - AVC) - TFC} \cdot \frac{Q}{\Delta Q} = \frac{Q(P - AVC)}{Q(P - AVC) - TFC}.$$

same pattern that Figure 7.12 shows graphically—that the profits of Firm C, the company with the most operating leverage, are most sensitive to changes in sales volume, while those of Firm A, which has only a small amount of operating leverage, are relatively insensitive to volume changes. Firm B, with an intermediate degree of leverage, lies between the two extremes.

PROFIT CONTRIBUTION ANALYSIS

In the short run, where many of a firm's costs are fixed and hence are invariant with respect to incremental sales and output decisions, management is often interested in determining the effects of a specific action on profits. Profit contribution analysis provides this information. Profit contribution is defined as the difference between revenues and variable costs and is therefore equal to price minus average variable cost on a per-unit basis. For example, if a product sells for $10 and average variable costs are constant at $7, then $3 (= $10 − $7) is the per-unit profit contribution of the product. The profit contribution can be applied to cover fixed costs or to increase reported profit.

Profit contribution analysis provides a convenient format for examining a variety of pricing and output decisions. To illustrate, consider again the textbook example discussed above. The variable costs of the proposed textbook are $14 a copy, and the price is $24. This means that each copy sold provides $10 in profit contribution. Assume now that the publisher is interested in determining how many copies must be sold in order to earn a $20,000 profit on the text. Because profit contribution is the amount available to cover fixed costs and provide profit, the answer is found by adding the profit requirement to the book's fixed costs, then dividing by the per-unit profit contribution. The sales volume required in this case is 7,000 books, found as follows:

$$Q = \frac{\text{Fixed Costs} + \text{Profit Requirement}}{\text{Profit Contribution}}$$

$$= \frac{\$50,000 + \$20,000}{\$10}$$

$$= 7,000 \text{ Units.}[16]$$

---

[16] To see that 7,000 units will indeed produce a profit of $20,000, note the following calculations:

Sales Revenue = $24 × 7,000 =	$168,000
Total Cost = FC + VC = $50,000 + $14(7,000) = $50,000 + $98,000 =	148,000
Profit = Sales Revenue − Total Cost =	$ 20,000

Consider a second decision problem that might confront the publisher. Assume that a book club has indicated an interest in purchasing the textbook for its members and has offered to buy 3,000 copies at $12 per copy. Profit contribution analysis can be used to determine the incremental effect of such a sale on the publisher's profits.

Since fixed costs are invariant with respect to changes in the number of textbooks sold, they should be ignored in the analysis. Variable costs per copy are $14, but note that $4.80 of this cost represents bookstore discounts. Since the 3,000 copies are being sold directly to the club, this cost will not be incurred, and hence the relevant variable cost is $9.20. Profit contribution per book sold to the book club then is $2.80 (= $12 − $9.20), and $2.80 times the 3,000 copies sold indicates that the order will result in a total profit contribution of $8,400. Assuming that these 3,000 copies would not have been sold through normal sales channels, the $8,400 profit contribution indicates the increase in profits to the publisher from accepting this order.

LIMITATIONS OF BREAKEVEN ANALYSIS

Breakeven analysis helps one understand the relationships among volume, prices, and cost structure; and it is useful in pricing, cost control, and other financial decisions. However, breakeven analysis has limitations as a guide to managerial actions.

Linear breakeven analysis is especially weak in what it implies about the sales possibilities for the firm. Any given linear breakeven chart is based on a constant selling price. Therefore, in order to study profit possibilities under different prices, a whole series of charts is necessary, one chart for each price. Nonlinear breakeven analysis can be used as an alternative method.

Breakeven analysis is also deficient with regard to costs. The linear relationships indicated by the chart do not hold at all output levels. As sales increase, existing plant and equipment are worked beyond capacity, thus reducing their productivity. This situation results in a need for additional workers and frequently longer work periods, which require the payment of overtime wage rates. All of these tend to cause variable costs to rise sharply. Additional equipment and plant may be required, thus increasing fixed costs. Finally, over a time the products sold by the firm change in quality and quantity. Such changes in product mix influence both the level and the slope of the cost function.

Although linear breakeven analysis has proved to be a useful tool for economic decision making, care must be taken to insure that it is not used in situations where its assumptions are violated so that the results are misleading. In short, this decision tool is like all others in that it must be employed with a good deal of judgment.

SUMMARY

Cost relationships play a key role in most managerial decisions. In this chapter we introduced a number of cost concepts, showed the relationship between cost functions and production functions, and examined several short-run and long-run cost relationships.

Although the definition of relevant costs varies from one decision to another, several important relationships are common in all cost analyses. First, relevant costs are typically based on the alternative-use concept: the relevant cost of a resource is determined by its value in its best alternative use. Second, the relevant cost of a decision includes only those costs which are affected by the action being contemplated. This is the incremental-cost concept. If a particular cost is unchanged by an action, the relevant incremental cost for decision purposes is zero. Finally, care must be taken to insure that all costs, both explicit and implicit, which are affected by a decision are included in the analysis.

Proper use of the relevant-cost concept requires an understanding of a firm's cost/output relationship or its cost function. Cost functions are determined by the production function and the market-supply function for its inputs, with the production function specifying the technical relationship between inputs and output and the prices of inputs converting this physical relationship to a cost/output function.

Two basic cost functions are used in managerial decision making—short-run cost functions, used in most day-to-day operating decisions, and long-run cost functions, used for planning purposes. The short run is the period during which some of the firm's productive facilities are unalterable; the long run is a period of sufficient length to permit the company to change its production system completely by adding, subtracting, or completely modifying its assets.

In the short run the shape of a firm's cost curves will be determined largely by the productivity of its variable input factors. Over that range of output where the marginal productivity of the variable inputs is increasing, costs will be increasing less than proportionately to output, so unit costs will be declining. Once diminishing returns to the variable factors set in, costs begin to increase faster than output, and unit costs will begin to rise.

A similar relationship holds for long-run cost curves. Here all inputs are variable, and the shape of the cost curve is determined by the presence of economies or diseconomies of scale. If economies of scale are present, the cost elasticity of output will be less than one ($\varepsilon_c < 1$), and unit costs will decline as output increases. Once diseconomies of scale begin to dominate, however, $\varepsilon_c > 1$, and average cost curves will turn up.

Cost functions may be developed both at the level of the plant and, for multiplant firms, at the level of the firm. Frequently, because of economies of multiplant operation, the cost function of the multiplant firm is lower than the sum of the cost functions of the individual plants. These economies typically result from centralized computer facilities, financial activities, purchasing, marketing, and the like.

Although a firm desires to produce its output at the minimum possible cost, the existence of uncertainty often dictates a trade-off between lower costs and production flexibility. In these cases, the firm must examine the probability distribution of demand and the relative cost differentials of alternative production techniques, then select as the optimal system the one which maximizes the value of the firm.

Breakeven analysis was shown to be an important tool for analyzing the relationships among fixed costs, variable costs, revenues, and profits. Its uses include analysis of the effects of varying the degree of operating leverage that a firm employs and analysis of incremental profit using the profit contribution concept.

QUESTIONS

7.1 The relevant cost for most managerial decision purposes is the *current* cost of an input. The relevant cost for computing income for taxes and stockholder reporting is the *historical* cost. Would it be preferable to use current costs for tax and stockholder reporting purposes?

7.2 What is the relationship among historical costs, current costs, and alternative opportunity costs?

7.3 Are implicit costs reflected in income-tax calculations?

7.4 What is the difference between marginal and incremental cost?

7.5 What is a sunk cost, and how is it related to a decision problem?

7.6 Explain in some detail the relationship between production functions and cost functions. Be sure to include in your discussion the impact of conditions in the input factor markets.

7.7 The president of a small firm has been complaining to his controller about rising labor and material costs. However, the controller notes that a recently completed cost study indicates that average costs have not increased during the past year. Is this possible? What factors might you examine to analyze this phenomenon?

7.8 Given the short-run total cost curve in Figure 7.1, explain why (a) Q_1 is the minimum of the *MC* curve, (b) Q_2 is the minimum of the *AVC* curve, (c) Q_3 is the minimum of the *ATC* curve, and (d) the *MC* curve cuts the *AVC* and *ATC* curves at their minimum points.

7.9 Will firms in industries where high levels of output are necessary for minimum efficient scale tend to have substantial degrees of operating leverage?

7.10 Will operating strategies of cost minimization and profit maximization always lead to identical levels of output?

7.11 Explain why an output elasticity > 1 and a cost elasticity < 1 both indicate increasing returns to scale. (See Chapter 6 for the definition of output elasticity.)

PROBLEMS

7.1 Assume that Output Q is a function of two inputs, or factors of production, X and Y. (In this problem, be *careful* with the geometry, as your graphs must reveal the required relationships.)

    a. Construct a set of production isoquants that exhibit (i) diminishing marginal substitutability and (ii) first increasing, then constant, and then decreasing returns to scale. Let the constant returns extend over a *range* of outputs. (Use a single two-dimensional graph.)

    b. Assuming that Factors X and Y are purchased in competitive markets, construct a *long-run total cost* curve that is consistent with the isoquant set constructed in Part a.

    c. Construct average and marginal cost curves that are consistent with the total cost curve shown in Part b.

    d. Explain what would happen to your graphs if the assumption of competitive factor markets in Part b is relaxed.

7.2 Using the total product curve shown below, which describes a production system in which X is the only variable input, answer the following questions relating production to costs.

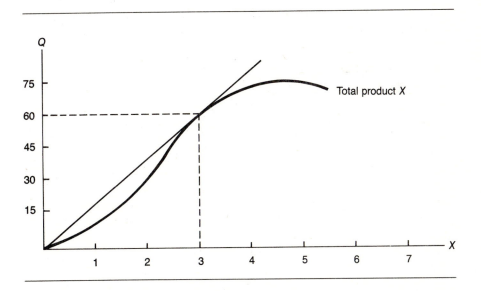

    a. Over approximately what range of input will marginal costs be falling if X is purchased in a competitive market?

    b. At approximately what level of employment of Input X will average variable costs be minimized?

c. If $P_x = \$25$ what is the minimum average variable cost in this production system?

d. What is the marginal cost of production at 60 units of output?

e. If the price of the output is $2 per unit, is employment of 3 units of X optimal for a profit maximizing firm (assuming again that X costs $25 per unit)? Explain your answer as fully as possible.

7.3 Last month, Geneseo Paint Company sold 20,000 gallons of paint, for which the variable manufacturing costs were $4.20 per gallon. Each gallon contributes 40 percent of its revenue to fixed costs and profits.

a. If the company reduces the price of this product by 5 percent, how many gallons will it have to sell this month in order to obtain the same profits as earned last month?

b. Geneseo's primary competition comes from Color-Lok, a firm whose product sells for $6. If Color-Lok's average profit contribution is 30 percent, what are that company's average variable costs?

7.4 Kansas Research Labs, Inc. (KRL), is evaluating a contract proposal for testing a new automobile fuel injection system. The contract calls for KRL to test the system for fuel efficiency gains, pollution emission control, and service reliability. Under terms of the contract KRL would receive $1,500,000 for carrying out the tests.

The following cost information is to be used in determining whether the contract should be accepted. KRL believes the testing can be completed using existing facilities and equipment, with the exception of one piece of emission test equipment which can be rented for a fee of $75,000. Labor requirements are estimated at 10,000 hours, and KRL calculates its labor cost at $110 per hour. This labor cost is derived by adding a 20 percent overhead charge to the actual direct labor costs, which is designed to spread the firm's fixed management expenses to the various jobs undertaken, and a 100 percent charge for the firm's required profit margin. The profit margin charge was developed on the basis of estimates of the profit contribution that management believes it can earn through employment of the firm's resources under normal conditions. KRL estimates that various materials, including fuels, costing $270,000 will be purchased explicitly for the tests. Additionally, KRL will use 100 ounces of an exotic catalytic agent which it currently has in inventory. This chemical cost KRL $40,000 when purchased one year ago. (It was acquired for a job that did not require the amount projected.) KRL estimates that its carrying cost (interest on investment, insurance, storage, etc.) for the catalyst has been 20 percent of the initial purchase cost. At the current time the catalyst has a market value of $600 per ounce.

Management of KRL has determined that although business is good and resources are fully employed, there would be no abnormal impact on other business if the fuel injection system test contract is accepted. That is, while other work is available, the acceptance of this job would not adversely affect future business with any customer.

A contract cost estimator for KRL has constructed the following cost projection for the fuel system test job.

1. Direct Labor Cost (10,000 hours @ $50 per hour)		$ 500,000
2. Direct Materials:		
Purchased Materials	$270,000	
Inventoried Catalyst	48,000	
		318,000
3. Equipment Rental		75,000
4. Overhead (20 percent of Direct Labor)		100,000
5. Required Profit Margin (100 percent of Direct Labor)		500,000
		$1,493,000

a. For each of the five numbered cost categories in the cost estimate determine: (1) whether the cost is relevant for the decision to accept or reject the contract, (2) whether the cost is an implicit or an explicit cost, and (3) whether the cost has been properly calculated given the information in the problem.

b. Determine KRL's true relevant cost (including all implicit as well as explicit costs) of accepting the contract.

c. How would an assumption that the economy was in a recession and that KRL didn't have enough business to keep its resources fully employed affect the relevant costs for this problem? Be specific and reestimate the costs of the job.

7.5 Two graduate business students are considering opening a business renting windsurfers next summer. The students view this as an alternative to taking summer employment with a local firm where they would each earn $2,500 during the three-month summer period. A preliminary market survey indicates that a rental price of $5 per hour is probably optimal. Thirty windsurfers can be leased from a manufacturer for $20,000 for the summer with lease payments being made monthly. Additional projected costs are $4,000 for insurance, $2,000 to rent a location for the business, and $2.50 per hour per rented windsurfer for repairs and maintenance.

a. What is the accounting cost function for this business?

b. What is the economic cost function for this business?

c. What is the breakeven number of rental hours for this operation? (Calculate an *economic* breakeven with all relevant costs accounted for, and assume a $5 per hour rental rate.)

7.6 PK Corporation manufactures ballpoint pens. The current price received by PK for its pens is $5 per gross, and unit variable profit, or profit contribution, is $1.50 per gross. Sales of the ballpoint pens have been disappointing, and PK is considering a quality improvement at a cost of 25¢ per gross. Advertising would be increased by $50,000 to promote the improvement. Current profit is $25,000 on sales of 200,000 gross of the ballpoint pens.

PK also sells another pen known as the rollarpoint. There is a relationship between sales of PK's ballpoint and rollarpoint pens. Specifically, PK estimates that every 10 gross of ballpoint pens sold leads to sales of one additional gross of the rollarpoint pens. The rollarpoint pens sell for $7.50 per gross and have an average variable cost of $5 per gross.

a. Determine the total cost to manufacture and sell ballpoint pens with the changes PK is considering.

b. What increase in sales of ballpoint pens must the quality improvement cause if PK is to earn total incremental profits of $30,000 from the project?

7.7 Hauschel Industrial Fasteners Company (HIF) operates in a relatively competitive market characterized by little product differentiation. HIF has fixed costs of $500,000 and average variable costs of $2.50 per gross of fasteners. The total industry demand for industrial fasteners is approximately 20 million gross annually.

a. Chris Hauschel, president of HIF, wants to operate so as to maintain the firm's 20 percent market share. What is the breakeven price for HIF under this pricing policy?

b. Given achievement of the market share policy stated above, at what price must HIF sell its fasteners if a profit of 15 percent of capital investment is to be earned (HIF has $1,250,000 of investment in plant and equipment)?

c. Will setting price at the level determined in Part b necessarily result in the firm earning zero economic profits (assuming 15 percent is the appropriate required return on capital)? Why?

d. A foreign air frame manufacturer who normally purchases fasteners outside the market served by HIF has a temporary shortage due to a strike by employees of its supplier. The firm has approached HIF with an offer to purchase 200,000 gross of fasteners at a price of $2.55 per gross. HIF has the additional capacity to produce these units without affecting fixed costs or the average variable costs of production. HIF's sales manager has rejected the offer, citing current average costs of $2.62 per gross as the reason. Do you agree with this decision? Why?

7.8 Marathon Motors, Inc., has developed a new car, dubbed the "Saver," as it has a mileage rating of 60 m.p.g. A preliminary market analysis suggests that 240,000 Savers could be sold during the first year of production at an average price of $10,000 each. Furthermore, a statistical analysis of industry cost-output data for plants which produce cars with physical characteristics similar to the Saver's revealed the following:

$$C = 300 + 10.5\,Q - 0.01\,Q^2$$

$$C = \text{total cost (in \$ millions)}$$

$$Q = \text{car production (in thousands of cars)}$$

a. Calculate the breakeven level of Saver production.

b. Calculate and interpret the anticipated elasticity of cost with respect to output at 240,000 in sales.

7.9 The Vernom Corporation, which produces and sells to wholesalers a highly successful line of summer lotions and insect repellents, has decided to diversify in order to stabilize sales throughout the year. A natural area for the company to consider is the production of winter lotions and creams to prevent dry and chapped skin.

After considerable research, a winter products line has been developed. However, because of the conservative nature of the company management, Vernom's president has decided to introduce only one of the new products for this coming winter. If the product is a success, further expansion in future years will be initiated.

The product selected (called Chap-off) is a lip balm that will be sold in a lipstick-type tube. The product will be sold to wholesalers in boxes of 24 tubes for $8 per box. Because of available capacity, no additional fixed charges will be incurred to produce the product. However, a $100,000 fixed charge will be absorbed by the product to allocate a share of the company's present fixed costs to the new product.

Using the estimated sales and production of 100,000 boxes of Chap-off as the standard volume, the accounting department has developed the following costs:

Direct Labor	$2.00/box
Direct Materials	$3.00/box
Total Overhead	$1.50/box
Total Cost	$6.50/box

Vernom has approached a cosmetics manufacturer to discuss the possibility of purchasing the tubes for Chap-off. The purchase price of the empty tubes from the cosmetics manufacturer would be 90¢ per 24 tubes. If the Vernom Corporation accepts the purchase proposal, it is estimated that direct labor and variable overhead costs would be reduced by 10 percent and direct material costs would be reduced by 20 percent.

a. Should the Vernom Corporation make or buy the tubes? Show calculations to support your answer.

b. What would be the maximum purchase price acceptable to the Vernom Corporation for the tubes? Support your answers with an appropriate explanation.

c. Instead of sales of 100,000 boxes, revised estimates show sales volume of 125,000 boxes. At this new volume, additional equipment to manufacture the tubes must be rented at an annual cost of $10,000. However, this incremental cost would be the only additional fixed cost required even if sales increased to 300,000 boxes. (The 300,000 level is the goal for the third year of production.)

The company has the option of making and buying at the same time. Under these circumstances how should Vernom Corporation acquire the tubes?

SELECTED REFERENCES

Anthony, Robert N. "What Should 'Cost' Mean?" *Harvard Business Review* 48 (May–June 1970): 121–131.

Bain, Joe S. "Survival-Ability as a Test of Efficiency." *American Economic Review* 59 (May 1969): 99–104.

Berndt, Ernst R., and Morrison, Catherine J. "Capacity Utilization Measures: Underlying Economic Theory and an Alternative Approach." *American Economic Review* 71 (May 1981): 48–52.

Duetsch, Larry L. "Geographic Market Size and the Extent of Multiplant Operations." *Review of Economics and Statistics* 64 (February 1982): 165–167.

Gupta, Vinod K. "Suboptimal Capacity and its Determinants in Canadian Manufacturing Industries." *Review of Economics and Statistics* 61 (November 1979): 506–512.

Hirshleifer, Jack. "The Firm's Cost Function: A Successful Reconstruction." *Journal of Business* (July 1962): 235–255.

Miller, Edward M. "The Extent of Economies of Scale: The Effect of Firm Size on Labor Productivity and Wage Rates." *Southern Economic Journal* 44 (January 1978): 470–487.

Oi, Walter Y. "Slack Capacity: Productive or Wasteful?" *American Economic Review* 71 (May 1981): 64–69.

Scherer, F. M. "The Determinants of Industry Plant Sizes in Six Nations." *Review of Economics and Statistics* 55 (May 1973): 135–145.

Stigler, George J. "The Economies of Scale." *Journal of Law and Economics* 1 (October 1958): 54–71.

Walters, A. A. "Production and Cost Functions: An Econometric Survey." *Econometrica* 31 (January–April 1963): 1–66.

Weiss, Leonard W. "The Survival Technique and the Extent of Suboptimal Capacity." *Journal of Political Economy* 72 (June 1964): 246–261.

———. "Optimal Plant Size and the Extent of Suboptimal Capacity." In Robert T. Masson and P. David Qualls, eds., *Essays on Industrial Organization in Honor of Joe S. Bain*. Cambridge: Ballinger Publishing Company, 1976: 123–141.

CHAPTER 8
EMPIRICAL COST ANALYSIS

The preceding chapter demonstrated the importance of a detailed knowledge of both long-run and short-run cost functions for many managerial decision purposes. The short-run cost curve provides useful information for short-run pricing and output decisions; with the long-run curve, the firm can do a better job of planning its capacity requirements and future plant configurations.

Public officials are also interested in long-run and short-run cost functions. As will be shown in Chapters 10, 11, and 12, regulatory authorities (including the Antitrust Division of the Justice Department) can influence the size of business enterprises. If the size of a firm is held down below the least-cost level, economic efficiency suffers. On the other hand, if economies of scale are not important, regulators create fewer problems with policies that limit firm size in order to stimulate competition.

A number of analytical techniques have proved useful in the empirical estimation of cost functions. In this chapter we examine several of these techniques, illustrating their particular strengths and noting some of their weaknesses and limitations.

SHORT-RUN COST ESTIMATION

By assuming that the firm has been operating efficiently, or at least that inefficiencies can be isolated and accounted for, it is possible to estimate cost functions by statistical analysis. Time-series and cross-sectional regression analyses are the most popular methods used for estimating a firm's short-run variable cost function.[1] In such regression studies, cost is regressed on output, typically in a model that includes a number of other variables whose effects on cost we wish to analyze or at least to account for. For estimating short-run cost relationships, the total variable cost function rather than the total cost function is estimated in order to remove the very difficult problem of allocating fixed costs to a particular production quantity. Since these allocated costs are invariant with respect to output, they cannot affect the important average variable cost function and the marginal cost function that are used for short-run decision making purposes and can therefore be safely eliminated from the analysis.

Cost Specification and Data Preparation

Most difficulties encountered in statistical cost analysis arise from two causes: (1) errors in the specification of the cost characteristics that are relevant for decision making purposes and (2) problems in the collection and modification of the data to be analyzed. Thus, before examining the types of regression models actually used to estimate short-run cost functions, we should consider several caveats regarding specification, collection, and modification of cost data.

Conceptual Problems. Managerial decision making pertains to future activities and events, so the relevant costs for managerial decisions are future costs, as opposed to current or historical costs. Cost estimates based on accounting data—which record actual current or past costs and are thus historical—must therefore be considered as only first approximations to the relevant costs in managerial economics. These accounting costs must be modified before they are used for decision making purposes. The most typical adjustment involves setting prices of input factors such as labor, materials, and energy at their current or projected levels.

A second conceptual problem that occurs when accounting data are used for cost analysis stems from the failure of accounting systems to record opportunity costs. Since opportunity costs are frequently the largest and the most important costs in a short-run decision problem, cost functions derived from accounting data are often inappropriate. As Joel Dean, a pioneer in the development of managerial economics, has so aptly stated: "In business problems the message of opportunity

---

[1]See Chapter 5 for a discussion of the least squares regression technique.

costs is that it is dangerous to confine cost knowledge to what the firm is doing. What the firm is not doing but could do is frequently the critical cost consideration which it is perilous but easy to ignore."[2]

Cost/Output Matching. A problem may arise in the attempt to relate certain costs to output. In short-run cost analysis, only the costs that vary with output should be included, but it is often difficult to distinguish between those costs which are and are not related to output. Economic depreciation of capital equipment is perhaps the best example of this difficulty. For most depreciable assets, both time and usage determine the rate of decline in value, but only the component related to usage should be included in short-run cost estimation. Both components, however, are generally embodied in accounting data on depreciation costs, and it is often impossible to separate the use costs from the obsolescence or time-related costs.

Semivariable costs also present a problem in cost/output matching. Some costs may not vary with output changes over certain ranges but may vary with output once a critical level has been exceeded for a long-enough period. These cost/output relationships must be accounted for if accurate short-run cost functions are to be estimated.

Timing of Costs. Another problem that arises from the use of accounting data is that of relating costs to the corresponding output. Care must be taken to adjust the data for leads and lags between cost reporting and output production. Maintenance expense provides a typical example of this problem: Production in one period causes additional maintenance expenses not in that period but, rather, in subsequent periods. During a period of high production, recorded maintenance expenses will be unusually low because the firm's equipment is being used at full capacity, so that maintenance must be postponed if possible. Repairs that are made will usually be temporary in nature, aimed at getting the equipment back into production rapidly until a period when some slack exists in the production system. Without careful adjustment, this problem can cause gross errors in statistically estimated cost functions.

Inflation. Price level changes present still another problem. In time-series analysis, recorded historical data are generally used for statistical cost analysis, and during most of the period for which data are available the costs of labor, raw materials, and other items have been rising. At the same time, an expanding population and greater affluence have caused the output of most firms to increase. The more recent output is therefore large and has a relatively high cost (in nominal or current dollar terms),

[2]Joel Dean, *Managerial Economics* (Englewood Cliffs, N.J.: Prentice-Hall, 1951), p. 260.

so a naïve cost study might suggest that costs rise rapidly with increases in output when this is not the case. To remove this bias, cost data must be deflated for price level changes. Because factor prices increase at different rates, the use of composite price indexes for this deflation often will not provide satisfactory results. Rather, an index for each category of inputs must be used. The problem of adjusting for price variation is further compounded by the fact that input price changes related to increases in demand for the input when the firm's output rate increases must not be removed. Only price changes that are independent of the production system under examination should be eliminated; otherwise, the statistically estimated cost function will understate the true cost of high-level production.[3]

Observation-Period Problems. Short-run cost curves are, by definition, cost/output relationships for a plant of specific scale and technology. If the short-run curve is to be accurately estimated, the period of examination must be one during which the product remains essentially unchanged and the plant facilities remain fixed. It should be noted that even though a firm's book value of assets remains relatively constant during the observation period, the plant may have actually changed significantly. Consider, for example, a firm that replaces a number of obsolete manual milling machines, which have been fully depreciated, with a single automated machine that it leases. The firm's production function, and hence its total cost function, could have changed substantially even though the book value of assets remains constant. The problem of changing plant and product can be minimized by limiting the length of the period over which data are analyzed. For satisfactory statistical estimation, however, the cost analyst needs an adequate sample size with a fairly broad range of outputs, and this requirement tends to lengthen the necessary period of data observations; this in turn necessitates a careful examination of a firm's total activities over the period of a cost study if accurate results are to be achieved.

Given the need for numerous data observations over a relatively short period, it is apparent that frequent data observations covering short production periods can improve the statistical results in empirical cost studies. Likewise, it is theoretically more satisfying to use frequent data observation points (for example, daily or weekly) so that output rates will be fairly constant *within* the observation period. At odds with this, however, is the fact that data collection and correction problems are magnified as the length of the observation period is shortened. Although the best length for the observation period will vary from situation to situation, one month is the period most frequently used. In other words, the various elements of variable

---

[3] A further difficulty encountered in statistical cost studies when prices fluctuate during the period of examination results from the substitution among the various input factors that takes place when their relative prices change. That is, price level changes rarely result in proportional changes in the prices of all goods and services and, as was shown in Chapter 6, optimal input combinations depend in part on the relative prices of resources. Changes in optimal input combinations will affect the cost projections that are relevant for managerial decision analysis.

costs incurred during each month are collected and compared with output produced during the month. A total period of perhaps two to three years (twenty-four to thirty-six months) can provide enough observations for statistical analysis, yet still be short enough that the plant and the product will have remained relatively unchanged. It is not possible to generalize about the best period of study for all cases as the facts of the individual case must always be taken into account.

This brief examination of some of the major data problems encountered in short-run statistical cost analysis points up the importance of proper data collection within the firm. That is, the value of statistical cost analysis to a firm is in large part a function of its cost accounting records. With this in mind, many firms are developing computerized management information systems in which cost and output data are recorded in sufficient detail to allow statistical analysis of their cost/output relations. It must be emphasized that, to be useful for managerial decision making purposes, these management information systems must go well beyond the collecting and reporting of data found in standard accounting systems. Thus, careful planning and a clear understanding of the relevant cost concepts used for various business decisions are required for establishing an information system that will provide the necessary inputs for proper decision analysis.

Statistical Short-Run Cost Functions

Once the data problems have been solved, cost analysts are faced with the problem of determining the proper functional form of the cost curve. A variety of linear and nonlinear models suitable for least squares regression analysis are available. If there are good theoretical or engineering reasons for using a particular model, that model will be selected. Often, however, there is no a priori reason for choosing one model over another, and in such cases the typical procedure is to fit several models to the cost/output data, then use the one that seems to fit best in terms of the statistical tests, especially R^2, the coefficient of determination. In other words, if one model has an R^2 of 0.80, indicating that the model explains 80 percent of the variation in total variable costs, and another model has an R^2 of 0.90, the second model will be relied upon for operating decisions.[4]

Linear Short-Run Cost Functions. For a great many production systems, a linear statistical cost curve of the form shown below provides an adequate fit of the cost/output data:

---

[4]This assumes that the independent variables in each model are the same; only the model structure is different. Without this proviso it would be possible to artificially inflate the R^2 for one model merely by adding additional explanatory variables. For this reason the adjusted coefficient of determination, $\bar{R}^2$, and the F-test described in Chapter 5 are typically used with the coefficient of determination in evaluating regression models.

$$C = a + bQ + \sum_{i=1}^{n} c_i X_i. \tag{8.1}$$

Here, C refers to the total variable cost during an observation period; Q is the quantity of output produced during that period; X_i designates all other independent variables whose cost effects the analyst wants to account for; and a, b, and c_i are the coefficients of the model as determined by the least squares regression technique. The other independent variables to be accounted for include such items as wage rates, fuel and materials costs, weather, input quality, production lot size, the product mix, and changes in product design. Including them in the model enables the analyst to obtain a better estimate of the relationship between cost and output.

The intercept coefficient a in this model is typically irrelevant. It cannot be interpreted as the firm's fixed costs because such costs are not included in the data. Even if total costs, as opposed to total variable costs, are used as the dependent variable, the intercept coefficient a may still not reflect the firm's fixed costs. This coefficient is simply the intercept of the estimated cost curve with the vertical axis. This intersection occurs where output is zero and usually lies far outside the range of cost/output data observation points.[5]

In those limited instances where firms or plants with very small levels of output are being considered and the measured costs are total costs, the a coefficient can be taken as an estimate, albeit an imperfect one, of fixed costs. In all instances, the interpretation of individual coefficient estimates must be restricted to the relevant range of observations.

Although a linear form for the cost/output relationship may be accurate for the range of available data, extrapolation far outside this range can lead to serious misstatements of the true relationship.[6] The problem of extrapolation outside the observation range is illustrated in Figure 8.1. Within the observed output range, Q_1 to Q_2, a linear function closely approximates the true cost/output relationship. Extrapolation beyond these limits, however, leads to inaccurate estimates of the firm's variable costs.

Coefficient b is the important one in a linear model of this type. As shown in both Figures 8.1 and 8.2, b provides an approximation to both marginal costs and average variable costs within the relevant output range.

Quadratic and Cubic Cost Functions. Two other forms, the quadratic and the cubic, are also widely used in empirical cost studies. Figures 8.3 and 8.4 illustrate the average variable cost curve and the marginal cost curve associated with quadratic

---

[5] As we pointed out in Chapter 5, extending the regression equation very far beyond the range of data observations is a hazardous procedure likely to result in significant errors.

[6] Since the short run is the period during which the law of diminishing returns is operative, we would expect such distortions to be the rule at very high output levels. That is, the estimated linear relationship should be taken only as an approximation, valid for a limited output range, to a true curvilinear relationship.

FIGURE 8.1

Linear Approximation of the Cost/Output Function

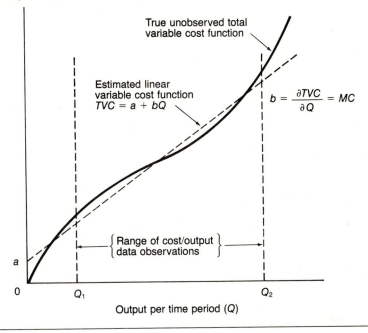

Total variable costs per time period ($)

True unobserved total variable cost function

Estimated linear variable cost function
$TVC = a + bQ$

$b = \dfrac{\partial TVC}{\partial Q} = MC$

$\left\{\begin{array}{c}\text{Range of cost/output}\\\text{data observations}\end{array}\right\}$

a

0 Q_1 Q_2

Output per time period (Q)

and cubic cost functions. Again, it should be emphasized that costs that are invariant with respect to output (fixed costs) are not typically included in the empirical estimates of short-run cost curves, so these curves are representative of variable costs only. An estimate of the fixed costs must be added to determine the firm's short-run total cost function.

Empirically Estimated Short-Run Cost Functions. Many empirical studies have been undertaken in attempts to ascertain the nature of cost/output relationships in the short run. Joel Dean's pioneering studies of short-run costs in a furniture factory, a hosiery mill, and a leather belt shop in the late 1930s and early 1940s all indicated that costs and output were linearly related and hence that marginal costs were constant over the observed output ranges.[7] In another cost study Dean estimated that

---

[7] These studies were originally reported in the following: Joel Dean, *Statistical Determination of Costs with Special Reference to Marginal Costs* (Chicago: University of Chicago Press, 1936); Joel Dean, *Statistical Cost Functions of a Hosiery Mill* (Chicago: University of Chicago Press, 1941); Joel Dean, "The Relation of Cost to Output for a Leather

FIGURE 8.2

Average Variable Cost and Marginal Cost for a Linear Cost Function—$TVC = a + bQ$

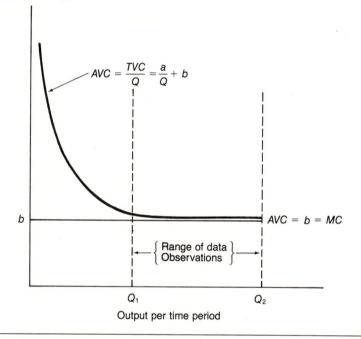

Cost per unit ($)

$$AVC = \frac{TVC}{Q} = \frac{a}{Q} + b$$

b

$AVC = b = MC$

Range of data Observations

Q_1 Q_2

Output per time period

Note: If $a = 0$, $AVC = b$, a constant. However, if $a > 0$, AVC declines continuously, but at a decreasing rate as output increases, because as Q becomes larger, a/Q becomes smaller and smaller.

marginal costs were constant in the hosiery and the shoe departments of a large department store, and slightly declining in the coat department.[8] Dean concluded his report of the latter study by noting that while the regression results indicated a linear cost function for two of the three departments, "the unexplained scatter of observations is great enough to permit a cubic of the traditional form to be fitted in each case. However, the curvature would be so slight as to be insignificant from a managerial viewpoint, so that it could scarcely affect any economic conclusions which might be derived from the linear functions."[9]

Belt Shop," National Bureau of Economic Research, Technical Paper No. 2, December 1941. They are also included in Joel Dean's *Statistical Cost Estimation* (Bloomington, Ind.: Indiana University Press, 1976), which provides an excellent discussion of empirical cost estimation techniques, uses, and limitations.

[8] Joel Dean, "Department Store Cost Functions," in *Studies in Mathematical Economics and Econometrics*, ed. Oskar Lange (London: Cambridge University Press, 1942).

[9] Dean, *Managerial Economics*, p. 254.

FIGURE 8.3

Average Variable Cost and Marginal Cost Curves for Quadratic Total Variable Cost Function—
TVC = a + bQ + cQ²

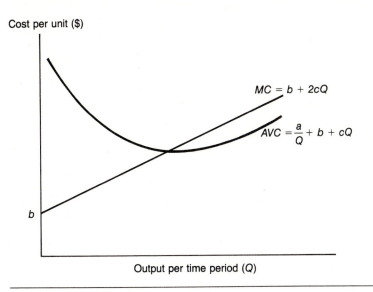

Cost per unit ($)

$MC = b + 2cQ$

$AVC = \dfrac{a}{Q} + b + cQ$

Output per time period (Q)

FIGURE 8.4

Average Variable Cost and Marginal Cost Curves for a Cubic Variable Cost Function—
TVC = a + bQ − cQ² + dQ³

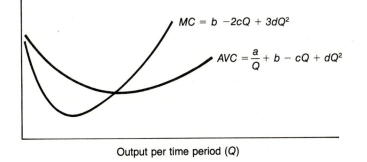

Cost per unit ($)

$MC = b - 2cQ + 3dQ^2$

$AVC = \dfrac{a}{Q} + b - cQ + dQ^2$

Output per time period (Q)

Another early cost study was that conducted by T. O. Yntema on costs at United States Steel Corporation.[10] The statistical cost function he estimated was:

$$\text{Total Cost} = \$132,100,000 + \$55.73Q,$$

where Q was a measure of output in tons of steel. Thus, Yntema found that the company's cost function was linear and that the marginal cost of producing an additional ton of steel was $55.73.

These early findings that short-run costs could be accurately estimated for many kinds of businesses by a linear function have been supported by more recent cost studies. By far the most complete statement of these empirical cost studies is found in J. Johnston's *Statistical Cost Analysis*, in which Johnston summarizes a considerable number of cost studies performed by others and then examines both short-run and long-run cost functions for a variety of firms and industries.[11] His short-run results tend to confirm the generality of the linear relationships reported earlier by Dean and by Yntema, and they lend further support to the hypothesis that marginal costs for many firms remain fairly constant over a substantial output range.

The empirical finding of constant marginal cost over a wide variety of production systems raises an interesting question. The law of diminishing productivity in microeconomic theory leads one to expect that short-run marginal costs would be increasing, imparting the traditional U shape to the average variable cost curve.[12] Why is it that this relationship is not observed in empirical studies?

Although a number of explanations for this phenomenon have been hypothesized, one of the most satisfying relates to the way input factors are utilized in a modern production system. In microeconomic theory, the quantity of the fixed factor *employed* in the production process is held constant in the short run, and varying quantities of the variable factor are used in conjunction with that fixed factor. In practice, the quantity of the fixed factor *actually used* often varies with output in some relatively constant ratio to the variable factor(s). Thus, only in theory is the fixed production factor truly fixed. The theory states that once a certain minimum level of production has been reached, additional units of the variable inputs exhibit diminishing productivity because of limitations imposed by the fixed factor. In actual production systems, however, capital equipment (the fixed factor) is frequently fixed with respect to cost (that is, costs are invariant with respect to output level) but quite variable with respect to actual usage. For example, a firm producing electronics devices may vary output by changing the number of assembly stations it operates, keeping the ratio of capital (fixed factor) to labor (variable factor) *actually employed* fixed over short-run production periods. Textile mills, where the number

---

[10] T. O. Yntema, "Steel Prices, Volume and Costs," *United States Steel Corporation Temporary National Economic Committee Papers*, vol. 2 (New York: U.S. Steel, 1940), p. 53.

[11] J. Johnston, *Statistical Cost Analysis* (New York: McGraw-Hill, 1960).

[12] The law of diminishing returns was examined in Chapter 6.

of spindles in operation varies with output, and electricity generation plants, where the number of generators in actual use is varied to increase or decrease output, provide other examples of variable employment of the "fixed" factor.

In these situations, the rate of utilization of each unit of the capital factor is nearly constant regardless of the production level.[13] Since fixed and variable inputs are being used in constant proportions over wide ranges of production output, the law of diminishing productivity does not hold, and the marginal cost of production remains constant. For these reasons the empirical findings are not particularly surprising.

LONG-RUN STATISTICAL COST ESTIMATION

Statistical estimation of long-run cost curves, although similar in many respects to short-run cost estimation, is typically somewhat more complex. In the long run, all costs are variable, and the problem is to determine the shape of the least-cost production curve for plants of different size. Total cost curves must be estimated, and this, in turn, introduces a number of additional difficulties.

As with short-run analysis, one can analyze the long-run cost/output relationship by examining a single firm over a long period. In this case the assumption that plant size is held constant during the examination period is removed, and total costs are regressed against output. The basic problem with this approach is that it is almost impossible to find a situation where the scale of a firm has been variable enough to allow statistical estimation of a long-run cost curve while, at the same time, technology and other extraneous conditions have remained constant. Without constant technology, the function estimated in this manner will bear little resemblance to the relevant long-run cost function necessary for planning purposes.

Because of the difficulties encountered in using time-series data to estimate long-run cost functions, a different procedure, cross-sectional regression analysis, is frequently employed. This procedure involves a comparison of different-size firms (or plants) at one point in time, regressing total costs against a set of independent variables. The key independent variable is again a measure of output, and other independent variables—such as regional wage rates, fuel costs, and the like— are included to account for the impact on cost of factors other than the level of output.

The use of cross-sectional analysis, as opposed to time-series analysis, for estimating long-run cost functions reduces some estimation problems and magnifies others. For example, since the data all represent factor prices at the same point in time, the problem of price inflation (or deflation) is removed. A new problem arises,

---

[13] Negotiated work rules also add to the fixity of capital and labor input ratios. Many labor contracts specify within narrow ranges the combinations of labor and capital equipment that can be utilized in a production system and the rate at which the capital equipment is operated.

however, because factor input prices vary in different regions of the country; unless all the firms in the sample are located in the same region, interregional price variations may distort the analysis.

A second difficulty in cross-sectional studies can be traced to variations in accounting procedures. Differing depreciation policies among firms and varying techniques for amortizing major expenses such as research and development costs can substantially distort the true cost/output relationship.

A similar distortion in statistical cost analysis can arise if the firms examined use different means of factor payment. For example, one firm might pay relatively low wages to its employees but may have a substantial profit-sharing program. If this firm's costs are compared with those of a firm that pays higher wages but has no profit sharing, and if shared profits are not included in wage costs, it is clear that an adjustment must be made prior to estimating the cost function for the industry.

Finally, even if all these data problems are solved so that the effects on costs of all factors other than output are held constant, a last requirement must also be met if we are to estimate accurately the long-run cost function. A basic assumption in the use of cross-sectional data is that all firms are operating at the point along the long-run curve at which costs are minimized. That is, the cross-sectional technique assumes that all firms are operating in an efficient manner and are using the most efficient plant available for producing whatever level of output they are producing. If this assumption holds, the cost/output relationship found in the analysis does trace a long-run cost curve, such as that shown as *LRAC* in Figure 8.5. If this assumption is violated, however, the least squares regression line will lie above the true *LRAC* curve, and costs will be overstated.

Even more important than the uniform overstatement of average cost is the possibility that the true curvature in the long-run average cost curve may be distorted

FIGURE 8.5

Estimating Long-Run Average Cost Curves with Cross-sectional Data

Cost per unit ($)

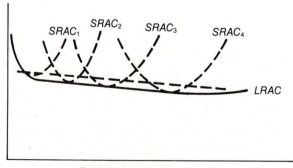

Output per time period (units)

and may thereby either under- or overstate any economies or diseconomies of scale in the industry being examined. For example, if the smaller firms in Figure 8.5 are operating well to the right of their optimal output, the estimated *LRAC* curve will have a downward slope much steeper than the true *LRAC* curve, and this bias will cause one to overestimate the extent of economies of scale in the industry. Similarly, scale economies may be underestimated due to a selection bias which results if small high-cost firms fail to compete successfully, become bankrupt, and thus fail to get included in the cost study.

Empirical Long-Run Cost Functions

The great majority of empirically estimated long-run cost functions exhibit sharply increasing returns to scale at low output levels, but the extent of these scale economies declines as output increases and constant returns appear to hold at a high output level. This means that the long-run average cost curve decreases at a decreasing rate as output increases, finally becoming horizontal. Very few studies have found evidence of decreasing returns to scale—an upturn in the average cost curve—at high output levels.

The results just discussed have caused researchers to hypothesize that typical long-run average cost curves are L-shaped as opposed to the U-shaped curves postulated in microeconomic theory. P. J. D. Wiles, for example, in discussing the results of his study of forty-four sets of data on long-run cost/output relationships, states that "average costs descend like the left-hand branch of a capital U, swiftly at first then more gently. Decreasing costs with size are almost universal. But the U seldom turns up. Sharply increasing costs with size are practically unknown and even slight increases are rare."[14] Wiles concludes that most of the cost functions "obey what we may call the law of L-shaped costs."

The study by Johnston led him to similar conclusions about the nature of long-run average costs. In examining the costs of electrical power generation in Great Britain, for example, Johnston found that average costs fell initially and then leveled off, indicating that "economies of scale in electricity generation can be fully exploited by firms of median size."[15]

In a recent study, one of the authors analyzed railroad freight service costs for light density and main railroad lines.[16] Light density lines are typically quite short (5 to 20 miles) and are used to connect a few shippers with the larger main line railroad track that connects towns and cities. Since fixed costs relating to track, train, and facility investments are usually quite high, light density railroad freight service is an example of service which is subject to increasing returns to scale. Variable labor,

---

[14]P. J. D. Wiles, *Prices, Cost, and Output* (Oxford: Basil, Blackwell and Mott, 1956).

[15]Johnston, *Statistical Cost Analysis*, p. 73.

[16]Mark Hirschey, "Estimation of Cost Elasticities for Light Density Railroad Freight Service," *Land Economics* (August 1979), pp. 366–378.

TABLE 8.1

Cost-Output Elasticity Estimates for Light Density and Main Line Railroad Freight Service, 1973 (Standard Errors in Parentheses)

	Cost-Output Elasticity	
Output Level	Light Density Service	Main Line Service
Sample Minimum	0.2384 (0.0021)	1.0787 (0.0112)
Sample Average − 1 Standard Deviation $(\bar{Q} - \sigma_Q)$	0.2666 (0.0006)	1.0565 (0.0334)
Sample Average $(\bar{Q})$	0.2660 (0.0002)	1.0122 (0.0361)
Sample Average + 1 Standard Deviation $(\bar{Q} + \sigma_Q)$	0.2423 (0.0003)	0.9998 (0.0413)
Sample Maximum	0.1431 (0.0007)	0.9638 (0.0502)

fuel, and equipment expenses constitute a more substantial share of total costs for main line service, and as a result, such service may not be subject to such increasing returns.

To empirically examine the nature of returns to scale for light density and main line railroad freight service, cost elasticities were analyzed. Elasticities were estimated at the sample average level of output $(\bar{Q})$, at the sample average plus and minus one standard deviation of output $(\bar{Q} + \sigma_q$ and $\bar{Q} - \sigma_q)$, and at the sample maximum and minimum output levels. Calculating a range of cost elasticity estimates enables one to determine how returns to scale vary over the output levels analyzed.

Table 8.1 reports these elasticity estimates and their standard errors.[17] As expected, increasing returns to scale are apparent at all output levels for light density railroad freight service. On the other hand, economies of scale for main line freight service appear to be essentially constant.

Alternative Cost Estimation Techniques

Because of the difficulty of obtaining satisfactory statistical estimates of long-run cost/output relationships, several alternative means of empirically examining cost

---

[17] Recall from Chapter 7 that when cost elasticity is less than 1 ($\varepsilon_C < 1$) increasing returns to scale are implied, $\varepsilon_C > 1$ implies decreasing returns to scale, and $\varepsilon_C = 1$ implies constant returns to scale.

functions have been developed. Two of these, the survivor technique and the engineering technique, have proved to be very useful in certain situations where statistical cost estimation is tenuous or impossible because of the absence of adequate data, or where checks on statistical cost estimates are sought. These techniques are discussed below.

Survivor Technique. The survivor principle was developed by George Stigler.[18] The basic idea behind this technique is that more efficient firms—that is, those with lower average costs—will survive through time. Therefore, by examining the size makeup of an industry over time, one can determine the nature of its cost/output relations.

More specifically, Stigler proposes that one classify the firms in an industry by size and calculate the share of the industry output or capacity provided by each size class over time. If the share of one class declines over time, that size production facility is assumed to be relatively inefficient. If the relative share increases, however, firms of that size are presumed to be relatively efficient and thus to have lower average costs.

The survivor technique has been applied to several industries to examine the question of returns to scale. Stigler examined the distribution of steel production among firms of varying size in 1930, 1938, and 1951.[19] He found that over this period the percentage of industry output accounted for by the smallest- and largest-size classes declined, while the output share of medium-size firms increased. These findings indicate a long-run average cost curve such as that illustrated in Figure 8.6. Returns to scale are increasing at low output levels, are nearly constant over a wide range of intermediate output, and are decreasing at higher output levels.

Stigler also applied the technique to the automobile industry. Again, he found that the smallest firms showed a continual decline in their share of total industry output; he concluded from this that average costs decline with size. The small firms' losses were distributed equally among medium-size and larger firms, indicating first increasing, then constant, returns to scale. Since there was no indication of diseconomies of scale at very high output levels, the conclusion was that the automobile industry's long-run average cost curve is L-shaped.

In a continuing study of economies of scale in the Portland cement industry Bruce T. Allen also finds an L-shaped long-run average cost curve.[20] Table 8.2 provides data on the composition of cement production by plant size for the years 1973 and 1980. The data indicate that plant-size classes of less than 700,000 tons a year accounted for smaller shares of industry capacity in 1980 than in 1973 and that

---

[18]George J. Stigler, "The Economies of Scale," *Journal of Law and Economics* 1 (October 1958), pp. 54–71.

[19]Ibid.

[20]Bruce T. Allen, "Economies of Scale in the Portland Cement Industry, 1973–1980," working paper, Michigan State University, 1971, revised April 8, 1981; and "Vertical Integration and Market Foreclosure: The Case of Cement and Concrete," *Journal of Law and Economics* 14 (April 1971), pp. 251–274.

FIGURE 8.6

Long-Run Average Costs for Steel Production as Determined by the Survivor Technique

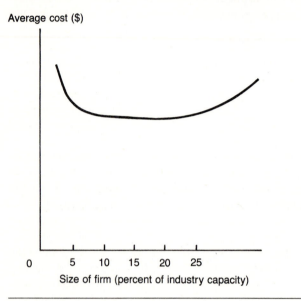

Average cost ($)

Size of firm (percent of industry capacity)

TABLE 8.2

Economies of Scale in the Portland Cement Industry, 1973–1980

Plant Capacity (thousand short tons per year)	Percent of Total Capacity	
	1973	1980
100– 299	7.21	4.22
300– 399	12.14	6.92
400– 499	13.36	13.02
500– 599	14.82	12.38
600– 699	12.71	11.92
700– 799	8.30	13.33
800– 899	5.55	6.98
900– 999	7.28	3.91
1000–1099	1.15	5.33
1100–1199	3.74	8.22
1200–1299	5.41	5.17
1300–1499	0.00	2.86
1500–1699	3.38	3.26
1700–1899	2.06	0.00
over 2000	2.88	2.47

Source: Reprinted by permission of the author from Bruce T. Allen, "Economies of Scale in the Portland Cement Industry, 1973–1980," working paper, Michigan State University, 1971, Revised, April 8, 1981.

plant-size classes between 700,000 and 1.5 million tons accounted for larger shares of industry capacity in 1980 than in 1973.

Allen's study does not reveal the conventional U-shaped long-run average cost curve; rather, it suggests that long-run average cost decreases as plant capacity increases to about 700,000 tons and that they are then flat at least up to a capacity of 1.5 million tons. Beyond 1.5 million tons there is slight evidence of diseconomies of scale. However, in these large capacity classes the data are dominated by single-firm activities and may be explained by area market conditions rather than scale economies. Thus, it appears that the minimum efficient scale in the Portland cement industry is about 700,000 tons per year and that any diseconomies are weak and exist only for plants above 1.5 million tons.

Although the survivor technique is a valuable tool for examining cost/output relations, it does have some severe limitations. First, its premise is the notion that survival is directly related to minimization of long-run average costs. As is demonstrated in more detail in Chapter 10, this premise implicitly assumes that the firms examined are operating in a highly competitive market structure. If markets are protected by regulation or various barriers to entry, even inefficient smaller firms can survive for extended periods. Second, high transportation costs can make survival possible for strategically located firms despite productive inefficiencies. Third, in many industries inefficient smaller firms survive by emphasizing personalized service or customized production. Successful product differentiation often makes it possible for smaller firms to not only survive but flourish in the face of competition from larger, more efficient rivals.

Finally, because of the very long-run nature of the analysis, the survivor technique is particularly susceptible to the problem of distorted results arising from inflation and changing technology. In many instances inventions or innovations over time favor firms in specific-size classes. Resulting changes in the distribution of industry output may reveal less about movements along industry long-run average cost curves (i.e., economies of scale) than they do about downward shifts in cost/output relationships.

Engineering Technique. The engineering method of cost analysis is based directly on the physical relationship expressed in the production function for a particular product or firm. On the basis of a knowledge of the production technology involved, the optimal input combination for producing any given output quantity is determined. The cost curve is then formulated by multiplying each input in these least-cost combinations by its price and summing to develop the cost function.

The engineering technique comes the closest of any of the estimation procedures to reflecting the timeless nature of theoretical cost functions. It is based on the currently available technology, and it alleviates the possibility of confounding the results through improper data observations. That is, while the cost observations used for statistical cost estimation may be contaminated by any number of extraneous factors, engineering estimation abstracts from these complications by coupling current price quotations from suppliers with estimates of required quantities of various inputs.

The engineering method of cost estimation has proved to be useful for examining cost/output relationships in such areas as oil refining, chemical production, and nuclear power generation. Leslie Cookenboo, Jr., for example, used the technique to estimate cost functions for oil pipeline systems.[21] Cookenboo first analyzed the input/output relationships for the three main factors in the system—pipe diameter, horsepower of pumps, and number of pumping stations—in order to determine the production function for the system. By adding input prices to the analysis, he was able to determine the least-cost combination of inputs for each production level and to develop the long-run cost curve for oil pipelines. His results showed that long-run costs decline continuously over the range of output levels examined.

The engineering method of cost estimation is not without pitfalls, and care must be exercised in using the method if accurate cost functions are to be developed. The difficulty often comes in trying to extend engineering production functions beyond the range of existing systems, or in going from pilot plant operations to full-scale production facilities. These problems are illustrated by the difficulties encountered by a major chemical company in developing a facility that made use of a new production technology. The firm completed an engineering cost study based on projected input/output relationships developed from a small pilot facility. The estimated cost of constructing the new plant was $100 million; and it was projected that output would have a marginal cost of approximately $100 a ton, substantially below the costs in existing facilities. Once construction got underway, however, it became clear that the projection of production relations beyond the pilot plant's size were woefully inadequate. A planned two-year construction period dragged on for five years, and construction costs ballooned to $300 million. After completion of the plant, actual marginal costs of production were $150 a ton, a 50 percent increase over the estimated level. Although this is an extreme case, it does illustrate that while the engineering method can provide a useful alternative to statistical cost estimation, it too must be applied with great care if accurate cost projection is to result.

SUMMARY

Empirical determination of a firm's cost function is a necessary requirement for optimal decision making. In this chapter a variety of techniques for analyzing both short-run and long-run cost/output relationships were examined.

---

[21]Leslie Cookenboo, Jr., *Crude Oil Pipe Lines and Competition in the Oil Industry* (Cambridge, Mass.: Harvard University Press, 1955).

The primary statistical methodology used for cost estimation is least squares regression analysis. Properly conducted time-series analysis of a single firm's cost/output relationship can provide an excellent estimate of the firm's short-run variable cost function. This function indicates the nature of marginal costs and average variable costs, the relevant-cost concepts for short-run decision making.

Statistical estimation of long-run costs typically involves cross-sectional analysis as opposed to time-series regression analysis. Here the cost/output relationships for many firms of varying size are analyzed to determine the nature of the total cost function for firms of different scale.

Two major findings dominate the work of researchers in the area of cost analysis. In the short run the relationship between cost and output appears to be best approximated in most cases by a linear function. This means that marginal costs are constant over a significant range of output for most firms. Long-run estimation has typically indicated that sharply increasing returns to scale (decreasing average cost) are available over low output ranges in most industries, giving way to constant returns (constant average cost) at higher output levels. Decreasing returns to scale (increasing average costs), even at very high output quantities, appear to be the exception rather than the rule for most long-run cost functions.

Because of the difficulties encountered in statistical cost estimation, alternative techniques of empirical analysis are frequently employed. The survivor technique and the engineering technique are two methods commonly used for this purpose.

The survivor technique is based on the assumption that more efficient firms—those with lower average costs—will have a greater probability of survival over time. Therefore, by examining the size makeup of an industry over time, one can determine the nature of its cost/output relationships.

The engineering technique is based on the physical relationships expressed in the production function for a firm. Using engineering estimates of input/output relationships, one determines the optimal production system and multiplies each required input by its cost to determine the cost function. This method is particularly useful for estimating cost relationships for new products or plants involving new technologies where the historical data necessary for statistical cost analysis are unavailable.

QUESTIONS

8.1 The law of diminishing productivity in microeconomic theory leads one to expect that short-run marginal (and average variable) cost curves would be U-shaped. What factors do you suppose lead to the empirical finding of constant marginal costs for most firms?

8.2 Name and briefly elaborate on three common problems encountered in short-run cost analysis.

8.3 Short-run statistical cost studies have been reported for a wide variety of industries, ranging from autos to Xerox machines. Long-run cost studies, on the other hand, have been restricted to a few industries, such as steel manufacturing, banks, savings and loans, insurance, and utilities. Why do you suppose so many more short-run than long-run studies have been conducted?

8.4 What conditions are necessary in order to estimate a long-run cost function?

8.5 For long-run statistical cost estimation, cross-sectional analysis, as opposed to time-series analysis, is used partly to overcome the problem of changing technology. Does the use of cross-sectional data necessarily eliminate this problem? Why or why not?

8.6 If the total cost/output relationship is analyzed using regression analysis, can the intercept term be interpreted as an unbiased estimate of fixed costs?

8.7 Does the survivor technique for estimating long-run cost/output relationships overcome the problem of changing technology?

PROBLEMS

8.1 Caufield Family Farms has just completed a cost study of its milk production operation. By regressing total variable costs on milk production the firm estimated the following equation:

$$\text{Cost} = \$10,500 + \$0.89 \; Q - \$0.005 \; Q^2$$
$$\phantom{\text{Cost} = }(6,000) \quad (0.18) \quad\;\; (0.093)$$

Here Q is milk production in gallons and the numbers in parentheses are the standard errors of the coefficients. The R^2 for the equation was 0.87, and the standard error of the estimate was 22. Monthly observations over a two-year period were used in the study.

    a. Interpret this estimated cost function. That is, explain the relationship between milk production and cost as depicted by this equation. Be as complete as possible.

8.2 Safeco, Inc., is a wholesaler of products designed to increase the safety of the home and work environment. Currently Safeco has an opportunity to offer its "Stay-Alert Smoke Detector" through a large chain of discount hardware stores located in southeastern states. Safeco executives anticipate that an initial order for 200,000 units can be placed, provided that a mutually agreeable price can be attained.

    In setting unit prices Safeco must consider estimates of production, warranty, and inventory expenses:

Expense Category	Estimated Unit Costs
Production	$C_P = 3 + .015\, Q$
Warranty	$C_W = 1 + .01\, Q$
Inventory	$C_I = 1$

Q is unit sales in thousands of units, and a 15 percent cost of capital is embedded in these costs. Total cost estimates are unbiased, and the standard error of the total cost estimate is $100,000.

Traditionally, Safeco has only entered into sales agreements which offer a 95 percent probability of at least covering total costs (including the cost of capital). Safeco's marketing department suggests that offering the above 200,000 units at a price of $10.50 each would be consistent with this policy.

a. Calculate expected total costs for 200,000 units.

b. Calculate the probability of at least covering these expected total costs given that the marketing department's proposal is adopted.

c. What price per unit should be charged if Safeco is to adhere to established corporate policy?

8.3 The federal government's decision during the late 1970s to decontrol oil prices is expected to affect immediate and future domestic oil production dramatically. In particular, a veritable explosion in the use of secondary (steam) and tertiary (chemical additive) methods of oil recovery is expected. This new drilling activity will undoubtedly increase demand for the products of the oil service industry. The current environment presents both a challenge and somewhat of a dilemma to Tulsa Drill Bit, Inc. While it currently dominates the market for high stress drill bits with a 40 percent share of the market, entry by new and highly sophisticated competitors is likely unless a substantial expansion program is undertaken. It seems that the time has come to "get big or get out." Petroleum Products, Inc., has made the exit alternative more palatable with an offer to purchase (privately held) Tulsa for $10 million (nearly double current book value).

Tulsa has retained you to advise it in its decision whether to accept the PPI offer. You have conducted an engineering cost analysis of industry plant data for 1982 and found:

$$C = 20 + 5\, Q + 0.25\, Q^2$$

$$C = \text{total cost (in millions of dollars)},$$

$$Q = \text{output (in thousands of drill bits)}.$$

Furthermore, you learn that in 1982 Tulsa sold 9,000 drill bits at $9,500 each. Future growth is expected to expand the size of the market for drill bits to 96,000 units by 1986.

    a. Calculate and fully interpret the current (1982) breakeven level of production.

    b. Determine the output level of the minimum efficient scale (MES) plant size.

    c. In light of the expected future size of the market for drill bits, how would you evaluate the future potential for competition in the industry? (Assume cost conditions don't change between now and 1986.)

    d. If the current cost of capital for firms in Tulsa's risk class is 20 percent, should Tulsa expand or should PPI's offer be accepted?

8.4 Jasper Batteries, Inc., is considering further expansion in the storage battery industry and has asked you to make an analysis of such a move's profit potential. In particular, the marketing department has suggested building a $10 million plant capable of producing 2 million batteries per year.

    To facilitate your analysis you consult a recent (1982) trade association study of plants in the industry which found (*t*-statistics in parentheses):

$$C = 4,000 + 18\,Q + 0.001\,Q^2 \qquad\qquad R^2 = 0.88$$
$$\quad\;\;(12.5)\quad(6.8)\qquad(5.2) \qquad\qquad\quad n = 39$$

C = total costs (in thousands of dollars) $\qquad F = 132$

Q = output (in thousands of batteries) $\qquad S.E.E. = 2,000$

During 1982 average plant fixed costs included capital costs of $2 million, reflecting an average 12 percent cost of capital.

    a. Define minimum efficient scale from a theoretical point of view, and discuss three aspects that determine its competitive consequences.

    b. Calculate 1982 minimum efficient scale for the storage battery industry.

    c. Calculate the current profit probability of the marketing department's proposal if industry prices are stable at $25 per battery and current capital costs are 24 percent per year.

SELECTED REFERENCES

Allen, Bruce T. "Vertical Integration and Market Foreclosure: The Case of Cement and Concrete." *Journal of Law and Economics* 14 (April 1971): 251–274.

Benston, George J. "Multiple Regression Analysis of Cost Behavior." *Accounting Review* (October 1966): 657–672.

Blair, Roger D., Jackson, Jerry R., and Vogel, Ronald J. "Economies of Scale in the Administration of Health Insurance." *Review of Economics and Statistics* 57 (May 1975): 185–189.

Christensen, Laurits R., and Greene, William H. "Economies of Scale in U.S. Electric Power Generation." *Journal of Political Economy* 84 (August 1976): 655–676.

Dean, Joel. *Statistical Cost Estimation.* Bloomington, Ind.: Indiana University Press, 1976.

Frech, H. E., and Ginsberg, Paul B. "Optimal Scale in Medical Practice: A Survivor Analysis." *Journal of Business* 47 (January 1974): 23–36.

Hirschey, Mark. "Estimation of Cost Elasticities for Light Density Railroad Freight Service." *Land Economics* 55 (August 1979): 366–378.

Hirshleifer, Jack A. "The Firm's Cost Function, A Successful Reconstruction." *Journal of Business* 35 (July 1962): 235–255.

Keeler, Theodore E. "Railroad Costs, Returns to Scale and Excess Capacity." *Review of Economics and Statistics* 56 (May 1974): 201–208.

Koot, Ronald S., and Walker, David A. "Short-Run Cost Functions of a Multiproduct Firm." *Journal of Industrial Economics* 18 (April 1970): 118–128.

Longbrake, William A. "Statistical Cost Analysis." *Financial Management* 2 (Spring 1973): 48–56.

Moore, Frederick T. "Economies of Scale: Some Statistical Evidence." *Quarterly Journal of Economics* 73 (May 1959): 232–245.

Stigler, George J. "The Economies of Scale." *Journal of Law and Economics* 1 (October 1958): 54–71.

CHAPTER 9
LINEAR PROGRAMMING

Linear programming is an analytical technique used to determine the optimal solution to a decision problem.[1] Like calculus, linear programming is a mathematical tool for solving maximization and minimization problems. It is particularly powerful in solving problems when constraints limit or restrict the course of action available to the decision maker. Since most managerial problems are of this nature, linear programming is a useful analytical technique for managerial decision making.

The value of linear programming in managerial decision making can be seen by considering a few of the many types of constrained optimization problems to which

---

[1]Linear programming is only one of a series of analytical techniques, known collectively as *mathematical programming*, that are used to solve constrained optimization problems. While knowledge of more advanced mathematical programming techniques is useful in many decision situations, an understanding of linear programming provides a solid base for examining the use of all these techniques, and it is appropriate that we restrict our discussion to this method in a managerial economics textbook.

it has been applied. Applications cover such diverse managerial problems as product design and product mix specification, input allocation in production systems (including job assignment of key personnel), product distribution analysis (including plant location and delivery routing), promotional mix in marketing activities, inventory and cash management, and capital budgeting (investment) decisions. Although quite different in terms of their focus, each of these problem structures involves the allocation of scarce resources to achieve some specific goal.

In the area of production-related decisions, firms are often faced with a variety of capacity limitations. Limited availability of skilled labor and specialized equipment, fixed plant size, and limits on raw materials or energy inputs can all constrain production. When such capacity constraints exist, managers must exercise careful judgment to insure that scarce resources are used in the most efficient manner possible to produce only the products that provide the greatest returns or profits.

For example, an oil company has a specified quantity of crude oil and a fixed refinery capacity. It can produce gasoline of different octane ratings, diesel fuel, heating oil, kerosene, or lubricants. Given its crude oil supplies and refinery capacity, what mix of outputs should it produce? Integrated forest products companies face a similar problem. Because they have a limited supply of logs and limited mill capacity, their problem is to determine the optimum output mix of lumber, plywood, paper, and other wood products.

A related production problem involves determining the best way of producing a given output. A firm owns two plants that can be used to produce its products. The plants employ somewhat different technologies, so their cost functions are different. How should production be allocated between the two plants to minimize the total cost of production, subject to these constraints: (1) Both plants must, because of a union contract, operate at least thirty hours a week; and (2) at least 100,000 units of output must be produced each week to satisfy the firm's supply contracts.

In marketing, a frequently encountered issue is: What is the optimal advertising mix among various media, where *optimal* is defined as that mix which minimizes the cost of reaching a specified number of potential customers with certain characteristics of age, income, education, and other factors?

In finance, firms may have a large number of investment opportunities but be limited in the funds available for investment. What set of projects will maximize the value of new long-term investments, subject to the constraint that the total capital budget not exceed some specified maximum? Moreover, firms must hold balances of cash, a nonearning asset. What is the minimum amount of cash that can be held, subject to the constraint that the probability of running short of cash must be kept below some minimum value?

In none of these problem situations is there a simple rule-of-thumb solution. The interrelationships involved are complex, and arriving at optimal solutions requires careful analysis of the alternatives. The fact that linear programming has proved useful in solving such a broad range of constrained maximization and minimization problems indicates its value as a managerial decision tool. Linear programming is indeed a powerful technique, one which promises to be applied to business problems with ever greater frequency in future years.

RELATIONSHIP OF LINEAR PROGRAMMING TO THE LAGRANGIAN TECHNIQUE

In Chapter 2 we described the Lagrangian-multiplier technique for solving constrained optimization problems. We have described linear programming as another methodology for constrained optimization. Accordingly, one might question the reason for developing linear programming. Why not just use the Lagrangian technique for solving all constrained optimization problems?

The answer is that linear programming can handle a class of problems that cannot be solved by the Lagrangian technique. Specifically, with the Lagrangian method, the constraints must be stated in the form of equalities and must be met *exactly*. For example, a Lagrangian problem might be to minimize cost in a production system subject to the constraint that *exactly* 40 hours of machine time be used. The corresponding linear programming problem would be to minimize costs subject to the constraint that *no more than* 40 hours of time be used. In other words, in the Lagrangian system the constraints must be *equalities* (machine-time use = 40 hours); in linear programming the constraints may be *inequalities* (machine-time ≤ 40 hours).

In managerial problems, many constraints are in fact inequalities rather than equalities. Constraints imposed are likely to involve either upper or lower limits on resource use or minimum product specifications which must be met but which can be exceeded. For this reason, linear programming can be more useful than Lagrangian calculus for many practical applications in management.

ASSUMPTION OF LINEARITY

Linear programming is more general than the Lagrangian technique in that it permits inequalities in the constraints, but it is also more restrictive in that all relationships are assumed to be linear. What relationships are involved, and how important is the assumption of linearity likely to be?

The basic relationship involved in linear programming problems typically encountered in business and economics revolves around revenue functions, cost functions, and their composite, the profit function. Each of these must be linear; that is, as output increases, revenues, costs, and profits must increase linearly. For revenues to increase linearly with output, product prices must be constant. For costs to rise linearly with output, two conditions are required: (1) The firm's production function must be linear (that is, it must be homogeneous of degree 1), meaning that returns to scale are constant; and (2) input prices must be constant. Constant input prices, when coupled with a linear production function, result in a linear total cost function.[2]

Under what conditions are product and factor prices likely to be constant? In other words, when can a firm buy unlimited quantities of its inputs, and sell unlimited amounts of its products, without having to change prices? The answer is, under conditions of pure competition. Does this mean that linear programming is applicable only for purely competitive industries and, further, only for competitive industries where returns to scale are constant? The answer is no, because linear programming is used for decision making over limited output ranges. Because input and product prices are approximately constant over these ranges, the profit function can be approximated by a linear relationship.

To illustrate, if an oil company is deciding the optimal output mix for a refinery with a capacity of 150,000 barrels of oil per day, it may be perfectly valid to assume that crude oil costs $40 a barrel, regardless of how much is purchased, and that products can be sold at constant prices, regardless of the quantities offered. The firm may have to pay more for crude oil and may have to sell its output at lower prices if it tries to expand the refinery by a factor of 10, but within the range of feasible outputs (up to 150,000 barrels a day) prices are approximately constant. Further, up to its capacity limits, it is reasonable to expect that a doubling of crude oil inputs leads to a doubling of output; therefore, returns to scale are constant. Roughly the same conditions hold for forest-product companies, office-equipment manufacturers, automobile producers, and most other firms.

We see, then, that in many instances the linearity assumptions are valid. Further, in many more cases, when the assumption does not hold precisely, linear approximations will not seriously distort the analysis.

LINEAR PROGRAMMING AND PRODUCTION PLANNING: ONE PRODUCT

Although linear programming has been applied in almost all aspects of business management, it has been developed most fully and is used most frequently in production decisions. Often the decision problem is to determine the least-cost combination of inputs needed to produce a particular product. In other cases, the problem may be concerned with obtaining the maximum level of output from a fixed

---

[2]The relationship between production and cost functions when input prices are constant is developed more fully in Chapter 7.

quantity of resources. Both problems can be readily solved by linear programming. To see this more clearly, we start with a simple case and examine the problem faced by a firm that can use two inputs in various combinations to produce a single product. Then, in later sections, we examine more realistic but necessarily more complex cases.

Production Processes

Assume that a firm produces a single product, Q, using two inputs, L and K, which might represent labor and capital. Further, instead of the possibility of continuous substitution between L and K, as was hypothesized in Chapter 6, assume that there are only four possible input combinations with which the firm can produce Q. In other words, four different production processes are available to the firm for making Q, each of which uses a different but fixed combination of the two inputs, L and K. In most industries, this is an entirely reasonable assumption, much more reasonable than continuous substitution. The four production processes discussed here, for example, might be thought of as being four different plants, each with its fixed asset configuration and each requiring a specific amount of labor to operate the equipment. Alternatively, they could be four different assembly stations or assembly lines, each using a slightly different combination of capital equipment and labor.

The four production processes are illustrated in Figure 9.1. Process A requires the combination of 15 units of L and 1 unit of K for each unit of Q produced. Process B uses 10 units of L and 2 units of K for each unit of output; while Processes C and D use 7.5 units of L with 3 units of K, and 5 units of L with 5 units of K, respectively, for each unit of Q produced. The four production processes are illustrated as rays in the figure. Each point along the production ray for Process A combines L and K in the ratio 15 to 1; and Process Rays B, C, and D are developed in the same way. Each point along a single production ray combines the two inputs in a fixed ratio, with the ratios differing from one production process to another. If we assume that L and K represent labor and capital inputs, we can view the four production processes as different plants employing different production techniques. Process A, for example, is very labor intensive in relation to the other production systems, while B, C, and D are based on increasingly capital-intensive technologies.

Examining Process A, we see that Point A_1 indicates the combination of L and K required to produce 1 unit of output using that production system. Doubling the quantities of both L and K doubles the quantity of Q produced; this is indicated by the distance moved along Ray A from A_1 to A_2. In other words, the line segment $0A_2$ is exactly twice the length of line segment $0A_1$ and thus represents twice as much output. Further, along Production Process Ray A, the distance $0A_1 = A_1A_2 = A_2A_3 = A_3A_4 = A_4A_5$. Each of these line segments indicates the addition of 1 unit of output, using increased quantities of L and K in the fixed ratio of 15 to 1.

Output along the ray increases proportionately with increases in the input fac-

FIGURE 9.1

Production Process Rays in Linear Programming

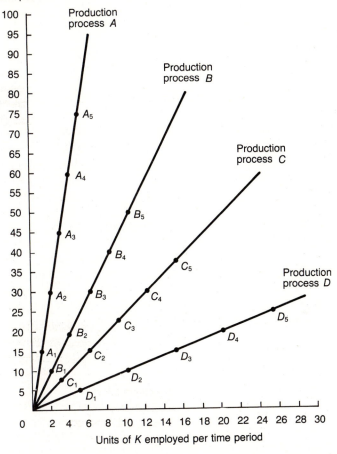

Units of L employed
per time period

Units of K employed per time period

tors. Thus, if each input is doubled, output is doubled; or if inputs are increased by a factor of 10 percent, output increases in the same proportion. This follows from the linearity assumption noted above: Each production process must exhibit constant returns to scale.

Output is measured in the same way along the other three production process rays in Figure 9.1. For example, Point C_1 indicates the combination of L and K required to produce 1 unit of Q using Process C. The production of 2 units of Q by that process requires the combination of L and K indicated at Point C_2, and the same is true for Points C_3, C_4, and C_5. Note that while the production of additional units by Process C is indicated by line segments of equal length, just as for Process A, the line segments are of different lengths between the various production systems. That is, although each production process exhibits constant returns to scale, allowing us to determine output quantities by measuring the length of the process ray in question, equal distances along *different* process rays do *not* ordinarily indicate equal output quantities.

Production Isoquants

Joining points of equal output on the four production process rays provides us with a set of isoquant curves, as illustrated in Figure 9.2, where isoquants for $Q = 1, 2, 3, 4,$ and 5 are shown. These curves have precisely the same interpretation as the isoquants developed in Chapter 6. They represent all possible combinations of Input Factors L and K that can be used to produce a given quantity of output. The production isoquants in linear programming are composed of linear segments connecting the various production processes, and the segments of the various isoquants are always parallel to one another. For example, Line Segment A_1B_1 is parallel to Segment A_2B_2; similarly, Isoquant Segment B_3C_3 is parallel to B_2C_2.

The points along each segment of an isoquant between two process rays represent a combination of output from each of the two adjoining production processes. Consider Point X in Figure 9.2, which represents production of a total of 4 units of Q using 25 units of L and 16 units of K. None of the available production processes can be used to manufacture Q using L and K in the ratio 25 to 16, but that combination is possible by producing part of the output with Process C and part with Process D. In this case, 2 units of Q can be produced using Process C and 2 units using Process D. Production of 2 units of Q with Process C utilizes 15 units of L and 6 units of K. For the production of 2 units of Q with Process D, 10 units each of L and K are necessary. Thus, although no single production system is available with which the firm can produce 4 units of Q using 25 units of L and 16 units of K, Processes C and D together can produce in that combination.

All points lying on the production isoquant segments can be interpreted in a similar manner. Each point represents a linear combination of output using the production process systems that bound the particular segment. Point Y in Figure 9.2 provides another illustration of this. At Y, 3 units of Q are being produced, using a total of 38.5 units of L and 4.3 units of K.[3] That input/output combination is possible through a linear combination of Processes A and B. The reader can verify from

[3]Another assumption of linear programming is that fractional variables are permissible. In many applications this assumption is not important. For example, in the present illustration we might be talking about labor-hours and machine-hours for the inputs. The solution value calling for $L = 38.5$ merely states that 38.5 hours of labor are required.

In some cases, however, where inputs are large—whole plants, for example—the fact that linear programming assumes divisible variables is important. In such cases linear programming as described herein may be inappropriate, and a more complex technique, integer programming, may be required.

FIGURE 9.2

Production Isoquants in Linear Programming

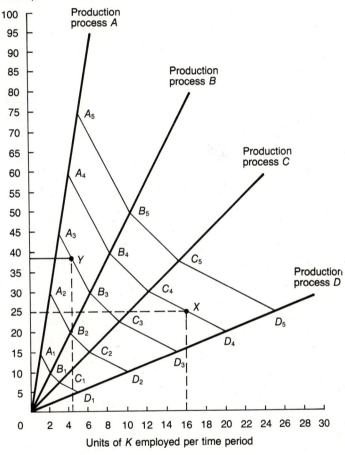

Units of L employed
per time period

Units of K employed per time period

Figure 9.2 that producing 1.7 units of Q using Process A and 1.3 units with Process B requires 38.5 units of L and 4.3 units of K.[4]

One method of determining the quantity to be produced by each production pro-

---

[4]This point can also be seen algebraically. To produce 1 unit of Q by Process A requires 15 units of L and 1 unit of K. Therefore, to produce 1.7 units of Q requires 25.5 (1.7 × 15) units of L and 1.7 (1.7 × 1) units of K. To produce a single unit of Q by Process B requires 10 units of L and 2 units of K, so 1.3 units of Q requires 13 (10 × 1.3) units of L and 2.6 (2 × 1.3) units of K. Thus, Point Y calls for the production of 3 units of Q in total, 1.7 units by Process A and 1.3 units by Process B, using a total of 38.5 units of L and 4.3 units of K.

cess at varying points along an isoquant is called the *relative distance method*. The relative distance method is based on the fact that the location of a point along an isoquant determines the relative shares of production for the adjacent processes. Consider Point X in Figure 9.2. If Point X were on Process Ray C, all output would be produced using Process C. Similarly, if Point X were on Process Ray D, all output would be produced using Process D. Since Point X lies between Process Rays C and D, both Processes C and D will be used in production of the output. Process C will be used relatively more than Process D if X is closer to Process Ray C than to Process Ray D. Conversely, Process D will be used relatively more than Process C if X is closer to Process Ray D than to Process Ray C. Since Point X in Figure 9.2 lies at the midpoint of the $Q = 4$ isoquant segment between C_4 and D_4, it implies production of equal proportions using Processes C and D. Thus, at Point X, $Q = 4$ and $Q_C = 2$ and $Q_D = 2$.

The relative proportions of Process A and Process B used to produce $Q = 3$ at Point Y can be determined in a similar manner. Since Y lies closer to Process Ray A than to Process Ray B, we know that Point Y entails relatively more output using Production Process A than using Production Process B. The share of total output produced using Process A can be calculated by considering the distance B_3Y relative to B_3A_3. The share of total output produced using Process B can be calculated by considering the distance A_3Y relative to A_3B_3. For example, starting from Point B_3, we note that the segment B_3Y covers approximately 56.6 percent of the total distance B_3A_3. This means that at Point Y, about 56.6 percent of total output is produced using Process A ($Q_A = .566 \times 3 = 1.7$), and roughly 43.3 percent ($= 1.0 - .566$) of total output is produced using Process B ($Q_B = .433 \times 3 = 1.3$). Alternatively, starting from Point A_3, we note that the segment A_3Y covers roughly 43.3 percent of the total distance A_3B_3. Thus, at Point Y, 43.3 percent of total output is produced using Process B, and 56.6 percent of total output is produced using Process A. While extreme accuracy would require painstaking graphic detail, in many instances the relative distance method can be used to provide adequate approximations of production intensities along isoquants.

Least-Cost Input Combinations

Adding isocost curves to the set of isoquants permits one to determine least-cost input combinations for the production of Product Q. This is shown in Figure 9.3, under the assumption that each unit of L costs $3 and each unit of K costs $10. The isocost curve illustrated indicates a total expenditure of $150.

The tangency between the isocost curve and the isoquant curve for $Q = 3$, at Point B_3, indicates that Production Process B, which combines Inputs L and K in the ratio 5 to 1, is the least-cost method of producing Q. For any expenditure level, production is maximized by using Process B. Alternatively, Production Process B is the least-cost method for producing any quantity of Q, given the assumed prices for L and K.

FIGURE 9.3

Determination of Least-Cost Production Process

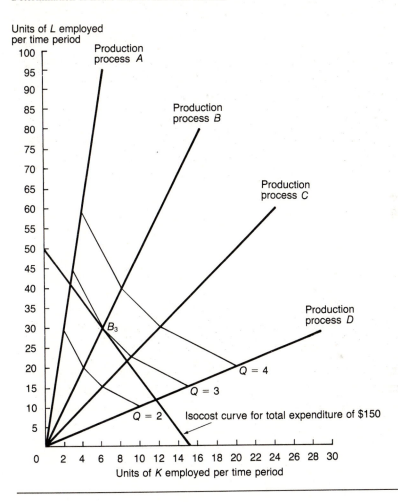

Units of L employed per time period

Units of K employed per time period

Optimal Input Combinations with Limited Resources

Frequently, firms are faced with limited inputs during a production period and because of this may find it optimal to use inputs in proportions other than the least-cost combination. Examples of such constraints on resources include limitations on the man-hours of skilled labor available, shortages of pieces of a particular type of equipment, insufficient raw materials, limited warehouse space, and other factors. In these cases the linear programming problem must be stated in terms of the

FIGURE 9.4

Optimal Input Combination with Limited Resources

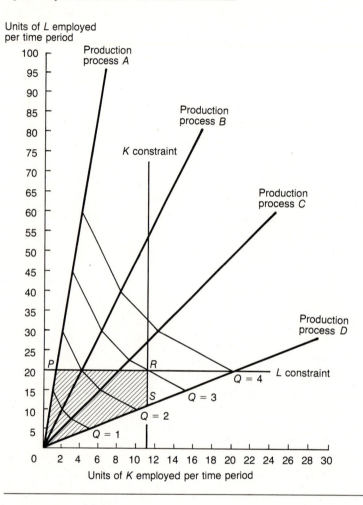

physical constraints on inputs rather than in terms of the constraints on total expenditures.

To illustrate, consider the effect of limits on the quantities of L and K available in our example. Specifically, assume that only 20 units of L and 11 units of K are available during the current production period and that the firm seeks to maximize the output of Q. These constraints are shown in Figure 9.4. The horizontal line drawn at $L = 20$ indicates the upper limit on the quantity of L that can be employed during the production period; the vertical line at $K = 11$ indicates a similar limit on the quantity of K.

We can determine the production possibilities for this problem by noting that, in addition to the limitations on Inputs L and K, the firm must operate within the area bounded by Production Process Rays A and D. In other words, the firm is unable to combine L and K in ratios that lie either above Production Process Ray A or below Production Process Ray D. There are no combinations of production systems that result in those input ratios. Thus, we see that combining the production possibilities with the input constraints restricts the firm to operations within the shaded area $0PRS$ in Figure 9.4. This area is known as the *feasible space* in the programming problem. Any point within the space combines L and K in a technically feasible ratio, and availability limits on L and K are not exceeded.

Since the firm is trying to maximize the production of Q, subject to constraints on the use of L and K, it should operate at that point in the feasible space that touches the highest possible isoquant. This is Point R in Figure 9.4, where $Q = 3$.

Although it is possible to solve problems like the foregoing example by using carefully constructed graphs, it is typically more useful to combine graphic analysis with analytical procedures to obtain accurate solutions in an efficient manner. For example, consider again Figure 9.4. Even if the isoquant for $Q = 3$ were not drawn, it would be apparent from the slopes of the isoquants for 2 or 4 units of output that the optimal solution to the problem must be at Point R. That is, it is readily apparent from the graph that the maximum production will be obtained by operating at the point where both inputs are fully employed. Since R lies between Production Processes C and D, we know that the output-maximizing production combination will make use of only these two production processes. We also know that all 20 units of L and 11 units of K will be employed, since Point R lies at the intersection of the two input constraints.

With this information from the graph we can solve for the optimal quantities to be produced using Processes C and D as follows. First, recall that each unit of output produced using Process C requires 7.5 units of L. Thus, the total L required in Process C will be equal to $7.5 \cdot Q_C$. Similarly, each unit produced using Process D requires 5 units of L so that total L used in Process D equals $5 \cdot Q_D$. At Point R, 20 units of L are being used in Processes C and D together, and thus the following relationship must hold:

$$7.5Q_C + 5Q_D = 20. \tag{9.1}$$

A similar relationship can be developed for the use of K. Each unit of output produced from Process C requires 3 units of K, while in Process D, 5 units of K are used to produce each unit of output. The total use of K equals 11 units at Point R, and these 11 units are used in Processes C and D such that

$$3Q_C + 5Q_D = 11. \tag{9.2}$$

Equations 9.1 and 9.2 must both hold at Point R; therefore, by solving them simultaneously we can determine the output quantities from Processes C and D at that location. Subtracting Equation 9.2 from Equation 9.1 provides

$$7.5Q_C + 5Q_D = 20 \qquad\qquad (9.1)$$

$$\text{minus } \underline{3.0Q_C + 5Q_D = 11} \qquad\qquad (9.2)$$

$$4.5Q_C \qquad\quad = \quad 9$$

$$Q_C \qquad\quad = \quad 2 \,.$$

Substituting 2 for Q_C in Equation 9.2 allows us to determine the output from Process D:

$$3(2) + 5Q_D = 11$$

$$5Q_D = \quad 5$$

$$Q_D = \quad 1.$$

Total output at Point R is 3 units, composed of 2 units from Process C and 1 unit from Process D.

The ability to combine graphic and analytical representations of the relationships in a linear programming problem allows one to obtain precise solutions in many cases with relative ease. This approach to solving linear programming problems is developed more fully in the following section.

LINEAR PROGRAMMING AND PRODUCTION PLANNING: MULTIPLE PRODUCTS

Most production decisions, as well as decisions in other areas, are considerably more complex than the preceding example. Accordingly, we expand our discussion, moving first to the problem of the optimal output mix for a multiproduct firm facing restrictions on productive facilities and other inputs. This problem, which is precisely the one faced by oil refineries, cereal-processing firms, and forest-products companies, among others, is readily solved by linear programming, as the following example reveals.

Consider a firm that produces Products X and Y and uses Inputs A, B, and C. To maximize its total profits, the firm must determine the optimal quantities of each product to produce, subject to the constraints imposed by limitations on input availability.[5]

[5] In the typical linear programming problem we seek to maximize *profit contribution*, defined as total revenue minus the *variable cost* of production. Fixed costs must be subtracted from the profit contribution to determine net profits. How-

TABLE 9.1

Inputs Available for Production of X and Y

Input	Quantity Available per Time Period	Quantity Required per Unit of Output	
		X	Y
A	32	4	2
B	10	1	1
C	21	0	3

Specification of the Objective Function

We assume that the firm wishes to maximize total profits from the two products, X and Y, during each time period. If per-unit profit contribution, the excess of price over average variable cost, is \$12 for Product X and \$9 for Product Y, we can write the objective function as:

$$\text{Maximize} \qquad\qquad \pi = 12Q_x + 9Q_y. \qquad\qquad \textbf{(9.3)}$$

Here Q_x and Q_y represent the quantities of each product produced. The per-unit profit contribution of X times the units of X produced and sold, plus the unit contribution of Y times Q_y, is the total profit contribution, π, earned by the firm. It is this total profit contribution that the firm wishes to maximize, for by maximizing profit contribution the firm also maximizes its net profit.

Specification of the Constraint Equations

Table 9.1, which specifies the available quantities of each input, as well as their usage in the production of X and Y, provides all the information necessary to construct the constraint relationships for this problem.

From the table we see that 32 units of Input A are available in each period, and that 4 units of A are required in the production of each unit of X, while 2 units of A are necessary to produce 1 unit of Y.

Since 4 units of A are required for the production of a single unit of X, the total amount of A used to manufacture X can be written as $4Q_x$. Similarly, 2 units of A are required to produce each unit of Y, so $2Q_y$ represents the total quantity of A used in the production of Product Y. Summing the quantities of A used in the production of

---

ever, since fixed costs are constant, regardless of how much or how little output is produced, maximizing profit contribution is tantamount to maximizing profit, and the output mix that maximizes profit contribution also maximizes net profit. This concept of profit contribution was developed more fully in Chapter 7.

X and Y provides an expression for the total usage of A, and since this total cannot exceed the 32 units available, we can write the constraint condition for Input A as:

$$4Q_x + 2Q_y \le 32. \tag{9.4}$$

The constraint for Input B can be determined in a like manner. One unit of Input B is necessary for the production of each unit of either X or Y, so the total amount of B that will be expended is $1Q_x + 1Q_y$. The maximum quantity of B available for production in each time period is 10 units; thus, the constraint requirement associated with Input B is:

$$1Q_x + 1Q_y \le 10. \tag{9.5}$$

Finally, there is the constraint relationship for Input C, which is used only in the production of Y. Each unit of Y requires an input of 3 units of C, and 21 units of Input C are available. Total usage of C, then, is given by the expression $3Q_y$, and the constraint can be written as:

$$3Q_y \le 21. \tag{9.6}$$

Constraint equations play major roles in solving linear programming problems. One further concept must be introduced, however, before we can completely specify the linear programming problem and examine how the constraints are used to obtain its solution.

Nonnegativity Requirement

Because linear programming is nothing more than a mathematical tool for solving constrained optimization problems, nothing in the technique itself insures that an answer will make economic sense. For example, in a production problem, for some very unprofitable product the mathematically optimal output level may be a *negative* quantity, clearly an impossible solution. Likewise, in a distribution problem, an optimal solution might include negative shipments from one point to another, again an impossible act.

To prevent such nonsensical results, we must include a nonnegativity requirement. This is merely a statement that all variables in the problem must be equal to or greater than zero. Thus, for the production problem we are examining, we must add the expressions:

$$Q_x \ge 0$$

and

$$Q_y \ge 0.$$

GRAPHIC SPECIFICATION AND SOLUTION OF THE LINEAR PROGRAMMING PROBLEM

Having specified all the component parts of the firm's linear programming problem, we first examine this problem graphically, then analyze it algebraically. Let us begin by restating the decision problem in terms of the system of expressions for the objective function and input constraints. The firm wishes to maximize its total profit contribution, π, subject to constraints imposed by limitations on its resources. This can be expressed as:

Maximize

$$\pi = 12Q_X + 9Q_Y, \tag{9.3}$$

subject to the following constraints:

$$\text{Input } A: 4Q_X + 2Q_Y \leq 32, \tag{9.4}$$

$$\text{Input } B: 1Q_X + 1Q_Y \leq 10, \tag{9.5}$$

$$\text{Input } C: \qquad 3Q_Y \leq 21, \tag{9.6}$$

where

$$Q_X \geq 0 \text{ and } Q_Y \geq 0.$$

Determining the Feasible Space

Figure 9.5 is a graph of the constraint equation for Input A, $4Q_X + 2Q_Y = 32$, which indicates the maximum quantities of X and Y that can be produced, given the limitation on the availability of Input A. A maximum of 16 units of Y can be produced if no X is manufactured; 8 units of X can be produced if the output of Y is zero. Any point along the line connecting these two outputs represents the maximum combination of X and Y that can be produced with no more than 32 units of A.

This constraint equation divides the XY plane into two half-spaces. Every point lying on the line or to the left of it satisfies the constraint expressed by the equation $4Q_X + 2Q_Y \leq 32$; every point to the right of the line violates that expression. Thus, only points on the constraint line or to the left of it can be in the feasible space. The shaded area of Figure 9.5 represents the feasible area as delimited by the constraint on Input A.[6]

---

[6] Although the half-space in the XY plane that satisfies the constraint conditions on Input A extends into the second, third, and fourth quadrants, only in the first are the nonnegativity requirements on the variables Q_X and Q_Y satisfied.

FIGURE 9.5

Constraint Imposed by Limitations in Input A

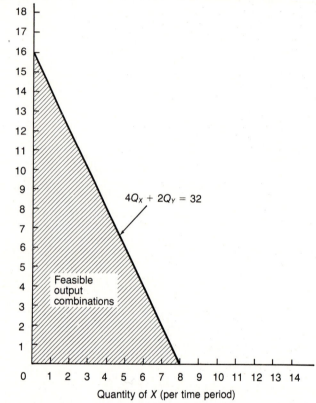

In Figure 9.6 we have further limited the feasible space by adding the constraints for Inputs B and C. The constraint on Input B can be expressed as $Q_x + Q_y = 10$. Thus, if no Y is produced, a maximum of 10 units of X can be produced; if output of X is zero, 10 units of Y can be manufactured. All combinations of X and Y lying on, or to the left of, the line connecting these two points are feasible with respect to utilization of Input B.

The horizontal line at $Q_y = 7$ in Figure 9.6 represents the constraint imposed by Input C. Since C is used only in the production of Y, it does not constrain the

---

Therefore, we can restrict the feasible space to those points in the first quadrant which satisfy the constraint conditions imposed by input restrictions.

production of X at all. Seven units of Y, however, are the maximum quantity that can be produced with the 21 units of C available.

The three input constraints, together with the nonnegativity requirement, completely delimit the feasible space of our linear programming problem, which is the shaded area of Figure 9.6. Only those points within this area meet all the constraints.

Graphing the Objective Function

The objective function in our example, $\pi = 12Q_x + 9Q_y$, can be graphed in the Q_xQ_y space as a series of isoprofit curves. This is illustrated in Figure 9.7, where

FIGURE 9.6

Feasible Space

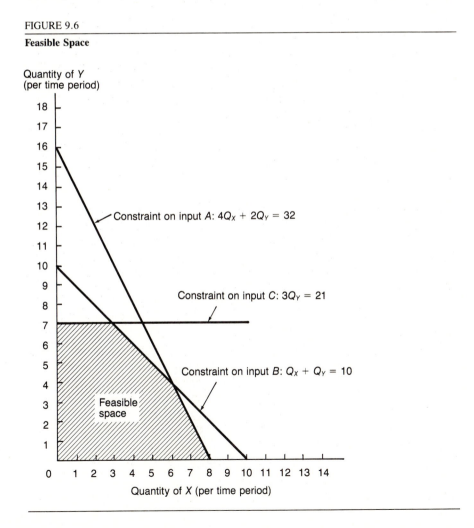

Quantity of Y
(per time period)

Constraint on input A: $4Q_x + 2Q_y = 32$

Constraint on input C: $3Q_y = 21$

Constraint on input B: $Q_x + Q_y = 10$

Feasible space

Quantity of X (per time period)

FIGURE 9.7

Isoprofit Contribution Curves

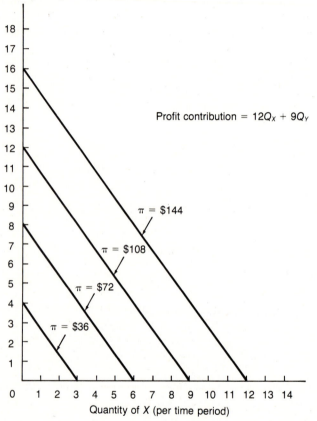

Quantity of Y
(per time period)

Profit contribution = $12Q_X + 9Q_Y$

$\pi = \$144$

$\pi = \$108$

$\pi = \$72$

$\pi = \$36$

Quantity of X (per time period)

isoprofit curves for $36, $72, $108, and $144 are shown. Each isoprofit curve illustrates all possible combinations of X and Y that result in a constant total profit. For example, the isoprofit curve labeled $\pi = \$36$ is the locus of all points that satisfy the equation $\pi = 36 = 12Q_x + 9Q_y$. Alternatively stated, each *combination* of X and Y lying along that curve results in a total profit of $36. Similarly, all output combinations along the $\pi = \$72$ curve satisfy the equation $72 = 12Q_x + 9Q_y$ and thus provide a total profit contribution of $72. It is clear from Figure 9.7 that the isoprofit curves are a series of parallel lines that take on higher values as we move upward and to the right.

Isoprofit curves are identical in form to the isocost curves developed in Chapter

6. Here, the profit function $\pi = aQ_X + bQ_Y$, where a and b are the profit contributions of Products X and Y respectively, is solved for Q_Y, resulting in an equation of the form:

$$Q_Y = \frac{\pi}{b} - \frac{a}{b} Q_X.$$

Given the individual profit contributions, a and b, the Q_Y intercept is determined by the profit level of the isoprofit curve, while the slope is given by the relative profitabilities of the products. Since the relative profitability of the products is unaffected by the output level, isoprofit curves in a linear programming problem will always be a series of parallel lines. In the example, all the isoprofit curves have a slope of $-12/9$, or -1.33.

Graphic Solution of the Linear Programming Problem

Since the firm's objective is to maximize total profit, it should operate on the highest isoprofit curve obtainable. Combining the feasible space limitations shown in Figure 9.6 with the family of isoprofit curves from Figure 9.7 allows us to obtain the graphic solution to our linear programming problem. The combined graph is illustrated in Figure 9.8.

Point M in the figure indicates the solution to the problem. Here, the firm produces 6 units of X and 4 units of Y, and the total profit is $108 [(12 \times 6) + (9 \times 4)]$, which is the maximum available under the conditions stated in the problem. No other point within the feasible space touches as high an isoprofit curve.[7]

Notice that the optimal solution to the linear programming problem occurs at a corner of the feasible space. This is not a chance result; rather, it is a feature of the linearity assumptions underlying the linear programming technique. When the objective function and all constraint relationships are specified in linear form, there

---

[7]Using the combined graphic and analytical procedure introduced in the preceding section, we can obtain the result that $Q_X = 6$ and $Q_Y = 4$ at Point M as follows. At M the constraints on Inputs A and B are both binding. That is, at M the 32 units of Input A and 10 units of Input B are being completely utilized in the production of X and Y. Thus, Expressions 9.4 and 9.5 can be written as equations and solved simultaneously for Q_X and Q_Y:

$$
\begin{array}{lll}
& 4Q_X + 2Q_Y = 32 & \text{(9.4)} \\
\text{minus} & \underline{2Q_X + 2Q_Y = 20} & 2 \times \text{(9.5)} \\
& 2Q_X \qquad\quad = 12 & \\
& Q_X \qquad\quad = 6. &
\end{array}
$$

Substituting 6 for Q_X in Equation 9.5 results in

$$6 + Q_Y = 10 \qquad\qquad \text{(9.5)}$$

$$Q_Y = 4.$$

FIGURE 9.8

Graphic Solution to the Linear Programming Problem

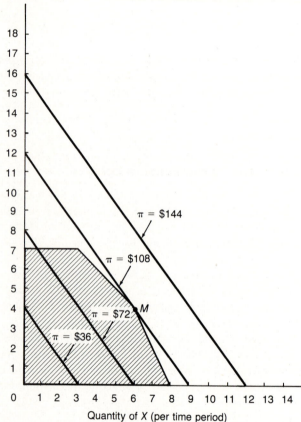

Quantity of Y
(per time period)

Quantity of X (per time period)

must be constant returns to scale. Because input and output prices do not change as production expands, it will always prove optimal to move as far as possible in the direction of higher outputs, provided that sales prices exceed variable costs per unit. This means that the firm will always move to a point where some capacity limit is reached; that is, to a boundary of the feasible space.

A final step is necessary to show that an optimal solution to any linear programming problem always lies at a corner of the feasible space. Since all the relationships in a linear programming problem must be linear by definition, every boundary of the feasible space is linear. Furthermore, the objective function is linear. Thus, the constrained optimization of the objective function takes place either at a corner of the feasible space, as in Figure 9.8, or at one boundary face, as is illustrated by Figure 9.9.

In Figure 9.9 we have modified the linear programming example by assuming that each unit of either X or Y produced yields a profit of $5. In this case, the optimal solution to the problem includes any of the combinations of X and Y found along Line Segment LM, since all these combinations are feasible and all result in a total profit of $50. If all points along Line LM provide optimal combinations of output, the combinations found at Corners L and M are also optimal. That is, since the firm is indifferent whether it produces the combination of X and Y indicated at Point L or at Point M, or at any point between them, either corner location provides an optimal solution to the production problem. Thus, even when the highest obtainable isoprofit curve lies along a bounding face of the feasible space, it is possible to achieve an optimal solution to the problem at a corner of the feasible space.

From this result it follows that in linear programming problems we can limit our analysis to just the corners of the feasible space. In other words, we can ignore

FIGURE 9.9

Graphic Solution of a Linear Programming Problem Where the Objective Function Coincides with a Boundary of the Feasible Space

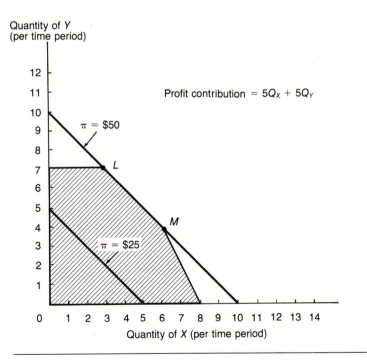

the infinite number of points lying within the feasible space and concentrate our efforts solely on the corner solutions. This greatly reduces the computations necessary to solve linear programming problems that are too large to solve by graphic methods.

ALGEBRAIC SPECIFICATION AND SOLUTION OF THE LINEAR PROGRAMMING PROBLEM

The graphic technique described above is useful to illustrate the nature of linear programming, but it can be applied only in the two-output case. Since most linear programming problems contain far too many variables and constraints to allow solution by graphic analysis, we must use algebraic methods. These algebraic techniques are especially valuable in that they permit us to solve large, complex linear programming problems on computers, and this greatly extends the usefulness of linear programming.

Slack Variables

In order to specify a linear programming problem algebraically we must introduce one additional concept, that of *slack variables*. These variables are added to a linear programming problem to account for the amount of any input that is *unused* at a solution point. One slack variable is introduced for each constraint in the problem. In our illustrative problem, the firm is faced with capacity constraints on Input Factors A, B, an C, so the algebraic specification of the problem contains three slack variables: S_A, indicating the units of Input A that are not used in any given solution; S_B, representing unused units of B; and S_C, which measures the unused units of C.

The introduction of these slack variables allows us to write each constraint relationship as an equation rather than as an inequality. Thus, the constraint on Input A, $4Q_X + 2Q_Y \leq 32$, can be written as:

$$4Q_X + 2Q_Y + S_A = 32. \tag{9.7}$$

Here $S_A = 32 - 4Q_X - 2Q_Y$, which is the amount of Input A not used in the production of X or Y. Similar equality constraints can be specified for Inputs B and C. Specifically, the equality form of the constraint on Input B is:

$$1Q_X + 1Q_Y + S_B = 10, \tag{9.8}$$

while for C the constraint equation is:

$$3Q_Y + S_C = 21. \tag{9.9}$$

Note that the slack variables not only allow us to state the constraint conditions in equality form, thus simplifying algebraic analysis, but also provide us with valuable information. In the production problem, for example, slack variables whose values are *zero* at the optimal solution indicate inputs that cause bottlenecks or are limiting factors. Slack variables with *positive* values, on the other hand, provide measures of excess capacity in the related factor.[8] In either case, the information provided by slack variables is important, and we return to this subject when we examine the dual linear programming problem later in this chapter.

Algebraic Solution

The complete specification of our illustrative programming problem can now be stated as follows:

Maximize

$$\pi = 12Q_X + 9Q_Y, \tag{9.3}$$

subject to these constraints:

$$4Q_X + 2Q_Y + S_A = 32, \tag{9.7}$$

$$1Q_X + 1Q_Y + S_B = 10, \tag{9.8}$$

$$3Q_Y + S_C = 21, \tag{9.9}$$

where

$$Q_X \geq 0, \, Q_Y \geq 0, \, S_A \geq 0, \, S_B \geq 0, \, S_C \geq 0.$$

In words, the problem is to find the set of values for Variables Q_X, Q_Y, S_A, S_B, and S_C that maximizes Equation 9.3 and at the same time satisfies the constraints imposed by Equations 9.7, 9.8, and 9.9.

The problem stated in this form is underdetermined: We must obtain a simultaneous solution to the constraint equations, but there are more unknowns (five) than constraint equations (three), so we cannot solve the system for unique values of the variables. However, the requirement that the solution to any linear programming problem must occur at a corner of the feasible space provides enough information to allow one to obtain the solution. To see how, let us first state the following facts:

---

[8] Slack variables obviously can never take on negative values, since this would imply that the amount of the resource used exceeds the amount available. Thus, slack variables are included in the general nonnegativity requirements for all variables.

1. The optimal output occurs at a corner point. Accordingly, we need examine only the corner locations of the feasible space.

2. There are a total of $M + N$ variables in the system, where M equals the number of products and N equals the number of constraints. Thus, in our example, $M = X + Y = 2$, and $N = A + B + C = 3$, so we have a total of five variables.

3. Each variable must be equal to or greater than zero.

4. At each corner point the number of non-zero-valued variables is equal to the number of constraint equations.[9] Consider Figure 9.10, where the feasible space for our illustrative problem has been regraphed. At the origin, where neither X nor Y is produced, Q_X and Q_Y both equal zero. Slack exists in all inputs, however, so S_A, S_B, and S_C are all greater than zero. Now move up the vertical axis to Point K. Here Q_X and S_C both equal zero, because no X is being produced and Input C is being used to the fullest possible extent. However, Q_Y, S_A, and S_B all exceed zero. At Point L, Q_X, Q_Y, and S_A are all positive; but S_B and S_C are equal to zero. The remaining corners, M and N, can be examined similarly, and at each of them the number of non-zero-valued variables is exactly equal to the number of constraints.

We see then that the optimal solution to a linear programming problem occurs at a corner of the feasible space, and that at each corner the number of non-zero variables is exactly equal to the number of constraints. These properties enable us to rewrite the constraints as a system with three equations and three unknowns for each corner point; such a system can be solved.

Solving the constraint equations at each corner point provides values for Q_X and Q_Y as well as for S_A, S_B, and S_C. The profit contribution at each corner can be determined by inserting the values for Q_X and Q_Y into the objective function (Equation 9.3). The corner solution that produces the maximum profit is the constrained profit maximizing output, the solution to the linear programming problem.

The procedure described above is followed in actual applications of linear programming. Computer programs are available that find solution values of the variables at a corner point, evaluate profits at that point, and then iterate to an adjacent corner point with a higher profit, continuing until the optimal corner point is located.

We can illustrate the technique somewhat more fully by examining the algebraic determination of the corner solutions in our present example. Although we could set any two of the variables equal to zero, it is convenient to begin by setting Q_X and Q_Y equal to zero and examining the solution to the programming problem at

---

[9]In almost all linear programming problems, the number of non-zero-valued variables in all corner solutions is *exactly* equal to the number of constraints in the problem. Only under a particular condition known as *degeneracy*, when more than two constraints coincide at a single corner of the feasible space, are there fewer non-zero-valued variables. This condition does not hinder the technique of solution considered in this chapter.

FIGURE 9.10

Determination of Zero-Valued Variables at Corners of the Feasible Space

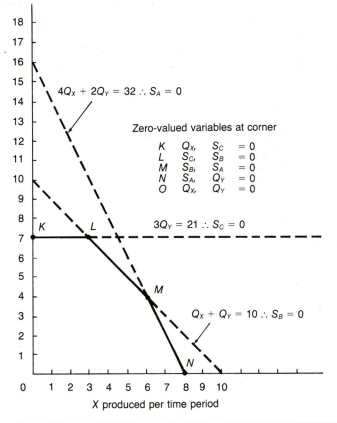

Y produced per
time period

$4Q_X + 2Q_Y = 32 \therefore S_A = 0$

Zero-valued variables at corner

K	$Q_X,$	S_C	$= 0$
L	$S_C,$	S_B	$= 0$
M	$S_B,$	S_A	$= 0$
N	$S_A,$	Q_Y	$= 0$
O	$Q_X,$	Q_Y	$= 0$

$3Q_Y = 21 \therefore S_C = 0$

$Q_X + Q_Y = 10 \therefore S_B = 0$

X produced per time period

the origin. Substituting those values into the three constraint equations—9.7, 9.8, and 9.9—indicates that the three slack variables are equal to the total units of their respective inputs available to the firm; that is, $S_A = 32$, $S_B = 10$, and $S_C = 21$. This result is not unexpected, because at the origin neither X nor Y is produced, and, therefore, none of the inputs is expended for production. The total profit contribution at the origin corner of the feasible space is zero.

Now let us examine the solution at a second corner, N in Figure 9.10, where Q_Y and S_A equal zero. Substituting into Constraint Equation 9.7 permits us to solve for Q_X:

$$4Q_x + 2Q_Y + S_A = 32 \qquad\qquad \textbf{(9.7)}$$

$$4 \cdot Q_x + 2 \cdot 0 + 0 = 32$$

$$4Q_x = 32$$

$$Q_x = 8.$$

With the value of Q_x determined, we can substitute into Equations 9.8 and 9.9 to determine values S_B and S_C:

$$Q_x + Q_Y + S_B = 10 \qquad\qquad \textbf{(9.8)}$$

$$8 + 0 + S_B = 10$$

$$S_B = 2,$$

and

$$3Q_Y + S_C = 21 \qquad\qquad \textbf{(9.9)}$$

$$3 \cdot 0 + S_C = 21$$

$$S_C = 21.$$

The total profit contribution is:

$$\pi = 12Q_x + 9Q_Y \qquad\qquad \textbf{(9.3)}$$

$$= 12 \cdot 8 + 9 \cdot 0$$

$$= \$96.$$

Next, we assign zero values to S_B and S_A, which permits us to reach solution values for Point M. Substituting zero values for S_A and S_B in Equations 9.7 and 9.8 gives us two equations in two unknowns:

$$4Q_x + 2Q_Y + 0 = 32. \qquad\qquad \textbf{(9.7)}$$

$$Q_x + Q_Y + 0 = 10. \qquad\qquad \textbf{(9.8)}$$

Multiplying Equation 9.8 by two and subtracting the result from Equation 9.7 provides the value for Q_x:

TABLE 9.2

Algebraic Solution to a Linear Programming Problem

Solution at Corner	Value of Variable					Total Profit Contribution
	Q_X	Q_Y	S_A	S_B	S_C	
O	0	0	32	10	21	$ 0
N	8	0	0	2	21	96
M	6	4	0	0	9	108
L	3	7	6	0	0	99
K	0	7	18	3	0	63

$$4Q_X + 2Q_Y = 32 \qquad (9.7)$$
$$\text{minus } \underline{2Q_X + 2Q_Y = 20} \qquad 2 \times (9.8)$$
$$2Q_X \qquad = 12$$
$$Q_X \qquad = 6.$$

Then, substituting 6 for Q_X in Equation 9.8, we find that $Q_Y = 4$. Total profit contribution in this case is $108 [($12 \cdot 6) + ($9 \cdot 4)]$.

Similar algebraic analysis would provide the solution for the remaining two corners of the feasible space. However, rather than work through those corner solutions, we present the results in Table 9.2. Here it is apparent, just as we illustrated in the earlier graphic analysis, that the optimal solution occurs at Point M, where 6 units of X and 4 units of Y are produced. Total profit is $108, which exceeds the profit at any other corner of the feasible space.

Slack Variables at the Solution Point

At each corner solution the values of the slack variables are determined by the linear programming process. For example, at the optimal solution (Corner M) reached in the preceding section, S_A and S_B are both equal to zero, meaning that Inputs A and B are used to the fullest extent possible, but the value of S_C is determined as follows. First, note that $Q_Y = 4$ at the optimal corner. Next, substitute this value into Constraint Equation 9.9 to find the solution value of S_C:

$$3 \cdot Q_Y + S_C = 21$$
$$3 \cdot 4 + S_C = 21$$
$$S_C = 9.$$

Production of the optimal combination of X and Y completely exhausts the available quantities of Inputs A and B, but 9 units of Input C remain unused. Thus, because

Inputs *A* and *B* impose effective constraints on the firm's profit level, it may wish to acquire more of one or both of them in order to expand output. Input *C*, on the other hand, is in excess supply, so the firm would certainly not want more capacity of *C*; it might even attempt to reduce its purchases of *C* during future production periods. Alternatively, if *C* is a fixed facility, such as a computer, the firm might attempt to sell some of that excess capacity to other computer users.

Complex Linear Programming Problems

Our illustrative linear programming problem is a simple one by design—we chose a problem that can be solved both graphically and algebraically so that we could first explain the theory of linear programming through the use of graphs, then rework the problem algebraically to show the symmetry between the two methods. The kinds of linear programming problems encountered in the real world, however, are quite complex, frequently involving very many constraints and output variables. Such problems are obviously too complex to solve geometrically—the geometry is messy if we have three outputs, impossible for four or more. However, computer programs, which use the algebraic techniques, can handle very large numbers of variables and constraints. While it is not necessary for our purposes to extend the discussion to use of these computer-based solution algorithms, we call attention to them to indicate the potential problem solving capability of the technique.

THE DUAL IN LINEAR PROGRAMMING

For every maximization problem in linear programming there exists a symmetrical minimization problem; for every minimization problem there exists a symmetrical maximization problem. These pairs of related maximization and minimization problems are known as *dual linear programming problems*. Convention specifies that for clarity we call one the primal problem and the other the dual problem. The symmetry or duality between constrained maximization and constrained minimization problems is a key concept in managerial economics. While the concept of duality has been implied in earlier material, explicitly examining duality in our discussion of linear programming will prove useful to show the equivalence of alternative approaches to constrained optimization.

Duality Theory

The concept of duality is important in managerial economics for several reasons. First, duality concepts demonstrate the symmetry between the value of a firm's products and the value of its resources or inputs. For example, with duality we can show that value maximization can be attained by focusing on either the revenue generating capability and resource requirements of a firm's products or on the cost of resources and their productivity.

In addition to providing valuable insight about the economics of optimal resource employment, duality provides the key to solving some very difficult constrained optimization problems. Because of the symmetry between primal and dual problem specifications, either one can be constructed from the other and the solution to either problem is the solution to both. This is beneficial because it is sometimes easier to obtain the solution to the dual problem than to the original or primal problem.

Finally, duality allows one to evaluate the solution of a constrained decision problem in terms of both the activities required for optimization of the firm's objective and the economic impact of the constraint conditions under which the decisions must be made. Analysis of the constraint conditions frequently provides important information for long-range planning or strategic decisions. Thus, one often sees the primal of a programming problem described as a tool for short-run operating decision making and the dual as a tool for long-run planning. Duality demonstrates the symmetry between these two activities and, therefore, the need to recognize that operating decisions and long-range planning are inextricably related.

Imputed Values or Shadow Prices

To further examine duality, we must introduce the concept of imputed values or shadow prices. In the primal programming problem discussed above, we sought the values of Q_X and Q_Y that would maximize the firm's profit subject to constraints on production imposed by limitations of Input Factors A, B, and C. Duality theory tells us that an identical operating decision would result if we instead had chosen to minimize the costs of the resources employed in producing Q_X and Q_Y, subject to an output constraint.

The key to this duality is that the costs we are concerned with are not the acquisition costs of the inputs but rather the economic costs of using them. For a resource that is available in a fixed amount, this cost is not the acquisition cost but the opportunity cost of not being able to use it for some alternative purpose. Consider, for example, a skilled labor force employed by a firm. If the workers are fully utilized producing valuable products for the firm, then a reduction in skilled labor will reduce valuable output, and an increase in skilled labor will increase the production of valuable output. Similarly, if some of the labor is shifted from the production of one product to another, the cost of using skilled labor in this new activity is the value of the original product that can no longer be produced. Thus, the marginal cost of a constrained resource that is fully utilized is its opportunity cost as measured by the value of the product produced.

If, on the other hand, a limited resource such as skilled labor is not fully utilized, then at least the last unit of the resource is not productive and its marginal value to the firm is zero. Acquiring an additional unit of the resource would not increase valuable output, since the firm already has excess, or unused, units of that resource. Similarly, the firm would incur a zero opportunity cost if it utilized the currently unused units of the resource in a different activity.

Thus, the economic value, or opportunity cost, of a constrained resource depends upon the extent to which it is utilized. When a constrained resource is fully utilized, its marginal value in use (opportunity cost) is positive. When a constrained resource is not fully utilized, its marginal value in use is zero. From this we see that minimizing the value of constrained resources used to produce valuable output is nothing more than minimizing the opportunity costs of employing those resources for that output. Such minimization of opportunity costs is equivalent to maximizing the value of the output produced with those resources.

Since the economic value of constrained resources is determined by their value in use rather than by historical acquisition costs, we call such amounts *imputed* values or *shadow prices*. The term *shadow price* is used because it represents the price that a manager should be willing to pay for additional units of a constrained resource. Comparing the shadow price of a resource with its acquisition price indicates whether the firm has an incentive to increase or decrease the amount of the resource that it acquires in future production periods. If shadow prices exceed acquisition prices, the resource's marginal value to the firm exceeds its cost and the firm has an incentive to expand employment of the resource. If, on the other hand, the acquisition cost exceeds the shadow price, there is an incentive to reduce the employment of that resource. These relationships and the importance of duality can be further clarified by considering the dual to the linear programming problem discussed above.

Dual Objective Function [10]

In our original primal problem, where the goal was to maximize profits, the objective function was stated in this way.

Primal Objective Function. Maximize

$$\pi = 12Q_X + 9Q_Y. \tag{9.3}$$

----

[10]Rules for constructing the dual linear programming problem from its related primal are provided in Appendix 9A at the end of this chapter.

In the dual problem we seek to minimize the imputed values, or the shadow prices, of the firm's resources. Defining V_A, V_B, and V_C as the shadow prices for Inputs A, B, and C, respectively, and π^* as the total imputed value of the firm's fixed resources, we can write the dual objective function this way.

Dual Objective Function. Minimize

$$\pi^* = 32V_A + 10V_B + 21V_C. \tag{9.10}$$

Since the firm has 32 units of A, the total imputed value of Input A is 32 times A's shadow price, or $32V_A$. If V_A, or Input A's shadow price, is found to be $1.50 when the dual equations are solved, then the imputed value of A is $48 ($= 32 \times \$1.50$). Inputs B and C are handled in the same way.

The Dual Constraints

In the primal problem the constraints stated that the total units of each input used in the production of X and Y must be equal to or less than the available quantity of the input. In the dual, the constraints state that the total value of inputs used in the production of 1 unit of X or 1 unit of Y must not be less than the profit contribution provided by a unit of these products. In other words, the shadow prices of A, B, and C times the amount of each of the inputs needed to produce a unit of X or Y must be equal to or greater than the unit profit of X or of Y. Recall that unit profit is defined as the excess of price over variable cost, that price and variable cost are both assumed to be constant, and that in our example the profit per unit of X is $12 while that of Y is $9.

As was shown in Table 9.1, each unit of X requires 4 units of A, 1 unit of B, and 0 units of C. Therefore, the total imputed value of the resources used to produce X is $4V_A + 1V_B$. The constraint requiring that this imputed cost of producing X be equal to or greater than the profit contribution of X can be written as:

$$4V_A + 1V_B \geq 12, \tag{9.11}$$

where $12 is the profit per unit of Product X. Moreover, since 2 units of A, 1 unit of B, and 3 units of C are required to produce each unit of Y, and the profit per unit of Y is $9, the second dual constraint is written as:

$$2V_A + 1V_B + 3V_C \geq \$9. \tag{9.12}$$

Because the firm produces only two products, the dual problem has but two constraint equations.

The Dual Slack Variables

Dual slack variables can be incorporated in the problem, enabling us to express the constraint requirements as equalities. Letting L_x and L_y represent the two slacks, Constraint Equations 9.11 and 9.12 can be rewritten as:

$$4V_A + 1V_B - L_x = 12 \qquad\qquad (9.13)$$

and

$$2V_A + 1V_B + 3V_C - L_y = 9. \qquad\qquad (9.14)$$

Here the slack variables are *subtracted* from the constraint equations, since we are dealing with equal-to or greater-than inequalities. The dual slack variables measure the opportunity cost associated with production of the two products X and Y. This can be seen by examining the two constraint equations. Solving Constraint Equation 9.13 for L_x, for example, provides:

$$L_x = 4V_A + 1V_B - 12.$$

This expression states that L_x is equal to the imputed cost of producing 1 unit of X minus the profit contribution provided by that product. Thus, L_x, the dual slack variable associated with Product X, is a measure of the opportunity cost of producing Product X. It compares the profit contribution of Product X, \$12, with the value to the firm of the resources necessary to produce it.

A zero value for L_x indicates that at the margin the imputed value of the resources going into producing a unit of X is exactly equal to the profit contribution received from it. This is similar to marginal costs being equal to marginal revenue where profits are maximized. A positive value for L_x indicates that the resources expended in the production of X are more valuable in terms of the profit contribution they can generate when used to produce the other product. A non-zero value of L_x then measures the firm's opportunity cost (profit loss) associated with production of Product X.

The slack variable for the second dual constraint has a similar interpretation. That is, L_y is the opportunity cost of producing Product Y. It will take on a value of zero if the imputed value of the resources used to produce 1 unit of Y exactly equals the \$9 profit contribution provided by that product. A positive value for L_y measures the opportunity loss in terms of the forgone profit contribution associated with the production of Y.

Since a firm would not choose to produce a product if the value of the resources needed to produce it were greater than the value of the resulting product, it follows that a product with a positive opportunity cost will not be included in the optimal production combination in a linear programming problem. The importance of this relationship is shown below when we interpret the dual solution to our linear programming example.

Solving the Dual Problem

The dual programming problem can be solved with the same algebraic technique that was employed to obtain the solution of the primal problem. Let us restate the equality form of the dual programming problem and examine possible corner solutions to that problem. The dual problem is expressed by the following system:

Minimize

$$\pi^* = 32V_A + 10V_B + 21V_C, \tag{9.10}$$

subject to

$$4V_A + 1V_B - L_X = 12, \tag{9.13}$$

and

$$2V_A + 1V_B + 3V_C - L_Y = 9, \tag{9.14}$$

where

$$V_A, V_B, V_C, L_X, L_Y \text{ all} \geq 0.$$

Since there are only two constraints in this programming problem, the maximum number of non-zero-valued variables at any corner solution will be two. Therefore, we can proceed by setting three of the variables equal to zero and solving the constraint equations for the values of the remaining two. By comparing the value of the objective function at each feasible solution, we can determine the point at which the function is minimized.

To illustrate the process, let us first set $V_A = V_B = V_C = 0$, and solve for L_X and L_Y:

$$4 \cdot 0 + 1 \cdot 0 - L_X = 12 \tag{9.13}$$

$$L_X = -12.$$

$$2 \cdot 0 + 1 \cdot 0 + 0 + 3 \cdot 0 - L_Y = 9 \tag{9.14}$$

$$L_Y = -9.$$

TABLE 9.3

Solutions for the Dual Programming Problem

Solution Number	Value of the Variable					Total Value Imputed to the Firm's Resources
	V_A	V_B	V_C	L_X	L_Y	
1	0	0	0	−12	−9	a
2	0	0	3	−12	0	a
3	0	0	b	0	b	a
4	0	9	0	−3	0	a
5	0	12	0	0	3	$120
6	0	12	−1	0	0	a
7	4.5	0	0	6	0	$144
8	3	0	0	0	−3	a
9	3	0	1	0	0	$117
10	1.5	6	0	0	0	$108

[a] Outside the feasible space.
[b] No real solution.

Since L_X and L_Y cannot be negative, this solution is outside the feasible set.

The values obtained above are inserted into Table 9.3 as Solution 1. All other solution values were calculated in a similar manner and used to complete Table 9.3. It is apparent from the table that not all the solutions lie within the feasible space of our linear programming problem. Specifically, only Solutions 5, 7, 9, and 10 meet the nonnegativity requirement of the programming specification while simultaneously providing solutions in which the number of non-zero-valued variables is exactly equal to the number of constraints in the problem. Thus, these four solutions coincide with the corners of the dual problem's feasible space.[11]

At Solution 10 the total value imputed to Inputs A, B, and C is minimized. Accordingly, Solution 10 is the optimum solution, about which we can make the following observations:

1. The total imputed value of the firm's resources is exactly equal to the $108 maximum profit contribution which we found by solving the primal problem. Thus, the solutions to the primal and the dual programming problems are identical.

2. The shadow price for Input C, V_C, is zero. Since the shadow price measures the *marginal* value of the input to the firm, a zero shadow price implies that the re-

---

[11] Note that while the number of non-zero-valued variables at a corner of the feasible space in a linear programming problem is equal to the number of constraints, this does not mean that all solutions to the constraint set where the number of non-zero-valued variables is equal to the number of constraints will necessarily be corner points of the feasible space. This is because there exists the possibility of solutions involving negative values for the variables, and these solutions must obviously lie outside the feasible space since they violate the nonnegative restrictions on the variables.

source in question has a zero marginal value to the firm. This means that adding another unit of this input would add nothing to the firm's maximum obtainable profits. Thus, a zero shadow price for Input C is entirely consistent with our findings in the primal problem: Input C is not a binding constraint. Excess capacity exists in C, so additional units of C will not result in increased production of either X or Y.

3. The shadow price of Input A is \$1.50. A positive shadow price implies that this fixed resource imposes a binding constraint on the firm, and that, if an additional unit of A is added, the firm can increase its total profit by \$1.50. The firm can afford to pay up to \$1.50 for a marginal unit of Input A.[12]

4. The interpretation of Input B's shadow price is similar to that for A's. Since B imposes an effective constraint on the firm's production, an additional unit of B would allow increased production of X and Y, with total profit increasing by \$6. Thus, the firm can afford to pay up to \$6 for a marginal unit of B.

5. Both of the dual slack variables are zero. This means that the imputed value of the resources required to produce a single unit of X or Y is exactly equal to the profit contribution provided by each of them. Thus, the opportunity cost of both X and Y is zero, indicating that the resources required for their production are *not* more valuable to the firm in some alternative use. Again, this is entirely consistent with the solution of the primal programming problem, as both X and Y were produced at the optimal solution. Any product with a positive opportunity cost would be non-optimal and would not be produced in the profit maximizing primal solution.

Use of the Dual Solution to Solve the Primal Problem

The dual solution, as we have developed it thus far, does not give us the optimal amounts of X and Y; it does, however, provide all the information necessary to determine the optimum output mix. First, note that the dual solution informs us that Input C does not impose a binding constraint on output of X and Y. Further, it tells us that at the optimum output of X and Y, $\pi = \pi^* = \$108$. Now consider again the three constraints in the primal problem.

$$\text{Constraint on } A: 4Q_X + 2Q_Y + S_A = 32,$$

$$\text{Constraint on } B: 1Q_X + 1Q_Y + S_B = 10,$$

$$\text{Constraint on } C: 3Q_Y + S_C = 21.$$

[12]It would pay the firm to buy additional units of Input A at any price less than \$1.50 per unit until A is no longer a binding constraint. This statement concerning the interpretation of a shadow price assumes that the cost of the quantity of Input A used in the production of each unit of Products X and Y *was not* deducted from their selling prices to obtain the profit contribution figures used in the primal programming problem. If, in fact, those costs were included in the calculation of the profit contributions, then the shadow price must be interpreted as the amount *above* the current price of Input A that the firm could afford to pay for additional units.

We know that the constraints on A and B are binding, *because the dual solution found both of these inputs to have positive shadow prices*. (Recall that only resources that are fully utilized will have a non-zero marginal value in use.) Accordingly, the slack variables S_A and S_B are equal to zero, and the binding constraints can be rewritten as follows:

$$4Q_X + 2Q_Y = 32,$$

and

$$1Q_X + 1Q_Y = 10.$$

We have two equations in two unknowns, so the system can be solved for values of Q_X and Q_Y:

$$
\begin{array}{rr}
4Q_X + 2Q_Y = & 32 \\
-2Q_X - 2Q_Y = & -20 \\
\hline
2Q_X = & 12 \\
Q_X = & 6,
\end{array}
$$

and

$$6 + Q_Y = 10,$$

$$Q_Y = 4.$$

These values of Q_X and Q_Y, which were found after learning from the dual which constraints were binding, are identical to the values found by solving the primal problem. Further, having obtained the value for Q_Y, it is possible to substitute into the equation for Constraint C and solve for the amount of slack in that resource:

$$3Q_Y + S_C = 21$$

$$S_C = 21 - 3 \cdot 4 = 9.$$

These relationships, which allow one to solve either the primal or dual specification of a linear programming problem and then quickly obtain the solution to the other, can be generalized by the following two expressions:

$$\text{Primal Objective Variable}_i \times \text{Dual Slack Variable}_i \equiv 0. \qquad \textbf{(9.15)}$$

$$\text{Primal Slack Variable}_j \times \text{Dual Objective Variable}_j \equiv 0. \qquad \textbf{(9.16)}$$

Equation 9.15 states that if an ordinary variable in the primal problem takes on a non-zero value in the optimal solution to that problem, its related dual slack variable must be zero. Only if a particular Q_i is zero-valued in the solution to the primal can its related dual slack, L_i, take on a non-zero value.

A similar relationship holds between the slack variables in the primal problem and their related ordinary variables in the dual, as indicated by Equation 9.16. If the primal slack is non-zero-valued, then the related dual variable will be zero-valued and vice versa.

CONSTRAINED COST MINIMIZATION: AN ADDITIONAL LINEAR PROGRAMMING PROBLEM EXAMPLE

The use of linear programming to solve constrained optimization problems is relatively complex, as is developing an understanding of the economic significance of the results. Gaining facility with the use of the technique requires substantial exposure and practice. Accordingly, in this section we provide an additional example of a typical managerial problem that can be solved with linear programming.

Constrained cost-minimization problems are frequently encountered in managerial decision making. One interesting example associated with a firm's marketing activities is the problem of minimizing advertising expenditures subject to meeting certain audience-exposure requirements. Consider, for example, a firm that is planning an advertising campaign for a new product. The goals that have been set for the campaign include exposure to at least 100,000 individuals, with no fewer than 80,000 of those individuals having incomes of at least $25,000 annually and no fewer than 40,000 of them being unmarried. For simplicity we will assume that the firm has only two media, radio and television, available for this campaign. One television ad costs $10,000 and is estimated to reach an audience numbering, on the average, 20,000 persons. Ten thousand of these individuals will have incomes of $25,000 or more, while 4,000 of them will be single. A radio ad, on the other hand, costs $6,000 and reaches a total audience of 10,000 individuals, all of whom have at least $25,000 in income. Eight thousand of the persons exposed to a radio ad will be unmarried. Table 9.4 summarizes these data.

TABLE 9.4

Advertising Media Relationships

	Radio	Television
Cost per ad	$ 6,000	$10,000
Total audience per ad	10,000	20,000
Audience per ad with income $\geq$ $25,000	10,000	10,000
Audience per ad single	8,000	4,000

The Primal Problem

The linear programming problem the firm would use to solve this constrained-optimization problem is developed as follows. The objective is to minimize the cost of the advertising campaign. Since total cost is merely the sum of the amounts spent on radio and television ads, the objective function is given by the expression:

Minimize   Cost = $6,000R + $10,000TV,

where R and TV represent the number of radio and television ads, respectively, that are to be employed in the advertising campaign.

The linear programming problem will have a total of three constraint equations: (1) the requirement for total audience exposure, (2) the income-related exposure requirement, and (3) the requirement that at least 40,000 single persons be among those exposed to the advertising campaign.

The restriction on the minimum number of individuals that must be reached by the ad campaign can be expressed as: [13]

$$10,000R + 20,000TV \geq 100,000.$$

This equation states that the number of persons exposed to radio ads (10,000 times the number of radio ads) plus the number exposed to television ads (20,000 times the number of television ads) must be equal to or greater than 100,000.

The remaining two constraints can be constructed similarly from the data in Table 9.4. The constraint on exposures to individuals with incomes of at least $25,000 is written:

$$10,000R + 10,000TV \geq 80,000,$$

while the marital status constraint is given by:

$$8,000R + 4,000TV \geq 40,000.$$

Combining the cost-minimization objective function with the three constraints—written in their equality form through the introduction of slack variables—allows us to write the programming problem as:

Minimize

$$Cost = $6,000R + $10,000TV,$$

---

[13]There is an implicit assumption in this formulation of the constraint that individuals are exposed *only once to either* a radio or a television ad. This could be accomplished by coordinating the times at which the ads are to run.

subject to

$$10,000R + 20,000TV - S_A = 100,000,$$

$$10,000R + 10,000TV - S_I = 80,000,$$

and

$$8,000R + 4,000TV - S_S = 40,000.$$

$$R, TV, S_A, S_I, S_S \geq 0.$$

Here S_A, S_I, and S_S are the slack variables indicating the extent to which the minimums on total audience exposure, on exposure to individuals with incomes of at least $25,000, and on exposure to single individuals, respectively, have been exceeded. Note that the slack variables are *subtracted* from the constraint equations in this situation since we are dealing with equal-to or greater-than inequalities. That is, excess capacity or slack in any of the constraints implies that the audience exposure is greater than required. Thus, in order to make the exposures exactly equal to the required quantity, one must subtract the slack from the total.

The solution to this linear programming problem is easily obtained graphically. Figure 9.11 illustrates that solution. There the feasible space for the programming problem is delimited by the three constraint equations and the nonnegativity requirements. Addition of an isocost curve allows one to determine that costs are minimized at Point M, where the constraints on total audience exposure and exposures to individuals meeting the income requirement are binding. The solution to the problem indicates that the firm should employ 6 radio and 2 television ads in its campaign in order to minimize its expenditure while meeting the audience goals set for the program. The total cost for such a campaign would be $56,000.

The Dual Problem

The dual linear programming problem for the advertising-mix decision provides some very interesting and valuable information to the firm's management. It will prove instructive to formulate, solve, and interpret that form of the problem.

The dual programming problem in this situation will be a constrained-maximization problem, since the primal problem was a minimization problem. Also, we know that the objective function of the dual problem will be expressed in terms of shadow prices or imputed values for the constraints or restrictions in the primal problem. Thus, the dual objective function will contain three variables: (1) the imputed value, or shadow price, for the total audience exposure requirement, (2) the shadow price of the high-income audience requirement, and (3) the shadow price associated with the marital status constraint. Since the constraint limits in the pri-

FIGURE 9.11

Advertising Cost-Minimization Linear Programming Problem

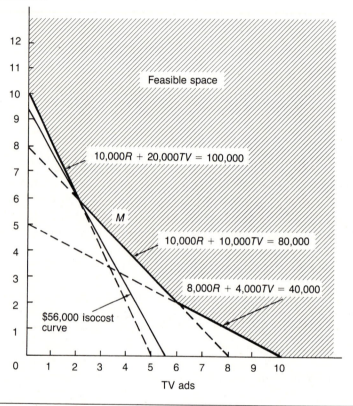

Radio ads

mal problem become the objective function parameters in the dual, the dual objective function can be written as:

Maximize $C^* = 100,000V_A + 80,000V_I + 40,000V_S,$

where V_A, V_I, and V_S are the three shadow prices described above.

The constraints in the dual problem are developed in terms of the objective function variables from the primal. Thus, there will be only two constraint conditions in the problem, the first associated with radio ads and the second with television ads. Both of these constraints will be of an equal-to or *less-than* nature since the constraints in the primal were of an equal-to or *greater-than* form.

The limit on the constraint associated with radio advertising is the $6,000 coefficient of radio ads found in the objective function of the primal problem. The coefficients for the three shadow prices in the constraint equation are the numbers of exposures within each category provided by a single radio ad. The coefficient for the total audience exposure shadow price, V_A, therefore, will be 10,000, the number of individuals exposed to a radio ad. Similarly, the coefficient for V_I is 10,000, and that for V_S is 8,000. The constraint for radio ads, then, is given by:

$$10{,}000V_A + 10{,}000V_I + 8{,}000V_S \leq 6{,}000.$$

The constraint associated with television advertising is constructed in the same fashion. Since each TV ad reaches a total audience of 20,000, this is the parameter for the V_A variable in the second constraint equation. The coefficients for V_I and V_S are 10,000 and 4,000, respectively, because these are the numbers of individuals in the income and marital categories exposed to one TV ad. With the $10,000 cost of a television ad providing a limit to the constraint, the second constraint equation for the dual problem is:

$$20{,}000V_A + 10{,}000V_I + 4{,}000V_S \leq 10{,}000.$$

With the introduction of slack variables in the constraints, the dual programming problem can be stated:

Maximize

$$C^* = 100{,}000V_A + 80{,}000V_I + 40{,}000V_S,$$

subject to

$$10{,}000V_A + 10{,}000V_I + 8{,}000V_S + L_R = 6{,}000,$$

and

$$20{,}000V_A + 10{,}000V_I + 4{,}000V_S + L_{TV} = 10{,}000.$$

$$V_A, V_I, V_S, L_R, L_{TV} \geq 0.$$

Solving the Dual. While it would be possible, although difficult, to solve the dual programming problem using either a three-dimensional graph or the complete enumeration technique developed earlier in this chapter, there is a much easier way to obtain the solution, since we have already solved the primal problem. Recall that the solution to both the primal and dual statements of a single linear programming problem will always be identical, and that the following relationships must always hold:

Primal Objective Variable$_i$ × Dual Slack Variable$_i$ ≡ 0.

Primal Slack Variable$_j$ × Dual Objective Variable$_j$ ≡ 0.

Thus, in this programming problem:

$$R \times L_R = 0 \text{ and } TV \times L_{TV} = 0,$$

and

$$S_A \times V_A = 0, \ S_I \times V_I = 0, \text{ and } S_S \times V_S = 0.$$

Since we know from the primal problem that both R and TV are non-zero-valued variables, L_R and L_{TV} in the dual problem must both be zero at the optimal solution. Further, since there was excess audience exposure in the unmarried category in the solution to the primal—that is, $S_S \neq 0$—we know that V_S in the dual must take on a value of zero in the optimal solution. This leaves only V_A and V_I as unknowns in the dual programming problem, and their values can be easily obtained by solving the two-equation constraint system for the two unknowns:

$$10,000V_A + 10,000V_I = \ \ 6,000,$$

$$20,000V_A + 10,000V_I = 10,000.$$

Subtracting the second constraint equation from the first results in:

$$-10,000V_A = -4,000,$$

$$V_A = 0.4.$$

Substituting the value 0.4 for V_A in either constraint equation produces a value of 0.2 for V_I. Finally, substituting the values for V_A, V_I, and V_S into the objective function of the dual problem results in a value for C^* of $56,000 (0.4 × 100,000 + 0.2 × 80,000 + 0 × 40,000), exactly the same as the minimum cost figure obtained in the solution of the primal problem.

Interpreting the Dual Problem Results. The solution to the primal of our linear programming problem tells management which advertising mix meets the various goals of its marketing program at the least cost and, thereby, allows the firm to move ahead with the promotional campaign. However, the results of the dual problem are equally valuable for effective management. This is due to the fact that the dual program solution allows management to evaluate the goals that are being used to determine how best to advertise the new product.

Recall that the dual problem objective function variables, the various shadow prices, provide a measure of how the constraints affect the primal problem's objective function *at the margin*. That is, each shadow price indicates the change in the optimal solution value of the primal (and also dual) problem objective function that would accompany a marginal change in the related constraint.

Thus, in the problem we are examining, each dual problem shadow price indicates the change in total cost that would accompany a 1-unit change in the various audience-exposure requirements. They are, therefore, the marginal costs of the last audience exposure gained in each of the three categories; total, with incomes $\geq \$25,000$, and single. For example, the value of V_A is the marginal cost of reaching the last individual in the total audience that is exposed to the firm's ads. In this case V_A is 0.4, indicating that if the firm were to reduce by one the number of total individuals who must come in contact with an ad, there would be a \$0.40 reduction in the \$56,000 total cost of the advertising program. Similarly, the marginal cost of increasing total audience exposure from 100,000 to 100,001 individuals is 40¢.

V_I, the shadow price of reaching individuals with incomes of at least \$25,000, is 0.2, or 20¢. This means that it would cost the firm an extra 20¢ per individual to reach more persons in the high-income category.

The zero value found for V_S, the shadow price for the requirement on exposures to unmarried individuals, indicates that the proposed advertising campaign already reaches more than the 40,000 required individuals in this category. Thus, a small change in that constraint will have no effect on the total cost of the promotion.

By comparing these marginal costs with the benefits it expects to derive from additional audience exposures in the various classes, the firm's management will be able to determine whether the goals on audience exposures are appropriate. If the expected return (profit) from one additional individual seeing an ad exceeded 40¢, it would prove profitable to design an advertising campaign for a larger audience. Likewise, if the expected return from an additional exposure to an individual in the \$25,000 and above income class were greater than the 20¢ marginal cost of reaching one more person in that class, then again, the lower limit on exposures to that group should be raised. In both cases a determination that the marginal profitability of the last audience exposure was less than its marginal cost (shadow price) would indicate that the firm should reduce the size of the audience requirement for that particular category. Such a reduction would increase profits, since the costs of the advertising campaign would fall faster than the profits on lost sales.

The two slack variables in the dual problem also have an interesting interpretation. They represent the opportunity costs of using a specific advertising medium. L_R is thus a measure of the inefficiency associated with using radio in the promotion, while the value of L_{TV} indicates the added cost of including television in the media mix employed. Both L_R and L_{TV} were zero in the solution to the dual problem, which indicates that neither medium is cost inefficient and that, in fact, both should be included in the promotional mix. This was also what we found in the solution to the primal problem.

This example has again demonstrated the symmetry of the primal and dual specifications of a linear programming problem. Either can be used to solve the basic problem, and the interpretations of both provide much valuable information for decision making purposes.

Postscript on the Relation of Linear Programming to the Lagrangian Technique

In an earlier section we pointed out that linear programming is used to solve maximization and minimization problems, subject to inequality constraints, just as the Lagrangian technique was used to solve optimization problems, subject to constraints that can be stated as equalities. Recall from Chapter 2 that the Lagrangian multiplier, λ, is the marginal gain in the objective function obtained by relaxing the constraint by 1 unit. In the preceding section we learned that the values of the dual variables, the shadow prices, measure the value of relaxing input constraints by 1 unit. Thus, the shadow prices are the linear programming equivalents to Lagrangian multipliers.

SUMMARY

Linear programming is a technique for solving maximization or minimization problems in which inequality constraints are imposed on the decision maker. This kind of problem occurs frequently in both business and government, so linear programming is rapidly becoming one of the most widely used tools in the sophisticated decision maker's kit.

Although linear programming has been applied to a wide variety of business problems, it has been developed most fully, and is used most frequently, in production problems. Accordingly, we used two production problems to explain the basic elements of the theory of linear programming. First, we presented the theory in graphic form, and then we showed that the same solution can be reached by an algebraic technique. The graphic method is useful to explain the theory; but the algebraic method is the one used in actual practice, because it can be adapted for solution by computers and used to solve the large, complex problems actually faced by managers.

After discussing the *primal* linear programming problem, we showed that for every primal problem there exists an equivalent *dual* problem. The primal is of interest because it provides us with values for the controllable variables—the output mix in our first illustrative problem. The dual is useful because the shadow prices that it generates for each input are an indication of the marginal value of adding additional capacity for each fixed input.

QUESTIONS

9.1 Can firms whose output is produced using a fixed-coefficients production system ignore input prices in determining optimal input proportions?

9.2 What managerial problems can be solved by linear programming? Give some illustrations of situations where you think the technique is useful.

9.3 Why can linear programming *not* be used in each of the following situations?
    a. Strong economies of scale exist.
    b. As the firm expands output, the prices of variable factors of production increase.
    c. As output increases, product prices decline.

9.4 What is the major similarity between linear programming and the Lagrangian multiplier technique? The major difference?

9.5 At corners of the feasible space why is the fact that the number of non-zero-valued variables exactly equals the number of constraints so important in linear programming?

9.6 If the primal problem calls for determining the set of outputs that will maximize profits, subject to constraints on inputs:
    a. What is the dual objective function?
    b. What interpretation can be given to the dual variables, defined as the shadow prices or imputed values?
    c. What does it mean if a dual variable or shadow price is zero?

PROBLEMS

9.1 Assume that production of a particular product, Q, makes use of two input factors, L and K, and that the production function can be expressed as $Q = (1/6)K^{0.5}L^{0.5}$.
    a. Explain the difference between *returns to factors of input* and *returns to scale*. What is the nature of each in the production system described in this problem?
    b. Assuming that each unit of L costs $4 and each unit of K costs $12, what is the optimal ratio in which to combine L and K in this production system?
    c. Assume now and throughout the remainder of the problem that while the production function given above indicates the output produced from this system, it is valid only for input combinations in the ratio of $9L$ to $4K$. (Note that this means that 1 unit of Q could be produced with 9 units of L and 4 units of K, 2 units of Q would require 18 units of L and 8 units of K, and so forth.) What are the returns to factors of input and returns to scale under these conditions?

d. Assuming each unit of L costs \$4 and each unit of K costs \$12, what combination of L and K would be used to produce 4 units of Q? Determine the quantity of L and K that would be used to produce 16 units of Q.

e. Assume that the firm producing this product has 45 units of L and 36 units of K available during the next production period. What is the maximum quantity of output the firm can produce with these limits on input availability?

f. Given the assumptions in Part e, what are the marginal products of additional units of L and K?

9.2 Suntron Electronics has just received an order for a large quantity of ripple control switches (an electronic switch triggered by FM signals sent through the electric wires which supply power to a piece of equipment). The company has been offered a substantial premium on the contract for rush delivery, but it must supply the switches at a rate of no fewer than 20 units a day to receive the premium. Because the production manager knows that the only production bottleneck will come in the final-assembly department, he is concentrating on maximizing output from that department.

Final assembly of the switches requires two input factors, labor and a test facility. Since it is impossible either to hire more labor with the proper skills or to purchase an additional test facility in time to meet this contract, the quantities of these two inputs available for use are limited to the amounts on hand: a total of 150 labor hours and of 40 test facility hours available each day.

The company is able to combine these two input factors in three different ratios using different production techniques. These input ratios are fixed for each production method regardless of the output level, and each method exhibits constant returns to scale. The input requirements for each method are provided in the table below:

	Input Requirement per Ripple Control Switch Using Process		
Resource	A	B	C
Labor (hours)	10	8	6
Test facility (hours)	1	1.4	2.4

a. The optimal usage of inputs in the final-assembly department for this problem can be determined by using linear programming methods. Set up the appropriate linear programming problem. (Define Q_A, Q_B, and Q_C as the quantity of switches produced by Processes A, B, and C respectively. Use the equality form for expressing the constraint conditions.)

b. Solve the primal problem using graphic techniques. (*Hint*: Draw an isoquant for 20 switches, then use the fact that all isoquants are parallel to determine the corner solution.)

c. Formulate the related dual linear programming problem, again using the equality form for stating constraint requirements.

d. Use your solution of the primal (that is, your knowledge from the primal of which variables are zero) to obtain the solution to the dual.

e. Interpret all variables *and* equations in both the primal and the dual linear programming problems.

f. Carefully examine the graph you constructed for Part b, then answer the following questions: (i) Will Process *B* or *C* be used more intensively if more labor is made available? (ii) How many additional units of labor will be required to make Suntron cease to use Process *C*?

9.3 Dallas Legal Clinic provides a variety of legal services. The Clinic is operated by 3 lawyers, 5 paralegals, and 3 secretaries. The Clinic currently has a large backlog of two types of jobs. The first type is unfair trade practice or consumer protection actions; the second is divorce proceedings. The firm has decided that it must clean up the backlog. Therefore, they want to maximize the number of these actions handled each day. The completion of each consumer protection job requires 4 hours of time by a lawyer, 3 hours of paralegal effort, and 3 hours of secretarial work. Each divorce action requires on average 1.5 hours of a lawyer's time, 4 hours of work by a paralegal, and 1.5 hours of secretarial effort.

a. Formulate a linear programming problem that Dallas Legal Clinic could use to determine how best to employ its resources. Assume that the lawyers and paralegals each work 10-hour days while the secretaries work only 8 hours per day.

b. Formulate the dual problem specification.

c. Solve both the primal and dual linear programming problems you constructed.

d. Assuming the firm's owners believe that completing another job in a day is worth $80, how much would they be willing to pay a secretary for working an hour of overtime?

9.4 Jackson Hole Mining Company has two mines with different production capacities for producing the same type of ore. After mining and crushing, the ore is graded into three classes: high, medium, and low. The company has contracted to provide a smelter with 48 tons of high-grade, 32 tons of medium-grade, and 96 tons of low-grade ore each week. It costs JHM $4,000 per day to operate Mine A and $3,200 per day to run Mine B. In a day's time, Mine A produces 12 tons of high-grade, 4 tons of medium-grade, and 8 tons of low-grade ore. Mine B produces 4, 4, and 24 tons per day of each grade respectively. The problem faced by JHM's management is to determine how many days a week to operate each mine.

a. Use a linear programming approach to solve this problem. Set up the problem algebraically, using both the inequality and equality forms of the constraint equations. Use a graph to determine the optimal solution (corner point), and then check your solution algebraically.

9.5 Midwest Hog Growers, Inc. (MHG), operates a number of hog farms in midwestern states. MHG's operating profits have declined sharply over the past month due to substantial price increases for both corn and soybeans, the prime ingredients in the feed mixture used by MHG. Jeremy Andrews, production manager of MHG, believes that the firm's profits might be improved by altering the firm's standard feed mixture. The daily feed mixture currently being used at a typical hog farm with 80 breeder sows with litters is composed of 300 pounds of corn gluten feed and 200 pounds of soybean meal. The corn has a cost of $300 per hundred, and the soybean meal costs $240 per hundred. Andrews has obtained data from a state university agriculture extensionist indicating that 80 sows with litters require at least 500 pounds of feed per day and that the feed mixture should contain at least 3,000 units of protein, 3,200 units of carbohydrates, and 9,000 units of roughage.

   a. Assuming that each 100 pounds of the corn mix contains 500 units of protein, 800 units of carbohydrates, and 3,000 units of roughage, and that each 100 pounds of soybean meal has 1,000 units of protein, 400 units of carbohydrates, and 1,000 units of roughage, set up the linear programming problem that Andrews would use to determine the best feed mixture for MHG.

   b. Solve the linear programming problem that you constructed in Part a.

   c. Set up and solve the related dual programming problem.

   d. Interpret your results in Parts b and c explicitly, explaining precisely what each variable in your linear programming problem relates to and how you would make use of the information provided by your results.

9.6 Designed for Style, Inc. (DFS), is a small architectural firm that designs single-family and multifamily housing units for real estate developers, building contractors, etc. DFS offers custom designs for single-family units, Q_1, for $3,000 and custom designs for multifamily units (duplexes, fourplexes, etc.), Q_2, for $2,000 each. Both types of output make use of scarce drafting, artwork, and architectural resources. Each custom design for single-family units requires 12 hours of drafting, 2 hours of artwork, and 6 hours of architectural input. Each custom design for multifamily units requires 4 hours of drafting, 5 hours of artwork, and 6 hours of architectural input. Currently DFS has 72 hours of drafting, 30 hours of artwork, and 48 hours of architectural services available on a weekly basis.

   What output mix would be optimal if DFS wishes to maximize its total sales revenue?

   a. Set up and interpret the primal and dual linear programs that DFS might use to determine an optimal weekly product mix. (*Note*: You may assume that basic linearity assumptions hold.)

   b. Solve for and interpret all solution values.

   c. Would DFS's optimal product mix be different with a profit maximization rather than sales revenue maximization goal? Why or why not?

9.7 Jeanne Danco operates an income tax service. Working for Danco are two tax return preparers and two secretary–typists. Danco's tax service concentrates on personal income tax returns and charges $50 to prepare a complex return and $20 to prepare a simple return. Each complex return requires 3 hours of Danco's time plus 2 hours of time from one of the tax preparers and 4 hours of typing. A simple return requires 1 hour of Danco's time, 2 hours of a tax preparer's time, and 1 hour of typing.

    a. Set up the primal and dual linear programming problem that Danco would use to maximize weekly total revenue subject to a 75 hour per week limit on her work, a 50 hour per week limit on the availability of each of the two tax return preparers, and a 40 hour per week limit on each of the two secretary–typists.

    b. Solve both the primal and dual problems.

    c. Assume that the secretary–typists each earn $5 per hour. How much would Danco be able to pay for another hour of tax preparer time without reducing *profits*? (Assume no other variable costs.)

    d. With the current mix of employees, what is the opportunity cost in terms of forgone *revenue* of an hour of Danco's time?

    e. Would the cost you calculated in Part d be an implicit or an explicit cost? Explain.

9.8 AB Corporation manufactures two products, A and B. Production and sale of the products are independent of each other except that they make use of the same inputs in their production. The production functions for both products exhibit constant returns to scale. Three inputs are used to produce A and B. These inputs are designated X, Y, and Z. Production of each unit of A requires 2 units of X, 1 unit of Y, and 1 unit of Z. Each unit of B requires 1 unit of X and 2 units of Z. Profit contributions of A and B are $8 and $6 respectively regardless of output levels.

    a. Formulate the linear programming problem AB would use to maximize short-run profits assuming the firm has 100 units of X, 40 units of Y, and 110 units of Z available during the current production period. Provide both a primal and a dual problem specification.

    b. Graph the problem and then solve it completely.

    c. Interpret the problem. Be as explicit and complete as possible with your answer.

    d. Assume now that AB is offered $6 for each unit of Resource Y that it doesn't use in its own production of A and B. If AB Corporation wants to maximize short-run profits, what should it do? Why?

9.9 Data Processors, Inc., is a small but rapidly growing firm located in Portland, Oregon. Historically, DPI's business products division has offered various types of programming services including Inventory (I), Budget (B), and Marketing (M) information processing. Each type of program service requires the use of junior (J) and senior (P) programming personnel, as well as computing facilities (C). Input requirements are as follows:

Output	Input Hours Required per Unit of Output		
	J	P	C
I	15	5	1
B	10	2	4
M	10	2	2

Junior programmers are readily available in the Portland area, but DPI has only been able to retain a single senior programmer on a part-time basis (80 hours per month). While junior programmers earn an average $10 per hour, DPI pays its senior programmer a $19,200 annual salary. Furthermore, DPI has signed a $216,000 contract with a time-sharing company making available a maximum of 60 hours of computer time per month. This agreement covers a 24-month period. DPI is currently re-evaluating the monthly product mix of its business products division in light of prevailing output prices of $750 for inventory, $1000 for budget, and $900 for marketing programs. DPI has an explicit organizational objective of profit maximization.

a. Set up and interpret the primal and dual linear programs that DPI might use to determine an optimal monthly product mix. (*Note*: You may assume that basic linearity assumptions hold.)

b. Solve for and interpret all solution values.

c. Given an optimal output mix, determine the business products division's monthly net profit before taxes. The division has $6,000 per month in fixed expenses unrelated to programming personnel or computing facilities.

d. What output and input combinations would occur if DPI wished to reduce programming staff in order to specialize in only one type of business product? Be sure to consider all relevant alternatives.

e. Determine the short- and long-run profit opportunity costs of such a strategy. Again, consider all relevant alternatives.

SELECTED REFERENCES

Baumol, William J. *Economic Theory and Operations Analysis*, 3d ed., Chapters 5 and 6. Englewood Cliffs, N.J.: Prentice-Hall, 1972.

Dantzig, George B. *Linear Programming and Extensions*. Princeton, N.J.: Princeton University Press, 1963.

Dorfman, Robert. "Mathematical, or Linear, Programming: A Nonmathematical Approach." *American Economic Review* 43 (December 1953): 797–825.

Dorfman, Robert, Samuelson, Paul A., and Solow, Robert M. *Linear Programming and Economic Analysis*. New York: McGraw-Hill, 1958.

Harvey, Charles M. *An Introduction to Linear Optimization*. New York: North-Holland, 1979.

Rau, Nicholas. *Matrices and Mathematical Programming: An Introduction for Economists*. New York: St. Martin's Press, 1981.

Rothenberg, Ronald I. *Linear Programming*. New York: North-Holland, 1980.

Wu, Yuan-Li, and Kwang, Ching-Wen. "An Analytical Comparison of Marginal Analysis and Mathematical Programming in the Theory of the Firm." in *Linear Programming and the Theory of the Firm*, eds. Kenneth E. Boulding and W. Allen Spivey. New York: McGraw-Hill, 1960.

APPENDIX 9A

RULES FOR FORMING THE DUAL LINEAR PROGRAMMING PROBLEM

Given the importance of duality, a list of simple rules that can be used to form the dual program to any given primal program would be useful. Five such rules exist. They are as follows:

1. Change a maximize objective to minimize and vice versa.

2. Reverse primal constraint inequality signs in dual constraints (i.e., $\geq$ to $\leq$, or $\leq$ to $\geq$).

3. Transpose primal constraint coefficients to get dual constraint coefficients.

4. Transpose objective function coefficients to get limits in dual constraints and vice versa.

Here the word *transpose* is a term that simply means that each row of coefficients is rearranged into columns so that row one becomes column one, row two becomes column two, and so on.

To illustrate the rules for transformation from primal and dual, consider the following simple example.

Primal Program

Maximize

$$\pi = \pi_1 Q_1 + \pi_2 Q_2$$

subject to

$$a_{11}Q_1 + a_{12}Q_2 \leq r_1$$

$$a_{21}Q_1 + a_{22}Q_2 \leq r_2$$

$$Q_1, Q_2 \geq 0.$$

Here π is profits and Q is output. Thus, π_1 and π_2 are unit profits for Q_1 and Q_2, respectively. The resource constraints are given by r_1 and r_2. The constants in the primal constraints reflect the input requirements for each type of output. For example, a_{11} is the amount of resource r_1 in one unit of output Q_1. Similarly, a_{12} is the amount of resource r_1 in one unit of output Q_2. Thus, $a_{11}Q_1 + a_{12}Q_2$ is the total amount of resource r_1 used in production. The remaining input requirements, a_{21} and a_{22}, have a similar interpretation. For convenience, the primal program described above can be rewritten in matrix notation as:

Primal Program

Maximize

$$\pi = \pi_1 Q_1 + \pi_2 Q_2$$

subject to

$$\begin{bmatrix} a_{11} & a_{12} \\ a_{21} & a_{22} \end{bmatrix} \cdot \begin{bmatrix} Q_1 \\ Q_2 \end{bmatrix} \le \begin{bmatrix} r_1 \\ r_2 \end{bmatrix}$$

$$Q_1, Q_2 \ge 0.$$

Matrix notation is just a convenient form for writing large numbers of equations. In going from matrix back to algebraic notation, one just multiplies each row element by each column element. Thus, the left-hand side of the first constraint equation is $a_{11} \times Q_1$ plus $a_{12} \times Q_2$, or $a_{11}Q_1 + a_{12}Q_2$, and this sum must be less than or equal to r_1.

Given the expression of the primal program in matrix notation, we can now apply the four rules for transformation from primal to dual. Following these rules, we have:

Dual Program

Minimize

$$\pi^* = r_1 V_1 + r_2 V_2$$

subject to

$$\begin{bmatrix} a_{11} & a_{21} \\ a_{12} & a_{22} \end{bmatrix} \cdot \begin{bmatrix} V_1 \\ V_2 \end{bmatrix} \ge \begin{bmatrix} \pi_1 \\ \pi_2 \end{bmatrix}$$

$$V_1, V_2 \ge 0$$

and converting from matrix back to algebraic notation we have:

Dual Program

Minimize

$$\pi^* = r_1V_1 + r_2V_2$$

subject to

$$a_{11}V_1 + a_{21}V_2 \geq \pi_1$$

$$a_{12}V_1 + a_{22}V_2 \geq \pi_2$$

$$V_1, V_2 \geq 0.$$

Here V_1 and V_2 are the shadow prices for resources one and two respectively. Since r_1 and r_2 represent the quantities of the two resources available, the objective function measures the total imputed value of the resources available. Recalling the interpretation of a_{11} and a_{21} from the primal, we see that $a_{11}V_1 + a_{21}V_2$ is the total value of inputs used in production of one unit of output Q_1. Similarly, $a_{12}V_1 + a_{22}V_2$ is the total value of inputs used in production of a unit of output Q_2.

Finally, the primal and dual linear programming problems shown above can be fully specified through the introduction of slack variables. Remember that with less-than or equal-to constraints, the left-hand side of the constraint equation must be brought up to equal the right-hand side. Thus, slack variables must be *added to* the left-hand side of such constraint equations. With greater-than or equal-to constraints, the left-hand side of the constraint equation must be brought down to equal the right-hand side. Thus, slack variables must be *subtracted from* the left-hand side of such constraint equations. With this, the full specification of the above primal and dual linear programs can be written:

Primal Program	**Dual Program**
Maximize	Minimize
$$\pi = \pi_1Q_1 + \pi_2Q_2$$	$$\pi^* = r_1V_1 + r_2V_2$$
subject to	subject to
$$a_{11}Q_1 + a_{12}Q_2 + S_1 = r_1$$	$$a_{11}V_1 + a_{21}V_2 - L_1 = \pi_1$$
$$a_{21}Q_1 + a_{22}Q_2 + S_2 = r_2$$	$$a_{12}V_1 + a_{22}V_2 - L_2 = \pi_2$$
$$Q_1, Q_2, S_1, S_2 \geq 0,$$	$$V_1, V_2, L_1, L_2 \geq 0,$$

where S_1 and S_2 are slack variables representing excess capacity of resource r_1 and r_2 respectively. L_1 and L_2 are also slack variables; they represent the amount by which the value of resources used in the production of Q_1 and Q_2 exceeds the value of output as measured by π_1 and π_2 respectively. Thus, L_1 and L_2 measure the opportunity cost or profit forgone as a result of producing the last unit of Q_1 and Q_2.

Understanding the simple rules for transformation discussed above will both simplify construction of the dual given a primal program and facilitate the understanding and interpretation of the constraints and coefficients found in primal and dual linear programming problems.

CHAPTER 10
MARKET STRUCTURE

We began our study of managerial economics by examining the microeconomic model of the firm. That model assumes the maximization of value—subject to constraints imposed by technology, resource limitations, and the economic and political environments in which the firm operates—to be the primary objective of management. This maximization process is extremely complex, involving the full range of business functions. Thus far, we have (1) examined the principles of optimization, (2) considered the nature of risk and its effect on the value of the firm and on managerial decision making, (3) studied the characteristics of demand and ways of estimating the demand function, (4) analyzed the process of production, (5) developed an understanding of optimal resource employment, and (6) investigated the nature of cost/output relationships and the role of costs in managerial decision making.

Having examined these components of managerial economics, we are now in a position to integrate the various topics to show how demand, production, and cost characteristics interact to determine both the market structure within which a firm operates and the nature of the price/output decision faced by the firm. In this chapter we develop the basic microeconomic models of market structure and optimal price/output determination. The empirical relevance of the various models of market structure is also discussed in the final section, where the industrial organization of U.S. industry is examined.

CLASSIFICATION OF MARKET STRUCTURES

Market structure refers to the degree of competition in the market for a particular good or service. A market consists of all firms and individuals who are willing and able to buy or sell a particular product. The most important characteristics of markets are the number and size distribution of buyers and sellers and the extent of product differentiation. Markets are traditionally divided into four classifications; these four prototypic structures are defined below and elaborated on in the remainder of the chapter.

Perfect (pure) competition is a market structure characterized by a large number of buyers and sellers, each of whose transactions are so small in relation to total industry output that they cannot affect the price of the product. Individual buyers and sellers are *price takers*. No firm earns above-normal profits in the long run.

Perfect (pure) monopoly is a market structure characterized by the existence of a single producer. A monopolistic firm simultaneously determines product price and output. It is possible for a monopoly to earn above-normal profits, even in the long run.

Monopolistic competition is a market structure quite similar to pure competition, but distinguished from it by the fact that consumers perceive differences among the products of different firms. Firms have some control over the prices at which they sell their products. As in pure competition, above-normal profits are attainable only in the short run.

Oligopoly is a market structure in which a small number of firms produce most of the industry's output. Oligopoly is subdivided into *differentiated oligopoly*, in which the product is not standardized (automobiles), and *undifferentiated oligopoly*, in which the product is standardized (steel). Under either class, the price/output decisions of firms are interdependent in the sense that if one firm changes its price, the other firms will react, and this knowledge is incorporated into the firm's price/output decision problem.

FACTORS DETERMINING MARKET STRUCTURE

Two key elements are involved in determining market structure: the number of buyers and sellers in the market and the extent to which the product is standardized.

These factors, in turn, are influenced by the nature of the product, the form of the industry's production function, and the characteristics of consumers. These relationships are described in the following subsections.

Effect of Product Characteristics on Market Structure

A product's characteristics can affect the structure of the market in which it is sold. If other products are good substitutes for the one in question, this will increase the degree of competition in the market. To illustrate, rail service between two points is typically supplied by only one railroad. Transportation service is available from several sources, however, and railroads compete with bus lines, truck companies, barges, airlines, and private autos. The substitutability of these other modes of transportation for rail service increases the degree of competition in the transportation service market.[1]

The physical characteristics of a product can also influence the competitive structure of its market. A low ratio of distribution cost to total cost, for example, tends to increase competition by widening the geographic range over which any particular producer can compete. Rapid perishability of a product produces the opposite effect.

Effect of Production Functions on Market Structure

The nature of the production function is perhaps the most fundamental determinant of market structure. Industries whose production functions exhibit increasing returns to scale out to a large output level in relation to total market demand are characterized by fewer producers and thus by less competition than are industries where constant or decreasing returns enter at an output that is small relative to total product demand.

Effect of Buyers on Market Structure

The degree of competition in a market is affected by buyers as well as sellers. If there are only a few buyers, there will be less competition than if there are many buyers. This situation, which is defined as *monopsony* (only one buyer) or *oligopsony* (a few large buyers), sometimes exists in local labor markets dominated by a

---

[1] It is important to note that market structures are not static. In the 1800s and early 1900s—before the introduction of trucks, buses, autos, and airplanes—the railroads were subject to very little competition. Railroads could therefore charge excessive prices and earn monopoly profits. Because of this exploitation, laws were passed giving public authorities permission to regulate the prices railroads charge (a topic discussed in detail in Chapter 12). Additionally, other firms were enticed by the railroads' profits to develop the competing transportation service systems, which led ultimately to a much more competitive market structure.

single firm, in local agricultural markets dominated by a few large processors, in governmental purchases of complex systems, and in markets for certain components, such as auto parts used by the major auto manufacturers.

Consumer education and mobility also affect the degree of competition in a market. Increasing consumer awareness of price and product differentials, coupled with the possibility of geographic mobility, increases competition by removing the constraints that allow isolated (perhaps noncompetitive) submarkets to exist.

PURE COMPETITION

The market characteristics described in the preceding section, together with certain other factors, determine the degree of competition in the market for any good or service.[2] In this section we discuss pure competition in some detail; the other prototypic market structures defined above are discussed in subsequent sections.

Pure competition exists when the individual producers in a market have no influence on prices—they are price takers as opposed to price makers. This absence of influence on price requires the following conditions:

Large numbers of buyers and sellers. Each firm in the industry produces a small portion of the industry output, and each customer buys only a small part of the total.

Product homogeneity. The output of each firm is perceived by customers to be precisely equivalent to the output of any other firm in the industry.

Free entry and exit. Firms are not restricted from entering or leaving the industry.

Perfect dissemination of information. Cost, price, and quality information is known by all buyers and all sellers in the market.

These four basic conditions, which are necessary for the existence of a purely competitive market structure, are far too restrictive for pure competition to be commonplace in the real world. While security and commodity exchanges approach the requirements, imperfections occur even there.[3] Nonetheless, for some firms, pricing decisions must be made under circumstances in which they have no control over price, and an examination of a purely competitive market structure provides insights into pricing decisions in these cases. More importantly, a clear understanding of pure competition provides a reference point from which to analyze the more typically encountered market structures—oligopoly and monopolistic competition.

---

[2] The legal constraint on competition introduced by patents and copyrights is one obvious element that enters into this determination. The ability of certain groups—for example, physicians and certain labor unions—to limit entry into their professions by controlling licensing practices is another element that affects market structure.

[3] The sale by AT&T of $1.5 billion of new securities, for example, clearly affects the price of its stocks and bonds.

TABLE 10.1

Market Supply Schedule Determination

Price ($)	Quantity Supplied by Firm						Partial Market Supply	× 1,000 =	Total Market Supply
	1 +	2 +	3 +	4 +	5 =				
1	5	0	5	10	30	50		50,000
2	15	0	5	25	45	90		90,000
3	20	20	10	30	50	130		130,000
4	25	35	20	35	55	170		170,000
5	30	55	25	40	60	210		210,000
6	35	75	30	45	65	250		250,000
7	40	95	35	50	70	290		290,000
8	45	115	40	55	75	330		330,000
9	50	130	45	65	80	370		370,000
10	55	145	50	75	85	410		410,000

Market Price Determination

Although the individual firms have no control over price, the market price for a competitive industry is determined by supply and demand. There is a total industry demand curve for the product—an aggregation of the quantities that individual purchasers will buy at each price—and an industry supply curve—the summation of the quantities that individual firms are willing to supply at different prices. The intersection of the industry supply and demand curves determines the market price.

The data in Table 10.1 illustrate the process by which an industry supply curve is constructed. First, suppose there are five firms in an industry and that each firm is willing to supply varying quantities of the product at different prices. The summing of the individual supply quantities of these five firms for each price determines their combined supply schedule, shown in the Partial Market Supply column. For example, at a price of $2 the output quantities supplied by the five firms are 15, 0, 5, 25, and 45 units, respectively, resulting in a combined supply of 90 units at that price. With a product price of $8, the supply quantities become 45, 115, 40, 55, and 75 for a total supply by the five firms of 330 units.

Now assume that the five firms, while representative of firms in the industry, account for only a small portion of the industry's total output. Assume specifically that there is actually a total of 5,000 firms in the industry, each with an individual supply schedule identical to one of the five firms illustrated in the table. That is, there are 1,000 firms just like each one illustrated in Table 10.1, so the total market supply—the total quantity supplied at each price—will be 1,000 times that shown under the Partial Market Supply schedule. This supply schedule is illustrated in Figure 10.1, and adding the market demand curve to the industry supply curve, as in Figure 10.2, allows us to determine the equilibrium market price.

FIGURE 10.1

Hypothetical Industry Supply Curve

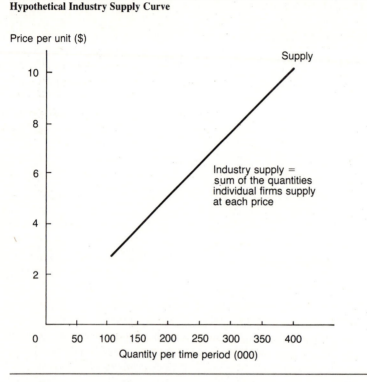

Price per unit ($)

While it is apparent from Figure 10.2 that both the quantity demanded and total supplied are dependent on price, a simple example should demonstrate the inability of an individual firm to affect price. Assume that the total demand function in Figure 10.2, which again represents the summation at each price of the quantities demanded by individual purchasers, can be described by the equation:

$$\text{Quantity Demanded} = Q = 400{,}000 - 10{,}000P, \qquad \textbf{(10.1)}$$

or, solving for price:

$$\$10{,}000P = \$400{,}000 - Q \qquad \textbf{(10.1a)}$$

$$P = \$40 - 0.0001Q.$$

According to Equation 10.1a, a 100-unit change in output would cause only a $0.01 change in price, or, alternatively, a $0.01 price increase (reduction) would lead to a decrease (increase) in total market demand of 100 units.

FIGURE 10.2

Market Price Determination in Perfect Competition

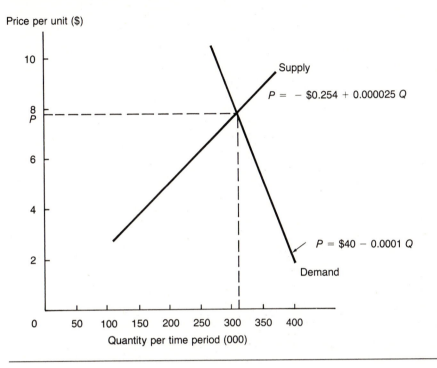

The demand curve shown in Figure 10.2 is redrawn for an individual firm in Figure 10.3. The slope of the curve is -0.0001, the same as in Figure 10.3; it is the marginal of Equation 10.1a in both cases.

The intercept $7.80 is the going market price as determined by the intersection of the market supply and demand curves in Figure 10.2.[4] At the scale shown in Figure 10.3, the firm's demand curve is seen to be a horizontal line, for all practical purposes. An output change of even 100 units by the individual firm results in only a $0.01 change in market price, and the data in Table 10.1 indicate that the typical firm would not vary output by this amount unless the market price changed by more than $10 a unit. Thus, it is clear that under pure competition the individual firm's output decisions do not affect price in any meaningful way, and for pricing decisions the demand curve is taken to be perfectly horizontal. That is, price is assumed to be constant irrespective of the output level at which the firm chooses to operate.

---

[4]The slopes of the demand curves in Figures 10.2 and 10.3 are identical; only the scales have been changed. Note also that at the equilibrium output shown in Figure 10.2, $P = \$40 - \$0.0001 \ (322,000) = \$40 - \$32.20 = \$7.80$.

FIGURE 10.3

Demand Curve Faced by a Single Firm in Perfect Competition

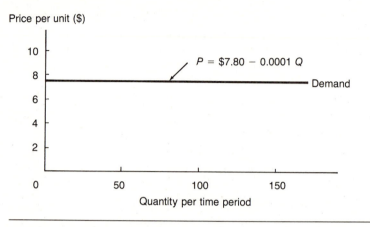

note: With price constant at, say, P^*, $TR = P^* \cdot Q$, $AR = P^* \cdot Q/Q = P^*$, and $MR = dTR/dQ = d(P^* \cdot Q)/dQ = P^*$.

The Firm's Price/Output Decision

Figure 10.4 illustrates the firm's price/output decision in a competitive market.[5] Profit maximization was shown in Chapter 2 to require that a firm operate at an output level where marginal revenue and marginal cost are equal to each other. With price a constant, average revenue, or price, and marginal revenue must always be equal, so the profit maximization requirement for a firm operating in a perfectly competitive market is that market price must be equal to marginal cost. In the example depicted in Figure 10.4, the firm chooses to operate at output level Q^*, where price (and hence marginal revenue) equals marginal cost and profits are maximized.

Notice that above-normal profits may exist in the short run even under conditions of pure competition.[6] For example, in Figure 10.4 the firm produces and sells Q^* units of output at an average cost of C dollars; and with a market price P, the firm earns economic profits of $P - C$ dollars per unit. Total economic profit, $(P - C)Q^*$, is shown by the shaded rectangle $PMNC$.

---

[5] We assume for simplicity in setting up graphic models in the sections on pure competition and monopolistic competition that the firm whose curves are graphed is a representative firm. Thus, the cost curves in Figure 10.4 are representative of an average firm in the industry.

[6] A normal profit, defined as a rate of return on capital just sufficient to attract the capital investment necessary to develop and operate a firm (see Chapter 1) is included as a part of economic costs. Therefore, any profit shown in a graph such as Figure 10.4 or 10.5 is defined as economic profit, and it represents an above-normal profit. Notice also that economic losses are incurred whenever the firm fails to earn a normal profit. Thus, a firm might show a small accounting profit but be suffering economic losses because these profits are below normal and are thus insufficient to provide an adequate return to the firm's stockholders.

FIGURE 10.4

Competitive Firm's Optimal Price/Output Combination

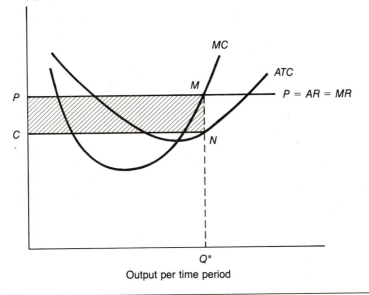

Output per time period

Over the longer run, however, positive economic profits will attract additional firms into the industry, will lead to increased output by existing firms, or will perhaps bring about both situations. As the industry supply is expanded, there will be a downward pressure on the market price for the industry as a whole—output for the industry can be expanded only by offering the product at a lower price—and simultaneously an upward pressure on cost, because of increased demand for factors of production. Long-run equilibrium will be reached when all economic profits and losses have been eliminated and each firm in the industry is operating at an output that minimizes average cost. The long-run equilibrium situation for a firm under pure competition is graphed in Figure 10.5. At the profit maximizing output, price, or average revenue, equals average cost, so the firm neither earns economic profits nor incurs economic losses. When this condition exists for all firms in the industry, new firms are not encouraged to enter the industry nor are existing ones pressured into leaving it. Prices are stable, and each firm is operating at the minimum point on its short-run average cost curve.[7]

---

[7] All firms must also be operating at the minimum cost point on the long-run average cost curve; otherwise firms would make production changes, decrease costs, and affect industry output and prices. Accordingly, a stable equilibrium requires that firms be operating with optimal-sized plants.

FIGURE 10.5

Long-Run Equilibrium in a Competitive Market

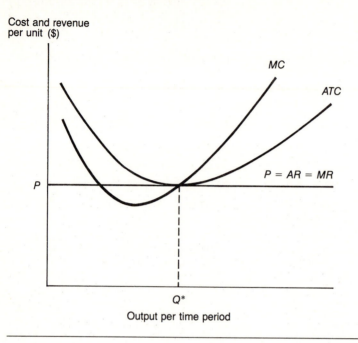

Cost and revenue
per unit ($)

MC

ATC

P = AR = MR

P

Q*

Output per time period

FIGURE 10.6

The Competitive Firm's Short-Run Supply Curve

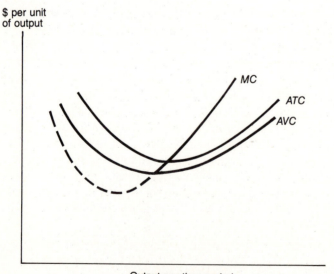

$ per unit
of output

MC

ATC

AVC

Output per time period

The Firm's Supply Curve

Market supply curves were seen above to be the summation of supply quantities of individual firms at various prices. We are now in a position to examine how the supply schedules for individual firms are determined.

In Figure 10.6 we add the firm's average variable cost curve to the average and marginal cost curves of Figure 10.4. *In the short run the competitive firm's supply schedule will correspond to that portion of the marginal cost curve which lies above the average variable cost curve—that is, the solid portion of the marginal cost curve in Figure 10.6.*

To understand the reason for this, consider the options available to the firm. Profit maximization under pure competition requires that the firm operate at the output where marginal revenue equals marginal cost—if it produces any output at all. That is, the firm will either (1) produce nothing and incur a loss equal to its fixed costs, or (2) produce an output determined by the intersection of the horizontal demand curve and the marginal cost curve. It will choose the alternative that maximizes profits or, if losses must be incurred, minimizes losses. If the price is less than average variable costs, the firm should produce nothing and incur a loss equal to its total fixed cost; if the firm produces any product under this condition, its losses will increase. But if price exceeds average variable costs, then each unit of output provides some profit contribution which can be applied to cover fixed costs and provide profit; the firm should produce and sell its product, because this production reduces losses or leads to profits. Accordingly, the minimum point on the firm's average variable cost curve determines the cutoff point, or the lower limit, of its supply schedule. This conclusion is illustrated in Figure 10.7. At a very low price such as $1, $MR = MC$ at 100 units of output. But notice that at 100 units the firm has a total cost per unit of $2 and a price of only $1, so it is incurring a loss of $1 a unit. Notice also that the total loss consists of a fixed cost component, $2.00 - $1.40 = $0.60, and a variable cost component, $1.40 - $1.00 = $0.40.[8] Thus, the total loss is:

$$\text{Total Loss} = (100 \text{ units}) \cdot (\$0.60 \text{ Fixed Cost Loss} + \$0.40 \text{ Variable Cost Loss})$$

$$= \$100.$$

If the firm simply shuts down and terminates production, it would cease to incur variable costs, and its loss would be reduced to the level of the fixed cost loss; that is, to 100($0.60) = $60.

Variable cost losses will occur at any price less than $1.25, the minimum point on the *AVC* curve, so this is the lowest price at which the firm will operate. Above $1.25, the price more than covers variable costs. Therefore, even though total costs

---

[8]The difference between the *ATC* and the *AVC* curves represents the fixed cost per unit of output.

FIGURE 10.7

Prices, Cost, and Optimal Supply Decisions for a Firm under Pure Competition

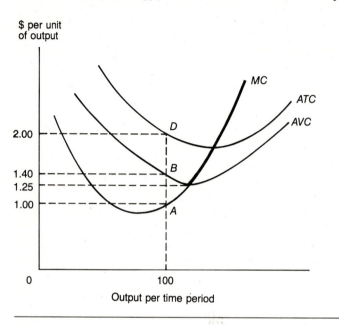

are not covered, it is preferable to operate and provide some contribution to cover a portion of fixed costs rather than to shut down and incur losses equal to total fixed costs.

To recapitulate, the *short-run supply curve is that portion of the marginal cost curve which lies above the* AVC *curve*. Where marginal cost is below average cost, but above average variable cost, the firm will incur losses but will produce, nonetheless. Positive economic profits occur over that part of the supply function where marginal cost (and price) is greater than average total cost.

The firm's long-run supply function is similarly determined. Since all costs are variable in the long run, a firm will choose to shut down unless total costs are completely covered. Accordingly, that portion of the firm's long-run marginal cost curve which lies above its long-run average total cost curve represents its long-run supply schedule.

MONOPOLY

Pure monopoly lies at the opposite extreme from pure competition on the market structure continuum. Monopoly exists when a single firm is the sole producer of a good that has no close substitutes—in other words, a single firm is the industry. Pure monopoly, like pure competition, exists primarily in economic theory—few goods are produced by a single producer, and fewer still are free from competition of a close substitute. Even the public utilities are imperfect monopolists in most of their markets. Electric companies, for example, typically approach a pure monopoly in their residential lighting market, but they face strong competition from gas and oil suppliers in the heating market. Further, in all phases of the industrial and commercial power markets, electric utilities face competition from gas- and oil-powered private generators.[9]

Even though pure monopoly rarely exists, it is still worthy of careful examination. Many of the economic relationships found under monopoly can be used to estimate optimal firm behavior in the less precise, but more prevalent, partly competitive and partly monopolistic market structures that dominate the real world. In addition, an understanding of monopoly market relationships provides the background necessary to examine the economics of regulation, a topic of prime importance to business managers.

Price/Output Decision under Monopoly

Under monopoly, the industry demand curve is identical to the demand curve of the firm, and because industry demand curves typically slope downward, monopolists also face downward-sloping demand curves. In Figure 10.8, for example, 100 units can be sold at a price of $10 a unit. At an $8 price, 150 units will be demanded. If the firm decides to sell 100 units, it will receive $10 a unit; if it wishes to sell 150 units, it must accept an $8 price. We see then that the monopolist can set either price or quantity, but not both. Given one, the value of the other is determined by the relationship expressed in the demand curve.

A monopolistic firm uses the same profit maximization rule as a firm in a competitive industry; it operates at the output where marginal revenue equals marginal cost. The demand curve facing the monopolistic firm, however, is not horizontal, or perfectly elastic, so marginal revenue will not coincide with price at any but the first unit of output. Marginal revenue is always less than price for output quantities greater than one.[10]

When the monopolistic firm equates marginal revenue and marginal cost, it simultaneously determines its output level and the market price for its product. This decision is illustrated in Figure 10.9. Here the firm produces Q units of output at a

---

[9]During the late 1960s, as electric rates climbed rapidly and future supply capabilities became questionable, some of the larger apartment- and office-building complexes began installing their own power-generating facilities. This practice has long been followed by large industrial firms.

[10]Marginal revenue is less than price because of the negatively sloped demand curve. Since the demand (average revenue) curve is negatively sloped, the marginal revenue curve must lie below it. This relationship was examined earlier in Chapters 2 and 4.

FIGURE 10.8

The Firm's Demand Curve under Monopoly

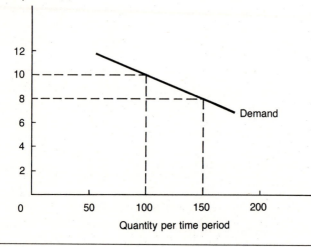

FIGURE 10.9

Price/Output Decision under Monopoly

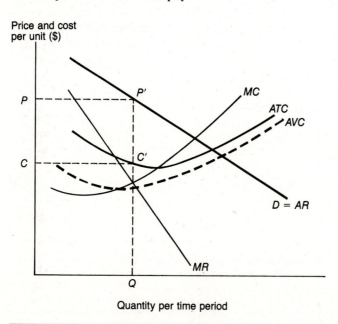

cost of C per unit, and it sells this output at price, P. Profits, which are equal to $(P - C)$ times (Q), are represented by the area $PP'C'C$, and are at a maximum.

While Q is the optimal short-run output, the firm will engage in production only if average revenue, or price, is greater than average variable cost. This condition holds in Figure 10.9, but if the price had been below the average variable cost, losses would have been minimized by shutting down.

Long-Run Equilibrium under Monopoly

In the long run a monopolistic firm will operate only if its price exceeds its long-run average cost. Because all costs are variable in the long run, the firm will not operate unless all costs are covered. No firm, monopolistic or competitive, will operate in the long run if it is suffering losses.

As was shown earlier, purely competitive firms must, in the long run, operate at the minimum point on the *LRAC* curve. This condition does not necessarily hold under monopoly. For example, consider again Figure 10.9 and assume that the *ATC* curve represents the long-run average total cost curve of the firm.[11] Here the firm will produce Q units of output at an average cost of C per unit, somewhat above the minimum point on the *ATC* curve. This firm is a *natural monopolist*, an entity that appears when the profit maximizing output for a monopolist occurs at a point where *long-run* average costs are declining. A single firm can produce the total market supply at a lower total cost than could any number of smaller firms, hence the term *natural*. Utility companies are the classic examples of natural monopoly, as the duplication of production and distribution facilities would greatly increase costs if more than one firm served a given area. The case of natural monopoly is discussed in Chapter 12.

Regulation of Monopoly

The existence of natural monopolies presents something of a dilemma. On the one hand, economic efficiency could be enhanced by restricting the number of producing firms to one; on the other hand, where only one firm serves a market, the possibility of economic exploitation exists. Specifically, monopolistic firms tend to earn excessive profits and to underproduce. The term *excessive profits* is defined as profits so large that the firm earns a rate of return on invested capital that exceeds the risk-adjusted normal or required rate. Profits serve a useful function in providing incentives and in allocating resources, but it is difficult to justify above-normal profits that are the result of market power, as opposed to exceptional performance. *Un-*

---

[11] All costs are variable in the long run and, therefore, average variable costs are equal to average total costs. Here, the *AVC* curve should be disregarded.

derproduction is defined as a situation where the firm curtails production at a level where the value of the resources needed to produce an additional unit of output, as measured by the marginal cost of production, is less than the social benefit derived from the additional unit, which is measured by the price someone is willing to pay for the additional unit. Under monopoly, marginal cost is clearly less than price at the firm's profit maximizing output level.

How can we escape from the dilemma posed by the twin facts (1) that monopoly can be efficient but (2) that monopoly can lead to excessive profits and underproduction? The answer lies in regulation, a topic discussed in Chapter 12.

MONOPOLISTIC COMPETITION

Pure competition and pure monopoly rarely exist in the real world; most firms are subject to some competition, but not to the extent that would exist under pure competition. Even though most firms are faced with a large number of competitors producing highly substitutable products, firms still have some control over the price of their output—they cannot sell all they want at a fixed price, nor would they lose all their sales if they raised prices slightly. In other words, most firms face downward-sloping demand curves, signifying less than perfect competition.

In 1933 Edward H. Chamberlain presented a theory of monopolistic competition that provided a more realistic explanation of the actual market structure faced by most firms. Chamberlain's theory retains two assumptions of a purely competitive market structure: (1) Each firm makes its decisions independently of all others; that is, each producer assumes that competitors' prices, advertising, and so on are invariant with respect to its own actions. Thus, price changes by one firm are assumed not to cause other firms to react by changing their prices.[12] (2) There are a large number of firms in the industry all producing the same basic product. The assumption of completely homogeneous products is removed, however, so each firm is assumed to be able to differentiate its product to at least some degree from those of rival firms.

The assumption of no direct reactions by competitors should not be misconstrued as implying an independence among firms in a monopolistically competitive market. There is an assumed independence in decision making, just as in a perfectly competitive market. However, the demand function faced by each firm in such an industry is significantly affected by: (1) the existence of numerous firms all producing goods that consumers view as reasonably close substitutes and (2) the fact that many demand and cost factors have a simultaneous impact on all firms, leading fre-

---

[12]If reactions occur, then the market structure is defined to be oligopolistic, a market structure examined later in this chapter. For Chamberlain's original work, see *The Theory of Monopolistic Competition* (Cambridge, Mass.: Harvard University Press, 1933).

FIGURE 10.10

Relationship between Product Differentiation and Elasticity of Demand

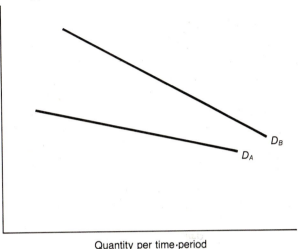

Price per unit ($)

D_B

D_A

Quantity per time·period

quently to similar price movements by them. As Chamberlain pointed out, this latter phenomenon causes each firm's demand to be more price inelastic than would be the case if total interfirm independence prevailed.

Product differentiation takes many forms. A tube of Crest toothpaste at a nearby drugstore is different from an identical tube available at a distant store. Quality differentials, packaging, credit terms, or superior maintenance service, such as IBM is reputed to supply, can lead to product differentiation, as can advertising and brand-name identification. The important factor in all these forms of product differentiation, however, is that some consumers prefer the product of one seller to that of others.

The effect of product differentiation is to remove the perfect elasticity of the firm's demand curve. Instead of being a price taker facing a horizontal demand curve, the firm determines its optimal price/output combination. The degree of price flexibility depends on the strength of a firm's product differentiation. Strong differentiation results in greater consumer loyalty and hence in more control over price. Alternatively stated, the more differentiated a firm's product, the lower the substitutability of other products for it. This is illustrated in Figure 10.10, which shows the demand curves of Firms A and B. Consumers view Firm A's product as being only slightly differentiated from the bulk of the industry's output, and since many other brands are suitable replacements for its own output, Firm A is close to being a price taker. Firm B, on the other hand, has successfully differentiated its

FIGURE 10.11

Price/Output Combinations under Monopolistic Competition

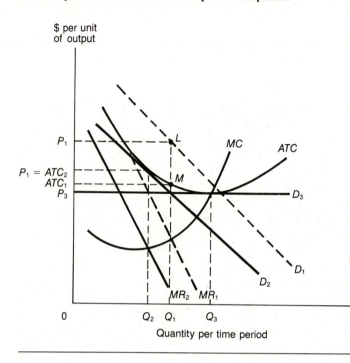

product, and consumers are therefore less willing to substitute for B's output. Accordingly, B's demand is not so sensitive to changes in price.

Price/Output Decisions under Monopolistic Competition

As its name suggests, monopolistic competition embodies elements of both monopoly and perfect competition. The monopoly aspect of monopolistic competition is observed in the short run. Consider Figure 10.11. There, with the demand curve, D_1, and its related marginal revenue curve, MR_1, the optimum output, Q_1, is found at the point where $MR_1 = MC$. Here, short-run monopoly profits equal to the area P_1LMATC_1 are earned. These profits may be the result of the introduction of a patented invention, an unpatented but valuable innovation, or simply an unexpected rise in demand.

With time, however, competition is attracted by these short-run monopoly profits, and entry into the industry is observed. Therefore, the competitive aspect of monopolistic competition is seen in the long run. As more firms enter and offer close (but imperfect) substitutes, the market share of the initial and leading firm is reduced. This means that firm demand and marginal revenue will shift to the left, as for example to D_2 and MR_2 in Figure 10.11. The firm's optimal output (the point where $MR_2 = MC$) shifts to Q_2; and the price, P_2, is equal to ATC_2, so economic profits are zero.[13] If perfect rather than close substitutes were offered by new entrants, D_2 would become more nearly horizontal, and the perfectly competitive situation, D_3 with P_3 and Q_3, would be approached.

Note that in equilibrium a monopolistically competitive firm will never be operating at the minimum point on its average cost curve—the demand curve is downward sloping, so it can be tangent to the ATC curve only at a point above the minimum of the ATC curve. Does this mean that a monopolistically competitive industry is inefficient? The answer is no, except in a superficial sense. The very existence of the downward-sloping demand curve implies that some consumers value the firm's products more highly than they do products of other producers. If the number of producers were reduced—perhaps by government edict—so that all the remaining firms could operate at their minimum cost point, some consumers would clearly suffer a loss in welfare, *because the product variety they desired would no longer be available*.

While the perfectly competitive and pure monopoly settings are comparatively rare in real-world markets, monopolistic competition is frequently observed. For example, in 1960 a small ($37 million in sales) office-machine company, Haloid Xerox, Inc., revolutionized the copy industry with the introduction of the Xerox 914 copier. Xerography was a tremendous improvement on electrofax and other coated paper copiers. It permitted the use of untreated paper, which not only resulted in a more desirable copy product but one that was less expensive on a cost-per-copy basis as well. Invention of the dry copier established what is now Xerox Corporation at the forefront of a rapidly growing office-copier industry and propelled the firm to a position of virtual monopoly by 1970. Between 1970 and 1980 the industry's structure changed dramatically due to an influx of competition as many of Xerox's original patents expired. IBM entered the copier market in April of 1970 with its Copier I model and expanded its participation in November 1972 with Copier II. Eastman Kodak made its entry into the market in 1975 with its Ektaprint model. Of course, Minnesota Mining and Manufacturing (3M) has long been a factor in the electrofax copier segment of the market. A partial list of smaller domestic firms with rapidly growing participation in the industry would include Addressograph-Multigraph, Nashua, and Savin Business Machines Company. A more complete list of Xerox's recent domestic and international competitors would include at least 30 firms. The effect of this entry on Xerox's market share and profitability has

---

[13]Recall that the term *cost* includes a normal profit sufficient to compensate the owners of the firm for their capital investment.

been substantial. Between 1970 and 1978 Xerox's share of the domestic copier market fell from 98 to 56 percent, and its return on stockholders' equity fell from 23.6 to 18.2 percent.

Therefore, the monopolistic dry-copier market of 1970 has evolved into a much more competitive industry as we enter the mid-1980s. Because IBM, Kodak, 3M, and Savin copiers are only close rather than perfect substitutes for Xerox machines, each company retains some price discretion, and they are therefore described as monopolistically rather than perfectly competitive.

OLIGOPOLY

The theory of monopolistic competition borrows heavily from those of pure competition and pure monopoly, but it provides a more accurate picture of the actual markets in which most businesses operate because it recognizes that firms have some control over price, but their actions are limited by the large number of close substitutes for their products. The theory assumes, however, that firms make decisions without explicitly taking into account competitive reactions. Such a behavioral assumption is appropriate for some industries but inappropriate for others, and when an individual firm's actions will in fact produce reactions on the part of its competitors, *oligopoly* exists.

Examples of oligopolistic industries abound in the United States. Aluminum, automobiles, electrical equipment, glass, and steel—all are produced and sold under conditions of oligopoly. Notice that in each of these industries a small number of firms produce all, or at least a very large percentage of, the total output. In the automobile industry, for example, General Motors, Ford, Chrysler, Volkswagen, and American Motors account for almost all auto production in the United States. Even the primary competition from imported automobiles is limited to a relatively small number of firms. Aluminum production is also highly concentrated, with Alcoa, Reynolds, and Kaiser producing almost all domestic output.

Oligopoly market structures also exist in a number of other industries where the market area for a single firm is quite small. Examples of this type of local oligopolistic structure include the markets for gasoline and food. Here, only a few sellers (service stations and grocery stores) compete within a small geographic area.

It is the fewness of sellers that introduces interactions into the price/output decision problem under oligopoly. Consider *duopoly*, a special form of oligopoly, under which only two firms produce a particular product. For simplicity, assume that the product is homogeneous and customers choose between the firms solely on the basis of price. Assume also that both firms charge the same price and that each has an equal share of the market. Now suppose Firm A attempts to increase its sales by lowering its price. All buyers will attempt to switch to Firm A, and Firm B will lose a substantial share of its market. To retain customers, B will react by lowering its price. Thus, neither firm is free to act independently—actions taken by one will lead to reactions by the other.

Price/Output Decisions under Oligopoly

Demand curves relate the quantity of a product demanded to price, *holding constant the effect of all other variables*. One variable that is assumed to remain fixed is the price charged by competing firms. In an oligopolistic market structure, however, if one firm changes the price it charges, other firms will react by changing their prices. The demand curve for the initial firm shifts position, so that instead of moving along a single demand curve as it changes price, the firm moves to an entirely new demand curve.

This phenomenon of shifting demand curves is illustrated in Figure 10.12(a). Firm A is initially producing Q_1 units of output and selling them at a price, P_1. Demand Curve D_1 applies here, *assuming* prices charged by other firms remain fixed. Under this assumption, a price cut from P_1 to P_2 would increase demand to Q_2. Assume, however, that only a few firms operate in the market and that each has a fairly large share of total sales. Therefore, if one firm cuts its price and obtains a substantial increase in volume, the other firms must lose a large part of their business. Further, they know exactly why their sales have fallen, and they react by cutting their own prices. This action shifts Firm A down to the second demand curve, D_2, which causes a reduction in Firm A's demand at P_2 from Q_2 to Q_3 units. The new curve is just as unstable as the old one, so a knowledge of its shape is useless to Firm A; if it tries to move along D_2, competitors will react, forcing the company to yet another curve.

Shifting demand curves would present no real difficulty in making price/output decisions *if Firm A knew for sure how its rivals would react to price changes*. The reactions would just be built into the price/demand relationship, and a new demand curve could be constructed to include interactions among firms. Curve D_3 in Figure 10.12(b) represents such a reaction-based demand curve; it shows how price reductions affect quantity demanded after competitive reactions have been taken into account. The problem with this approach, however, lies in the fact that there are many different theories about interfirm behavior, and each theory leads to a different pricing model and thereby to different decision rules.

Cartel Arrangements

In an oligopolistic market it would benefit all the firms in an industry if they got together and set prices so as to maximize total industry profits. The firms could reach an agreement whereby they set the same prices as would a monopolist and thereby extract the maximum amount of profits from consumers. If such a formal, overt agreement were made, the group would be defined as a *cartel*; if a covert,

FIGURE 10.12

Shifting Demand under Oligopoly

Price per unit ($)

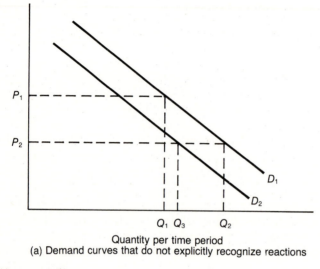

(a) Demand curves that do not explicitly recognize reactions

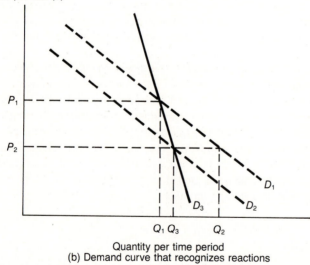

(b) Demand curve that recognizes reactions

FIGURE 10.13

Price/Output Determination for a Cartel

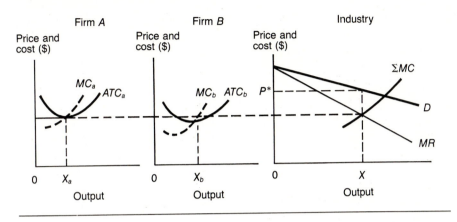

informal agreement were reached, the firms would be operating in collusion. Both practices are generally illegal in the United States.[14]

If a cartel has absolute control over all the firms in the industry, it can operate as a monopoly. To illustrate, consider the situation shown in Figure 10.13. The marginal cost curves of each firm are summed horizontally to arrive at an industry marginal cost curve. Equating the cartel's total marginal cost with the industry marginal revenue curve determines the profit maximizing output and, simultaneously, the price, P^*, to be charged. Once this profit maximizing price/output level has been determined, each individual firm finds its output by equating its own marginal cost to the previously determined industry profit maximizing marginal cost level.

While profits are often divided among firms on the basis of their individual outputs, other allocating techniques can be used. Historical market shares, capacity as determined in a number of ways, and a bargained solution based on economic power have all been used in the past.

For numerous reasons cartels have typically been rather short-lived. In addition to the long-run problems of changing products and of entry into the market by new producers, cartels are subject to much disagreement among the members. While firms usually agree that maximizing joint profits is mutually beneficial, they seldom agree on the equity of various profit allocation schemes, a problem leading to attempts to subvert the agreement.

Subversion of the cartel by an individual firm can be extremely profitable to

[14]Cartels are legal, however, in many parts of the world, and multinational United States corporations often become involved in them in foreign markets. Additionally, several important domestic markets are in effect cartels, through producer associations, and appear to operate without interference from the government. Certain farm products, including milk, are prime examples of products marketed under cartel-like arrangements.

that firm. With the industry operating at the monopoly price/output level, the demand curve facing an individual firm is highly elastic, provided it can lower its price without other cartel members learning of this action and retaliating. The availability of significant profits to a firm that cheats on the cartel, coupled with the ease with which secret price concessions can be made, makes policing a cartel agreement extremely difficult. These problems combine to make cartel survival difficult.

Price Leadership

A less formal but nonetheless effective means of reducing oligopolistic uncertainty is through price leadership. Price leadership results when one firm establishes itself as the industry leader and all other firms in the industry accept its pricing policy. This leadership may result from the size and strength of the leader firm, from cost efficiency, or as a result of the recognized ability of the leader to forecast market conditions accurately and to establish a price that produces satisfactory profits for all firms in the industry.

   A typical case is price leadership by a dominant firm, usually the largest firm in the industry. Here the leader faces a price/output problem similar to a monopolist, while the other firms face a competitive price/output problem.[15] This is illustrated in Figure 10.14, where the total market demand curve is D_T, the marginal cost curve of the leader is MC_L, and the horizontal summation of the marginal cost curves for all the price followers is labeled MC_f. Because the price followers take prices as given, they choose to operate at that output level at which their individual marginal costs equal price, just as they would in a purely competitive market structure. Accordingly, the MC_f curve represents the supply curve for the follower firms. This means that at price P_1, the followers would supply the entire market, leaving nothing for the dominant firm. At all prices below P_1, however, the horizontal distance between the summed MC_f curve and the market demand curve represents the demand faced by the price leader. At a price of P_2, for example, the price followers will provide Q_2 units of output, leaving a demand of $Q_4 - Q_2$ for the price leader.[16] Plotting of all the residual demand quantities for prices below P_1 results in the demand curve faced by the price leader, D_L in Figure 10.14, and the related marginal revenue curve, MR_L.

   Since the price leader faces the demand curve D_L as a monopolist, it maximizes profit by operating where marginal revenue equals marginal cost; that is, where

---

[15] The leader allows the followers to sell as much as they please at the established price. This presents no problem for the price leader, since the followers' output is constrained by their marginal cost curves.

[16] More generally, the leader faces a demand curve of the form:

$$D_L = D_T - S_f,$$

where D_L is the leader's demand, D_T is total demand, and S_f is the followers' supply curve found by setting price = MC_f and solving for Q_f, the quantity that will be supplied by the price followers. Since D_T and S_f are both functions of price, D_L is likewise determined by price.

FIGURE 10.14

Oligopoly Pricing with Dominant Firm Price Leadership

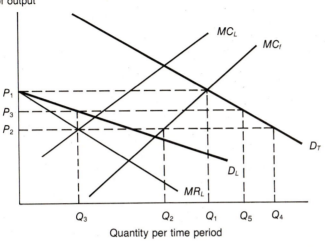

$MR_L = MC_L$. At this output for the leader, Q_3, the market price is established to be P_3. The price followers will supply a combined output of $Q_5 - Q_3$ units. If no one challenges the price leader, a stable short-run equilibrium has been reached.

A second type of price leadership is *barometric price leadership*. In this case one firm announces a price change in response to what it perceives as a change in industry supply and demand conditions. This change could stem from cost increases that result from a new industry labor agreement, higher energy or material input prices, and changes in taxes, or it might result from a substantial increase or decrease in demand. With barometric price leadership the price leader will not necessarily be the largest or the dominant firm in the industry. The price leader role varies from one firm to another over time. It is important, however, that the price leader accurately read the prevailing industry view of the need for a price adjustment and the appropriate new price level. If a firm is incorrect in its assessment of the desire for a price change by other firms, then its price move will not be followed, and it may have to rescind or modify the announced price change in order to retain its market share or perhaps, if the price change involved a reduction, in order to prevent other firms from retaliating with an even lower price.

Kinked Demand Curve

An often-noted characteristic of oligopolistic markets is that once a general price level has been established, whether through a cartel or through some less formal

FIGURE 10.15

Kinked Demand Curve

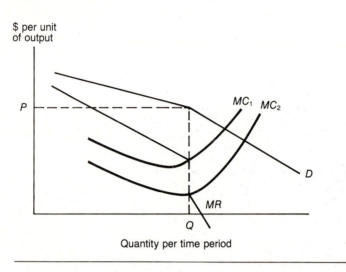

Quantity per time period

arrangement, it tends to remain fixed for an extended period. This rigidity of prices is typically explained by yet another set of assumptions about firm behavior under conditions of price interdependence, which is known as the *kinked demand curve theory of oligopoly prices*.

The kinked demand curve theory describes a behavior pattern in which rival firms are assumed to follow any decrease in price in order to maintain their respective market shares but to refrain from following price increases, thereby allowing their market shares to increase at the expense of the price raiser. Thus, the demand curve facing an individual firm is kinked at the current price/output combination as illustrated in Figure 10.15. The firm is producing Q units of output and selling them at a price of P per unit; if it lowers its price, competing firms will retaliate by lowering their prices. The result of a price cut, therefore, is a relatively small increase in sales; that is, the demand curve associated with price reductions has very low elasticity.[17] Price increases, on the other hand, result in significant reductions in quantities demanded and in related decreases in total revenue, because customers will shift to competing firms that do not follow the price increases.

Associated with the kink in the demand curve is a point of discontinuity in the marginal revenue curve. That is, the firm's marginal revenue curve has a gap at the current price/output level, and it is this gap in the marginal revenue curve that explains the rigidity of price. The profit maximizing firm always chooses to operate at

[17] The reader is referred to Figure 10.12, where the shift in demand curves which results from a price cut was explained. The curve D_3 in Figure 10.12 is the counterpart of the steeper segment of D in Figure 10.15.

the point where marginal cost equals marginal revenue, and because of this gap in the marginal revenue curve, the price/output combination at the kink can remain optimal even though marginal cost fluctuates considerably. Thus, as illustrated in Figure 10.15, the firm's marginal cost curve can fluctuate between MC_1 and MC_2 without causing a change in the firm's optimal price/output combination.

NONPRICE COMPETITION

Because rival firms are likely to retaliate against price cuts, oligopolists tend to use nonprice competitive techniques to boost demand. What does nonprice competition mean? To explain the concept, let us first assume that a firm's demand function is given by Equation 10.2:

$$Q_A = f(P_A, P_X, Ad_A, Ad_X, SQ_A, SQ_X, I, Pop, \ldots) \qquad (10.2)$$

$$= a - bP_A + cP_X + dAd_A - eAd_X + fSQ_A$$
$$- gSQ_X + hI + iPop + \ldots,$$

where Q_A is the quantity of output demanded from Firm A, P_A is A's price, P_X is the average price charged by other firms in the industry, Ad is advertising expenditures, SQ denotes an index of styling and quality, I represents income, and Pop is population.[18] The firm can control three of the variables in Equation 10.2: P_A, Ad_A, and SQ_A. If it reduces P_A in an effort to stimulate demand, it will probably cause a reduction in P_X, offsetting the hoped-for effects of the initial price cut. Rather than get a substantial boost in sales, Firm A may have simply started a price war.

Now consider the effects of changing the other controllable variables in the demand function, Ad_A and SQ_A. Increased advertising could be expected to shift the demand curve to the right, thus enabling the firm to increase sales at a given price or to sell a constant quantity at a higher price. An improvement in styling or quality would have the same effect as a boost in the advertising budget; and similar results would follow from easing credit terms, training salespersons to be more courteous, providing more convenient retail locations, or any other improvement in the product. Competitors can be expected to react to changes in nonprice variables, but the reaction rate is likely to be slower than for price changes. For one thing, these changes are generally less obvious, at least initially, to rival firms, so it will take them longer to recognize that changes have occurred. Then, too, advertising campaigns have to be designed, and media time and space must be purchased. Styling and quality changes frequently require long lead times, as do training programs for

---

[18]There may be other variables such as credit terms, number of outlets (stores for a grocery chain or branches for a bank), and the like in the demand function.

salespeople, the opening of new facilities, and the like. Further, all these nonprice activities tend to differentiate the firm's products in the minds of consumers from those of other firms in the industry, and rivals may therefore find it difficult to regain lost customers even after they have reacted. While it may take longer to build up a reputation through the use of nonprice competition, once the demand curve has been shifted outward, it will take rivals longer to counteract that shift. Thus, the advantageous effects of nonprice competition are likely to be more persistent than the fleeting benefits of a price cut.

How far should nonprice competition be carried? The answer is that such activities should be carried to the point where the marginal cost of the action is just equal to the marginal revenue produced by it. For example, suppose widgets sell for $10 per unit and the variable cost per unit is $8. If less than $2 of additional advertising expenditures will boost sales by 1 unit, the additional expenditure should be made.[19]

DEFINING MARKET STRUCTURE

We have seen that a firm's price/output strategies will vary markedly depending on the market structures encountered. Similarly, profit rates are affected by the level of competitive pressures.

In order to design and carry out effective production, pricing, and promotion strategies a firm must define its relevant economic markets and characterize the market structure of each. To do this, firms in the United States make extensive use of economic data collected by the U.S. Bureau of the Census. Since these data pro-

---

[19] In theory, the firm should operate where the change in profit (π) associated with changing any variable (X_i) is zero: $\partial \pi / \partial X_i = 0$. To see this, consider the following:

1. $\pi = TR - TC$.

2. $TR = P \cdot Q$, where $Q = f_1(X_i)$. The X_i's include advertising expenditures, expenditures on quality improvements, and so on.

3. $TC = f_2(X_i)$.

4. Therefore, $\pi = P \cdot f_1(X_i) - f_2(X_i)$.

5. To maximize profits, set $\partial \pi / \partial X_j = 0$ for all controllable variables X_j. This is equivalent to setting $\partial TR / \partial X_j - \partial TC / \partial X_j = 0$, or, alternatively, $MR_{X_j} - MC_{X_j} = 0$, which is the same as setting $MR_{X_j} = MC_{X_j}$.

This process requires that the cost and demand functions be specified and used to construct the profit function. The profit function is partially differentiated for every controllable variable X_j to obtain a set of j equations in j unknowns. The simultaneous solution of this system of equations provides the optimal value of all controllable variables: price, advertising expenditures, quality, and the like.

It is much easier to say what to do than to do it. Nevertheless, a thorough understanding of the theoretical model provides us with insights about the probable direction if not magnitude of specific changes. Further, an understanding of the theory helps us to recognize what information would be most useful for decision purposes and, accordingly, what data we should attempt to collect.

vide valuable information on economic activity across the broad spectrum of U.S. industry, we will briefly consider the method and scope of the economic censuses, then examine how census data is used to provide valuable information on market structure within industries.

The Economic Censuses

U.S. economic censuses provide comprehensive statistical profiles of large segments of the economy, including: manufacturing, retail trade, wholesale trade, services, mining, and construction. In 1977, these sectors accounted for approximately 60 percent of the $1,918.0 billion U.S. gross national product (GNP). Important industry groups that were not covered were finance, insurance, real estate, agriculture, forestry, communications, transportation, and electric, gas, and sanitary services.

Across fields of economic activity that are covered by the U.S. economic censuses, manufacturing is clearly the largest sector. In 1977, manufacturing employed nearly 20 million persons, or 20 percent of the civilian labor force, and it accounted for about 24 percent of GNP. Every five years the Bureau of the Census provides a wealth of detailed information on this important sector in its *Census of Manufacturers*. It provides information covering almost every measurable aspect of industrial activity, such as employment; payroll; hours worked; production; prices; inventories; orders; investment in structures, machinery, and equipment; and consumption of raw materials, fuels, and water. To present this information in a meaningful fashion, the Bureau disaggregates these data into various levels of distinction. These levels proceed from very general two-digit industry groups to very specific seven-digit product classifications. Table 10.2 indicates the disaggregation provided by this Standard Industrial Classification (SIC) scheme and illustrates the finer breakdown that occurs as one moves from two-digit to seven-digit levels of classification. Most economists agree that the four-digit level classifications corre-

TABLE 10.2

Census Product Classification

Digit Level	Number of Classifications	Example SIC Code	Description
Two	20	20	Food and Kindred Products
Three	144	202	Dairy Products
Four	452	2023	Condensed and Evaporated Milk Industry
Five	1,500	20232	Canned Milk
Six			(Not Currently Utilized)
Seven	13,000	2023212	Canned Evaporated Milk

TABLE 10.3

Sample of 4-Digit Census Industries (1977 Data)

Standard Industrial Classification (SIC) Code	Description	Number of Firms	Industry Sales (millions of dollars)	Market Share (Percent)	
				Top Four Firms (CR_4)	Top Eight Firms (CR_8)
2043	Cereal Breakfast Foods	32	$ 2,497.5	89	98
2047	Dog, Cat, and Other Pet Food	218	3,086.7	58	74
2095	Roasted Coffee	133	5,616.4	61	73
2371	Fur Goods	620	383.4	11	19
2387	Apparel Belts	281	286.9	21	32
2621	Paper Mills	171	12,613.3	23	42
3425	Handsaws and Saw Blades	105	363.3	53	69
3711	Motor Vehicles and Car Bodies	254	76,517.8	93	99
3721	Aircraft	151	14,834.2	59	81
3732	Boat Building and Repairing	2,148	1,822.6	11	19

spond quite closely with the economic definition of a market and therefore use four-digit data in analyses of industrial competition.

Market Concentration

Industries fall along a continuum from perfect competition to monopoly. In order to understand where a particular industry falls along this continuum, one must not only consider numbers of competitors but their relative sizes as well. The relative market share of leading firms in monopoly and oligopoly markets will tend to be greater than in the case of monopolistically and perfectly competitive markets.

Table 10.3 shows numbers of competitors, industry sales, and leading firm market-share data for a small cross section of four-digit census industries. Here, as is generally the case, leading firm market shares are calculated using sales data for the top four or eight firms in an industry. These market-share data are called *concentration ratios* because they measure the percentage market share held by (concentrated in) an industry's top four or eight firms. Typically, industries where the four leading firms control less than 25 to 30 percent of total industry sales—i.e., $CR_4 < 30$—are highly competitive. Industries where leading firms control greater than 80 or 90 percent of industry sales—i.e., $CR_4 > 80$—are less competitive and generally quite profitable.

Caution is required, however, in interpreting census data on market structures for several reasons. First, only data on total *domestic production*, not total domestic sales, are reported. Domestic sales by foreign competitors (imports) as well as exports are ignored. This means, for example, that if foreign-car manufacturers have a market share of 25 percent, the four leading domestic car manufacturers account for only about 70 percent (= 93 percent of 75 percent) rather than 93 percent of total U.S. (foreign plus domestic) car sales. Second, only *national*, not regional or local, markets are considered.

For example, average four-firm concentration ratios in metropolitan newspaper markets fall in the 60 to 80 percent range, if not higher. Thus, the 1977 national CR_4 for newspapers (SIC 2711), which was only 19 percent, significantly understates localized market power in that industry. Third, recall that an economic market includes those firms willing and able to sell an identifiable product. This includes firms currently active in an industry, as well as firms which can be regarded as *potential entrants*. A potential entrant is a firm with both the knowledge and resources for successful entry. Often the mere presence of one or more potential entrants constitutes a sufficient threat to force competitive market behavior in industries with only a handful of established competitors. Major retailers such as K-Mart and Sears, for example, use their positions as potential entrants into manufacturing to obtain attractive prices on a wide range of private label merchandise, like clothing, lawn mowers, washing machines, and so on. And finally, considering market-share data in isolation may result in misleading conclusions regarding the vigor of competition or ease of entry in an industry. Under certain circumstances, even a very few large competitors will compete vigorously. Considering Chrysler Corporation's difficulties during the late 1970s and early 1980s, competition in an admittedly oligopolistic automobile industry (SIC 3711) appears extensive. In this instance, foreign imports undoubtedly provide an important stimulus to greater competition. Therefore, in addition to industry structure as measured by concentration levels, firms must consider foreign competition, regional product differences, advertising, research and development, growth, customer loyalty, and economies of scale in production—among other factors—if accurate pricing and output decisions are to be made.

SUMMARY

Demand functions and cost functions interact to determine market structures, and this chapter has explained the process by which this determination is made. If the average cost curve turns up at an output that is small in relation to total demand, then a large number of firms will operate, and a *competitive* market structure will emerge. However, if unit costs decline throughout the entire range of outputs, then in the absence of external controls (such as antitrust legislation) the industry is likely to consist of but one firm, a *monopolist*.

If a large number of firms exist in the industry and if a homogeneous product is produced, the result is likely to be *pure competition*, in which firms face horizontal demand curves. On the other hand, if the product is somewhat differentiated, each firm will face a downward-sloping demand curve, and the market structure will be *monopolistic competition*.

Under competition, either pure or monopolistic, no individual firm is enough of a factor in the market so that its actions affect other firms seriously enough to cause them to respond. Accordingly, competitive firms do not take into account reactions of other firms when making their price and output decisions. However, if only a few firms operate in the market, each of them will have a sizable share of the total market, and an action by one firm will have a noticeable effect on other firms. Therefore, other firms will react to the actions of any individual firm, and all firms will recognize this fact and will take such reactions into consideration in their pricing decisions. This situation is defined as *oligopoly*.

The profit maximizing decision rules are relatively simple and straightforward under monopoly, pure competition, and monopolistic competition. Under oligopoly, however, the rules become complex, almost to the point of being indeterminate. Firms recognize that profits could be maximized by some form of cooperative behavior, so *cartels*, *price leadership arrangements*, and stable prices as explained by the *kinked demand curve* may develop. Also, because reactions may be delayed, oligopolistic firms are likely to engage in such forms of nonprice competition as advertising, styling and quality changes, and service improvements as much as or more than firms in direct price competition.

Knowledge of market structure is important for many managerial decisions. Industrial concentration ratios provide useful information concerning the relative importance of leading firms in an industry. Although concentration ratios are helpful in indicating potential market power, it must be remembered that concentration in an industry does not necessarily mean lack of competition. In some instances, competition among the few can be vigorous.

QUESTIONS

10.1 Explain the process through which above-normal profits are eliminated in a purely competitive industry and in a monopolistically competitive industry.

10.2 Would the demand curve for a firm in a monopolistically competitive industry be more or less elastic after any above-normal profits have been eliminated?

10.3 Assume that a Congressional committee is holding hearings on a proposed bill that would restrict the number of firms in monopolistically competitive industries, the idea being to help firms reach the minimum points on their *ATC* curves. (See

Figure 10.11.) You have been retained as an economic consultant to analyze the proposal.

    a. What disadvantages can you see in the proposal?

    b. Consider how the trend from "mom and pop" grocery stores to super-markets (with large parking lots) might be used as evidence in the hearing.

10.4 "One might expect firms in a competitive industry to experience greater swings in the price of their products over the business cycle than those in an oligopolistic industry. However, fluctuations in profits will not necessarily follow the same pattern." Do you agree with this statement? Why or why not?

10.5 Explain how the following cost curve could be consistent with monopoly, oligopoly, or competition.

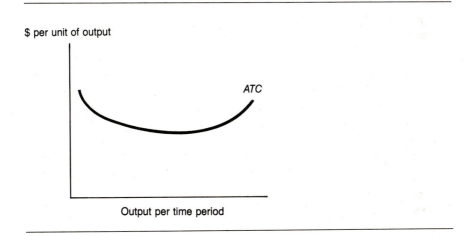

$ per unit of output

ATC

Output per time period

10.6 When a single seller faces a large number of buyers, a condition known as *monopoly* exists.

    a. Give an illustration of this form of market structure in U.S. labor markets.

    b. Discuss the impact of such a structure on inflation.

    c. Discuss the feasibility of modifying the antitrust laws to deal with such situations.

10.7 Why is the four-firm concentration ratio only an imperfect measure of monopoly power?

10.8 Will revenue maximizing firms have profits as large or larger than profit maximizing firms? If so, when? If not, why not?

10.9 Is a revenue maximizing firm necessarily inconsistent with the more traditional long-run profit maximizing model of firm behavior? Why or why not?

PROBLEMS

10.1 Given the following market supply and demand equations for a certain Product X:

$$Q_S = 20,000P_X$$

$$Q_D = 60,000 - 12,000P_X,$$

a. Graph the demand and supply equations.
b. Determine both algebraically and graphically the equilibrium price for the industry—that is, the point where quantity supplied equals quantity demanded.

10.2 Armstrong Corporation operates in a perfectly competitive industry. Armstrong's cost function is $TC = 40,000 + 200Q + Q^2$. (This cost function also describes all other producers in the industry.)
a. The industry is in long-run equilibrium. What is the market price for Armstrong's product?

10.3 Watercraft, Inc., is a small firm in the boat industry, which is purely competitive. The market price for fourteen-foot fishing boats is $640; the company's cost function is given by the equation $TC = \$240Q - \$20Q^2 + 1Q^3$. A normal profit is included in the cost function.
a. Determine
   (i) the output at which profit is maximized,
   (ii) the average cost per unit at this output, and
   (iii) total profits.
b. If this firm is typical of all firms in the industry, is the industry in equilibrium? How do you know?
c. Assume that this firm's input factors are perfectly unspecialized such that there is no difference between the short-run and the long-run cost curves. If the firm and the industry are not now in equilibrium, when they do reach an equilibrium what will be:
   (i) the output per firm,
   (ii) the cost per unit of output, and
   (iii) the price per unit of output?
d. Describe the process that will drive the industry into equilibrium.

10.4 The Skyhawk Trailer Company has just obtained a patent covering important design features of the Tomahawk II, a new ultra-light camper trailer that can be safely towed behind high-mileage subcompact cars. Skyhawk expects that its patent protection will make it quite difficult for competitors to offer similar ultra-light trailers during the next two or three years. If the Tomahawk II is as successful as early reports indicate, however, a veritable flood of similar products can be expected within five years.

Skyhawk has asked its financial planning committee to analyze short- and long-run pricing and production levels for the new Tomahawk II. To facilitate the decision making process, the committee has been provided the following price and cost data by Skyhawk's marketing and production departments:

$$P = 7000 - 5Q$$

$$TC = 225{,}000 + 1000Q + 10Q^2$$

$$P = \text{Price (in dollars)}$$

$$Q = \text{Quantity (in hundreds)}$$

$$TC = \text{Total Cost (in dollars)}.$$

a. What short-run price and output combination would be recommended if the committee decided that Skyhawk should take full advantage of its short-run monopoly position and maximize profits?

b. What long-run price and output combination would result if Tomahawk II's current brand loyalty and cost/output relationship can be maintained despite competitor offerings of several varieties of similar (not identical) trailers, but the firm cannot earn any economic profits? (*Note*: For simplicity, assume Tomahawk II sales decline because of a parallel leftward shift in the demand curve and the cost/output relationship, which includes a normal profit, remains unchanged.)

c. What long-run price and output combination would result if Skyhawk's patent protection were to expire (and/or be circumvented) and competitors offered trailers identical to the Tomahawk II such that a perfectly competitive market existed? Again, assume that the current cost-output relationship can be maintained.

10.5 The solar-heating industry in a southwestern state is composed of just two firms. The market for solar-heating devices is such that the actions of each firm affect the profits of the other firm; that is, the profit of each firm is a function of the output decision of the other firm. The profit functions for the two firms are as follows:

$$\pi_1 = 5Q_1 - Q_1^2 - 0.5Q_2^2 + 12$$

$$\pi_2 = 9Q_2 - 1.5Q_2^2 - Q_1^2 + 20.$$

a. Assuming that each firm continuously assumes that the other firm will not react to its output decisions, what will be the output and profits of each firm, and what will be the total industry output and profits?

b. Demonstrate that there is a strong economic rationale for collusion between these two firms.

c. What economic considerations are likely to make such collusion difficult?

10.6 The Cocoa Corporation of America faces the following segmented demand curve:

$$P = 30 - 0.1Q \text{ over the range of } 0-50 \text{ units of output,}$$

$$P = 40 - 0.3Q \text{ when output exceeds 50 units.}$$

The company's total cost function is:

$$TC_1 = 100 + 3Q + 0.1Q^2.$$

a. Graph the demand, marginal revenue, and marginal cost curves.

b. How would you describe the market structure of Cocoa's industry? Explain your answer in detail, including an explanation of why the demand curve takes the shape given above.

c. What is the firm's optimal price and quantity, and what will its profits (or losses) be at this output?

d. Assume Cocoa's costs change to $TC_2 = 100 + 3Q + 0.3Q^2$; will their optimal price/output level change? If so, to what? If not, why not?

e. Would your answer to Part d change if you knew the cost increase facing Cocoa had been industry-wide? Why?

10.7 Consider an industry with 100 small firms and a single large, dominant, price-leading firm. The industry demand curve is $Q_t = 450 - 5P$. Each small firm operates a plant with marginal costs equal to 2.5 times its output level. That is, the marginal cost function for *each* small firm is given by the expression $MC = 2.5Q$. The small firms in this industry all act as price takers.

a. Develop the equation for the aggregate supply function of the price following firms.

b. What is the demand curve facing the price leader?

c. Determine the price leader's profit maximizing price/output level. Assume that the price leader's cost curve is:

$$TC = 5 + Q + 0.225Q^2.$$

Prove that your solution is consistent with a short-run equilibrium for this market.

10.8 Three firms make up the industry for a product sold in Florida. Alpha Corporation is the largest firm and it operates as a dominant firm price leader. Beta and

Delta Corporations are significantly smaller and operate as price followers. The cost functions for Beta and Delta respectively are:

$$TC_B = 100 + 500Q_B + 0.50Q_B{}^2$$

$$TC_D = 200 - 150Q_D + 0.625Q_D{}^2.$$

Alpha Corporation's cost function is:

$$TC_A = 500 + 5Q_A + 0.01Q_A{}^2.$$

The industry demand curve is:

$$P = 1620 - Q.$$

a. Determine the supply curves for Beta and Delta Corporations.
b. What is the demand curve faced by Alpha Corporation?
c. Assuming Alpha operates as a profit maximizer, what will the market price be for the product of this industry?
d. Assuming the cost functions for the three firms include the required return on capital, is the industry in long-run equilibrium? Explain.

SELECTED REFERENCES

Bain, Joe S. *Barriers to New Competition*. Cambridge, Mass.: Harvard University Press, 1956.

Baumol, William J. "Contestable Markets: An Uprising in the Theory of Industry Structure." *American Economic Review* 72 (March 1982): 1–15.

Comanor, William S., and Wilson, Thomas N. "Advertising, Market Structure and Performance." *Review of Economics and Statistics* 49 (November 1967): 423–440.

Demsetz, Harold. "Barriers to Entry." *American Economic Review* 72 (March 1982): 47–57.

Hirschey, Mark. "The Effect of Advertising on Industrial Mobility, 1947–1972." *Journal of Business* 54 (April 1981): 329–339.

———. "Market Power and Foreign Involvement by U.S. Multinationals." *Review of Economics and Statistics* 64 (May 1982): 343–346.

———, and Pappas, James L. "Market Power and Manufacturer Leasing." *Journal of Industrial Economics* 30 (September 1980): 39–47.

Lindenberg, Eric B., and Ross, Stephen A. "Tobin's *q* Ratio and Industrial Organization." *Journal of Business* 54 (January 1981): 1–32.

Peltzman, Sam. "The Gains and Losses From Industrial Concentration." *Journal of Law and Economics* 20 (October 1977): 229–263.

Qualls, P. David. "Market Structure and the Cyclical Flexibility of Price-Cost Margins." *Journal of Business* 52 (April 1979): 305–325.

Stonebraker, Robert J. "Turnover and Mobility Among the 100 Largest Firms: An Update." *American Economic Review* 69 (December 1979): 968–973.

Strickland, Allyn D., and Weiss, Leonard W. "Advertising, Concentration, and Price-Cost Margins." *Journal of Political Economy* 84 (October 1976): 1109–1121.

White, Lawrence J. "What Has Been Happening to Aggregate Concentration in the United States?" *Journal of Industrial Economics* 29 (March 1981): 223–230.

CHAPTER 11
PRICING PRACTICES

Chapter 10 demonstrated that regardless of the market structure within which the firm operates, pricing for profit maximization is based on a careful analysis of the relationship between marginal cost and marginal revenue. Research into the question of actual pricing practices, however, indicates that many firms set prices without an explicit analysis of the marginal relationships. Hall and Hitch, for example, found that most firms use *cost-plus pricing*, setting prices to cover all direct costs plus a percentage markup for overhead and profit instead of determining the specific price at which $MR = MC$.[1] Similar findings were reported by Kaplan, Dirlam, and

---

[1] R. L. Hall and C. J. Hitch, "Price Theory and Business Behavior," in *Oxford Economic Papers* (Oxford: Clarendon Press, 1939), p. 19.

Lanzillotti in their study of pricing practices in big business,[2] and by Haynes in his analysis of small-business pricing decisions.[3]

How can this conflict between economic theory and observed pricing practices be reconciled? If one thoroughly understands microeconomic theory, particularly its limitations, and fully comprehends the procedures used in actual pricing decisions, one can see that the conflict between theory and practice is more apparent than real. In this chapter we examine a variety of pricing practices, indicate their value in real-world situations, and demonstrate the economic rationale for their use.

COST-PLUS PRICING

Surveys of actual business pricing indicate that cost-plus pricing, or full-cost pricing as it is sometimes called, is by far the most prevalent pricing method employed by business firms. There are many varieties of cost-plus pricing, but a typical one involves estimating the average variable costs of producing and marketing a particular product, adding a charge for overhead, and then adding a percentage markup, or margin, for profits. The charge for indirect costs, or overhead, is usually determined by allocating these costs among the firm's products on the basis of their average variable costs. For example, if a firm's total overhead for a year was projected to be $1.3 million, and the estimated total variable costs of its planned production was $1.0 million, then overhead would be allocated to products at the rate of 130 percent of variable cost. Thus, if the average variable costs of a product are estimated to be $1, the firm would add a charge of 130 percent of that variable cost, or $1.30, for overhead, obtaining an estimated fully allocated average cost of $2.30. To this figure the firm might add a 30 percent markup for profits, or $0.69, to obtain a price of $2.99 per unit.[4]

---

[2]A. D. H. Kaplan, Joel B. Dirlam, and Robert F. Lanzillotti, *Pricing in Big Business* (Washington, D.C.: Brookings Institution, 1958). *See also* Robert F. Lanzillotti, "Pricing Objectives in Large Companies," *American Economic Review* 48 (December 1958): 921–940.

[3]W. W. Haynes, *Pricing Decisions in Small Business* (Lexington: University of Kentucky Press, 1962).

[4]Profit margins, or markups, are often calculated as a percentage of price instead of cost. It is a simple matter to convert from one to the other by use of the following expressions:

$$\text{Markup on Price} = \frac{\text{Markup on Cost}}{1 + \text{Markup on Cost}}. \tag{11.1}$$

$$\text{Markup on Cost} = \frac{\text{Markup on Price}}{1 - \text{Markup on Price}}. \tag{11.2}$$

Thus, a 30 percent profit margin on a cost basis is equivalent to a 23 percent margin on price:

$$\text{Markup on Price} = \frac{0.3}{1 + 0.3} = 0.23.$$

Cost-plus pricing has long been criticized as a naïve pricing technique based solely on cost considerations—and the wrong costs at that. The failure of the technique to examine demand conditions, coupled with its emphasis on fully allocated accounting costs rather than marginal costs, is said to lead to suboptimal price decisions. While it is true that firms which use cost-plus pricing naïvely may fail to make optimal decisions, the widespread use of the technique by many successful firms must cause one to question the charge that it has no place in managerial decision making. In fact, a closer examination of the technique indicates both its value and its limitations in pricing analysis.

Role of Costs in Cost-Plus Pricing

Although several different cost concepts are employed in cost-plus pricing, most firms use a standard, or normal, cost concept. These fully allocated costs are determined by first estimating the per-unit direct costs, then allocating the firm's expected indirect expenses, or overhead, assuming a standard or normal output level. The resulting standard cost per unit is then used for price determination, irrespective of short-term variations in actual unit costs.

The standard cost concept is typically based on historical accounting costs, with adjustments to account for wage and price changes that are expected to affect costs during the period for which prices are being established. The use of historical accounting costs as the basis for cost-plus pricing gives rise to several potential problems. First, firms sometimes fail to properly adjust the historical cost data to reflect recent or *expected* price changes for key input factors. Unadjusted historical accounting costs have little relevance for decision making. The firm should use estimates of future costs; that is, costs that will be incurred during the period for which prices are being set. A further problem is that accounting costs seldom reflect true economic costs. The concept of opportunity, or alternative, costs must be employed for optimal decision making. Additionally, the use of fully allocated costs is erroneous for many pricing decisions where incremental costs, rather than full costs, should be used for optimization in pricing decisions.

Role of Demand in Cost-Plus Pricing

The structure of profit margins among different products for firms using cost-plus pricing provides clear evidence that demand analysis does, in fact, play an important role in price determination. James S. Earley, for example, reported that most of the firms he examined differentiated their markups for different product lines on the basis of competitive pressure and demand elasticities.[5] Kaplan, Dirlam, and Lan-

---

[5] James S. Earley, "Marginal Policies of Excellently Managed Companies," *American Economic Review* 46 (March 1956): 44–70.

zillotti reported a similar finding in their study of pricing practices.[6] A relatively recent *BusinessWeek* article on flexible pricing also stressed this point. It noted that "While companies have always shown some willingness to adjust prices or profit margins on specific products as market conditions varied, this kind of flexibility is [now] being carried to a state of high art."[7] The airline and automobile industries were cited as examples of industries where changes in competitive relationships have forced a more careful and thorough analysis of demand conditions for pricing. The widespread introduction of discounts and special fares by airlines as federal regulation was relaxed indicates close attention to demand conditions and competition. U.S. automobile manufacturers are also paying increased attention to demand conditions in their pricing. An economist for one major auto manufacturer stated it this way: "And this [pricing approach] means a more sensitive effort to assess the competitive relationship of products and the cost of making them."

That demand analysis plays an important role in cost-plus pricing is clear. There is no evidence, however, that the markups used in cost-plus pricing result in the same prices that would be established through marginal analysis; that is, by operating where $MR = MC$. Cost-plus pricing may not produce optimal results.

Explanation for the Existence of Cost-Plus Pricing

Given the possibility that cost-plus pricing might result in a nonoptimal price/output decision, is there a rationale for its continued use by many firms? There are, indeed, reasons for this use, and an examination of the deviations between the basic microeconomic model of the firm and the actual environment faced by businesses explains why cost-plus pricing is so popular.

Although microeconomic theory is based on an assumed goal of value maximization, much of it is developed around a static construct in which the firm is assumed to operate so as to maximize *short-run* profits. Implicit in this is the assumption that continual maximization of short-run profits, coupled with proper adjustments to the physical plant as technology, factor prices, and demand change, will lead to long-run profit and value maximization.

The real world is more complicated than this model suggests. Actions taken at one time affect results in subsequent times, and wise business managers recognize this fact. Accordingly, because short-run profit maximization is seldom entirely consistent with long-run wealth maximization, firms do not focus solely on short-run profit maximization.

An illustration will help to clarify the point. Consider the case of a firm that sets the current price of its product below the short-run profit maximizing level in

[6] Kaplan, Dirlam, and Lanzillotti, *Pricing in Big Business.*

[7] "Flexible Pricing," *BusinessWeek* (December 12, 1977): 78–88.

order to expand its market rapidly. Such a policy can lead to long-run profit maximization if the firm is able to secure a larger permanent market share by its action. A similar policy might also be used to forestall competitive entry into the market. From a legal standpoint, a policy of accepting less than maximum short-run profits could reduce the threat of antitrust suits or government regulations, thereby again leading to long-run profit and wealth maximization.

The pricing practices of U.S. automobile manufacturers in the years just after World War II provide an example of this kind of behavior. Prices on most models were maintained well below the short-run profit maximizing level. Automobile manufacturers felt that the rapid expansion of both private automobile ownership and their dealership networks that would result from this policy would lead to higher long-run profits. Further, there was some fear of alienating customers by charging high prices during this period of extremely heavy demand; moreover, the possibility of antitrust action also affected automobile-pricing decisions.

The existence of uncertainty in the real world is another complication that causes firms to depart from the theoretical microeconomic pricing solution. Pricing under microeconomic theory is based on the assumption that firms have precise knowledge of the marginal relationships in their demand and cost functions. Given this knowledge, it would be easy to operate so as to equate marginal revenue and marginal cost. However, firms know their cost and revenue functions only to an approximation. Consider first the demand function. In addition to the statistical problems of empirical demand estimation, the element of product interdependence discussed under the section on oligopoly in Chapter 10 is a most severe barrier to precise demand function estimation. The same statistical problems plague cost-function estimation, and such considerations as joint costs, overhead costs, and the like present additional difficulties. When the uncertainties of the future—economic conditions, the weather, labor contract settlements, and so on—are added, it is abundantly clear why managers might do something other than equate marginal revenue and marginal cost when making price/output decisions.

Although the pricing corollaries of microeconomic theory are far too limited to be applied without modification in actual pricing problems, the theory does provide a useful basis for analyzing a firm's pricing decision. For example, any attempt to reduce uncertainty and to estimate more precisely the marginal revenue and cost relationships results in added costs. Marginal analysis indicates that the firm must weigh the added expense against the possible gain and act accordingly. That is, the firm must determine whether the added expense associated with obtaining better estimates of the marginal relationships is more than offset by the gain in profits expected to result. It follows from this that short-cut decision techniques may actually result in maximum profits when full consideration is given to the added expense of obtaining the data necessary for complete marginal analysis.

INCREMENTAL ANALYSIS IN PRICING

For many pricing decisions the correct approach involves *incremental profit analysis*, which deals with the relationship between the *changes* in revenues and costs associated with managerial decisions. The emphasis on only the costs or revenues that are actually affected by the decision insures proper economic reasoning in decision analysis. That is, proper use of incremental profit analysis results in accepting any action that increases net profits and in rejecting any action that reduces profits.[8]

The fact that incremental analysis involves only those factors that are affected by a particular decision does not mean that the concept is easy to apply. Proper use of incremental analysis requires a wide-ranging examination of the *total* effect of the decision. Consider, for example, a firm's decision to introduce a new product. Incremental analysis requires that the decision be based on the net effect of changes in revenues and costs. An analysis of the effect on revenues involves an estimate of the net revenues to be received for the product and, additionally, a study of how sales of the new product will affect the firm's other products. It may well be that the new product will, in fact, compete with the firm's existing products; if so, even though the new product has a high individual revenue potential, the net effect on revenue might not justify the added expense. At the other extreme, although a new product may not be expected to produce much profit on its own—if it is complementary to the firm's other products—the expected gain in sales of these other products could result in a large incremental increase in total profit. Kodak's Instamatic camera series is an example of a product introduced, in part at least, because of the complementarity between it and a major component of the firm's existing product line, photographic film.

Incremental cost analysis is just as far-reaching. In addition to the direct incremental costs associated with the new product, the firm must consider any impact on the costs of existing products. For example, introduction of a new product might cause production bottlenecks that would raise the cost of other products.

Incremental analysis involves long-run as well as short-run effects. A new product may appear to be profitable in an incremental sense in the short run because the firm has excess capacity in its existing plant and equipment. Over the long run, however, this commitment to produce the new item may require a substantial investment when the necessary equipment wears out and must be replaced. There may also be high opportunity costs associated with future production if either expansion of other product lines or development of future alternative products is restricted by the decision to produce the new product.

It is important to stress once again that incremental analysis is based on the

---

[8]In this section we abstract from changing the firm's risk posture. However, the primary economic goal of the firm is wealth maximization, and, as was pointed out in Chapter 1, an action might increase expected profits but be so risky that it would raise the firm's capitalization rate to a point where the value of the firm might decline. The question of risk is considered in Chapter 13.

TABLE 11.1

Incremental Analysis as Employed by Continental Airlines

Problem: Shall Continental run an extra daily flight from City X to City Y?

Facts:	Fully-allocated costs of this flight	$4,500
	Out-of-pocket costs of this flight	$2,000
	Flight should gross	$3,100

Decision: Run the flight. It will add $1,100 to net profit by adding $3,100 to revenues and only $2,000 to costs. Overhead and other costs totaling $2,500 ($4,500 minus $2,000) would be incurred whether the flight is run or not. Therefore, fully-allocated or average costs of $4,500 are not relevant to this business decision. It is the out-of-pocket, or incremental, costs that count.

changes associated with the decision. For short-run analysis, fixed cost (overhead) is irrelevant and must not be included in incremental analysis.

An Illustration of Incremental Analysis

The *BusinessWeek* article on flexible pricing (cited in footnote 7) reports on pricing practices that reflect the use of incremental logic by numerous firms. The value of this approach is also demonstrated by an example of how Continental Airlines has used incremental analysis in its flight service decisions.[9] When considering adding a new flight (or dropping an existing one that appears to be doing poorly), Continental engaged in a very thorough incremental analysis along the lines of Table 11.1. The corporate philosophy was clear: "If revenues exceed out-of-pocket costs, put the flight on." In other words, Continental compared the out-of-pocket, or incremental, costs associated with each proposed flight to the total revenues generated by that flight. An excess of revenues over incremental costs led to a decision to add the flight to Continental's schedule.

The out-of-pocket costs figure that Continental used was obtained by circulating a proposed schedule for the new flight to every operating department concerned and finding out what added expenses would be incurred by each of them. Here, an alternative cost concept was used. If a ground crew was on duty and between work on other flights, the proposed flight was not charged a penny of their salary. Some costs may even have been reduced by the additional flight. For example, on a late-night round trip flight between Colorado Springs and Denver, Continental often flew without any passengers and with only a small amount of freight. Even without passenger revenues, these flights were profitable because their net costs were less than the rent for overnight hangar space at Colorado Springs.

[9]Adapted from the April 20, 1963, issue of *BusinessWeek* by special permission. Copyright © 1963 by McGraw-Hill, Inc., New York, N.Y. 10020. All rights reserved.

On the revenue side, Continental considered not only the projected revenues for the flight but also the effect on revenues of competing and connecting flights on the Continental schedule. Several Continental flights that failed to cover their out-of-pocket costs directly brought in passengers for connecting long-haul service. When the excess of additional revenue over cost on the long-haul flight was considered, Continental earned a positive net profit on the feeder service.

Continental's use of incremental analysis extended to its scheduling of airport arrival and departure times. A proposed schedule for the Kansas City Municipal Airport, for example, had two planes landing at the same time. This was expensive for Continental, because its facilities in Kansas City at that time were not sufficient to service two planes simultaneously. Continental would have been forced to lease an extra fuel truck and to hire three new employees at an additional monthly cost of $1,800. However, when Continental began shifting around proposed departure times in other cities to avoid the congestion at Kansas City, it appeared that the company might lose as much as $10,000 in monthly revenues if passengers switched to competing flights leaving at more convenient hours. Needless to say, the two flights were scheduled to be on the ground in Kansas City at the same time.

PRICE DISCRIMINATION

Additional complexities are introduced into the pricing decision when the firm sells its products in multiple markets. The existence of more than one market, or customer grouping, gives rise to the possibility of price discrimination, or differential pricing.

In a general sense price discrimination can be said to exist whenever different classes of customers are charged different prices for the same product, or when a multiproduct firm prices closely related products in such a manner that the differences in their prices are not proportional to the differences in their costs. In other words, price discrimination occurs whenever a given firm's prices in different markets are not related to differentials in production and distribution costs. For example, a practice of nationwide uniform pricing for fountain pens by the Parker Pen Company of Janesville, Wisconsin, would be a form of price discrimination. The transportation cost of selling these pens in Chicago is lower than transportation cost to the Los Angeles market; thus a uniform price for the product reflects a lower markup in Los Angeles than in Chicago.

Price discrimination does not carry an evil connotation in a moral sense. It is merely a term used in economics to describe a particular condition that must be judged good or bad on other grounds. In some situations price discrimination can actually lead to lower costs and prices and to the provision of more goods and services than would otherwise be available. For example, an opera company that charges lower prices for students than for nonstudents may through this pricing practice both provide an opportunity for students who could not afford the usual price to attend performances and also, because of the incremental revenues provided by students, be able to stage productions that could not be supported by ticket sales to nonstudents alone. Of course, price discrimination can also be used by a predatory monopolist to increase already excessive profits, in which case most of us would agree with the antitrust laws designed to thwart such behavior.

Requirements for Profitable Price Discrimination

There are two necessary conditions for profitable price discrimination. First, the firm must be able to segment the market for a product; that is, to identify submarkets and to prevent transfers among customers in the different submarkets. When markets are segmented, the firm can isolate one group of buyers from another. If this is possible, the firm can sell at one price to some buyers and at a different price to others without the possibility of intermarket leakages.

Second, different price elasticities of demand for the product must exist in the various submarkets. Unless price elasticities differ among the submarkets, there is no point in segmenting the market; with identical elasticities, the profit maximizing price policy calls for charging the same price in all the segments. This point is elaborated in a later section.

Types of Price Discrimination

The extent, or *degree*, to which a firm can engage in price discrimination has been classified into three major categories. Under *first-degree price discrimination* the firm extracts the maximum amount each and every purchaser is willing to pay for its product. The firm prices each unit of output separately at the level indicated at successive quantities along a demand curve. (In effect, the demand curve becomes the firm's marginal revenue curve.) Although there are some cases where price discrimination of the first degree actually occurs—primarily in the provision of personal services, such as legal services, medical care, and personal finance advising—the formidable demand information requirements (the seller must know the maximum price each buyer will pay for each unit of output) and problems of market segmentation associated with this type of price discrimination prevent its use in most situations.[10]

Second-degree price discrimination, a more frequently employed type of price discrimination, involves the setting of prices on the basis of quantity purchased.

---

[10]Doctors' fee schedules, which often discriminate on an ability (and willingness) to pay basis, are cited as the classic example of first-degree price discrimination. The medical profession asserts that such discrimination—if it exists—is philanthropic and actually leads to the provision of better service. This assertion may be correct, but one can be equally sure that it leads to higher income for the doctors as well and represents profit maximizing behavior.

Typically, prices are *blocked*, with a high price set for the first unit or block of units purchased by each consumer and lower prices set for successive units or blocks. Public utilities, such as electric companies, gas companies, and water companies, frequently use block rates that are discriminatory.[11] The use of second-degree price discrimination is also somewhat limited, since it can be applied only to products whose use is metered in some fashion—which explains its use by electric, gas, and water utilities. Office equipment such as copiers or time-sharing computer systems, which lend themselves to such metering, are other examples of products where second-degree price discrimination is practiced.

The most commonly observed form of price discrimination is *third-degree price discrimination*; this results when a firm separates its customers into several classes and sets a different price for each class. These customer classifications can be based on a variety of factors. Geographical differentials may be used when a product's supplier feels that regional markets can be isolated through control of the product distribution system. For example, in 1978 General Motors set a lower price on its Chevette model in the western United States than in the rest of the country, because Japanese competition made the West Coast small-car automobile market more price-elastic than the markets in other parts of the United States. (Price differentials among geographically separated markets that are proportional to transportation costs are not classified as discriminatory.)

Product use provides another basis for third-degree price discrimination. Railroads, for example, typically charge different prices per ton-mile depending on the value of the product being hauled. Electric, gas, water, and telephone utilities' rate differentials between commercial and private consumers is another example of price discrimination based on product use. The utilities face very different demand elasticities in the residential and the industrial sectors of their markets.[12] The demand for electricity from residential users is inelastic, because these customers have no good substitutes for the electricity supplied by the power utility. Industrial buyers, on the other hand, have a much more elastic demand, because many of them could generate their own power if electricity prices should rise above the cost of operating in-plant generating equipment.

Time, either clock or calendar, provides another common basis for this form of price discrimination. Segmenting the day for long-distance telephone rates is one example of such price discrimination; rates are higher during periods of the day when demand is greatest—for example, during business hours. Theater pricing provides another example of price discrimination based on clock time. Calendar-time

---

[11] Remember that in order for differential prices to be discriminatory in an economic sense, they cannot be related to cost differences. Therefore, block rates based strictly on different costs of service would not be classified as price discrimination.

[12] Utility users are prohibited from selling services to other users; otherwise, those paying low rates could make sales to those who are charged high rates by the utility.

price discrimination is often reflected in peak-season and off-season pricing for resort facilities.

Age, sex, and income provide still other bases of discrimination, particularly for services as opposed to physical products. For example, lower prices for children's haircuts and movie tickets are discriminatory practices based on age; ladies'-day admission prices for sports events illustrate price discrimination based on sex. Discrimination on the bases of age, sex, and income is controversial, both popularly and legally, so this pricing topic should be closely monitored for changes.

Profit Maximization under Price Discrimination

The firm that can segment its market will maximize profits by operating in such a way that marginal revenue equals marginal cost *in each market segment*. This can be demonstrated by an example. Suppose a firm is selling the same product in two separate markets, A and B. The demand curves for the two markets are given by Equations 11.3 and 11.4:

$$\text{Market A: } P_A = 60 - 0.5Q_A. \tag{11.3}$$

$$\text{Market B: } P_B = 110 - 3Q_B. \tag{11.4}$$

P_A and P_B are the prices charged in the two markets, and Q_A and Q_B are the quantities demanded. The firm's total cost function for its single homogeneous product is:

$$TC = 1,000 + 9Q + 0.1Q^2. \tag{11.5}$$

Here, Q equals the sum of the quantities sold in Markets A and B; that is, $Q = Q_A + Q_B$.

Figure 11.1 illustrates this pricing situation. The demand curve for Market A is shown in the first panel, that for Market B in the second. The aggregate demand curve shown in the third panel represents the horizontal sum of the quantities demanded at each price in Markets A and B. The associated marginal revenue curve, MR_{A+B}, has a similar interpretation. For example, marginal revenue equals $20 at 40 units of output in Market A and $20 at 15 units of output in Market B. Accordingly, one point on the firm's total marginal revenue curve will have output equal to 55 units and marginal revenue equal to $20. From a production standpoint it does not matter whether the product is being sold in Market A or Market B; therefore, the single marginal cost curve shown in the third panel is applicable to both markets. If distribution costs had differed between the two markets, this fact would have had to be taken into account.

FIGURE 11.1

Price Discrimination for an Identical Product Sold in Two Markets

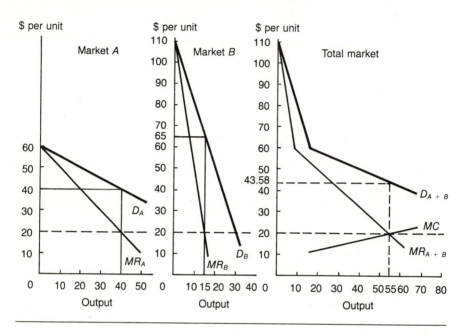

Obtaining the solution to this pricing problem can be thought of as a two-part process. First, the firm must determine the profit maximizing total output level. Profit maximization occurs at that aggregate output level at which marginal cost and marginal revenue are equal. As shown in Figure 11.1, the profit maximizing output is 55 units, where marginal cost and marginal revenue are both equal to $20. Second, the firm must allocate this output between the two submarkets. Proper allocation of the total output between the two submarkets can be determined graphically by drawing a horizontal line through the graphs in the first two panels at $20 to indicate that $20 is the marginal cost in *each* market at the indicated aggregate output. The intersection of this horizontal line with the marginal revenue curve in each submarket indicates the distribution of sales and the optimal pricing structure. According to the figures, our illustrative firm maximizes profits by producing a total of 55 units, then selling 40 units in Market A at a price of $40 and 15 units in Market B at a price of $65.

The price charged in the less elastic Market B is over 50 percent higher than the price charged in Market A, where demand is relatively elastic, and this differential adds significantly to the firm's profits. This can be seen by comparing profits earned with discrimination to profits earned if the firm were unable to segment the market. In the nondiscrimination case the firm acts as though it were facing only the single total market demand curve shown in the third panel of Figure 11.1. Profit maximization requires that the firm operate at the output level where $MR = MC$; that is, at 55 units. Here, however, the single price that would prevail is $43.58, the price determined by the intersection of a vertical line at 55 units of output with the total market demand curve.

Because the optimal output level for the firm is 55 units irrespective of whether the firm can engage in price discrimination, total costs are the same in either case, and we need only consider the total revenues to determine the effect of price discrimination on the firm's profits. With price discrimination, the firm's total revenue is equal to $2,575, found as $40 × 40 units = $1,600 revenue in Market A plus $65 × 15 units = $975 revenue in Market B. Without price discrimination total revenue is $2,397 (= $43.58 × 55 units). The difference between these total revenue figures, $178, indicates that the firm gains an additional $178 profit by segmenting its markets and charging a higher price in that segment where demand is relatively inelastic.[13]

Calculus of Price Discrimination

Since the effect of price discrimination on profits can be illustrated through the use of calculus as well as through graphs, this technique is employed below to reexamine the economics of differential pricing.

Step 1: Set Up the Total Revenue Function. The firm seeks to maximize the total profits from the sale of its product in Markets A and B. The total revenue function is given by Equation 11.6:

$$TR = P_A \cdot Q_A + P_B \cdot Q_B. \tag{11.6}$$

Substituting Equations 11.3 and 11.4 into Equation 11.6, we obtain:

$$TR = 60Q_A - 0.5Q_A^2 + 110Q_B - 3Q_B^2. \tag{11.7}$$

Step 2: Set Up the Total Cost Function. Total costs were previously given in Equation 11.5. Recognizing that Q in Equation 11.5 equals the sum $Q_A + Q_B$, the total cost function can be rewritten as:

$$TC = 1,000 + 9(Q_A + Q_B) + 0.1(Q_A + Q_B)^2 \tag{11.8}$$

$$= 1,000 + 9Q_A + 9Q_B + 0.1Q_A^2 + 0.2Q_AQ_B + 0.1Q_B^2.$$

---

[13]The extra profit of $178 in this case is a single period short-run profit. The firm might well want to analyze the long-run effects of discriminatory pricing before embarking on such a strategy.

Step 3: Set Up the Total Profit Function. Combining Equations 11.7 and 11.8, we can express the firm's total profit function as follows:

$$\pi = TR - TC \tag{11.9}$$

$$= \text{Equation } 11.7 - \text{Equation } 11.8$$

$$= 60Q_A - 0.5Q_A{}^2 + 110Q_B - 3Q_B{}^2 - 1{,}000 - 9Q_A$$
$$- 9Q_B - 0.1Q_A{}^2 - 0.2Q_AQ_B - 0.1Q_B{}^2$$

$$= 51Q_A - 0.6Q_A{}^2 + 101Q_B - 3.1Q_B{}^2 - 0.2Q_AQ_B - 1{,}000.$$

Step 4: Determine the Marginal Profit Functions for Each Market. Taking the partial derivatives of this profit function with respect to Q_A and Q_B, we obtain the following expressions:

$$\frac{\partial \pi}{\partial Q_A} = 51 - 1.2Q_A - 0.2Q_B$$

$$\frac{\partial \pi}{\partial Q_B} = 101 - 6.2Q_B - 0.2Q_A.$$

Step 5: Determine Profit Maximizing Output Quantities. Setting these partial derivatives equal to zero and solving the two equations simultaneously, we can determine the profit maximizing quantities to be sold in each market:

(a) $$51 - 1.2Q_A - 0.2Q_B = 0 \tag{11.10}$$

$$101 - 0.2Q_A - 6.2Q_B = 0. \tag{11.11}$$

(b) Multiply Equation 11.11 by 6 and subtract the result from Equation 11.10 to eliminate Q_A, then solve for Q_B:

$$51 - 1.2Q_A - 0.2Q_B = 0$$
$$\underline{-(606 - 1.2Q_A - 37.2Q_B = 0)}$$
$$-555 + 37Q_B = 0$$
$$37Q_B = 555$$
$$Q_B = 15 \text{ units.}$$

(c) Substitute the 15 units of output for Market B into Equation 11.10, then solve for Q_A:

$$51 - 1.2Q_A - 0.2(15) = 0$$

$$51 - 1.2Q_A - 3 = 0$$

$$1.2Q_A = 48$$

$$Q_A = 40 \text{ units.}$$

Step 6: Determine the Optimal Prices in Each Market. As in the graphic analysis, we see that profits are maximized by selling 40 units of the product in Market A and 15 units in Market B. Substituting these values into the two demand equations, we calculate the price for each market:

$$P_A = 60 - 0.5(40)$$

$$= 60 - 20$$

$$= \$40,$$

and

$$P_B = 110 - 3(15)$$

$$= 110 - 45$$

$$= \$65.$$

These prices correspond to those found graphically in Figure 11.1, as they must.

Step 7: Determine the Total Profits. The firm's total profits are found by substituting the optimal values of Q_A and Q_B into the profit function, Equation 11.9:

$$\pi = 51(40) - 0.6(40)^2 + 101(15) - 3.1(15)^2 - 0.2(40)(15) - 1,000$$

$$= \$777.50.$$

Step 8: Compare Total Profits with and without Price Discrimination. It is possible to illustrate the value of differential pricing by examining the maximum profits that could be achieved without price discrimination. Analytically, the problem is similar to the one just completed. The firm attempts to maximize its profit function as given by Equation 11.9, but here it must operate under the constraint that the price charged in Market A must be equal to the price charged in Market B; that is,

$P_A = P_B$. Substituting Equations 11.3 and 11.4 for P_A and P_B, this constraint can be written as:

$$P_A = P_B$$

$$60 - 0.5Q_A = 110 - 3Q_B$$

or

$$-50 - 0.5Q_A + 3Q_B = 0. \qquad (11.12)$$

Writing the price constraint in this form allows us to use the Lagrangian multiplier technique for constrained optimization. Thus, we want to maximize the following Lagrangian function:

$$L\pi = 51Q_A - 0.6Q_A{}^2 + 101Q_B - 3.1Q_B{}^2 - 0.2Q_AQ_B \qquad (11.13)$$
$$- 1,000 + \lambda(-50 - 0.5Q_A + 3Q_B).$$

Taking the partial derivatives of this expression with respect to Q_A, Q_B, and λ and setting them equal to zero results in the following system of equations: [14]

$$\frac{\partial L\pi}{\partial Q_A} = 51 - 1.2Q_A - 0.2Q_B - 0.5\lambda = 0. \qquad (11.14)$$

$$\frac{\partial L\pi}{\partial Q_A} = 101 - 6.2Q_B - 0.2Q_A + 3\lambda = 0. \qquad (11.15)$$

$$\frac{\partial L\pi}{\partial \lambda} = -50 - 0.5Q_A + 3Q_B = 0. \qquad (11.16)$$

The system can be solved by first multiplying Equation 11.14 by 6 and adding the result to Equation 11.15, obtaining:

$$407 - 7.4Q_A - 7.4Q_B = 0. \qquad (11.17)$$

Solving Equation 11.16 for Q_A results in:

$$Q_A = 6Q_B - 100, \qquad (11.18)$$

---

[14]Notice that setting the partial derivative of $L\pi$ with respect to λ equal to zero insures that the constraint expressed in Equation 11.12 must be met at the optimum. That is, at the profit maximizing solution, Equation 11.16 = Equation 11.12, so the prices are equal in the two markets.

and substituting this into Equation 11.17 allows us to determine Q_B:

$$407 - 7.4(6Q_B - 100) - 7.4Q_B = 0$$

$$407 - 44.4Q_B + 740 - 7.4Q_B = 0$$

$$51.8Q_B = 1,147$$

$$Q_B = 22.14.$$

Substituting the 22.14 units of Q_B into Equation 11.18 provides the quantity that will be sold in Market A: [15]

$$Q_A = 6(22.14) - 100$$

$$Q_A = 32.84.$$

Examination of the prices at which these quantities can be sold in each market reveals that a single price for the product, $43.58, does in fact exist:

$$P_A = 60 - 0.5 (32.84) = \$43.58.$$

$$P_B = 110 - 3.0 (22.14) = \$43.58.$$

Total profit for the nondiscrimination solution is found as follows:

$$\pi = 51(32.84) - 0.6(32.84)^2 + 101(22.14) - 3.1(22.14)^2$$
$$- 0.2(32.84) (22.14) - 1,000$$

$$= \$598,$$

or $178 less than the maximum profits obtained with differential pricing. Thus, we see that the firm gains an additional $178 profit by segmenting its markets and charging a higher price in that segment where demand is relatively inelastic.

Optimal price discrimination in this case, where an identical product is being sold in two markets, requires that the firm operate so that the marginal revenues in both markets are equated not only to marginal costs but also to one another; that is, $MR_A = MR_B = MC$. This is the result of the products being indistinguishable from a production standpoint. If the marginal costs of production and distribution of the

[15] $Q_A + Q_B = 54.98$ rather than 55 units because of rounding.

product in the two markets were different, profit maximization would have required the equating of marginal revenues to marginal costs in *each separate market*.

MULTIPLE-PRODUCT PRICING

The basic microeconomic model of the firm typically assumes that the firm produces a single homogeneous product. Yet most of us would be hard-pressed to name even one firm that does not produce a variety of products. Almost all firms produce at least multiple models, styles, or sizes of their output, and for pricing purposes each of these variations should be considered a separate product. Although multiple-product pricing requires the same analysis as for a single product, the analysis is complicated by demand and production interrelationships.

Demand Interrelationships

Demand interrelationships arise because of competition or complementarity among the firm's various products. Consider, for example, a firm that produces two products. If the products are interrelated, either as substitutes or as complements, a change in the price of one will affect the demand for the other. This means that in multiple-product pricing decisions these interrelationships—perhaps among dozens of products—must be taken into account.

Analysis of Demand Interrelationships. In the case of a two-product firm, the total revenue function can be specified as:

$$TR = f(P_A, Q_A, P_B, Q_B), \tag{11.19}$$

where P_A, P_B and Q_A, Q_B are the prices and quantities of the two products, respectively. The marginal revenues of the products can be obtained by partially differentiating Equation 11.19 with respect to Q_A and Q_B:

$$MR_A = \frac{\partial TR}{\partial Q_A} = P_A + Q_A \frac{\partial P_A}{\partial Q_A} + P_B \frac{\partial Q_B}{\partial Q_A} + Q_B \frac{\partial P_B}{\partial Q_A}. \tag{11.20}$$

$$MR_B = \frac{\partial TR}{\partial Q_B} = P_B + Q_B \frac{\partial P_B}{\partial Q_B} + P_A \frac{\partial Q_A}{\partial Q_B} + Q_A \frac{\partial P_A}{\partial Q_B}. \tag{11.21}$$

Equations 11.20 and 11.21 are completely general statements describing the revenue/output relationships for the two products. The first two terms on the right-hand side of each equation represent the marginal revenue directly associated with each product. The last two terms illustrate the problem of demand interrelationships. They indicate the change in total revenues associated with the second product that results from a change in the sales of the first. For example, the terms $P_B(\partial Q_B/\partial Q_A)$ and $Q_B(\partial P_B/\partial Q_A)$ in Equation 11.20 show the effect on the revenues generated by Product B when an additional unit of Product A is sold. Likewise, $P_A(\partial Q_A/\partial Q_B)$ and $Q_A(\partial P_A/\partial Q_B)$ in Equation 11.21 represent the change in revenues received from the sale of Product A when an additional unit of Product B is sold.

These cross-marginal revenue terms showing the demand interrelationships between two products can be positive or negative, depending on the nature of the relationship. For complementary products the net impact will be positive, demonstrating that increased sales of one product will lead to increased revenues associated with the other. For competitive products the reverse is true: Increased sales of one product will reduce demand for the second, and hence the cross-marginal revenue term will be negative.

This brief examination of demand interrelationships demonstrates that proper price determination in the multiple-product case requires a thorough analysis of the total effect of the decision on the firm's revenues. In practice this implies that optimal pricing must be based on a proper application of incremental reasoning so that the total impact of the decision is considered.

Production Interrelationships

Just as the multiple products of a firm can be related through their demand functions, so too are they often interrelated in production. Products may be jointly produced in a fixed ratio, for example in the case of cattle, where hide and beef are obtained from each animal, or in variable proportions as in the refining of crude oil into gasoline and fuel oil. Products may compete with one another for the resources of the firm, as in the case of alternative products; or they may be complementary, as when one product uses wastes generated in the production of another or when increased production of one results in lower costs of another because of economies of scale at the firm level. In each case the production interrelationships must be considered if proper pricing decisions are to be made.

Joint Products Produced in Fixed Proportions. The simplest case of joint production is that of joint products produced in fixed proportions. In this situation it makes no sense to attempt to separate the products from a production or cost standpoint. That is, if the products must be produced in fixed proportions with no possibility of adjusting the ratio of output, they are not really multiple products from a production standpoint but should be considered as a package of output. The reason for this stems from the impossibility of determining the costs for the individual

FIGURE 11.2

Optimal Pricing for Joint Products Produced in Fixed Proportions

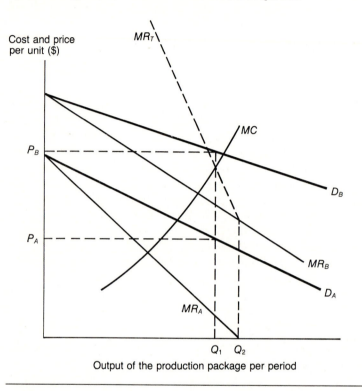

Output of the production package per period

products in the package. Since the products are jointly produced, all costs are incurred in the production of the *package*, and there is no economically sound way of allocating them to the individual products.

Optimal price/output determination requires an analysis of the relationship between the marginal revenue of the output package and its marginal cost of production. So long as the total marginal revenue of the combination—the sum of the marginal revenues obtained from each product in the package—is greater than the marginal cost of producing it, the firm gains by expanding output.

Figure 11.2 illustrates the pricing problem for the case of two joint products produced in fixed proportions. The demand and the marginal revenue curves for the two products and the single marginal cost curve associated with the production of the combined output package are shown. A *vertical* summation of the two marginal revenue curves indicates the total marginal revenue generated by the package of products. (The marginal revenue curves are summed vertically because each unit of output provides revenues from the sale of both of the joint products.) Thus, it is the intersection of this total marginal revenue curve, MR_T in the figure, with the marginal cost curve that locates the profit maximizing output level.

The optimal price for each product is determined by the intersection of a vertical line at the profit maximizing output quantity with the demand curves for each separate product. Q_1 represents the optimal quantity of the output package to be produced, and P_A and P_B are the prices to be charged for the individual products.[16]

Note that the MR_T curve in Figure 11.2 coincides with the marginal revenue curve for Product B at all output quantities greater than Q_2. This is so because MR_A becomes negative at that point, and hence the firm would never sell more than the quantity of Product A represented by Output Package Q_2. That is, the total revenues generated by Product A are maximized at Output Q_2, and, therefore, sales of any larger quantity must reduce revenues and profits.

If the marginal cost curve for producing the package of output intersects the total marginal revenue curve to the right of Q_2, profit maximization requires that the firm raise output up to this point of intersection—price Product B as indicated by its demand curve at that point, and price Product A so as to maximize its total revenue. This pricing situation is illustrated in Figure 11.3, where the same demand and marginal revenue curves presented in Figure 11.2 are shown, along with a new marginal cost curve. The optimal output quantity is Q_3, determined by the intersection of the marginal cost curve and the total marginal revenue curve. Product B is sold in the amount indicated by Output Package Q_3 and is priced at P_B. The sales quantity of Product A is limited to the amount in Output Q_2 and is priced at P_A. The excess quantity of Product A contained in the production, $Q_3 - Q_2$, must be destroyed or otherwise kept out of the market so that its price—and total revenue—is not lowered from that indicated at Q_2.[17]

Pricing Example for Products Produced in Fixed Proportions. An example of a price/output decision for two products produced in fixed proportions will clarify the relationships developed above. Consider a firm that produces two products in a joint production process where we assume output must be in the ratio of $1:1$. That is, the two products, say, A and B, must always be produced in equal quantities because of the nature of the production process. The total cost function for this system is:

[16]To illustrate, if we are dealing with cattle, the joint package would consist of one hide and two sides of beef. Q_1 for the firm in question, a cattle feed lot, might be 3,000 steers, resulting in 6,000 sides of beef sold at a price of P_A and 3,000 hides sold at P_B per unit.

[17]A case in point involves pineapple, where sliced pineapple and pineapple juice are joint products, the juice being produced as a by-product as pineapples are peeled and sliced. An excessive amount of juice was produced, and rather than put it on the market and depress prices, the excess was destroyed. This did not continue long, however; Dole, Del Monte, and other producers advertised heavily to shift the demand curve for juice and created new products, such as pineapple-grapefruit juice, to bring about a demand for the waste product. Moreover, the canning machinery was improved to reduce the percentage of the product going into juice. The proportions of sliced pineapple and juice were fixed in the short run but not in the long run.

FIGURE 11.3

**Optimal Pricing for Joint Products Produced in Fixed Proportions
with Excess Production of One Product**

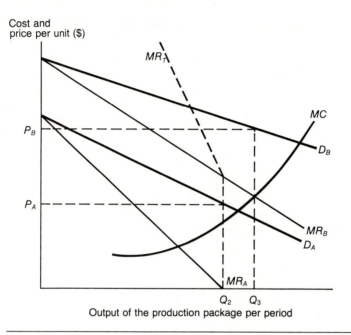

Output of the production package per period

$$TC = 500 + 5Q + 2Q^2, \qquad \qquad (11.22)$$

where Q is a unit of output consisting of one unit of Product A and one unit of
Product B. Assume further that the price/demand relationship for the two products,
given current market conditions, can be described by the demand curves:

$$P_A = \$395 - Q_A \qquad \qquad (11.23)$$

and

$$P_B = \$100 - 0.5Q_B. \qquad \qquad (11.24)$$

The profit maximizing firm would view its price/output decision as being one of
determining the optimal quantity of Q (the units of production—composed of equal
quantities of A and B) to produce and of setting prices and sales quantities for the
individual products, A and B. The problem is most conveniently analyzed by developing the proper profit function for the firm.

Although there are several ways in which one could express the profit function for this pricing problem, the most appropriate is an expression in terms of Q, the unit of production, since the individual products, A and B, must be produced in $1:1$ *fixed* proportions. Consider first the revenues associated with the firm's output. For each unit of Q produced, the firm obtains one unit of Product A and one unit of Product B for sale to its customers. Therefore, the revenue derived from the production and sale of a unit of Q (again the combined product package consisting of one unit each of A and B) is a simple summation of the revenues obtained from the sales of a unit of Product A and a unit of Product B. Similarly, the total revenue function for the firm expressed as a function of Q is merely the summation of the revenue functions for Products A and B. This relationship can be developed algebraically as:

$$TR_{FIRM} = TR_A + TR_B$$

$$= P_A \cdot Q_A + P_B \cdot Q_B.$$

Substituting Equations 11.23 and 11.24 for P_A and P_B, respectively, results in the total revenue function:

$$TR_{FIRM} = (395 - Q_A)\, Q_A + (100 - 0.5Q_B)\, Q_B \qquad \textbf{(11.25)}$$

$$= 395Q_A - Q_A^2 + 100Q_B - 0.5Q_B^2.$$

Now, since one unit of Product A and one unit of Product B are contained in each unit of Q produced by the firm, Q_A, Q_B, and Q must all be equal. This means that we can substitute Q for Q_A and Q_B in Equation 11.25 to develop a total revenue function in terms of Q, the unit of production:

$$TR = 395Q - Q^2 + 100Q - 0.5Q^2 \qquad \textbf{(11.26)}$$

$$= 495Q - 1.5Q^2.$$

Note that this revenue function is constructed under the assumption that equal quantities of Products A and B are *sold*. That is, it assumes no dumping or other withholding from the market of either product. Thus, it is the appropriate revenue function for use if the solution to the output determination problem is as shown in Figure 11.2—that is, with no excess production of one product. The only way to determine whether in fact this condition holds is to solve the problem and then check to ascertain that the marginal revenues of both products are in fact positive at the indicated profit maximizing output level.

Because the firm's total cost function for the production of these joint products was expressed in terms of Q, the unit of production, in Equation 11.22, the profit function can be formed by combining that cost function with the total revenue function, Equation 11.26:

$$Profit = \pi = TR - TC$$

$$= 495Q - 1.5Q^2 - (500 + 5Q + 2Q^2)$$

$$= 490Q - 3.5Q^2 - 500.$$

Differentiating the profit function to solve for the profit maximizing output level results in:

$$\frac{d\pi}{dQ} = 490 - 7Q = 0$$

$$7Q = 490$$

$$Q = 70 \text{ units.}$$

The optimal solution to the output quantity decision will be 70 units of production—70 units each of Products A and B—*provided that at a 70-unit output level the marginal revenues of both* A *and* B *are nonnegative*. This condition can be checked by evaluating the derivatives of the revenue functions for the two products at the 70-unit sales level:

$$TR_A = 395Q_A - Q_A^2$$

$$MR_A = \frac{dTR_A}{dQ_A} = 395 - 2Q_A$$

$$= 395 - 2(70) \quad \text{(at 70 Units)}$$

$$= +225.$$

$$TR_B = 100Q_B - 0.5Q_B$$

$$MR_B = \frac{dTR_B}{dQ_B} = 100 - Q_B$$

$$= 100 - 70 \quad \text{(at 70 Units)}$$

$$= +30.$$

Since the marginal revenues are both positive, the solution to the problem is correct and one can then proceed with the determination of the proper prices for the two products.[18] The prices are obtained by substituting into the two demand curves, Equations 11.23 and 11.24:

$$P_A = 395 - Q_A \qquad\qquad (11.23)$$

$$P_A = 395 - 70$$

$$= \$325$$

and

$$P_B = 100 - 0.5Q_B \qquad\qquad (11.24)$$

$$= 100 - 0.5(70)$$

$$= \$65.$$

Thus, in this example, the firm should produce 70 units of output, selling the resultant 70 units of Product A at \$325 per unit and the 70 units of B at a price of \$65 per unit.

Joint Products Produced in Variable Proportions. Typically, the firm has the ability to vary the proportions in which joint products are produced. Even the classic example of fixed proportions in the joint production of beef and hides holds only over short periods, because cattle can be bred to provide an output package with differing proportions of these two products.

When the firm can vary the proportions in which the joint output is produced, it is possible to construct separate marginal cost relationships for each of the joint products. This is illustrated in Table 11.2, a matrix of the total cost/output relationships for two joint products, A and B. Since the marginal cost of either product is defined as the increase in total costs associated with a unit increase in that product, *holding constant the quantity of the other product produced*, the marginal costs of

---

[18] Had one product's marginal revenue been negative at 70 units of output, a problem solution with excess production of one product, as illustrated in Figure 11.3, would have been indicated. In such a situation the firm stops selling additional units of the product with a negative marginal revenue at the point where marginal revenue is zero. Hence, the relevant marginal revenue figure for use in determining the optimal output level is that associated with the other product. This would require use of the revenue function for only the one product being sold at the margin in the profit function used to determine the optimal output level. Equating the marginal revenue of that product to the marginal cost of producing a unit of output results in the optimal output determination, as is illustrated in Figure 11.3.

TABLE 11.2

Cost/Output Matrix for Two Joint Products

			Output of A		
Output of B	1	2	3	4	5
1	\$ 5	\$ 7	\$10	\$15	\$ 22
2	10	13	18	23	31
3	20	25	33	40	50
4	35	43	53	63	75
5	55	67	78	90	105

producing A can be determined by examining the data in the rows of the table, and the marginal costs of B are obtained from the columns. For example, the marginal cost of the 4th unit of A, holding the production of B at 2 units, is \$5(= \$23 − \$18); the marginal cost of the 5th unit of B when output of A is 3 units is \$25(= \$78 − \$53).

Optimal price/output determination for joint products in this case requires a simultaneous solution of their cost and revenue relationships. The procedure can be illustrated graphically through the construction of isorevenue and isocost curves as in Figure 11.4. The isocost curves map out the locus of all production combinations that can be produced for a given total cost; the isorevenue curves indicate all combinations of the products which, when sold, result in a given revenue.[19] At the points of tangency between the isocost and the isorevenue curves, the marginal costs of producing the products are proportionate to their marginal revenues. The tangencies therefore indicate the optimal proportions in which to produce the products. Since profits are equal to revenue minus cost, the firm maximizes profits by operating at the tangency between the isorevenue and isocost curves whose positive difference is greatest. At that tangency the marginal cost of producing each product is just equal to the marginal revenue it generates.

Point Q^* in Figure 11.4 indicates the profit-maximizing combination of Products A and B in the example illustrated in the figure. Production and sale of A^* units of A and B^* units of B result in a profit of 12, the maximum possible under the conditions shown here.

We should note that while the preceding discussion demonstrates the possibility of determining the separate marginal costs of production for goods produced jointly in variable proportions, it is impossible to determine the individual average costs.

---

[19] The isorevenue relationships in Figure 11.4 have been drawn as straight lines for simplicity. This implies that the products are sold in competitive markets; only if the demand curve is horizontal will prices be invariant with respect to changing quantities of the two products. If pure competition does not exist and prices change as output changes, the isorevenue curves will not be straight lines, but the optimum output combinations will still be indicated by tangencies between isocost and isorevenue curves.

These individual costs cannot be determined because the common costs of production—costs associated with raw materials and equipment used for both products, management expenses, and other overhead—cannot be allocated to the individual products on any economically sound basis. Therefore, any allocation of common costs that affects the price/output decision is necessarily arbitrary and possibly irrational. This point is stressed because of the frequency with which businesses and government regulatory bodies use fully allocated average costs in pricing problems of this kind.

Optimal multiple-product pricing requires a complete marginal (or incremental) analysis of the total effect of the decision on the firm's profitability. This analysis must include an examination of the demand interrelationships of the products to be sure that a complete picture of the marginal revenue to be derived from a decision is drawn. Likewise, complementarity and competition in production must be accounted for in the analysis of marginal costs. For alternative goods produced from a common production facility, this means that opportunity costs of forgone production

FIGURE 11.4

Optimal Price/Output Combinations for Joint Products Produced in Variable Proportions

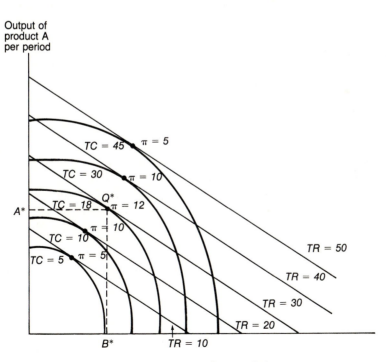

Output of product B per period

must be considered in determining the relevant marginal costs of a decision. Linear programming has proved useful for cost/output analysis of this type when common facilities must be allocated among a variety of products.

SUMMARY

In this chapter a number of pricing topics were examined. *Cost-plus pricing*, a pricing technique frequently used in practice, was shown to be closely related to marginal analysis. Proper use of cost-plus pricing requires that close attention be paid to both cost and demand relationships, but the wide variation in product margins, coupled with the empirical finding of an inverse relationship between the size of a product's margin and the competitiveness of the market in which it is sold, indicates such analysis does, in fact, play a major role in cost-plus pricing as applied by successful managers.

Incremental profit analysis was also shown to be a powerful tool for optimal pricing decisions. Its emphasis on only the costs and revenues associated with the decision under consideration insures proper economic reasoning in decision analysis.

When a firm sells its product in multiple markets, it may be able to increase profits by charging different prices in the various markets, a practice known as *price discrimination*. In order to engage successfully in price discrimination, the firm (1) must be able to segment its market and isolate the various submarkets to prevent transfers and (2) must face differing price elasticities of demand in the various market segments. Profit maximization under discrimination requires that the firm operate so as to equate marginal revenue and marginal cost in each separate submarket.

Multiple-product pricing was shown to be based on the same economic concepts used for single-product pricing. The pricing analysis is complicated, however, by demand and production externalities, which arise because of competition or complementarity among the products on either the demand or the production side. Proper use of the incremental profit concept to insure that the total impact of a pricing decision on the firm is analyzed leads to optimal pricing in the multiple-product case, just as with a single product.

QUESTIONS

11.1 "Marginal cost pricing, as well as the use of incremental analysis illustrated by the example of Continental Airlines, is looked upon with favor by economists, especially those on the staffs of regulatory agencies. With this encouragement, regulated industries do indeed employ these 'rational' techniques quite frequently. Unregulated firms, on the other hand, use marginal or incremental cost pricing much less frequently, sticking to cost-plus, or full-cost, pricing except under exceptional circumstances. In my opinion, this goes a long way toward explaining the problems of the regulated firms, especially the airlines, vis-a-vis unregulated industry." Discuss this statement.

11.2 What are the necessary conditions for price discrimination? Why is price discrimination profitable for a monopolist?

11.3 Why is it possible to determine the marginal costs associated with the production of joint products produced in variable proportions, but not joint products produced in fixed proportions?

PROBLEMS

11.1 Meditek, Inc., produces a line of disposable thermometers that it sells primarily to hospitals. The company's pricing policy currently consists of a cost-plus procedure. Prices are typically set at 200 percent of average variable cost; that is, the margin is 100 percent. The firm has just received a special offer for the sale of 200,000 disposable thermometers at a price of $.80 each to a chain of for-profit hospitals located in southeastern states.

The production manager has estimated production of costs for this special order at

Raw Materials	$ 20,000
Direct Labor	50,000
Variable Overhead	45,000
Fixed Overhead Allocation	
(40% of direct labor)	20,000
Production Setup Costs	5,000
Total Cost	$140,000

The offer specifies that delivery of the 200,000 units must be made within the next six months. To meet this schedule, Meditek will have to forgo 80,000 units to regular customers at a price of $1.25 each because of the limited excess capacity currently available at the firm. This inability to supply regular customers will not affect future demand from them.

    a. Using this information, determine whether Meditek should accept the special order.

    b. What is the minimum unit price Meditek should accept for the special order of 200,000 thermometers?

11.2 Storrs University recently received an invitation to submit a proposal to the

U.S. Department of Energy (DOE) for the construction of a computerized information system for energy consumption analysis in the northeastern region. In developing its proposal, Storrs spent $80,000 in design and development costs and had submitted a proposal of $322,000 for the job. The proposal was based on the following projected cost budget:

Costs:	
Design and Development Expenses	$ 80,000
Materials	50,000
Labor	120,000
Overhead (60% of direct labor)	72,000
Total Costs and Proposal	$322,000

DOE has just notified the university that it is enthusiastic about the submitted design, but that it is unwilling to pay more than $300,000 for the job. Assuming that the university has adequate capacity for the effort so that acceptance of the order will not require any increase in fixed expenses, should it accept this offer at the $300,000 price? Why? Or why not?

11.3 Jolly Good Beverage Company is a local producer of a variety of discount-priced soft drinks. Among the company's products is a drink called Sun Spot, which has been marketed for the past five years. Sales of Sun Spot were strong during the first three years, but they have declined substantially during the last two. Heavy advertising of competing flavors by other soft drink companies is believed to have been the major cause of this decline in sales. Sun Spot's retail price is $1.80 for an eight-bottle package with the retailer paying $1.50 for the eight-pack. The principal competing brands of soft drink are retailed at $2.00 for an eight-pack with retailers paying $1.60 a pack.

   Jolly Good's sales manager believes that sales of Sun Spot will continue to decline unless the retail price difference between it and the competing brands is increased. He has therefore undertaken an examination of the cost and revenue relationships of the product in order to formulate a new pricing policy. This examination has provided the following cost data. Variable production and distribution costs appear to be approximately constant at $.60 a pack. The fixed production overhead is allocated among the firm's various soft drinks at a rate of $.10 for each eight-pack produced, and fixed selling and administrative costs are allocated to all soft drink brands at a rate of 15 percent of total sales revenue. Jolly Good's production facilities are common to all soft drinks. The only fixed distribution costs directly traceable to Sun Spot are annual promotional expenses of $40,000. These advertising expenses are believed to be necessary to generate any significant sales volume for Sun Spot.

a. What is the company's breakeven point to retailers for Sun Spot, assuming a 200,000 eight-pack volume annually?

b. Assuming that $.20 a can is the maximum price at which Sun Spot can effectively compete with other soft drinks and that retailers will not stock and push Sun Spot unless their percentage gross margin on it is as large as on competing brands, what price to retailers should Jolly Good set on this product?

c. What factors should Jolly Good's sales manager consider in his final price decisions?

11.4 Gormet Appliance Company manufactures a popular food processor. Sales of the appliance have increased steadily during the past five years and, because of its recently completed expansion program, annual capacity is now 550,000 units. Production and sales for next year are forecasted at 400,000 units, and projected standard production costs are estimated as:

Materials	$30.00
Direct Labor	20.00
Variable Indirect Labor	10.00
Overhead	15.00
Standard Costs per Unit	$75.00

In addition to production costs, Gormet projects fixed selling expenses and variable warranty repair expenses of $7.50 and $6.00 a unit respectively. Gormet is currently receiving $120 a unit from its customers (primarily retail appliance stores) and expects this price to hold during the coming year.

After making these projections, Gormet received an inquiry for the purchase of a large quantity of processors from a discount department store chain. The discount chain's inquiry contained two purchase offers:

Offer 1. The chain would purchase 160,000 units at $100 a unit. These units would bear the Gormet label and the Gormet warranty would be provided.

Offer 2. The chain would purchase 240,000 units at $90 a unit. These units would be sold under the buyer's private label and Gormet would not provide warranty service.

a. Evaluate the effect of each offer on net income (pretax) for next year.

b. Should other factors be considered in deciding whether to accept one or the other of these offers?

c. Which offer (if either) should Gormet accept? Why?

11.5 Universal Cinema Corporation, a small theater chain in the Los Angeles area, is contemplating charging a different price for a ticket to an afternoon show than for the same film that evening. In adopting a pricing strategy, Universal must consider that fixed costs are $1,500 per week and variable (maintenance, ticket taking, etc.) costs are 20 cents per customer. Furthermore, a study of weekly demand for afternoon and evening shows has revealed:

$$P_A = 10.2 - .5Q_A$$

$$P_B = 5.2 - .25Q_B$$

$$P_A, P_B = \text{Ticket prices (in dollars)}$$

$$Q_A, Q_B = \text{Number of customers (in hundreds)}.$$

a. If Universal charges separate prices for afternoon and evening shows it may be engaging in what is known as *third-degree price discrimination*. Under what conditions will such discrimination be profitable?
b. Which demand curve do you think describes the afternoon market, A or B? Why?
c. Calculate Universal's prices, output, and profit with price discrimination.
d. Calculate Universal's prices, output, and profit without price discrimination.

11.6 Mazo Cheese Company manufactures cheddar cheese. Whey is a byproduct of the production process. The demand for Mazo's cheddar cheese is described by the function $P_c = 500 - Q_c$. Whey has little market value but can be sold as indicated by its demand curve, $P_w = 100 - 2Q_w$. Whey not sold can be disposed of at a cost of $20 per unit. Cheese and whey are produced in a fixed $1:1$ ratio. Mazo's cost function is $TC = 50,000 + 2Q + .5Q^2$.
a. What is Mazo's optimal production level?
b. How many units of cheese and whey will Mazo sell and at what prices?

11.7 Ray Krebbs is a Montana rancher in the sheep-raising business. Each year Krebbs raises a large number of lambs for sale to a Boise, Idaho, stock buyer. Because of the growing scale of his operation, Krebbs is considering personally marketing the joint meat and hide outputs to grocery wholesalers and hide processors.

On average, each lamb processed yields 50 pounds of meat in addition to one hide. Based on data published by the Montana Sheep Raisers Association, Krebbs predicts an average wholesale price for processed meat of $1.00 per pound during the coming year. While local prices for hides are somewhat less stable, Krebbs feels that hide demand can be described by the relationship:

$$P_H = 50 - 0.03Q_H$$

where P_H is hide price in dollars and Q_H is the quantity of hides .

And finally, Krebbs predicts that total costs for his operation can be described by the relationship:

$$TC = 20{,}000 + 20Q + 0.01Q^2,$$

where TC is total cost in dollars and Q is lamb output.

a. How many lambs should Krebbs raise during the coming year assuming that the current relationship with the Boise wholesaler is maintained?

b. How many lambs should be raised if Krebbs personally markets his meat and hide outputs?

11.8 International Control Machinery, Inc. (ICM), is the sole manufacturer of a unique computer system that is used to control distilling processes. ICM has two customers for this product. The Delta Company buys the computer and integrates it into a production system that it sells to beverage firms. The demand for Delta's system (including the control computer) is described by the function $P_D = 9{,}000 - 8Q_D$. Delta's cost function is $TC_D = 500{,}000 + 1{,}000Q_D + 2Q_D^2 + P_{ICM}Q_D$, where P_{ICM} represents the price paid to ICM for its computer.

ICM's second customer, Epsilon Corporation, uses the control computer in a fuel processing system that it sells to agriculture operations. These complex systems require *two* of the computers. Demand for Epsilon's product is given by the equation $P_E = 12{,}000 - Q_E$. Epsilon's cost function *without including the cost of the control computer* is $TC_E = 300{,}000 + 400Q_E + Q_E^2$.

ICM's cost of producing the computer is $300Q + 10Q^2$.

a. Determine the demand for ICM's computer from each of the two customers.

b. Express the demand curve facing ICM assuming it is unable to segment the market and therefore cannot engage in price discrimination.

c. What is the profit maximizing price and output for ICM given the assumption of a single market price?

d. Calculate ICM's optimal prices for the computer assuming that it can engage in price discrimination.

e. Would you expect the acquisition of Epsilon Corporation by ICM to be more profitable (valuable) in (1) the case where ICM can engage in price discrimination or (2) the case where it cannot engage in price discrimination? Explain.

SELECTED REFERENCES

Carlson, John A., and Pescatrice, Donn R. "Persistent Price Distributions." *Journal of Economics and Business* 33 (Fall 1980): 21–27.

Day, R. H.; Morley, S.; and Smith, K. R. "Myopic Optimizing and Rules of Thumb in a Micro Model of Industrial Growth." *American Economic Review* 64 (March 1974): 11–23.

Earley, James S. "Marginal Policies of Excellently Managed Companies." *American Economic Review* 46 (March 1956): 44–70.

Hall, R. L., and Hitch, C. J. "Price Theory and Business Behavior." *Oxford Economic Papers*. Oxford: Clarendon Press, 1939.

Haynes, W. Warren. *Pricing Decisions in Small Firms*. Lexington, Ky.: University of Kentucky Press, 1962.

Hirshleifer, Jack. "On the Economics of Transfer Pricing." *Journal of Business* 29 (July 1956): 172–184.

———. "Economics of the Divisionalized Firm." *Journal of Business* 30 (April 1957): 96–108.

Kaplan, A. D. H.; Dirlam, Joel B.; and Lanzillotti, Robert F. *Pricing in Big Business*. Washington, D.C.: Brookings Institution, 1958.

Lanzillotti, Robert F. "Pricing Objectives in Large Companies." *American Economic Review* 48 (December 1958): 921–940.

Stigler, George J. "The Economics of Information." *Journal of Political Economy* 64 (June 1961): 213–225.

Scherer, F. M. *Industrial Pricing*. Chicago: Rand-McNally, 1972.

Von Grebmer, Klaus. "International Pharmaceutical Supply Prices: Definitions-Problems-Policy Implications." *Managerial and Decision Economics* 2 (June 1981): 74–81.

Yunker, James A., and Yunker, Penelope J. "Cost-Volume-Profit Analysis under Uncertainty: An Integration of Economic and Accounting Concepts." *Journal of Economics and Business* 34 (Number 1, 1982): 21–37.

APPENDIX 11A

TRANSFER PRICING

Technological advances and expanding markets brought on by a continually larger and wealthier population have, over time, led to the development of large, multi-product firms. This trend has been accelerated by financial factors—large, diversified firms have greater access to capital markets and are frequently thought to be less risky than small, undiversified companies; both these factors cause larger firms to have a lower cost of capital than smaller ones. Larger size results in increasing costs of internal communications and coordination, so if production, marketing, and financial economies of scale are to be realized, these coordination costs must be kept within reasonable bounds.

Perhaps the most significant management innovations in recent years—the establishment of divisional profit centers and decentralized operations—were designed to combat the problem of increasing costs of coordinating large-scale enterprises. Here separate profit centers are established for different products, and the individual profit centers are kept small enough so that their managers can control them without the need for excessive, expensive staffs to coordinate the various phases of the operation.

Decentralization into semiautonomous profit centers, while absolutely necessary for large-scale enterprises, creates problems of its own. Perhaps the most critical of these is that of *transfer pricing* or the pricing of products transferred between divisions. United States Steel, for example, owns coal mines and iron mines as well as steel mills, and the coal and iron divisions sell to the steel division as well as to outsiders.[1] How much should the steel division pay for the coal and iron ore it obtains internally? Should it buy its entire requirements of these materials from the coal and iron divisions, or should it meet part of its needs from outside sources? Further, should the coal and iron divisions be expected to produce whatever amounts of coal and iron the steel division requires? Suppose the steel division offers to pay $15 a ton for coal, but the coal division can sell to outsiders for $20; should the coal divisions be required to sell to the steel mills?

The answers to these questions are critically important for at least two reasons. First, the way they are answered will influence the output of each division, hence the output of the firm as a whole. If they are answered incorrectly, the firm will not produce at the optimal level. Second, transfer prices are an important determinant of divisional profits, and since promotions, bonuses, stock options, and so on are typically based on divisional performance, if a system of transfer prices is arbitrary and inequitable, it can completely wreck morale and literally destroy the firm.

While the topic of transfer pricing is one of the more complex in managerial economics, and we cannot hope to more than scratch the surface in an introductory book of this kind, its importance dictates that we at least demonstrate the nature of the problem and point the direction toward optimal transfer rules. For the reader who wishes to pursue the topic further, the works of Jack Hirshleifer[2] and David Solomons[3] provide excellent expositions of both the theoretical and the practical problems in transfer pricing.

TRANSFER PRICING WITH NO EXTERNAL MARKET FOR THE INTERMEDIATE PRODUCT

The basic criterion by which to judge any internal transfer pricing scheme is the impact it will have on the operating efficiency of the firm. Optimally, a transfer pricing system will lead to activity levels in each division of the firm that are consistent with profit maximization for the entire enterprise. Alternatively stated, a well-designed transfer pricing scheme will lead to activity levels for the various decentralized divisions of a firm that are precisely identical to the activity levels that

---

[1] United States Steel also owns steamship lines, cement mills, coking ovens, construction companies, and other concerns; and all these divisions buy and sell among one another.

[2] Jack Hirshleifer, "On the Economics of Transfer Pricing," *Journal of Business* 29 (July 1956): 172–184; and "Economies of the Divisionalized Firm," *Journal of Business* 30 (April 1957): 96–108.

[3] David Solomons, *Divisional Performance: Measurement and Control* (New York: Financial Executives Research Foundation, 1965).

FIGURE 11A.1

Profit Maximizing Price/Output Combination

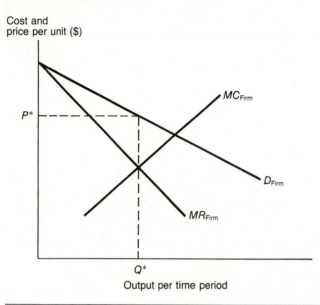

Output per time period

would prevail in centralized decision making without provision for divisional profit centers.

This relationship can be examined in the context of a two-division firm producing a single product. Such a case is illustrated in Figure 11A.1, which shows the demand, marginal revenue, and marginal cost curves for the entire operation of the firm.

Profit maximization requires that the firm expand its output so long as the marginal revenue of additional units is greater than their marginal costs. In terms of Figure 11A.1, this means that the firm's profits are maximized at output Q^*, indicating a market price of P^* for the firm's product.

To clarify the relationship we are developing, it will prove useful to introduce a specific set of cost and demand functions. Assume that the demand curve illustrated in Figure 11A.1 is:

$$P = 100 - Q, \tag{11A.1}$$

and that the firm's total cost function is:

$$TC = 70 + 10Q + 1.5Q^2. \tag{11A.2}$$

The marginal revenue and marginal cost curves in Figure 11A.1 are then found as: [4]

$$MR = 100 - 2Q. \qquad \textbf{(11A.3)}$$

$$MC = 10 + 3Q. \qquad \textbf{(11A.4)}$$

Profit maximization occurs at the point where marginal revenue equals marginal cost, so the optimal output level is found as:

$$MR = MC$$

$$100 - 2Q = 10 + 3Q$$

$$90 = 5Q$$

$$Q = 18.$$

Thus, Q^* in Figure 11A.1 is 18 units and P^* is \$82 (100 − 18).

Consider now the situation if the firm we are examining is divisionalized into a manufacturing and a distribution division. The demand curve facing the distribution division is precisely the same demand curve the firm faced initially. The total cost function of the firm is unchanged, but it can be broken down into the costs of manufacture and the costs of distribution. Assume that such a breakdown results in the divisional cost functions:

$$TC_{MFG.} = 50 + 7Q + 0.5Q^2$$

and

$$TC_{DISTR.} = 20 + 3Q + Q^2.$$

---

[4] The marginal revenue function is found as the derivative of the total revenue function; that is:

$$TR = P \cdot Q$$
$$= (100 - Q)Q$$
$$= 100Q - Q^2.$$

$$MR = \frac{dTR}{dQ} = 100 - 2Q.$$

The marginal cost curve is given by the derivative of the total cost curve, so:

$$MC = \frac{dTC}{dQ} = 10 + 3Q.$$

FIGURE 11A.2

Transfer Pricing with No External Market for the Intermediate Product

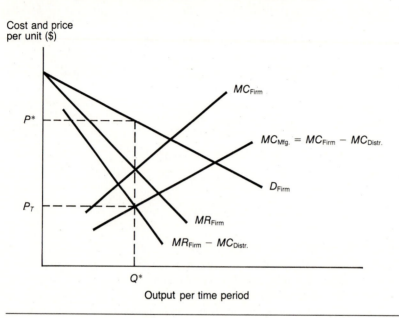

The total cost function for the firm would be:

$$TC_{FIRM} = TC_{MFG.} + TC_{DISTR.}$$

$$= 50 + 7Q + 0.5Q^2 + 20 + 3Q + Q^2$$

$$= 70 + 10Q + 1.5Q^2,$$

precisely the same as Equation 11A.2 above. Obviously in this situation no substantive changes have taken place, and the firm should still operate at an 18-unit output level for profit maximization.

When no external market exists for the intermediate product (that is, if the manufacturing division is not able to sell its product externally), it can be shown that intrafirm transfers should take place based on prices that are set equal to the marginal costs of the transferring division—the manufacturing division in this case. This relationship is shown in Figure 11A.2, which adds the net marginal revenue $(MR_{FIRM} - MC_{DISTR.})$ curve for the distribution division and the marginal cost curve for the manufacturing division to the revenue and cost curves illustrated in Figure 11A.1. The *net marginal revenue curve* for the distribution division is found by subtracting the marginal costs of that division from the marginal revenues generated by its marketing activities. It is essentially nothing more than a net marginal profits curve for that division prior to taking account of the cost of the product that has been transferred to it from the manufacturing division.

Note that in Figure 11A.2 the net marginal revenue curve for the distribution division intersects the marginal cost curve for the manufacturing division at Q^*, the firm's profit maximizing activity level. This is not mere happenstance but must always occur. The reason is simple. Recall that the distribution division's net marginal revenue curve is nothing more than the firm's marginal revenue curve less the marginal cost of the distribution division. Similarly, the manufacturing division's marginal cost curve is nothing more than the firm's marginal cost curve less the marginal cost of the distribution division. If the firm's marginal revenue and marginal costs are equal at Q^* units of output, then obviously the distribution division's net marginal revenue must be equal to the manufacturing division's marginal cost at that same output level. Algebraically, if:

$$MR_{FIRM} = MC_{FIRM},$$

then:

$$MR_{FIRM} - MC_{DISTR.} = MC_{FIRM} - MC_{DISTR.} = MC_{MFG.}.$$

This means that the correct transfer price for intermediate products for which there is no external market is the marginal cost of production. In Figure 11A.2 this transfer price is P_T.

Continuing with the numerical example, the net marginal revenue curve for the distribution division is given by the expression:

$$MR_{FIRM} - MC_{DISTR.} = 100 - 2Q - (3 + 2Q)$$

$$= 97 - 4Q.$$

Equating this to the marginal cost curve of the manufacturing division results in:

$$MR_{FIRM} - MC_{DISTR.} = MC_{MFG.}$$

$$97 - 4Q = 7 + Q$$

$$90 = 5Q$$

$$Q = 18.$$

This result indicates once again that at an optimal activity level the net marginal revenue of the distribution division will equal the marginal cost of the manufacturing division. This leads to the profit maximizing condition that internal transfers of intermediate products for which no external market exists must take place at marginal production costs.

It still remains to demonstrate that by setting the transfer price equal to the marginal cost of production, the two decentralized divisions will choose to operate at the firm's profit maximizing activity level. Consider first the manufacturing division. If the firm's central management specifies that transfers are to take place at marginal manufacturing costs, then the marginal cost curve of the manufacturing division becomes its supply curve, just as the marginal cost curve is the supply curve for a firm operating as a price taker, such as a firm in pure competition. Given a transfer price, P_T, the manufacturing division *must* supply a quantity such that $MC_{MFG.} = P_T$.

Now consider the distribution division. The profit function for that division can be written as:

$$Profit = TR_{FIRM} - TC_{DISTR.} \tag{11A.5}$$

$$= 100Q - Q^2 - [20 + 3Q + Q^2 + (P_T \cdot Q)]$$

$$= 97Q - 2Q^2 - 20 - [P_T \cdot Q].$$

Notice that in this expression we have added the term $P_T \cdot Q$ to the total cost function for the distribution division to account for the fact that this division must now pay a price of P_T for each unit of product it receives from the manufacturing division.

Since profit maximization requires that marginal profit be zero, the profit maximization requirement for the distribution division is that the derivative of Equation 11A.5 be set to zero; that is:

$$M\pi = 97 - 4Q - P_T = 0,$$

or, solving for P_T, the transfer price:

$$P_T = 97 - 4Q. \tag{11A.6}$$

Thus, profit maximization for the distribution division requires that the transfer price be equal to $97 - 4Q$. Therefore, $97 - 4Q$ can be considered a demand function indicating how the transfer price of the product is related to the quantity that the distribution division will seek to purchase. Note, however, that this demand function is identical to the net marginal revenue curve for the distribution division developed above.

Now if the distribution division determines the quantity it will purchase by movement along the net marginal revenue curve, and the manufacturing division is supplying output along its marginal cost curve, then the only market clearing transfer price is that price which occurs where $MR_{FIRM} - MC_{DISTR.} = MC_{MFG.}$ In the example, this is at 18 units of output with a transfer price, P_T, equal to \$25 ($MC_{MFG.}$ $= 7 + Q = 25$ at $Q = 18$). At a transfer price above \$25 the distribution division will accept fewer units of output than the manufacturing division wants to supply, while if P_T is less than \$25, the distribution division will seek to purchase more units than the manufacturing division desires to produce. Only at a \$25 transfer price are the supply and demand forces in balance.

The marginal cost pricing rule can be implemented in actual practice in either of two ways. First, the distribution division could be given the manufacturing division's marginal cost curve and told that this is the supply function it must use in determining the quantity it desires to purchase internally. Alternatively, the manufacturing division could be supplied with data on the net marginal revenue curve for the distribution division and told to use this as its relevant marginal revenue curve in determining the quantity it should supply. In either case the divisions should choose to operate at Output Q^*, and a transfer price of $P_T = MC_{MFG}$ should prevail.

TRANSFER PRICING OF A PRODUCT HAVING A COMPETITIVE MARKET

A second transfer pricing problem involves goods that can be sold externally in a competitive market. In this case, where the transferred good is sold in a competitive market, the market price of the good is also the appropriate transfer price; its use will lead to firm profit maximizing levels of operation for all the divisions involved in the transfer.

Figure 11A.3 illustrates the economics of the competitive case. There, the demand, D_F, and the marginal revenue, MR_F, curves for the final product, F, are shown along with the demand, D_T, marginal revenue, MR_T, and marginal cost, MC_T, curves for T, the intermediate or transferred product. The line $MR_F - MC_F$ represents the net marginal contribution to overhead and profits of the final product *before the transfer price is deducted.*[5] That is, $MR_F - MC_F$ shows the excess of the marginal revenue of F over its marginal cost prior to a payment for the transferred good, T. At output Q_1, for example, Product F would sell at a price of \$100 and would have a marginal revenue equal to \$90. Since $MR_F - MC_F = \$70$, MC_F, *before any charge for the intermediate product*, is equal to \$20. The marginal cost of the transferred product at Output Q_1 is \$30. Since the firm earns a contribution margin of \$70 on the final product at Q_1, and since the intermediate good costs only \$30, output should be expanded beyond Q_1.

Profit maximization requires that both the final product and the intermediate

---

[5]The area under the curve $MR_F - MC_F$ represents the total contribution *before* paying for the transferred product.

FIGURE 11A.3

Transfer Price Determination with the Intermediate Product Sold Externally in a Competitive Market: Excess Internal Demand

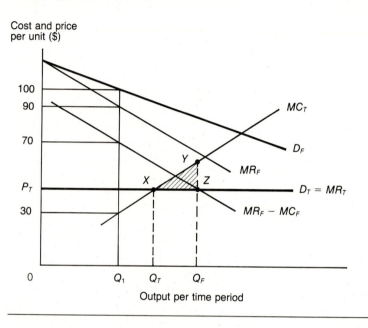

Cost and price
per unit ($)

product divisions operate at the output levels at which their marginal costs equal their marginal revenues. At any lower output level the marginal revenue obtained from sales of additional units is greater than the marginal costs of their production, and profits are increased by expanded production. At higher output levels the reverse is true; marginal costs exceed marginal revenues, and a reduction of output increases profits.

The optimal outputs for the two divisions are shown in Figure 11A.3. Division F should purchase Q_F units of the intermediate good, paying the market price P_T for it.[6] At that point the marginal cost of producing F is equal to its marginal revenue, and divisional profits—the area under the $MR_F - MC_F$ curve which lies above the horizontal line P_TD_T—are maximized. Division T should supply Q_T units of the product, the quantity at which its marginal cost equals its marginal revenue.[7] At Q_T units of output its divisional profits—the area under the curve D_T which lies above the curve MC_T—are maximized.

Note that this solution to the transfer pricing problem results in Division F

[6]$D_T = MR_T$ is the relevant marginal cost of T for use in producing F. Note that this is not the same as MC_T, the marginal cost of physically producing an added unit of T.

[7]Since the intermediate product is defined to be a purely competitive good, $MR_T = P_T$.

demanding more units of the intermediate product than Division T is willing to supply at price P_T. This situation presents no problem to the firm; it merely indicates that profit maximization requires Division F to purchase Q_T units of the intermediate product internally from Division T and $Q_F - Q_T$ units in the marketplace. No other solution results in as great a total profit for the firm. For example, if Division T attempts to supply the entire quantity demanded by F, the cost to the firm would exceed the cost incurred by purchasing it in the market. The shaded triangle XYZ in Figure 11A.3 indicates the excess cost, and hence the reduction in profits, that would result from such a decision.

The use of the market price for transferring the intermediate product remains optimal even if the quantity of the intermediate product supplied by Division T is greater than the demand by Division F at the market price. Division T merely transfers the quantity demanded by F and sells the remainder in the market. This situation is depicted in Figure 11A.4.

Here, although the marginal cost of producing the intermediate product, T, is below the net marginal revenue obtainable from an additional unit of F at the optimal quantity, Q_F, the marginal cost of producing T, *plus* the opportunity cost of not selling that additional unit in the competitive market, is greater than the net marginal revenue received from F. Therefore, the transfer of additional units to Division F would result in lower total firm profits.

FIGURE 11A.4

Transfer Price Determination with the Intermediate Product Sold Externally in a Competitive Market: Excess Internal Supply

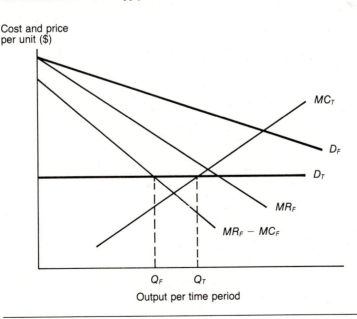

FIGURE 11A.5

Transfer Pricing with an Imperfect Market for the Intermediate Product

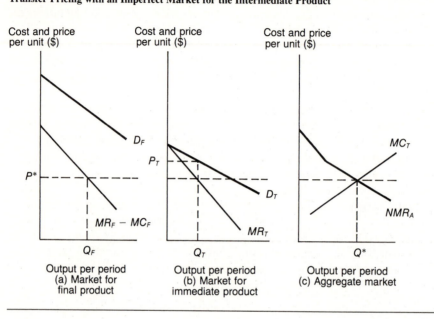

So long as the intermediate product being transferred within the firm can be sold in a competitive market, the market price remains the proper transfer price. Only by transferring at that price can the firm's management insure that the level of activities in both the supplying and the using divisions will be optimal for firm, as opposed to divisional, profit maximization.

TRANSFER PRICING WITH AN IMPERFECT EXTERNAL MARKET FOR THE INTERMEDIATE PRODUCT

Where an imperfect outside market exists for the intermediate product, transfer pricing is only slightly more complex than the case cited above. Again, transfer pricing at marginal costs results in optimal activity levels for both the supplying and the using divisions of the firm.

This case is illustrated in Figure 11A.5. In Figure 11A.5, (a) shows the demand and the net marginal revenue curves for the final product, F; (b) contains the external demand and the marginal revenue curves for the intermediate product, T. In (c) the net marginal revenue curve for Product F and the marginal revenue curve for T have been horizontally summed to arrive at an aggregate net marginal revenue curve, NMR_A, for Product T. The marginal cost of producing T is also shown in Figure 11A.5 (c).

The profit maximizing output of T occurs where the marginal cost of producing it and the aggregate net marginal revenue obtained from it are equal: Output Q^* in Figure 11A.5(c). That output is divided between internal transfers and external sales by equating the net marginal revenue in Part (a) of the figure and the marginal revenue in Part (b) to the marginal cost of the optimal output as determined in Part (c).[9] Setting an internal transfer price equal to that marginal cost, P^*, insures that Division F will demand the quantity of T that leads to profit maximization not only of that division but also of the firm as a whole. The price to be charged in the external market—P_T in Figure 11A.5(b)—is determined by the height of the demand curve for the product at a point directly above the intersection of the marginal revenue curve and the transfer price, or marginal cost of production.

SUMMARY

The material we have presented on transfer pricing barely scratches the surface of this important but complex subject. It by no means exhausts the possible cases for intrafirm transfers of goods and services. There are, for example, situations where several internal divisions are competing for the products of yet another division, or where two or more divisions supply intermediate products to a third. Still another whole set of transfer pricing problems arises when the demand and production externalities in multiple-product firms are considered.[10] Nonetheless, the material we have presented introduces the basic problem and demonstrates the kind of economic analysis necessary to obtain optimal solutions. To the extent that we can generalize, our analysis suggests that transfers should take place at the market price for intermediate products that are traded externally in a competitive market and at marginal cost in most other cases.

PROBLEMS

11A.1 Allen Manufacturing produces and retails a single product. The monthly demand relationship for the product has been estimated to be:

[9] Note that the distribution of the intermediate product follows the same pattern as a discriminating monopolist allocating output among available segmented markets. In this case T acts as a monopolist, selling part of its output in one internal market at the transfer price P^* and part in the external market at P_T.

[10] Mathematical programming has been shown to be a useful analytical tool for these more complex cases. See, for example, William J. Baumol and Tibor Fabian, "Decomposition, Pricing for Decentralization and External Economies," *Management Science* 11 (September 1964): 1–32.

$$P = 60 - 0.35Q.$$

The firm's cost analysts have estimated that the total manufacturing cost, TC_M, and the total distribution cost, TC_D, can be represented by the expressions:

$$TC_M = 1,000 + 8Q + 0.1Q^2$$

$$TC_D = 100 + 2Q + 0.05Q^2.$$

These cost functions pertain to monthly cost and output levels.

    a. On the basis of the above cost and demand estimates:

        (i) What quantity of output should the corporate management of Allen schedule for production each month?

        (ii) What price should be established?

        (iii) What will be the firm's monthly profits at this output level?

    b. Suppose the management of Allen decides to decentralize the decision making process by setting up a manufacturing division and a distribution division. Each division constitutes a profit center, and each division manager is to be rewarded on the basis of profit performance. To handle the intrafirm transfer of the product between the manufacturing and the distribution divisions, the manufacturing division is to have the right to set a transfer price on the product it will sell to the distribution division. The distribution division will then have the right to buy any quantity of the product it desires at that price for resale to the outside market. Under this arrangement, the quantity of the product demanded by the division at each transfer price, P_T, is given by the expression:

$$P_T = 58 - 0.8Q.$$

(Consider this expression, which is the demand curve facing the manufacturing division given at this point; you will be asked to analyze it later.)

        (i) Assuming that the management of the manufacturing division has knowledge of this demand curve, what transfer price would it set to maximize its own (the manufacturing division's) profits, and how many units would be sold to the distribution division at this price?

        (ii) What total monthly profit would each division report if the internal transfer price is established at this level?

        (iii) How does this compare with the monthly profits determined in Part a?

        (iv) What modification to the manufacturing division's price determination will result in an optimal transfer price from a firm, as opposed to divisional, profit standpoint?

        (v) What is the optimal transfer price?

(vi) What profits or losses will each division have with the transfer price developed in (v)? What problems might this cause, and how might the problems be solved?

(vii) Explain why the distribution division would make purchases in accordance with the demand expression given above, $P_T = 58 - 0.8Q$.

11A.2 Among the products manufactured and sold by Frontier Engineering Corporation is a digital clock radio. The demand curve facing the firm for this product is $P = 610 - 9Q$. Manufacture and sale of the radio is done by FEC's Home Products Division (HPD), with a major component part being supplied by a second division, the Electronics Specialty Division (ESD). The cost functions for the radio and the electronic component are:

$$\text{Total Cost}_{HPD} = 3,000 + 10Q$$

$$\text{Total Cost}_{ESD} = 7,000 + 10Q + Q^2.$$

a. The divisions are operated as separate profit centers. Internal transfers of goods and services are accomplished by allowing the using division to offer a given price and the supplying division to determine the quantity that it will sell. Assuming that there is no outside market for the component supplied by the ESD, what is the optimal quantity (from the firm's standpoint) of product that should be transferred, and what transfer price will lead to operation at this level?

b. Assume that the electronic component supplied by ESD could be sold to an outside firm for use in another product (one that doesn't compete with FEC's) for $190. This firm will purchase up to 100 units at this price. What is the optimal transfer price in this situation? How many units will ESD sell to HPD? How many will it sell to the outside firm?

c. Assume now that external demand for the component manufactured by ESD is described by the function $P = 410 - 9.1Q$. What is the optimal transfer price? The optimal price in the external market? How many units will ESD supply to each of these two markets?

d. Explain how the following assumptions would influence the analysis of this problem: Sales of the electronic component in the external market affect sales of the radios, and production of the component by ESD affects the cost of other products of that division.

11A.3 MicroTech manufactures and sells a microprocessor that is used primarily as a control device in sophisticated manufacturing robots. The market for this microprocessor has in the past been described by the demand curve $Q_D = 11,000 - 1.25P_D$. Recently, however, a new firm has begun manufacturing robots. This firm, Robo Inc., uses one microprocessor of the type manufactured by MicroTech in each robot produced. Demand for Robo's robots is given by the function $Q_R = 1,000$

$- .01P_R$, and Robo's cost function *before accounting for the cost of the micro-processor* is $TC_R = 750,000 + 1,000Q_R$. Thus, the total demand is now the sum of the demand given by the Q_D function and Robo's demand.

In addition to MicroTech, there are 50 small firms that manufacture competing microprocessors. These 50 firms each operate with a cost function $TC = 60,000 + 700Q + 10Q^2$, and each acts as a price taker. MicroTech recognizes this price-taking behavior and operates as a price leader.

a. Determine the demand for microprocessors by Robo Inc.

b. Assuming the market *cannot* be segmented, determine the total domestic demand for the microprocessor.

c. Determine the aggregate microprocessor supply function for the 50 price takers.

d. Determine the demand faced by MicroTech in the total market.

e. Determine the price at which MicroTech would sell its microprocessor. MicroTech's cost function is $TC = 200,000 + 500Q + 2.5Q^2$.

f. Assume that MicroTech acquires Robo Inc. and operates it as a separate division. There are no synergistic impacts on the costs of either firm (division). What is the model that you would use to determine the optimal allocation of MicroTech's microprocessor production between transfers to Robo and the external market?

g. What transfer price would you set as president of MicroTech if each division operated as a profit center and if you wanted to maximize total *firm* profits?

CHAPTER 12

REGULATION AND ANTITRUST: THE ROLE OF GOVERNMENT IN THE MARKET ECONOMY

The history of government involvement in the economy is both long and substantial. Government acts to stimulate and assist private enterprise and to regulate or control business practices so that firm operations are consistent with the public interest. We have discussed some of the interactions between government and business throughout the text; however, a closer examination is worthwhile because the government's role in the operations of the private sector of the economy has grown substantially over the past several decades.

While no sector of the U.S. economy can be considered unregulated as we enter the mid-1980s, both the scope and the methods of control vary widely. For example, makers of industrial products typically escape price and profit restraint (except during periods of general wage-price control) but are subject to operating regulations governing plant and product pollutant emissions, product packaging and labeling, worker safety and health, and so on. On the other hand, many firms, particularly in the financial and the public utility sectors, face financial regulation in addition to such operating controls. Banks, for example, are subject to both state and federal regulation of product prices (interest rates, loan fees, etc.) and financial soundness. Unlike power and communications utilities, however, banks face no explicit controls on the level of profits they earn. For this reason, regulation in the financial sector (banking, insurance, securities, etc.), although more encompassing than regulation in the industrial sector, is less comprehensive than the regulation of public utilities.

The growing importance of government involvement in the economy makes an examination of its causes, means, and ends an important component of managerial economics. To provide effective leadership, managers must fully understand the nature of government-business interaction in a modern economic environment. In this chapter we analyze the role of government in the private economy by considering (1) the economic and political rationale for regulation; (2) grant policy, which provides firms with positive incentives for "desirable" activity; (3) tax policy, which constrains the nature of goods and services that are marketed and the production processes used to produce them; (4) direct regulation of firms which possess substantial market power; and (5) antitrust policy, designed to maintain a workable level of competition in the economy.

THE RATIONALE FOR REGULATION

Both economic and political considerations enter into decisions of what and how to regulate. Economic considerations relate to cost and efficiency implications of various regulatory methods. From an economic standpoint, a given mode of regulation, or change in regulatory policy, is desirable to the extent that benefits exceed costs. Here the question is not so much whether or not to regulate, but rather what type of regulation (market competition or otherwise) is most desirable. On the other hand, equity rather than efficiency criteria must be carefully weighed when political considerations bear on the regulatory decision making process. Here the *incidence* of costs and benefits of regulatory decisions are considered. For example, if a given change in regulatory policy provides significant benefits to the poor, substantial costs in terms of lost efficiency may be borne willingly by society.

In most decisions regarding regulatory policy the tradeoff between efficiency- and equity-related criteria is a most difficult one. While we can't hope to resolve the conflict between economic and political rationales for regulation, it is useful to consider more carefully each argument as a basis for regulation. The material that follows addresses the question, "Why *should* society regulate?" In later sections we see that some economists suggest far different reasons for why sectors of the private economy actually are regulated.

Economic Considerations

Regulation of production and marketing activities of firms began and perseveres in part because of the public's perception of market imperfections. It is often believed that unregulated market activity could lead to inefficiency and waste or to market failure. An early analysis by Francis M. Bator characterized market failure as "the failure of a more or less idealized system of price-market institutions to sustain 'desirable' activities or to estop [limit] 'undesirable' activities." [1]

A first type (or cause) of market failure is called failure by market *structure*. In order for the beneficial results of competition to be attained, there must be many producers (sellers) and consumers (buyers) within each market, or at least the ready potential of many to enter the market. This condition is unfulfilled in some markets. Consider, for example, water, power, and telecommunications markets. If customers in a given market area can be most efficiently serviced by a single firm (a natural monopoly situation), providers of these services could possess market power and have an ability to achieve excess profits by limiting output and charging high prices. As a result, regulatory control of utility prices and profits were instituted and have continued with the goal of preserving the efficiency of large-scale production while preventing the higher prices and excess profits of monopoly. Where the advantages of large size are not thought to be as great (industrial manufacturing, retailing, etc.), antitrust policy is used to limit the growth and size of large competitors.

A second kind of market failure is failure by *incentive*. In the production and consumption of goods and services, social values and costs often differ significantly from the private costs and values of producers and consumers. Differences between social and private costs, or benefits, are called *externalities*. A negative externality is a cost of producing, marketing, or consuming a product which is not borne by the product's producers or consumers. A positive externality is a benefit of production, marketing, or consumption which is not reflected in the product pricing structure, and, hence, does not accrue to the product's producers or consumers.

Environmental pollution is one well-known example of a negative externality. Negative externalities also arise when employees are exposed to hazardous working conditions for which they are not fully compensated. Similarly, if a firm dams a river or builds a solar collector to produce energy, and in so doing limits the access of others to hydropower or solar power, a negative externality is created.

Positive externalities can arise if an increase in a firm's productive activity causes lower costs for its suppliers, thereby reducing costs of a supplier's products to all its customers. The expansion of automobile production by Ford Motor Company conferred this type of external benefit on early users of steel. Economies of scale in steel production, which were achieved through the increased demand for steel brought about by Ford's mass production of automobiles, resulted in cheaper

---

[1] Francis M. Bator, "The Anatomy of Market Failure," *Quarterly Journal of Economics* 72 (August 1958): 351–379.

steel being available for all firms using steel. Positive externalities in production also result when a firm trains employees who then are available to work for other firms that incur no training costs. They can also come from a firm's improvement of production methods which is later transferred to other firms and industries without compensation. The dam cited above for its potential negative externalities might also provide positive externalities through flood control or creation of new recreational facilities.

In sum, externalities lead to differing levels of private and social costs and benefits. These divergencies have a significant impact on the workings of the economy. Firms that provide substantial positive externalities for which they are not compensated are unlikely to carry their activities out to the socially optimal level. Likewise, consumers whose consumption activities confer positive externalities may not use as much of the particular good or service as would be socially optimal. On the other hand, the existence of negative externalities can result in too many resources being allocated to a particular activity. This follows from the fact that producers or consumers generating negative externalities do not pay the full cost of their activities and will most likely carry them out beyond the level that maximizes social benefits. These market imperfections, or market failures—situations where the market does not provide the appropriate cost or benefit signals—give rise to an active government role in the economy.

Political Considerations

Economic considerations play a prominent role in the design of regulatory policies. But political considerations are also important.

From an efficiency standpoint, a most desirable feature of competition is that firms have substantial incentives to produce products consumers want, and to produce them in desired quantities. Furthermore, competitive pressures force each firm to use its resources wisely so that at least a normal profit will be earned. An important aspect of a market-based resource allocation system is that it is efficient because it responds quickly and accurately to consumer preferences. In other words, the preservation of *consumer choice* or *consumer sovereignty* is an important aspect of competitive markets. By retaining individual initiative in the market, competition does much to enhance personal freedom. For this reason, reductions in the vigor of competitive pressures are seen as an indication of lessening consumer sovereignty. Remember: Firms with market power can limit output and raise prices to earn excess profits, while firms in competitive markets refer to market prices in order to determine optimal output quantities. In other words, monopoly firms have far more discretion as actors than do the reactor firms in competitive markets. Therefore, in cases of monopoly, regulatory policy can be a valuable tool to restore control over the price and quantity decision making process to the public.

A second political purpose for regulatory intervention into the market process is a desire to limit *concentration of economic and political power*. It has long been recognized that economic and political relationships can and do become intertwined. Concentrations of economic power are generally inconsistent with the democratic process. In fact, it has been asserted that one of the most important institutional reforms to characterize the American economic system was the incorporation laws of the 1850s.[2] With these laws it became possible for owners of capital (stockholders) to pool economic resources without also pooling political resources, thereby allowing big business and democracy to coexist. Of course, the large scale of modern corporations has at times diminished the controlling influence of individual stockholders. In these instances, regulatory policy—particularly antitrust policy—has been used to limit the growth or size of large firms in order to avoid undue concentrations of political power.

In conclusion, important political considerations often constitute compelling justification for government intervention in the marketplace. Deciding whether or not a particular reform in regulatory policy is or is not warranted is compounded by the fact that such political considerations can run counter to efficiency considerations. This is not to say that policies where expected benefits are exceeded by expected costs should never be pursued. Costs in the form of lost efficiency may sometimes be borne so that more equitable solutions might be achieved.

REGULATORY RESPONSE TO INCENTIVE FAILURES

Government intervention in the market economy is designed in part to respond to the problems created by both positive and negative externalities of production, marketing, and consumption. In its effort to limit the frequency of market failure due to incentive problems, government makes frequent use of both grant and tax policies. The granting of patents and operating subsidies, for example, are two frequently used methods by which government recognizes positive externalities and provides compensation to reward activities which provide such externalities. Local, state, and federal governments also use taxes (a form of negative subsidy) along with operating requirements, or controls, to limit the creation of negative externalities. Although grant, tax, and operating-control policies are by no means the only government responses to incentive failures, they are among the most widely employed; and they provide a good introduction to this area of government-business interaction.

Operating Right Grants

The regulation of operating rights is a common, though seldom-discussed, method of providing firms with an incentive to promote service "in the public interest."

[2]John R. Commons, "Marx Today: Capitalism and Socialism," *Atlantic Monthly* (November 1925): 3–14.

Common examples would be Federal Communications Commission (FCC) control of local television- and radio-broadcasting rights; federal and state regulatory bodies, which govern national or state chartering of banks and savings institutions; and insurance commissions, which oversee insurance company licensing at the state level. In each of these instances firms must be able to demonstrate fiscal responsibility and financial soundness and to provide evidence that they are meeting the needs of their service areas. Should firms fail to meet these established criteria, public franchises—in the form of broadcasting rights, charters, or licenses—can be withdrawn, or new franchises can be offered to potential competitors. While such drastic action is rare, the mere threat of such action is often sufficient to compel compliance with prescribed regulations.

Although control of operating rights can be an effective form of regulation, it often falls short of its full potential due to the imprecise nature of many operating criteria. For example, is a television station which broadcasts poorly rated local programming 20 hours per week responding better to the needs of its service area than a station which airs highly popular reruns of hit shows? How progressive in electronic fund-transfer services should a local bank be in order to be sufficiently progressive? Without clear, consistent, and workable standards of performance, policies in the area of operating grant regulation will be hampered by inefficiency and waste. The magnitude of these costs is measured not only by the low quality and limited quantity of desired goods and services, but also by the excessive profits and/or higher costs of producers sheltered by little or no competition.

Patent Grants

Patents are a prime example of a type of limited operating grant that can be conferred by government. Unlike most operating grants (e.g., local broadcasting rights), however, patent rights do not originate from the public domain but from the private domain of the firm. Patents are a government grant of the exclusive right to produce, use, or sell an invention or idea for a limited period of time (17 years in the United States). As such, they are a valuable grant of legal monopoly power designed to stimulate research and development. Without patents, firms would be less likely to reap the full benefit of technological breakthroughs, as competitors would quickly exploit and develop close—if not identical—substitutes.

Patent policy is a regulatory attempt to achieve the benefits of both monopoly and competition in the field of research and development. In granting the patent monopoly, the public wishes to stimulate research activity and the economic growth which it creates. By limiting the patent monopoly, competition is encouraged to extend and develop existent bodies of knowledge. These limits on the patent monopoly are not restricted to time-period considerations but include limitations on the use of the patent monopoly as well. Firms may not use patenting as a method of monopolizing or limiting competition. For example, on January 29, 1973, the Federal Trade Commission (FTC) charged Xerox with dominating the office-copier industry by engaging in unfair marketing and patent practices.[3] In its complaint the FTC alleged that Xerox—in association with Battelle Memorial Institute, a private research corporation—had created an artificial "patent barrier to competition." A final consent order was accepted on April 16, 1975, which resolved the FTC's monopolization suit against Xerox. The consent order required Xerox to license competitors to use its more than 1,700 copier patents on a little or no royalty basis and restricted Xerox's freedom to acquire such rights from its competitors. Partially due to this action, small-firm entry into the copier industry grew rapidly during the 1970s. Thus, the regulatory response to abuse of the patent monopoly grant can be both swift and effective.

Subsidies

Government also responds to positive externalities by providing subsidies to private business firms. These subsidies can be indirect, as in the case of government construction and highway maintenance grants, which benefit the trucking industry. They can also take the form of direct payments, such as special tax treatments and government-provided low-cost financing.

Investment tax credits, allowed for certain types of business investments, and depletion allowances, provided to promote natural resource development, are examples of tax subsidies given in recognition of production externalities which provide benefits to society (e.g., job creation, energy independence, etc.). In addition, positive externalities associated with locating a major manufacturing facility in an industrial park have given rise to local government financing of such facilities. Such low-cost financing is thought to provide compensation for the external benefits provided.

Tax Policies

Although subsidy policy is a method of providing firms with positive incentives for desirable performance, tax policy is a system of penalties, or negative subsidies, which can be designed to limit undesirable performance. Under tax policy regular and anticipated tax payments are considered, as are fines or penalties which may be assessed on an intermittent or irregular basis.

Local, state, or federal fines for truckers who exceed specified weight limits, pollution taxes, and effluent charges or fines are common examples of tax policies intended to limit negative externalities by shifting external costs of production onto firms and their customers. Determination of an appropriate tax level is extremely difficult because of the problems associated with estimating the magnitude of nega-

---

[3]U.S. Bureau of National Affairs, *Patent, Trademark and Copyright Journal* (Washington, D.C.: 12–14–72), No. 107, A16.

tive externalities. While determining some of the social costs of air pollution, such as more frequent house painting, may be quite straightforward, calculating the costs of increased discomfort—even death—for emphysema patients is less so. Nevertheless, attempts must be made to consider the full range of consequences associated with negative externalities if appropriate and effective incentives are to be created.

Although tax policy may appear simply as a mirror image of subsidy and other grant policies, an important distinction should not be overlooked. If society wishes to limit the harmful consequences of pollution, for example, either subsidies for pollution reduction or taxes on pollution levels can provide effective incentives. There is, however, a significant difference in implied property rights under the two approaches. Under the subsidy mechanism, a firm's right to pollute is implied, in that society pays to have pollution reduced. In contrast, a system of pollution-tax penalties is an assertion of society's right to a clean environment. Here, firms must reimburse society for damage that results from their emissions. The difference is a distinction in who "owns" the environment. Many prefer tax policy as a method for pollution reduction on the simple grounds that it makes explicit recognition of the public's property right to a clean environment.

Operating Controls

Operating control regulation, or control by government directive, is an important and growing form of regulation. Operating controls are designed to limit undesirable behavior by compelling certain actions while prohibiting others. If operating control regulation results in 100 percent compliance, a situation is created similar to that resulting when a prohibitive tax policy is instituted. In each instance the undesirable activity in question is completely eliminated, and no tax revenues are collected. When operating controls result in less than full compliance, operating control regulation becomes much like tax policy regulation as fines and levies are instituted to punish violators.

What kinds of operating controls are imposed on business firms? Controls over environmental pollution immediately come to mind, but businesses are also subject to many other kinds of constraints. For example, federal legislation sets limits for automobile emissions, fuel efficiency, and safety standards; and firms handling food products, drugs, and other substances that could harm consumers are constrained under the Pure Food and Drug Act. Industrial work conditions are governed under various labor laws and health regulations; included are provisions relating to noise levels, noxious gases and chemicals, and safety standards. Antidiscrimination laws designed to protect minority groups and women also cause some firms to modify their hiring and promotional policies. Wage and price controls, imposed at various times in attempts to reduce high rates of inflation, restrict the freedom of firms in setting prices and affect the usage of resources throughout the economic system.

Like operating grants regulation, the effectiveness of operating control regulations is often limited by statutory specifications which are vague or imprecise. Similarly, if the punitive sanctions taken against violators are overly lenient or poorly defined, effective incentives for compliance are not created. Beyond the difficulties created by poorly defined regulations and sanctions, problems can also result if operating controls are imposed which conflict with one another. For example, Ford Motor Company estimated that mandatory safety standards raised the cost of producing the average 1974 passenger car by $325. The added cost of pollution control equipment required on 1975 automobiles was estimated at an additional $160.[4] Although such costs were undoubtedly anticipated by those designing auto safety and pollution regulations, it was perhaps less obvious that these regulations would result in important reductions in auto fuel efficiency. Thus, safety and pollution regulations were in direct conflict with other regulations mandating increases in the fuel efficiency of cars to reduce U.S. dependence on foreign-produced oil.

Perhaps the clearest difference between operating control regulation and regulation via tax or subsidy policies is the reliance on nonmonetary incentives for compliance. There are no easy alternatives to operating control regulation in those instances where the social costs of an activity are prohibitively great (e.g., nuclear disaster, giant oil slicks, etc.) or difficult if not impossible to measure (e.g., public health, worker death, or serious injury). In some instances, however, operating control regulations can cause firms to direct their efforts toward being exempted or dismissed from regulation rather than toward reducing the negative externalities of concern to society. It is not clear that operating controls are more effective than tax and subsidy policies in insuring that the results of regulatory efforts are both effective and equitable.

The "Who Pays?" Issue

The question of who pays for regulations intended to mitigate the problems associated with market failure due to incentive problems is an important one. While the *incidence* of pollution charges may fall on a heavily polluting foundry, for example, the *burden* of those charges may be passed on by the offending firm to its customers or suppliers. In fact, the question of who pays for specific regulations can seldom be determined by merely considering the fined, taxed, or otherwise regulated party.

In general, who "pays" for operating control regulation depends on the elasticity of demand for the final products of affected firms. Figure 12.1 illustrates this issue by considering the theoretically polar extremes of perfectly elastic demand for final products (Figure 12.1[a]) and perfectly inelastic demand for final products (Figure 12.1[b]). Identically upward-sloping *MC* curves are assumed in each in-

---

[4]Murray L. Weidenbaum, *Business, Government and the Public* (Englewood Cliffs, N.J.: Prentice-Hall, 1977), p. 49.

FIGURE 12.1

Regulatory Burden Allocation under Elastic and Inelastic Demand

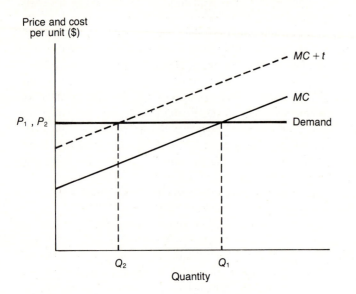

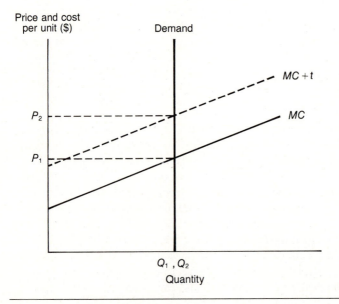

stance. Here, as is often the case, regulation is assumed to increase marginal costs by a fixed amount per unit. This amount, t, can reflect pollution taxes per unit of output or regulatory induced cost increases.

In Figure 12.1(a) we see that if good substitutes for a firm's product exist and demand is highly elastic, producers will be incapable of passing regulatory induced cost increases or taxes on to customers. As a result, producers (including investors, employees, and suppliers) will be forced to bear the burden of regulatory costs, at least in the short run. In these instances, falling industry rates of return on invested capital and high rates of industry unemployment will be symptomatic of regulatory influences.

In Figure 12.1(b) we consider the effect of regulatory induced cost or tax increases in the case of perfectly inelastic final product demand. Without effective substitute products, producers can be successful in passing the burden of regulation on to customers. In contrast to the perfectly elastic demand case, producers may encounter relatively few disadvantages due to regulatory induced cost increases.

The above analysis is greatly simplified. Nevertheless, it points out that regulatory taxes or induced cost increases can have widely differing effects on industries if demand relationships vary. Similarly, the effect of regulation on industries with similar product demand elasticities will vary to the extent that supply characteristics are different. For example, in industries where marginal costs per unit are constant, per-unit regulatory taxes will result in output prices rising by an amount greater than in the case of rising marginal costs, but by less than in the instance of falling marginal costs.

In general, regulations which affect the marginal costs of production will usually have some combination of adverse price and output effects for producers and consumers. A realization of this fact has, in some instances, caused policymakers to promote taxes or regulations which result in fixed or "lump sum" charges for products. (Recall that increases in fixed costs affect neither price nor output levels for profit maximizing firms in the short run.) Even this approach to regulation is far from painless, however, since heavily regulated producers may be forced to leave the industry in the long run, should industry profitability be forced below the cost of capital. It is clear that the costs of regulation must be weighed carefully against its benefits.

REGULATORY RESPONSE TO STRUCTURAL FAILURES

In Chapter 10 we saw that, under certain conditions, monopoly or oligopoly may develop in an industry with the result that too little output is produced and excess profits are created. Regulatory policies to reduce or eliminate the socially harmful consequences of such structural failures can be aimed at controlling already existent monopoly power or at the prevention of its emergence. Public utility regulation, which controls prices and profits of established monopolies, is an important example of attempts to enjoy the benefits of low-cost production by large firms while avoiding the social costs of unregulated monopoly. Both tax and antitrust policies are used to address the problem of structural failures by attempting to limit not only the abuse of monopoly but also its growth.

The Dilemma of Natural Monopoly

Recall that under perfect competition many firms, perhaps of roughly comparable size, are able to produce with equal efficiency. It is significant that for effective competition, large firms must not be more efficient than their smaller rivals. This condition does not necessarily hold in all industries.

Evidence indicates that in some industries average costs of production decline continuously as output expands. That means that a single large firm has the potential to produce total industry output more efficiently than any group of smaller producers. This situation is called *natural monopoly* and is defined as the case where the profit maximizing level of output in an industry occurs at a point where long-run average costs for a single firm are still declining. The term *natural* is used because monopoly would naturally result from the superior efficiency of the single large producer and not necessarily because of anticompetitive or predatory practices.

For example, consider Figure 12.2. Here the firm will produce Q units of output at an average cost of C per unit. Note that this cost level is above the minimum point on the long-run average cost curve, and average costs are still declining. As a monopolist, the firm can earn an economic profit equal to the rectangle $PP'C'C$, or $Q(P - C)$. Electric, gas, and water companies are the classic examples of natural monopolies, as the duplication of production and distribution facilities would greatly increase costs if more than one firm served a given area.

This situation presents somewhat of a dilemma. Economic efficiency could be enhanced by restricting the number of firms to one, but where only one firm serves a market the possibility of monopolistic inefficiency exists. Specifically, unregulated monopolists tend to earn excessive profits and to underproduce. Excessive profits are defined as profits so large that the firm earns a rate of return on invested capital that exceeds the risk-adjusted normal, or required, rate. Profits are useful both for allocating resources and as an incentive for efficiency, but it is difficult to justify above-normal profits caused by market power rather than by exceptional performance.

Underproduction occurs when the firm curtails production to a level where the value of the marginal resources needed to produce an additional unit of output (marginal cost) is less than the benefit derived from the additional unit, as measured by the price that consumers are willing to pay for it. In other words, at outputs just greater than Q in Figure 12.2, consumers are willing to pay approximately P dollars

FIGURE 12.2

Price/Output Decision under Monopoly

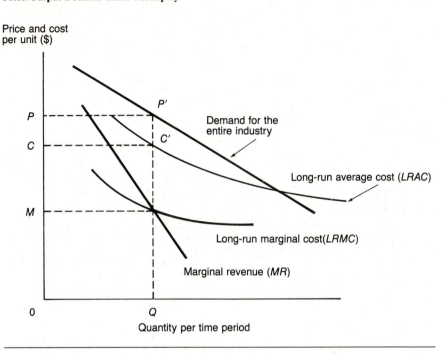

Price and cost
per unit ($)

P'

P

C

C'

Demand for the
entire industry

Long-run average cost (*LRAC*)

M

Long-run marginal cost(*LRMC*)

Marginal revenue (*MR*)

0   *Q*

Quantity per time period

per unit, so the value of additional units is *P*. However, the marginal cost of producing an additional unit is only slightly greater than *M* dollars and well below *P*, so cost is not equal to value. Accordingly, an expansion of output is desirable from society's point of view.

In addition to possibly earning excessive profits and withholding production, an unregulated natural monopolist could be susceptible to operating inefficiency. In competitive markets, firms must operate efficiently to remain in business. Pressure for cost-efficiency from established competitors, however, is absent in the case of natural monopoly. This means that the market power of the natural monopolist would permit some inefficiency and waste in production. While excessive amounts of operating inefficiency would surely attract new competition (entry), significant losses in economic efficiency may persist for extended periods in the case of natural monopoly.

How can we escape from the dilemma posed by the fact that monopoly may have the potential for greatest efficiency, but that unregulated monopoly could lead to excess profits, underproduction, and resource waste? One answer is to permit natural monopolies to persist but to subject them to price and profit regulation.

FIGURE 12.3

Price Regulation and Monopoly: Optimal Price/Output Decision Making

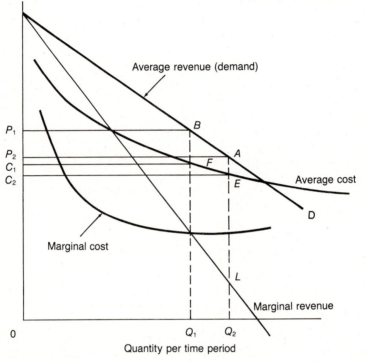

Utility Price Regulation

The most common method of monopoly regulation is through price controls. Price regulation typically results (1) in a larger quantity of the product being sold than would be the case with an unrestricted monopoly, (2) in a reduced dollar profit, and (3) in a lower rate of return on investment by the firm's owners. This situation is illustrated in Figure 12.3. A monopolist operating without regulation would pro-duce Q_1 units of output and charge a price, P_1. If regulators set a ceiling on prices at P_2, the firm's effective demand curve would become the kinked curve P_2AD. Since price is a constant from 0 to Q_2 units of output, marginal revenue equals price in this range; that is, P_2A is the marginal revenue curve over the output range $0Q2$. For output beyond Q_2, marginal revenue is given by the original marginal revenue func-tion, the line LM. Thus, the marginal revenue curve is now discontinuous at Output

Q, with a gap between Points A and L. This regulated firm will maximize profits by operating at Output Q_2 and by charging the ceiling price, P_2. Marginal revenue is greater than marginal cost up to that output, but less than marginal cost beyond it.

Profits are also reduced by the regulatory action. Without price regulation, price P_1 is charged; a cost of C_1 per unit is incurred; and Output Q_1 is produced. Profit will be $(P_1 - C_1)(Q_1)$, which is equal to the area P_1BFC_1. With price regulation, the price is P_2; the cost is C_2; Q_2 units are sold; and profits are represented by the smaller area P_2AEC_2.

How does the regulatory authority determine a fair price? In essence, the theory is as follows. The regulatory commission has in mind a fair or normal rate of return, given the risk inherent in the enterprise. The regulators also know how much capital investment will be required to produce a given output. The commission then approves prices such that the profits earned, when divided by the required investment at the resultant output level, will produce the target rate of return. In the case illustrated in Figure 12.3, if the profit at Price P_2, when divided by the investment required to produce Q_2, produces a rate of return greater than the target, the price would be reduced until the actual and the target rates of return are equalized.[5]

Problems in Utility Price Regulation

Pricing Problems. Although the concept of price regulation is simple, serious problems exist in the regulation of public utilities. First, it is impossible to exactly determine cost and the demand schedules, as well as the asset base necessary to support a specified level of output. Utilities also serve several classes of customers, which means that a number of different demand schedules with varying price elasticities are involved. Therefore, any number of different rate schedules could be used to produce the desired profit level. If telephone company profits are too low, should rates be raised for business subscribers or for residential customers; should they be raised on local calls or on long-distance calls? If electric utilities need more profits, should industrial, commercial, or residential users bear the burden? An appeal to cost considerations for a solution to this problem is often of no avail, because the services provided are joint products, a factor that makes it extremely difficult, if not impossible, to separate costs and allocate them to specific classes of customers.

Output Level Problems. A second problem with price regulation is that regulators can make mistakes with regard to the optimal level and growth of service. For example, if a telephone utility is permitted to charge excessive rates, more funds will be allocated to system expansion, and communication services will grow at a faster

---

[5]This treatment assumes that the cost curves in Figures 12.3 and 12.4 do not include capital costs. That is, the profit referred to is business profit, not economic profit.

FIGURE 12.4

Efficient and Inefficient Utility Companies

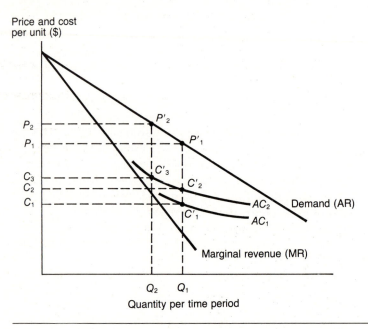

Quantity per time period

than optimal rate. Similarly, if prices allowed to natural-gas producers are too low, consumers will be encouraged to use gas at a high rate, producers will not seek new gas supplies, and a shortage of gas will occur. Too low a price structure for electricity will likewise encourage the use of power but discourage the addition of new generating equipment.

Inefficiency. Price regulation can also lead to inefficiency. If the regulated companies are guaranteed a minimum return on their invested capital, then, provided demand conditions permit, operating inefficiencies can be offset by higher prices. To illustrate, consider the situation depicted in Figure 12.4. A regulated utility faces the demand curve AR and the marginal revenue curve MR. If the utility operates at peak efficiency, the average cost curve AC_1 will apply. At a regulated price, P_1, Q_1 units will be demanded; cost per unit will be C_1; and profits equal to the rectangle $P_1P_1'C_1'C_1$ will be earned. These profits are, let us assume, just sufficient to provide a reasonable return on invested capital.

   Now suppose that another company, one with less capable managers, is operating under similar conditions. Because this management is less efficient than that of the first company, its cost curve is represented by AC_2. If its price is set at P_1, it too will sell Q_1 units, but average cost will be C_2; profits will be only $P_1P_1'C_2'C_2$; and the company will be earning less than its required rate of return. In the absence of regulation, inefficiency and low profits go together, but under regulation the inefficient company can request—and probably be granted—a rate increase to P_2. Here it can sell Q_2 units of output, incur an average cost of C_3 per unit, and earn profits of $P_2P_2'C_3'C_3$, resulting in a rate of return on investment approximately equal to that of the efficient company. We see, then, that regulation can reduce the profit incentive for efficiency.[6]

Investment Level. A fourth problem with regulation is that it can lead to overinvestment or underinvestment in fixed assets. Allowed profits are calculated as a percentage of the rate base, which is approximately equal to fixed assets. If the allowed rate of return exceeds the cost of capital, it will benefit the firm to expand fixed assets and to shift to capital-intensive methods of production. Conversely, if the allowed rate of return is less than the cost of capital, the firm will not expand capacity rapidly enough and will produce by methods that require relatively little capital but perhaps excessive amounts of fuel. Thus, regulation can lead to suboptimal input combinations.

Regulatory Lag and Political Problems. A related problem is that of *regulatory lag*, which is defined as the period between the time a price increase (or decrease) is appropriate and the effective date of the allowed price change. Because of the often lengthy legal proceedings involved in these price decisions, long periods can pass between the time when the need for utility rate level adjustments is recognized and when they are implemented.

The problem of regulatory lag is particularly acute during periods of rapidly rising prices. During the late 1960s and the 1970s, for example, inflationary pressures exerted a constant upward thrust on costs. If normal profits and a fair rate of return on capital are to be maintained in such a time, expeditious price increases have to be implemented.

However, public utility commissioners are either political appointees or elected officials, and either those who appoint them or the commissioners themselves must

---

[6]Utility commissions could attempt to consider efficiency when setting rates. For example, a particular commission might feel that 11 percent is a reasonable rate of return, but might allow efficient companies within its jurisdiction to earn up to 11.5 percent and penalize inefficient companies by holding them to a return of less than 11 percent. The difficulty with this approach is that each utility operates in a unique setting, so it is extremely difficult to make valid comparisons. One electric company might have a cost of 2 mils per kilowatt hour, while another in the same state might have a cost of 2.5 mils. Is the first company more efficient than the second, or is the cost difference due to fuel cost differences, different plant sizes, labor cost differentials, and differing depreciation charges caused by construction during a more or less inflated period? Because of these difficulties, utility commissions do not frequently make explicit use of efficiency differentials in setting profit rates.

periodically stand for election. Further, most voters are consumers of utility services and naturally dislike price increases, whether these increases are justified or not. Utility customers can and do exert great pressure on public utility commissioners to deny or at least delay even reasonable rate increases.

At least in part because of regulatory lag, a number of major utility companies experienced severe financial difficulties during the mid-1970s. The largest U.S. electric utility, Consolidated Edison (which serves New York City and the surrounding area), was almost forced into bankruptcy, and many other companies were forced to curtail construction programs because they were unable to obtain the funds necessary to purchase new plants and equipment. Profits were simply inadequate to induce investors to purchase the companies' stocks and bonds.

Cost of Regulation. By this time a sixth problem with price regulation should be obvious. A great deal of careful and costly analysis must be conducted before regulatory decisions can be made. Maintaining public utility commission staffs is expensive, as is maintaining required records and processing rate cases, costs borne directly by companies. Ultimately the cost of both the commissions' and the companies' regulation-related activities are borne by consumers.

While most economists can see no reasonable alternative to utility regulation for electric, gas, telephone, and private water companies, serious problems arise from efforts to regulate industry through price determination. If competition is present, the market system is a much more efficient allocator of goods and services, and it is for this reason that efforts are made to maintain a workable level of competition in the economy through tax and antitrust policies.

Excess or Windfall Profit Taxes

In recent years, tax policy has been increasingly used to limit perceived abuses of monopoly power and, to a lesser extent, to encourage the growth of small as opposed to large business. *Excess* or *windfall profit taxes* are examples of tax policies intended to limit perceived abuses of economic power. Normal profit is defined as the risk-adjusted rate of return necessary to maintain investment in an industry. Excess profit, therefore, is profit above and beyond necessary minimums. The term *windfall profit* is commonly used to distinguish excess profit, which is due to the unexpected and unwarranted good fortune of firms, from profits resulting from such factors as superior operating efficiency, innovation, economies of scale, and so on.

Excess profit taxes have been frequently imposed during wartime both to help finance the high level of government expenditure and to reduce the substantial profits accruing to providers of critical goods and services. More recently, in 1980 the United States imposed a windfall profit tax on domestic oil company profits. The intent was to reduce oil company profits resulting from the very rapid increase in crude oil prices.

One of the most serious challenges to a successful excess or windfall tax policy is the problem of correctly defining the magnitude of unwarranted profits. This means that prices, operating expenses, and investment policies of affected firms must be carefully scrutinized. Therefore, substantial industry expertise is necessary if potential abuses of a windfall tax policy are to be avoided. If firms perceive that a windfall profit tax policy is only a temporary phenomenon, unnecessary operating expenses may be incurred or unwarranted investments may be undertaken if future benefits from such expenditure are anticipated. For example, the railroad industry substantially rebuilt or replaced its right-of-way (track and related) investments during World War II. Although some reinvestment in plant and equipment was undoubtedly necessary if wartime demands for freight and passenger service were to be met, one can only speculate as to how much investment was undertaken simply to avoid wartime windfall profit taxes. Newer plant and equipment, rather than increased tax payments, were obviously preferable to railroad executives. Quite different problems may result from the windfall taxes on oil company profits. Beyond the obvious problem of defining the magnitude of excess profit, windfall profit taxes can increase the level of risk or uncertainty in doing business. If oil company executives perceive that profits from successful exploration activities will be taxed severely, the risk of obtaining a satisfactory return from the firm's entire drilling program could rise. Higher industry averages for both required profit and product prices would naturally result.

Small Company Tax Preferences

During recent years the corporate income tax has become somewhat more progressive, favoring small as opposed to large business. In 1980 the corporation income tax rate was 17 percent on the first $25,000 in profits; 20 percent between $25,000 and $50,000; 30 percent between $50,000 and $75,000; 40 percent between $75,000 and $100,000; and 46 percent on profits over $100,000. Therefore, firms paid a total of $26,750 in taxes on the first $100,000 of profit, but $46,000 in taxes for each additional $100,000.

The rationale provided for these tax preferences is quite diverse. Growth in small business is seen as consistent with democratic principles of self-determination and individual decision making. Growth in small business is also important because small firms often form a "competitive fringe" in industries, thereby exerting downward pressure on prices and profits of leading firms. Furthermore, recent evidence suggests that small firms are the source of substantial amounts of invention and technological innovation. To some extent, progressive taxes might also be considered a partial offset to the relatively high costs that government-regulation reporting requirements impose on small businesses.

That small business plays a vital role in our economy is quite clear. This is even true in manufacturing, which tends to be characterized by relatively large-scale operations. The *1977 Census of Manufacturers* reports that while the largest 200 corporations account for 44 percent of the industrial output (value added) and 31 percent of industrial employment, 90 percent of all manufacturing establishments have fewer than 100 employees. These relatively small industrial plants account for 20 percent of industrial output. The relative importance of small business in agriculture, construction, retail trade, real estate, and other services is even greater. *Forbes* magazine reported in 1979 that, according to Small Business Administration standards, 97 percent of the 10.7 million businesses in the United States are small. Interestingly, both the number of small companies and the small business share of total industry employment is growing steadily. For example, from 1969 through 1979 the top 1,000 companies in the United States failed to increase their employment, while small business employment grew by 6 million jobs.[7]

A partial explanation of this trend is given by the changing makeup of the U.S. gross national product. During recent years, the service portion of the U.S. economy has grown rapidly, whereas the goods sector has grown more slowly. This trend tends to favor small as opposed to big business, because fewer advantages to large-scale production exist in the provision of services as compared to goods.

Whatever the causes, it is clear that small business is an important part of the U.S. economy. The extent to which tax and other regulatory preferences enhance the competitive position of small firms is not fully known, but their use to insure a continued role of small business seems likely.

ANTITRUST POLICY

In the late nineteenth century a movement toward industrial consolidation developed in the United States. Industrial growth was rapid, and because of economies of scale or unfair competitive practices, an oligopolistic structure emerged in certain industries. In some instances, pricing decisions were made by industry leaders who concluded that higher profits could be attained through cooperation rather than competition. As a result, voting trusts were formed. In these trusts, voting rights to the stocks of various firms in an industry were consolidated so that a monopoly price/output solution could be achieved. The oil and tobacco trusts of the 1880s are well-known examples.

Although profitable to the firms, the trusts were socially undesirable, and public indignation resulted in the 1890 passage of the Sherman Act, the first significant U.S. antitrust measure. Other important legislation subsequently passed includes the Clayton Act (1914), the Federal Trade Commission Act (1914), the Robinson–Patman Act (1936), and the Celler–Kefauver Act (1950). Each of these acts was designed to prevent anticompetitive actions, whose impact is more likely to

---

[7] *See* Thomas P. Murphy, "Wait 'till Next Year," *Forbes* (Aug. 20, 1979).

reduce competition than to lower costs by increasing operating efficiency. In this section we present an overview of antitrust law, as well as a brief chronology of major antitrust legislation.

Overview of Antitrust Law

As is the case with any body of law or legal principles, multiple purposes of federal antitrust law are apparent. Antitrust law is essentially concerned with the control of economic and political power through the force of competitive markets. The purpose of such control is not only to improve economic efficiency, but to enhance consumer sovereignty and the impartiality of resource allocation while limiting concentrations in both economic and political power.

There is no single antitrust statute in U.S. law. Rather, federal antitrust law is founded on two basic statutes—the Sherman Act and the Clayton Act—and their amendments. An important characteristic of these laws is that they tend to be quite broad and somewhat vague in banning "restraints of trade," monopolization, "unfair competition," and so on. By never precisely defining the nature of monopolizing, for example, the statutes left it to judicial interpretation to determine prohibited behavior. Because of this, many principles in antitrust law rest on judicial interpretation in key decisions. For this reason, individual court decisions (case law) must be consulted in addition to statutory standards (statutory law) to determine the legality of business practices.

Sherman Act

The Sherman Act of 1890 was the first piece of federal antitrust legislation. In substance, it was brief and to the point. Section 1 forbade contracts, combinations, or conspiracies in restraint of trade (then offenses under common law), and Section 2 forbade monopolization. Both sections could be enforced by civil court decrees or by criminal proceedings, with the guilty liable to fines or jail sentences.

Despite some landmark decisions against the tobacco, powder, and Standard Oil trusts, enforcement proved to be sporadic. Moreover, the Sherman Act was alleged to be too vague. On the one hand, business people claimed not to know what was illegal; on the other, it was widely felt that the Justice Department was ignorant of monopoly-creating practices and did not bring suit against them until it was too late and monopoly was a fait accompli.

In 1974 the Sherman Act was amended to make violations felonies rather than misdemeanors. That statute also increased the maximum penalties that could be levied. Instead of $50,000 against a corporation and $50,000 and one year in prison against an individual, the act now provides for $1 million maximum fines against corporations and up to $100,000 fines and three years' imprisonment for individuals. In addition to criminal fines and prison sentences, firms and individuals violating the Sherman Act face the possibility of triple-damage civil suits from those injured by the antitrust violation.

Despite its shortcomings, the Sherman Act remains one of the government's main weapons against anticompetitive behavior. In February 1978 a federal judge imposed some of the stiffest penalties in the history of U.S. antitrust actions on eight firms and eleven of their officers who were convicted of violating the Sherman Act. These convictions for price fixing in the electrical wiring devices industry resulted in fines totaling nearly $900,000 and jail terms for nine of the eleven officers charged.

Clayton Act

Congress passed two measures in 1914 designed to overcome weaknesses in the Sherman Act. The most important of these was the Clayton Act, which addressed problems of mergers, interlocking directorships, price discrimination, and tying contracts. Also enacted in 1914 was the Federal Trade Commission (FTC) Act, which outlawed unfair methods of competition in commerce and established the FTC, an agency intended to enforce both the Clayton and Sherman Acts.

Section 2 of the Clayton Act made it illegal for a seller to discriminate in prices among its business customers unless (1) cost differentials in serving the various customers justified the price differentials or (2) the lower prices charged in certain markets were offered to meet competition in the area. The primary concern was that a strong regional or national firm might employ selective price cuts in local markets to eliminate weak local firms. Once the competitors in one market were eliminated, monopoly prices would be charged in the area, and the excessive profits could be used to subsidize cut-throat competition in other areas. The Robinson–Patman Act was passed in 1936 as an amendment to the section of the Clayton Act dealing with price discrimination. Specific forms of price discrimination, especially related to chain-store purchasing practices, were declared to be illegal.

Section 3 of the Clayton Act forbade tying contracts that reduce competition. A firm, particularly one with the patent on a vital process or a monopoly on a natural resource, could use licensing or other arrangements to restrict competition. One such procedure was the tying contract, through which a firm tied the acquisition of one item to an agreement to purchase other items. For example, the International Business Machines Corporation (IBM) for many years refused to sell its business machines. It rented these machines to customers, who were required to buy IBM punch cards and related materials as well as machine maintenance from the company. This clearly had the effect of reducing competition in the maintenance and service industry, as well as in the punch card and related products industry. After the IBM lease agreement was declared illegal under the Clayton Act, the company was forced to offer its machines for sale and to cease leasing arrangements that tied firms to agreements to purchase other IBM materials and services.

And finally, while voting trusts that lessened competition were prohibited by the Sherman Act, interpretation of the act did not always prevent one corporation from acquiring the stock of competing firms and then merging them into itself. Section 7 of the Clayton Act prohibited such mergers if they were found to reduce competition. Either the Antitrust Division of the Justice Department or the FTC can bring suit under Section 7, and mergers can be prevented. If they have been consummated prior to the suit, divestiture can be ordered. The Clayton Act also prevented individuals from serving on the boards of directors of two competing companies. Two so-called competitors having common directors would obviously not compete very hard. Although the Clayton Act made it illegal for firms to merge through stock transactions when the effect would be to lessen competition, a loophole in the law existed. A firm could purchase the assets of a competing firm, integrate the operations into its own, and effectively reduce competition. The Celler–Kefauver Act closed this loophole, making asset acqusitions illegal when the effect of such purchases was to reduce competition. By a slight change in wording, it made clear that the policy of Congress was to attack all mergers between a buyer and a seller (vertical), between potential competitors (horizontal or product and market extension), and between entirely unrelated firms (pure conglomerate), whenever competition was threatened.

Enforcement

Public enforcement of the antitrust laws is the dual responsibility of the Antitrust Division of the Department of Justice and the Federal Trade Commission (FTC). Generally speaking, the Justice Department concerns itself with significant or flagrant offenses against the Sherman Act, as well as with mergers for monopoly covered by Section 7 of the Clayton Act. In most instances, the Justice Department will only bring charges under the Clayton Act when broader Sherman Act violations are also being addressed. In addition to policing law violations, the Sherman Act also charges the Justice Department with the duty of restraining possible future violations. Thus, firms found in violation of the law often receive from the federal courts detailed injunctions regulating future business activity. In fact, "injunctive relief" (e.g., dissolution or divestiture decrees, etc.) is a much more typical outcome of Justice Department suits than are criminal penalties.

While the Justice Department can also institute civil proceedings in addition to the criminal proceedings discussed above, civil proceedings are typically the responsibility of the FTC. The FTC is an administrative agency of the executive branch with quasijudicial powers used to enforce compliance with the Clayton Act. Because the substantive provisions of the Clayton Act do not create criminal offenses, the FTC has no criminal jurisdiction. The FTC holds hearings if law violations are suspected, and issues "cease and desist" orders if violations are found. Such "cease and desist" orders under the Clayton Act are subject to review by appellate courts.

Economic Analyses in Antitrust Actions

The various antitrust provisions listed above apply if a particular action would tend to lessen competition substantially. Mergers are attacked if they would alter industry structure in a manner that reduces competition, but they are not illegal if competition is not reduced. When is competition reduced? If two firms merge—each with 1 percent of a market served by 100 competitors—few would argue that the merger reduces competition, for 99 firms would still remain after the merger. However, if each of the firms had 5 percent of the market and only 19 firms would remain, the merger might affect competition. Surely competition would be affected if the merging firms each had 20 percent of a market served by only four or five firms. But where should the line be drawn?

Further, if it is judged that a *particular* merger would not in and of itself reduce competition but that a series of similar mergers would do so, should the merger in question be permitted? Suppose 20 firms, each with a 5 percent share of the market, are in competition. A judgment is made, perhaps in a court of law that has heard much economic evidence, that a particular merger will not harm competition. If the merger is approved, however, other firms will also seek to merge, and the result will be a reduction in competition. When should the trend toward concentration be stopped?[8]

Market concentration is a key element in making judgments about the effect of a merger on the competitive posture of an industry, but how should an industry or a market be determined? To illustrate, suppose two banks in lower Manhattan seek to merge. There are about 14,000 banks in the United States, and the national banking concentration ratio is low. However, the entire United States is not a relevant market for most banking services—a local area is the relevant market. But what local area? Should metropolitan New York be deemed the market? The City of New York? The Borough of Manhattan? Or lower Manhattan only? The answer really depends on the nature of the banks. For certain classes of services, especially loans to major national corporations, the nation as a whole constitutes the market. But for small checking account and personal loan services, the local area is the relevant market.

The problem is even more complex when competing products or industries are considered. A particular bank might, for example, be the only one serving a given neighborhood, but the bank might still face intense competition from savings and loan associations, credit unions, and distant banks that offer mail-deposit service.

Similar problems are found in other aspects of antitrust policy. Given the difficulties we have noted in determining costs, what situations create opportunities for

---

[8]As discussed in Chapter 10, industrial concentration is usually measured by the percentage share of a given market served by the four largest firms in an industry. The higher the concentration ratio, the less likely that workable competition will exist in an industry. The classic work in this area is by Joe S. Bain, *Industrial Organization* (New York: Wiley, 1959). Bain distinguishes among "highly concentrated oligopoly" (75 to 100 percent of sales by the top four firms in an industry), "moderately concentrated oligopoly" (50 to 75 percent concentration ratio), "slightly concentrated (or low-grade) oligopoly" (25 to 50 percent concentration ratio), and "atomistic oligopoly" (for concentration ratios below 25 percent).

legal price discrimination based on quantity discounts because of low production costs on large orders? Here, just as in merger cases, the answer is not likely to be clear-cut. A comprehensive economic cost analysis is required before a determination can be made, and even then the decision is likely to be somewhat arbitrary.

Antitrust is quite complex, with its complete coverage being well beyond the scope of this text. Additionally, generalizations are difficult. The fact that so many antitrust decisions are made in the courts is testimony to this point. Nevertheless, because antitrust policy does constitute a serious constraint to many business decisions, antitrust considerations are an important, if nebulous, aspect of managerial economics.

THE REGULATED ENVIRONMENT: A SECOND LOOK

For effective decision making in the regulated environment, managers must be aware of both the rationale and the means of modern regulatory processes. We have briefly addressed this need by considering both economic and political considerations stimulating regulatory responses to perceived market failures caused by incentive or structural problems. Both positive and negative aspects of current regulatory methods were briefly examined. Rather than summarizing this material immediately, we think it will prove useful to look somewhat more closely at both the problems and promise of regulation. Seldom is the issue one of regulation versus deregulation; rather it is one of how much and what type or kind of regulation is most appropriate.

The "Capture" Problem

In our earlier discussion of the "why regulate" question, we considered both economic and noneconomic factors which influence regulatory decisions. This discussion presented the widely held belief that regulation is in the "public interest" and is used to firm behavior toward socially desirable ends. This view is not universally held, however, and the compelling nature of counter-arguments requires that they be considered.

In a 1971 study, George Stigler presented what may be called the *capture theory* of economic regulation.[9] According to Stigler, the machinery and power of the state is a potential resource to every industry in society. With its power to prohibit or compel, to take or give money, the state can and does selectively help or hurt a vast number of industries. Because of this, regulation may be actively *sought* by an industry. Stigler contends that, as a rule, regulation is acquired by industry and is

---

[9]George J. Stigler, "The Theory of Economic Regulation," *Bell Journal of Economics and Management Science* 2 (Spring 1971): 3–20.

designed and operated primarily for industry's benefit. Although some regulations are undeniably onerous, these examples are thought to be exceptional rather than usual cases.

Stigler asserts that the types of state favors commonly sought by regulated industries include: direct money subsidies, control over entry by new rivals, control over offerings of substitutes and complements, and price-fixing. Therefore, domestic airline "air-mail" subsidies, Federal Deposit Insurance Corporation (FDIC) regulation reducing the rate of entry into commercial banking, suppression of margarine sales by butter producers, price-fixing in motor carrier (trucking) regulation, and American Medical Association control of medical training and licensing can be interpreted as examples of regulatory process control by regulated industries.

In summarizing his views on regulation, Stigler suggests that criticism of the Interstate Commerce Commission's (ICC) pro-industry policies is as misplaced as would be criticism of the Great Atlantic and Pacific Tea Company (A&P) for selling groceries, or of politicians for seeking popular support. Given current methods of enacting and carrying out regulation, pro-industry policies made by regulatory bodies are to be expected. Stigler contends that the only way to get different results from regulation would be to change the political process of regulator selection and to reward regulators on a basis unrelated to their services on behalf of regulated industries.

The Size-Efficiency Problem

The discussion of the dilemma of natural monopoly suggested that, in some instances, a single seller has the potential for superior cost efficiency. A potentially important negative consequence, however, is that such natural monopolists would have a tendency to restrict output, resulting in higher prices and excess profits. This conflict between the superior efficiency of large firms and the harmful consequences of limited numbers of competitors is one of the oldest controversies in antitrust and regulation.

During recent years, federal legislation has been proposed that would prohibit all mergers between firms of a certain size, say, $100 million or more in sales. These proposals are a reflection of the belief that such mergers increase monopoly power, and that the sizes reached by the largest firms in our economy cannot be justified on the basis of scale-associated advantages in production. While such views remain widespread, some counterevidence has emerged in several recent studies which suggest that the commonly observed link between leading firm market shares (concentration) and profitability can be explained by lower costs made possible by superior efficiency rather than by higher prices due to collusion. These findings are as controversial as they are important and suggest the need to continue research on the size-efficiency question. In the meantime, the controversy will persist, as the dilemma is real. Perhaps Peter Finley Nunne's characterization of Theodore Roosevelt's attitude says it best:

"Th' trusts," [says T.R.], "are heejous monsthers built up by th' enlightened inthrprise [of] th' men that have done so much to advance progress in our beloved country . . . on wan hand I wud stamp them undher fut; on th' other hand not so fast." [10]

Costs of Regulation

Milton Friedman, Nobel prize-winning economist, is often credited with coining the phrase, "There is no such thing as a free lunch." With respect to regulation, this can be interpreted to mean that every government program and policy has economic costs. The economic costs of regulatory policies are measured in terms of administrative burdens for regulatory agencies, deviations from optimal methods of production, and the general effect that regulation has on the allocation of economic resources.

A first, and most obvious, cost of business regulation is the cost to local, state, and federal governments for supervisory agencies. Although no recent data on such costs for local and state governments are currently available, Murray Weidenbaum estimated 1976 federal expenditures for business regulation at $3 billion.[11] Interestingly, he found that the largest regulatory budgets were not those of traditional regulatory agencies, such as the ICC ($50 million) or the CAB ($85 million), but those devoted to the broader regulatory activities of the Departments of Labor ($397 million for employment and job safety standards) and Agriculture ($381 million, mainly for food inspection).

While these "direct" costs of regulation are substantial, they may be far less than hidden or "indirect" costs. For example, if the Occupational Safety and Health Administration (OSHA) requires manufacturers to employ safer methods of production, increases in affected product prices will surely occur. Similarly, the cost of Environmental Protection Agency (EPA) mandated reductions in auto emissions will ultimately be borne by consumers. In the case of auto emissions, the National Academy of Sciences and the National Academy of Engineering estimated the annual benefits of the catalytic converter at $5 billion and annual costs at $11 billion.[12] In a social sense, one might ask if the noneconomic advantages of this method of pollution reduction are sufficient to offset what appear to be significant economic disadvantages. Similarly, the economic and noneconomic advantages of regulation must be sufficient to offset annual private costs for pollution control ($24.1 billion), OSHA-mandated noise reductions ($13.5 billion), health and safety equipment ($3.4 billion), and FTC-mandated business reports ($13.8 million).[13]

The magnitude of the economic costs of regulation suggests that neither busi-

---

[10] Cited in William Letwin, *Law and Economic Policy in America* (New York: Random House, 1965), p. 205.

[11] Weidenbaum, *Business, Government and the Public*, pp. 17–19.

[12] Ibid., p. 54.

[13] Ibid., pp. 78, 69, 67, and 147.

ness nor the public may regard them as trivial or unimportant. Where important concerns for the public's health and safety are apparent, for example, business and government can accomplish much through cooperative effort. It is the public's role to supervise this process to insure that government-business interactions yield regulatory results in the public interest, rather than in the narrow self-interest of the regulated industry or of the regulators.

SUMMARY

Promises of Regulation

Our earlier discussion suggested that an important problem of regulation, particularly utility regulation, was that regulators seldom have the information or expertise necessary to accurately specify, for example, the correct level of utility investment, the minimum necessary regulated carrier costs, or the optimal method of pollution control. In fact, because technology is rapidly changing in many industries, often only those industry personnel currently working at the frontier of technology have the type of specialized knowledge necessary to deal satisfactorily with such issues.

One possible method for dealing with the technical expertise problem of current regulation is to have regulators focus on the preferred outcomes (ends) of regulatory processes, rather than on the technical means industry adopts in achieving those outcomes. Such an innovation in regulation would allow regulators to specialize in defining the public interest in regulation, while industry specialized in meeting those objectives in a least-cost fashion. If regulator rewards and regulated industry profits were tied to objective output-oriented performance criteria, desirable incentives for minimizing the costs of necessary regulations could be created.

For example, there is a real public interest in safe, reliable, and low-cost electric power. State and federal regulators which oversee the operations of utilities could develop objective standards for measuring utility safety, reliability, and cost efficiency. If firm profit rates were tied to such performance-oriented criteria, real improvements in utility operations could result.

Rationalizing The Regulatory Process

Although some feel there is simply a question of regulation versus deregulation, this is seldom the case. Most often it will prove valuable to consider methods of improving regulation instead of focusing on the perhaps unrealistic no-regulation alternative.

Competitive forces provide a persistent and socially desirable constraining influence on firm behavior. In those instances where the vigorous influences of competition are diminished or absent, government regulation can be justified on the grounds of both efficiency and equity. Where regulation is warranted, business, government, and the public must work together to insure that regulatory processes represent not only large or special interests, but also those with an individually small but collectively large stake in regulatory decisions.

QUESTIONS

12.1 What role does the price elasticity of demand play in determining the effect of operating controls on an industry if these controls lead to increased fixed costs and to increased variable costs?

12.2 It has been suggested that given the difficulties encountered in regulating the various utility industries in the United States, nationalization might lead to a more socially optimal allocation of resources. Do you agree? Why or why not?

12.3 The antitrust statutes in the United States have been used primarily to attack monopolization by big business. Should monopolization of labor supply by giant unions be as vigorously prosecuted?

12.4 Do bigness in business and absence of competition necessarily go hand in hand?

12.5 Do the U.S. antitrust statutes protect competition or competitors? What is the distinction between the two?

12.6 One of the major airlines recently proposed a modified standby fare scheme. A passenger would be able to buy a ticket without a reservation for half-fare but would have to wait until the last minute to board. If he or she were "bumped" (that is, if all seats were reserved and claimed), the passenger would have a guaranteed seat on the next flight.

    a. What are the necessary preconditions for price discrimination?
    b. How are they met (or might they be met) in this case?
    c. In what sense is this scheme *not* price discrimination?

12.7 The Brown Shoe Company was a retailer of shoes, primarily in central-city areas. In 1955, it bought the Kinney Shoe Company, which sold shoes at roadside outlets and in suburban shopping centers. The Justice Department sued to prevent the merger, charging that it substantially lessened competition, in violation of Section 7 of the Clayton Act. Brown lost in the District Court, which held, inter alia, that the Justice Department's depiction of the (horizontal) relevant market was correct. On appeal, the Supreme Court noted:

> *The District Court found that the effects of this aspect of the merger must be analyzed in every city with a population exceeding 10,000 and its immediate contiguous surrounding territory in which both Brown and Kinney sold shoes at retail*

. . . [Brown] claims that such areas should, in some cases, be defined so as to include only the central business districts of large cities, and, in others, so as to encompass the "standard Metropolitan areas" within which smaller communities are found. . . . [370 U.S. 294, 338-39 (1962)]

    a. Why did the company try to define the relevant market in the ways it did?
    b. Why did the government try to define the relevant market the way it did?
    c. Which market structure do you think is more appropriate?

12.8 Explain why state tax rates on personal income vary more on a state-by-state basis than do corresponding rates on corporate income.

12.9 In recent years return on stockholders' equity has averaged between 14½ and 15 percent per year for U.S. industrials. Average returns for stockholders of many bank-holding companies, however, were persistently higher during the 1970s despite the fact that no superior operating efficiency was apparent. This suggests that large bank-holding companies may have enjoyed some market power. During the period in question:

    a. Cite and describe factors that made entry into banking difficult during the 1970s.

    b. In Wisconsin an electronic funds transfer system (TYME—Take Your Money Everywhere) is available to all banks. Large banks may have feared prosecution by the Justice Department if they refused to "deal" with smaller banks wishing to adopt the system. Carefully describe how such a refusal to deal might violate U.S. antitrust law.

    c. Describe the likely effect of changing financial regulation for both the efficiency and profitability of bank-holding companies.

12.10 On January 29, 1973, the federal government charged Xerox Corporation with dominating the office-copier industry by engaging in certain restrictive patent practices while preventing foreign affiliates from competing with it in the United States. In its complaint the government alleged that Xerox—in association with Battelle Memorial Institute, a private research corporation—had created an artificial "patent barrier to competition."

    a. Carefully describe how creation of an artificial patent barrier to competition could directly violate at least *two* distinct antitrust laws.

    b. Describe and defend an appropriate antitrust remedy. In other words, what should the government do?

PROBLEMS

12.1 In a recent hearing before the State Pollution Control Board, members of the Environmental Society argued with representatives of the paper industry over the extent to which the companies should be permitted to discharge wastes into the Neuse

River. The Environmental Society, whose representatives were supported by the Resort Owners League, argued for quite stringent rules, whereas the paper companies sought less severe control regulation and more time in which to implement the rules. The companies were backed by representatives of Greensboro and Smithfield, the two largest towns on the river and both sites of several large paper mills.

There was no argument about the need for *some* controls—everyone agreed that mercury emissions must cease and also that organic wastes should be reduced. The arguments were over the *extent* of controls, with the conservationists calling for a return of the river to its preindustrial state and the companies arguing that such tight controls would cause (1) a severe reduction in production, (2) industry to move to other states with less severe restrictions, and (3) large losses both to stockholders and to property owners in the mill towns. Besides, the companies argued, many other rivers in the state were still unspoiled, and it made good sense to industrialize some areas and keep others pure.

As the hearings progressed, it became clear that insufficient facts were available. The companies suggested that the costs of tight pollution controls would be quite high and would drive industry out. The conservationists argued that the companies were overstating costs and understating the probability that other states would pass similarly tough control laws making it impossible for paper mills to escape pollution control laws by relocating. The companies retorted that if all states passed legislation similar to that backed by the Environmental Society, the companies could not pass their cost increases on to customers because of an elastic demand for paper products and because of foreign imports, especially from Canada.

After several days of emotion-packed debate, the Pollution Control Board adjourned the hearings, commissioned a team of economists and engineers from the state university to develop some facts on the case, and rescheduled the hearings for a later date when this information would be available.

As a result of this analysis, the following data were developed:

1. Demand curve for raw paper facing all U.S. producers (Q in millions of tons):

$$P_A = \$650 - \$10Q.$$

2. Aggregate total and marginal cost curves (ignoring the required return on capital) facing all U.S. producers (dollars in millions, Q in million-unit increments):

$$TC = \$1,800 + \$200Q + \$5Q^2.$$

$$MC = \$200 + \$10Q.$$

3. Total equity investment of all 200 U.S. paper producers: $5 billion. A normal rate of return is 10 percent. The state in question has eight percent of the U.S. paper industry. Assume all firms operate with similar cost functions.

4. Demand curve facing each individual producer:

$$P = \$425 - \$0.0Q.$$

5. Increased operating costs of $1 billion a year, excluding any return on the required new investment, would be required to bring the U.S. paper industry pollution standards up to the level recommended by the Environmental Society.

> **a.** What price/output solution would be reached in the paper industry given the above information?
> **b.** What profits would be earned?
> **c.** Would above-normal or below-normal profits be earned? What would the economic profits amount to?
> **d.** What would happen to the paper industry if the Environmental Society recommendation were adopted nationwide, assuming all data given thus far were valid and the firms all continued to operate?
> **e.** In fact, what would be likely to occur? What assumptions in the data would likely be incorrect, causing the result in Part d *not* to occur?
> **f.** What market structure would you judge the paper industry to have, assuming the facts given above?
> **g.** What would become of the state paper industry if only this one state put in pollution control restrictions? What bearing does this have on federal pollution control legislation?

12.2 Don's Floor Refinishing Service operates in a competitive market where the price per square foot for floor refinishing is $.75. Don's has a crew of 10 experienced floor refinishers working for the company, and he has determined that output could be increased by hiring some unskilled labor to assist his crew. Don's estimates that the marginal product of unskilled labor is $MP = 20 \, (Q_U + Q_S)/Q_U$, where MP = square feet of refinished floor per 8-hour day, Q_U = number of unskilled laborers, and Q_S = skilled floor refinishers. The per square foot marginal cost of floor refinishing before inclusion of the unskilled labor's cost is $.45.

> **a.** Assume that unskilled laborers would be willing to accept employment at Don's at a wage of $2.00 per hour. Determine the impact on employment of a $3.75 per hour minimum wage.
> **b.** A lower minimum wage requirement for teenagers has been proposed as a means of providing more jobs for this group without reducing the income of older workers receiving the standard minimum wage. Would you expect it to be the case that a lower minimum wage for teenagers would expand their employment opportunities without affecting older workers? Explain.

12.3 The Long Beach Telephone Company is currently engaged in a rate case with the regulatory commission under whose jurisdiction it operates. At issue is the annual rate for local telephone service to be charged Long Beach customers. The firm has assets of $3 million, and the utility commission desires that the firm earn a 14 percent return on investment. The demand curve faced by Long Beach is given by:

$$P = \$2000 - 0.06Q$$

and its total cost (excluding capital costs) function is:

$$TC = \$1,200,000 + 150Q.$$

a. Long Beach has requested an annual rate of $215 (or $17.92 per month). What will Long Beach's return on investment be if the commission allows that price?

b. What rate should the commission set if it wishes to limit Long Beach's return on investment to 10 percent?

12.4 Omega Enterprises produces two products in a joint production process. The products are produced in fixed proportions in a $1:1$ ratio. The total cost function for this production process is: $TC = 50 + 2Q + 2Q^2$, where Q is a unit of output consisting of one unit of Product A and one unit of Product B.

a. Assuming that the demand curves for Omega's two products are:

$$P_A = 252 - Q_A$$

and

$$P_B = 100 - 2Q_B,$$

what are the optimal sales quantities and prices for each of these products?

b. Assume now that Omega incurs an added disposal cost of $20Q^*$, where Q^* is the number of units A and/or B manufactured but not sold. What are the optimal sales quantities and product prices under these conditions?

c. Assume now that a fine of $200 for disposal of unsold (dumped) products is imposed on Omega. What are the optimal production and sales quantities for A and B?

12.5 Colorado Coal, Inc., has a number of surface coal mines in western states. The demand function for coal is given by the equation $Q = 5000 - 2P$. CCI's cost function is $TC = 150,000 + 1000Q + 2Q^2$. Q in each equation is measured in hundred tons of coal.

a. Determine CCI's short-run profit maximizing price and output combination.

b. The states in which CCI operates apply a 50 percent profits tax and a $1 per ton extraction tax. The firm has argued that a removal of the extraction tax will result in significant benefit to these states and their citizens. A state legislator has argued that the benefits to the states in terms of increased employment from the higher activity (output) level of CCI's operations without the extraction tax, while quite large (perhaps as great as $20,000), are less than the approximately $30,000 currently being collected by that tax. Hence, this legislator is arguing against providing this tax reduction. Evaluate the legislator's position. Is retention of the tax in the states' best interest? Why or why not? (*Note*: The cost function given above includes the extraction tax but not the profits tax.)

12.6 RCH Nuclear reprocesses radioactive wastes from nuclear power plants. Two joint outputs result from RCH's recycling process, including industrial grade uranium for use in nuclear fuel rods, Q_A, and a waste by-product called radioactive slag, Q_B. There is a market for each output since utilities can readily use reprocessed uranium and specialized firms can further reprocess RCH's radioactive slag. Demand conditions for each product can be described as follows:

$$P_A = 150 - Q_A$$

$$P_B = 5 - 0.2Q_B,$$

where

$$P_A = \text{industrial grade uranium price (in dollars)}$$

$$P_B = \text{radioactive slag price (in dollars)}$$

$$Q_A = \text{industrial grade uranium (in pounds)}$$

$$Q_B = \text{radioactive slag (in pounds)}$$

RCH's recycling process results in Q_A and Q_B production in a $1:4$ ratio. In other words, for every 1 pound of radioactive waste reprocessed, 0.2 pounds of industrial grade uranium are produced and 0.8 pounds of radioactive slag are created. And finally, RCH estimates a marginal cost of $10 per pound for radioactive waste reprocessing.

   a. Calculate optimal production Q_A and Q_B if RCH plans to sell all of its production.

   b. Calculate optimal production and sales of Q_A and Q_B if RCH has the option of not selling (dumping) some of its output.

   c. What pollution tax or disposal cost would make RCH indifferent to selling or dumping excess production?

12.7 Briefly explain:

   a. The causes and consequences of regulation according to the "public interest" theory of regulation.

b. The causes and consequences of regulation according to the "capture" theory of regulation.

c. How the following discussion of gas mileage regulation in the auto industry both supports *and* contradicts the capture theory.

Executives at a smaller U.S. automobile manufacturer admitted in 1980 that they could not finance internally a fuel efficiency conversion program necessary to meet U.S. regulations for 1982. It could cost as much as $6 billion, and "It would take dough that just isn't in the cards for us," said a company spokesman. "We have to find a better way."

Apparently, this manufacturer has staked its future in cars by agreeing to assemble and sell high-mileage cars designed and produced in Europe. But the plan is risky. It anticipates a change in U.S. law that would allow these foreign cars to be included in the corporate average fuel economy (CAFE) rating so that the company's overall fleet could meet a required average of 24 mpg by 1982.

The company lobbied furiously for a change in the rules during 1980. At that time, bills were pending in both houses of Congress that would have allowed the company to include 150,000 foreign cars per year in CAFE figures. The Senate version would have expanded that privilege to all auto makers, but that did not satisfy Detroit's "Big Three." They wanted to include all the cars they sold in computing CAFE, with no import limit and no required percentage of U.S. content. If the smaller auto producer were to win its point in Washington, it could continue to be an exception to hard times in Detroit. The company currently makes an estimated profit of $300 when it sells an imported, fully assembled car. By selling one assembled in the U.S., it could earn roughly twice that.

12.8 On Monday, December 5, 1977, *The Wall Street Journal* carried a short article titled "Detroit's New Drive against Imported Cars To Be an Uphill Battle." The following is an excerpt from that article.

In the West, where Japanese imports are especially popular, the auto makers are pinning their hopes on a new pricing scheme, which puts a lower price tag on their cars. Thus, a two-door Chevette Hatchback will cost $118 less in seven western states than anywhere else in the U.S. Similarly, a Ford Pinto is $122 less than in the rest of the country, and an AMC Gremlin is $120 cheaper.

This two-tier pricing has already raised the ire of some eastern dealers who view it as discriminatory and a violation of antitrust laws.

a. Is this pricing scheme discriminatory in the economic sense? What would be necessary in order for it to be profitable to the auto makers?

b. Carefully describe how price discrimination could violate U.S. antitrust laws, and be sure to mention which laws in particular might be violated.

SELECTED REFERENCES

Armstrong, Alan G. "Consumer Safety and the Regulation of Industry." *Managerial and Decision Economics* 2 (June 1981): 67–73.

Bailey, Elizabeth E. "Contestability and the Design of Regulatory and Antitrust Policy." *American Economic Review* 71 (May 1981): 178–183.

Bator, Francis M. "The Anatomy of Market Failure." *Quarterly Journal of Economics* 72 (August 1958): 351–379.

Baumol, William J. "Contestable Markets: An Uprising in the Theory of Industry Structure." *American Economic Review* 72 (March 1982): 1–15.

Christainsen, Gregory B., and Haveman, Robert H. "Public Regulations and the Slowdown in Productivity Growth." *American Economic Review* 71 (May 1981): 320–325.

Gatti, James F. *The Limits of Government Regulation*. New York: Academic Press, 1981.

Hirschey, Mark. "Incentive Contracting for Railroad Subsidies: A Statistical Approach to Cost Control." *Land Economics* 56 (August 1980): 366–379.

Neale, A. D. *The Antitrust Laws of the U.S.A., A Study of Competition Enforced by Law*. New York: Cambridge University Press, 1970.

Oster, Sharon. "Product Regulations: A Measure of the Benefits." *Journal of Industrial Economics* 29 (June 1981): 395–409.

Peltzman, Sam. "The Gains and Losses from Industrial Concentration." *Journal of Law and Economics* 20 (October 1977): 229–263.

———. "The Effects of FTC Advertising Regulation." *Journal of Law and Economics* 24 (December 1981): 403–448.

Stigler, George J. "The Theory of Economic Regulation." *Bell Journal of Economics and Management Science* 2 (Spring 1971): 3–21.

Stonebraker, Robert J. "Turnover and Mobility among the 100 Largest Firms: An Update." *American Economic Review* 69 (December 1979): 968–971.

Strickland, Allyn D. *Government Regulation and Business*. Boston: Houghton Mifflin, 1981.

Ulen, Thomas S. "The Market for Regulation: The ICC from 1887 to 1920." *American Economic Review* 70 (May 1980): 306–310.

Weidenbaum, Murray L. *Business, Government and the Public*. Englewood Cliffs, N.J.: Prentice-Hall, 1979.

CHAPTER 13

LONG-TERM INVESTMENT DECISIONS: CAPITAL BUDGETING

Management faces two separate but related tasks in working toward its goal of maximizing the value of the firm: (1) It must use existing resources in an optimal manner. (2) It must decide when to increase or reduce the firm's stock of resources. We have not yet explicitly separated these tasks, although our emphasis has been on the first one. Now we explicitly consider the decision to add to the stock of resources, or the decision process known as *capital budgeting*.

Capital budgeting consists of the entire process of planning expenditures whose returns are expected to extend beyond one year. The choice of one year is arbitrary, of course, but it is a convenient cutoff for distinguishing between classes of expenditures. Obvious examples of capital outlays are expenditures for land, buildings, and equipment and for permanent additions to working capital (especially inventories) associated with plant expansion. An advertising or promotion campaign or a program of research and development is also likely to have an impact beyond one year, and hence to come within the classification of capital budgeting expenditures.

In a very real sense capital budgeting integrates and fuses the various elements of the firm. Although the financial manager generally has administrative control of the capital budgeting process, the effectiveness of the process itself is fundamentally dependent on inputs from all major departments. Because a sales forecast is always required, the marketing department has a key role in the process. Because operating costs must be estimated, the accounting, production, engineering, and purchasing departments are involved. The initial outlay, or investment cost, must be estimated; again engineering and purchasing must supply inputs. Funds must be procured to finance the project, and obtaining these funds and estimating their cost are major tasks of the financial manager. Finally, these various estimates must be drawn together in the form of a project evaluation. Although the finance department generally writes up the evaluation report, top management sets the standards of acceptability and ultimately makes the decision to accept or reject the project.

Our first task in this chapter is to describe the mechanics of the capital budgeting process. Then we discuss in some detail the key roles of the marketing, production, and finance departments in the process.

A SIMPLIFIED VIEW OF CAPITAL BUDGETING

Capital budgeting is essentially an application of a classic proposition from the economic theory of the firm; that is, a firm should operate at the point where its marginal revenue is just equal to its marginal cost. When this rule is applied to the capital budgeting decision, marginal revenue is taken to be the rate of return on investments, and marginal cost is the firm's cost of capital.

A simplified version of the concept is depicted in Figure 13.1(a). The horizontal axis measures the dollars of investment during a year; the vertical axis shows both the percentage cost of capital and the rate of return on projects. The projects are denoted by the boxes—Project A, for example, calls for an outlay of $3 million and promises a 17 percent rate of return; Project B requires $1 million and yields about 16 percent; and so on. The last investment, Project E, simply involves buying 9 percent government bonds, which may be purchased in unlimited quantities. In Figure 13.1(b) the concept is generalized to show a smoothed investment opportunity schedule, the curve labeled *IRR*.[1]

The curve *MCC* designates the marginal cost of capital, or the cost of each additional dollar acquired for purposes of making capital expenditures. As it is drawn in Figure 13.1(a), the marginal cost of capital is constant at 10 percent until the firm has raised $8 million, after which the cost of capital begins to rise. To maximize value, the firm should accept Projects A through D, obtaining and investing

---

[1]The investment opportunity schedule measures the yield or rate of return on each project. The rate of return on a project is generally called the *internal rate of return* (*IRR*). This is why we label the investment opportunity schedules *IRR*. The process of calculating the *IRR* is explained later in this chapter.

FIGURE 13.1

Illustrative Capital Budgeting Decision Process

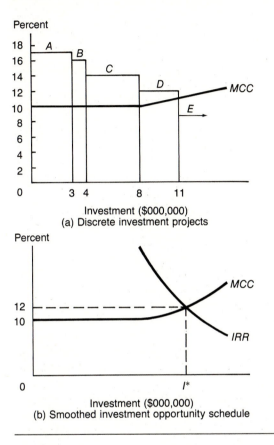

Percent

(a) Discrete investment projects

Investment ($000,000)

Percent

(b) Smoothed investment opportunity schedule

Investment ($000,000)

$11 million, and reject E, the investment in government bonds. The smoothed gen-
eralized curves in Figure 13.1(b) indicate that the firm should invest $I*$ dollars.
Here, the marginal cost of capital, the cost of the last dollar raised, is 12 percent,
the same as the rate on the last project accepted.

At the applied level, the capital budgeting process is much more complex than
the preceding example would suggest. Projects do not just appear. A continuing
stream of good investment opportunities results from hard thinking, careful planning, and, often, large outlays for research and development. In addition, some
very difficult measurement problems are involved—the revenues and costs associated with particular projects must be estimated, frequently for many years into the
future, in the face of great uncertainty. Finally, some difficult conceptual and empirical problems arise over the methods of calculating rates of return and the cost of

capital. Managers are required to take action, however, even in the face of problems such as these, and the capital budgeting procedure described in this chapter is designed to aid in this decision process.

Investment Proposals

The capital budgeting process begins with the generation of ideas—capital investment proposals must be created. This development of investment proposals is no small task. A firm's growth and development, even its ability to remain competitive and to survive, depend upon a constant flow of new investment ideas. Accordingly, a well-managed firm will go to great lengths to develop good capital budgeting proposals. For example, the executive vice president of one major corporation indicated that his company takes the following steps to generate projects:

Our R & D department is constantly searching for new products, or for ways to improve existing products. In addition, our Executive Committee, which consists of senior executives in marketing, production, and finance, identifies the products and markets in which our company will compete, and the Committee sets long-run targets for each division. These targets, which are formalized in the corporate budget, provide a general guide to the operating executives who must meet them. These executives then seek new products, set expansion plans for existing products, and look for ways to reduce production and distribution costs. Since bonuses and promotions are based in large part on each unit's ability to meet or exceed its targets, these economic incentives encourage our operating executives to seek profitable investment opportunities.

While our senior executives are judged and rewarded on the basis of how well their units perform, people further down the line are given bonuses for specific suggestions, including ideas that lead to profitable investments. Additionally, a percentage of our corporate profit is set aside for distribution to nonexecutive employees. Our objective is to encourage lower-level workers to keep on the lookout for good ideas, including those that lead to capital investments.

Project Classification

If the firm has capable and imaginative executives and employees, and if its incentive system is working properly, its personnel will advance many ideas for capital investment. Since only some ideas will be good, project-screening procedures must be established. The first step in this screening process is to assemble a list of the proposed new investments together with the data necessary to evaluate them.

Benefits can be gained from a careful capital expenditure analysis, but such an evaluation is expensive. For certain types of projects, a refined analysis may be warranted; for others, cost/benefit studies will suggest a simpler procedure. Accordingly, firms frequently classify projects into the following categories:

1. *Replacement—Maintenance of Business*: Investments necessary to replace worn-out or damaged equipment.

2. *Replacement—Cost Reduction*: Investments to replace working, but obsolete, equipment.

3. *Expansion of Existing Products or Markets*: Investments to increase output of existing products or to expand outlets or distribution facilities in markets now being served.

4. *Expansion into New Products or Markets*: Investments necessary to produce a new product or to expand into a geographic area not currently served.

5. *Safety and/or Environmental*: Investments necessary to comply with government requirements, labor agreements, or insurance policy terms.

6. *Other*: A catch-all for investments that do not fall in one of the other categories.

Ordinarily, maintenance-type replacement decisions are the simplest to make. Assets wear out and become obsolete, and they must be replaced if production is to continue. The firm has a very good idea of the savings in cost obtained by replacing an old asset, and it knows the consequences of nonreplacement. Relatively simple calculations and only a few supporting documents are required for these investment decisions in profitable plants. More detailed analysis is required for cost reduction replacements, for expansion of existing product lines, and for investments into new products or areas. Also, within each category, projects are broken down by their dollar costs: the larger the required investment, the more detailed the analysis and the higher the level of the officer who must authorize the expenditure. Thus, while a plant manager may be authorized to approve maintenance expenditures up to $10,000 on the basis of a rather unsophisticated analysis, the full board of directors may have to approve decisions which involve amounts over $1 million or expansions into new products or markets. A very detailed, refined analysis will be required to support these latter decisions. Investments in the *safety and/or environmental* and *other* categories are frequently treated separately from the regular capital budget because of the complexities involved in their evaluation.

Estimating Cash Flows

The most important and the most difficult step in capital expenditure proposal analysis is the estimation of cash flows associated with the project—the outflows associ-

TABLE 13.1

Estimated Investment Requirements for Project X

Capital Investment	1983	1984	1985	1986	Total
Capital					
1. Land	$ 0	$ 0	$	$	$ 0
2. Land Improvements	0	0			0
3. Buildings	300,000	790,700			1,090,700
4. Process Equipment	900,000	1,602,000			2,502,000
5. Mobile Equipment	0	175,000			175,000
6. Less: Investment Tax Credit	(90,000)	(177,700)			(267,700)
7. Subtotal	$1,110,000	$2,390,000			$3,500,000
Working Capital					
8. Accounts Receivable	$	$ 652,500	$238,500	$ 86,000	$ 977,000
9. Raw Materials Inventory		107,500	52,500	19,000	179,000
10. Goods in Process		170,000	39,000	47,000	256,000
11. Finished Materials Inventory		232,500	45,500	17,000	295,000
12. Operating Materials and Supplies		140,500	12,000	5,000	157,500
13. Payables/Accruals	( )	(270,000)	(72,500)	(22,000)	(364,500)
14. Net Working Capital	$	$1,033,000	$315,000	$152,000	$1,500,000
Total Investment (lines 7 + 14)					$5,000,000

ated with building and equipping the new facility and the annual cash inflows the project will produce after it goes into operation. A great many variables are involved in the cash flow forecast, and many individuals and departments participate in developing them. We cannot in this book develop fully the techniques and methodologies used in cash flow analysis, but an examination of Tables 13.1 and 13.2 will provide an idea of what is entailed.

Table 13.1 summarizes the outlay required for an investment project which involves construction of a facility to manufacture a new product. A total outlay of $5 million is necessary: $3.5 million for land, buildings, and equipment, and $1.5 million for the net investment in working capital. These expenditures will be incurred over the four-year period from 1983 to 1986. The plant will be constructed and equipped in 1983 and 1984, while working capital will be built up during 1984, 1985, and 1986.

Table 13.2 shows a series of income statements detailing the expected cash flows during certain years of the project's anticipated 15-year life. Sales in both units and dollars are shown, after which the various types of expenses and taxes are deducted to produce the net income expected from the project as shown on the third line from the bottom. These incremental profits are before all financing charges; the cost of the capital used to finance an investment project is accounted for when the cash flows are evaluated. Depreciation, which is not a cash outlay, is added to profits to produce the bottom line figures, the net cash flows from the project.[2]

The new plant will go into service in 1983, and it is expected to generate a net cash flow of $581,564 in that year. Cash flows are expected to climb during the next two years as the plant is broken in and the market developed, but to decline thereafter because of rising taxes caused by declining deductions for depreciation.[3]

Although the estimation of cash flows for capital budgeting analysis is a difficult task, there are a number of key relationships that help insure an appropriate

[2]If the treatment of depreciation is not clear, recognize that net sales represent cash received, and that all expenses *except depreciation* represent cash outlays during the year. Thus, the project is expected to generate cash from net sales of $4,275,000 and to incur cash costs for taxes and all expenses shown except depreciation, so that $4,275,000 cash from net sales, minus cash costs totaling $2,898,000 + $662,500 = $3,560,500, minus $132,936 income taxes, equals $581,564. The $581,564 cash flow is, of course, also equal to net income after taxes plus depreciation.

[3]The firm in our example, like most firms, uses accelerated depreciation for tax calculations. This causes depreciation charges (a noncash expense) to be high early in the project's life and lower later on. The high initial depreciation results in lower tax payments, hence higher cash flows during the early years.

Two other points are worth mentioning here. First, the question of what happens to the cash flows shown at the bottom of Table 13.2 can be raised. The answer is that they are available for payment of dividends and interest on capital and for reinvestment in other projects. The second point has to do with the recovery of working capital. Some amount of working capital—cash, receivables, inventories, less trade credit (accounts payable) and other accruals—must be held to support sales. In the example, $1.5 million is the investment in working capital, and this investment must be maintained as long as the operations continue. Thus the $1.5 million will be needed until 1998, the year the project is expected to end. As operations are phased out during that year, inventories will be worked down; receivables will be collected with no new ones created because sales will cease; and the cash balances to operate the plant will no longer be needed. Thus, during 1998 the $1.5 million of working capital will be recovered and presumably paid to providers of capital (debt and equity) or reinvested elsewhere in the company.

TABLE 13.2

Cash Flow Analysis for Project X

			Estimated Profits and Cash Flows				
	1984	1985	1986	1987		1997	1998
Quantity Shipped, Tons	75,000	90,000	100,000	100,000	Years 1988 through 1996 not shown here	100,000	100,000
Gross Sales, Dollars	$4,336,000	$5,203,000	$5,781,000	$5,781,000		$5,781,000	$5,781,000
Less: Freight	(44,000)	(52,000)	(58,000)	(58,000)		(58,000)	(58,000)
Cash Discounts	(17,000)	(21,000)	(23,000)	(23,000)		(23,000)	(23,000)
Total Deductions	(61,000)	(73,000)	(81,000)	(81,000)		(81,000)	(81,000)
Net Sales	$4,275,000	$5,130,000	$5,700,000	$5,700,000		$5,700,000	$5,700,000
Cost of Sales							
Variable	$2,223,000	$2,736,000	$3,078,000	$3,078,000		$3,078,000	$3,078,000
Fixed, Excluding Depreciation and Depletion	342,000	342,000	342,000	342,000		342,000	342,000
Break-in Costs	333,000	137,000	—	—		—	—
Total	2,898,000	3,215,000	3,420,000	3,420,000		3,420,000	3,420,000
Depreciation	437,550	408,380	379,210	350,040		58,290	29,120
Total Cost of Sales	$3,335,550	$3,623,380	$3,799,210	$3,770,040		$3,478,290	$3,449,120
Gross Profit	$1,939,450	$1,506,620	$1,904,790	$1,930,960		$2,222,710	$2,251,880

Selling Expenses	228,000	228,000	228,000	228,000	228,000	228,000
Advertising	124,000	100,000	86,000	86,000	86,000	86,000
Administrative	285,000	285,000	285,000	285,000	285,000	285,000
Provision for Bad Debts	25,500	29,800	32,600	32,600	32,600	32,600
Total: Selling and Administrative	662,500	642,800	631,600	631,600	631,600	631,600
Net Income before Tax	276,950	863,820	1,273,190	1,299,360	1,591,110	1,620,280
Income Tax @ 48%	132,936	414,634	611,131	623,693	763,733	777,734
Net Income	144,014	449,186	662,059	675,667	827,377	842,546
Depreciation	437,550	408,380	379,210	350,040	58,290	29,120
Net Cash Flow	$ 581,564	$ 857,566	$1,041,269	$1,025,707	$ 885,667	$ 871,666

Salvage Value, Buildings and Machines = 0
Recovery of Working Capital = $1,500,000
Net Cash Flow, Year 15 = $2,371,666

effort in this area of the capital budgeting process. First, cash flows must be constructed on an incremental basis. Only cash flows that will differ with or without acceptance of the project are relevant for inclusion in the analysis. Second, care must be taken to include *all* incremental cash flows, including revenue and cost changes for other activities of the firm that are affected by a particular capital investment. The impact of a new product on the sales revenue of an existing product is an example of a frequently important indirect cash flow. Third, cash flows should be constructed on an aftertax basis. Fourth, depreciation should not be included in the relevant cash flows—except to account for its impact on taxes—as it is a noncash expense.

EVALUATING PROPOSED PROJECTS

Once cash flow estimates for a proposed investment have been generated, an evaluation must be performed to determine the worth of the project to the firm.[4] Although a number of different methods are used to rank projects and decide whether they should be accepted, the economically sound approaches are all based on the discounted present value concept.[5] We can see this by noting that capital investment analysis is essentially an application of the basic valuation model introduced in Chapter 1.

$$\text{Value} = \sum_{t=1}^{n} \frac{\text{Total Revenue}_t - \text{Total Cost}_t}{(1+k)^t} = \sum_{t=1}^{n} \frac{\text{Net Cash Flow}_t}{(1+k)^t}. \quad \textbf{(13.1)}$$

Equation 13.1 was developed earlier in the text to apply to the entire firm. In this equation Net Cash Flow$_t$ represents the firm's total after-tax profit plus noncash expenses such as depreciation; and k, which is based on an appraisal of the firm's overall riskiness, represents the average cost of capital to the firm.[6]

[4] A knowledge of compound interest is necessary for an understanding of this evaluation. Students who have not covered compound interest in other courses or who could use a review should read through the relevant sections of Appendix A.

[5] Other evaluation methods, generally shortcut or rule-of-thumb techniques designed to simplify the capital budgeting process, include payback and accounting, or average rate of return. Under certain conditions these techniques result in reasonably good evaluations in the sense that they lead to the same accept-reject decisions as the discounted present value method. However, these shortcut procedures have severe shortcomings and cannot in general be expected to provide a sound basis for project evaluation and selection. For a detailed discussion of these methods for evaluating capital investment proposals, see an introductory corporation finance textbook such as E. F. Brigham, *Financial Management: Theory and Practice*, 3d ed. (Hinsdale, Ill.: The Dryden Press, 1982).

[6] In order to avoid unnecessary complications that might hinder an understanding of the fundamental elements of capital budgeting, we shall generally assume in this chapter (1) that all sales are for cash and (2) that all costs except depreciation are cash expenses. This permits us to abstract from a myriad of accounting details and to concentrate on the basic elements of capital budgeting theory.

The Net Present Value Technique

When the present value model is used in capital budgeting, it is applied to a single project rather than to the firm as a whole.[7] In brief, the procedure is as described below:

1. Estimate the expected net cash flows from the project. Depending on the nature of the project, these estimates will have a greater or lesser degree of riskiness. For example, the benefits from replacing a piece of equipment used to produce a stable, established product can be estimated more accurately than those from an investment in equipment to produce a new and untried product.

2. Estimate the expected cost, or investment outlay, of the project. This cost estimate will be quite accurate for purchased equipment since cost is equal to the invoice price plus delivery and installation charges; but cost estimates for other kinds of projects may be highly uncertain or speculative. To illustrate, in 1968 Rolls-Royce estimated that it could develop a jet engine for a new aircraft at a cost of about $156 million and signed a contract to develop the engine. By 1970 the company had spent in excess of the original estimate and made a new cost projection of $324 million. In 1971 the estimated cost of development was increased once again to $600 million before the company went bankrupt, with the engine still far from completion.

3. Determine an appropriate discount rate, or cost of capital, for the project. The cost of capital is considered in detail later in this chapter, but for now it may be thought of as being determined by the riskiness of the project; that is, by the uncertainty of the expected cash flows and the investment outlay.

4. Find the present value of the expected cash flows and subtract from this figure the estimated cost of the project.[8] The resulting figure is defined as the net present value (*NPV*) of the project. If the *NPV* is greater than zero, the project should be accepted; if it is less than zero, the project should be rejected. In equation form:

$$NPV_i = \sum_{t=1}^{n} \frac{R_{it}}{(1 + k_i)^t} - C_i, \qquad (13.2)$$

---

[7] Note that a project can consist of a single asset such as a truck, a group of similar assets such as a new fleet of trucks, or a group of dissimilar assets which are used in concert and are therefore evaluated as a single project. An example of the last group is a proposal to invest in a fleet of trucks, a warehouse, and a maintenance shop—all for the purpose of establishing an in-house delivery system as a replacement for a contract delivery service presently being used.

[8] If costs are spread over several years, this fact must be taken into account. Suppose, for example, that a firm bought land in 1983, erected a building in 1984, installed equipment in 1985, and started production in 1986. One could treat 1983 as the base year, comparing the present value of the costs as of 1983 to the present value of the benefit stream as of that same date. For ease in exposition we shall assume in this chapter that all costs are incurred immediately and that profits occur annually at the end of each future year.

where NPV_i is the NPV of the ith project, R_{it} represents the expected net cash flows of the ith project in the tth year, k_i is the risk-adjusted discount rate applicable to the ith project, and C_i is the project's investment outlay, or cost.[9]

NPV as an Application of Marginal Analysis

To see that this procedure of accepting only investment projects for which the net present value is positive is in fact an application of the marginal analysis illustrated in Figure 13.1, consider briefly the determination of the yield or internal rate of return on an investment. The *internal rate of return* is defined as that interest or discount rate which equates the present value of the future receipts of a project to the initial cost or outlay. The equation for calculating the internal rate of return is simply the NPV formula set equal to zero. That is:

$$NPV_i = \sum_{t=1}^{n} \frac{R_{it}}{(1 + k_i^*)^t} - C_i = 0. \tag{13.3}$$

Here the equation is solved for the discount rate, k_i^*, which produces a zero net present value or which causes the sum of the discounted future receipts to equal the initial cost. That discount rate is the internal rate of return earned by the project.

Because the net present value equation is a complex polynomial, it is extremely difficult to actually solve for the internal rate of return on an investment. For this reason a trial-and-error method is typically employed. One begins by arbitrarily selecting a discount rate with which to calculate the net present value of the project. If the NPV is positive, then the internal rate of return must be greater than the interest or discount rate used, and another *higher* rate would be tried. Similarly, if the NPV is negative, this implies that the internal rate of return on the project is lower than the discount rate, and the NPV calculation must be repeated, using a lower discount rate. This process of changing the discount rate and recalculating the net present value is continued until the discounted present value of the future cash flows is approximately equal to the initial cost. The interest rate that brings about this equality is the yield, or internal, rate of return on the project.[10]

Now consider again the decision rule, which states that a firm should accept only projects whose net present values are positive when the firm's risk-adjusted

[9] If the cost of capital is expected to vary over time, this fact could be taken into account by designating k_{it} as the cost of capital for the ith project in the tth year.

[10] This trial-and-error procedure is a bit tedious if done by hand for a project that extends over a long time horizon. Computers, however (and even some of the more powerful hand-held calculators), can evaluate numerous trial discount rates very rapidly, and thus the computational side of calculating internal rates of return presents no difficulty for capital budgeting analysis.

cost of capital, k_i, is used as the discount rate. In this model, k_i, the risk-adjusted discount factor, is the firm's marginal cost of capital and is, therefore, the rate of interest that must be paid on the funds invested in a project. As we have seen from the discussion of the calculation of internal rates of return or yields on an investment, if the net present value of a project, calculated using the firm's cost of capital as the discount rate, is positive, this implies that the rate of return on the project is greater than the cost of capital. Likewise, if the *NPV* is negative, the implication is that the internal rate of return is less than the cost of capital. Thus it is clear that the *NPV* decision technique, which limits acceptable projects to those whose net present values, using k_i as the discount rate, are positive, is one based essentially on a comparison of the marginal cost of capital and the marginal yield, or return, on the investment.

Illustration of the *NPV* Technique

To illustrate the *NPV* evaluation technique, assume that a firm has two investment opportunities, each costing \$1,000 and each having the expected profits shown in Table 13.3.

Let us further assume that the cost of each project is known with certainty, but the expected cash flows of Project B are riskier than are those of Project A. After giving due consideration to the risks inherent in each project, management has determined that A should be evaluated with a 10 percent cost of capital, with a 15 percent cost of capital for the riskier Project B.

Equation 13.2 can be restated as Equation 13.3, using Project A as an example:

$$NPV_A = \sum_{t=1}^{n} \frac{R_{At}}{(1 + k_A)^t} - C_A \tag{13.3}$$

$$= \left[\frac{R_{A1}}{(1 + k_A)^1} + \frac{R_{A2}}{(1 + k_A)^2} + \frac{R_{A3}}{(1 + k_A)^3} + \frac{R_{A4}}{(1 + k_A)^4} \right] - C_A$$

$$= \left[(R_{A1}) \left(\frac{1}{1 + k_A} \right)^1 + (R_{A2}) \left(\frac{1}{1 + k_A} \right)^2 + (R_{A3}) \left(\frac{1}{1 + k_A} \right)^3 \right.$$

$$\left. + (R_{A4}) \left(\frac{1}{1 + k_A} \right)^4 \right] - C_A$$

$$= [R_{A1} (PVIF_{A1}) + R_{A2} (PVIF_{A2}) + R_{A3} (PVIF_{A3}) + R_{A4} (PVIF_{A4})] - C_A.$$

Values for the interest factors, the *PVIF* terms, are found in Appendix C. For example, $PVIF_{A1}$, the interest factor for the present value of \$1 due in one year dis-

TABLE 13.3

Expected Cash Flows from Projects A and B

Year	A	B
1	$500	$200
2	400	400
3	300	500
4	100	600

TABLE 13.4

Calculating the Net Present Value (*NPV*) of Projects with $1,000 Cost

	Project A				Project B		
Year	Cash Flow	PVIF (10%)	PV of Cash Flow	Year	Cash Flow	PVIF (15%)	PV of Cash Flow
1	$500	0.91	$ 455	1	$200	0.87	$ 174
2	400	0.83	332	2	400	0.76	304
3	300	0.75	225	3	500	0.66	330
4	100	0.68	68	4	600	0.57	342
	PV		$1,080		PV		$1,150
	Less Cost		−1,000		Less Cost		−1,000
	NPV_A		$ 80		NPV_B		$ 150

counted at a 10 percent rate, is 0.909; $PVIF_{A2}$, the interest factor for the present value of $1 received in two years discounted at a 10 percent rate, is 0.826; and so on.

Equation 13.3 for both projects is given in tabular form in Table 13.4. Project A's *NPV* is $80 and Project B's is $150. Since both projects have positive *NPV*s, both earn a rate of return in excess of their costs of capital—the marginal rate of return is greater than the marginal cost of capital, in the sense of Figure 13.1. If the two projects are independent, they should both be accepted, because each adds more to the value of the firm than its cost: Project A increases the value of the firm by $80 over what it would be if the project is not accepted; Project B increases the firm's value by $150. If the projects are mutually exclusive, B should be selected, because it adds more to the firm's value than does A.[11]

---

[11] Some firms use the internal rate of return (*IRR*) approach for selecting capital investment projects rather than the *NPV* method. Under the *IRR* criterion, projects are ranked according to their *IRR*; and projects whose *IRR* exceeds the appropriate risk-adjusted discount rate (cost of capital) are accepted. Although the *IRR* and *NPV* methods will lead to the same accept-reject decisions for an individual project, they can provide contradictory signals concerning the choice

OTHER ISSUES IN PROJECT EVALUATION

Ordinarily, firms operate as illustrated in Figure 13.1; that is, they take on investments to the point where the marginal returns from investment are just equal to their marginal cost of capital. For firms operating in this way the decision process is as described above—they make investments having positive net present values, reject those whose net present values are negative, and choose between mutually exclusive investments on the basis of the higher net present value. For many capital budgeting problems, however, the use of the *NPV* concept for analyzing capital budgeting decisions is far more complex than the illustration suggests. For example, the capital budgeting problem may require analysis of mutually exclusive projects with different expected lives or with substantially different initial costs. When these conditions exist, the net present value criterion as discussed above may not result in the selection of projects that maximize the value of the firm.

A similar complication arises when the firm sets an absolute limit on the size of its capital budget that is less than the level of investment that would be undertaken on the basis of the criteria described above. The rationale behind such *capital rationing*, as it is called, stems from a number of factors. First, it is sometimes a fallacy to consider that what is true of the individual parts will be true of the whole. Although individual projects appear to promise a relatively attractive yield, when they are taken together unforeseen difficulties can prevent the achievement of all the favorable results. One problem is that other firms in the same industry may engage in similar capital expenditure programs in attempts to increase their capacity or, by cost and price reductions, to obtain larger shares of the product market. For a given growth rate in the industry, it is obviously impossible for every firm to obtain increases in sales that would fully utilize all the capital expenditure projects being undertaken.

A second problem is that, although individual projects promise favorable yields, to undertake a large number of projects simultaneously might involve a very high rate of expansion by the individual firm. Such substantial additional personnel requirements and organizational problems may be involved that overall rates of return will be diminished. Top management, at some point in the capital budgeting process, must therefore make a decision regarding the total volume of favorable projects that may be successfully undertaken without causing a significant reduction in the prospective returns from individual projects.

A third reason for limiting the capital budget, and one that perhaps better meets

---

between mutually exclusive projects. That is, one project can have a higher *IRR* but lower *NPV* when discounted at the firm's cost of capital. This problem arises because the *IRR* is the implied reinvestment rate for cash flows under the *IRR* method while the discount rate used in the *NPV* model is the implicit reinvestment rate with that methodology. In most situations the reinvestment of cash flows at a rate close to the cost of capital is more realistic; therefore, the *NPV* method is generally superior. A further discussion of the difference between the reinvestment rate assumptions is found in Brigham, *Financial Management: Theory and Practice*, 3d ed.

the strict definition of capital rationing, is the reluctance of some managements to engage in external financing (borrowing or selling stock). One management, recalling the plight of firms with substantial amounts of debt in the 1930s, may simply refuse to use debt. Another management, which has no objection to selling debt, may not wish to sell equity capital for fear of losing some measure of voting control. Still others may refuse to use any form of outside financing, considering safety and control to be more important than additional profits. These are all cases of capital rationing, and they result in limiting the rate of expansion to a slower pace than would be dictated by purely wealth maximizing behavior.

Under conditions of capital rationing, the net present value criterion may again give a ranking of projects that does not maximize the value of the firm. Further, when the possibility that investment opportunities in the future may provide substantially better (or worse) returns than those available today is coupled with capital rationing, the capital budgeting process is complicated even further. Complication arises because the reinvestment of cash flows from current projects is dependent on investment opportunities that become available over their lives.[12]

Mathematical Programming Approaches to Project Evaluation

Correct capital budgeting decisions under the more complex conditions cited above require that the net present value concept be expanded through a mathematical programming approach. As a first step in examining such a programming method, consider a procedure that can at least conceptually improve our decision in the capital rationing case. Figure 13.2 gives a matrix of investments in alternative projects, as well as cash flows from the projects. The values in the cells of the matrix are the net cash flows attributable to the Projects A, B, . . . Z over Years 1, 2, . . . n. The rows of the matrix thus represent the investment opportunities available during the relevant time horizon, and the columns represent the net cash flows from all projects during a given year. The cash flows in a particular cell can be either positive or negative. A negative cash flow represents an investment; a positive cash flow represents the benefits resulting from the investment.

Figure 13.2 simply describes the investment opportunities open to the firm— the capital projects it can take on. If no capital rationing is imposed, the firm will be able to take on all economically desirable projects. If it is further assumed that the cost of capital is constant, the straightforward *NPV* method can be used to determine which of the available projects should be accepted in each year. The whole concept of Figure 13.2 is totally unnecessary in this case.

Suppose, however, that the firm is subject to capital rationing. Specifically, assume that it has an initial amount of money available for investment at the beginning

---

[12]The *NPV* criterion assumes implicitly that these cash flows are reinvested at the cost of capital, an assumption that is clearly inappropriate when capital rationing prevents the firm from investing up to the point at which the internal rate of return, or yield on investment, is just equal to the marginal cost of capital.

FIGURE 13.2

Matrix of Future Investment Opportunities

Years

Projects	1	2	3	4	5	6	7	8	9	10	11	12	13	14	15
A	R_{a1}	R_{a2}	R_{a3}												
B	R_{b1}	R_{b2}	R_{b3}	R_{b4}											
C	R_{c1}	R_{c2}	R_{c3}	R_{c4}	R_{c5}	R_{c6}	R_{c7}								
D		R_{d2}	R_{d3}	R_{d4}	R_{d5}	R_{d6}	$\rightarrow$								
E		R_{e2}	R_{e3}	...											
F		R_{f2}	R_{f3}	...											
G		R_{g2}	R_{g3}	...											
H			R_{h3}	...											
I			R_{i3}	...											
J			R_{j3}	...											
K				R_{k4}	...										
L				R_{l4}	...										
M				R_{m4}	...										
N					R_{n5}										
O					R_{o5}										
P					R_{p5}										
					$\vdots$										

of Year 1. It can invest this amount but no more. Further assume that the funds available for investment in future years must come from cash generated by past investments. The funds available for investment in Year 2 will therefore depend on the set of investments chosen in Year 1; investment funds available in Year 3 will depend on cash throw-off from investments in Years 1 and 2; and so the process continues.

If the projects available for investment in Year 2 are more profitable than those available in Year 1—that is, if they have higher internal rates of return—the firm should perhaps select investments in Year 1 that will have fast paybacks, making funds available for the profitable investment opportunities in Year 2. This is, however, only an approximation. Conceptually, the firm should select its investments in each year (subject to the capital rationing constraint) so as to maximize the net present value of all future cash flows. These cash flows should be discounted at the firm's cost of capital.[13]

If the investment opportunities are infinitely divisible—for example, if the investment opportunities are securities such as stocks or bonds that could be pur-

---

[13] Actually, all projects should be discounted at an appropriate risk-adjusted discount rate if they vary in riskiness.

chased in larger or smaller quantities—the firm could use linear programming to determine the optimal set of investment opportunities. If such opportunities are not infinitely divisible—and in capital budgeting they often are not—a more complex procedure known as *integer programming* must be used to find the optimum investment strategy.[14] Regardless of the computational process used to solve the problem, the firm should seek the set of investment opportunities that maximizes the *NPV* of the firm as a whole without exceeding the capital rationing constraint.

The mathematical programming approach can also handle the difficulties that arise because of interdependence between capital budgeting projects. For example, the program can be structured to insure that only one of a set of mutually exclusive projects is included in the final capital budget selection. This is done by adding a constraint equation to the problem that limits the total selection from those mutually exclusive projects to no more than one.[15]

Likewise, the selection of projects whose inclusion in the capital budget is dependent on selection of a second project can also be handled within a mathematical programming approach. An investment in jet engine maintenance equipment by an airline that is considering investing in its first jet aircraft is an example of such a project. The firm can invest in the maintenance equipment and perform its own engine maintenance, or it can contract with an outside concern for engine upkeep. The choice between these two alternatives is dependent on a number of factors, including their relative costs and the availability of other uses for investment funds. It is also totally dependent on a decision to purchase jet aircraft, because without them the maintenance equipment would be of little value to the airline. A constraint equation in the programming model can insure that the maintenance equipment investment is accepted only if jet aircraft are also included in the capital budget.[16]

In summary, the mathematical programming extension of the *NPV* provides a conceptual capital budgeting model that allows a firm to explicitly take into account the many complexities that can arise in actual investment decision problems. Its implementation in real-world capital budgeting processes has been limited in the past because of limitations on input information and computational difficulties. These problems are being rapidly overcome as management information systems are developed to improve the informational flow for managerial decision making and as computer technology advances, thus making the complex analysis practicable. The programming approach to capital budgeting is likely to become an important management decision tool in the near future.

---

[14]H. Martin Weingartner—in *Mathematical Programming and the Analysis of Capital Budgeting Problems* (Englewood Cliffs, N.J.: Prentice-Hall, 1963)—has shown how integer programming can be used in capital budgeting decisions. To this point, however, information and computer processing requirements have limited the use of the approach on real-world capital budgeting problems.

[15]It is possible that none of those projects would be included in the optimal package of investments.

[16]This does not mean that the engine maintenance equipment will be automatically included if the jets are selected; it merely means that without the jets the maintenance equipment investment will be ruled out.

STEPS IN THE CAPITAL BUDGETING PROCESS

The information requirements referred to above indicate that the complexity of the capital budgeting decision extends far beyond the mechanical process required to evaluate investment alternatives. In fact, almost all the topics covered in this book must be brought to bear on important capital budgeting decisions. Demand functions, production functions, and cost functions must all be estimated and analyzed. Market structures may have to be appraised, both for use in determining how competitors are likely to react to major decisions and for the antitrust implications of particular courses of action; antitrust analysis is especially important if the action involves an investment in another firm or a joint venture with another company. Regulated firms are subject to special problems in their long-term investment programs, and almost all manufacturing companies are undergoing appraisals of the costs of and benefits accruing from investments in pollution-control equipment.

Demand Forecasts

The first step in most capital budgeting decisions is to make an estimate of future demand. The need for this step is obvious in expansion decisions, but it is also a vital part of replacement, modernization, and pollution-control investments. A worn-out machine should not be replaced unless demand for its output will continue for some time into the future; a plant should be closed rather than equipped with pollution-control equipment if demand for the plant's output is weak.

Cost Forecasts

Once the demand function has been estimated, the next step is to determine the operating cost function. This procedure frequently involves a knowledge of production theory, input factor markets, and statistical cost estimation. And, although we do not take up these considerations in this chapter, accurate cost analysis is also heavily dependent on such accounting-based topics as depreciation, inventory valuation procedures, and tax considerations.

Cash Flow Forecasts

The third step in the process is to integrate the demand and cost relationships in order to determine the optimal output level and the expected annual cash flows resulting from operation at this output. Many firms have set up systems to generate the data necessary for thorough analyses of options, and many of them construct simulation models, with demand and cost functions as key components, to appraise major investment proposals.

Cost of Capital

Determining the firm's cost of capital for use as the appropriate discount rate is an essential part of the capital budgeting process. The cost of capital is a complex subject, which is discussed in detail in finance courses, and a thorough treatment of the topic is beyond the scope of this book. Accordingly, we shall merely summarize some of the important elements of the cost of capital theory as it is developed in finance.

Firms raise funds in the form of long-term and short-term debt, the sale of preferred stock, the sale of common stock, and by retaining earnings.[17] Each source of funds has a cost, and these costs are the basic inputs in the cost of capital determination.

Capital is a necessary factor of production, and like any other factor, it has a cost. The cost of each type of capital employed by the firm is defined as the *component cost* of that particular capital. For example, if a firm can borrow money at a 14 percent interest rate, the component cost of debt is defined as 14 percent. Although firms obtain capital funds through the use of many financial instruments, we concentrate on debt and equity capital components in this discussion of capital costs. These are the major capital resource categories, and limiting our discussion to them will enable us to examine the basic cost-of-capital concept without getting mired down in too much financial, accounting, and legal detail.

Cost of Debt. The component cost of debt is based on the interest rate investors require on debt issues, adjusted for taxes. If a firm borrows $100,000 for one year at 14 percent interest, its before-tax dollar cost is $14,000, and its before-tax percentage cost is 14 percent. However, interest payments on debt are deductible for income tax purposes. It is necessary to account for this tax deductibility by adjusting the cost of debt to an after-tax basis. The deductibility of interest payments means, in effect, that the government pays part of a firm's interest charges. This reduces the cost of debt capital as follows:

After-Tax Component Cost of Debt = (Interest Rate) × (1.0 − Tax Rate).

Assuming that the firm's marginal tax rate is 50 percent, the after-tax cost of debt will be one-half the interest rate.

Note that the cost of debt is applicable only to *new* debt, not to the interest on old, previously outstanding debt. In other words, we are interested in the cost of new debt, or the *marginal cost of debt*. The primary concern with the cost of capital is to use it in a decision making process—the decision being whether to obtain capi-

---

[17] Funds are also obtained by sales of convertibles and warrants, by leasing, from government agencies, and so on.

tal to make new investments. The fact that the firm borrowed at high or low rates in the past is irrelevant.[18]

Cost of Equity. The *component cost of equity* is defined as the rate of return stockholders require on the common stock of a firm. Because dividends paid to stockholders are not deductible as a business expense for income tax purposes (dividend payments must be made with after-tax dollars), there is no tax adjustment for the component cost of equity capital.

Although empirical estimation of the cost of equity capital is a complex and often difficult process, most methods employed in this effort are based on one of two relatively simple concepts. The first of these is to recognize that the cost of capital of a risky security such as a common stock consists of a riskless rate of return (R_F) plus a risk premium (P):

$$k = R_F + P.$$

The risk-free return is typically taken to be the interest rate on U.S. government securities. Various procedures are available for estimating P for different securities.

One frequently encountered procedure involves adding a premium of about four to five percentage points to the interest rate on a firm's long-term bonds so that the total risk premium on equity is equal to the difference between the yield on the firm's debt and that on government bonds *plus* four to five percentage points. For example, if government bonds are priced to yield 12 percent and the bonds of a firm yield 14 percent, then Cost of Equity, k_e, would be estimated as:

$$k_e = \text{Bond Rate} + 4\% \text{ to } 5\% \text{ Risk Premium}$$

$$= 14\% + 4\% \text{ to } 5\% = 18\% \text{ to } 19\%.$$

Since

$$k_e = R_F + P,$$

where R_F = Yield on Government Bonds = 12 percent

$$18\% \text{ to } 19\% = 12\% + P$$

$$P = 6\% \text{ to } 7\%.$$

---

[18]The fact that the firm borrowed at high or low rates in the past is obviously important in terms of the effect of the interest charges on current profits, but this past decision is not relevant for current decisions. For current financial decisions, only current interest rates are relevant.

Analysts who use this procedure generally cite studies of historical returns on stocks and bonds and use the difference between the average yield (dividends plus capital gains) on stocks and the average yield on bonds as the risk premium of stocks over bonds. The primary difficulties with using historical returns to estimate risk premiums are that (1) historical returns differ depending on the beginning and ending dates used to estimate them and (2) there is no reason to think that past differences in stock and bond yields precisely indicate future required risk premiums.

A second procedure for estimating P is based on a construct known as the Capital Asset Pricing Model (CAPM). This approach assumes that the risk of a stock is based on the sensitivity of its return to changes in the level of return on all securities in the market.

To use this procedure for estimating the required return on a stock we proceed as follows:

Step 1 Estimate the riskless rate, R_F, generally taken to be the U.S. Treasury bond rate.

Step 2 Estimate the stock's risk by calculating the variability of its return relative to variability of return on the capital market as a whole. This risk index, known as the stock's beta coefficient, b, is a measure of the risk of one security relative to the average risk on the market, or average, stock. Thus, a stock with average risk will have a beta of 1.0; low-risk stocks will have betas less than 1.0; and high-risk stocks will have betas greater than 1.0.[19]

Step 3 Estimate the rate of return on the market, or average, stock. This return, K_M, provides a benchmark for determining how investors are pricing risk as measured by the betas of individual stocks.

Step 4 Estimate the required rate of return on the firm's stock as:

$$K_e = R_F + b(K_M - R_F).$$

The value $(K_M - R_F)$ is the risk premium on the average stock. (Recall that the average stock has a beta of 1.0.) Multiplying this price of risk by the index of risk for a particular stock, b, gives us the risk premium for that stock. To illustrate, assume that $R_F = 9\%$, $K_M = 13\%$, and $b = 0.8$ for a given stock. The stock's required return is calculated as follows:

$$k_e = 9 + 0.8(13 - 9) = 9 + 3.2 = 12.2\%.$$

---

[19]Estimation of betas is a complex task involving regressing of returns for a stock on the average return to all securities. Securities analysts and investment advisory services publish estimates of betas that can be used for estimating equity capital costs.

Had b been 1.7, indicating that the stock was more risky than the average security, k_e would have been estimated as

$$k_e = 9 + 1.7(13 - 9) = 9 + 6.8 = 15.8\%.$$

Yet another procedure for determining the cost of equity is to estimate the basic required rate of return as:[20]

$$\text{Rate of Return} = \frac{\text{Dividends}}{\text{Price}} + \text{Expected Growth Rate}$$

$$k = \frac{D}{P} + g.$$

The rationale for this equation is that stockholder returns are derived from dividends and capital gains. If past growth rates in earnings and dividends have been relatively stable, and if investors appear to be projecting a continuation of past trends, then g may be based on the firm's historic growth rate. However, if the company's growth has been abnormally high or low, either because of its own unique situation or because of general economic conditions, then investors will not project the past growth rate into the future. In this case, g must be estimated in some other manner. Security analysts regularly make earnings growth forecasts, looking at such factors as projected sales, profit margins, and competitive factors. Someone making a cost of capital estimate can obtain such analysts' forecasts and use them as a proxy for the growth expectations of investors in general, then combine g with the expected dividend yield, to estimate k_e as

$$k_e = \frac{D}{P} + \text{Growth Rate as Projected by Security Analysts.}$$

In practical work it is best to use all the methods described above and then apply judgment when the methods produce different results. People experienced in estimating equity capital costs recognize that both careful analysis and some very fine judgments are required.

Weighted Cost of Capital. Suppose a particular firm's after-tax cost of debt is estimated to be 6 percent (the interest rate on new debt issues is 12 percent and the firm's marginal income tax rate is 50 percent); its cost of equity is estimated to be 15 percent; and the decision has been made to finance next year's projects by selling

---

[20]The growth rate here is the growth in the price of the firm's stock, but if the dividend payout rate is constant, and if the dividend capitalization rate (k) remains unchanged, earnings, dividends, and the stock price all grow at the same rate.

debt. The argument is sometimes advanced that the cost of these projects is 6 percent, because debt will be used to finance them.

This position contains a basic fallacy. To finance a particular set of projects with debt implies that the firm is also using up some of its potential for obtaining new low-cost debt. As expansion takes place in subsequent years, at some point the firm will find it necessary to use additional equity financing or else the debt ratio will become too large. In other words, the interest rate or component cost on debt is not the firm's true opportunity cost of this kind of capital.

To illustrate, suppose the firm has a 6 percent cost of debt and a 15 percent cost of equity. In the first year it borrows heavily, using up its debt capacity in the process, to finance projects yielding 7 percent. In the second year it has projects available that yield 13 percent, almost twice the return on first-year projects, but it cannot accept them because they would have to be financed with 15 percent equity money. To avoid this problem the firm should be viewed as an ongoing concern, and its cost of capital should be calculated as a weighted average of the various types of funds it uses. The proper set of weights to be employed in computing the weighted average cost of capital is determined by the optimal financial structure of the firm.

In general, the risk to investors is lower on debt and higher on common stock; because of risk aversion, therefore, debt is the lowest-cost source of funds and equity the highest-cost source. Risk increases as the percentage of total capital obtained in the form of debt increases, since the higher the debt level, the greater the probability that adverse conditions will lower earnings to the point where the firm is unable to pay its interest charges and to pay off debt issues as they mature. The fact that interest rates on debt are lower than the expected rate of return (dividends plus capital gains) on common stock causes the overall, or average, cost of capital to the firm to decline as the percentage of capital raised as debt increases. However, the fact that more debt means higher risk offsets this effect to some extent. As a result, it is generally felt that the average cost of capital (1) declines at first as a firm moves from zero debt to some positive amount of debt; (2) hits a minimum (perhaps over a range rather than at some specific amount of debt); and then (3) rises as an increase in the level of debt drives the firm's risk position beyond acceptable levels. Thus, there is an optimal amount of debt for each firm, an amount of debt that minimizes its cost of capital and maximizes its value.

Figure 13.3 shows, for a hypothetical industry, how the cost of capital changes as the debt ratio increases. (The average cost of capital figures in the graph are calculated in Table 13.5.) In the figure each dot represents one of the firms in the industry. For example, the dot labeled 1 represents Firm 1, a company with no debt. Since it is financed entirely with 20 percent equity money, Firm 1's average cost of capital is 20 percent. Firm 2 uses 10 percent debt in its capital structure, and it too has a 6 percent after-tax cost of debt and 20 percent cost of equity. Firm 3 also has a 6 percent cost of debt and a 20 percent cost of equity even though it uses 20 percent debt. Firm 4 has a 21 percent cost of equity and a 7 percent cost of debt. It uses 30

FIGURE 13.3

Hypothetical Cost of Capital Schedules for an Industry

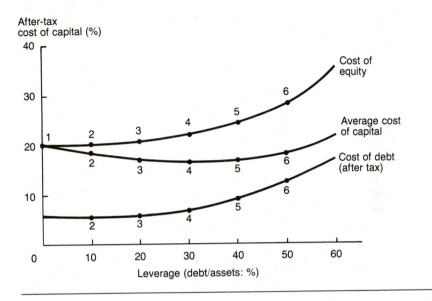

percent debt, and a risk premium of 1 percent has been added to the required return on equity to account for the additional risk of financial leverage. Providers of debt capital also feel that because of the added risk of financial leverage at this debt level, they should obtain higher yields on the firm's securities. In this particular industry the threshold debt ratio that begins to worry creditors is about 20 percent. Below 20 percent debt, creditors are totally unconcerned about any risk induced by debt; above 20 percent they are aware of the higher risk and require compensation in the form of higher rates of return.

In Table 13.5 the debt and equity costs of the various firms are averaged on the basis of their respective proportions of the firm's total capital. Firm 1 has a weighted average cost equal to 20 percent; Firm 2 has a weighted average cost of 18.6 percent; Firm 3 has a weighted cost of 17.2 percent; and Firm 4 has a weighted cost of 16.8 percent. These weighted costs, together with those of the other firms in the industry, are also plotted in Figure 13.3. We can see that firms with approximately 30 percent debt in their capital structure have the lowest weighted average cost of capital. Accordingly, proper calculation of the cost of capital requires that the cost of equity for a firm in the industry be given a weight of 0.70 and that debt be given a weight of 0.30.

TABLE 13.5

Calculation of Average Cost of Capital for Hypothetical Firms with Different Debt Ratios

		Percent of Total (1)	Component Cost (2)	Weighted Cost $\frac{(1) \times (2)}{100}$ (3)
Firm 1	Debt	0	6.0	0.00
	Equity	100	20.0	20.00
		100%	Average Cost	20.00%
Firm 2	Debt	10	6.0	0.60
	Equity	90	20.0	18.00
		100%	Average Cost	18.60%
Firm 3	Debt	20	6.0	1.20
	Equity	80	20.0	16.00
		100%	Average Cost	17.20%
Firm 4	Debt	30	7.0	2.10
	Equity	70	21.0	14.70
		100%	Average Cost	16.80%
Firm 5	Debt	40	9.0	3.60
	Equity	60	22.5	13.50
		100%	Average Cost	17.10%
Firm 6	Debt	50	12.0	6.00
	Equity	50	24.0	12.00
		100%	Average Cost	18.00%
Firm 7	Debt	60	17.0	10.20
	Equity	40	27.5	11.00
		100%	Average Cost	21.20%

The Post-Audit

A discussion of the *post-completion audit*, or *post-audit*, is necessary in any treatment of capital budgeting. The post-audit involves (1) a comparison of actual results to those predicted in the investment proposal and (2) an explanation of observed differences.

The post-audit has several purposes, including the following:

1. *Improving Forecasts*. When decision makers systematically compare their projections to actual outcomes, estimates tend to improve. Conscious or unconscious biases are observed and eliminated; new forecasting methods will be sought as their need becomes apparent; and people simply tend to work better if they know that their actions are being monitored.

2. *Improving Operations.* Businesses are run by people, and people can perform at higher or lower levels of efficiency. When a divisional team has made a forecast about a new installation, it is, in a sense, putting its reputation on the line. Because of the post-audit these executives have every incentive to make it happen, to fulfill their prophecies. If costs are above predicted levels, sales below expectations, and so on, then managers in production, sales, and related areas will strive to improve operations and bring results into line with forecasts.

The post-audit is a complex process. First, we must recognize that each element of the cash flow forecast is subject to uncertainty, so a percentage of all projects undertaken by any reasonably venturesome firm will prove unsuccessful. This fact must be considered when appraising the performances of the operating executives who submit capital expenditure requests. Second, projects sometimes fail to meet expectations for reasons beyond the control of the operating executives and for reasons that no one could realistically be expected to anticipate. For example, the imposition of price controls in 1971 adversely affected many projects for which price increases had been projected, and the quadrupling of oil prices in 1973 hurt others. Third, it is often difficult to separate the operating results of one investment from those of a larger system. Fourth, if the post-audit process is not used carefully, executives may be reluctant to suggest potentially profitable but risky projects.

Because of these difficulties, some firms tend to play down the importance of the post-audit. However, observations of both businesses and governmental units suggest that the best-run and most successful organizations are those that put the greatest stress on post-audits. Accordingly, the post-audit is one of the most important elements in a good capital budgeting system.

SUMMARY

Capital budgeting is the process of planning expenditures where the returns or benefits are expected to extend beyond one year. Capital budgeting decisions are among the most important faced by a firm's management because of both the size of the expenditures and the long-run nature of the commitments involved. It is a difficult process because one is dealing with estimates of events which are going to occur some distance in the future.

Capital budgeting decision making requires an integration of all the elements of the firm. Demand projections must be developed for the firm's products. Production and cost relationships have to be analyzed. Personnel requirements must be estimated. The funds necessary to support the investment project have to be procured.

Capital budgeting decisions should be made by comparing the marginal return on investment with the marginal cost of capital. The net present value (*NPV*) technique was shown to be a theoretically correct method for analyzing investment proposals.

For certain complex capital budgeting situations—those involving capital rationing, mutually exclusive, and closely interrelated projects—the *NPV* approach may be inappropriate for project selection. Mathematical programming techniques are being developed that will improve decision making in these complex circumstances.

Calculation of the cost of capital for use in the net present value model is a difficult problem. Proper decision making requires that a weighted average of the costs of the various types of capital employed by the firm should be used for all capital budgeting decisions.

QUESTIONS

13.1 The economics of input combination tell us that factors should be used in proportions such that the marginal product/price ratios for all inputs are equal. For capital management policy, this implies that the marginal net cost of debt should equal the marginal net cost of equity at the optimal capital structure. Yet we typically see firms issuing debt at interest rates significantly below the yields that investors require on the firm's equity shares. Does this mean that these firms are not operating with optimal capital structures? Explain.

13.2 New York City licenses taxicabs in two classes: (1) for operation by companies with fleets and (2) for operation by independent driver-owners having only one cab. It also fixes the rates that taxis charge. For many years now no new licenses have been issued in either class. There is an unofficial market in the medallions that signify the possession of a license. A medallion for an independent cab recently sold for about $37,000 in this market.

    a. Discuss the factors determining the price of a medallion. To make your answer concrete, estimate the numerical values of the various components that together can be summarized in a price of $37,000.

    b. What factors would determine whether a change in the fare fixed by the city would raise or lower the price of a medallion?

    c. Cab drivers, whether hired by companies or as owners of their own cabs, seem unanimous in opposing any increase in the number of cabs licensed. They argue that an increase in the number of cabs would increase their competition for customers, thereby driving down what they regard as an already unduly low return to drivers. Is their economic analysis correct? Who would benefit and who would lose from an expansion in the number of licenses issued at a nominal fee?

PROBLEMS

13.1 Michigan Printing, Inc., plans to bid on three printing jobs in the state of Ohio, each requiring a different production setup and having a different variable cost, a different projected winning per-unit bid, and a different expected annual sales volume. Relevant data on each job are given below:

	Job A	Job B	Job C
Projected Winning Bid (per unit)	$5.00	$6.00	$7.00
Direct Cost per Unit	$2.00	$2.30	$2.50
Annual Unit Sales Volume	800,000	650,000	450,000
Annual Marketing Costs	$90,000	$75,000	$55,000
Investment Required to Produce Annual Sales Volume	$3,000,000	$2,500,000	$2,000,000

Assume the following facts: (1) The company's marginal tax rate is 50 percent; (2) each project is expected to have a six-year life; (3) the firm uses straight-line depreciation; (4) the average cost of capital is 14 percent; (5) the projects are of about the same riskiness as the firm's other business; and (6) the company has already spent $60,000 on research for the new venture—this amount has been capitalized and will be written off over the life of the project.

    a. What is the expected net cash flow each year? (*Hint*: Cash flow equals net profits after taxes plus depreciation and amortization charges.)

    b. What is the net present value of each project? Which project, if any, should be selected?

    c. Suppose that MPI's primary business is quite cyclical, moving up and down with the economy, while Job A is expected to be countercyclical. Might this have any bearing on your decision?

13.2 Ventrock Corporation is considering investing $50,000 in facilities to produce a new product. The product is sold in an essentially competitive market structure at a price of $390 per unit. Assume that the facility will have a total cost function with fixed costs of $5,000 annually (in addition to depreciation on the facility, which is computed in a straight-line manner) and variable costs given by the equation:

$$\text{Variable Costs} = -\$10X + \$2X^2.$$

If the facility is expected to have an economic life of ten years (and a salvage value of $0), should the firm make the investment if its after-tax cost of capital is 16 percent? (Assume a 50 percent income tax rate for Ventrock Corporation.)

13.3 John Alfred must choose between two mutually exclusive investment projects. Each project costs $6,000 and has an expected life of four years. Annual net cash flows from each project begin one year after the initial investment is made and have the following characteristics:

	Probability	Annual Net Cash Flow
Project A	0.05	$2,200
	0.40	3,300
	0.30	3,600
	0.25	3,800
	1.00	
Project B	0.15	$ 300
	0.35	3,700
	0.28	6,200
	0.22	6,900
	1.00	

Alfred has decided to evaluate the riskier project at a 16 percent cost of capital and the less risky project at 12 percent.

a. What is the expected value of the annual net cash flows from each project?

b. What is the risk-adjusted *NPV* of each project?

13.4 Burger Brothers, Inc., is a small restaurant located near the main dormitory complex at a large midwestern university. The latest weekly operating statement for the restaurant is presented below.

Revenues		$2,500
Costs:		
Rent	$300	
Maintenance	200	
Foodstuffs	750	
Labor	950	
Miscellaneous Expenses	100	
Total		$2,300
Profit		$ 200

The week represented by this statement is typical of the average week over the entire year, although there is considerable variation from week to week. Of the expenses incurred in the operation of the restaurant, only foodstuffs, labor, and miscellaneous expenses are directly related to the restaurant's traffic. (The maintenance is done under a service contract for a fixed fee.)

Currently the restaurant is considering the purchase of additional cooking equipment in order to offer Italian food specialties. There is space available for the equipment in the current facility. The equipment costs $15,000 and has an expected life of three years with zero salvage value. With this new equipment available, Burger Brothers expects to be able to sell Italian specialties (pizza, spaghetti, etc.) at the rate of $1,000 per week. Unfortunately, 30 percent of these sales will be to Burger Brothers' current customers. Burger Brothers expects variable costs to increase by 30 percent if the new equipment is purchased. Assume a 17 percent income tax rate and straight line depreciation.

a. Develop the relevant cash flows for the analysis of this decision.

b. Assume Burger Brothers has the capital necessary to purchase the equipment and that it places a 16 percent opportunity cost on those funds. Should the equipment be purchased? Why or why not?

SELECTED REFERENCES

Bierman, Harold, Jr. *Strategic Financial Planning*. New York: Free Press, 1980.

Brigham, Eugene F. *Financial Management Theory and Practice*, 3rd ed. Hinsdale, Ill.: The Dryden Press, 1982.

————. *Fundamentals of Financial Management*, 3rd ed. Hinsdale, Ill.: The Dryden Press, 1983.

Durand, David. "Comprehensiveness in Capital Budgeting." *Financial Management* 10 (Winter 1981): 7–13.

Rappaport, Alfred, and Taggart, Robert A., Jr. "Evaluation of Capital Expenditure Proposals Under Inflation." *Financial Management* 11 (Spring 1982): 5–13.

Schall, Lawrence D., Sudem, Gary L., and Geijsbeek, William R., Jr. "Survey and Analysis of Capital Budgeting Methods." *Journal of Finance* (March 1978): 281–287.

Singhvi, Surendra S. *Planning for Capital Investments*. Oxford, Ohio: Planning Executives Institute, 1979.

Weston, J. Fred, and Brigham, Eugene F. *Essentials of Managerial Finance*, 6th ed. Hinsdale, Ill.: The Dryden Press, 1982.

————. *Managerial Finance*, 7th ed. Hinsdale, Ill.: The Dryden Press, 1981.

CHAPTER 14
JCF COMPUTER: AN INTEGRATED CASE IN MANAGERIAL DECISION MAKING

JCF Computer Company is a computer design and manufacturing firm with head-quarters in the Chicago area. This innovative electronics firm builds computers for special industrial applications and has extensive experience and expertise in both hardware (computer) and software (computer program) development.

1982 is a strategically important year for JCF. To remain at the forefront of computer applications in manufacturing, the board of directors of JCF has decided to join the "robot revolution." The company previously designed sophisticated as-sembly robots with limited sensory capabilities (vision, touch) for its own manufac-turing plant. This experience, a rapidly growing market, and potentially valuable synergy between computers and robots all create an interesting opportunity for JCF in the robotics industry.

Two key developments have worked to bring the industrial robot to the com-mercial marketplace; one was technology. The development of microprocessors, computers so small that they fit onto a tiny silicon chip, made the computer practical as the "brain" to run a robot. The second development was wage inflation. In the past, typical industrial robots have cost more to purchase and operate than the labor they replaced. Today the average industrial robot costs about $40,000 and it can be paid for and operated at a cost of approximately $4.80 per hour; the labor replaced has an average cost of $15 to $20 per hour. These two developments have poised robotics for substantial growth in the next decade.

Wall Street analysts predict that robot sales by U.S. companies will grow on the order of 35 percent a year throughout the 1980s. That gives the U.S. robotics industry a sales potential by 1990 of about $2 billion out of a projected $4.4 billion worldwide market.

Besides its high market growth potential, JCF's management believes that robotics is an area where the firm has unique synergistic advantages over most potential competitors. The mechanics involved in making robots have been largely perfected, which minimizes the value of machine-tool expertise and makes it increasingly important for a robot company to have electronic and software capabilities, areas where JCF excels. Industrial robots have control and memory systems, in the form of microcomputers of the type JCF produces. The company has also developed technology to integrate computer software with sensory systems that will enable robots to make limited decisions. All of this adds up to a wealth of computer hardware and software technology that can be used in the production of sophisticated robots.

Over the past six months JCF management has extensively examined the robotics decision from a strategic planning perspective and has decided to push ahead to develop a specific plan to enter the industry. Tentative objectives for the robot project are:

1. Establish a new Robotics Division that operates as a decentralized profit center.

2. Develop and manufacture assembly robots with advanced "thinking" capabilities by integrating sophisticated software with visual and tactile sensors.

3. Capture five to ten percent of the market for advanced industrial robots within three years of initiating production.

Because of the size and importance of the initial capital investment required to enter this new field, the corporate financial analysis staff, headed by its manager, Carson L. Dadler, has been asked to carefully analyze the options available to the firm. The report of this group will provide the basis for the proposals that top management will present to the board of directors for final approval to begin commercial robotics development.

CAPITAL BUDGETING PROCESS

Normal capital budgeting procedures at JCF require that department managers have their own staff prepare capital expenditure requests. The managers review these proposals, then forward them to the corporate financial analysis staff. The corporate staff can approve projects involving less than $25,000 and all replacement projects costing less than $100,000. Projects exceeding these limits, but under $200,000, can be approved by the financial vice-president. Projects costing between $200,000 and $1 million are approved by the executive committee consisting of the president, executive vice-president, and financial vice-president. Projects involving over $1 million are first cleared by the executive committee, then referred to the board of directors for final approval.

Budget officers in each department write the formal funds requests, review them with their respective departmental manager and present them to the corporate staff. Department operating personnel, especially the production people, initiate most expenditure requests by providing budget officers with cost and revenue data on standard forms. If the request is for the replacement of inoperative equipment, it is typically approved with only a cursory evaluation on the assumption that revenues would certainly exceed costs.[1] Requests for funds to replace obsolete equipment with newer, more efficient machines require estimates of cost savings and equipment costs, which are used to calculate the project's net present value. JCF Computer Company has recently changed their project evaluation method. Previously, the internal rate of return was used as a capital rationing device, since JCF had more high-return projects than it could implement. However, access to capital markets has improved, justifying the use of the net present value evaluation technique. The firm's cost of capital, 18 percent, is used to evaluate most projects.[2] Projects with exceptional risks are evaluated at a higher rate.

Another major area of capital expenditure at JCF is research and development (R & D). R & D expenditures at JCF are budgeted at approximately 10 percent of gross revenues. These funds are used to support product improvement and research about new product applications and advanced technological developments. The R & D department prepares reports enumerating their findings and sends them on to the marketing manager, Jack L. Roomey. Roomey and the production manager evaluate product desirability and feasibility. If proposals pass inspection at this level, they are sent on for approval by top management.

---

[1] The standard argument against formal evaluation of such requests is to ask what the incremental costs and revenues would be if a broken drive motor is replaced on the main assembly line. The motor would cost about $1,500, while the incremental profits resulting from its purchase would be the *entire* profit from the plant because the plant could not operate without the drive motor. Obviously, the present value of these incremental profits far exceeds the $1,500 cost of the motor.

[2] JCF determines its cost of capital in the following manner: It believes that its optimal capital structure calls for 70 percent equity and 30 percent debt. The company currently pays 15 percent for debt (7.5 percent after taxes), and the estimated equity capitalization rate is 22.5 percent. Using these figures, the weighted average cost of capital is determined:

$$30\% \times 7.5 = 2.25$$
$$70\% \times 22.5 = \underline{15.75}$$
$$\text{Weighted Average} \quad 18\,\%$$

Auditors from the corporate staff check the accepted projects to see that the actual cost and revenue figures are reasonably close to the projected figures. It is expected that even though individual projects may deviate from the estimates, departmental figures, on the average, should approximate the projections. If any department consistently overestimates revenues or underestimates costs, this indicates an optimistic bias that will cause too much of JCF's available funds to be invested in that department. Conversely, if revenues are consistently underestimated or costs overestimated, this indicates a conservative bias and an underallocation of funds to the department. When the auditor finds such biases, he alerts the department manager who initiates corrective action.

For the robotics proposal, JCF Computer Company is deviating from normal capital budgeting procedures. The corporate staff is directly handling the analysis because of the size of the investment and the overall strategic importance of the proposal. Dadler and his corporate financial analysis staff have already received preliminary estimates of incremental sales revenue, operating costs, capital outlays, and the useful life of new production facilities for robot manufacturing. The staff spent several hours collecting cost and revenue data in order to prepare earlier reports for the strategic planning analysis, reports that prompted the move into robotics. Because the robot production project is so important to the future profitability of JCF, Dadler knows he cannot rely totally on the judgments of production and sales personnel to develop the key variables required for the analysis. Further, he wants to carefully examine the question of what cost of capital to use in evaluating the project's cash flows.

In addition to analyzing the revenue from the robot product, Dadler must consider alternative forms of facility expansion and their costs. Engineers on the production staff have narrowed the expansion options to two. JCF could build one plant in Harrisburg, Pennsylvania, or two plants over a three to five year period, one in Pennsylvania and the other in Illinois. The latter method of expansion is appealing for several reasons. First, JCF could match production capacity more closely to actual demand during the critical growth years; the single plant, to realize its full cost-saving potential, would have to be built with its full capacity installed at the time of its completion.[3] Second, some of the high technological obsolesence risk that is associated with the robotics industry can be alleviated by constructing two plants over a period of years. Third, total transportation costs would be reduced by locating plants in two major markets instead of one. Fourth, constructing two smaller plants, with construction phased over several years, would place a lighter burden on the corporation's available investment funds, and thus might slightly reduce the cost of capital.

---

[3]This statement somewhat oversimplifies the case, but the reader should *assume* that the Harrisburg plant must be built with full capacity and that it is not feasible to install additional capacity to meet increases in demand in this plant.

DEMAND ESTIMATES

Dadler recognized that estimating the revenue potential from the robotics project would be both critical and difficult. The size of the capital investment involved and the project's significant impact on the entire future of JCF dictated a careful and thorough consideration of the demand and revenue analyses.

Dadler decided to attack the question of demand estimation by assigning S. W. Brolaw, a recent MBA with extensive training in managerial economics, to research and analyze industry demand relationships. From this Dadler planned to develop an estimated demand relationship for JCF robots.

Based on prior demand analysis of similar high-technology industrial products, Brolaw began by hypothesizing an industry demand function for sophisticated "thinking" (sensory systems integrated with extensive software) robots. A great many factors affect the demand for "thinking" robots, but Brolaw believed the key variables to be the following:

1. Price: P = Industry average price of sophisticated industrial "thinking robots."

2. Labor Cost: L = Average hourly wages in manufacturing.

3. Interest Rate: i = Long-term interest rate on corporate AA bonds.

4. Corporate Profits: π = Aggregate corporate profits.

5. Time: T = A trend factor that accounts for the acceptance through time of new technological innovations.

Using annual data on high-technology products from an industry trade association, corporate reports, the U.S. Department of Commerce, and various other sources, Brolaw fitted the following models to determine which one seemed to provide a superior functional form for demand analysis:

$$Q = a - bP + cL - di + e\pi + fT \qquad (14.1)$$

$$Q = aP^bL^ci^d\pi^eT^f. \qquad (14.2)$$

The linear model, Equation 14.1, provides the better fit—its R^2 and t ratios were higher for most of the historical relationships examined.

On this basis Brolaw estimated a linear industry demand curve for sophisticated robots. From this and company data on their experience in similar high-technology markets, Brolaw developed a demand function for JCF robots. The estimated demand function is:

$$Q_r = -1{,}450 - 0.02P + 163.6L - 10i + 4.23\pi + 320T. \qquad (14.3)$$
$$(0.85) \quad (2.01) \quad (1.96) \quad (1.75) \quad (2.79) \quad (3.13)$$

TABLE 14.1

Demand Function Variable Values

Variable	1983	1990
P	$225,000	$386,500
L	$11.00	$21.43
i	15%	15%
π	$213 (billion)	$340 (billion)
T	11	18

TABLE 14.2

"Thinking" Robot Demand Calculations for 1983 and 1990

Variable	Variable Coefficient	1983 Independent Variable	1983 Product (2) × (3)	1990 Independent Variable	1990 Product (2) × (5)
(1)	(2)	(3)	(4)	(5)	(6)
Intercept	−1,450		−1,450		−1,450
P	−0.02	225,000	(4,500)	386,500	(7,730)
L	163.6	11.00	1,800	21.43	3,506
i	−10	15	(150)	15	(150)
π	4.23	213	900	340	1,440
T	320	11	3,520	8	5,760
		Projected Demand	120		1,376
				≈	1,400

Here variables are as defined above with price and labor wages measured in dollars, interest measured as a percent, and corporate profits measured in billions of dollars. The trend term, T, equals 10 in 1982 and increases by 1 in each successive year. The terms in parentheses are t-statistics for the coefficients.

The demand function was used to obtain demand projections for each year between 1983 and 1990. The estimates were obtained by projecting the independent variables for each of the years in the planning period. Labor rates are assumed to grow at 10 percent annually, the interest rate is assumed to remain at the 1982 level of 15 percent, and corporate profits are assumed to increase annually at a 6 percent rate. The values used for each of the independent variables in 1983 and 1990 are shown in Table 14.1.

Next, the demand function, Equation 14.3, was combined with the data given in Table 14.1 to generate the demand projections for 1983 and 1990 that appear in Table 14.2. Projections for other years (1984–1989) in the forecast period were

TABLE 14.3

Demand Projections (1984–1989)

Year:	1984	1985	1986	1987	1988	1989
Demand:	290	465	645	830	1,020	1,200

generated in the same way. Projected demand for the new Robotics Division for the period 1983–1990 is shown in Table 14.3. In these projections a forecasted price for robots was used. Brolaw recognized that this price was just a first approximation and would require modification later when cost and revenue analyses were combined to determine appropriate price and activity levels.

Brolaw also used the demand function to generate demand curves and revenue functions for the JCF robot. The procedure used is shown below for 1983.

$$Q_r = -1,450 - 0.02P + 163.6L - 10i + 4.23\pi + 320T$$

$$Q_r = -1,450 - 0.02P + 163.6(11) - 10(15) + 4.23(213) + 320(1)$$

$$Q_r = 4,620 - 0.02P \ or \ P = 231,000 - 50Q_r.$$

From the demand curves Brolaw calculated the related total revenue functions. Again using 1983 as an example, the procedure is:

$$TR = P \cdot Q$$

$$= (231,000 - 50Q)Q$$

$$= 231,000Q - 50Q^2.$$

The derivative of the total revenue function provides the important marginal revenue function that Brolaw needed to determine the appropriate price and output levels:

$$MR = \frac{\partial TR}{\partial Q} = 231,000 - 100Q.$$

The JCF robot demand curves and marginal revenue functions for 1983 and 1990 are shown in Table 14.4. Similar curves were prepared for each intervening year.

TABLE 14.4

Demand Curves and Marginal Revenue Functions for 1983 and 1990

1983		1990	
	$P = \$231{,}000 - \$50Q$		$P = \$455{,}300 - \$50Q$
	$MR = \$231{,}000 - 100Q$		$MR = \$455{,}300 - 100Q$

COST ESTIMATES

Cost estimates for sophisticated robots were needed for the proposed large Harrisburg plant and for dual plants located in Pennsylvania and Illinois. After extended discussions, Dadler and his staff decided to approach the question of cost estimation in two ways: (1) They would themselves conduct a statistical cost analysis for the production of sophisticated robots, and (2) they would have the JCF engineering department develop an engineering cost study to generate functions showing the total and average costs for different plant sizes and different operating levels. They planned to compare the two sets of estimates and to use any major differences as indications that further study was necessary.

Statistical Cost Analysis

Several members of the financial analysis staff had prior work experience and educational backgrounds that would provide useful insights into the question of statistical cost estimation. They agreed that the best approach, from a theoretical standpoint, would be to follow these steps: (1) examine the production function for sophisticated robot manufacturing; (2) examine the nature of input prices; (3) combine the results of these two examinations to derive a theoretical cost function; (4) statistically estimate the parameters of the cost function, using least squares regression analysis.

Production Function. In the production of sophisticated robots, as in most other manufacturing operations, it seems reasonable to assume that the production function of a single plant will be of the form shown in Figure 14.1. Here the production function exhibits first increasing, then decreasing, returns to scale.

Cost Functions. A preliminary investigation suggested that the prices of inputs other than the fixed plant and equipment would be approximately equal in the geographic areas of the potential plant sites. Further, since JCF would not be an especially large employer in either area, the staff decided that it would be appropriate to assume that

FIGURE 14.1

Assumed Form of the Production Function for a Single Plant

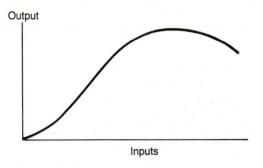

input prices remain constant with respect to output. Labor and materials costs were, however, expected to rise over time because of inflationary pressures.

Fixed costs would be higher for the large Harrisburg plant than for either single small plant, but it was not clear at this stage of the analysis whether total fixed costs would be greater for the single large plant or for the two smaller plants. Also, the staff noted that certain elements of fixed costs would be constant over time, but other elements would rise. Depreciation charges were placed in the first category; property taxes, supervisory personnel salaries, and utilities were placed in the second.

On the basis of these assumptions about the production functions and input prices, the analysts concluded that the total cost function for the large plant would probably have the general shape of the hypothetical TC_L curve shown in Figure 14.2. FC_L represents the fixed costs. The slope of TC_L first declines, then rises, indicating that marginal costs first decline, and then rise. The average cost per unit—measured by the slope of a line from the origin to TC—declines until output reaches about 1,300; it is equal to marginal costs (the slope of the TC curve) at this output, and then begins to rise.

The situation is somewhat different for the two small plants. The curve TC_{S1} in Figure 14.2 designates the total cost function for one small plant. TC_{S1} has the same general shape as TC_L, but the fixed costs for the small plant (FC_S) are lower, and the curve turns up sharply at a lower output. The optimal, or minimum average cost output, is about 700 units; average cost per unit rises rather sharply beyond this production level.

Suppose JCF builds one small plant, then adds another similar plant when the first one is operating at its minimum average cost output. Total cost will jump by the amount of fixed costs (FC_S) incurred by the second plant, plus any variable costs incurred by the second plant. Accordingly, the total costs of the firm will be represented by TC_{S2} for outputs beyond about 900 units. *It is important to keep in mind that Figure 14.2 is strictly hypothetical—the cost curves were constructed purely to illustrate intuitively the general nature of the cost functions that the financial analysis staff expected to find in their later empirical studies.*

Changes in Cost Functions Over Time. Although input prices are assumed to remain constant with respect to output in any given production period, inflationary pressures may be expected to cause input prices to rise over time. A rise in input prices will shift all the cost functions upward. If fixed input prices (plant managers' salaries, property taxes, and so on) rise by the same percentage as variable factor prices, the shifts will be parallel. If fixed input prices rise less than proportionately to increases in variable factor prices, the shifts will not be parallel.

FIGURE 14.2

Hypothetical Total Cost Functions for a Large Plant and Dual Small Plants

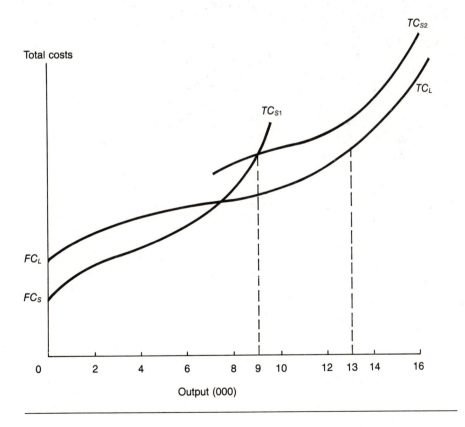

Fitting Long-Run Statistical Cost Functions. When Dadler first began this project with the financial analysis staff, several of the group members were convinced that they could fit a statistical cost curve that would provide a great deal of insight into their decision problem. This initial feeling was reinforced by a related experience with statistical cost functions. The financial analysis group, with the assistance of the management services department of a large accounting firm, had recently completed a short-run statistical cost study for use in setting standard costs on various JCF products. Their analysis employed multiple regression techniques to study the relationship between monthly variable costs and monthly output, holding constant other factors—such as wage rates, materials costs, and machine down-time. Their analysis proved quite useful for short-run planning purposes. The regression statistics had been good—the R^2 was high; the standard errors of the coefficients were low; and the model had proved to be an accurate predictor.

The results of the long-run statistical cost study were quite different. It was initially decided, on the basis of theoretical considerations, to fit a cubic cost function of the following kind:

$$TC = a + bQ - cQ^2 + dQ^3 + eX_1 + fX_2 + \ldots \qquad (14.4)$$

Here TC is total costs, Q is output in units, and the X variables represent other independent variables included in the cost function to hold constant such factors as wage rates for firms operating in different areas, age of plant facilities, and the like.

Twila Fisher, a statistician in the group, pointed out that they would need data on at least 10 observations, or preferably 15 to 20 similar production facilities, and that they could use the standard regression program available in JCF's central computer facilities to estimate the parameters a, b, c, and so on. Further, Fisher believed that they should estimate the parameters for a number of different years— say, each year from 1975 through 1981—to determine whether the parameters were stable. If they were, then more confidence could be placed in the use of the cost function as a predictor of the cost/output relationship in the years ahead. "Where," asked Dadler, "could they possibly get the required data for such a study?" Although he knew of several firms that manufactured industrial robots, cost data of the required type would not be available from even one of them. Further, the sophisticated robots JCF planned to manufacture were far more complex than the robots produced by firms currently in the industry, and even if their costs were available it was not clear that they would reveal much about the cost function of JCF.

With that assessment, the financial analysis staff abandoned the idea of a statistical cost study and turned their attention to the engineering cost estimates.

Engineering Cost Estimates

The engineering staff, at the request of Dadler, worked with equipment manufacturers to determine the optimum kinds of machinery, assembly-line setups, and so forth for various levels of operation. Labor requirements, raw materials usage, power costs, transportation charges, and the like were then calculated for the optimum plant associated with each production level. The total of these variable costs, divided by the various output figures, resulted in an engineering estimate of the average variable cost curve.

Some amount of fixed cost is associated with each plant size—the larger the plant, the higher the fixed costs. The total fixed costs plus total variable costs *at the output for which the plant was designed* divided by the optimal output gives the average total cost (*ATC*) for that output, and the set of minimum *ATC*s for various outputs defines the long-run average cost curve.

Relatively early in the analysis, JCF's chief engineer pointed out the need to approximate a target output figure before he could develop a cost function. In view of time limitations, not to mention the costs of making the estimates, it was simply not feasible to develop very many short-run cost functions for use in constructing a long-run cost function that covered a wide range of output. The *LRAC* curve would have to be estimated over a more limited range.

After much discussion it was decided that the engineers would design the plants and develop short-run cost functions based on target outputs of 1,000 and 1,500 units for the large plant and 500 and 700 for each small plant respectively. Based on preliminary estimates of 1983 and 1990 demand, these seemed to be reasonable ranges of plant outputs.

Preliminary cost function analyses revealed that the 1,500-unit design would clearly be the most efficient plant for Harrisburg, and that the 700-unit plant would be optimal if two facilities were constructed. Accordingly, the engineering department fully developed only two cost functions for each year, namely: (1) a single 1,500-unit per year facility and (2) a small-plant configuration with one 700-unit facility operating in 1983 and a second facility of similar size scheduled to come on line during 1987. Table 14.5 presents the resulting cost functions for 1983 and 1990 under these two production alternatives. The marginal cost curve associated with each total cost curve in Table 14.5 is simply the first derivative of the related

TABLE 14.5

Engineering Cost Functions

Large Plant

1983	$TC_{L83} = \$3,500,000 + \$200,000Q + \$90Q^2$
1990	$TC_{L90} = \$50,000,000 + \$220,000Q + \$40Q^2$

Small Plant(s)[a]

1983	$TC_{S83} = \$2,250,000 + \$180,000Q + \$150Q^2$
1990	$TC_{S90} = \$95,000,000 + \$210,000Q + \$50Q^2$

[a] Assumes one plant in 1983 with the second coming on line during 1987. The 1990 production assumes an optimal allocation of production between the two plants.

TABLE 14.6

Marginal Cost Curves

Large Plant

1983	$MC_{L83} = \$200,000 + \$180Q$
1990	$MC_{L90} = \$220,000 + \$80Q$

Small Plant(s)

1983	$MC_{S83} = \$180,000 + \$300Q$
1990	$MC_{S90} = \$210,000 + \$100Q$

total cost curve. Thus, for the large plant in 1983, the marginal cost function is calculated as:

$$TC_{L83} = \$3,500,000 + \$200,000Q + \$90Q^2.$$

$$MC_{L83} = \frac{\partial TC_{L83}}{\partial Q} = \$200,000 + \$180Q.$$

The remaining marginal cost curves were calculated similarly and are shown in Table 14.6.

ESTIMATING NET PRESENT VALUES FOR ALTERNATIVE PLANTS

Given the demand and cost functions, Dadler directed the financial staff to next calculate the expected profits for each of the two production alternatives. This calculation was made by setting $MR = MC$ to estimate the optimal output for the robots, which was then used to determine revenues, costs, and profits.[4]

To illustrate, the marginal revenue curve for 1983 (Table 14.4) can be used with the large plant's 1983 marginal cost function (Table 14.6) to determine the optimal production level for that facility:

---

[4]This case is simplified by ignoring the difficulties presented by depreciation and other noncash charges. We assume, for simplicity, that all costs other than depreciation are paid as they occur and that a depreciation reserve fund is set up and increased each year by a "depreciation payment" calculated to permit replacement of assets as they wear out. Making these assumptions permits us to concentrate on *economic* issues rather than on issues covered in accounting and finance courses.

Also, as will be noted later, revenues and costs are determined for three different economic conditions: good, normal, and poor. The equations presented in this section are all based on normal conditions, but it should be realized that the corporate staff conducted a similar analysis for good and poor conditions.

$$MR_{83} = MC_{L83}$$

$$231,000 - 100Q = 200,000 + 180Q$$

$$Q = 111.$$

An output of 111 units could be sold at a price of $225,450, calculated from the demand function as follows:

$$P_{83} = \$231,000 - \$50(111)$$

$$= \$225,450.$$

The costs, revenues, and profits at the optimal price/output points were estimated next. The calculations for sophisticated robot production, 1983, Harrisburg plant, are given below as an illustration:[5]

Step 1 Revenue $= PQ = (\$225,450)(111)$

$$= \$25,025,000$$

Step 2 Costs $= \$3,500,000 + \$200,000(111) + \$90(111)^2$

$$= \$26,809,000$$

Step 3 Before-Tax Profit (Loss) $= \$25,025,000 - \$26,809,000$

$$= (\$1,784,000)$$

Step 4 After-Tax Profit (Loss) $= (\$1,784,000) \times 0.5$

$$= (\$892,000)$$

Thus, an after-tax loss of $892,000 was projected for the first year of operations, assuming (1) normal economic conditions, and (2) that a large plant is built in Harrisburg to produce sophisticated "thinking" robots. Similar calculations were performed to determine the projected after-tax profits for the other processes. After-tax profit projections for each year (1983–1990) under all three economic conditions are displayed in Table 14.7.

---

[5]The tax calculation assumes (1) a 50 percent tax rate and (2) that losses are offset by profitable operations in other divisions.

TABLE 14.7

Robotics After-Tax Profit (Cash Flow) Projections for Normal, Good, and Poor Economic Conditions ($000)

	1983	1984	1985	1986	1987	1988	1989	1990	1991–2000
Normal Conditions									
One Plant									
(Harrisburg)	($ 892)	$3,542	$11,415	$20,938	$29,487	$37,510	$45,662	$51,897	$51,897
Two Plants	$ 501	$4,211	$ 8,582	$13,149	$17,066	$21,699	$24,862	$27,465	$27,465
Good Conditions									
One Plant									
(Harrisburg)	($ 535)	$3,959	$14,981	$29,313	$43,282	$52,514	$60,927	$67,656	$67,656
Two Plants	$ 701	$5,895	$13,215	$19,409	$25,892	$30,379	$34,807	$36,451	$36,451
Poor Conditions									
One Plant									
(Harrisburg)	($1,159)	$2,979	$ 7,994	$14,657	$21,641	$26,957	$31,963	$35,328	$35,328
Two Plants	$ 351	$4,001	$ 6,918	$10,804	$13,946	$16,789	$19,403	$21,225	$21,225

Project Life

The engineering department estimated that the effective service life of the equipment would be 15 to 20 years; however, because of uncertainties about the rate of obsolescence they admitted that this was only a rough guess. Also, the engineers suggested that the plant structures, regardless of the production process adopted, would probably require extensive modifications to render them suitable for continual operations after 20 years. These considerations, combined with questions about the long-run nature of the demand for sophisticated robots, suggested to Dadler that they should use the year 2000 as the estimated terminal date for the project. It was decided to project the 1990 profits for an additional 10 years under an assumption that growth beyond that point was highly speculative and would require substantial new investment, as plant capacity would be reached at that point.

Terminal Value

The land, buildings, and equipment would undoubtedly have some value in the year 2000, the projected terminal date of the project, but how much value? If JCF should modernize the plant and continue the operation, the value could be quite high; in view of the probable level of inflation, land value could easily be three times the 1982 purchase price, and buildings could be worth close to their cost of construction, even considering necessary renovation. On the other hand, if technology should change to the extent that the buildings were no longer usable, and if the neighborhood in which the plant is located should deteriorate, the cost of closing the plant could exceed its worth, leading to a *negative* terminal value. On the basis of the experience of JCF's other operations, Dadler decided that a conservative, but not unrealistic, assumption would be that the net salvage value of the plant and equipment in 2000 would be zero. That is, he assumed that any realizable revenue would no more than offset disposal costs.

Project Costs

Estimates of the required outlays for plant and equipment shown in Table 14.8 were obtained from the engineering department. The cost of the raw land for the Harrisburg plant is known with certainty, but there is a degree of uncertainty about the

TABLE 14.8

Estimated Investment Costs

Large Plant	$90,000,000
Small Plant (each)	$30,000,000

land cost in Illinois. Site preparation costs, as well as the cost of completing the buildings, could vary considerably depending on soil conditions, weather, and strikes during construction. Some equipment would be purchased at known catalogue prices, but other equipment would be built on contract, and these costs could vary greatly, depending on technical problems that might be encountered. Finally, break-in costs would be incurred as "bugs" were worked out of the processing and assembly facilities, and again, depending on technical factors, these costs could range from modest to quite high.

For the dual plant project, the cost of one plant was estimated. Only one plant would be built in 1982, with the other scheduled for construction in 1986. The cost of the later plant must be discounted back to the present to determine a present value cost-of-investment figure comparable to the cost given for the Harrisburg plant. For reasons explained in the following section, a 20 percent discount rate was used to determine the present value of these costs. The present value of the cost of constructing the two small plants was determined to be $44.5 million.

Dadler and his staff attempted to pin down the engineers to a somewhat narrower range of possible costs, but the engineers stated flatly that this was the best they could do in view of the time constraints, and that even if the time constraints were relaxed, they would not be able to estimate costs much more precisely.

Cost of Capital

Although the weighted average cost of capital for JCF was approximately 18 percent, Dadler felt that this cost was too low for evaluating the robot development decision. He based this on an analysis of the relative risks of the new activity and on the capital structure of several new firms that had been started strictly to enter this field. Dadler believed that an appropriate capital structure for a new venture of the type being contemplated would be 25 percent debt and 75 percent equity. Current corporate debt for ventures similar to high-technology robot manufacture yielded 16 percent with an aftertax cost of 8 percent. The return on equity Dadler imposed on the project was 24 percent. This resulted in a 20 percent aftertax weighted average cost of capital calculated as:

Component	Cost	Weight	Weighted Cost
Equity	24%	75%	18%
Debt	8%	25%	2%
		Weighted Average Cost	20%

Dadler used the 20 percent capital cost to evaluate both production alternatives.

Present Value Calculations

The next step in the decision process was to calculate the net present values for the various possible alternatives and outcomes. The calculation for the large plant under normal economic conditions is found as follows:

$$NPV(000) = \sum_{t=1}^{18} \frac{\text{Aftertax Cash Flow}_t}{(1+k)^t} - \text{Investment}$$

$$= \frac{(\$892)}{1.20} + \frac{\$3,542}{(1.20)^2} + \frac{\$11,415}{(1.20)^3} + \frac{\$20,938}{(1.20)^4} + \frac{\$29,487}{(1.20)^5}$$

$$+ \frac{\$37,510}{(1.20)^6} + \frac{\$45,662}{(1.20)^7} + \sum_{t=8}^{18} \frac{\$51,897}{(1.20)^t}$$

$$= \$28,246.$$

The other net present values were developed in a like manner and are presented in Column 1 of the decision tree shown in Figure 14.3.

Decision Tree

The information developed thus far was used to construct the decision tree shown in Figure 14.3. From the initial decision point, two branches emerge: the Harrisburg plant and the dual plant alternative. Regardless of which branch is taken, the probability is 0.25 that economic conditions in the sophisticated robot industry will be good, 0.50 that conditions will be normal, and 0.25 that conditions will be bad. Depending on the state of the economy, the profits will vary, as will the *NPV* of the profit streams; these figures are given in Column 4 of the tree diagrams. The probabilities that represent the various economic climates are multiplied by the possible *NPV*s to develop Column 6, and the sum of the Column 6 figures for each branch represents the expected value of the branch. For the Harrisburg plant, the expected *NPV* is $29.348 million.

FINAL DECISION

The final task faced by Dadler was to decide on a recommended course of action, prepare the formal report, and present (and defend) that choice to the top management committee, who would present the decision to the board of directors.

FIGURE 14.3

Decision Tree for Sophisticated "Thinking" Robot Production

Decision point (1)	Plant configuration (2)	Economic state (3)	Probability (4)	Possible net present value ($000) (5)	(5) × (4) (6)	Expected present value ($000) (7)
	Harrisburg plant	Good	0.25	$ 68,795	$17,199	
		Normal	0.50	$ 28,246	$14,123	$29,348
		Bad	0.25	($ 7,895)	($ 1,974)	
	Dual plants	Good	0.25	$ 51,497	$12,874	
		Normal	0.50	$ 24,380	$12,190	$27,578
		Bad	0.25	$ 10,058	$ 2,514	

QUESTIONS

14.1 The potential return from robotics looks quite attractive. What major risks face JCF as it enters the field?

14.2 Evaluate the capital budgeting procedures used by JCF. What are the strengths and weaknesses of the system? Do you see any problems concerning the allocation of capital to various departments?

14.3 Evaluate the procedure used to determine a cost of capital for the Robotics Division. Specifically:

    a. Is the weighted average approach reasonable?

    b. Suppose that JCF's management strongly believes that the stock market is wrong and that less risk should be assigned to robotics production than is implied by the 20 percent equity return requirement. Would this affect the way the firm should calculate its divisional cost of capital?

    c. Suppose the reverse is true—investors assign a low degree of risk to robot production, but management considers robotics to be a very risky operation. What effect should this have on the assigned cost of capital to that division?

14.4 How would each of the following affect the cost of capital that should be used by the firm?

    a. Interest rates rise because the Federal Reserve System tightens the money supply.

    b. The stock market suffers a sharp decline, and JCF stock falls from $75 to $30 a share without, in management's judgment, any decline in the company's future earnings expectations.

    c. The firm decides that it can move from 30 percent to 50 percent debt without affecting the interest rate on debt or the cost of equity capital.

    d. The firm's rate of expansion increases to the point where it must raise substantial sums of new equity capital by selling common stock. Previously, only retained earnings and debt had been used to finance expansion. (The cost of floating new stock issues is estimated to be 20 percent of the funds raised, giving consideration to necessary underpricing that will be required to sell new stock issues.)

14.5 JCF executives, as well as investors, are concerned about possible overinvestment in the robotics industry. Do you think that the industry trade association could perform a service for the firms in the industry by collecting statistics on existing capacity and planned expansions and supplying this information to member firms? How would firms use such information, and might there be any antitrust implications?

14.6 Consider the demand equation for sophisticated industrial robots and answer the following questions.

a. Are there additional variables which you believe might improve the function for decision making purposes?

b. Suppose corporate profits in 1990 were actually twice the projected amount. What effect would this have on demand for JCF's robots? What caveats would you mention in estimating the impact of corporate profits of that magnitude?

c. How would you interpret the trend variable in the regression equation, and what do you think accounts for the relationship between it and robot demand?

d. Would you classify the demand for industrial robots as price sensitive?

e. One might hypothesize that labor wage rates and corporate profits affect robot demand in an interactive fashion. If you felt this was likely to be the case, would it affect your choice of a linear model for the demand function? What alternative might you use?

14.7 Short-run statistical cost studies have been reported for a wide variety of industries, ranging from autos to photocopy machines. Long-run cost studies, on the other hand, have been restricted to a handful of industries such as banks, savings and loans, insurance companies, utilities, and steel. Why do you suppose so many more short-run than long-run studies have been conducted?

14.8 What transfer pricing problems will JCF face with the new Robotics Division? What suggestions do you have for establishing a transfer pricing system for the firm?

14.9 Do you think that the engineers were justified in developing just the four cost functions shown in Table 14.5, or should they have developed a more complete set of functions? Explain the advantages and disadvantages of developing these additional functions.

14.10 The present value investment cost for the two-plant option is $44.5 million and the *NPV* analysis assumes construction of both plants. Is this assumption appropriate?

14.11 How might you improve the decision tree branch for the two-plant option by considering abandonment possibilities? (That is, consider what you as a manager of JCF might do if, after constructing the initial plant, demand turned out to be very low.)

14.12 Do you think Dadler's decision to use the same discount rate to evaluate the two options is appropriate?

14.13 What recommendation should Dadler make to top management?

APPENDIX A
COMPOUNDING AND THE TIME VALUE OF MONEY

The concepts of compound growth and the time value of money are widely used in all aspects of business and economics. Compounding is the principle that underlies growth, whether it is growth in value, growth in sales, or growth in assets. The time value of money—the fact that a dollar received in the future is worth less than a dollar in hand today—also plays an important role in managerial economics. Cash flows occurring in different periods must be adjusted to their value at a common point in time if they are to be analyzed and compared. Because of the importance of these concepts in economic analysis, a thorough understanding of the material on future (compound) and present values in this appendix is vital.

FUTURE VALUE (OR COMPOUND VALUE)

Suppose you deposit $100 in a bank savings account that pays 5 percent interest compounded annually. How much will you have at the end of one year? Let us define terms as follows:

PV = present value of your account, or the beginning amount, $100.

i = interest rate the bank pays you = 5 percent per year, or, expressed as a decimal, 0.05.

I = dollars of interest you earn during the year.

FV_n = future value, or ending amount, of your account at the end of n years. Whereas PV is the value now, at the *present* time, FV_n is the value n years into the future, after compound interest has been earned. Note also that FV_0 is the future value *zero* years into the future, which is the *present*, so FV_0 = PV.

In our example, n = 1, so $FV_n = FV_1$, and it is calculated as follows:

$$FV_1 = PV + I \qquad\qquad\qquad (A.1)$$

$$= PV + (PV)(i)$$

$$= PV(1 + i).$$

We can now use Equation A.1 to find how much the account is worth at the end of one year:

$$FV_1 = \$100(1 + 0.05) = \$100(1.05) = \$105.$$

Your account earned $5 of interest ($I$ = $5), so you have $105 at the end of the year.

Now suppose you leave your funds on deposit for five years; how much will you have at the end of the fifth year? The answer is $127.63; this value is worked out in Table A.1.

Notice that the Table A.1 value for FV_2, the value of the account at the end of Year 2, is equal to

$$FV_2 = FV_1(1 + i) = PV(1 + i)(1 + i) = PV(1 + i)^2.$$

TABLE A.1

Compound Interest Calculations

Year	Beginning Amount, PV	×	$(1 + i)$	=	Ending Amount, FV_n
1	$100.00		1.05		$105.00
2	105.00		1.05		110.25
3	110.25		1.05		115.76
4	115.76		1.05		121.55
5	121.55		1.05		127.63

Continuing, we see that FV_3, the balance after three years, is

$$FV_3 = FV_2(1 + i) = PV(1 + i)^3.$$

In general, FV_n, the future value at the end of n years, is found as:

$$FV_n = PV(1 + i)^n. \tag{A.2}$$

Applying Equation A.2 to our five-year, 5 percent case, we obtain

$$FV_5 = \$100(1.05)^5$$

$$= \$100(1.2763)$$

$$= \$127.63,$$

which is the same as the value worked out in Table A.1.

If an electronic calculator is handy, it is easy enough to calculate $(1 + i)^n$ directly.[1] However, tables have been constructed for values of $(1 + i)^n$ for wide ranges of i and n. Table A.2 is illustrative. Table C.1 in Appendix C contains a more complete set of compound value interest factors. Notice that we have used the term *period* rather than *year* in Table A.2. As we shall see later in the appendix, compounding can occur over periods of time different from one year. Thus, while compounding is often on an annual basis, it can be quarterly, semiannually, monthly, or for any other period.

We define the term *future value interest factor* ($FVIF_{i,n}$) to equal $(1 + i)^n$. Therefore Equation A.2 may be written as $FV_n = PV(FVIF_{i,n})$. One need only to go to an appropriate interest table to find the proper interest factor. For example, the correct interest factor for our five-year, 5 percent illustration can be found in Table A.2. We look down the period column to 5, then across this row to the 5 percent column to find the interest factor, 1.2763. Then, using this interest factor, we find the value of $100 after five years as $FV_n = PV(FVIF_{i,n}) = \$100(1.2763) = \$127.63$, which is identical to the value obtained by the long method in Table A.1.

Graphic View of the Compounding Process: Growth

Figure A.1 shows how $1 (or any other initial quantity) grows over time at various rates of interest, or growth. The higher the rate of interest, the faster the rate of

---

[1]For example, to calculate $(1 + i)^n$ for $i = 5\% = 0.05$ and $n = 5$ years, we multiply $(1 + i) = (1.05)$ times (1.05); multiply this product by (1.05); and so on:

$$(1 + i)^n = (1.05)(1.05)(1.05)(1.05)(1.05) = (1.05)^5 = 1.2763.$$

TABLE A.2

Future Value of \$1 at the End of _n_ Periods: $FVIF_{i,n} = (1 + i)^n$

Period (n)	1%	2%	3%	4%	5%	6%	7%	8%	9%	10%
0	1.0000	1.0000	1.0000	1.0000	1.0000	1.0000	1.0000	1.0000	1.0000	1.0000
1	1.0100	1.0200	1.0300	1.0400	1.0500	1.0600	1.0700	1.0800	1.0900	1.1000
2	1.0201	1.0404	1.0609	1.0816	1.1025	1.1236	1.1449	1.1664	1.1881	1.2100
3	1.0303	1.0612	1.0927	1.1249	1.1576	1.1910	1.2250	1.2597	1.2950	1.3310
4	1.0406	1.0824	1.1255	1.1699	1.2155	1.2625	1.3108	1.3605	1.4116	1.4641
5	1.0510	1.1041	1.1593	1.2167	1.2763	1.3382	1.4026	1.4693	1.5386	1.6105
6	1.0615	1.1262	1.1941	1.2653	1.3401	1.4185	1.5007	1.5869	1.6771	1.7716
7	1.0721	1.1487	1.2299	1.3159	1.4071	1.5036	1.6058	1.7138	1.8280	1.9487
8	1.0829	1.1717	1.2668	1.3686	1.4775	1.5938	1.7182	1.8509	1.9926	2.1436
9	1.0937	1.1951	1.3048	1.4233	1.5513	1.6895	1.8385	1.9990	2.1719	2.3579
10	1.1046	1.2190	1.3439	1.4802	1.6289	1.7908	1.9672	2.1589	2.3674	2.5937
11	1.1157	1.2434	1.3842	1.5395	1.7103	1.8983	2.1049	2.3316	2.5804	2.8531
12	1.1268	1.2682	1.4258	1.6010	1.7959	2.0122	2.2522	2.5182	2.8127	3.1384
13	1.1381	1.2936	1.4685	1.6651	1.8856	2.1329	2.4098	2.7196	3.0658	3.4523
14	1.1495	1.3195	1.5126	1.7317	1.9799	2.2609	2.5785	2.9372	3.3417	3.7975
15	1.1610	1.3459	1.5580	1.8009	2.0789	2.3966	2.7590	3.1722	3.6425	4.1772

FIGURE A.1

Relationships among Future Value Interest Factors, Interest Rates, and Time: Amount to Which Interest Factor Grows after _n_ Periods at Various Interest Rates

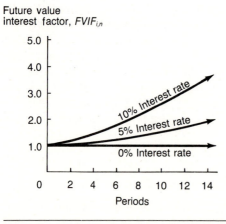

Future value interest factor, $FVIF_{i,n}$

growth. The interest rate is, in fact, the growth rate: If a sum is deposited and earns 5 percent, then the funds on deposit grow at the rate of 5 percent per period. Similarly, the sales of a firm or the gross national product (GNP) of a country might be expected to grow at a constant rate. Projections of future sales or GNP could be obtained using the compound value process.

Future value curves could be drawn for any interest rate, including fractional rates. In Figure A.1, we have plotted curves for 0 percent, 5 percent, and 10 percent, using the data from Table A.2.

PRESENT VALUE

Suppose you are offered the alternative of receiving either $127.63 at the end of five years or X dollars today. There is no question that the $127.63 will be paid in full (perhaps the payer is the U.S. government). Having no current need for the money, you would deposit it in a bank account that pays 5 percent interest. (Five percent is defined to be your *opportunity cost*, or the rate of interest you could earn on alternative investments of equal risk.) What value of X will make you indifferent between X dollars today or the promise of $127.63 five years hence?

Table A.1 shows that the initial amount of $100 growing at 5 percent a year yields $127.63 at the end of five years. Thus, you should be indifferent in your choice between $100 today and $127.63 at the end of five years. The $100 is defined as the present value, or *PV*, of $127.63 due in five years when the applicable interest rate is 5 percent. Therefore, if X is anything less than $100, you would prefer the promise of $127.63 in five years to $X today.

In general, the present value of a sum due n years in the future is the amount which, if it were on hand today, would grow to equal the future sum over a period of n years. Since $100 would grow to $127.63 in five years at a 5 percent interest rate, $100 is defined to be the present value of $127.63 due five years in the future when the appropriate interest rate is 5 percent.

Finding present values (or *discounting*, as it is commonly called) is simply the reverse of compounding, and Equation A.2 can readily be transformed into a present value formula:

$$FV_n = PV(1 + i)^n,$$

which, when solved for *PV*, gives

$$PV = \frac{FV_n}{(1 + i)^n} = FV_n \left[\frac{1}{(1 + i)} \right]^n. \qquad \textbf{(A.3)}$$

Tables have been constructed for the term in brackets for various values of *i* and *n*; Table A.3 is an example. For a more complete table, see Table C.2 in Appendix C.

TABLE A.3

Present Values of $1 Due at the End of *n* Periods

$$PVIF_{i,n} = \frac{1}{(1 + i)^n} = \left[\frac{1}{(1 + i)} \right]^n$$

Period (*n*)	1%	2%	3%	4%	5%	6%	7%	8%	9%	10%	12%	14%	15%
1	.9901	.9804	.9709	.9615	.9524	.9434	.9346	.9259	.9174	.9091	.8929	.8772	.8696
2	.9803	.9612	.9426	.9246	.9070	.8900	.8734	.8573	.8417	.8264	.7972	.7695	.7561
3	.9706	.9423	.9151	.8890	.8638	.8396	.8163	.7938	.7722	.7513	.7118	.6750	.6575
4	.9610	.9238	.8885	.8548	.8227	.7921	.7629	.7350	.7084	.6830	.6355	.5921	.5718
5	.9515	.9057	.8626	.8219	.7835	.7473	.7130	.6806	.6499	.6209	.5674	.5194	.4972
6	.9420	.8880	.8375	.7903	.7462	.7050	.6663	.6302	.5963	.5645	.5066	.4556	.4323
7	.9327	.8706	.8131	.7599	.7107	.6651	.6227	.5835	.5470	.5132	.4523	.3996	.3759
8	.9235	.8535	.7894	.7307	.6768	.6274	.5820	.5403	.5019	.4665	.4039	.3506	.3269
9	.9143	.8368	.7664	.7026	.6446	.5919	.5439	.5002	.4604	.4241	.3606	.3075	.2843
10	.9053	.8203	.7441	.6756	.6139	.5584	.5083	.4632	.4224	.3855	.3220	.2697	.2472

For the illustrative case being considered, look down the 5 percent column in Table A.3 to the fifth row. The figure shown there, 0.7835, is the *present value interest factor (PVIF_{i,n})* used to determine the present value of $127.63 payable in five years, discounted at 5 percent:

$$PV = FV_5(PVIF_{i,n})$$

$$= \$127.63(0.7835)$$

$$= \$100.$$

Graphic View of the Discounting Process

Figure A.2 shows how the interest factors for discounting decrease as the discounting period increases. The curves in the figure were plotted with data taken from Table A.3; they show that the present value of a sum to be received at some future date decreases (1) as the payment date is extended further into the future and (2) as the discount rate increases. If relatively high discount rates apply, funds due in the future are worth very little today. Even at relatively low discount rates, the present values of funds due in the distant future are quite small. For example, $1.00 due in ten years is worth about $0.61 today if the discount rate is 5 percent. It is worth only $0.25 today at a 15 percent discount rate. Similarly, $1.00 due in five years at 10 percent is worth $0.62 today, but at the same discount rate $1.00 due in ten years is worth only $0.39 today.

FUTURE VALUE VERSUS PRESENT VALUE

Notice that Equation A.2, the basic equation for compounding, was developed from the logical sequence set forth in Table A.1; the equation merely presents in mathematical form the steps outlined in the table. The present value interest factor ($PVIF_{i,n}$) in Equation A.3, the basic equation for discounting or finding present values, was found as the *reciprocal* of the future value interest factor ($FVIF_{i,n}$) for the same i,n combination:

$$PVIF_{i,n} = \frac{1}{FVIF_{i,n}}.$$

For example, the *future value* interest factor for 5 percent over five years is seen in Table A.2 to be 1.2763. The *present value* interest factor for 5 percent over five years must be the reciprocal of 1.2763:

$$PVIF_{5\%, 5\,years} = \frac{1}{1.2763} = 0.7835.$$

The $PVIF_{i,n}$ found in this manner does, of course, correspond with the $PVIF_{i,n}$ shown in Table A.3.

The reciprocal nature of the relationship between present value and future

FIGURE A.2

Relationships among Present Value Interest Factors, Interest Rates, and Time

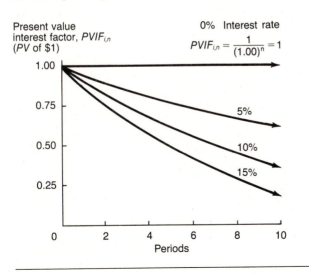

FIGURE A.3

Time Line for an Annuity: Future Value ($i = 4\%$)

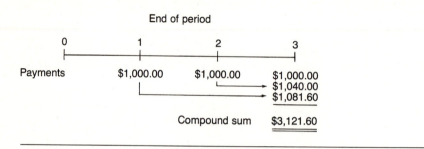

value permits us to find present values in two ways—by multiplying or by dividing. Thus, the present value of $1,000 due in five years and discounted at 5 percent may be found as

$$PV = FV_n \left[\frac{1}{1 + i} \right]^n = FV_n(PVIF_{i,n}) = \$1,000(0.7835) = \$783.50,$$

or as

$$PV = \frac{FV_n}{(1 + i)^n} = \frac{FV_n}{FVIF_{i,n}} = \frac{\$1,000}{1.2763} = \$783.50.$$

To conclude this comparison of present and future values, compare Figures A.1 and A.2.[2] Notice that the vertical intercept is at 1.0 in each case, but future value interest factors rise, while present value interest factors decline.

FUTURE VALUE OF AN ANNUITY

An annuity is defined as a series of payments of a fixed amount for a specified number of periods. Each payment occurs at the end of the period.[3] For example, a promise to pay $1,000 a year for three years is a three-year annuity. If you were to receive such an annuity and were to deposit each annual payment in a savings account paying 4 percent interest, how much would you have at the end of three years? The answer is shown graphically as a *time line* in Figure A.3. The first payment is made

[2]Notice that Figure A.2 is not a mirror image of Figure A.1. The curves in Figure A.1 approach ∞ as n increases; in Figure A.2 the curves approach zero, not −∞.

[3]Had the payment been made at the beginning of the period, each receipt would simply have been shifted back one year.

at the end of Year 1, the second at the end of Year 2, and the third at the end of Year 3. The last payment is not compounded at all; the second payment is compounded for one year; and the first is compounded for two years. When the future values of each of the payments are added, their total is the sum of the annuity. In the example, this total is $3,121.60.

Expressed algebraically, with S_n defined as the future value, R as the periodic receipt, n as the length of the annuity, and $FVIFA_{i,n}$ as the future value interest factor for an annuity, the formula for S_n is

$$S_n = R(1 + i)^{n-1} + R(1 + i)^{n-2} + \ldots + R(1 + i)^1 + R(1 + i)^0 \qquad \textbf{(A.4)}$$

$$= R[(1 + i)^{n-1} + (1 + i)^{n-2} + \ldots + (1 + i)^1 + (1 + i)^0]$$

$$= R \sum_{t=1}^{n} (1 + i)^{n-t}, \text{ or } = R \sum_{t=1}^{n} (1 + i)^{t-1}$$

$$= R(FVIFA_{i,n}).$$

The expression in parentheses, $FVIFA_{i,n}$, has been calculated for various combinations of i and n.[4] An illustrative set of these annuity interest factors is given in Table A.4.[5] To find the answer to the three-year, $1,000 annuity problem, simply refer to Table A.4, look down the four percent column to the row of the third period, and multiply the factor 3.1216 by $1,000. The answer is the same as the one derived by the long method illustrated in Figure A.3:

$$S_n = R(FVIFA_{i,n})$$

$$S_3 = \$1,000(3.1216) = \$3,121.60.$$

Notice that for all positive interest rates, the $FVIFA_{i,n}$ for the sum of an annuity is always equal to or greater than the number of periods the annuity runs.[6]

The annuity would have been called an *annuity due*; the one in the present discussion, where payments are made at the end of each period, is called a *regular annuity* or, sometimes, a *deferred annuity*.

[4] The third equation is simply a shorthand expression in which sigma (Σ) signifies *sum up* or add the values of n factors. The symbol $\sum_{t=1}^{n}$ simply says, "Go through the following process: Let $t = 1$ and find the first factor. Then let $t = 2$ and find the second factor. Continue until each individual factor has been found, and then add these individual factors to find the value of the annuity."

[5] The equation given in Table A.4 recognizes that the *FVIFA* factor is the sum of a geometric progression. The proof of this equation is given in all college algebra texts. Notice that it is easy to use the equation to develop annuity factors. This is especially useful if you need the *FVIFA* for some interest rate not given in the tables (for example, 6.5 percent).

[6] It is worth noting that the entry for each period t in Table A.4 is equal to the sum of the entries in Table A.2 up to

TABLE A.4

Sum of an Annuity of $1 per Period for n Periods:

$$FVIFA_{i,n} = \sum_{t=1}^{n} (1 + i)^{t-1}$$

$$= \frac{(1 + i)^n - 1}{i}$$

Number of Periods	1%	2%	3%	4%	5%	6%	7%	8%
1	1.0000	1.0000	1.0000	1.0000	1.0000	1.0000	1.0000	1.0000
2	2.0100	2.0200	2.0300	2.0400	2.0500	2.0600	2.0700	2.0800
3	3.0301	3.0604	3.0909	3.1216	3.1525	3.1836	3.2149	3.2464
4	4.0604	4.1216	4.1836	4.2465	4.3101	4.3746	4.4399	4.5061
5	5.1010	5.2040	5.3091	5.4163	5.5256	5.6371	5.7507	5.8666
6	6.1520	6.3081	6.4684	6.6330	6.8019	6.9753	7.1533	7.3359
7	7.2135	7.4343	7.6625	7.8983	8.1420	8.3938	8.6540	8.9228
8	8.2857	8.5830	8.8923	9.2142	9.5491	9.8975	10.2598	10.6366
9	9.3685	9.7546	10.1591	10.5828	11.0266	11.4913	11.9780	12.4876
10	10.4622	10.9497	11.4639	12.0061	12.5779	13.1808	13.8164	14.4866

PRESENT VALUE OF AN ANNUITY

Suppose you were offered the following alternatives: a three-year annuity of $1,000 per year or a lump sum payment today. You have no need for the money during the next three years, so if you accept the annuity you would simply deposit the receipts in a savings account paying 4 percent interest. How large must the lump sum payment be to make it equivalent to the annuity? The time line shown in Figure A.4 will help explain the problem.

The present value of the first receipt is $R[1/(1 + i)]$, the second is $R[1/(1 + i)]^2$, and so on. Defining the present value of an annuity of n years as A_n, and with $PVIFA_{i,n}$ defined as the present value interest factor for an annuity, we may write the following equation:

---

period $n - 1$. For example, the entry for Period 3 under the 4 percent column in Table A.4 is equal to $1.000 + 1.0400 + 1.0816 = 3.1216$.

Also, had the annuity been an *annuity due*, with payments received at the beginning rather than the end of each period, then the three payments would have occurred at $t = 0$, $t = 1$, and $t = 2$. To find the future value of an annuity due, (1) Look up the $FVIFA_{i,n}$ for $n + 1$ years, then (2) subtract 1.0 from the amount to get the $FVIFA_{i,n}$ for the annuity due. In the example, the annuity due $FVIFA_{i,n}$ is $4.2465 - 1.0 = 3.2465$ versus 3.1216 for a regular annuity. Because payments on an annuity due come earlier, it is a little more valuable than a regular annuity.

$$A_n = R\left(\frac{1}{1+i}\right)^1 + R\left(\frac{1}{1+i}\right)^2 + \ldots + R\left(\frac{1}{1+i}\right)^n \qquad \text{(A.5)}$$

$$= R\left(\frac{1}{(1+i)^1} + \frac{1}{(1+i)^2} + \ldots + \frac{1}{(1+i)^n}\right)$$

$$= R\sum_{t=1}^{n}\left(\frac{1}{1+i}\right)^t$$

$$= R(PVIFA_{i,n}). \qquad \text{(A.6)}$$

Again, tables have been worked out for $PVIFA_{i,n}$, the term in parentheses in Equation A.6. Table A.5 is illustrative; a more complete listing is found in Table C.4 in Appendix C. From Table A.5, the $PVIFA_{i,n}$ for a three-year, 4 percent annuity is found to be 2.7751. Multiplying this factor by the $1,000 annual receipt gives $2,775.10, the present value of the annuity. This figure is identical to the long-method answer shown in Figure A.4:

$$A_n = R(PVIFA_{i,n})$$

$$A_3 = \$1,000(2.7751)$$

$$= \$2,775.10.$$

Notice that the entry for each period n in Table A.5 is equal to the sum of the entries in Table A.3 up to and including period n. For example, the $PVIFA$ for 4 percent, three periods as shown in Table A.5 could have been calculated by summing values from Table A.3:

FIGURE A.4

Time Line for an Annuity: Present Value ($i = 4\%$)

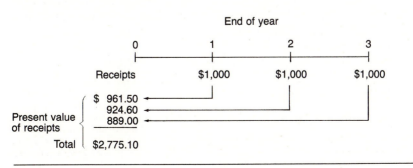

TABLE A.5

Present Value of an Annuity of $1 per Period for *n* Periods:

$$PVIFA_{i,n} = \sum_{t=1}^{n} \frac{1}{(1 + i)^t} = \frac{1 - \dfrac{1}{(1 + i)^n}}{i}$$

Period	1%	2%	3%	4%	5%	6%	7%	8%	9%	10%
1	0.9901	0.9804	0.9709	0.9615	0.9524	0.9434	0.9346	0.9259	0.9174	0.9091
2	1.9704	1.9416	1.9135	1.8861	1.8594	1.8334	1.8080	1.7833	1.7591	1.7355
3	2.9410	2.8839	2.8286	2.7751	2.7232	2.6730	2.6243	2.5771	2.5313	2.4869
4	3.9020	3.8077	3.7171	3.6299	3.5460	3.4651	3.3872	3.3121	3.2397	3.1699
5	4.8534	4.7135	4.5797	4.4518	4.3295	4.2124	4.1002	3.9927	3.8897	3.7908
6	5.7955	5.6014	5.4172	5.2421	5.0757	4.9173	4.7665	4.6229	4.4859	4.3553
7	6.7282	6.4720	6.2303	6.0021	5.7864	5.5824	5.3893	5.2064	5.0330	4.8684
8	7.6517	7.3255	7.0197	6.7327	6.4632	6.2098	5.9713	5.7466	5.5348	5.3349
9	8.5660	8.1622	7.7861	7.4353	7.1078	6.8017	6.5152	6.2469	5.9952	5.7590
10	9.4713	8.9826	8.5302	8.1109	7.7217	7.3601	7.0236	6.7101	6.4177	6.1446

$$0.9615 + 0.9246 + 0.8890 = 2.7751.$$

Notice also that for all positive interest rates, $PVIFA_{i,n}$ for the *present value* of an annuity is always less than the number of periods and annuity runs, whereas $FVIFA_{i,n}$ for the *sum* of an annuity is equal to or greater than the number of periods.[7]

PRESENT VALUE OF AN UNEVEN SERIES OF RECEIPTS

The definition of an annuity includes the words *fixed amount*—in other words, annuities involve situations where cash flows are *identical* in every year. Although many managerial decisions involve constant cash flows, some important decisions are concerned with uneven flows of cash. Consequently, it is necessary to expand our analysis to deal with varying payments streams.

The *PV* of an uneven stream of future income is found as the sum of the *PV*s of the individual components of the stream. For example, suppose we are trying to find the *PV* of the stream of receipts shown in Table A.6, discounted at 6 percent. As shown in the table, we multiply each receipt by the appropriate $PVIF_{i,n}$, then sum these products to obtain the *PV* of the stream, $1,413.24. Figure A.5 gives a graphic view of the cash flow stream.

---

[7]To find the $PVIFA_{i,n}$ for an *annuity due*, go through these steps: (1) Look up the $PVIFA_{i,n}$ for $n - 1$ periods, then (2) add 1.0 to this amount to obtain the $PVIFA_{i,n}$ for the annuity due. In the example, the $PVIFA_{i,n}$ for a 4 percent, three-year annuity due is $1.8861 + 1.0 = 2.8861$.

TABLE A.6

Present Value of an Uneven Stream of Receipts

	Stream of Receipts	×	$PVIF_{i,n}$ (6%)	=	PV of Individual Receipts
Year 1	$ 100		0.9434		$ 94.34
Year 2	200		0.8900		178.00
Year 3	200		0.8396		167.92
Year 4	200		0.7921		158.42
Year 5	200		0.7473		149.46
Year 6	0		0.7050		0
Year 7	1,000		0.6651		665.10
				PV = Sum =	$1,413.24

The *PV* of the receipts shown in Table A.6 and Figure A.5 can also be found by using the annuity equation; the steps in this alternative solution process are outlined below:

Step 1 Find *PV* of $100 due in one year:

$$\$100(0.9434) = \$94.34.$$

Step 2 Recognize that a $200 annuity will be received during Years 2 through 5. Thus, we could determine the value of a five-year annuity, subtract from it the value of a one-year annuity, and have remaining the value of a four-year annuity whose first payment is due in two years. This result is achieved by subtracting the *PVIFA* for a one-year, 6 percent annuity from the *PVIFA* for a five-year annuity and then multiplying the difference by $200:

$$PV \text{ of the Annuity} = (PVIFA_{6\%, 5\,yrs.} - PVIFA_{6\%, 1\,yr.})(\$200)$$

$$= (4.2124 - 0.9434)(\$200)$$

$$= \$653.80.$$

Thus, the present value of the annuity component of the uneven stream is $653.80.

Step 3 Find the *PV* of the $1,000 due in Year 7:

$$\$1,000(0.6651) = \$665.10.$$

Step 4 Sum the components:

$$\$94.34 + \$653.80 + \$665.10 = \$1,413.24.$$

FIGURE A.5

Time Line for an Uneven Cash Flow Stream ($i = 6\%$)

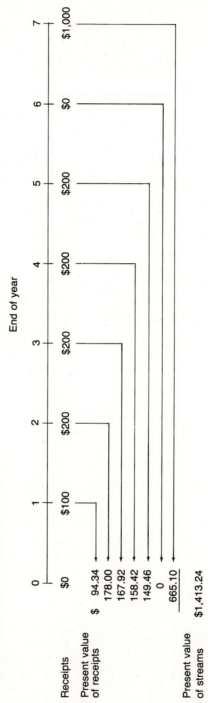

Either of the two methods can be used to solve problems of this type. However, the alternative (annuity) solution is easier if the annuity component runs for many years. For example, the alternative solution would be clearly superior for finding the *PV* of a stream consisting of $100 in Year 1, $200 in Years 2 through 29, and $1,000 in Year 30.

ANNUAL PAYMENTS FOR ACCUMULATION OF A FUTURE SUM

Suppose we want to know the amount of money that must be deposited at 5 percent for each of the next five years in order to have $10,000 available to pay off a debt at the end of the fifth year. Dividing both sides of Equation A.4 by *FVIFA*, we obtain:

$$R = \frac{S_n}{FVIFA_{i,n}} \,. \tag{A.7}$$

Looking up the future value of an annuity interest factor for five years at 5 percent in Table A.4 and dividing this figure into $10,000, we find:

$$R = \frac{\$10,000}{5.5256} = \$1,810.$$

Thus, if $1,810 is deposited each year in an account paying 5 percent interest, at the end of five years the account will have accumulated $10,000.

ANNUAL RECEIPTS FROM AN ANNUITY

Suppose that on September 1, 1979, you receive an inheritance of $7,000. The money is to be used for your education and is to be spent during the academic years beginning September 1980, 1981, and 1982. If you place the money in a bank account paying 4 percent annual interest and make three equal withdrawals at each of the specified dates, how large can each withdrawal be so as to leave you with exactly a zero balance after the last one has been made?

The solution requires application of the present value of an annuity formula, Equation A.6. Here, however, we know that the present value of the annuity is $7,000, and the problem is to find the three equal annual payments when the interest rate is 4 percent. This calls for dividing both sides of Equation A.6 by $PVIFA_{i,n}$ to derive Equation A.8:

$$R = \frac{A_n}{PVIFA_{i,n}} \cdot \qquad \qquad \text{(A.8)}$$

The interest factor is found in Table A.5 to be 2.775, and substituting this value into Equation A.8, we find the three annual withdrawals to be $2,523:

$$R = \frac{\$7,000}{2.775} = \$2,523.$$

This particular calculation is used frequently to set up insurance and pension plan benefit schedules and to find the periodic payments necessary to retire a loan within a specified period. For example, if you want to retire in three equal annual payments a $7,000 bank loan drawing interest at 4 percent on the unpaid balance, each payment would be $2,523. In this case the bank is acquiring an annuity with a present value of $7,000.

DETERMINING INTEREST RATES

We can use the basic equations developed earlier to determine the interest rates implicit in financial contracts.

Example 1. A bank offers to lend you $1,000 if you sign a note to repay $1,610.50 at the end of five years. What rate of interest are you paying? To solve the problem, recognize that $1,000 is the *PV* of $1,610.50 due in five years, and solve Equation A.3 for the present value interest factor ($PVIF_{i,n}$).

$$PV = FV_n \left[\frac{1}{(1 + i)^n} \right] = FV_n(PVIF_{i,n}) \qquad \qquad \text{(A.3)}$$

$$\$1,000 = \$1,610.50(PVIF_{i,n} \text{ for 5 years})$$

$$\$1,000/\$1,610.50 = 0.6209 = PVIF_{i,5}.$$

Now, go to Table A.3 and look across the row for Year 5 until you find 0.6209. It is in the 10 percent column, so you would be paying a 10 percent rate of interest.

Example 2. A bank offers to lend you $75,000 to buy a house. You must sign a mortgage calling for payments of $9,562.67 at the end of each of the next 25 years. What interest rate is the bank charging you?

1. Recognize that $75,000 is the *PV* of a 25-year, $9,562.67 annuity:

$$\$75{,}000 = PV = \sum_{t=1}^{25} \$9{,}562.67 \left[\frac{1}{(1+i)^t} \right] = \$9{,}562.67(PVIFA_{i,n}).$$

2. Solve for $PVIFA_{i,n}$:

$$PVIFA_{i,n} = \$75{,}000/\$9{,}562.67 = 7.843.$$

3. Turn to Table C.4 in Appendix C, since Table A.4 does not cover a 25-year period. Looking across the row for 25 periods, we find 7.843 under the column for 12 percent. Therefore, the rate of interest on this mortgage loan is 12 percent.

SEMIANNUAL AND OTHER COMPOUNDING PERIODS

In all the examples used thus far, it has been assumed that returns were received once a year, or annually. Suppose, however, that you put your $1,000 in a bank that advertises that it pays 6 percent interest *semiannually*. How much will you have at the end of one year? Semiannual compounding means that interest is actually paid every six months, a fact taken into account in the tabular calculations in Table A.7. Here the annual interest rate is divided by two, but twice as many compounding periods are used, because interest is paid twice a year. Comparing the amount on hand at the end of the second six-month period, $1,060.90, with what would have been on hand under annual compounding, $1,060, shows that semiannual compounding is better from the standpoint of the saver. This result occurs because you earn interest on interest more frequently.

Throughout the economy, different types of investments use different compounding periods. For example, bank and savings and loan accounts generally pay interest quarterly, some bonds pay interest semiannually, and other bonds pay annual interest. Thus, if we are to compare securities with different compounding periods, we need to put them on a common basis. This need has led to the development of the terms *nominal*, or *stated*, *interest rate* and *effective annual*, or *annual percentage*, *rate* (APR). The stated, or nominal, rate is the quoted rate; thus, in our

TABLE A.7

Compound Interest Calculations with Semiannual Compounding

Period	Beginning Amount (PV)	×	$(1 + i/2)$	=	Ending Amount, FV_n
1	$1,000.00		(1.03)		$1,030.00
2	1,030.00		(1.03)		1,060.90

example the nominal rate is 6 percent. The annual percentage rate is the rate that would have produced the final compound value, $1,060.90, under annual rather than semiannual compounding. In this case, the effective annual rate is 6.09 percent:

$$\$1,000(1 + i) = \$1,060.90$$

$$i = \frac{\$1,060.90}{\$1,000} - 1 = 0.0609 = 6.09\%.$$

Thus, if one bank offered 6 percent with semiannual compounding, while another offered 6.09 percent with annual compounding, they would both be paying the same effective rate of interest. In general, we can determine the effective annual rate of interest, given the nominal rate, as follows:

Step 1 Find the *FV* of $1 at the end of one year, using the equation

$$FV = 1\left(1 + \frac{i_n}{m}\right)^m.$$

Here i_n is the nominal rate, and m is the number of compounding periods per year.

Step 2 Subtract 1.0 from the result in Step 1, then multiply by 100. The final result is the effective annual rate.

Example. Find the effective annual rate if the nominal rate is 6 percent, compounded semiannually:

$$\text{Effective Annual Rate} = \left(1 + \frac{0.06}{2}\right)^2 - 1.0$$

$$= (1.03)^2 - 1.0$$

$$= 1.0609 - 1.0$$

$$= 0.0609$$

$$= 6.09\%.$$

The points made about semiannual compounding can be generalized as follows. When compounding periods are more frequent than once a year, we use a modified version of Equation A.2:

$$FV_n = PV(1 + i)^n. \qquad\qquad\qquad \text{(A.2)}$$

$$FV_n = PV\left(1 + \frac{i}{m}\right)^{mn}. \qquad\qquad \text{(A.2a)}$$

Here m is the number of times per year compounding occurs. When banks compute daily interest, the value of m is set at 365, and Equation A.2a is applied.

The interest tables can be used when compounding occurs more than once a year. Simply divide the nominal, or stated, interest rate by the number of times compounding occurs, and multiply the years by the number of compounding periods per year. For example, to find the amount to which $1,000 will grow after six years if semiannual compounding is applied to a stated 8 percent interest rate, divide 8 percent by 2 and multiply the six years by 2. Then look in Table A.2 under the 4 percent column and in the row for Period 12. You find an interest factor of 1.6010. Multiplying this by the initial $1,000 gives a value of $1,601, the amount to which $1,000 will grow in six years at 8 percent compounded semiannually. This compares with $1,586.90 for annual compounding.

The same procedure is applied in all the cases covered—compounding, discounting, single payments, and annuities. To illustrate semiannual discounting in finding the present value of an annuity, consider the case described in the section "Present Value of an Annuity": $1,000 a year for three years, discounted at 4 percent. With annual discounting, the interest factor is 2.7751, and the present value of the annuity is $2,775.10. For semiannual discounting, look under the 2 percent column and in the Period 6 row of Table A.5 to find an interest factor of 5.6014. This is now multiplied by half of $1,000, or the $500 received each six months, to get the present value of the annuity, $2,800.70. The payments come a little more rapidly— the first $500 is paid after only six months (similarly with other payments)—so the annuity is a little more valuable if payments are received semiannually rather than annually.

SUMMARY

Managerial decisions often involve determining the present value of a stream of future cash flows. Also, we often need to know the amount to which an initial quantity will grow during a specified time period, and at other times we must calculate the interest rate built into a financial contract. The basic concepts involved in these processes are called compounding and the time value of money.

The key procedures covered in this appendix are summarized below:

Future Value: $FV_n = PV(1 + i)^n$, where FV_n is the future value of an initial amount, PV, compounded at the rate of i percent for n periods. The term $(1 + i)^n$ is defined as $FVIF_{i,n}$, the *future value interest factor*. Values for $FVIF$ are contained in tables.

Present Value: $PV = FV_n[1/(1 + i)]^n$. This equation is simply a transformation of the future value equation. The term $[1/(1 + i)]^n$ is defined as $PVIF_{i,n}$, the present value interest factor.

Future Value of an Annuity: An annuity is defined as a series of constant or equal payments of R dollars per period. The sum, or future value of an annuity, is given the symbol S_n, and it is found as follows: $S_n = R[\sum_{t=1}^{n} (1 + i)^{t-1}]$. The term $[\sum_{t=1}^{n} (1 + i)^{t-1}]$ is defined as $FVIFA_{i,n}$, the future value interest factor for an annuity.

Present Value of an Annuity: The present value of an annuity is given the symbol A_n, and it is found as follows: $A_n = R[\sum_{t=1}^{n} (1/1 + i)^t]$. The term $[\sum_{t=1}^{n} (1/1 + i)^t] = PVIFA_{i,n}$ is defined as the present value interest factor for an annuity.

APPENDIX B
FORECASTING

Two key functions of management for any organization are *planning* and *control*. The firm must plan for the future. Planning for the future involves the following steps:

1. Determine the product and geographic markets where the firm can earn the highest returns.

2. Forecast the level of demand in these markets under different conditions of price, promotional activities, competition, and general economic activity levels.

3. Forecast the cost of producing different levels of output under conditions of changing technology, wage rates, and raw materials prices.

4. Decide on the optimum operating plan; that is, the value-maximizing plan.

5. Engage in capital acquisition programs, labor training programs, and so forth in order to implement the general corporate plan.

Once the plan has been determined, it must be carried out in the *control*, or *operating*, phase of the activity of the enterprise. Quite obviously, planning and control are closely related; in practice, they are often inseparable. Operating procedures, or the process of control, must be geared to the firm's plans. If the forecasts about demand or about the cost of the input factors of production, technology, and the like that go into the plan are seriously in error, then the plan will be no good and the control phase will also break down.

In view of the key role of forecasting in managerial decisions, it is not surprising that forecasting per se is emphasized in managerial economics. In this appendix we describe and illustrate several of the more useful techniques employed in forecasting.

FORECASTING METHODOLOGIES

Many techniques are available for use in forecasting economic variables. They range from simple, often somewhat naïve, and relatively inexpensive procedures to methods that are quite complex and very expensive. Some forecasting techniques are basically quantitative; others are qualitative. Forecasting techniques can be divided into the following three broad categories:

1. Qualitative Analyses
2. Time Series Analysis and Projection
3. Econometric Models

It is impossible to state unequivocally that one or another of these basic forecasting approaches is superior to all others. The best one for a particular task depends in large part on a number of factors in each specific forecasting problem. Some of the important factors that must be considered include:

1. The distance into the future that one must forecast.
2. The lead time available for making decisions.
3. The level of accuracy required.
4. The quality of data available for analysis.
5. The nature of the relationships included in the forecasting problem.
6. The cost and benefits associated with the forecasting problem.

Some techniques—for example, certain time series, barometric, and survey methodologies—are well suited for short-term projections. Others require more lead time and are therefore more useful for long-run forecasting. Within each class of forecasting techniques, the level of sophistication also varies. Typically, the greater the level of sophistication required for a given level of forecast accuracy, the higher the cost. If the level of accuracy desired in projection is low, less sophisticated methods may provide adequate results at minimal cost. Therefore, the choice of an appropriate forecasting methodology depends upon both the underlying characteristics of the forecasting problem as well as the level of accuracy desired.

In order to determine an appropriate level of forecast accuracy, one must compare the costs and benefits of increased forecast accuracy. When forecast accuracy is low, the probability of significant forecasting error is high as is the chance of making erroneous managerial decisions. Conversely, when forecast accuracy is high, the probability of substantial forecasting error is reduced and the chance of making erroneous managerial decisions is low. Thus, it is reasonable to require a relatively high level of forecast accuracy when the dollar costs of forecast error are high. When only minor costs result from forecast error, only inexpensive and typically less accurate methods can be justified.

In the material that follows, we examine both the advantages and limitations of various forecasting techniques. By understanding the strengths and weaknesses of various forecasting methodologies, managers can select an appropriate method or combination of methods to generate required forecast values.

QUALITATIVE ANALYSES

When quantitative information in unavailable, qualitative analysis must be relied upon to prepare required forecasts. Qualitative analysis can be a highly useful forecasting technique if the approach adopted allows for the systematic collection and organization of data derived from unbiased informed opinion. However, qualitative methods can produce biased results in instances where specific individuals dominate the forecasting process through reputation, force of personality, or strategic position within the organization.

Expert Opinion

The most basic form of qualitative analysis used in forecasting is *personal insight*. Here an informed individual uses personal or organizational experience as a basis for projecting future expectations. While this approach is highly subjective and non-scientific, it cannot be rejected out-of-hand since the reasoned judgment of informed individuals often provides invaluable insight. Because this approach is highly subjective, it is important that the underlying assumptions involved in various forecast scenarios be stated explicitly so that changes in basic conditions can be accounted for in the analysis. When the informed opinion of several individuals is relied upon, the approach is called forecasting through use of *panel consensus*. The panel consensus method assumes that several experts can arrive at forecasts that are superior to those that individuals generate. Direct interaction among the experts is used in the panel consensus method, with the hope that resulting forecasts embody all available objective and subjective evidence.

While the panel consensus method often results in forecasts which embody the collective wisdom of consulted experts, it can sometimes be unfavorably affected by the force of personality of one or a few key individuals. A related approach, the *delphi method*, has been developed to counter this disadvantage of the panel consensus method. In the delphi method a panel of experts is individually presented a series of questions relating to the underlying forecasting problem. Responses are analyzed by an independent party who then tries to elicit the apparent consensus opinion by providing feedback to the panel members in a manner that prevents direct identification of individual positions. This approach can prove useful in limiting problems associated with the steamroller or bandwagon possibilities of the panel consensus approach.

Survey Techniques

Survey techniques constitute another important forecasting tool, especially for short-term projections. Surveys generally involve use of interviews or mailed questionnaires asking business firms, government agencies, and individuals about their future plans. Business firms plan and budget virtually all their expenditures in advance of actual purchases or production. Surveys asking about capital budgets, sales budgets, and operating budgets can thus provide much useful information for forecasting. Government units also prepare formal budgets well before the actual spending is done, and surveys of budget material, congressional appropriations hearings, and the like can provide a wealth of information to the forecaster. Finally, even individual consumers usually plan expenditures for such major items as automobiles, furniture, housing, vacations, and education well ahead of the purchase date, so consumer intention surveys can accurately predict future spending on consumer goods.

While surveys do provide an alternative to quantitative forecasting techniques, they are frequently used to supplement rather than replace quantitative analysis. Survey information may be all that is obtainable in certain forecasting situations— for example, when a firm is attempting to project the demand for a new product. More often, surveys are used in conjunction with the quantitative methods. The value of survey techniques as a supplement to quantitative methods stems from two factors. First, a nonquantifiable psychological element is inherent in most economic behavior, and surveys and other qualitative methods are especially well suited to pick up this phenomenon. Second, econometric models generally assume stable consumer tastes and the like, and if these factors are actually changing, survey data may reveal such changes.

Surveys for Forecasting Various Classes of Expenditures

Many useful surveys for forecasting business activity in various sectors of the U.S. economy are published periodically by private and government units. Some of these are:

Plant and Equipment Expenditures. Surveys of businesses' intentions to expand plant and equipment are conducted by the U.S. Department of Commerce, the Securities and Exchange Commission, the National Industrial Conference Board, McGraw-Hill, Inc., *Fortune* magazine, and various trade associations such as the Edison Electric Institute and the American Gas Association.

Inventory Changes and Sales Expectations. The U.S. Commerce Department, *Fortune* magazine, McGraw-Hill, Inc., Dun and Bradstreet, and the National Association of Purchasing Agents all survey businesspeople's expectations about future sales levels and their plans for inventory changes. These surveys, while not nearly so accurate as those for long-term investment, provide a useful check on other forecasting methods.

Consumer Expenditures. The consumer intentions surveys of the Census Bureau, the University of Michigan Research Center, and the Sindlinger-National Industrial Conference Board all provide information on planned purchases of specific products—such as automobiles, housing, and appliances. In addition, these surveys often indicate consumer confidence in the economy and, thereby, spending expectations in general. Attempts are being made to quantify all aspects of survey data and to incorporate this information directly into econometric models. Although some success is being achieved with these attempts, a great deal of judgment is still required. Forecasting is becoming a science, but it still contains elements of art.

TIME-SERIES ANALYSIS AND PROJECTION

Probably the most frequently employed forecasting methodology is one variously known as *trend projection*, *extrapolation*, or *curve fitting*. The technique is based on an assumption that future events will follow along an established path or, alternatively, that past patterns of economic behavior prevail sufficiently to justify using historical data to predict the future. The economic forecaster who uses this technique looks at the historical pattern of the variable of interest and then projects, or forecasts, that it will continue moving along the path described by its past movement.

The many variations of forecasting by trend projection are all predicated by assuming a continuing relationship between the variable being projected and the passage of time, so all of them employ time-series data. An economic time series is a sequential array of the values of an economic variable. Weekly, monthly, or annual series of sales and cost data, income statistics, population, labor force participation rates, and the gross national product (GNP) are all examples of economic time series.

All time series, regardless of the nature of the economic variable involved, can be described by the following four characteristics:

1. *Secular trend*, or the long-run increase or decrease in the series.

2. *Cyclical fluctuations*, or rhythmic variations in the economic series.

3. *Seasonal variation*, or variations caused by weather patterns and/or social habits that produce an *annual* pattern in the time series.

4. *Irregular or random influences*, or unpredictable shocks to the system—such as wars, strikes, natural catastrophes, and so on.

These four patterns are illustrated in Figure B.1, where (a) shows secular and cyclical trends in sales of women's clothing and (b) shows (1) the seasonal pattern superimposed over the long-run trend (which, in this case, is a composite of the secular and cyclical trends) and (2) random fluctuations around the seasonal curve.

Time-series analysis can be as simple as projecting or extrapolating the unadjusted trend. Applying either graphic analysis (by *eye* fitting) or least squares regression techniques, one can use historical data to determine the average increase or decrease in the series during each time period and then project this rate of change into the future.

Time-series analysis can also be considerably more complex and sophisticated, allowing examination of seasonal and cyclical patterns as well as the basic trend. The X-11 procedure developed by the U.S. Census Bureau and the Box-Jenkins method are two of the more useful and used of these techniques.

Since extrapolation techniques assume that a variable will follow its established path, the problem is to determine accurately the appropriate trend curve. In theory, one could fit any complex mathematical function to the historical data and extrapolate to estimate future values. In practice, however, one typically finds linear, simple power, or exponential curves used for economic forecasting.

Selection of the appropriate curve is guided by both empirical and theoretical considerations. Empirically, it is a question of finding the curve that best fits the

FIGURE B.1

Time-Series Characteristics: (a) Secular Trend and Cyclical Variation in Women's Clothing Sales; (b) Seasonal Pattern and Random Fluctuations

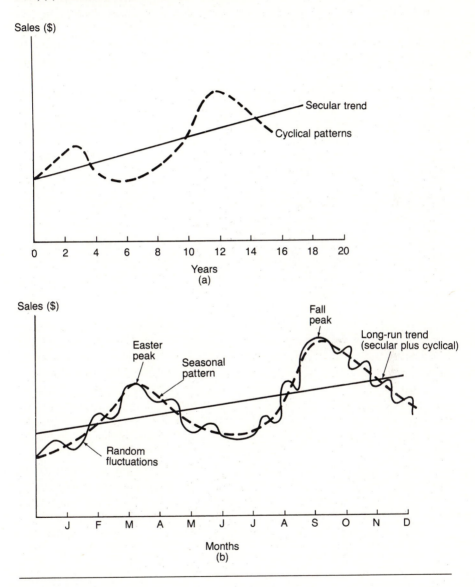

FIGURE B.2

U.S. Gross National Product, 1966–1980 (current dollars)

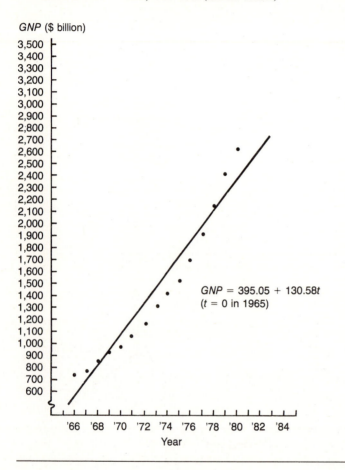

GNP = 395.05 + 130.58t
(t = 0 in 1965)

historical movement of the data. Theoretical considerations intervene when logic dictates that a particular pattern of future events must prevail. For example, output in a particular industry may have been expanding at a constant rate historically, but because of known resource limitations, one might use a declining growth rate model to reflect the slowing down of growth that must ultimately prevail.

A simple trending procedure is illustrated in Figure B.2. There the gross national product (GNP) time-series data given in Table B.1 are displayed along with a curve representing a linear relationship between GNP and time. This linear relationship can be written as:

$$GNP = a + b \cdot t. \tag{B.1}$$

TABLE B.1

U.S. Gross National Product, 1966–1980 (current dollars)

Year	GNP (Billions)
1980	2,626.1
1979	2,413.9
1978	2,156.1
1977	1,899.5
1976	1,702.2
1975	1,528.8
1974	1,412.9
1973	1,306.6
1972	1,171.1
1971	1,063.4
1970	982.4
1969	930.2
1968	865.7
1967	793.5
1966	743.3

Sources: U.S. Bureau of the Census, *Statistical Abstract of the United States*, Washington, D.C. (various years); *Federal Reserve Bulletin*, Vol. 67, No. 11 (November 1981), p. A52.

The coefficients of this linear relationship were estimated using least squares regression as (*t*-statistics in parentheses):

$$GNP = 395.05 + 130.58t \qquad R^2 = .94. \qquad \textbf{(B.2)}$$
$$(4.66) \quad (14.00)$$

While a linear trending procedure for GNP is obviously naive, there is an important trend element in GNP. Using the naive linear trend equation estimated over the 1966–1980 period, one can estimate GNP for future time periods. To do so one must realize that in the above model $t = 1$ for 1966, $t = 2$ for 1967, and so on. This means that $t = 0$ in a 1965 base period. To forecast GNP in any future period we simply subtract 1965 from the year in question to determine a relevant value for t.

For example, a GNP forecast for 1985 using Equation B.2 would be:

$$t = 1985 - 1965 = 20$$

$$GNP_{1985} = 395.05 + 130.58 \, (20)$$

$$= 395.05 + 2,611.60$$

$$= \$3,006.65 \text{ billion}$$

Similarly, a GNP forecast for 1990 could be calculated as:

$$t = 1990 - 1965 = 25$$

$$GNP_{1990} = 395.05 + 130.58 \, (25)$$

$$= 395.05 + 3,264.50$$

$$= \$3,659.55 \text{ billion}$$

Note that these projections of future GNP are based upon a *linear* trend line, which implies that GNP is increasing by a constant dollar amount each year. There are important reasons for believing that the underlying trend relationship for GNP is nonlinear and that the GNP forecasts generated above will be relatively poor estimates of actual values. To see why a linear trend relationship may not be accurate in the case of GNP projection, consider the relationship between actual GNP data and the linear trend relationship shown in Figure B.2. Remember that the least squares regression line is the line that minimizes the sum of squared residuals between actual and fitted values over the sample period. As is typical, actual data points lie both above and below the fitted regression lines. Note, however, that the pattern of the differences between actual and fitted values varies dramatically over the sample period. Differences between actual and fitted values are positive in both early (1966–1969) and late (1978–1980) periods, while being negative in the intervening period. This suggests that the slope of the GNP and time relationship is not constant, but rather increases over the sample period.

While an assumption of a constant absolute annual change is quite appropriate for some economic variables, there are several alternative assumptions that more accurately describe the way many economic series such as GNP change over time. One widely used alternative model is the constant growth rate, or constant rate of change, model. Sales revenues for many products—as well as GNP, per capita income, and population—are all examples of economic variables whose change over time appears to be proportional rather than constant in absolute amount.

The constant *rate* of change, or proportional change model, involves determining the average historical rate of change in the variable and projecting that rate into the future. This is essentially identical to the compounding of value model used in finance.[1] For example, if a firm is projecting its sales for five years into the future and if it has determined that sales are increasing at an annual rate of 10 percent, the projection would simply involve multiplying the 10 percent compound value interest factor for five years times current sales. Assuming current sales are $1 million, the forecast of sales five years from now would be:

---

[1] *See* Appendix A section entitled "Future Value (or Compound Value)" for more on compound value growth models.

$$\text{Sales in Year 5} = \text{Current Sales} \times (1 + \text{Growth Rate})^5$$

$$= \$1,000,000 \times (1.10)^5$$

$$= \$1,000,000 \times 1.61$$

$$= \$1,610,000.$$

More generally, the constant rate of change projection model can be stated as follows:

$$\text{Value } t \text{ Years in the Future} = \text{Current Value} \times (1 + \text{Rate of Change})^t.$$

Just as one can estimate the constant annual change in an economic time series by fitting historical data to a linear regression model of the form $Y = a + bt$, so, too, can one estimate the annual growth rate in a constant rate of change projection model using the same technique. In this case the growth rate is estimated using linear regression by fitting historical data to the logarithmic transformation of the basic model. For example, if one were to formulate a constant growth rate model for GNP it would take the form:

$$GNP_t = GNP_0 \cdot (1 + g)^t. \tag{B.3}$$

Here GNP t years in the future is assumed to be equal to GNP today, GNP_0, compounded at a growth rate, g, for a period of t years. Taking logarithms of both sides of Equation B.3 results in the expression:

$$ln\ GNP_t = ln\ GNP_0 + ln(1 + g) \cdot t. \tag{B.4}$$

Note that Equation B.4 is an expression of the form:

$$Y_t = a + bt,$$

where $Y_t = ln\ GNP_t$, $a = ln\ GNP_0$, and $b = ln\ (1 + g)$; hence, its coefficients, $ln\ GNP_0$ and $ln\ (1 + g)$, can be estimated using the least squares regression technique.

Applying this technique to the GNP data in Table B.1 results in the regression (t-statistics in parenthesis)

$$ln\ GNP_t = 6.46 + 0.091t \qquad\qquad R^2 = .99, \tag{B.5}$$
$$(323.83)\ \ (41.46)$$

or, equivalently, by transforming this estimated equation back to its original form:

$$GNP_t = [\text{Antilog } 6.46] \times [\text{Antilog } 0.091]^t = 639.06(1.095)^t. \qquad \textbf{(B.6)}$$

In this model, \$639.06 billion is the adjusted GNP for $t = 0$ (which would be 1965, since the first year of data used in the regression estimation [$t = 1$] was 1966); and 1.095 is the quantity one plus the average annual rate of growth, or increase in GNP, indicating that GNP has been increasing by 9.5 percent annually over the 1966–1980 period.[2]

As before, to forecast GNP in any future year using this model, we subtract 1965 from the year being forecast to determine t. Thus, a constant growth model forecast of GNP in 1985 is:

$$t = 1985 - 1965 = 20$$

$$GNP_{1985} = 693.06 \, (1.095)^{20}$$

$$= 693.06 \cdot 6.1416$$

$$= \$4,256.51 \text{ billion.}$$

Similarly, a constant growth model forecast of GNP in 1990 is:

$$t = 1990 - 1965 = 25$$

$$GNP_{1990} = 693.06 \, (1.095)^{25}$$

$$= 693.06 \cdot 9.6684$$

$$= \$6,700.76 \text{ billion.}$$

The importance of selecting the correct structural form for a trending model can be demonstrated by comparing the GNP projections that result from the two models we have examined. Recall that with the constant absolute annual change model, GNP

---

[2]Another frequently used form of the constant growth rate model is based on a *continuous* (as opposed to annual) compounding assumption. This model is expressed by the exponential equation

$$Y_t = Y_0 e^{gt},$$

and its logarithmic equivalent is:

$$ln \, Y_t = ln \, Y_0 + gt.$$

Thus, with the exponential growth assumption, the regression model's estimate of the slope coefficient, g, is a direct estimate of the continuous rate of growth. For example, in the GNP regression model, Equation B.3, the coefficient 0.091 (= 9.1%) is a direct estimate of a continuous compounding growth rate for GNP.

was projected to be $3 trillion and $3.7 trillion in 1985 and 1990, respectively. These projections compare with the $4.3 trillion GNP projection for 1985 and $6.7 trillion forecast for 1990 obtained with the constant growth rate model. Notice the difference in the near-term forecasts (1985) is small relative to the difference in the 1990 projections. This points up the fact that if an economic time series is growing at a constant rate rather than increasing by a constant absolute amount—and GNP does appear to exhibit this characteristic—then forecasts based on a linear trend model will tend to become less and less accurate the further out into the future one projects.

Although trend projections can provide very adequate estimates for some forecasting purposes, a number of serious shortcomings in the technique limit its usefulness for many purposes. First, trend projections are typically more useful for intermediate to long-term forecasting than for short-run estimation. The reason lies in the inability of the technique to predict cyclical turning points or fluctuations. Second, trend projections implicitly assume that the historical relationships involved in the time series will continue into the future. This is not always the case. There are many examples of the disastrous effects of using this forecasting method just prior to the economic reversals of 1929, 1937, 1975, and 1982. Finally, trend analysis entails no analysis of causal relationships and hence offers no help in analyzing either why a particular series moves as it does or what the impact of a particular policy decision would be on the future movement of the series.

Seasonal and Cyclical Variations

Many important economic time series are regularly influenced by seasonal and cyclical variations. Figure B.1 illustrated how such variations can influence demand patterns for a typical consumer product. It is worthwhile to consider these influences further since the treatment of seasonal and cyclical variations plays an important role in time-series analysis and projection.

New housing starts constitute an important economic time series which is regularly influenced by seasonal and cyclical variations. Table B.2 provides data on the number of new privately owned housing units started in the United States during a recent fifteen-year period, 1965–1979. Thousands of housing units started are reported in Table B.2(a), while seasonally adjusted annual rates are shown in Table B.2(b). From B.2(a) it is clear that there is an important seasonal element in the total variation of housing starts. Quite understandably, housing starts tend to be high in the months of May, June, and July and relatively low in November, December, and January. The obvious source of such variations is the weather. In many northern states it is difficult if not impossible to maintain a high level of housing starts during colder winter months. After adjusting for the seasonal element in housing starts, a regular pattern of cyclical variations becomes apparent. Seasonally adjusted annual data provided in Table B.2(b) show that housing starts declined precipitously in

TABLE B.2

New Privately Owned Housing Units Started, 1965–1979

(a)   Unadjusted Monthly Data
                                                  Thousands

	Jan.	Feb.	Mar.	Apr.	May	June	July	Aug.	Sept.	Oct.	Nov.	Dec.	Total
1979	73.9	84.5	152.9	142.3	170.5	173.1	144.5	145.4	144.7	152.6	106.9	91.6	1582.9
1978	75.6	84.7	141.9	163.9	174.6	172.8	154.6	156.0	149.2	158.0	158.6	102.5	1692.4
1977	81.3	112.5	173.5	182.2	201.3	197.6	189.8	194.0	177.7	193.1	154.8	129.2	1987.1
1976	72.5	89.9	118.4	137.2	147.9	154.2	136.6	145.9	151.8	148.4	128.1	108.6	1539.7
1975	56.1	54.7	80.2	97.9	116.1	110.3	119.3	117.3	111.9	123.6	96.2	76.1	1160.4
1974	84.5	109.4	124.8	159.5	149.0	147.6	126.6	111.1	98.3	96.7	75.1	55.1	1337.7
1973	146.6	138.0	200.0	205.0	234.0	202.6	202.6	197.2	148.4	147.1	133.3	90.4	2045.3
1972	149.1	152.2	203.9	211.6	225.8	223.1	206.5	228.6	203.0	216.5	185.7	150.5	2356.6
1971	110.6	102.2	167.9	201.1	198.5	193.8	194.3	204.5	173.8	179.7	173.7	152.1	2052.2
1970	66.4	74.3	114.7	128.4	125.0	135.2	140.8	128.7	130.9	140.9	126.9	121.4	1433.6
1969	101.5	90.1	131.9	159.0	155.5	147.3	125.2	124.9	129.3	123.4	94.6	84.1	1466.8
1968	80.5	84.6	126.6	162.0	140.9	137.9	139.8	136.6	134.3	140.8	127.1	96.4	1507.6
1967	59.1	61.4	91.5	113.7	132.0	125.4	125.3	127.4	121.9	135.4	118.4	80.1	1291.6
1966	79.4	76.2	118.1	140.9	130.0	120.6	99.3	101.8	89.1	76.6	72.8	60.2	1164.9
1965	81.7	80.9	119.9	148.6	153.3	151.8	139.1	128.3	124.6	133.1	110.5	110.1	1472.8

(b)   Seasonally Adjusted Annual Rates
                                                  Thousands

	Jan.	Feb.	Mar.	Apr.	May	June	July	Aug.	Sept.	Oct.	Nov.	Dec.
1979	1,727	1,469	1,800	1,750	1,801	1,910	1,764	1,788	1,874	1,710	1,522	1,548
1978	1,779	1,762	2,028	2,182	2,018	2,092	2,090	1,983	2,014	2,001	2,111	2,052
1977	1,527	1,943	2,063	1,892	1,971	1,893	2,058	2,020	1,949	2,042	2,042	2,142
1976	1,262	1,452	1,427	1,405	1,468	1,508	1,410	1,546	1,753	1,662	1,680	1,824
1975	1,032	904	993	1,005	1,121	1,087	1,226	1,260	1,264	1,344	1,360	1,321
1974	1,453	1,784	1,553	1,571	1,415	1,526	1,290	1,145	1,180	1,100	1,028	940
1973	2,481	2,289	2,365	2,084	2,266	2,067	2,123	2,051	1,874	1,677	1,724	1,526
1972	2,494	2,390	2,334	2,249	2,221	2,254	2,252	2,382	2,481	2,485	2,421	2,366
1971	1,828	1,741	1,910	1,986	2,049	2,026	2,083	2,158	2,041	2,128	2,182	2,295
1970	1,108	1,322	1,364	1,230	1,280	1,396	1,506	1,401	1,531	1,589	1,621	1,944
1969	1,769	1,705	1,561	1,524	1,583	1,528	1,368	1,358	1,507	1,381	1,229	1,327
1968	1,344	1,498	1,472	1,532	1,384	1,393	1,561	1,501	1,527	1,579	1,690	1,618
1967	1,111	1,149	1,094	1,116	1,274	1,233	1,369	1,407	1,445	1,496	1,569	1,354
1966	1,433	1,408	1,430	1,377	1,262	1,185	1,079	1,108	1,048	845	975	931
1965	1,409	1,434	1,451	1,453	1,484	1,503	1,508	1,399	1,472	1,467	1,460	1,570

Source: Standard and Poor's Industry Surveys, *Basic Statistics, Building and Building Materials*. New York: Standard and Poor's Corporation, 1980, p. 137.

1966 and 1974. Because these declines preceded the economic downturns of 1967 and 1975, respectively, housing starts are considered a leading economic indicator.

While housing starts are an obvious and classic example of economic data subject to seasonal and cyclical variations, it is by no means a unique case. For example, economic activity in the clothing, recreation, travel, automobile, and related industries are all affected by such variations. As a result, controlling for seasonal and cyclical variations is an important aspect of time-series analysis and projection. For many economic projections an analysis of seasonal and cyclical fluctuations can vastly improve forecasting results, especially short-run forecasting results.

There are several techniques for estimating seasonal variations. A simple one examines the ratio of the actual monthly data to the trend projection. For example, if monthly sales data for a product indicate that, on the average, December sales are 20 percent above the trend line, a seasonal adjustment factor of 1.20 can be applied to that trend projection to forecast sales in that month. Likewise, if it is found that February sales had on average been 15 percent below the trend, an adjustment factor of 0.85 would be applied in projecting February sales. To illustrate, annual sales might be forecast at $1.2 million, or $100,000 a month. When the seasonal factor is introduced, however, December sales would be projected at $120,000 (= $100,000 × 1.20) and February sales at $85,000 (= $100,000 × 0.85). Production, inventory, and financing requirements could be scheduled accordingly.

Determination of cyclical patterns is very similar to that for seasonal patterns. Here the interest is on rhythmic patterns that occur over a period of years. While a few industries appear to have rhythmic oscillations that repeat with enough regularity to be considered cycles—home construction is frequently cited—these are probably the exception rather than the rule. Further, statistical problems make any breakdown of a time series into trend and cycle components tenuous at best. Most analysts today recognize that both secular trend and cycle are typically generated by a common causal mechanism, and therefore separation of the two does not lead to unambiguous forecasts. Moreover, the timing and amplitude of cycles are inconsistent over time, making cyclical adjustments difficult.

The relatively new Box-Jenkins technique for time-series analysis provides a very sophisticated approach to analyzing the various components—trend, seasonal, cyclical, random—which make up an economic time series. This technique enables one to analyze complex patterns that exist in an ordered data set. For many forecasting purposes it provides a very substantial improvement over simpler extrapolation procedures.

BAROMETRIC METHODS

Although cyclical patterns in most economic time series are so erratic as to make simple projection a hazardous short-term forecasting technique, there is evidence that a relatively consistent relationship exists between the movements of *different* economic variables over time. In other words, even though an economic series may not exhibit a consistent pattern over time, it is often possible to find a second series (or group of series) whose movement is closely correlated to that of the first. Should the forecaster have the good fortune to discover an economic series that *leads* the one he or she is attempting to forecast, the leading series can be used as a barometer for forecasting short-term change, just as a meteorologist uses changes in a mercury barometer to forecast changes in the weather.

There is evidence that this barometric, or leading, indicator approach to business forecasting is nearly as old as business itself. More than 2,000 years ago merchants used the arrival of trading ships as indicators of business activity. Over 100 years ago Andrew Carnegie is reported to have used the number of smoking industrial chimneys to forecast business activity and hence the demand for steel. Today, the barometric approach to forecasting has been refined considerably, primarily through the work of the National Bureau of Economic Research and the U.S. Department of Commerce. *Business Conditions Digest*, a monthly publication of the Department of Commerce, provides extensive data on a large number of business

TABLE B.3

Leading, Coincident, and Lagging Economic Time Series

Leading Indicators

Average Workweek—Production Workers, Manufacturing
Average Weekly Initial Claims—State Unemployment Insurance
Index of Net Business Formation
New Orders—Durable Goods Industries
Contracts and Orders—Plant and Equipment
New Building Permits—Private Housing
Change in Manufacturing and Trade Inventories
Industrial Materials Prices
Stock Prices—500 Common Stocks
Corporate Profits, After Taxes
Ratio of Price to Unit Labor Cost—Manufacturing
Changes in Consumer Installment Debt

Roughly Coincident Indicators

Employees on Nonagricultural Payrolls
Unemployment Rate—Total
GNP in Current Dollars
Industrial Production
Personal Income
Manufacturing and Trade Sales
Sales of Retail Stores

Lagging Indicators

Unemployment Rate—15 Weeks and Over
Business Expenditures—New Plant and Equipment
Book Value—Manufacturing and Trade Inventories
Labor Cost per Unit of Output—Manufacturing
Commercial and Industrial Loans Outstanding
Bank Rates on Short-Term Business Loans

indicators. Table B.3 lists 25 leading, coincident, and lagging economic time series which are contained in that data.

Barometric Forecasting

As indicated above, barometric, or indicator, forecasting is based on the observation that there are lagged relationships among many economic time series. Changes in some series appear to consistently follow changes in one or more other series. The theoretical basis for some of these leads and lags is obvious. For example, building permits issued precede housing starts, and orders for plant and equipment lead production in durable goods industries. The reason is that each of these indicators refers to plans or commitments for the activity that follows. Other barometers are not so directly related to the economic variables they forecast. An index of common stock prices, for example, is a good leading indicator of general business activity. Although the causal relationship here is not readily apparent, stock prices reflect an aggregation of profit expectations by business managers and others and hence a composite expectation of the level of business activity.

Theoretically, barometric forecasting requires the isolation of an economic time series that consistently leads the series being forecast. Once this relationship is established, forecasting directional changes in the lagged series is simply a matter of keeping track of movement in the leading indicator. Actually, several problems prevent such an easy solution to the forecasting problem. First, few series *always* correctly indicate changes in another economic variable. Even the best leading indicators of general business conditions forecast with only 80 to 90 percent accuracy. Second, even the indicators that have good records of forecasting directional changes generally fail to lead by a consistent period. If a series is to be an adequate barometer, it not only must indicate directional changes but, additionally, must provide a constant lead time. Few series meet the test of lead time consistency. Finally, barometric forecasting suffers in that, even when leading indicators prove to be satisfactory from the standpoint of consistently indicating directional change with a stable lead time, they provide very little information about the magnitude of change in the forecast variable.

Composite and Diffusion Indexes

Two techniques that have been used with some success to overcome at least partially the difficulties in barometric forecasting are composite indexes and diffusion indexes. *Composite indexes* are weighted averages of several leading indicators. The combining of individual series into a composite index results in a series with less random fluctuation, or *noise*. The smoother composite series has a lower tendency to produce false signals of change in the predicted variable.

Diffusion indexes are similar to composite indexes. Here, instead of combining a number of leading indicators into a single standardized index, the methodology consists of noting the percentage of the total number of leading indicators that are rising at a given point in time. For example, if twelve individual indicators have all proved to be relatively reliable leading indicators of steel sales, a diffusion, or *pressure*, index would show the percentage of those indicators which are increasing at the present time. If seven are rising, the diffusion index would be seven-twelfths, or 58 percent; with only three rising, the index would register 25 percent. Forecasting with diffusion indexes typically involves projecting an increase in the economic variable if the index is above fifty—that is, when over one-half of the individual leading indicators are rising—and a decline when it is below fifty.

Even with the use of composite and diffusion indexes, the barometric forecasting technique is a relatively poor tool for estimating the magnitude of change in an economic variable. Thus, although it represents a significant improvement over simple extrapolation techniques for short-term forecasting, where calling the turning points is necessary, the barometric methodology is not the solution to all forecasting problems.

ECONOMETRIC MODELS

Econometric methods of forecasting combine economic theory with mathematical and statistical tools to analyze economic relationships. The use of econometric forecasting techniques has several distinct advantages over alternative methods. For one, it forces the forecaster to make explicit assumptions about the interrelationships among the variables in the economic system being examined. In other words, the forecaster must deal with *causal* relationships. This process reduces the probability of logical inconsistencies in the model and thus increases the reliability and acceptability of the results.

A second advantage of econometric methods lies in the consistency of the technique from period to period. The forecaster can compare forecasts with actual results and use the insights gained from this comparison to improve the model. That is, by feeding past forecasting errors back into the model, the forecaster can obtain new parameters which should improve future forecasting results.

The output form of econometric forecasts is another major advantage of this technique. Since econometric models provide estimates of the actual values for the forecasted variables, the models indicate not only the direction of change but also the magnitude of change. This is a significant improvement over the barometric approach, which provides little information about the magnitude of changes.

Perhaps the most important advantage of econometric models relates to their basic characteristic of *explaining* economic phenomena. In the vast majority of business forecasting problems, management has some degree of control over many of the variables present in the relationship being examined. For example, in forecasting sales of a product, the firm must take into account both the price it will charge and the amount it has spent and will spend on advertising, as well as many other variables over which it may or may not have any influence. Only by thoroughly understanding the interrelationships involved can management hope to forecast accurately and to make optimal decisions as it selects values for the controllable variables.

Single Equation Models

Many of the firm's forecasting problems can be solved adequately with single equation econometric models. The first step in developing an econometric model is to express the hypothesized economic relationship in the form of an equation. For example, in constructing a model for forecasting sales of new personal computers, one might hypothesize that demand (Q) is determined by price (P), disposable income (Y_d), population (Pop), availability of credit (C), and advertising expenditures (AD). A linear model expressing this relationship could be written as follows:

$$Q = a_0 + a_1P + a_2Y_d + a_3Pop + a_4C + a_5AD. \qquad \textbf{(B.7)}$$

Once the economic relationship has been expressed in equation form, the next step in econometric modeling is to estimate the parameters of the system, or values of the a's in Equation B.7. The most frequently used technique for parameter estimation is the application of the method of least squares regression analysis with either time-series or cross-sectional data.

Once the coefficients of the model have been estimated, forecasting with a single equation model consists of obtaining the values for the independent variables in the equation and then evaluating the equation for those values. This means that an econometric model that is to be used for forecasting purposes must contain independent or explanatory variables whose values for the forecast period can be readily obtained.

Multiple Equation Systems

Although in numerous instances forecasting problems can be analyzed adequately with a single equation model, in many other cases the interrelationships involved are so complex that they require the use of multiple equation systems. In these systems we refer to the variables whose values are determined by the model through the simultaneous solution of the equations as *endogenous*, meaning originating from within, and to those determined outside, or external to, the system as *exogenous*. The values of endogenous variables are determined with the model; the values of exogenous variables are given externally. Endogenous variables are equivalent to the dependent variable in a single equation system; the exogenous variables are equivalent to the independent variables.

Multiple equation econometric models are composed of two basic kinds of equations, identities and behavioral equations. Identities, or definitional, equations express relationships that are true by definition. The statement that profits (π) are equal to total revenue (TR) minus cost (TC) is an example of an identity:

$$\pi = TR - TC. \qquad (B.8)$$

Profits are *defined* by the relationship expressed in Equation B.8; the equation is true by definition.

The second group of equations encountered in econometric models, behavioral equations, reflects hypotheses about how the variables in the system interact with one another. Behavioral equations may indicate how individuals and institutions are expected to react to various stimuli, or they may be technical as, for example, a production function that indicates the technical relationships in the production system.

Perhaps the easiest way to illustrate the use of a multiple equation system is to examine a simple three-equation model of a national economy. Actual econometric models used for forecasting general business conditions have many more variables and equations than this, but the three-equation system provides insight into the technique without being so complex as to become confusing. The three equations are:

$$C_t = a_1 + b_1 GNP_t + u_1, \qquad (B.9)$$

$$I_t = a_2 + b_2 \pi_{t-1} + u_2, \qquad (B.10)$$

$$GNP_t = C_t + I_t + G_t, \qquad (B.11)$$

where: C = personal consumption expenditures; I = net capital investment; π = profits; G = government expenditures for goods and services; GNP = gross national product; a, b = parameters to be estimated; u = stochastic disturbance terms; t = current time period; and $t - 1$ = previous time period.

Equations B.9 and B.10 are behavioral hypotheses. The first hypothesizes that current period consumption is a function of the current level of gross national product; the second, that current net capital investment depends on profits in the previous period. The last equation in the system is an identity. It defines gross national product as being equal to the sum of personal consumption expenditures, net capital investment, and government expenditures.

The stochastic terms in the behavioral equations—the u's—are included because the hypothesized relationships are not exact. In other words, other factors, including random disturbances, are not accounted for in the system, and these factors affect the size of personal consumption expenditures and of net capital investment. So long as these stochastic elements are randomly distributed and their net effects are canceled—that is, the expected value of each stochastic term is zero—they do not present a barrier to empirical estimation of the parameters. However, if the error terms are not randomly distributed, the parameter estimates will be biased and the reliability of forecasts made with the model will be questionable. Furthermore, even though the error terms are random, if the error terms are large the model will not forecast very accurately.

Empirical estimation of the parameters—that is, the a's and b's in Equations B.9 and B.10—of multiple equation systems often requires the use of statistical techniques that go beyond the scope of the text.[3] We can, however, illustrate the use of such a system for forecasting purposes after the parameters have been estimated.

To forecast next year's consumption, investment, and gross national product for the economic system represented by our illustrative model, we must express C, I, and GNP in terms of only those variables whose values are known at the moment the forecast is generated. In other words, each endogenous variable (C, I, and GNP) must be expressed in terms of all exogenous and predetermined variables (π_{t-1} and G). Such relationships are called *reduced-form equations*, because they reduce complex simultaneous relationships to their most basic and simple form. Consider the manipulations of equations in the system necessary to solve for GNP via its reduced-form equation.

Substituting Equation B.9 into B.11—that is, replacing C_t with Equation B.9—results in:[4]

$$GNP_t = a_1 + b_1 GNP_t + I_t + G_t. \tag{B.12}$$

A similar substitution of Equation B.10 for the variable I_t produces:

$$GNP_t = a_1 + b_1 GNP_t + a_2 + b_2 \pi_{t-1} + G_t. \tag{B.13}$$

Collecting terms and isolating GNP in Equation B.13 gives:

$$(1 - b_1)GNP_t = a_1 + a_2 + b_2 \pi_{t-1} + G_t,$$

or, alternatively:

$$GNP_t = \frac{a_1 + a_2 + b_2 \pi_{t-1} + G_t}{1 - b_1} \tag{B.14}$$

$$= \frac{a_1 + a_2}{1 - b_1} + \frac{b_2}{1 - b_1} \pi_{t-1} + \frac{1}{1 - b_1} G_t.$$

---

[3] *See* Chapter 10 of W. J. Baumol's text, *Economic Theory and Operations Analysis*, 4th ed. (Englewood Cliffs, N.J.: Prentice-Hall, 1977), for an introduction to several of these techniques.

[4] The stochastic terms (u's) have been dropped from the illustration since their expected values are zero. The final equation for GNP, however, is stochastic in nature.

Equation B.14 now relates current GNP to the previous period's profits and to current government expenditure. Assuming that profits and government spending on goods and services, which are predetermined and exogenous to the system, respectively, can be obtained from data currently available, Equation B.14 provides us with a forecasting model that takes into account the simultaneous relationships expressed in the multiple equation system.

Econometric models are playing an increasingly important role in business forecasting. Firms use models of the national or regional economy as a base for analyzing and forecasting demand for their products. Many larger companies have developed their own capabilities to forecast using econometric models, although most firms purchase econometric forecasts and analyses from organizations that provide such services.

INPUT-OUTPUT ANALYSIS [5]

A forecasting method known as *input-output analysis* provides perhaps the most complete examination of all the complex interrelationships within an economic system. Input-output analysis shows how an increase or a decrease in the demand for one's industry output will affect other industries. For example, an increase in the demand for trucks will lead to increased production of steel, plastics, tires, glass, and other materials. The increase in the demand for these materials will have secondary effects. The increase in the demand for glass will lead to a further increase in the demand for steel, as well as for trucks used in the manufacture of glass, steel, and so on. Input-output analysis traces through all these interindustry relationships to provide information about the total impact on all industries of the original increase in the demand for trucks.

Input-output forecasting is based on a set of tables that describe the interrelationships among all the component parts of the economy. The construction of input-output tables is a most formidable task; fortunately, however, such tables are available for the United States from the Office of Business Economics, U.S. Department of Commerce. To use the tables effectively, one must understand their construction. Accordingly, the construction of these tables, as well as the use of input-output tables, is examined in this section.

Input-Output Tables

The starting point for constructing input-output tables is the set of accounts on which the nation's GNP is based; the basic accounts are listed in Table B.4. The

[5] This section draws heavily from "Input-Output Structure of the U.S. Economy: 1967," *Survey of Current Business*, February 1974.

TABLE B.4

List of National Income and Product Accounts Used to Construct GNP

National Income Accounts

  1. Compensation of Employees
  2. Proprietors' Income
  3. Rental Income of Persons
  4. Corporate Profits and Inventory Valuation Adjustment
  5. Net Interest   } Gross National Product
  6. Business Transfer Payments
  7. Indirect Business Tax and Nontax Liability
  8. Less: Subsidies Less Current Surplus of Government Enterprises
  9. Capital Consumption Allowances

Final Product Accounts

  10. Personal Consumption Expenditures
  11. Gross Private Domestic Investment   } Gross National Product
  12. Net Export of Goods and Services
  13. Government Purchases of Goods and Services

table shows that GNP is equal to the sum of the national income accounts, Items 1–9, or, alternatively, to the sum of final product flows to consuming sectors, Items 10–13.

Input-output tables break down the income and the product account data and provide information about interindustry transactions. Table B.5 is an example of a simplified input-output table. It is a matrix of the same gross national product data contained in Table B.4, but with the addition of a (shaded) section showing all the interindustry transactions as well.[6] The industry-to-industry flows in the shaded area depict the intput-output structure of the economy. For example, the manufacturing row, Row 4, shows the sales by manufacturing firms to other manufacturing firms, to each of the other industries, and also to final users. Thus, Cell 4, 2 shows sales from manufacturers to mining companies; Cell 4, 4 from manufacturers to other manufacturers; and Cell 4, 7 from manufacturers to service firms such as banks, entertainment companies, and the like. The manufacturing column, Column 4, shows the sources of goods and services purchased by manufacturers for production, as well as the value added in their production of output. For example, Cell 2, 4 shows manufacturing firms' purchases from mining companies; and Cell 6, 4 shows the manufacturing firms' purchases from the transportation industry.

Since interindustry sales are included in the value of the products sold to various final consumers, they must be omitted from the measurement of total gross national product. That is, to avoid double counting, producer-to-producer sales must

---

[6] Although the illustrated input-output table has only eight industry classifications, actual 1972 Office of Business Economics input-output tables are far more complex, containing nearly 500 separate industry classifications.

TABLE B.5

Input-Output Flow Table

| | | Interindustry Transactions | | | | | | | | Final Markets (National Product Accounts) | | | |
		Agriculture (1)	Mining (2)	Construction (3)	Manufacturing (4)	Trade (5)	Transportation (6)	Services (7)	Other (8)	Persons (9) Personal Consumption Expenditures (Account 10)	Investors (10) Gross Private Domestic Investment (Account 11)	Foreigners (11) Net Exports of Goods and Services (Account 12)	Government (12) Government Purchase of Goods and Services (Account 13)
Interindustry Transactions	Agriculture (1)												
	Mining (2)				2,4								
	Construction (3)												
	Manufacturing (4)		4,2		4,4			4,7					
	Trade (5)												
	Transportation (6)				6,4								
	Services (7)												
	Other (8)												
Value Added (National Income Accounts)	Employees (9) Compensation of Employees (Account 1)												
	Owners of Business and Capital (10) Profit-type Income and Capital Consumption Allowances (Accounts 2, 3, 4, 5, 6, 9)[a]												
	Government (11) Indirect Business Taxes and Current Surplus of Government Enterprises, and So Forth (Accounts 7, 8)												

Gross National Product (spanning the Final Markets accounts — Accounts 10, 11, 12, 13)

[a] Account numbers refer to the national income and product accounts of Table B.4.

be excluded from the determination of GNP. The same is true when calculating GNP by use of the national income accounts; interindustry transactions must be eliminated to avoid redundancy. Accordingly, the entire shaded area of Table B.5 is ignored when GNP is determined: GNP is calculated either as the total of all the cells shown in the Final Markets columns or as the total of cells in the Value Added rows.

Uses of Input-Output Analysis

Input-output analysis has a variety of applications, ranging from forecasting the sales of an individual firm to probing the implications of national economic programs and policies. The major contribution of input-output analysis is that it facilitates measurement of the effects on all industrial sectors of changes in activity in any one sector.

The usefulness of input-output analysis can be illustrated by the following example, which shows the effect of an increase in consumer demand for passenger cars. The first effect of the change in demand is an increase in the output of the automobile industry; there are further effects, however. The increase in auto output requires more steel production, which in turn requires more chemicals, more iron ore, more limestone, and more coal. Auto production also requires other products, and demand will increase for upholstery fabrics, synthetic fibers, plastics, and glass. There will be still further reactions; for example, the production of synthetic fibers and other chemicals will lead to increased demand for electricity, containers, and transportation services. Input-output analysis traces this intricate chain reaction throughout all industrial sectors and measures the effects, both direct and indirect, on the output of each of the industries.

The industry outputs derived in this way can be used for estimating related industry requirements. For example, with supplementary data the estimated output of each industry can be translated into requirements for employment or for additional plant and equipment. Or, bolstered by information on the geographic distribution of industries, input-output analysis can also shed light on the regional implications of changes in national GNP.

Recognizing the unique ability of input-output analysis to account completely for the complex interaction among industries, many businesses have been guided in their decision making by this analysis. For example, input-output has been used to evaluate market prospects for established products, to identify potential markets for new products, to spot prospective shortages in supplies, to add new dimensions and greater depth to the analysis of the economic environment in which the firms can expect to operate, and to evaluate investment prospects in various industries.

Input-output analysis has also been employed in the decision making processes of government agencies at every level. A notable federal application has been in the study of the long-term growth of the economy and its implications for manpower requirements. Input-output has also been used to calculate the impact of U.S. exports and imports on employment in various industries and regions. A number of state and local governments have sponsored the construction of input-output tables for use in evaluating the effects of different paths of economic development. Others have used input-output to study the industrial impact of alternative tax programs. In one state input-output is the central element in a large-scale system for forecasting demographic and economic variables and also serves as an aid in planning land use, expenditure and revenue programs, industrial development, and so on.

Moreover, many regions throughout the country have been increasingly concerned about the adequacy of water resources. Input-output is being used as part of a total system to measure the industrial requirements for water. The analysis is particularly helpful in identifying the activities that generate important demands for water, not only as direct users but also because their suppliers of materials, power, and other inputs also require water.

Forecasting with Input-Output Tables

It should be obvious that the data required to construct an input-output system are numerous, and the analysis necessary to trace the intricate interrelationships is overwhelming. Because of the enormous costs of constructing and maintaining input-output tables, individual firms, even the largest ones, typically rely on U.S. Department of Commerce tables rather than construct their own. But firms can and do extend the published tables and apply them to their own unique situations.

To use input-output tables, it is necessary to understand thoroughly the nature of an input-output system. To facilitate such an understanding we trace through a very simple hypothetical economy containing only three producing sectors. Table B.6 provides the basic national accounting data for the hypothetical system. The upper section contains the detailed interindustry relationships necessary for construction of input-output tables; the lower section gives the national income and product accounts that make up GNP.

Table B.7 shows all this information reformulated in an input-output matrix for the system. The Producers rows contain information about the distribution of output. For example, Industry A produces and sells a total of $130 billion, with $10 billion going to other firms in Industry A, $2 billion to Industry B, $50 billion to Industry C, $40 billion to individuals for personal consumption, and $28 billion to the government. As is shown in the Producers columns, firms in Industry A buy $10 billion of goods and services from other A firms and $3 billion from B firms, pay $100 billion in wages, and have $17 billion left for depreciation and profits. Gross national product can be obtained from the input-output table by summing either the Value Added section or the Final Markets section. Cells in the producer-to-producer section of the matrix are eliminated to avoid double counting.

For forecasting purposes, two additional types of matrices are constructed from

TABLE B.6

National Accounting Data for a Hypothetical Economy (billions of dollars)

	Industry Production Accounts			
	Receipts		Expenses + Profits	
Industry A	Sales to Industry A	$ 10	Purchases from Industry A	$ 10
	Sales to Industry B	2	Purchases from Industry B	3
	Sales to Industry C	50	Wages (employee compensation)	100
	Sales to Persons	40	Depreciation	10
	Sales to Government	28	Profits	7
		$130		$130
Industry B	Sales to Industry A	$ 3	Purchases from Industry A	$ 2
	Sales to Industry C	15	Purchases from Industry C	25
	Sales to Persons	30	Wages (employee compensation)	25
	Sales to Government	20	Depreciation	8
	Sales to Exports	2	Profits	10
		$ 70		$ 70
Industry C	Sales to Industry B	$ 25	Purchases from Industry A	$ 50
	Sales to Persons	65	Purchases from Industry B	15
			Wages (employee compensation)	20
			Profits	5
		$ 90		$ 90

	National Income and Product Accounts			
	Wages	$145	Personal Consumption Expenditures	$135
	Profits	22	Government	48
	Depreciation	18	Exports	2
		$185		$185

the Producers section of Table B.7. One is the percentage distribution of gross output matrix, which indicates where each industry sells its products and, thus, how dependent it is on various sectors of the system. Table B.8 shows the percentage distribution matrix for this hypothetical economy. Each element in that table is found by dividing the corresponding element in Table B.7 by its row total. For example, the 8 percent in element A, A was found by dividing the $10 billion of sales Industry A makes for itself by the $130 billion total sales of that industry. The 4 percent in Cell B, A indicates that Industry B sells 4 percent of its output to Industry A.

A second type of input-output matrix derived from the producer-to-producer sector of Table B.7, the *direct* and *total requirement* tables, is especially useful when individual firms are making demand forecasts. Table B.9 is the direct require-

TABLE B.7

Input-Output Matrix for a Hypothetical Economy (billions of dollars)

| | | Producers | | | Final Markets | | | |
		A	B	C	Personal Consumption	Government	Exports	Row Totals
	A	10	2	50	40	28		130
Producers	B	3		15	30	20	2	70
	C		25		65			90
Value Added	Wages	100	25	20				145
	Profit plus Depreciation	17	18	5				40
	Column Total	130	70	90	135	48	2	

GNP = $185

GNP = $185

TABLE B.8

Percentage Distribution of Gross Output

| | Percentage Sales to Each Consuming Sector | | | | | | |
Producing Industry	Industry A	Industry B	Industry C	Persons	Government	Export	Total
A	8	1	38	31	22	0	100
B	4	0	21	43	29	3	100
C	0	28	0	72	0	0	100

ments table for the hypothetical economy. The entries in each column show the dollar inputs required directly from each industry given in the rows to produce $1 of output. Industry C, for example, requires direct inputs costing $0.56 from Industry A and $0.17 from Industry B to produce an additional $1 of output. These direct requirement figures are found by dividing each element in the industry columns in Table B.7 by the column total. Thus, the 0.08 figure for the first-row, first-column element in Table B.9 is found by dividing the $10 billion of purchases among Industry A firms by the $130 billion total found in the first column of Table B.7.

The direct requirements matrix in Table B.9 permits systematic examination of all the interrelationships among the various industries and final demand sectors. For example, assume that Industry A is expected to produce $1 million of output for sale to final consumers. Using the first column of Table B.9, we can see that Industry A

TABLE B.9

Direct Requirements per Dollar of Gross Output

	Producing Industry		
Supplying Industry	A	B	C
A	0.08	0.03	0.56
B	0.02	0.00	0.17
C	0.00	0.36	0.00

TABLE B.10

Total Requirements (Direct plus Indirect) per Dollar of Output for Final Consumption

	Producing Industry		
Supplying Industry	A	B	C
A	1.09	0.27	0.66
B	0.03	1.07	0.19
C	0.01	0.39	1.07

will use $80,000 ($1,000,000 × 0.08) of its own production in the process of manufacturing the $1 million of output for final consumption. Thus, the industry must actually produce a minimum of $1.080 million of output. Production of $1.080 million of output by A also requires $21,600 ($1,080,000 × 0.02) from Industry B. As shown by the 0.00 element in the last row of the first column, Industry A requires no direct inputs from Industry C. Calculating the total effect of the original $1 million final demand for A's output requires further analysis. Note that Industry A requires $21,600 in inputs from Industry B. To meet this requirement, B needs inputs of $648 ($21,600 × 0.03) from Industry A and $7,776 ($21,600 × 0.36) from Industry C. These requirements, in turn, must be fed back into the system to determine the second-round effects, which in turn produce further reactions as the cycle continues. Each successive reaction is smaller than the preceding one, and the reactions converge on the final effects of the original demand.

Table B.10 presents the *total requirements*—direct plus indirect—for the hypothetical economy.[7] Each column in the table shows the inputs required, both direct and indirect, by the producing industry; each row shows the demand that sup-

[7]The total requirements tables provide the solution values, or the values on which the chain reaction converges. The mathematics of the solution is described in W. H. Miernyk, *The Elements of Input-Output Analysis*, New York: Random House, 1965.

plying industries can expect per dollar of final consumption demand. To continue our illustration of a $1 million final consumer demand for the output of Industry A, we see that, in order to produce the $1 million to meet final demand, Industry A production must total $1.09 million; Industry B, $.03 million; and Industry C, $.01 million. In total, production must amount to $1.13 million to supply $1 million of final output of Product A, with the $0.13 million being the product required to produce the $1 million final output.

This illustration of the construction and use of input-output tables indicates the versatility of the technique in a variety of forecasting situations. It should be apparent at this point that a large part of that versatility depends on the detail contained in the basic input-output matrix. That is, the finer the industry distinctions in the input-output tables, the more valuable they are for forecasting purposes.

The 1972 input-output table for the U.S. economy, completed by the Office of Business Economics, segments the industrial sector of the system into 496 industry categories. This compares with a classification into only 367 and 86 separate industries for successively earlier input-output tables. The much greater detail provided by these latest tables vastly increases their value to managerial decision makers and should lead to much greater use of the techniques of input-output analysis for industry and firm forecasting purposes.

JUDGING FORECAST RELIABILITY

One of the most challenging aspects of forecasting is testing the reliability of forecasts obtained from various basic forecasting techniques. How well do various methodologies deal with specific forecasting problems? In comparing forecast and actual values, how close is close enough? Is forecast reliability over one sample or time period necessarily transferable to other samples and time periods? Each of these questions is fundamentally important and must be adequately addressed prior to the implementation of any successful forecasting program.

Ideally, to test predictive capability, a model generated from data of one sample or period is used to forecast data for some alternative sample or period. Thus, the reliability of a model for predicting GNP, such as that shown in Equation B.5, can be tested by examining the relationship between forecast and actual data for years beyond 1980, given that the model was generated using data from the 1966–1980 period. At times, it may be desirable to test a model without waiting for new data to become available. In such instances one can divide the available data into two subsamples, called a test group and a forecast group. The forecaster then estimates a forecasting model using data from the test group, and uses the resulting model to forecast the data of interest in the forecast group. A comparison of forecast and actual values can then be conducted to test the stability of the underlying cost or demand relationship.

In analyzing a model's forecast capability the correlation between forecast and actual values is of substantial interest. The formula for the simple correlation coefficient, r, for forecast and actual values, f and x, respectively, is:

$$r = \frac{\sigma_{fx}}{\sigma_f \sigma_x}, \tag{B.15}$$

where σ_{fx} is the covariance between the forecast and actual series, and σ_f and σ_x are the sample standard deviations of the forecast and actual series, respectively. It is seldom necessary to calculate r since most computer system statistical packages and many hand-held calculators can readily calculate such coefficients. Generally speaking, correlations between forecast and actual values in excess of 0.99 (99 percent) are highly desirable and indicate that the forecast model being considered constitutes an effective tool for analysis. However, in cross-sectional analysis where the important trend element in most economic data is held constant, a correlation of 99 percent between forecast and actual values would be quite rare. In instances where unusually difficult forecasting problems are being addressed, correlations between forecast and actual data of 90 percent or 95 percent may prove satisfactory. On the other hand, in critical decision situations forecast values may have to be estimated at very precise levels. In such instances, forecast and actual data may have to exhibit an extremely high level of correlation, 99.5 percent or 99.75 percent, in order to generate a high level of confidence in forecast reliability. In summary, the correlation between forecast and actual values necessary to reach a threshold reliability acceptance level depends, in large part, upon the difficulty of the forecasting problem being analyzed and the cost of forecast error.

Further evaluation of a model's predictive capability can be made through consideration of a common measure of forecast error, the sample mean squared forecast error. The sample mean squared forecast error, denoted by the symbol U^2, is calculated as:

$$U^2 = \frac{1}{n} \sum_{i=1}^{n} (f_i - x_i)^2, \tag{B.16}$$

where n is the number of sample observations, f_i is a forecast value, and x_i is the corresponding actual value. The deviations between forecast and actual values are squared in the calculation of the mean squared forecast error to prevent positive and negative deviations between forecast and actual values from canceling one another out.

Henri Theil, a noted econometrician, suggested that a specific decomposition of forecast error can provide useful insight into its causes.[8] According to Theil, forecast error can be decomposed as follows:

Mean Squared Forecast Error	=	Error Due To Unequal Central Tendency (*Bias*)	+	Error Due To Unequal Variation (*Inefficiency*)	+	Error Due To Imperfect Covariation (*Residual Variation*)

Symbolically, this relationship can be written:

$$U^2 = (\bar{f} - \bar{x})^2 + (\sigma_f - r\sigma_x)^2 + (1 - r^2)\sigma_x^2 \tag{B.17}$$

where $\bar{f}$ and $\bar{x}$ are the sample means of the forecast and actual data series, σ_f and σ_x are the sample standard deviations, and r is the sample correlation between the forecast and actual data series. To consider the sources of mean squared forecast error in percentage terms, we can divide both sides of Equation (B.17) by U^2 and find that:

$$\frac{U^2}{U^2} = \frac{(\bar{f} - \bar{x})^2}{U^2} + \frac{(\sigma_f - r\sigma_x)^2}{U^2} + \frac{(1 - r)^2 \, \sigma_x^2}{U^2} \, , \tag{B.18}$$

or, $1 = U^B + U^I + U^R,$

where U^B is the percentage of error due to unequal central tendency (*bias*), U^I is the percentage of error due to unequal variation (*inefficiency*), and U^R is the percentage of error due to imperfect covariation (*residual variation*).

If we found $U^B = 0$, then the forecasts would be unbiased in the sense that mean forecast and actual values would be equal. If $U^I = 0$, then the forecast series would be efficient in that the forecast and the actual series would have equal variation when perfectly correlated. In order for $U^R = 0$ the predicted series would have to have either zero variation or perfect positive correlation with the forecast series. In this case there would be no residual variation. If perfect forecasts, $U^2 = 0$, are not possible, then it would seem desirable to have a source of error distribution where $U^B + U^I = 0$ and $U^R = 1$. This is because small proportions of U^B and U^I indicate that systematic errors play a small role in the overall level of forecast error. When U^B and U^I are large, one can enhance forecast reliability by considering a number of new predictor variables or by considering alternative functional specifications of the forecast model. On the other hand, when both U^B and U^R are relatively small, it may be difficult to improve forecast reliability. Analysis of the

---

[8] *See* Henry Theil, *Economic Forecasts and Policy*, Amsterdam: North-Holland, 1961.

sources of forecast error can be very useful in determining the cause of error and improving both the application and interpretation of forecasting models.

FORECASTING COLOR TELEVISION DEMAND: AN ILLUSTRATIVE FORECASTING PROBLEM

In early 1982 Boulger Imports, Inc., entered into a long-term licensing agreement with Tsuruoka Manufacturing, Ltd., a medium-sized manufacturer of color televisions. In order to avoid stockouts of excessive inventory charges, Boulger's marketing department must develop accurate forecasts of color television demand during coming periods.

As is typical with durable consumer products, the demand for color televisions is subject to a secular trend, cyclical fluctuations, seasonal variation, and irregular or random influences. The production and marketing of color televisions has definitely been a growth industry. During the late 1970s and early 1980s, there has been a veritable explosion in both the number and variety of products sold in the United States. Many expect this secular trend to continue well into the 1990s due to increases in both leisure-time activities and personal incomes. Being a durable product, the demand for color televisions is affected by the overall level of economic activity as reflected by the level of GNP, interest rates, employment levels, etc. Thus, there is an important cyclical element to color television demand. Seasonal variations also play an important role in the demand for color televisions, since many are bought in November and December, just prior to the Christmas season. Finally, no forecast methodology can be expected to provide perfectly accurate demand estimates because of irregular or random influences.

Table B.11 shows some recent data on television manufacturer shipments in the United States in terms of thousands of units and millions of dollars of retail value. A casual analysis of these data suggests that demand for black and white televisions has been stagnate or declining recently, while demand for color televisions has been growing quite rapidly. This has led to a somewhat irregular pattern of growth for television demand in general.

Clearly, projecting future television demand constitutes a difficult forecasting problem. For example, in examining the data one would expect that a constant growth model would more successfully project demand in the case of color televisions than in the case of black and white televisions. Furthermore, the pattern of growth in color television demand may be tied quite closely to the overall pace of economic activity as measured by GNP, while any link between demand for black and white televisions and GNP is likely to be weaker.

As a first step in their secular trend analysis, Boulger's marketing staff decided to examine a simple econometric approach to color television demand forecasting. The general form of the model used incorporates the effects of color television

TABLE B.11

Television Manufacturer Shipments, 1965–1979

Year	Manufacturer Shipments (thousands of units)			Retail Value (millions of dollars)			GNP (billions of dollars)
	Black & White	Color	Total	Black & White	Color	Total	
1979	6,281	9,793	16,074	682	4,618	5,300	2,413.9
1978	6,064	10,236	16,300	701	4,993	5,694	2,156.1
1977	5,664	9,107	14,771	651	4,438	5,089	1,899.5
1976	5,196	7,700	12,896	567	3,933	4,500	1,702.2
1975	4,968	6,485	11,453	529	3,271	3,800	1,528.8
1974	6,868	8,411	15,279	881	3,922	4,451	1,412.9
1973	7,297	10,071	17,368	753	4,530	5,283	1,306.6
1972	5,600	7,908	13,508	692	4,032	4,724	1,171.1
1971	4,848	6,349	11,197	627	3,333	3,960	1,063.4
1970	4,546	4,822	9,368	611	2,479	3,090	982.4
1969	5,309	5,962	11,271	701	3,073	3,774	930.2
1968	5,813	5,981	11,794	769	3,115	3,884	865.7
1967	5,105	5,777	10,882	678	3,033	3,711	.793.5
1966	7,288	5,892	13,180	1,024	2,724	3,748	743.3
1965	8,382	2,646	11,028	1,336	1,482	2,818	683.9

Sources: U.S. Bureau of the Census, *Statistical Abstract of the United States*, Washington, D.C. (various years), *Federal Reserve Bulletin*, Vol. 67, No. 11 (November 1981).

prices, black and white television prices, and income; the model can be expressed as follows:

$$Q_c = f(P_c, P_B, GNP) \qquad \textbf{(B.19)}$$

where Q_c is color television demand, P_c and P_B are average prices for color and black and white televisions, respectively, and GNP is gross national product. It is expected that $\partial Q_c/\partial P_c < 0$ since higher average prices should reduce the quantity of color televisions demanded, that $\partial Q_c/\partial P_B > 0$ if, as seems reasonable, consumers perceive black and white and color televisions as substitutes, and finally that $\partial Q_c/\partial GNP > 0$ since higher incomes should cause an increase in the overall level of color television demand. Equation B.19 was estimated over the 1965–1974 period and then used to forecast demand over the subsequent 1975–1979 period. This approach allows one to examine the model's ability to forecast demand during recent years and indicates its reliability for future projections.

Least squares estimation results for the simple linear form of Equation B.19 over the 1965–1974 period were as follows (*t*-statistics in parenthesis):

$$Q_c = 22527.0 - 15.901P_c - 79.306P_B + 2.329GNP \quad R^2 = .95 \qquad \textbf{(B.20)}$$
$$\quad\;\;(4.91) \qquad (-2.18) \qquad (-3.56) \qquad\;\; (1.94) \qquad\quad F = 38.0$$

On an overall basis, the explanatory power of this simple econometric model is quite good, with 95 percent of the variation in Q_c explained by the model. An F-statistic of 38.0 is highly significant ($F^*_{3,6,\alpha=.01} = 9.79$), and we can reject the hypothesis that color television sales are not related to the variables in the model with 99 percent confidence. This implies that the regression variables as a group explain a significant share of the total variation in Q_c over the period 1964–1974. The estimated coefficient for P_c is negative and significant as expected, indicating that price increases will decrease the quantity of color televisions demanded, while price decreases will increase the quantity demanded. Again as expected, the estimated coefficient for GNP is positive and significant, which suggests that color televisions can be classified as a normal or superior good. Contrary to previous expectations, however, the estimated coefficient for P_B is negative and significant. The finding is *not* consistent with the notion that black and white and color televisions can be viewed as substitutes. This finding is perplexing and may suggest some potential problems for the analysis due to the very small sample size being analyzed.

For exploratory purposes, the estimation results reported in Equation (B.20) can be used to generate color television demand forecasts over the 1975–1979 period for comparison with actual shipment data. Table B.12 presents this data. Of particular interest is the fact that annual demand forecasts tend to exceed actual demand, and often by substantial amounts. Indeed, using Equation B.18 to analyze the sources of forecasting error reveals that roughly three quarters of total forecast error is due to the unequal central tendency of the forecast and actual demand series. The average annual forecast error—often called the *root mean squared forecast error*—is 2,022.68 units (calculated as $\sqrt{U^2}$), or 23.2 percent of average actual demand. For most forecasting purposes, this is an unacceptably high level of forecasting error. The low level of correlation between forecast and actual demand, $r = .635$, also raises some question about the use of Equation B.20 as a forecasting

TABLE B.12

Color Television Demand Forecast Analysis

Year	Forecast Demand, f_i	Actual Demand, x_i	Squared Forecast Error, $(f_i - x_i)^2$
1979	12,039.52	9,793	5,046,840.0
1978	10,624.44	10,236	150,887.4
1977	10,086.95	9,107	960,304.8
1976	9,715.46	7,700	4,062,088.0
1975	10,044.39	6,485	10,236,102.0
Average:	$\bar{f} = 10,502.20$	$\bar{x} = 8,736.20$	$U^2 = 4,091,240$
Standard Deviation:	$\sigma_f = 919.14$	$\sigma_x = 1,427.77$	
Correlation Between Forecast and Actual Demand:		$r = .635$	

FIGURE B.3

Color Television Manufacturer Shipments, 1965–1979 (in thousands of units)

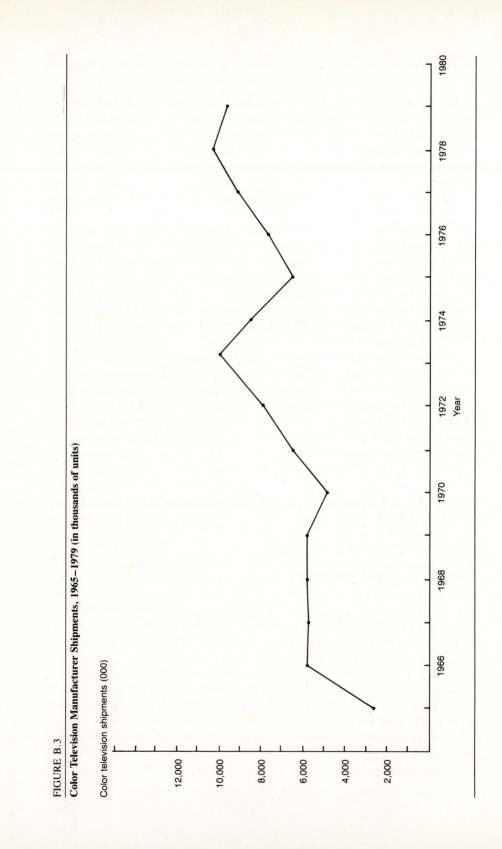

device. These findings may be somewhat surprising in light of the simple econometric model's ability to closely fit annual demand data over the 1965–1974 period. In fact, the level of R^2 for the forecast model over the 1965–1974 period and the model's apparent inability to forecast demand between 1975–1979 suggest that an important change in color television demand occurred between these two time periods.

To gain some insight regarding the nature of such a change, Boulger's marketing staff constructed a simple plot of color television demand over the entire 1965–1979 period. As shown in Figure B.3, while color television demand seems to be growing over time, its growth has been temporarily interrupted by economic downturns in 1970 and 1975. The recession of 1975 was particularly severe and caused a sharp contraction in color television demand. Indeed, it was not until 1978 that manufacturer shipments of 10.2 million units exceeded the earlier peak of 10.1 million units reached in 1973. The simple econometric approach to color television demand forecasting may have failed, because it did not adequately incorporate the effects of changing economic conditions.

The lessons from this illustrative color television forecasting problem are quite simple. First, while accurate forecasts are often possible when economic data have an important trend element, as is true with GNP, forecasts are seldom accurate when demand is strongly affected by changing economic conditions. Second, modeling the effects of changing economic conditions is especially difficult when only limited series of data are available. For these reasons, demand forecasting is a very challenging aspect of managerial decision making.

SUMMARY

Managerial decision making requires forecasts of many future events. In this appendix we examined several techniques that are used for economic forecasting. These included qualitative analysis, time-series analysis and projection, econometric models, and input-output methods.

All of these forecasting procedures have their particular strengths and shortcomings. The appropriate method for a given forecasting problem will depend on such factors as the distance into the future being forecasted, the lead time available, the accuracy required, the quality of data available for analysis, and the nature of relationships involved in the forecasting problem. When little quantitative information is available, qualitative analysis must be relied upon to form the basis for forecasts. Time-series approaches are appropriate for forecasting in those situations when it is thought that the historical pattern of the economic series being analyzed provides the best clues about future movement of the variable. Barometric methods make use of consistent lead and lag relationships between economic variables to project directional changes in the time series. Although it is difficult to forecast the magnitude of a change using these procedures, they have proven useful for calling turning points in economic activity. Composite and diffusion indexes combine various leading indicators, thereby reducing random fluctuations and providing a smoother series, which reduces the generation of false signals.

Econometric methods move beyond pure forecasting to provide estimates of important relationships that affect the outcomes in an economic system. This explanatory characteristic of econometric methods allows them to be used to determine the impact on the economic variable being examined of changes in specific key variables, such as product price, advertising, consumer incomes, and so on. Specification of these important interrelationships allows econometric methods to forecast economic conditions under a variety of assumptions. Input-output analysis is another forecasting tool that focuses on the interrelationships in an economic system. By tracing out the flows between sectors, input-output analysis provides a basis for examining how changes in one sector of the economy will affect other sectors. It is useful for examining aggregate requirements for such various key resources as energy, labor, water, etc.

An important aspect of forecasting is testing the reliability of forecasts obtained from various basic forecasting techniques. Two statistics used in reliability analysis are the simple correlation between forecast and actual values and the average amount of forecasting error (root mean squared error). In addition, a useful technique proposed by Henri Theil can be used to determine the amount of forecasting error caused by *bias*, *inefficiency*, and *residual variation*. Such analyses can provide invaluable insight into the limitations of models currently employed, as well as suggest methods for improving forecast reliability.

QUESTIONS

B.1 Discuss the basic advantages and limitations of the three broad categories of basic forecasting techniques.

B.2 Why does trend projection seem to be particularly relevant for GNP forecasting?

B.3 What is the shortcoming of trend projection that barometric approaches improve on?

B.4 When should single equation versus multiequation models be adopted in the econometric approach to forecasting?

B.5 Discuss the comparative strengths and limitations of the simple correlation between forecast and actual values and average forecast error (root mean squared forecast error) measures of forecast reliability.

PROBLEMS

B.1 You are presented with the following time-series data for the gross national product (GNP):

Year	GNP (in billions)
1960	503.7
1965	683.9
1970	982.4
1975	1,528.8
1980	2,626.1

    a. Determine the GNP growth rate for the years 1960–1965, 1960–1970, 1960–1975, and 1960–1980. Use the constant growth model with annual compounding.

    b. Use the 1960–1980 growth rate to forecast 1982 GNP, then check a current reference to compare your forecast with the actual GNP.

B.2 The following figures constitute annual sales for Ray's Restaurant:

Year	Sales
1969	$239,000
1970	266,000
1971	287,000
1972	315,000
1973	353,000
1974	384,000
1975	427,000
1976	462,000
1977	520,000
1978	575,000
1979	628,000

    a. Forecast sales for 1980 and 1985, using the constant rate of change model with annual compounding.

    b. Forecast sales for 1980 and 1985 by graphic analysis.

B.3 To convince potential investors of the viability of your new store, Nite Life Fashions, Ltd., you would like to generate a sales forecast. Based on your assumption that next-period sales are a function of current-period local disposable income, own advertising, and competitor advertising (i.e., advertising by a competing retailer):

    a. Specify a demand equation.

    b. Write an equation for predicting sales if you assume that the percentage growth (or decline) in sales is twice as large as the sum of the current period's percentage changes in local disposable income and own advertising, plus one-half of the current period's percentage change in competitor advertising.

    c. Forecast sales if during the current period sales total $300,000, disposable income is $204 million, own advertising is $24,000, and competitor advertising is $66,000. Previous period levels were $200 million (disposable income), $30,000 (own advertising), and $60,000 (competitor advertising).

B.4 Joe Braun, operations manager at Apple Video Games Company, believes that sales in any given month are related to consumers' incomes during the preceding month.

    a. Write an equation for next month's sales, using the symbols S = sales, Y = income, t = time, a_0 = constant term, a_1 = regression slope coefficient, and u = random disturbance.

    b. Now assume that sales in this month increase by the same percentage as income increased during the preceding month. Write an equation for predicting sales.

    c. If last month's income was $2 billion and this month's sales are $400,000, what should sales amount to next month if income this month is $2.1 billion? Use the equation developed in Part b.

B.5 The quantity demanded of Product A in any given week is inversely proportional to the sales of Product B in the previous week; that is, if sales of B rose by X percent last week, sales of A can be expected to fall by X percent this week.

    a. Write the equation for next week's sales of A, using the symbols A = sales of Product A, B = sales of Product B, and t = time. Assume there will be no shortages of either product.

    b. Two weeks ago 200 units of Product A and 150 units of Product B were sold. Last week 160 units of A and 180 units of B were sold. What would you predict the sales of A to be this week?

    c. What is the significance of the error term? What property must the error term have to allow use of regression results in forecasting?

B.6 In July 1982 the management of Paulisa Manufacturing was evaluating the merits of building a new plant in order to fulfill a new contract with the federal government. The alternative to expansion is to use additional overtime or to reduce other production or to do both. The company manufactures a wide range of parts for aircraft, automotive, and agricultural equipment industries and will want to add new capacity only if the economy appears to be expanding. Forecasting the general economic activity of the United States, therefore, is of obvious interest to the company as an input in the decision process.

The firm has collected the data and has estimated the relationships for the U.S. economy shown below:

Last Year's Total Profits (all corporations) P_{t-1} = \$300 billion

This Year's Government Expenditures G = \$500 billion

Annual Consumption Expenditures C = \$60 billion + 0.70(Y) + u

Annual Investment Expenditures I = \$4 billion + 0.85 (P_{t-1}) + u

Annual Tax Receipts T = 0.25 (GNP)

National Income Y = $GNP - T$

Gross National Product GNP = $C + I + G$.

Assume that all random disturbances average out to zero, and forecast each of the above variables through the simultaneous relationships expressed in the multiple equation system.

SELECTED REFERENCES

Armstrong, J. Scott. "Forecasting with Econometric Methods: Folklore Versus Fact." *Journal of Business* 51 (October 1978): 549–564.

Beardsley, George, and Mansfield, Edwin. "A Note on the Accuracy of Industrial Forecasts of the Profitability of New Products and Processes." *Journal of Business* 51 (January 1978): 127–135.

Box, G. E. P., and Jenkins, G. M. *Time Series Analysis, Forecasting and Control*, 2d ed. San Francisco: Holden-Day, 1976.

Butler, William F., Kavesh, Robert A., and Platt, Robert B. *Methods and Techniques of Business Forecasting*. Englewood Cliffs, N.J.: Prentice-Hall, 1974.

Chambers, John C., Mullick, Satinder K., and Smith, Donald D. "How to Choose the Right Forecasting Technique." *Harvard Business Review* 49 (July–August 1971): 45–74.

Chow, Gregory C. "Are Econometric Methods Useful for Forecasting?" *Journal of Business* 51 (October 1978): 565–571.

Freedman, David. "Some Pitfalls in Large Econometric Models: A Case Study." *Journal of Business* 54 (July 1981): 479–500.

Granger, C. W. J., and Newbold, P. *Forecasting Economic Time Series*. New York: Academic Press, 1977.

Hirschey, Mark. "Incentive Contracting for Railroad Subsidies: A Statistical Approach to Cost Control." *Land Economics* 56 (August 1980): 366–379.

Makridakis, Spyros, and Wheelwright, Steven C. *Interactive Forecasting*, 2d ed. San Francisco: Holden-Day, 1978.

Sobek, Robert S. "A Manager's Primer on Forecasting." *Harvard Business Review* 51 (May–June 1973): 1–9.

Theil, Henri. *Economic Forecasts and Policy.* Amsterdam: North-Holland, 1961.

Zarnowitz, Victor. "An Analysis of Annual and Multiperiod Quarterly Forecasts of Aggregate Income, Output, and the Price Level." *Journal of Business* 52 (January 1979): 1–33.

———, and Moore, Geoffrey H. "Sequential Signals of Recession and Recovery." *Journal of Business* 55 (January 1982): 57–85.

APPENDIX C
INTEREST FACTOR TABLES[1]

TABLE C.1

Compound Sum of \$1: $FVIF_{i,n} = (1 + i)^n$

Period	1%	2%	3%	4%	5%	6%	7%	8%	9%	10%
1	1.0100	1.0200	1.0300	1.0400	1.0500	1.0600	1.0700	1.0800	1.0900	1.1000
2	1.0201	1.0404	1.0609	1.0816	1.1025	1.1236	1.1449	1.1664	1.1881	1.2100
3	1.0303	1.0612	1.0927	1.1249	1.1576	1.1910	1.2250	1.2597	1.2950	1.3310
4	1.0406	1.0824	1.1255	1.1699	1.2155	1.2625	1.3108	1.3605	1.4116	1.4641
5	1.0510	1.1041	1.1593	1.2167	1.2763	1.3382	1.4026	1.4693	1.5386	1.6105
6	1.0615	1.1262	1.1941	1.2653	1.3401	1.4185	1.5007	1.5869	1.6771	1.7716
7	1.0721	1.1487	1.2299	1.3159	1.4071	1.5036	1.6058	1.7138	1.8280	1.9487
8	1.0829	1.1717	1.2668	1.3686	1.4775	1.5938	1.7182	1.8509	1.9926	2.1436
9	1.0937	1.1951	1.3048	1.4233	1.5513	1.6895	1.8385	1.9990	2.1719	2.3579
10	1.1046	1.2190	1.3439	1.4802	1.6289	1.7908	1.9672	2.1589	2.3674	2.5937
11	1.1157	1.2434	1.3842	1.5395	1.7103	1.8983	2.1049	2.3316	2.5804	2.8531
12	1.1268	1.2682	1.4258	1.6010	1.7959	2.0122	2.2522	2.5182	2.8127	3.1384
13	1.1381	1.2936	1.4685	1.6651	1.8856	2.1329	2.4098	2.7196	3.0658	3.4523
14	1.1495	1.3195	1.5126	1.7317	1.9799	2.2609	2.5785	2.9372	3.3417	3.7975
15	1.1610	1.3459	1.5580	1.8009	2.0789	2.3966	2.7590	3.1722	3.6425	4.1772
16	1.1726	1.3728	1.6047	1.8730	2.1829	2.5404	2.9522	3.4259	3.9703	4.5950
17	1.1843	1.4002	1.6528	1.9479	2.2920	2.6928	3.1588	3.7000	4.3276	5.0545
18	1,1961	1.4282	1.7024	2.0258	2.4066	2.8543	3.3799	3.9960	4.7171	5.5599
19	1.2081	1.4568	1.7535	2.1068	2.5270	3.0256	3.6165	4.3157	5.1417	6.1159
20	1.2202	1.4859	1.8061	2.1911	2.6533	3.2071	3.8697	4.6610	5.6044	6.7275
21	1.2324	1.5157	1.8603	2.2788	2.7860	3.3996	4.1406	5.0338	6.1088	7.4002
22	1.2447	1.5460	1.9161	2.3699	2.9253	3.6035	4.4304	5.4365	6.6586	8.1403
23	1.2572	1.5769	1.9736	2.4647	3.0715	3.8197	4.7405	5.8715	7.2579	8.9543
24	1.2697	1.6084	2.0328	2.5633	3.2251	4.0489	5.0724	6.3412	7.9111	9.8497
25	1.2824	1.6406	2.0938	2.6658	3.3864	4.2919	5.4274	6.8485	8.6231	10.834
26	1.2953	1.6734	2.1566	2.7725	3.5557	4.5494	5.8074	7.3964	9.3992	11.918
27	1.3082	1.7069	2.2213	2.8834	3.7335	4.8223	6.2139	7.9881	10.245	13.110
28	1.3213	1.7410	2.2879	2.9987	3.9201	5.1117	6.6488	8.6271	11.167	14.421
29	1.3345	1.7758	2.3566	3.1187	4.1161	5.4184	7.1143	9.3173	12.172	15.863
30	1.3478	1.8114	2.4273	3.2434	4.3219	5.7435	7.6123	10.062	13.267	17.449
40	1.4889	2.2080	3.2620	4.8010	7.0400	10.285	14.974	21.724	31.409	45.259
50	1.6446	2.6916	4.3839	7.1067	11.467	18.420	29.457	46.901	74.357	117.39
60	1.8167	3.2810	5.8916	10.519	18.679	32.987	57.946	101.25	176.03	304.48

Table C.1   **607**

TABLE C.1

(continued)

Period	12%	14%	15%	16%	18%	20%	24%	28%	32%	36%
1	1.1200	1.1400	1.1500	1.1600	1.1800	1.2000	1.2400	1.2800	1.3200	1.3600
2	1.2544	1.2996	1.3225	1.3456	1.3924	1.4400	1.5376	1.6384	1.7424	1.8496
3	1.4049	1.4815	1.5209	1.5609	1.6430	1.7280	1.9066	2.0972	2.3000	2.5155
4	1.5735	1.6890	1.7490	1.8106	1.9388	2.0736	2.3642	2.6844	3.0360	3.4210
5	1.7623	1.9254	2.0114	2.1003	2.2878	2.4883	2.9316	3.4360	4.0075	4.6526
6	1.9738	2.1950	2.3131	2.4364	2.6996	2.9860	3.6352	4.3980	5.2899	6.3275
7	2.2107	2.5023	2.6600	2.8262	3.1855	3.5832	4.5077	5.6295	6.9826	8.6054
8	2.4760	2.8526	3.0590	3.2784	3.7589	4.2998	5.5895	7.2058	9.2170	11.703
9	2.7731	3.2519	3.5179	3.8030	4.4355	5.1598	6.9310	9.2234	12.166	15.916
10	3.1058	3.7072	4.0456	4.4114	5.2338	6.1917	8.5944	11.805	16.059	21.646
11	3.4785	4.2262	4.6524	5.1173	6.1759	7.4301	10.657	15.111	21.198	29.439
12	3.8960	4.8179	5.3502	5.9360	7.2876	8.9161	13.214	19.342	27.982	40.037
13	4.3635	5.4924	6.1528	6.8858	8.5994	10.699	16.386	24.758	36.937	54.451
14	4.8871	6.2613	7.0757	7.9875	10.147	12.839	20.319	31.691	48.756	74.053
15	5.4736	7.1379	8.1371	9.2655	11.973	15.407	25.195	40.564	64.358	100.71
16	6.1304	8.1372	9.3576	10.748	14.129	18.488	31.242	51.923	84.953	136.96
17	6.8660	9.2765	10.761	12.467	16.672	22.186	38.740	66.461	112.13	186.27
18	7.6900	10.575	12.375	14.462	19.673	26.623	48.038	85.070	148.02	253.33
19	8.6128	12.055	14.231	16.776	23.214	31.948	59.567	108.89	195.39	344.53
20	9.6463	13.743	16.366	19.460	27.393	38.337	73.864	139.37	257.91	468.57
21	10.803	15.667	18.821	22.574	32.323	46.005	91.591	178.40	340.44	637.26
22	12.100	17.861	21.644	26.186	38.142	55.206	113.57	228.35	449.39	866.67
23	13.552	20.361	24.891	30.376	45.007	66.247	140.83	292.30	593.19	1178.6
24	15.178	23.212	28.625	35.236	53.108	79.496	174.63	374.14	783.02	1602.9
25	17.000	26.461	32.918	40.874	62.668	95.396	216.54	478.90	1033.5	2180.0
26	19.040	30.166	37.856	47.414	73.948	114.47	268.51	612.99	1364.3	2964.9
27	21.324	34.389	43.535	55.000	87.259	137.37	332.95	784.63	1800.9	4032.2
28	23.883	39.204	50.065	63.800	102.96	164.84	412.86	1004.3	2377.2	5483.8
29	26.749	44.693	57.575	74.008	121.50	197.81	511.95	1285.5	3137.9	7458.0
30	29.959	50.950	66.211	85.849	143.37	237.37	634.81	1645.5	4142.0	10143.
40	93.050	188.88	267.86	378.72	750.37	1469.7	5455.9	19426.	66520.	*
50	289.00	700.23	1083.6	1670.7	3927.3	9100.4	46890.	*	*	*
60	897.59	2595.9	4383.9	7370.1	20555.	56347.	*	*	*	*

*$FVIF > 99,999$.

TABLE C.2

Present Value of \$1: $PVIF_{i,n} = 1/(1 + i)^n = 1/FVIF_{i,n}$

Period	1%	2%	3%	4%	5%	6%	7%	8%	9%	10%
1	.9901	.9804	.9709	.9615	.9524	.9434	.9346	.9259	.9174	.9091
2	.9803	.9612	.9426	.9246	.9070	.8900	.8734	.8573	.8417	.8264
3	.9706	.9423	.9151	.8890	.8638	.8396	.8163	.7938	.7722	.7513
4	.9610	.9238	.8885	.8548	.8227	.7921	.7629	.7350	.7084	.6830
5	.9515	.9057	.8626	.8219	.7835	.7473	.7130	.6806	.6499	.6209
6	.9420	.8880	.8375	.7903	.7462	.7050	.6663	.6302	.5963	.5645
7	.9327	.8706	.8131	.7599	.7107	.6651	.6227	.5835	.5470	.5132
8	.9235	.8535	.7894	.7307	.6768	.6274	.5820	.5403	.5019	.4665
9	.9143	.8368	.7664	.7026	.6446	.5919	.5439	.5002	.4604	.4241
10	.9053	.8203	.7441	.6756	.6139	.5584	.5083	.4632	.4224	.3855
11	.8963	.8043	.7224	.6496	.5847	.5268	.4751	.4289	.3875	.3505
12	.8874	.7885	.7014	.6246	.5568	.4970	.4440	.3971	.3555	.3186
13	.8787	.7730	.6810	.6006	.5303	.4688	.4150	.3677	.3262	.2897
14	.8700	.7579	.6611	.5775	.5051	.4423	.3878	.3405	.2992	.2633
15	.8613	.7430	.6419	.5553	.4810	.4173	.3624	.3152	.2745	.2394
16	.8528	.7284	.6232	.5339	.4581	.3936	.3387	.2919	.2519	.2176
17	.8444	.7142	.6050	.5134	.4363	.3714	.3166	.2703	.2311	.1978
18	.8360	.7002	.5874	.4936	.4155	.3503	.2959	.2502	.2120	.1799
19	.8277	.6864	.5703	.4746	.3957	.3305	.2765	.2317	.1945	.1635
20	.8195	.6730	.5537	.4564	.3769	.3118	.2584	.2145	.1784	.1486
21	.8114	.6598	.5375	.4388	.3589	.2942	.2415	.1987	.1637	.1351
22	.8034	.6468	.5219	.4220	.3418	.2775	.2257	.1839	.1502	.1228
23	.7954	.6342	.5067	.4057	.3256	.2618	.2109	.1703	.1378	.1117
24	.7876	.6217	.4919	.3901	.3101	.2470	.1971	.1577	.1264	.1015
25	.7798	.6095	.4776	.3751	.2953	.2330	.1842	.1460	.1160	.0923
26	.7720	.5976	.4637	.3607	.2812	.2198	.1722	.1352	.1064	.0839
27	.7644	.5859	.4502	.3468	.2678	.2074	.1609	.1252	.0976	.0763
28	.7568	.5744	.4371	.3335	.2551	.1956	.1504	.1159	.0895	.0693
29	.7493	.5631	.4243	.3207	.2429	.1846	.1406	.1073	.0822	.0630
30	.7419	.5521	.4120	.3083	.2314	.1741	.1314	.0994	.0754	.0573
35	.7059	.5000	.3554	.2534	.1813	.1301	.0937	.0676	.0490	.0356
40	.6717	.4529	.3066	.2083	.1420	.0972	.0668	.0460	.0318	.0221
45	.6391	.4102	.2644	.1712	.1113	.0727	.0476	.0313	.0207	.0137
50	.6080	.3715	.2281	.1407	.0872	.0543	.0339	.0213	.0134	.0085
55	.5785	.3365	.1968	.1157	.0683	.0406	.0242	.0145	.0087	.0053

Table C.2   609

TABLE C.2

(continued)

Period	12%	14%	15%	16%	18%	20%	24%	28%	32%	36%
1	.8929	.8772	.8696	.8621	.8475	.8333	.8065	.7813	.7576	.7353
2	.7972	.7695	.7561	.7432	.7182	.6944	.6504	.6104	.5739	.5407
3	.7118	.6750	.6575	.6407	.6086	.5787	.5245	.4768	.4348	.3975
4	.6355	.5921	.5718	.5523	.5158	.4823	.4230	.3725	.3294	.2923
5	.5674	.5194	.4972	.4761	.4371	.4019	.3411	.2910	.2495	.2149
6	.5066	.4556	.4323	.4104	.3704	.3349	.2751	.2274	.1890	.1580
7	.4523	.3996	.3759	.3538	.3139	.2791	.2218	.1776	.1432	.1162
8	.4039	.3506	.3269	.3050	.2660	.2326	.1789	.1388	.1085	.0854
9	.3606	.3075	.2843	.2630	.2255	.1938	.1443	.1084	.0822	.0628
10	.3220	.2697	.2472	.2267	.1911	.1615	.1164	.0847	.0623	.0462
11	.2875	.2366	.2149	.1954	.1619	.1346	.0938	.0662	.0472	.0340
12	.2567	.2076	.1869	.1685	.1372	.1122	.0757	.0517	.0357	.0250
13	.2292	.1821	.1625	.1452	.1163	.0935	.0610	.0404	.0271	.0184
14	.2046	.1597	.1413	.1252	.0985	.0779	.0492	.0316	.0205	.0135
15	.1827	.1401	.1229	.1079	.0835	.0649	.0397	.0247	.0155	.0099
16	.1631	.1229	.1069	.0930	.0708	.0541	.0320	.0193	.0118	.0073
17	.1456	.1078	.0929	.0802	.0600	.0451	.0258	.0150	.0089	.0054
18	.1300	.0946	.0808	.0691	.0508	.0376	.0208	.0118	.0068	.0039
19	.1161	.0829	.0703	.0596	.0431	.0313	.0168	.0092	.0051	.0029
20	.1037	.0728	.0611	.0514	.0365	.0261	.0135	.0072	.0039	.0021
21	.0926	.0638	.0531	.0443	.0309	.0217	.0109	.0056	.0029	.0016
22	.0826	.0560	.0462	.0382	.0262	.0181	.0088	.0044	.0022	.0012
23	.0738	.0491	.0402	.0329	.0222	.0151	.0071	.0034	.0017	.0008
24	.0659	.0431	.0349	.0284	.0188	.0126	.0057	.0027	.0013	.0006
25	.0588	.0378	.0304	.0245	.0160	.0105	.0046	.0021	.0010	.0005
26	.0525	.0331	.0264	.0211	.0135	.0087	.0037	.0016	.0007	.0003
27	.0469	.0291	.0230	.0182	.0115	.0073	.0030	.0013	.0006	.0002
28	.0419	.0255	.0200	.0157	.0097	.0061	.0024	.0010	.0004	.0002
29	.0374	.0224	.0174	.0135	.0082	.0051	.0020	.0008	.0003	.0001
30	.0334	.00196	.0151	.0116	.0070	.0042	.0016	.0006	.0002	.0001
35	.0189	.0102	.0075	.0055	.0030	.0017	.0005	.0002	.0001	*
40	.0107	.0053	.0037	.0026	.0013	.0007	.0002	.0001	*	*
45	.0061	.0027	.0019	.0013	.0006	.0003	.0001	*	*	*
50	.0035	.0014	.0009	.0006	.0003	.0001	*	*	*	*
55	.0020	.0007	.0005	.0003	.0001	*	*	*	*	*

*The factor is zero to four decimal places.

TABLE C.3

Sum of an Annuity of \$1 for N Periods: $FVIFA_{i,n} = \sum_{t=1}^{n} (1 + i)^{t-1}$

$$= \frac{(1 + i)^n - 1}{i}$$

Number of Periods	1%	2%	3%	4%	5%	6%	7%	8%	9%	10%
1	1.0000	1.0000	1.0000	1.0000	1.0000	1.0000	1.0000	1.0000	1.0000	1.0000
2	2.0100	2.0200	2.0300	2.0400	2.0500	2.0600	2.0700	2.0800	2.0900	2.1000
3	3.0301	3.0604	3.0909	3.1216	3.1525	3.1836	3.2149	3.2464	3.2781	3.3100
4	4.0604	4.1216	4.1836	4.2465	4.3101	4.3746	4.4399	4.5061	4.5731	4.6410
5	5.1010	5.2040	5.3091	5.4163	5.5256	5.6371	5.7507	5.8666	5.9847	6.1051
6	6.1520	6.3081	6.4684	6.6330	6.8019	6.9753	7.1533	7.3359	7.5233	7.7156
7	7.2135	7.4343	7.6625	7.8983	8.1420	8.3938	8.6540	8.9228	9.2004	9.4872
8	8.2857	8.5830	8.8923	9.2142	9.5491	9.8975	10.259	10.636	11.028	11.435
9	9.3685	9.7546	10.159	10.582	11.026	11.491	11.978	12.487	13.021	13.579
10	10.462	10.949	11.463	12.006	12.577	13.180	13.816	14.486	15.192	15.937
11	11.566	12.168	12.807	13.486	14.206	14.971	15.783	16.645	17.560	18.531
12	12.682	13.412	14.192	15.025	15.917	16.869	17.888	18.977	20.140	21.384
13	13.809	14.680	15.617	16.626	17.713	18.882	20.140	21.495	22.953	24.522
14	14.947	15.973	17.086	18.291	19.598	21.015	22.550	24.214	26.019	27.975
15	16.096	17.293	18.598	20.023	21.578	23.276	25.129	27.152	29.360	31.772
16	17.257	18.639	20.156	21.824	23.657	25.672	27.888	30.324	33.003	35.949
17	18.430	20.012	21.761	23.697	25.840	28.212	30.840	33.750	36.973	40.544
18	19.614	21.412	23.414	25.645	28.132	30.905	33.999	37.450	41.301	45.599
19	20.810	22.840	25.116	27.671	30.539	33.760	37.379	41.446	46.018	51.159
20	22.019	24.297	26.870	29.778	33.066	36.785	40.995	45.762	51.160	57.275
21	23.239	25.783	28.676	31.969	35.719	39.992	44.865	50.422	56.764	64.002
22	24.471	27.299	30.536	34.248	38.505	43.392	49.005	55.456	62.873	71.402
23	25.716	28.845	32.452	36.617	41.430	46.995	53.436	60.893	69.531	79.543
24	26.973	30.421	34.426	39.082	44.502	50.815	58.176	66.764	76.789	88.497
25	28.243	32.030	36.459	41.645	47.727	54.864	63.249	73.105	84.700	98.347
26	29.525	33.670	38.553	44.311	51.113	59.156	68,676	79.954	93.323	109.18
27	30.820	35.344	40.709	47.084	54.669	63.705	74.483	87.350	102.72	121.09
28	32.129	37.051	42.930	49.967	58.402	68.528	80.697	95.338	112.96	134.20
29	33.450	38.792	45.218	52.966	62.322	73.639	87.346	103.96	124.13	148.63
30	34.784	40.568	47.575	56.084	66.438	79.058	94.460	113.28	136.30	164.49
40	48.886	60.402	75.401	95.025	120.79	154.76	199.63	259.05	337.88	442.59
50	64.463	84.579	112.79	152.66	209.34	290.33	406.52	573.76	815.08	1163.9
60	81.669	114.05	163.05	237.99	353.58	533.12	813.52	1253.2	1944.7	3034.8

Table C.3   **611**

TABLE C.3

(continued)

Number of Periods	12%	14%	15%	16%	18%	20%	24%	28%	32%	36%
1	1.0000	1.0000	1.0000	1.0000	1.0000	1.0000	1.0000	1.0000	1.0000	1.0000
2	2.1200	2.1400	2.1500	2.1600	2.1800	2.2000	2.2400	2.2800	2.3200	2.3600
3	3.3744	3.4396	3.4725	3.5056	3.5724	3.6400	3.7776	3.9184	4.0624	4.2096
4	4.7793	4.9211	4.9934	5.0665	5.2154	5.3680	5.6842	6.0156	6.3624	6.7251
5	6.3528	6.6101	6.7424	6.8771	7.1542	7.4416	8.0484	8.6999	9.3983	10.146
6	8.1152	8.5355	8.7537	8.9775	9.4420	9.9299	10.980	12.135	13.405	14.798
7	10.089	10.730	11.066	11.413	12.141	12.915	14.615	16.533	18.695	21.126
8	12.299	13.232	13.726	14.240	15.327	16.499	19.122	22.163	25.678	29.731
9	14.775	16.085	16.785	17.518	19.085	20.798	24.712	29.369	34.895	41.435
10	17.548	19.337	20.303	21.321	23.521	25.958	31.643	38.592	47.061	57.351
11	20.654	23.044	24.349	25.732	28.755	32.150	40.237	50.398	63.121	78.998
12	24.133	27.270	29.001	30.850	34.931	39.580	50.894	65.510	84.320	108.43
13	28.029	32.088	34.351	36.786	42.218	48.496	64.109	84.852	112.30	148.47
14	32.392	37.581	40.504	43.672	50.818	59.195	80.496	109.61	149.23	202.92
15	37.279	43.842	47.580	51.659	60.965	72.035	100.81	141.30	197.99	276.97
16	42.753	50.980	55.717	60.925	72.939	87.442	126.01	181.86	262.35	377.69
17	48.883	59.117	65.075	71.673	87.068	105.93	157.25	233.79	347.30	514.66
18	55.749	68.394	75.836	84.140	103.74	128.11	195.99	300.25	459.44	700.93
19	63.439	78.969	88.211	98.603	123.41	154.74	244.03	385.32	607.47	954.27
20	72.052	91.024	102.44	115.37	146.62	186.68	303.60	494.21	802.86	1298.8
21	81.698	104.76	118.81	134.84	174.02	225.02	377.46	633.59	1060.7	1767.3
22	92.502	120.43	137.63	157.41	206.34	271.03	469.05	811.99	1401.2	2404.6
23	104.60	138.29	159.27	183.60	244.48	326.23	582.62	1040.3	1850.6	3271.3
24	118.15	158.65	184.16	213.97	289.49	392.48	723.46	1332.6	2443.8	4449.9
25	133.33	181.87	212.79	249.21	342.60	471.98	898.09	1706.8	3226.8	6052.9
26	150.33	208.33	245.71	290.08	405.27	567.37	1114.6	2185.7	4260.4	8233.0
27	169.37	238.49	283.56	337.50	479.22	681.85	1383.1	2798.7	5624.7	11197.9
28	190.69	272.88	327.10	392.50	566.48	819.22	1716.0	3583.3	7425.6	15230.2
29	214.58	312.09	377.16	456.30	669.44	984.06	2128.9	4587.6	9802.9	20714.1
30	241.33	356.78	434.74	530.31	790.94	1181.8	2640.9	5873.2	12940.	28172.2
40	767.09	1342.0	1779.0	2360.7	4163.2	7343.8	22728.	69377.	*	*
50	2400.0	4994.5	7217.7	10435.	21813.	45497.	*	*	*	*
60	7471.6	18535.	29219.	46057.	*	*	*	*	*	*

*$FVIFA > 99,999$.

TABLE C.4

Present Value of an Annuity of $1 for *n* Periods: $PVIFA_{i,n} = \sum_{t=1}^{n} \frac{1}{(1+i)^t} = \frac{1 - \frac{1}{1+i^n}}{i}$

Number of Pay- ments	1%	2%	3%	4%	5%	6%	7%	8%	9%
1	0.9901	0.9804	0.9709	0.9615	0.9524	0.9434	0.9346	0.9259	0.9174
2	1.9704	1.9416	1.9135	1.8861	1.8594	1.8334	1.8080	1.7833	1.7591
3	2.9410	2.8839	2.8286	2.7751	2.7232	2.6730	2.6243	2.5771	2.5313
4	3.9020	3.8077	3.7171	3.6299	3.5460	3.4651	3.3872	3.3121	3.2397
5	4.8534	4.7135	4.5797	4.4518	4.3295	4.2124	4.1002	3.9927	3.8897
6	5.7955	5.6014	5.4172	5.2421	5.0757	4.9173	4.7665	4.6229	4.4859
7	6.7282	6.4720	6.2303	6.0021	5.7864	5.5824	5.3893	5.2064	5.0330
8	7.6517	7.3255	7.0197	6.7327	6.4632	6.2098	5.9713	5.7466	5.5348
9	8.5660	8.1622	7.7861	7.4353	7.1078	6.8017	6.5152	6.2469	5.9952
10	9.4713	8.9826	8.5302	8.1109	7.7217	7.3601	7.0236	6.7101	6.4177
11	10.3676	9.7868	9.2526	8.7605	8.3064	7.8869	7.4987	7.1390	6.8052
12	11.2551	10.5753	9.9540	9.3851	8.8633	8.3838	7.9427	7.5361	7.1607
13	12.1337	11.3484	10.6350	9.9856	9.3936	8.8527	8.3577	7.9038	7.4869
14	13.0037	12.1062	11.2961	10.5631	9.8986	9.2950	8.7455	8.2442	7.7862
15	13.8651	12.8493	11.9379	11.1184	10.3797	9.7122	9.1079	8.5595	8.0607
16	14.7179	13.5777	12.5611	11.6523	10.8378	10.1059	9.4466	8.8514	8.3126
17	15.5623	14.2919	13.1661	12.1657	11.2741	10.4773	9.7632	9.1216	8.5436
18	16.3983	14.9920	13.7535	12.6593	11.6896	10.8276	10.0591	9.3719	8.7556
19	17.2260	15.6785	14.3238	13.1339	12.0853	11.1581	10.3356	9.6036	8.9501
20	18.0456	16.3514	14.8775	13.5903	12.4622	11.4699	10.5940	9.8181	9.1285
21	18.8570	17.0112	15.4150	14.0292	12.8212	11.7641	10.8355	10.0168	9.2922
22	19.6604	17.6580	15.9369	14.4511	13.1630	12.0416	11.0612	10.2007	9.4424
23	20.4558	18.2922	16.4436	14.8568	13.4886	12.3034	11.2722	10.3711	9.5802
24	21.2434	18.9139	16.9355	15.2470	13.7986	12.5504	11.4693	10.5288	9.7066
25	22.0232	19.5235	17.4131	15.6221	14.0939	12.7834	11.6536	10.6748	9.8226
26	22.7952	20.1210	17.8768	15.9828	14.3752	13.0032	11.8258	10.8100	9.9290
27	23.5596	20.7069	18.3270	16.3296	14.6430	13.2105	11.9867	10.9352	10.0266
28	24.3164	21.2813	18.7641	16.6631	14.8981	13.4062	12.1371	11.0511	10.1161
29	25.0658	21.8444	19.1885	16.9837	15.1411	13.5907	12.2777	11.1584	10.1983
30	25.8077	22.3965	19.6004	17.2920	15.3725	13.7648	12.4090	11.2578	10.2737
35	29.4086	24.9986	21.4872	18.6646	16.3742	14.4982	12.9477	11.6546	10.5668
40	32.8347	27.3555	23.1148	19.7928	17.1591	15.0463	13.3317	11.9246	10.7574
45	36.0945	29.4902	24.5187	20.7200	17.7741	15.4558	13.6055	12.1084	10.8812
50	39.1961	31.4236	25.7298	21.4822	18.2559	15.7619	13.8007	12.2335	10.9617
55	42.1472	33.1748	26.7744	22.1086	18.6335	15.9905	13.9399	12.3186	11.0140

Table C.4   613

TABLE C.4

(continued)

Number of Pay-ments	10%	12%	14%	15%	16%	18%	20%	24%	28%	32%
1	0.9091	0.8929	0.8772	0.8696	0.8621	0.8475	0.8333	0.8065	0.7813	0.7576
2	1.7355	1.6901	1.6467	1.6257	1.6052	1.5656	1.5278	1.4568	1.3916	1.3315
3	2.4869	2.4018	2.3216	2.2832	2.2459	2.1743	2.1065	1.9813	1.8684	1.7663
4	3.1699	3.0373	2.9137	2.8550	2.7982	2.6901	2.5887	2.4043	2.2410	2.0957
5	3.7908	3.6048	3.4331	3.3522	3.2743	3.1272	2.9906	2.7454	2.5320	2.3452
6	4.3553	4.1114	3.8887	3.7845	3.6847	3.4976	3.3255	3.0205	2.7594	2.5342
7	4.8684	4.5638	4.2883	4.1604	4.0386	3.8115	3.6046	3.2423	2.9370	2.6775
8	5.3349	4.9676	4.6389	4.4873	4.3436	4.0776	3.8372	3.4212	3.0758	2.7860
9	5.7590	5.3282	4.9464	4.7716	4.6065	4.3030	4.0310	3.5655	3.1842	2.8681
10	6.1446	5.6502	5.2161	5.0188	4.8332	4.4941	4.1925	3.6819	3.2689	2.9304
11	6.4951	5.9377	5.4527	5.2337	5.0286	4.6560	4.3271	3.7757	3.3351	2.9776
12	6.8137	6.1944	5.6603	5.4206	5.1971	4.7932	4.4392	3.8514	3.3868	3.0133
13	7.1034	6.4235	5.8424	5.5831	5.3423	4.9095	4.5327	3.9124	3.4272	3.0404
14	7.3667	6.6282	6.0021	5.7245	5.4675	5.0081	4.6106	3.9616	3.4587	3.0609
15	7.6061	6.8109	6.1422	5.8474	5.5755	5.0916	4.6755	4.0013	3.4834	3.0764
16	7.8237	6.9740	6.2651	5.9542	5.6685	5.1624	4.7296	4.0333	3.5026	3.0882
16	8.0216	7.1196	6.3729	6.0472	5.7487	5.2223	4.7746	4.0591	3.5177	3.0971
18	8.2014	7.2497	6.4674	6.1280	5.8178	5.2732	4.8122	4.0799	3.5294	3.1039
19	8.3649	7.3658	6.5504	6.1982	5.8775	5.3162	4.8435	4.0967	3.5386	3.1090
20	8.5136	7.4694	6.6231	6.2593	5.9288	5.3527	4.8696	4.1103	3.5458	3.1129
21	8.6487	7.5620	6.6870	6.3125	5.9731	5.3837	4.8913	4.1212	3.5514	3.1158
22	8.7715	7.6446	6.7429	6.3587	6.0113	5.4099	4.9094	4.1300	3.5558	3.1180
23	8.8832	7.7184	6.7921	6.3988	6.0442	5.4321	4.9245	4.1371	3.5592	3.1197
24	8.9847	7.7843	6.8351	6.4338	6.0726	5.4510	4.9371	4.1428	3.5619	3.1210
25	9.0770	7.8431	6.8729	6.4642	6.0971	5.4669	4.9476	4.1474	3.5640	3.1220
26	9.1609	7.8957	6.9061	6.4906	6.1182	5.4804	4.9563	4.1511	3.5656	3.1227
27	9.2372	7.9426	6.9352	6.5135	6.1364	5.4919	4.9636	4.1542	3.5669	3.1233
28	9.3066	7.9844	6.9607	6.5335	6.1520	5.5016	4.9697	4.1566	3.5679	3.1237
29	9.3696	8.0218	6.9830	6.5509	6.1656	5.5098	4.9747	4.1585	3.5687	3.1240
30	9.4269	8.0552	7.0027	6.5660	6.1772	5.5168	4.9789	4.1601	3.5693	3.1242
35	9.6442	8.1755	7.0700	6.6166	6.2153	5.5386	4.9915	4.1644	3.5708	3.1248
40	9.7791	8.2438	7.1050	6.6418	6.2335	5.5482	4.9966	4.1659	3.5712	3.1250
45	9.8628	8.2825	7.1232	6.6543	6.2421	5.5523	4.9986	4.1664	3.5714	3.1250
50	9.9148	8.3045	7.1327	6.6605	6.2463	5.5541	4.9995	4.1666	3.5714	3.1250
55	9.9471	8.3170	7.1376	6.6636	6.2482	5.5549	4.9998	4.1666	3.5714	3.1250

APPENDIX D
STATISTICAL TABLES

TABLE D.1

Values of the Standard Normal Distribution Function

z	0.00	0.01	0.02	0.03	0.04	0.05	0.06	0.07	0.08	0.09
0.0	.0000	.0040	.0080	.0120	.0160	.0199	.0239	.0279	.0319	.0359
0.1	.0398	.0438	.0478	.0517	.0557	.0596	.0636	.0675	.0714	.0753
0.2	.0793	.0832	.0871	.0910	.0948	.0987	.1026	.1064	.1103	.1141
0.3	.1179	.1217	.1255	.1293	.1331	.1368	.1406	.1443	.1480	.1517
0.4	.1554	.1591	.1628	.1664	.1700	.1736	.1772	.1808	.1844	.1879
0.5	.1915	.1950	.1985	.2019	.2054	.2088	.2123	.2157	.2190	.2224
0.6	.2257	.2291	.2324	.2357	.2389	.2422	.2454	.2486	.2517	.2549
0.7	.2580	.2611	.2642	.2673	.2704	.2734	.2764	.2794	.2823	.2852
0.8	.2881	.2910	.2939	.2967	.2995	.3023	.3051	.3078	.3106	.3133
0.9	.3159	.3186	.3212	.3238	.3264	.3289	.3315	.3340	.3365	.3389
1.0	.3413	.3438	.3461	.3485	.3508	.3531	.3554	.3577	.3599	.3621
1.1	.3643	.3665	.3686	.3708	.3729	.3749	.3770	.3790	.3810	.3830
1.2	.3849	.3869	.3888	.3907	.3925	.3944	.3962	.3980	.3997	.4015
1.3	.4032	.4049	.4066	.4082	.4099	.4115	.4131	.4147	.4162	.4177
1.4	.4192	.4207	.4222	.4236	.4251	.4265	.4279	.4292	.4306	.4319
1.5	.4332	.4345	.4357	.4370	.4382	.4394	.4406	.4418	.4429	.4441
1.6	.4452	.4463	.4474	.4484	.4495	.4505	.4515	.4525	.4535	.4545
1.7	.4554	.4564	.4573	.4582	.4591	.4599	.4608	.4616	.4625	.4633
1.8	.4641	.4649	.4656	.4664	.4671	.4678	.4686	.4693	.4699	.4706
1.9	.4713	.4719	.4726	.4732	.4738	.4744	.4750	.4756	.4761	.4767
2.0	.4773	.4778	.4783	.4788	.4793	.4798	.4803	.4808	.4812	.4817
2.1	.4821	.4826	.4830	.4834	.4838	.4842	.4846	.4850	.4854	.4857
2.2	.4861	.4864	.4868	.4871	.4875	.4878	.4881	.4884	.4887	.4890
2.3	.4893	.4896	.4898	.4901	.4904	.4906	.4909	.4911	.4913	.4916
2.4	.4918	.4920	.4922	.4925	.4927	.4929	.4931	.4932	.4934	.4936
2.5	.4938	.4940	.4941	.4943	.4945	.4946	.4948	.4949	.4951	.4952
2.6	.4953	.4955	.4956	.4957	.4959	.4960	.4961	.4962	.4963	.4964
2.7	.4965	.4966	.4967	.4968	.4969	.4970	.4971	.4972	.4973	.4974
2.8	.4974	.4975	.4976	.4977	.4977	.4978	.4979	.4979	.4980	.4981
2.9	.4981	.4982	.4982	.4982	.4984	.4984	.4985	.4985	.4986	.4986
3.0	.4987	.4987	.4987	.4988	.4988	.4989	.4989	.4989	.4990	.4990

z is the number of standard deviations from the mean, or $z = (x - u)/\sigma$ where x is the point of interest, u is the mean, and σ is the standard deviation. Some area tables are set up to indicate the area to the left or right of the point of interest; in this book we indicate the area between the mean and the point of interest.

Source: E. F. Brigham, *Financial Management: Theory and Practice*, 3rd ed. (Hinsdale, Ill.: The Dryden Press, 1982), p. 844. Copyright © 1982 by The Dryden Press.

TABLE D.2

Critical F Values at the 90 Percent Confidence Level (α = .10)

Degrees of Freedom in the Numerator (d.f. = k − 1)

d.f. = n − k	1	2	3	4	5	6	7	8	9	10	12	15	20	24	30	40	60	120	∞
1	39.86	49.50	53.59	55.83	57.24	58.20	58.91	59.44	59.86	60.19	60.71	61.22	61.74	62.00	62.26	62.53	62.79	63.06	63.33
2	8.53	9.00	9.16	9.24	9.29	9.33	9.35	9.37	9.38	9.39	9.41	9.42	9.44	9.45	9.46	9.47	9.47	9.48	9.49
3	5.54	5.46	5.39	5.34	5.31	5.28	5.27	5.25	5.24	5.23	5.22	5.20	5.18	5.18	5.17	5.16	5.15	5.14	5.13
4	4.54	4.32	4.19	4.11	4.05	4.01	3.98	3.95	3.94	3.92	3.90	3.87	3.84	3.83	3.82	3.80	3.79	3.78	3.76
5	4.06	3.78	3.62	3.52	3.45	3.40	3.37	3.34	3.32	3.30	3.27	3.24	3.21	3.19	3.17	3.16	3.14	3.12	3.10
6	3.78	3.46	3.29	3.18	3.11	3.05	3.01	2.98	2.96	2.94	2.90	2.87	2.84	2.82	2.80	2.78	2.76	2.74	2.72
7	3.59	3.26	3.07	2.96	2.88	2.83	2.78	2.75	2.72	2.70	2.67	2.63	2.59	2.58	2.56	2.54	2.51	2.49	2.47
8	3.46	3.11	2.92	2.81	2.73	2.67	2.62	2.59	2.56	2.54	2.50	2.46	2.42	2.40	2.38	2.36	2.34	2.32	2.29
9	3.36	3.01	2.81	2.69	2.61	2.55	2.51	2.47	2.44	2.42	2.38	2.34	2.30	2.28	2.25	2.23	2.21	2.18	2.16
10	3.29	2.92	2.73	2.61	2.52	2.46	2.41	2.38	2.35	2.32	2.28	2.24	2.20	2.18	2.16	2.13	2.11	2.08	2.06
11	3.23	2.86	2.66	2.54	2.45	2.39	2.34	2.30	2.27	2.25	2.21	2.17	2.12	2.10	2.08	2.05	2.03	2.00	1.97
12	3.18	2.81	2.61	2.48	2.39	2.33	2.28	2.24	2.21	2.19	2.15	2.10	2.06	2.04	2.01	1.99	1.96	1.93	1.90
13	3.14	2.76	2.56	2.43	2.35	2.28	2.23	2.20	2.16	2.14	2.10	2.05	2.01	1.98	1.96	1.93	1.90	1.88	1.85
14	3.10	2.73	2.52	2.39	2.31	2.24	2.19	2.15	2.12	2.10	2.05	2.01	1.96	1.94	1.91	1.89	1.86	1.83	1.80
15	3.07	2.70	2.49	2.36	2.27	2.21	2.16	2.12	2.09	2.06	2.02	1.97	1.92	1.90	1.87	1.85	1.82	1.79	1.76
16	3.05	2.67	2.46	2.33	2.24	2.18	2.13	2.09	2.06	2.03	1.99	1.94	1.89	1.87	1.84	1.81	1.78	1.75	1.72
17	3.03	2.64	2.44	2.31	2.22	2.15	2.10	2.06	2.03	2.00	1.96	1.91	1.86	1.84	1.81	1.78	1.75	1.72	1.69
18	3.01	2.62	2.42	2.29	2.20	2.13	2.08	2.04	2.00	1.98	1.93	1.89	1.84	1.81	1.78	1.75	1.72	1.69	1.66
19	2.99	2.61	2.40	2.27	2.18	2.11	2.06	2.02	1.98	1.96	1.91	1.86	1.81	1.79	1.76	1.73	1.70	1.67	1.63

Degrees of Freedom in the Denominator (d.f. = n − k)

20	2.97	2.59	2.38	2.25	2.16	2.09	2.04	2.00	1.96	1.94	1.89	1.84	1.79	1.77	1.74	1.71	1.68	1.64	1.61
21	2.96	2.57	2.36	2.23	2.14	2.08	2.02	1.98	1.95	1.92	1.87	1.83	1.78	1.75	1.72	1.69	1.66	1.62	1.59
22	2.95	2.56	2.35	2.22	2.13	2.06	2.01	1.97	1.93	1.90	1.86	1.81	1.76	1.73	1.70	1.67	1.64	1.60	1.57
23	2.94	2.55	2.34	2.21	2.11	2.05	1.99	1.95	1.92	1.89	1.84	1.80	1.74	1.72	1.69	1.66	1.62	1.59	1.55
24	2.93	2.54	2.33	2.19	2.10	2.04	1.98	1.94	1.91	1.88	1.83	1.78	1.73	1.70	1.67	1.64	1.61	1.57	1.53
25	2.92	2.53	2.32	2.18	2.09	2.02	1.97	1.93	1.89	1.87	1.82	1.77	1.72	1.69	1.66	1.63	1.59	1.56	1.52
26	2.91	2.52	2.31	2.17	2.08	2.01	1.96	1.92	1.88	1.86	1.81	1.76	1.71	1.68	1.65	1.61	1.58	1.54	1.50
27	2.90	2.51	2.30	2.17	2.07	2.00	1.95	1.91	1.87	1.85	1.80	1.75	1.70	1.67	1.64	1.60	1.57	1.53	1.49
28	2.89	2.50	2.29	2.16	2.06	2.00	1.94	1.90	1.87	1.84	1.79	1.74	1.69	1.66	1.63	1.59	1.56	1.52	1.48
29	2.89	2.50	2.28	2.15	2.06	1.99	1.93	1.89	1.86	1.83	1.78	1.73	1.68	1.65	1.62	1.58	1.55	1.51	1.47
30	2.88	2.49	2.28	2.14	2.05	1.98	1.93	1.88	1.85	1.82	1.77	1.72	1.67	1.64	1.61	1.57	1.54	1.50	1.46
40	2.84	2.44	2.23	2.09	2.00	1.93	1.87	1.83	1.79	1.76	1.71	1.66	1.61	1.57	1.54	1.51	1.47	1.42	1.38
60	2.79	2.39	2.18	2.04	1.95	1.87	1.82	1.77	1.74	1.71	1.66	1.60	1.54	1.51	1.48	1.44	1.40	1.35	1.29
120	2.75	2.35	2.13	1.99	1.90	1.82	1.77	1.72	1.68	1.65	1.60	1.55	1.48	1.45	1.41	1.37	1.32	1.26	1.19
∞	2.71	2.30	2.08	1.94	1.85	1.77	1.72	1.67	1.63	1.60	1.55	1.49	1.42	1.38	1.34	1.30	1.24	1.17	1.00

Table 18 from *Biometrika Tables for Statisticians*, Volume 1, edited by E. S. Pearson and H. O. Hartley. By permission of the Biometrika Trustees.

TABLE D.2 (CONTINUED)

Critical F Values at the 95 Percent Confidence Level ($\alpha = .05$)

Degrees of Freedom in the Numerator ($d.f. = k - 1$)

	1	2	3	4	5	6	7	8	9	10	12	15	20	24	30	40	60	120	∞
1	161.4	199.5	215.7	224.6	230.2	234.0	236.8	238.9	240.5	241.9	243.9	245.9	248.0	249.1	250.1	251.1	252.2	253.3	254.3
2	18.51	19.00	19.16	19.25	19.30	19.33	19.35	19.37	19.38	19.40	19.41	19.43	19.45	19.45	19.46	19.47	19.48	19.49	19.50
3	10.13	9.55	9.28	9.12	9.01	8.94	8.89	8.85	8.81	8.79	8.74	8.70	8.66	8.64	8.62	8.59	8.57	8.55	8.53
4	7.71	6.94	6.59	6.39	6.26	6.16	6.09	6.04	6.00	5.96	5.91	5.86	5.80	5.77	5.75	5.72	5.69	5.66	5.63
5	6.61	5.79	5.41	5.19	5.05	4.95	4.88	4.82	4.77	4.74	4.68	4.62	4.56	4.53	4.50	4.46	4.43	4.40	4.36
6	5.99	5.14	4.76	4.53	4.39	4.28	4.21	4.15	4.10	4.06	4.00	3.94	3.87	3.84	3.81	3.77	3.74	3.70	3.67
7	5.59	4.74	4.35	4.12	3.97	3.87	3.79	3.73	3.68	3.64	3.57	3.51	3.44	3.41	3.38	3.34	3.30	3.27	3.23
8	5.32	4.46	4.07	3.84	3.69	3.58	3.50	3.44	3.39	3.35	3.28	3.22	3.15	3.12	3.08	3.04	3.01	2.97	2.93
9	5.12	4.26	3.86	3.63	3.48	3.37	3.29	3.23	3.18	3.14	3.07	3.01	2.94	2.90	2.86	2.83	2.79	2.75	2.71
10	4.96	4.10	3.71	3.48	3.33	3.22	3.14	3.07	3.02	2.98	2.91	2.85	2.77	2.74	2.70	2.66	2.62	2.58	2.54
11	4.84	3.98	3.59	3.36	3.20	3.09	3.01	2.95	2.90	2.85	2.79	2.72	2.65	2.61	2.57	2.53	2.49	2.45	2.40
12	4.75	3.89	3.49	3.26	3.11	3.00	2.91	2.85	2.80	2.75	2.69	2.62	2.54	2.51	2.47	2.43	2.38	2.34	2.30
13	4.67	3.81	3.41	3.18	3.03	2.92	2.83	2.77	2.71	2.67	2.60	2.53	2.46	2.42	2.38	2.34	2.30	2.25	2.21
14	4.60	3.74	3.34	3.11	2.96	2.85	2.76	2.70	2.65	2.60	2.53	2.46	2.39	2.35	2.31	2.27	2.22	2.18	2.13
15	4.54	3.68	3.29	3.06	2.90	2.79	2.71	2.64	2.59	2.54	2.48	2.40	2.33	2.29	2.25	2.20	2.16	2.11	2.07
16	4.49	3.63	3.24	3.01	2.85	2.74	2.66	2.59	2.54	2.49	2.42	2.35	2.28	2.24	2.19	2.15	2.11	2.06	2.01
17	4.45	3.59	3.20	2.96	2.81	2.70	2.61	2.55	2.49	2.45	2.38	2.31	2.23	2.19	2.15	2.10	2.06	2.01	1.96
18	4.41	3.55	3.16	2.93	2.77	2.66	2.58	2.51	2.46	2.41	2.34	2.27	2.19	2.15	2.11	2.06	2.02	1.97	1.92
19	4.38	3.52	3.13	2.90	2.74	2.63	2.54	2.48	2.42	2.38	2.31	2.23	2.16	2.11	2.07	2.03	1.98	1.93	1.88

Degrees of Freedom in the Denominator ($d.f. = n - k$)

20	4.35	3.49	3.10	2.87	2.71	2.60	2.51	2.45	2.39	2.35	2.28	2.20	2.12	2.08	2.04	1.99	1.95	1.90	1.84
21	4.32	3.47	3.07	2.84	2.68	2.57	2.49	2.42	2.37	2.32	2.25	2.18	2.10	2.05	2.01	1.96	1.92	1.87	1.81
22	4.30	3.44	3.05	2.82	2.66	2.55	2.46	2.40	2.34	2.30	2.23	2.15	2.07	2.03	1.98	1.94	1.89	1.84	1.78
23	4.28	3.42	3.03	2.80	2.64	2.53	2.44	2.37	2.32	2.27	2.20	2.13	2.05	2.01	1.96	1.91	1.86	1.81	1.76
24	4.26	3.40	3.01	2.78	2.62	2.51	2.42	2.36	2.30	2.25	2.18	2.11	2.03	1.98	1.94	1.89	1.84	1.79	1.73
25	4.24	3.39	2.99	2.76	2.60	2.49	2.40	2.34	2.28	2.24	2.16	2.09	2.01	1.96	1.92	1.87	1.82	1.77	1.71
26	4.23	3.37	2.98	2.74	2.59	2.47	2.39	2.32	2.27	2.22	2.15	2.07	1.99	1.95	1.90	1.85	1.80	1.75	1.69
27	4.21	3.35	2.96	2.73	2.57	2.46	2.37	2.31	2.25	2.20	2.13	2.06	1.97	1.93	1.88	1.84	1.79	1.73	1.67
28	4.20	3.34	2.95	2.71	2.56	2.45	2.36	2.29	2.24	2.19	2.12	2.04	1.96	1.91	1.87	1.82	1.77	1.71	1.65
29	4.18	3.33	2.93	2.70	2.55	2.43	2.35	2.28	2.22	2.18	2.10	2.03	1.94	1.90	1.85	1.81	1.75	1.70	1.64
30	4.17	3.32	2.92	2.69	2.53	2.42	2.33	2.27	2.21	2.16	2.09	2.01	1.93	1.89	1.84	1.79	1.74	1.68	1.62
40	4.08	3.23	2.84	2.61	2.45	2.34	2.25	2.18	2.12	2.08	2.00	1.92	1.84	1.79	1.74	1.69	1.64	1.58	1.51
60	4.00	3.15	2.76	2.53	2.37	2.25	2.17	2.10	2.04	1.99	1.92	1.84	1.75	1.70	1.65	1.59	1.53	1.47	1.39
120	3.92	3.07	2.68	2.45	2.29	2.17	2.09	2.02	1.96	1.91	1.83	1.75	1.66	1.61	1.55	1.50	1.43	1.35	1.25
∞	3.84	3.00	2.60	2.37	2.21	2.10	2.01	1.94	1.88	1.83	1.75	1.67	1.57	1.52	1.46	1.39	1.32	1.22	1.00

TABLE D.2 (CONTINUED)

Critical F Values at the 99 Percent Confidence Level ($\alpha = .01$)

Degrees of Freedom in the Numerator (d.f. = k − 1)

	1	2	3	4	5	6	7	8	9	10	12	15	20	24	30	40	60	120	∞
1	4052	4999.5	5403	5625	5764	5859	5928	5982	6022	6056	6106	6157	6209	6235	6261	6287	6313	6339	6366
2	98.50	99.00	99.17	99.25	99.30	99.33	99.36	99.37	99.39	99.40	99.42	99.43	99.45	99.46	99.47	99.47	99.48	99.49	99.50
3	34.12	30.82	29.46	28.71	28.24	27.91	27.67	27.49	27.35	27.23	27.05	26.87	26.69	26.60	26.50	26.41	26.32	26.22	26.13
4	21.20	18.00	16.69	15.98	15.52	15.21	14.98	14.80	14.66	14.55	14.37	14.20	14.02	13.93	13.84	13.75	13.65	13.56	13.46
5	16.26	13.27	12.06	11.39	10.97	10.67	10.46	10.29	10.16	10.05	9.89	9.72	9.55	9.47	9.38	9.29	9.20	9.11	9.02
6	13.75	10.92	9.78	9.15	8.75	8.47	8.26	8.10	7.98	7.87	7.72	7.56	7.40	7.31	7.23	7.14	7.06	6.97	6.88
7	12.25	9.55	8.45	7.85	7.46	7.19	6.99	6.84	6.72	6.62	6.47	6.31	6.16	6.07	5.99	5.91	5.82	5.74	5.65
8	11.26	8.65	7.59	7.01	6.63	6.37	6.18	6.03	5.91	5.81	5.67	5.52	5.36	5.28	5.20	5.12	5.03	4.95	4.86
9	10.56	8.02	6.99	6.42	6.06	5.80	5.61	5.47	5.35	5.26	5.11	4.96	4.81	4.73	4.65	4.57	4.48	4.40	4.31
10	10.04	7.56	6.55	5.99	5.64	5.39	5.20	5.06	4.94	4.85	4.71	4.56	4.41	4.33	4.25	4.17	4.08	4.00	3.91
11	9.65	7.21	6.22	5.67	5.32	5.07	4.89	4.74	4.63	4.54	4.40	4.25	4.10	4.02	3.94	3.86	3.78	3.69	3.60
12	9.33	6.93	5.95	5.41	5.06	4.82	4.64	4.50	4.39	4.30	4.16	4.01	3.86	3.78	3.70	3.62	3.54	3.45	3.36
13	9.07	6.70	5.74	5.21	4.86	4.62	4.44	4.30	4.19	4.10	3.96	3.82	3.66	3.59	3.51	3.43	3.34	3.25	3.17
14	8.86	6.51	5.56	5.04	4.69	4.46	4.28	4.14	4.03	3.94	3.80	3.66	3.51	3.43	3.35	3.27	3.18	3.09	3.00
15	8.68	6.36	5.42	4.89	4.56	4.32	4.14	4.00	3.89	3.80	3.67	3.52	3.37	3.29	3.21	3.13	3.05	2.96	2.87
16	8.53	6.23	5.29	4.77	4.44	4.20	4.03	3.89	3.78	3.69	3.55	3.41	3.26	3.18	3.10	3.02	2.93	2.84	2.75
17	8.40	6.11	5.18	4.67	4.34	4.10	3.93	3.79	3.68	3.59	3.46	3.31	3.16	3.08	3.00	2.92	2.83	2.75	2.65
18	8.29	6.01	5.09	4.58	4.25	4.01	3.84	3.71	3.60	3.51	3.37	3.23	3.08	3.00	2.92	2.84	2.75	2.66	2.57
19	8.18	5.93	5.01	4.50	4.17	3.94	3.77	3.63	3.52	3.43	3.30	3.15	3.00	2.92	2.84	2.76	2.67	2.58	2.49

Degrees of Freedom in the Denominator (d.f. = n − k)

20	8.10	5.85	4.94	4.43	4.10	3.87	3.70	3.56	3.46	3.37	3.23	3.09	2.94	2.86	2.78	2.69	2.61	2.52	2.42
21	8.02	5.78	4.87	4.37	4.04	3.81	3.64	3.51	3.40	3.31	3.17	3.03	2.88	2.80	2.72	2.64	2.55	2.46	2.36
22	7.95	5.72	4.82	4.31	3.99	3.76	3.59	3.45	3.35	3.26	3.12	2.98	2.83	2.75	2.67	2.58	2.50	2.40	2.31
23	7.88	5.66	4.76	4.26	3.94	3.71	3.54	3.41	3.30	3.21	3.07	2.93	2.78	2.70	2.62	2.54	2.45	2.35	2.26
24	7.82	5.61	4.72	4.22	3.90	3.67	3.50	3.36	3.26	3.17	3.03	2.89	2.74	2.66	2.58	2.49	2.40	2.31	2.21
25	7.77	5.57	4.68	4.18	3.85	3.63	3.46	3.32	3.22	3.13	2.99	2.85	2.70	2.62	2.54	2.45	2.36	2.27	2.17
26	7.72	5.53	4.64	4.14	3.82	3.59	3.42	3.29	3.18	3.09	2.96	2.81	2.66	2.58	2.50	2.42	2.33	2.23	2.13
27	7.68	5.49	4.60	4.11	3.78	3.56	3.39	3.26	3.15	3.06	2.93	2.78	2.63	2.55	2.47	2.38	2.29	2.20	2.10
28	7.64	5.45	4.57	4.07	3.75	3.53	3.36	3.23	3.12	3.03	2.90	2.75	2.60	2.52	2.44	2.35	2.26	2.17	2.06
29	7.60	5.42	4.54	4.04	3.73	3.50	3.33	3.20	3.09	3.00	2.87	2.73	2.57	2.49	2.41	2.33	2.23	2.14	2.03
30	7.56	5.39	4.51	4.02	3.70	3.47	3.30	3.17	3.07	2.98	2.84	2.70	2.55	2.47	2.39	2.30	2.21	2.11	2.01
40	7.31	5.18	4.31	3.83	3.51	3.29	3.12	2.99	2.89	2.80	2.66	2.52	2.37	2.29	2.20	2.11	2.02	1.92	1.80
60	7.08	4.98	4.13	3.65	3.34	3.12	2.95	2.82	2.72	2.63	2.50	2.35	2.20	2.12	2.03	1.94	1.84	1.73	1.60
120	6.85	4.79	3.95	3.48	3.17	2.96	2.79	2.66	2.56	2.47	2.34	2.19	2.03	1.95	1.86	1.76	1.66	1.53	1.38
∞	6.63	4.61	3.78	3.32	3.02	2.80	2.64	2.51	2.41	2.32	2.18	2.04	1.88	1.79	1.70	1.59	1.47	1.32	1.00

TABLE D.3

Students' t Distribution

Degrees of freedom	Area in the Rejection Region (two-tail test)[a]												
	0.9	0.8	0.7	0.6	0.5	0.4	0.3	0.2	0.1	0.05	0.02	0.01	0.001
1	0.158	0.325	0.510	0.727	1.000	1.376	1.963	3.078	6.314	12.706	31.821	63.657	636.619
2	0.142	0.289	0.445	0.617	0.816	1.061	1.386	1.886	2.920	4.303	6.965	9.925	31.598
3	0.137	0.277	0.424	0.584	0.765	0.978	1.250	1.638	2.353	3.182	4.541	5.841	12.924
4	0.134	0.271	0.414	0.569	0.741	0.941	1.190	1.533	2.132	2.776	3.747	4.604	8.610
5	0.132	0.267	0.408	0.559	0.727	0.920	1.156	1.476	2.015	2.571	3.365	4.032	6.869
6	0.131	0.265	0.404	0.553	0.718	0.906	1.134	1.440	1.943	2.447	3.143	3.707	5.959
7	0.130	0.263	0.402	0.549	0.711	0.896	1.119	1.415	1.895	2.365	2.998	3.499	5.408
8	0.130	0.262	0.399	0.546	0.706	0.889	1.108	1.397	1.860	2.306	2.896	3.355	5.041
9	0.129	0.261	0.398	0.543	0.703	0.883	1.100	1.383	1.833	2.262	2.821	3.250	4.781
10	0.129	0.260	0.397	0.542	0.700	0.879	1.093	1.372	1.812	2.228	2.764	3.169	4.587
11	0.129	0.260	0.396	0.540	0.697	0.876	1.088	1.363	1.796	2.201	2.718	3.106	4.437
12	0.128	0.259	0.395	0.539	0.695	0.873	1.083	1.356	1.782	2.179	2.681	3.055	4.318
13	0.128	0.259	0.394	0.538	0.694	0.870	1.079	1.350	1.771	2.160	2.650	3.012	4.221
14	0.128	0.258	0.393	0.537	0.692	0.868	1.076	1.345	1.761	2.145	2.624	2.977	4.140
15	0.128	0.258	0.393	0.536	0.691	0.866	1.074	1.341	1.753	2.131	2.602	2.947	4.073
16	0.128	0.258	0.392	0.535	0.690	0.865	1.071	1.337	1.746	2.120	2.583	2.921	4.015
17	0.128	0.257	0.392	0.534	0.689	0.863	1.069	1.333	1.740	2.110	2.567	2.898	3.965
18	0.127	0.257	0.392	0.534	0.688	0.862	1.067	1.330	1.734	2.101	2.552	2.878	3.922
19	0.127	0.257	0.391	0.533	0.688	0.861	1.066	1.328	1.729	2.093	2.539	2.861	3.883
20	0.127	0.257	0.391	0.533	0.687	0.860	1.064	1.325	1.725	2.086	2.528	2.845	3.850

21	0.127	0.257	0.391	0.532	0.686	0.859	1.063	**1.323**	**1.721**	**2.080**	2.518	**2.831**	3.819
22	0.127	0.256	0.390	0.532	0.686	0.858	1.061	**1.321**	**1.717**	**2.074**	2.508	**2.819**	3.792
23	0.127	0.256	0.390	0.532	0.685	0.858	1.060	**1.319**	**1.714**	**2.069**	2.500	**2.807**	3.767
24	0.127	0.256	0.390	0.531	0.685	0.857	1.059	**1.318**	**1.711**	**2.064**	2.492	**2.797**	3.745
25	0.127	0.256	0.390	0.531	0.684	0.856	1.058	**1.316**	**1.708**	**2.060**	2.485	**2.787**	3.725
26	0.127	0.256	0.390	0.531	0.684	0.856	1.058	**1.315**	**1.706**	**2.056**	2.479	**2.779**	3.707
27	0.127	0.256	0.389	0.531	0.684	0.855	1.057	**1.314**	**1.703**	**2.052**	2.473	**2.771**	3.690
28	0.127	0.256	0.389	0.530	0.683	0.855	1.056	**1.313**	**1.701**	**2.048**	2.467	**2.763**	3.674
29	0.127	0.256	0.389	0.530	0.683	0.854	1.055	**1.311**	**1.699**	**2.045**	2.462	**2.756**	3.659
30	0.127	0.256	0.389	0.530	0.683	0.854	1.055	**1.310**	**1.697**	**2.042**	2.457	**2.750**	3.646
40	0.126	0.255	0.388	0.529	0.681	0.851	1.050	**1.303**	**1.684**	**2.021**	2.423	**2.704**	3.551
60	0.126	0.254	0.387	0.527	0.679	0.848	1.046	**1.296**	**1.671**	**2.000**	2.390	**2.660**	3.460
120	0.126	0.254	0.386	0.526	0.677	0.845	1.041	**1.289**	**1.658**	**1.980**	2.358	**2.617**	3.373
∞	0.126	0.253	0.385	0.524	0.674	0.842	1.036	**1.282**	**1.645**	**1.960**	2.326	**2.576**	3.291

NAME INDEX

Allen, B. T., 303–305

Bain, J. S., 476 n
Bator, F. M., 455
Baumol, W. J., 185, 449 n
Brigham, E. F., 498 n, 503 n

Commons, J. R., 457 n
Cookenboo, L., Jr., 306

Dean, J., 295–296, 298
Dirlam, J. B., 405–406, 407–408
Draper, N. R., 189

Earley, J. S., 407

Fabian, T., 449 n
Friedman, M., 479

Hall, R. L., 405
Haynes, W. W., 406
Hirschey, M., 301 n
Hirshleifer, J., 439
Hitch, C. J., 405

Johnston, J., 187, 298, 301

Kaplan, A. D. H., 405–406,
    407–408

Lanzillotti, R. F., 406, 407–408

Murphy, T. P., 472 n

Nunne, P. F., 478

Smith, H., 189
Solomons, D., 439
Stigler, G. J., 303, 477

Weidenbaum, M. L., 461 n, 479
Weingartner, H. M., 306 n
Wiles, P. J. D., 301

Yntema, T. O., 298

SUBJECT INDEX

Alternative-use concept, 253, 254
Annual payments, for accumulation
    of a future sum, 557
Annual receipts, from an annuity,
    557–558
Annuity
    annual receipts from, 557–558
    future value of, 550–552
    present value of, 552–554
Antitrust legislation, 12, 13,
    472–475
Antitrust policy, 472–475
Arc elasticity, 131–133, 135
Assumption of linearity, 314–315
Autocorrelation, 186–189
Average costs, 265–268
Average product, 206, 207,
    209–211
Average relationship, 26–30

Barometric method of forecasting,
    577–580
Barometric price leadership, 391
Breakeven analysis, 271–280
    limitations of, 280
    linear, 272–274, 280
    and operating leverage, 276–279
Business, role of in society, 11–13
Business administration, relation-
    ship to managerial econom-
    ics, 5–6
Business indicators, 578–580
Business profit, 14
Buyers, effect of on market struc-
    ture, 369–370

Calculus
    differential, 30–52
    of price discrimination, 417–422
Capacity, 267
Capital, cost of, 499, 508–514, 536
Capital asset pricing model,
    510–511
Capital budgeting, 489–516,
    521–523
Capital budgeting process, steps in,
    507–515

Capital expenditure analysis, 493
Capital outlay, 489
Capital rationing, 503–504, 505
Capture theory of economic regula-
    tion, 477–478
Cartels, 387–390
Cash flow, estimation of, 493–498,
    515
Cash flow forecasts, 507
Celler–Kefauver Act, 475
Censuses, economic, 395–396
Certainty equivalent adjustments,
    84–89
Chain rule, in differential calculus,
    38–41
Clayton Act, 474–475
Coefficient of determination,
    174–178, 293
Coefficient of variation, 78–79, 93
Competition
    monopolistic, 368
    nonprice, 393–394
    pure, 368, 370–374
    substitutes for, 12
Component cost, of capital, debt,
    and equity, 508–509
Composite indexes, for forecasting,
    579–580
Compound value, 543–547
Compounding, 543–562
Compounding periods, 559–561
Computer simulation, in risk analy-
    sis, 92, 96–98
Concentration ratios, 396–397
Constants, in differential calculus, 34
Constrained cost minimization,
    349–356
Constrained optimization, 9, 52–58,
    246–249, 312–314, 326,
    333, 349
Constraint equations, 325–326,
    327–330, 334–340
Constraints, 325–329, 334, 343–
    349, 350–354
    dual, 343
Consumer interviews, 161–163

Control
    of business operations by gov-
        ernment, 457–463
    economic analysis of the effects
        of, 457–463
    of monopolies, 463–477
    of prices, 464–466
Cost
    average, 265–268
    capital, 499, 508–514, 536
    common, 431
    current, 252, 255
    debt, 508–509
    definitions of, 252–258
    equity, 509–511
    explicit, 253–254
    fixed, 254–255, 258–260,
        271–280, 377–378, 528,
        531
    historical, 252, 407
    implicit, 253–254
    incremental, 254–256, 258–260
    long-run, 256–257, 265–267
    marginal, 254, 258–260, 298–
        299, 374–378, 382
    opportunity, 253, 290–291, 407,
        547
    relevant, 252–253, 254, 255, 256
    role in cost-plus pricing, 407
    semivariable, 258
    short-run, 256–257
    standard cost concept, 407
    sunk, 254–256
    total, 258–260, 261–263, 271–
        276, 528, 530–531
    uncertainty, 117–119
    variable, 257–260, 271–274,
        280, 377–380
Cost-accounting records, 293
Cost analysis, empirical, 289–306
Cost curves
    long-run, 260–263, 266–268,
        301, 306
    short-run, 258–260, 266, 293–
        294, 298
Cost elasticity, 264–265